0349

D0142199

Techniques of Healthy Cooking

Techniques of
healthy
cooking

The Culinary Institute of America

1807
WILEY
2007

JOHN WILEY & SONS, INC.

The Culinary Institute of America

PRESIDENT	Dr. Tim Ryan
VICE-PRESIDENT, CONTINUING EDUCATION	Mark Erickson
DIRECTOR OF INTELLECTUAL PROPERTY	Nathalie Fischer
MANAGING EDITOR	Kate McBride
EDITORIAL PROJECT MANAGER	Mary Donovan
PRODUCTION ASSISTANT	Patrick Decker
WRITER	Martha Scheuneman
RECIPE DEVELOPMENT	David Kamen, Mark Ainsworth
CONTENT DEVELOPMENT	Marjorie Livingston, RD, Catherine H. Powers, MS, RD
PHOTOGRAPHER	Ben Fink
STYLISTS	Joseba Encabo, Michael Garnero, Lynn Gigliotti

This book is printed on acid-free paper. ∞

Published by John Wiley & Sons, Inc., Hoboken, New Jersey

Published simultaneously in Canada

Limit of Liability/Disclaimer of Warranty: While the publisher and author have used their best efforts in preparing this book, they make no representations or warranties with respect to the accuracy or completeness of the contents of this book and specifically disclaim any implied warranties of merchantability or fitness for a particular purpose. No warranty may be created or extended by sales representatives or written sales materials. The advice and strategies contained herein may not be suitable for your situation. You should consult with a professional where appropriate. Neither the publisher nor author shall be liable for any loss of profit or any other commercial damages, including but not limited to special, incidental, consequential, or other damages.

For general information on our other products and services or for technical support, please contact our Customer Care Department within the United States at (800) 762-2974, outside the United States at (317) 572-3993 or fax (317) 572-4002.

Wiley also publishes its books in a variety of electronic formats. Some content that appears in print may not be available in electronic books. For more information about Wiley products, visit our web site at www.wiley.com.

Library of Congress Cataloging-in-Publication Data:

Techniques of healthy cooking / the Culinary Institute of America.
     p. cm.
Includes bibliographical references and index.
ISBN 978-0-470-05232-7 (cloth)
1. Quantity cookery. 2. Nutrition. 3. Menus. I. Culinary Institute of America.
TX820.T384 2007
641.5'7—dc22
2006038750

Printed in the United States of America

10 9 8 7 6 5 4 3 2

Cover and Interior photography by Ben Fink
Cover and interior design by Vertigo Design NYC
Wiley bicentennial logo: Richard J. Pacifico

Contents

6 Main Dishes for Lunches and Dinners   243

7 Side Dishes 361

8 Breakfast and Beverages   409

9 Baked Goods and Desserts   435

10 Chef's Pantry   481

Acknowledgments

To our faculty, past and present, who teach the material to our students and make it come to life for our guests: Dr. Tim Ryan, Mark Erickson, Robert Briggs, Jonathan Zearfoss, Ron DeSantis, Victor Gielisse, Greg Fatigati, Eve Felder, Morey Kanner, David Kamen, Mark Ainsworth, Fred Brash, Dan Turgeon, Thomas Kief, Steven Kolpan, Anthony Ligouri, Richard Vergili, Marjorie Livingston, Marianne Turow, Elizabeth Briggs, Catherine Powers, Lynn Gigliotti, Michael Garnero, and Joseba Encabo.

The Worlds of Flavor and Worlds of Healthy Flavors conferences added another level of excitement and, ultimately, resulted in our Principles of Healthy Menu Development. We wish to acknowledge Greg Drescher and John Barkley for their important contributions, along with the inspiring recipes and thought-provoking conversations between food-service and nutrition experts they have made part of the national discussion of healthy cooking and eating in the twenty-first century.

Preface

Choosing a healthy eating pattern is vitally important, as diet directly influences health. Obesity causes at least 300,000 deaths a year, while the combination of excess weight and lack of physical activity are responsible for more than 400,000 deaths a year. The problem isn't limited to the United States—it affects both rich and poor countries around the world.

Americans need to understand that excess weight and obesity are literally killing us. Each small step makes a difference: A healthy diet (combined with regular exercise and not smoking) can help prevent not only excess weight and obesity, but also heart disease, diabetes, some cancers, and other chronic diseases. A healthy diet can also help control many health conditions.

The problem for most people is how to understand what constitutes healthy eating. It's a daunting task, even for people who consider themselves nutrition-savvy. Dozens of new diets books are published each year, but few are based on solid scientific principles. An independent team, led by Dr. Walter C. Willett, chairman of the Department of Nutrition at the Harvard School of Public Health, has been working to clear up the confusion by defining what constitutes a healthy diet according to the best scientific evidence available. Their work complements research from a range of leaders

Overweight and obesity may soon cause as much preventable disease and death as cigarette smoking.

—DAVID SATCHER, former U.S. Surgeon General

Obesity is almost entirely preventable through diet and exercise, as are the health problems that come with it.

—RICHARD CARMONA, current U.S. Surgeon General

in the field of nutrition from all over the world. In many cases, this work is running ahead of government policy-makers' ability to translate it into accurate, up-to-date public health messages.

The Culinary Institute of America's first Worlds of Healthy Flavors Leadership Retreat was held in 2004 on our Greystone campus to address the needs of leaders in the food-service industry. We invited several internationally-acclaimed chefs and cookbook authors to prepare meals and to showcase the healthful nature of their native kitchens. Aromatic, stimulating, and delicious beyond words, the lunches and dinners confirmed that the world's cuisines abound in healthful ideas: from India's spicy lemon broth with lentils to Mexico's green mole with vegetables to a Spanish salad of greens, figs, and gazpacho vinaigrette.

Obesity is an epidemic of global proportions.

—WORLD HEALTH ORGANIZATION

As food experts from Mexico, Greece, India, and Vietnam displayed the riches of their native table at the Worlds of Healthy Flavors gathering, one point crystallized: Americans still have a lot to discover. With the recipes and healthy cooking techniques in this book, and the drive to continue your study of how food and health are intertwined, the lessons of the world's most intriguing cuisines can translate into healthier menu options both in your restaurant and in your home.

Introduction

When The CIA first approached the idea of nutritional cooking, in 1990, we set out to prepare a manual for our students to use in the two courses we then offered in nutrition and nutritional cooking. That manual grew like Topsy to become the 500-plus page volume we are now proud to present in its third edition. Over the years and through each edition of this book, more information has come to the fore about healthy cooking. And with each passing year, our guests have continued to call for great-tasting food that is good for you in every sense of the word.

Our knowledge of nutrition continues to grow. Every day, it seems, the news features a newly released study on how the foods we eat affect our health. In addition, we have learned that the way foods are grown and distributed can also have a significant impact on our health and the health of our planet's farmland and overall food supply.

People have become increasingly aware that, as part of a lifestyle that also includes such elements as proper amounts of rest and exercise, good nutrition is important in maintaining physical health and overall well-being. Consequently, the demand for products and services designed to help support the quest for good health has increased dramatically.

Chefs, restaurateurs, and other food-service professionals are rising to the challenge of offering foods that appeal to patrons' desire for a healthy lifestyle. We now know that a healthy diet is based on eating a wide variety of high-quality foods that provide balanced nutrition. Chefs are in the vanguard of efforts to revitalize regional food systems and are urging a conscious evaluation of how we choose to buy, cook, and serve foods.

Chapter 1 covers some of the basics of nutrition by defining the various roles that foods play in sustaining life. This material is not intended as a replacement for more in-depth study of nutrition. We introduce a number of important concepts, including the importance of calories, and discuss dietary guidelines, healthy diets, and food guide pyramids. We know that a healthy, balanced diet plays a role in maintaining optimum health, along with regular physical activity. When we examine the diets and dining habits of cultures whose members exhibit low levels of heart disease, obesity, and other diet-related health concerns, we can begin to identify the foundations of healthy cooking.

Based on the combined knowledge of dozens of professional chefs, dietitians, and food-service professionals, and on the lessons of the pyramids, The Culinary Institute of America has revised its own set of principles for healthy cooking. These guidelines are an invitation to think about the foods you select, the cooking techniques you use, and the types of beverages you offer. They are not ironclad rules. Instead, they should be regarded as ways to explore the possibilities of flavor and healthy cooking.

To begin cooking for good health, we have to revise the way we think of meals and shift our focus to those foods that once were relegated to the side. The major challenge in such an undertaking is the preservation of flavor.

Our recipes offer practical solutions for putting healthy cooking into effect. The recipes in this book are written to help you learn, or relearn, how portion sizes and ingredient measurements look when using healthy cooking guidelines.

At first, it may seem cumbersome and time-consuming to measure out certain ingredients, but the extra time will pay off. As you grow familiar with the correct measures and portion sizes, using them consistently becomes easier. You will probably discover that it is always best to weigh or measure ingredients that could add extra calories, cholesterol, sodium, and fats not intended to be part of the dish.

The analysis provided at the end of each recipe is based on the exact measurements supplied in the ingredient list. Adding a few more teaspoons of butter, an extra ounce of heavy cream, or another slice of bacon is likely to have a negative effect on the dish's nutritional profile.

Not every component needs the same careful monitoring, though. Adding more basil to the pasta, for example, or increasing the amount of vegetable garnish in a soup will probably not make much difference, nutritionally speaking, but the flavor of the dish might benefit dramatically.

Many factors affect the nutrients in each ingredient (season, ripeness, soil conditions, etc.), and many factors affect the nutrients in the cooking process (how long, what temperature, storage conditions, etc.). The nutritional analysis we have provided for each recipe is a reliable estimation of the nutrients that are in that dish. The nutrients selected for analysis are based on the current food label and include calories, total fat, saturated fat, cholesterol, sodium, total carbohydrate, dietary fiber, sugars, and protein. To standardize the process and to ensure consistency in the nutritional analysis, the following standards were used:

Each analysis includes only the ingredients in the main ingredient list. Serving suggestions are not included in the analysis.

All ingredients were measured using the U.S. measurement system.

Nutrient values were rounded using the FDA food label standards.

When a range of ingredient measures is given, the smallest amount is used in the analysis.

When an ingredient, such as pepper, is listed as "to taste" or "optional," it is not included in the analysis.

When more than one ingredient is listed, such as "chicken or vegetable stock," the first ingredient is the one we used in the analysis.

A Healthy Diet

WHAT IS A HEALTHY DIET? The answer is rarely a simple one. Our individual needs differ greatly for a variety of reasons, including our age, gender, activity level, and the status of our health. As more studies are conducted and the results are analyzed, the media continue to report about miracle diets and wonder cures, but those don't necessarily lead to a healthy diet.

At its simplest, *diet* means the foods we normally eat and drink. The first two definitions of *diet* in *Merriam-Webster's Collegiate Dictionary, Eleventh Edition,* stress the idea of foods that are regularly or habitually eaten. The word also encompasses the notion of foods that are prescribed for an individual for a specific reason. However, the popular understanding of *diets* is that they are something a person "goes on" (and often "falls off") in order to drop extra pounds.

Diets are popularly thought of as restricting the foods someone might normally eat. Most popular weight-loss diets fall into this category. These diets are often described with an emphasis on "delicious and bountiful" aspects of the foods the dieter is permitted, to counteract the perception that diets are mainly about deprivation. Diets that are prescribed by a health care professional may also include a number of restrictions, eliminating or curtailing some foods, reducing portions, or even changing someone's typical eating pattern. Some of these restrictions, discussed in greater detail later, help to control the number of calories consumed, while others are meant to prevent disagreeable, harmful, or even potentially deadly consequences.

A "poor" diet used to mean a diet that did not supply enough of the basic nutrients to keep an individual from starving to death or developing deficiency diseases like rickets, scurvy, or beriberi. There are still many places in the world where these are issues of vital concern. In most of the industrialized nations, however, the reason a diet is described as "poor" has more to do with excess: too many calories, too much sodium, too much fat. Ironically, an excess in one area can also lead to a deficiency in another; too many calories in the form of sugary or fatty foods means that there is a corresponding deprivation in the form of not enough fiber or vitamins.

As an individual, you may want to know about diets in order to keep yourself healthy or to lose weight. As a professional, your motivation for knowing more about a healthy diet might be to develop entire menus for clients who do have specific dietary needs—clients with diabetes or hypertension, schoolchildren, or the residents of an assisted-livingfacility, for instance. If your clientele is composed of a group that has a variety of needs or desires when it comes to eating, your challenge is developing menu items that are good options for those who have a personal interest in healthier foods.

The history of medical and culinary science is littered with dietary plans and special foods and products meant to control weight, build muscle, or treat an illness. Graham crackers, for instance, were a health food when they first arrived on the market. Today, they are simply sweet crackers, not the cornerstone of a dietary program. Part of the issue is that the climate today is more frenetic. There are alarms about the dangers of foods that should be taken seriously, like mercury in seafood or trans fats in snack foods; there are others that are overturned almost before the ink is dry on the newspaper in which they are reported.

We know that schoolchildren are increasingly at risk for some very "adult" diseases, like diabetes and hypertension. Baby boomers now are nearly or well into their retirements and are waking up to the fact that staying healthy means learning new dietary behaviors. Chefs are not necessarily going to have all the answers about what foods are best to eat. But we believe firmly that they need to learn as much as they can about nutrition so that they can apply that knowledge in the kitchen—not as a laboratory exercise, but in the pursuit of foods and flavors that feed our hunger for satisfying, sustaining, and healthful dishes.

Chefs have a responsibility to offer foods that their patrons will want to eat that are also good for them to eat. No one has all the answers about which foods are best, but in order to do a good job, today's chefs are honor bound to learn about the basics of food and nutrition so they can apply that knowledge as part of the techniques of healthy cooking. In this chapter, we will examine basic nutrition concepts. If you are interested in learning more about nutrition, please review the Recommended Resources and Readings (page 547).

Nutrition 101

We eat because we must. Our bodies need food in order to function properly. Human beings eat for more reasons than actual hunger, however. Very often, we eat simply because we want to. Our love affair with food is at the basis of the culinary profession. Chefs have always been in the business of preparing and presenting foods that do much more than fill an empty belly. It is precisely because chefs have the job of enticing us to the table that they need to incorporate lessons from nutrition about food and health in the dishes they prepare.

At the same time that nearly every industrialized country is reporting a growing number of overweight and obese citizens, we are also growing increasingly aware of the relationship between the foods we eat and the consequences to our health. Nutrition is the study of how the foods we eat affect us. Simply eating "enough" is not sufficient to ensure that a diet is healthy. It is vital that we eat enough of the right foods.

The right foods are those that supply us with a full array of all the nutrients we need in order to be properly nourished. Escoffier used to talk about the "nutritive" aspects of a dish. However, at the time that Escoffier was writing—around the turn of the last century—we were just beginning to identify the elements in foods that we need to maintain or improve our health. Nutrition is a dynamic science. Our knowledge of it changes as studies unveil new and sometimes contradictory findings. Behind the controversies and inconsistencies there remain some basic principles. We know, for instance, that getting "the right foods" generally means eating a variety of foods because no single food contains enough of all the important nutrients our bodies need. This section is meant as a brief overview of those nutrients as well as some basic concepts in nutrition: calories, protein, fat, carbohydrates, vitamins, and minerals.

Calories Count

Foods provide our bodies with energy. We use this energy for physical activity as well as for basic functions like respiration, digestion, circulation, and temperature regulation. The energy used for these involuntary bodily functions is known as *resting energy expenditure*.

Energy from food is measured in kilocalories, or the amount of energy or heat required to raise the temperature of 1 kilogram of water by 1 degree Celsius. The term *calorie* is often substituted for kilocalorie.

Calories affect body weight directly: If we consume more calories than we burn, our bodies will convert the extra calories (energy) to fat, and will store it throughout the body. If we burn more calories than we consume, our bodies will draw on stored energy, or fat, to perform the basic functions and to fuel physical activities.

Sources of Calories

Calories come from four sources—carbohydrates, protein, fat, and alcohol. The majority of calories should come from carbohydrates, protein, and fat. (Alcohol does not provide any nutrients and is therefore considered non-nutritive.) Generally, experts recommend that most people get 55 to 60 percent of their total calories from carbohydrates, 12 to 15 percent from protein, and no more than 30 percent from fat. Similarly, the United States Department of Agriculture's Dietary Guidelines recommend ranges of 45 to 65 percent of calories from carbohydrates and 20 to 35 percent of calories from fat, with the remaining 20 to 35 percent coming from protein. This allows for flexibility based on individual or cultural preferences, and for some health conditions.

ALTHOUGH IT IS IMPOSSIBLE FOR CHEFS TO KNOW what customers will eat before they've entered an establishment, there are guidelines chefs can use in developing nutritious recipes and meals. Reference amounts customarily consumed per eating occasion (see chart on pages 514–29) can be used to determine appropriate portion sizes. You'll find more information about this in the Appendix, but in general:

A *main dish* weighs at least 6 ounces per serving, contains not less than two different 40-gram portions of foods from at least two of the food groups listed here, and is represented as a main dish. A *meal* weighs at least 10 ounces per serving, contains not less than three different 40-gram portions of food from at least two of the following food groups, and is represented as a breakfast, lunch, dinner, or meal.

Food Groups:

• **Bread, cereal, rice, and pasta**

• **Fruits and vegetables**

• **Milk, yogurt, and cheese**

• **Meat, poultry, fish, dried beans, eggs, and nuts**

Counting Calories

Not all sources of calories are created equal. Fat supplies more than two times the calories per gram that carbohydrates and protein do, so fats and foods that are high in fat are said to be calorie dense. But these foods may also be dense in nutrients. Alcohol also supplies significantly more calories per gram than carbohydrates and protein, but it contains no nutrients whatsoever.

CARBOHYDRATES	4 calories per gram
PROTEIN	4 calories per gram
FAT	9 calories per gram
ALCOHOL	7 calories per gram

(Note: There are 28 grams in an ounce.)

Factors That Influence Caloric Needs

Throughout this book, nutrition needs are discussed in the context of a 2,000-calorie day. This amount was chosen because it is the basis for the Nutrition Facts label that appears on all packaged food as mandated by federal law, and because it represents the average caloric needs for males and females between the ages of two and sixty. The actual number of calories an individual requires depends on a number of factors:

• **Weight:** In the same way that heavier vehicles use more fuel than lighter ones, heavier people require more calories than lighter individuals.

• **Age and life cycle:** People who are growing rapidly, especially infants and adolescents, as well as pregnant and nursing women, have greater caloric needs. As we age, our metabolisms often slow down and we require fewer calories.

• **Activity level:** Inactive people require fewer calories than people who move frequently. Physically demanding jobs, strenuous exercise, and even fidgeting translate into more calories expended.

• **Gender:** Men typically have leaner body mass than women, and thus have higher basal metabolic rates than women do because muscle burns more calories than fat.

THE GLYCEMIC INDEX, or GI, is a tool some scientists use to measure the effects of carbohydrates on blood sugar levels. Simple carbohydrates are digested rapidly, and they can cause blood sugar levels to rise and then drop rapidly. The GI measures how quickly 50 grams of carbohydrates from a particular food—not 50 grams of the food itself—raise blood sugar levels compared to 50 grams of glucose. A food's GI is expressed as a percentage, with pure glucose at 100 percent.

There are a few flaws with the GI, however. The first is that a GI value does not address the serving sizes of foods. Consider carrots and bagels. Carrots have a GI of 71, and bagels have a GI of 72. The logical conclusion is that eating carrots will raise your blood sugar as much as eating a bagel will. But, remember, the GI is based on the amount of carbohydrate in a food. One 4- to 5-ounce bagel contains about 70 grams of carbohydrates, but one cup of cooked carrots supplies only 13 grams. To eat 50 grams of carbohydrates from carrots, you'd have to eat about 1½ pounds of them. A serving of carrots, in fact, has a much lower impact on blood sugar levels than a bagel does.

In addition, eating foods in combination, whether that's butter or cream cheese on a bagel or carrots in a stew or as a side dish, can affect the rate at which the sugars from these foods enter the bloodstream.

Similar foods may have very different GIs. An oatmeal cookie may have a much lower GI than a chocolate-chip cookie. That's because complex carbohydrates are digested more slowly than simple carbohydrates, in part because fiber can slow down the rate at which sugar is absorbed by the bloodstream.

Determining GI is a labor-intensive process. To measure a food's effect on blood sugar, an actual person must eat the food, and then blood must be drawn and analyzed. Blood sugar levels must be noted before and after the food is consumed, and because individuals respond differently to foods, these tests must be conducted on several people before a GI can be determined. At present, only a limited number of foods have been tested.

Essential Nutrients

When nutrition scientists use the word *essential*, they don't just mean that a nutrient is important. An *essential nutrient* is one that the body does not manufacture. Cholesterol, for example, performs several important functions in the body and is critical for good health. However, the human body manufactures all the cholesterol it needs, so cholesterol is not an essential nutrient.

Carbohydrates, proteins, fats, vitamins, minerals, and water are all essential nutrients. The first three are considered nutritive—that is, they supply calories. The last three are non-nutritive because they are calorie-free.

Carbohydrates

Carbohydrates are the body's preferred source of energy. When we do not eat carbohydrates in sufficient amounts, the body uses protein as fuel, which is much less efficient. As carbohydrates are digested, they are broken down into sugars that the body can absorb, and use, easily. Carbohydrates provide energy for the nervous system and red blood cells. They fuel physical activity and basal metabolic functions and help burn fat efficiently. Carbohydrates should be 45 to 65 percent of the daily caloric intake.

Simple carbohydrates, also known as simple sugars, contain only one or two types of sugar molecules and are called monosaccharides or disaccharides. Easy to digest, simple carbohydrates are found in fruit, fruit juices, dairy products, and sweets. They are often lower in fiber than complex carbohydrates. Glucose, fructose, lactose, maltose, and sucrose are simple carbohydrates.

Complex carbohydrates contain chains of sugars and are called polysaccharides. They are more difficult to digest because they must be broken down into simple sugars first. Because complex carbohydrates take longer to digest than simple carbohydrates, they can provide a sense of fullness and satiety. Whole grains, legumes, nuts, and vegetables contain complex carbohydrates. It is important to note, however, that all carbohydrates influence blood sugar levels.

During digestion, carbohydrates are broken down into glucose, which is absorbed by the body and released into the blood. When blood sugar levels increase, the pancreas releases insulin, a hormone that makes it possible for glucose to enter the cells and to be used for energy.

Simple carbohydrates are often considered empty calories. Fruit, of course, contains nutrients like vitamins and fiber and has an advantage over honey or table sugar, but diets high in simple carbohydrates are often high in empty calories. Malnutrition may result. Excess sugar can contribute to tooth decay as well. (Sugar does not cause diabetes, hypoglycemia, or hyperactivity, although it can worsen an existing condition.)

Fiber

Fiber is a form of carbohydrate that is indigestible and non-nutritive. It is a mixture of several compounds, and the proportion of these compounds in a food varies. Fiber is divided into two basic types: soluble and insoluble.

Soluble fiber dissolves in water. Pectins and gums are components of soluble fiber. Soluble fiber regulates the body's use of sugars by slowing their digestion and release into the bloodstream. Soluble fiber binds with cholesterol-rich bile acids in the intestine, which may help to reduce serum cholesterol levels. Beans, fruits, oats, and barley are good sources of soluble fiber.

Insoluble fiber does not dissolve in water. Instead, it absorbs water and provides bulk in the diet. Cellulose, hemicellulose, and lignin are components of insoluble fiber. Insoluble fiber helps to clear out the intestinal tract and may reduce the risk of certain types of cancer and the risk of Type II diabetes. Fruits and vegetables, wheat bran, whole-grain flours, and popcorn are good sources of insoluble fiber.

The Health Effects of Fiber

HEALTH EFFECT	INSOLUBLE FIBER (CELLULOSE, LIGNIN, AND HEMICELLULOSE)	SOLUBLE FIBER (PECTIN, GUMS)
Decreases colon cancer risk	Yes	No
Lowers blood cholesterol	No	Yes
Lessens constipation and hemorrhoids (reduces pressure, softens stools)	Yes	No
Speeds up transit time in the colon (helps body eliminate waste)	Yes	No
Interferes with mineral absorption	Yes	No
Interferes with vitamin A	Not known	Yes, pectin does
Provides feeling of fullness	Yes	Yes

Protein

Protein is essential for growth. We use it to build, maintain, and repair tissues; to produce hormones, enzymes, and antibodies; to transport nutrients and oxygen throughout the body; and to regulate the balance of bodily fluids. If there are not sufficient carbohydrates available, protein can also be used for energy. However, carbohydrates cannot perform all of the functions protein does.

EATING SUGAR doesn't cause diabetes, but it can definitely make diabetes worse.

During digestion, carbohydrates are broken down into glucose, which goes into the bloodstream to become blood sugar. In a healthy person, insulin—a hormone produced by the pancreas—regulates blood sugar levels, and helps carry blood sugar into cells for energy.

In a diabetic person, insulin is either not produced in sufficient amounts or does not perform its functions. Rather than passing from the blood into the body's cells, glucose builds up in the bloodstream. Excess blood sugar goes into the kidneys to be excreted, causing more work for the kidneys. Over time, high blood sugar levels can cause damage to the kidneys, eyes, circulatory system, and nervous system.

Type I diabetes occurs when the cells in the pancreas responsible for producing insulin have been destroyed. It accounts for only 5 to 10 percent of all diabetes cases. Type II diabetes occurs most often in people who are overweight, physically inactive, and older.

There is no cure for diabetes, but it can be managed. Type I diabetes requires daily insulin, as well as a careful management of diet and physical activity. Type II diabetes can often be controlled through diet, physical activity, and weight management alone, but sometimes insulin is necessary.

For information about dietary recommendations for diabetics, see page 25.

The USDA recommends that only 20 to 35 percent of a day's total calories come from protein. In a 2,000-calorie diet, this means no more than 300 calories should come from protein, or no more than 75 grams. The average person in the United States consumes 100 to 120 grams of protein a day. Too much protein can be as detrimental as too little. Excess protein can contribute to osteoporosis, kidney failure, and gout (a painful inflammation of the joints, particularly in the hands and feet).

Proteins are made of amino acids. All of the proteins found in human cells are composed of about twenty amino acids. Essential amino acids are those that humans cannot produce on their own. Adult humans must acquire eight amino acids from their diets. From those acids, their bodies can produce the remaining twelve that are necessary to produce the proteins they need. Conditionally essential amino acids are those which our bodies are not currently producing for one of the following reasons: age (for instance, infants and children require histidine and arginine), stress, injury, disease, or physical exertion. Under those conditions, some other amino acids need to be introduced through appropriate dietary sources or supplements.

Foods are considered "complete" or "incomplete" sources of protein based on whether they supply all the essential amino acids in amounts required by humans. Meat, poultry, fish, eggs, and other animal sources are complete proteins. With the exception of soyfoods, quinoa, and amaranth, plant foods (grains, vegetables, nuts, legumes) are considered incomplete proteins.

The Amino Acids

ESSENTIAL	CONDITIONALLY ESSENTIAL*	NONESSENTIAL
Isoleucine	Arginine	Alanine
Leucine	Cysteine	Aspartic acid
Lysine	Histidine	Cystine
Methionine	Tyrosine **	Glutamic acid
Phenylalanine		Glutamine
Threonine		Glycine
Tryptophan		Proline
Valine		Serine

* Essential for infants and small children.
** Tyrosine is made from phenylalanine, so if there is a deficiency of phenylalanine, tryosine may be required.

THERE'S CURRENTLY A DEBATE RAGING over juice. One side says it's a healthy beverage—much better for you than sugary sodas. The other side says it can contribute to weight gain and tooth decay every bit as much as soda does.

The truth is that both sides are right. Compared to soda, "elixirs," and sport drinks, juice is a fairly nutritious choice. While they all contain sugars in comparable amounts, no-sugar-added juice gets its sweetness from naturally occurring fruit sugar called fructose, whereas sugar-added drinks get theirs from high-fructose corn syrup, but both types of sugar are simple carbohydrates that the body metabolizes in the same way. Juice, however, does supply some vitamins and minerals, as well as antioxidants and phytochemicals, which are found in the fruits they're made from.

Compare an 8-ounce glass of fruit juice to the medium-sized fruit it's made from, though, and it doesn't look so nutritious:

Food	Calories	Carbohydrates (grams)	Sugars (grams)	Fiber (grams)
ORANGE JUICE	112	26	20	0.5
ORANGE	62	15	12.2	3.1
APPLE JUICE	117	29	27	0.2
APPLE (W/SKIN)	81	21	18	3.7

Bottom line: Juice contains nutrients that other beverages don't, but it lacks the fiber that fruit contains.

Fat

Fat has been maligned for decades, but it is an essential nutrient that performs several vital functions within the body. It surrounds and cushions vital organs, helps to maintain body temperature, maintains structural elements in cells, helps the immune system to function properly, slows digestion, makes the fat-soluble vitamins (A, D, E, and K) available to the body, and supplies essential fatty acids necessary for normal growth and development. However, too much fat, or too much of the wrong types of fat, can increase the risk of coronary heart disease, obesity, and certain types of cancer.

Many experts recommend that fat be limited to 30 percent of daily calories, with no more than 10 percent of daily calories coming from saturated fats; the USDA's Dietary Guidelines allow for 20 to 35 percent of calories from fat. In a 2,000-calorie diet, about 600 calories should come from all fats, and 200 calories should come from saturated fats. Because fat supplies 9 calories per gram, this means that only 67 grams of fat (22 grams of saturated fat) should be consumed every day.

Though it makes sense to conclude that eating fat will cause you to become fat, this isn't necessarily true. Excess calories, whether from fat, carbohydrates, protein, or alcohol, combined with too little activity, are what cause weight gain and obesity. However, fat is calorie-dense, so it is easier to consume too many calories from fat than from protein or carbohydrates. In addition, fat is more readily stored as adipose (body) fat than carbohydrates and protein.

Fats are comprised of linked chains known as fatty acids. Each fatty acid is composed of carbon, hydrogen, and oxygen. The number of slots for hydrogen atoms to bond with carbon atoms determines whether a fat is considered saturated, monounsaturated, or polyunsaturated. If there is no room for any more hydrogen, the fatty acid is considered saturated. Monounsaturated fats have room for two hydrogen atoms on the chain, and polyunsaturated fats have more than two "slots" open.

Monounsaturated fats appear to raise levels of high-density lipoprotein (HDL) in the blood. Sometimes called "good cholesterol," HDL is associated with reduced health risks for circulatory diseases. Olive oil, canola oil, and some nut oils are monounsaturated. Brazil nuts, cashews, avocados, and pumpkin seeds are high in monounsaturated fats.

Polyunsaturated fats, like monounsaturated fats, are associated with reduced health risks and are liquid at room temperature. Cooking oils made from corn, safflower, sunflower, and soybeans are polyunsaturated. Omega-3 and omega-6 fatty acids are polyunsaturated (see table below).

Saturated fats can cause elevated levels of low-density lipoprotein (LDL) in the blood. (They also may cause high-density lipoprotein, or HDL, levels to rise, which can balance the high LDL to a certain extent.) Usually solid at room temperature, saturated fats include butter, lard, and other animal-based fats, as well as tropical oils such as coconut, palm, and palm kernel.

Trans fats are also usually solid at room temperature, and they can cause levels of LDL to increase—but unlike saturated fats, trans fats cause levels of HDL to decrease as well. They may also be carcinogenic. Trans fats are formed when liquid oils are processed into solids like shortening or margarine. Additional hydrogen atoms bond alongside the carbon atoms. This increases the smoke point of the fat and improves its shelf life, making trans fats a popular choice for commercial baked goods and frying.

Essential Fatty Acids

There are twenty fatty acids in the human body, and they are made from two: linoleic acid, also known as omega-6 fatty acid, and linolenic acid, also called omega-3 fatty acid. In addition to the functions below, these fatty acids are crucial in producing prostaglandins, hormone-like substances that control pain and inflammation, allergic reactions, and blood clotting; help to regulate blood pressure; and are used in making hormones.

ESSENTIAL FATTY ACID	FUNCTION	SOURCE
OMEGA-3	Reduces risk of heart attack by lowering the amount of cholesterol manufactured by the liver. Helps to prevent blood clots from forming in deposits of arterial plaque. May slow or prevent growth of tumors, stimulate the immune system, and lower blood pressure.	Fatty fish including mackerel, salmon, trout, anchovies, albacore tuna, and sardines; walnuts; canola, soy, and flaxseed oils
OMEGA-6	Reduces the risk of cardiovascular disease by lowering total and LDL cholesterol. May also reduce HDL cholesterol levels.	All polyunsaturated foods; corn, soy, and safflower oil

MANY EXPERTS RECOMMEND limiting fats to 30 or so percent of calories, but what often gets lost in communication is that this is over the course of a day, and could even be averaged over a few days. It does not mean that only foods that get 30 percent or less of their calories from fat should be eaten.

For example, salmon can vary considerably in fat content depending on where and when it is caught, but it typically gets at least 40 percent of its calories from fat—far above the 30 percent limit. Top the salmon with a fruit salsa and serve it with a whole-grain pilaf that's virtually fat free and some lightly sautéed vegetables, and the calories from fat can drop to 20 or 25 percent for the meal.

Cholesterol

Cholesterol is not a fat: It has no calories. It is a fat-related compound in the lipid family. Although cholesterol is essential to good health, it is not an essential nutrient because our bodies produce all the cholesterol we need. Cholesterol can be measured in two ways: in our blood (serum cholesterol) and in our foods (dietary cholesterol). Dietary cholesterol is found in animal foods. (Cholesterol does not exist in plant foods.)

The liver manufactures about 1,000 milligrams of cholesterol every day. Cholesterol protects nerves, produces vitamin D on the skin when exposed to sunlight, and is an important building block in the manufacture of hormones.

Cholesterol is transported throughout the body by lipoproteins in the bloodstream. Low-density lipoproteins (LDL) carry cholesterol from the liver to the body's cells, but they are not very efficient and also tend to "drop" cholesterol. These deposits, called plaque, may build up on the walls of arteries and blood vessels and eventually block them, obstructing the flow of blood. This can cause a condition called atherosclerosis, which can lead to coronary and cerebral thrombosis and embolisms. Plaque buildup happens gradually. It isn't until arteries are about 75 percent blocked that symptoms like chest pain or shortness of breath occur.

High-density lipoproteins (HDL) transport cholesterol from the body's cells back to the liver, where it is broken down and flushed out of the body or reassembled into other compounds. HDLs also "sweep up" the cholesterol in the bloodstream that LDLs have dropped, so high levels of HDL indicate a reduced health risk, whereas very low levels can leave cholesterol in the blood rather than ferrying it to the liver for removal.

Eating a diet high in cholesterol does not always translate into high levels of serum cholesterol. For most people, diets high in saturated fats and trans fats have a more direct impact on serum cholesterol levels. However, dietary cholesterol is found in animal products, which tend to be higher in saturated fats than plant foods. For this reason, it is recommended that the daily intake of dietary cholesterol not exceed 300 milligrams.

Studies show that people who eat more monounsaturated fat than saturated fat have lower serum cholesterol levels and lower incidences of heart disease. When total fat consumption is limited to 30 percent of daily calories and most of the fats consumed are monounsaturated, there appears to be a positive effect on HDL levels. Polyunsaturated fats have also been linked to lower serum cholesterol levels, but in large amounts they may also lower HDL, which can be detrimental.

Noncaloric Nutrients

There are some components of food that are essential to good nutrition but that do not supply calories: water, vitamins, and minerals.

Water

The adult human body is nearly 60 percent water. Water contains no calories and is not a significant source of nutrients, but without it humans can survive for only a few days. Water can be found in every cell in the human body and is critical to the body's chemical reactions. Water also:

- Dissolves water-soluble vitamins, minerals, and other compounds to transport them to each cell via the bloodstream
- Removes impurities from the bloodstream and the body
- Cushions joints, organs, and sensitive tissues such as the spinal cord
- Maintains pressure on the eyes' optic nerves for proper vision
- Stabilizes blood pressure
- Regulates body temperature

We typically lose about two to three quarts of water, or anywhere from 8 to 12 cups of water, each day as our bodies use it to cleanse and cool processes. When the weather is hot or humid, or during strenuous exercise, our need for fluids increases. We must replenish the water we lose every day because the body does not store excess water.

Most recommendations suggest a minimum of 8 glasses of water per day. It is possible to consider some of the foods we eat as a surprisingly good source of water. Some foods supply little to no water—vegetable oil is 100 percent fat and supplies no water, and other dense foods like nuts, honey, raisins, and Cheddar cheese are less than one-third water. Would you guess, though, that roast beef and chicken are two-thirds water? They are. And fruits and vegetables are all extremely good sources of water as well. Broccoli and carrots, for example, are comparable in water content to milk.

Fluids other than water can also contribute to the daily requirement. Milk and juice are adequate sources, and it appears that caffeinated beverages may be as well. People were told that caffeinated drinks didn't count because they were thought to cause a diuretic effect and could actually increase your body's need for additional water. A small study of eighteen adults demonstrated that there was no statistical difference in hydration levels when water or caffeinated beverages were consumed. Because this study was preliminary, it makes sense to moderate consumption of caffeinated and alcoholic beverages, since both are diuretics.

Our bodies also produce water through metabolic functions—about one cup a day. For most individuals, drinking eight glasses of water can be a challenge. A more reasonable, but still appropriate, goal of five or six cups of liquid in the form of water or other nonalcoholic beverages takes into account the three to four cups of water that foods with a high water content provide.

Vitamins and Minerals

Like water, vitamins and minerals do not supply calories. Although they are important to overall health, they are generally required in smaller quantities than energy-providing nutrients. Recommended Daily Values (DVs) have been established for many of the vitamins

DEPENDING ON YOUR SOURCE OF INFORMATION, you may have heard that fiber is good for you or that it has no effect on health. You may have heard that low-fat diets are the key to reducing cancer and heart disease or that the amount of fat you eat doesn't matter. And you will read in this chapter that caffeinated beverages might or might not increase dehydration.

Studies on human nutrition tend to be inconclusive at best and flawed at worst. They are rarely done in a carefully controlled laboratory setting, but instead rely on subjects' memories of what they consumed and when. It is often difficult to control for genetic or lifestyle factors that may affect results.

A study might show that people who eat whole grains have lower rates of diabetes and heart disease. But people who eat whole grains regularly might be more likely to get regular exercise, eat more fruits and vegetables, and have more nutrient-dense diets in general than those who don't consume whole grains regularly; and they may also be less likely to drink to excess or to smoke. Further studies would need to be done to screen out these other factors.

There are a few things to look for when evaluating research studies. Look for larger studies that are not underwritten by private organizations that may have an interest in the results. Those that are double-blind (where neither the researchers nor the subjects know the control group or the makeup of the test) usually give more accurate results.

and minerals known to be important to good health. These are listed in the Appendix (page 536–539).

Daily Values are the amounts listed on Nutrition Facts labels of packaged food, and they are based on the standard 2,000-calorie diet. They are not necessarily the amount a person needs to prevent disease or to enjoy or maintain health. The Dietary Reference Intake (DRI) for a food is based on age and gender and gives the amount each subgroup requires.

The DV for calcium, for example, is 1,000 milligrams. If a Nutrition Facts label says that one cup of yogurt supplies 35 percent of the DV for calcium, that food contains 350 milligrams. Not everyone needs only 1,000 milligrams of this mineral, though. Adolescents and young adults should get at least 1,300 milligrams, and people over fifty need at least 1,200. For them, that cup of yogurt supplies only 27 percent or 29 percent of the DV of calcium.

Water-Soluble Vitamins

Water-soluble vitamins dissolve in water and are easily transported throughout the body in the bloodstream. These vitamins include the B-complex vitamins (thiamin, riboflavin, niacin, folacin, biotin, pantothenic acid, B6, and B12) and vitamin C. B-complex vitamins are found in grains, legumes, vegetables, meats, and fortified cereals. They perform many functions: thiamin, riboflavin, niacin, and B6 are used in metabolizing nutrients; B12, which is found only in animal foods, is used to synthesize amino acids and in the formation of blood; folacin, also called folate (when it occurs naturally in foods) and folic acid (when it is synthetic), is used in blood formation and amino acid metabolism.

Deficiencies of the B-complex vitamins can range from reduced stamina and insomnia to nervous system damage, liver damage, ulcers, and death. Insufficient folacin is the most common vitamin deficiency and has been linked to birth defects such as spina bifida.

Vitamin C is found in fruits and vegetables. Although oranges are practically synonymous with vitamin C, they are not the richest source: guava, strawberries, broccoli, and red bell peppers supply more per serving. Vitamin C performs hundreds of functions in the body: It increases the body's absorption of iron and is imperative to the growth and maintenance of body tissues. Vitamin C is used to produce collagen, a protein substance that helps hold tissues together, like muscles to bone or teeth to gums. Vitamin C also boosts the immune system and has antioxidant properties that protect cells from damage caused by oxygen. It may also protect against heart disease and cancer.

The Exercise Equation

NUTRITION IS CRITICAL TO GOOD HEALTH, but it is by no means the only aspect. Regular physical activity makes an important contribution to our health and well-being, and can help to maintain a healthy body weight.

Physical activity doesn't have to be strenuous to provide benefits—in the USDA's Dietary Guidelines it is defined as "any bodily movement produced by skeletal muscles resulting in any expenditure of energy." People who are physically fit are at a lower risk for developing a host of diseases. Most people in the United States lead a sedentary lifestyle, and that can increase their risks for overweight and obesity, hypertension, Type II diabetes, osteoporosis, heart disease, and even some forms of cancer. Physical activity may also help to manage mild to moderate depression and anxiety.

So how much exercise do people need? That depends on goals.

- To reduce the risk of disease, 30 minutes of moderate-intensity activity most days a week is enough, but greater benefits come with longer sessions or with more vigorous activity.

- To manage weight and prevent weight gain related to aging and a slowing metabolism, 60 minutes of moderate- to vigorous-intensity exercise most days of the week is recommended.

- To sustain weight loss, engage in 60 to 90 minutes of moderate-intensity exercise most days of the week.

This activity should be above and beyond normal daily activities. Examples of moderate-intensity activities include hiking, dancing, gardening or yard work, golf (when you walk and carry clubs), bicycling at a rate of 10 miles or less per hour, walking at a rate of 3.5 miles per hour, light weight lifting, and stretching. Vigorous-intensity exercise includes jogging or running, swimming, bicycling at a rate of more than 10 miles per hour, walking at a rate of 4.5 miles per hour, aerobics, heavy yard work (such as chopping wood), vigorous weight lifting, and playing basketball.

Exercise can also help to meet nutrient needs. The more active a person is, the more calories he or she requires, and the easier it is to ensure that a wide variety of nutrient-rich foods is eaten.

A small amount of water-soluble vitamins can be stored briefly in lean tissue, such as muscles and organs, but the body's supplies must be replenished daily. Toxic levels of these vitamins are possible but unlikely because any excess is excreted from the body.

Water-soluble vitamins can be affected by ordinary food-handling techniques and cooking methods. B vitamins are somewhat more stable than vitamin C, but both can be lost through:

- **Exposure to air** (removing peels, cutting foods, or storing food uncovered)
- **Heat** (cooking or storing at room temperature)
- **Exposure to water** (rinsing cut foods before they are cooked, cooking foods in water, holding foods in water)
- **Time** (as foods age, they lose moisture and, along with the moisture, vitamins)

To retain water-soluble vitamins, observe the following recommendations:

- Keep cooking times to a minimum.
- Cook foods in as little water as possible, or choose a dry-heat technique like roasting.
- Prepare foods as close to their time of service as possible.
- Purchase foods in reasonable amounts to avoid prolonged storage.

Fat-Soluble Vitamins

Vitamins A, D, E, and K are fat-soluble—they are stored in fat tissues and, once ingested, cannot be easily flushed from the body. In the proper amounts, fat-soluble vitamins are basic to health, but exceeding the DVs for these vitamins can cause them to build up in the body, making it easy for toxic levels to accumulate. Once toxic levels are reached, a variety of dangerous and even fatal conditions may develop. These vary by vitamin, but kidney stones, nerve damage, and abnormal bone growth are just a few.

Fat-soluble vitamins are far more stable than water-soluble ones. They cannot be destroyed by contact with air or water, and are less affected by heat than water-soluble vitamins are. Some fat-soluble vitamins increase in bioavailablity when they are heated. Carotenoids such as lycopene in tomatoes and beta carotene in carrots are more available to the body after cooking. Cooking breaks down cellular walls, and it concentrates these nutrients.

The type of vitamin A present in animal foods is called retinol. Beef and chicken liver are excellent sources, as are fortified dairy products. Vitamin A itself is not found in plant foods, but beta carotene, a phytochemical that the body uses to produce vitamin A, is found in orange and deep yellow vegetables such as squash, sweet potatoes, and carrots, as well as in dark green leafy vegetables (the orange pigment is hidden by the chlorophyll these foods contain) like kale, collards, and spinach. Beta carotene cannot be quickly converted to vitamin A, so it is difficult for toxic levels to be reached. Excess beta carotene may, however, cause a person to appear jaundiced because the pigment is stored in fat layers just beneath the skin.

Vitamin D is responsible for proper bone formation. It works in concert with calcium and phosphorus and helps the body use these minerals. A deficiency of vitamin D causes rickets, a condition in which the bones grow abnormally. Vitamin D is present in foods such as fish-liver oils and egg yolks, as well as in fortified milk and cereals. The skin, when exposed to sunlight, produces vitamin D from cholesterol. Ten to fifteen minutes per day is often enough. People with limited exposure to sunlight may need to get the amounts needed through fortified foods or supplements. The body's ability to manufacture vitamin D declines with age, so people over age sixty should consider supplementation.

The USDA is currently reviewing its recommendations concerning appropriate levels of vitamin D in our diets. Recent studies show that our diets are deficient in this vitamin. Debate is under way concerning what we should consume on a daily basis. Some experts have suggested more than doubling the current DV.

Vitamin E, like vitamin C, is an antioxidant that protects the body from oxygen damage and may have cancer-fighting potential. It is found in a variety of foods, especially whole grains and nuts. It is usually not difficult to obtain adequate vitamin E with a healthy and varied diet, but followers of extremely low-fat diets may be deficient.

Vitamin K is associated with proper formation of blood clots and makes a protein that is necessary for strong bones. Although it is produced by bacteria found in the intestines, a person who eats a varied diet obtains about half of the DV from food, particularly dark green leafy vegetables. Those who take anticoagulants should avoid foods high in vitamin K because it can interfere with the action of these drugs.

MACROMINERALS

Calcium, magnesium, sodium, and potassium are called macrominerals because they are required in relatively large amounts. Calcium is the most abundant mineral in the body.

THREE MINERALS ARE CALLED ELECTROLYTES: sodium, chloride, and potassium. There are no minimum requirements for sodium or chloride. Because these two combine to make table salt, they are usually eaten in sufficient amounts.

Electrolytes transmit nerve impulses, regulate fluids in cells, and help balance body fluids, including blood and blood pressure. Deficiencies are rare but may result from illnesses whose symptoms include diarrhea and nausea, or from extreme water loss such as that experienced by performance athletes or people who work outdoors on hot humid days. Sodium deficiencies result in loss of appetite, muscle cramps, confusion, and forgetfulness. Potassium deficiencies result in weakness, falling blood pressure, and confusion.

Most athletes and people with normal amounts of physical activity are able to replace the electrolytes from the foods they normally eat, and restore fluid balance by drinking water to quench their thirst. Performance athletes and workers like roofers or road construction crews, may need to go out of their way to eat foods that are high in salt, such as pretzels or soda crackers. Sport drinks may also help to speed rehydration.

Ninety-nine percent of the calcium needed by the body is used in the development of bones and teeth; the remaining 1 percent is used to regulate blood pressure and to aid in muscle contractions, transmit nerve impulses, and clot the blood. A deficiency in calcium may cause stunted growth and a loss of bone density. Because the body requires so much calcium, excess calcium in the body is rare unless supplements are taken. Good sources of calcium include dairy products such as milk and yogurt, leafy greens such as collards and turnip greens, and canned fish with bones. Many foods are now fortified with calcium, including orange juice and cereal.

Phosphorus is used by the body in conjunction with calcium to maintain bone and tooth structure; it is also integral to releasing energy from food for the body to use. Deficiencies in this mineral are rare, but may result in weakness, decreased heart function, and neurological problems. Phosphorus is present in animal protein, nuts, cereals, and legumes.

Magnesium is used for bone and tooth structure, muscle contraction, nerve transmission, and bowel function. Too little magnesium can cause possible growth failure, behavioral disturbances, tremors, weakness, and seizures. The U.S. diet tends to be deficient in magnesium. Good sources include green vegetables, nuts, legumes, and whole grains.

Sodium and potassium are known as electrolytes. These are essential to regulating bodily functions, helping to maintain the balance of fluid in the body, and they are involved in nerve and muscle functions. Both are plentiful in food so dietary deficiencies are uncommon.

Diets that are high in sodium may aggravate pre-existing hypertension (high blood pressure) in people who suffer from this condition, but sodium does not appear to cause high blood pressure. Most experts recommend that healthy adults limit sodium consumption to 2,300 to 2,400 milligrams per day, or about a third less than what the typical adult consumes.

Salt performs many important culinary functions, and one of them is to enhance the flavor of foods. It may be tempting for a chef to limit salting during the cooking process, but this may backfire: if foods are not salted enough in the kitchen, customers may react by adding salt at the table—and often more salt after cooking is needed to attain the same level of flavor enhancement than if salting is done throughout cooking. At the same time, a chef may have built up a tolerance to salty flavors, and may add more salt during the cooking process than customers prefer.

Adequate potassium has been linked to lower blood pressure levels and reduced risk of stroke and heart disease. This mineral is widely available in foods. Bananas have a reputation for being a rich source, but they have almost half the amount of a baked potato. Avocados, white beans, yogurt, and tomato and orange juices are also good sources.

Nutraceuticals vs. Functional Foods

NUTRACEUTICALS ARE FOODS OR SUBSTANCES IN FOODS that provide health benefits, including preventing or treating diseases; vitamins, minerals, and phytochemicals can be considered nutraceuticals. Some foods come by their medical benefits naturally—oatmeal doesn't need to have substances added to it to help reduce cholesterol levels. Other foods may be enriched, enhanced, or engineered. Medicinal plants or herbs added to sport bars or soft drinks, compounds called stanols added to margarines to reduce blood cholesterol levels, or vitamins and minerals added to bread, cereals, and pastas are all examples of fortifications to food.

The phrase "enriched with eight essential vitamins and minerals" has been around so long that many of us do not think twice about how enriched foods first came about. The story of their origin began in 1936, when a survey revealed that the incidence of deficiency diseases resulting from inadequate supplies of certain nutrients was increasing. Until that time, whole wheat bread had supplied the majority of the daily requirements of iron, thiamin, niacin, riboflavin, magnesium, zinc, vitamin B6, folacin, and dietary fiber. With the advent of improved milling machinery, it became possible to make a whiter, smoother flour that produced a softer white bread. Unfortunately, highly refined flours lose significant amounts of nutrients. Niacin levels in unenriched white bread, for example, are only 2 percent of those found in whole-grain bread.

As white bread became cheap and readily available, the demand for whole-grain breads dropped. The prevalence of deficiencies made it obvious that something needed to be done to boost people's nutrient supply. The Enrichment Act of 1942 required enrichment of all grain products, including cereals, pastas, and breads, that were brought across state lines. Iron, thiamin, niacin, and riboflavin levels are required to be close to what they had been in the whole-grain versions.

As of January 1, 1998, an amendment to the law also requires that folic acid, a B vitamin shown to prevent birth defects, must be added. Other nutrients are added as part of the enrichment process, but it is not mandatory that their levels be raised to match those in whole-grain foods. There is no requirement for replacing dietary fiber.

Today, nutrition modification is going beyond fortifying foods with nutrients lost in processing. Foods are now fortified with nutrients they have never supplied. Orange juice, for example, may be fortified with calcium or with vitamins E and A as well as extra vitamin C. Hens are fed special diets high in flax, and the eggs they lay are rich in omega-3 fatty acids and somewhat lower in cholesterol than eggs from hens fed a traditional diet.

Enriched products are certainly a better nutritional bargain than unenriched, bleached, and refined ones. However, they are no match for whole grains. Replacing some of the nutrients does not make the product nutritionally complete, even if the label claims that a cereal offers 100 percent of eight or ten essential nutrients. The possible side effects from a diet that relies heavily upon highly processed grains and flours are still coming to light as scientists and researchers uncover more about the special roles played by each nutrient.

MICROMINERALS

Fluoride, iodine, and iron are known as trace minerals or microminerals because they are needed in minute amounts. Fluoride helps prevent tooth decay and may play a role in preventing osteoporosis. Many community water supplies contain fluoride. This mineral is also present in saltwater fish, shellfish, and tea.

Iodine is essential for the normal functioning of the thyroid gland, and it helps to regulate energy metabolism, cellular oxidation, and growth. Iodine is found most abundantly in saltwater fish and some dairy products; its content in fruits and vegetables depends on the soil they are grown in. A deficiency of iodine results in goiter, or enlargement of the thyroid gland. Since the early 1900s, when goiter was common in the midwestern United States, iodine has been added to table salt (iodized salt) to eliminate this deficiency.

Iron is a component of hemoglobin, the part of the red blood cells that carries oxygen from the lungs to the cells. About 75 percent of the body's iron is found in the blood. The remaining iron functions as a component of myoglobin, the oxygen-supplying molecule found in muscles, as part of certain enzymes involved in cellular energy metabolism. Iron deficiencies are a worldwide health problem, particularly for women of childbearing age, and cause a form of anemia in which blood cells lack sufficient hemoglobin. Someone who is anemic may appear pale and feel weak; they will also have an impaired immune system. The best food sources of iron are liver and red meat, but it is also found in whole grains, legumes, green leafy vegetables, dried fruit, and egg yolks.

Units of Measure for Daily Values of Vitamins and Minerals

GRAM (G)	The equivalent of ⅟₂₈ of an ounce. Few vitamins and minerals are measured in grams.
MILLIGRAM (MG)	One thousandth of a gram. The majority of vitamins and minerals are measured in milligrams.
MICROGRAM (µg)	One millionth of a gram. Folacin, vitamin B12, and vitamin A are measured in micrograms.

Phytochemicals and Antioxidants

Phytochemicals are compounds that occur naturally in plant foods such as fruits, vegetables, legumes, and grains, (phyto- is from the Greek word for plant). Like vitamins, they occur naturally, but unlike vitamins, they have not yet been recognized as essential. There are no deficiency levels or Daily Values yet determined for phytochemicals.

The study of phytochemicals is a very new science, and although it is tempting to take supplements of specific phytochemicals that appear to provide specific health benefits, this isn't always wise. The best way to capitalize on the benefits of phytochemicals is to eat a wide variety of fruits, vegetables, grains, and legumes.

Every plant food appears to have a different mix of phytochemicals that work in concert with each other, as well as with vitamins and minerals, hormones, and other compounds to provide health benefits. Tomatoes, for example, contain more than 100 phytochemicals. Researchers are continuing to identify the compounds in foods and their role in good health and proper nutrition.

Phytochemicals include flavonoids, which impart flavor (such as the sulfur compounds in onions or the capsaicin in peppers) and pigments (beta carotene and lycopene are carotenoid pigments; anthocyanin is a pigment that gives red cabbage and berries their deep red-to-purple hue). In general, phytochemicals seem to function in a combination of three ways: some have antioxidant properties, some affect hormone levels, and some change enzymes that may eliminate carcinogens. Phytochemicals like digitalis and quinine have been used for medical purposes for centuries; their anticancer effects are only beginning to be explored.

Antioxidants are a subcategory of phytochemicals. They are essential for combating the cellular damage caused by free radicals, which are reactive forms of oxygen produced by the body's metabolic processes. Free radicals are present in particularly great quantities during times of stress, illness, exposure to toxins, and are even a natural by-product of exercise.

Antioxidants include vitamins A, C, and E, the mineral selenium, and carotenoid pigments. More than 600 carotenoids are found in nature, and about fifty of these may be used by the body. Lycopene, found in watermelon and cooked tomatoes, is one type of carotenoid used by the body. Lutein and zeaxanthin, xanthophylls found in corn and in leafy greens such as kale and spinach, also types of carotenoids, are believed to protect the macular area of the eye. These antioxidants in general seem to interfere with the growth of cancer cells and may reduce the risk of some cancers.

One of the most intriguing aspects of phytochemicals for the cook is that they are associated with specific flavors in foods, from the pungency of onions (allyl sulfides) to the heat in chiles (capsaicin) to the sharp aromas of pine in some herbs (terpense).

Phytochemicals

PHYTOCHEMICAL FAMILY	FOOD SOURCE	POSSIBLE HEALTH BENEFIT
ALLYL SULFIDES	Onions, garlic, leeks, chives	Increase enzymes that affect cancer-causing substances and aid in their elimination from the body
CAPSAICIN	Chiles	Appears to prevent blood clotting; may interfere with development of cancer cells
CATECHINS	Apples, dark chocolate, grapes, raspberries, red wine, tea	May reduce the risk of cancers and help to prevent buildup of plaque on arterial walls
INDOLES	Cruciferous vegetables (kale, broccoli, cabbage, cauliflower)	Stimulate enzymes; make estrogen less effective, possibly reducing breast cancer risks
ISOFLAVONES	Soybeans (tofu, soymilk, soy nuts)	Inhibit cancer cell growth and division under some conditions
ISOTHIOCYANATES	Cruciferous vegetables	Protect against cancer through their effects on enzymes
PHENOLIC ACIDS (ELLAGIC ACID, FERULIC ACID)	Tomatoes, citrus fruits, carrots, nuts, strawberries, raspberries, whole grains, pomegranates	Reduce the genetic damage caused by carcinogens like tobacco smoke and air pollution
POLYPHENOLS	Green tea, grapes, wine	Help to prevent cancer
QUERCETIN	Apples, berries, red onions, red and purple grapes, tea, tomatoes	Antioxidant that may prevent some kinds of cancer; also may help to maintain beneficial levels of serum cholesterol and prevent cell damage
RESVERATROL	Grapes, especially the skins; red wine, peanuts	Inhibit all three stages of carcinogenesis (tumor initiation, promotion, and progression); lower serum cholesterol levels
SAPONINS	Beans, legumes	Prevent cancer cells from multiplying by influencing the genetic material in the cells
TERPENES (PERILLYL ALCOHOL, LIMONENE)	Cherries, citrus peel, lavender	Block development of breast tumors; cause existing tumors to regress

WALK INTO ANY HEALTH FOOD STORE
and you'll see what a huge business vitamin and mineral supplements are. But is it necessary—or even advisable—to get nutrients from a pill?

If a person eats a balanced diet that includes a variety of foods, supplements probably aren't necessary. While some health conditions may indicate the need for vitamin and mineral supplements, currently no strong evidence supports the claim that supplements provide real benefits to individuals who are in good health and who eat properly. And supplements probably won't counteract or correct health problems brought about by poor nutrition.

In fact, taking indiscriminate megadoses of vitamins and minerals can be risky. Toxic levels caused by overdosing can lead to a number of health problems, including nausea, depression, even death. And virtually all instances of toxic levels of vitamins are caused by supplementation.

There are situations where supplementation is warranted. Vitamin B12 is found only in animal foods. Vegetarians who eat dairy and eggs may obtain some, but they, and vegans, should consider taking supplemental B12, as should people over the age of fifty. The body's ability to absorb vitamin B12 declines with age. And the body's ability to synthesize vitamin D also declines significantly with age: seventy-year-olds produce about 30 percent of what people in their twenties do. People who are over sixty, who live in northern climates where the sun sets early in the winter, or who are housebound should also consider supplementing their diets. Women who may become pregnant should discuss folic acid supplements with their health care practitioner; this B vitamin has been shown to reduce some birth defects.

Assessing Foods Based Upon Nutrient or Calorie Density

Different foods contain different nutrients. The foods we choose to eat may be a rich source of a wide array of essential nutrients. Whole, minimally processed foods fall into this category. A steady diet of highly processed foods, on the other hand, can leave us shortchanged on certain important nutrients. When our nutrition needs are not met, our chances of developing diseases or chronic health conditions, including hypertension, heart disease, diabetes, osteoporosis, gingivitis, and even some types of cancer increase.

Foods that have a good supply of essential nutrients in relation to the number of calories they contain are considered *nutrient-dense*. Fruits and vegetables, lean meats and skinless poultry, low-fat dairy products, and whole grains supply a great deal of nutrients and are fairly low in calories, thus they are all nutrient-dense.

Foods that supply a great deal of calories per serving are considered *calorie-dense*. Nuts, for example, are a very concentrated source of calories and other nutrients. Foods with little or no nutritional value in relation to their caloric content are said to have *empty calories*. Alcoholic beverages, soda, breakfast pastries, desserts, and jams and jellies are examples of foods with empty calories.

Dietary Guidelines and Recommendations

If you find the amount of information in this chapter daunting, you're not alone. Translating all that information into balanced, nutritious menus for people who are in good health is a challenging task. Add diseases or health conditions like diabetes, high blood pressure, or heart disease to the mix, and it's easy to be overwhelmed.

Dietary guidelines can help simplify choosing the right foods and provide general recommendations for the total diet. They are issued by recognized governmental or private health organizations such as the United States Department of Agriculture, the American Diabetes Association, the Joslin Diabetes Center, the American Heart Association, the American Cancer Society, and the American Dietetic Association. Weight-loss companies may also sell eating plans to their customers.

As scientists learn more about the relationship between foods and well-being, various health organizations are able to make recommendations about which foods may be the most beneficial sources of calories and nutrients. These recommendations can address specific health conditions and diseases, allergies, and weight loss goals, and they can be adapted for food preferences.

The majority of these recommendations take the form of eating plans or dietary guidelines. Most group foods into categories, and a number of servings from each group is to be eaten every day or week. The groups may go by different names, but they typically are fruits, vegetables, breads and cereals, milk and milk products, and meat and meat alternatives. Some guidelines provide information for food quantities by weight, by piece, or by serving; others by a percentage of calories.

Grains and grain-based foods such as pasta, rice, cereals, and bread, as well as fruits and vegetables, usually comprise the bulk of the recommended daily food choices. The vegetable group is sometimes divided into subgroups based on color, with recommendations for dark green leafy vegetables, orange vegetables, legumes, starchy vegetables, and a catchall group of other vegetables. Some eating plans group starchy vegetables, such as potatoes, carrots, turnips, and beets, with starchy foods like grains. Legumes supply protein and complex carbohydrates, and different eating plans may group them in either category.

Foods like fats, oils, and sweets are included in some guidelines, typically with the recommendation that they can be added at an individual's discretion. These *discretionary calories* are usually small in portion and limited in amount, and if an individual is trying to lose weight, they should be among the first to be reduced.

The USDA Dietary Guidelines

Every five years, the United States Department of Agriculture (USDA) revises the Dietary Guidelines for Americans based on the latest medical and scientific findings. Although these guidelines are meant to address personal lifestyle and dietary choices, chefs and other culinary professionals use them to develop menus and recipes that meet the needs and requirements of their guests.

The Dietary Guidelines released in 2005 recommend that carbohydrates should supply 45 to 65 percent of the total daily calories, and fat should supply 20 to 35 percent; protein should contribute the balance. The ranges given are generous enough to allow for cultural and other preferences.

The Guidelines recognize that some foods are more nutrient-dense than others, and the USDA has created a pyramid that provides general information on distribution of calories. Grains, vegetables, fruits, and low-fat dairy are the wider bars of the pyramid; the Guidelines recommend choosing more whole grains and orange and dark green vegetables, and limiting fruit juices. The narrower bars indicate lean proteins and fats, with the recommendation that most fats come from fish, nuts, and vegetable oils. The number of recommended servings within each food group varies depending upon the number of calories an individual should consume each day.

The Dietary Guidelines for Americans 2005 is available as an eighty-page document online (www.healthierus.gov/dietaryguidelines). It provides a wealth of information, including recommendations for specific population groups, from infants to the elderly, as well as groups that are at risk for developing certain diseases or conditions. It addresses weight management, physical fitness, balancing a diet to ensure adequate nutrients, how to choose the most nutrient-rich sources of fats and carbohydrates, limiting sodium and alcoholic beverages, and food safety.

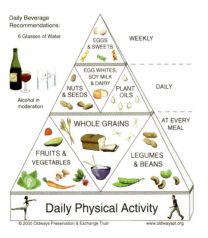

Other Dietary Pyramids

After the USDA first developed its Food Guide Pyramid in 1991, other organizations developed pyramid models of traditional cuisines or of diets for special population groups. Oldways Preservation & Exchange Trust, in conjunction with the Harvard School of Public Health, developed Asian, Latin American, and vegetarian pyramids. The American Dietetic Association has pyramids for vegetarians, older citizens, and children, as well as pyramids modeled on the cuisines of India, China, Italy, Mexico, and several North American cultures. The American Diabetic Association has developed a pyramid as well.

The Mediterranean pyramid represents a diet based on the traditional diets of Greece and southern Italy—areas where people once had the world's lowest rates of heart disease, obesity, and hypertension. Foods rich in carbohydrates make up the bulk of meals, and fruits, vegetables, legumes, and nuts round out the daily diet. Olive oil is the principal source of fat, and cheeses and yogurt are the most common dairy foods. Although these may be high in fat, they are rich in nutrients, so moderate amounts are justified. Fish, poultry, eggs, and sweets are consumed a few times a week, and red meats are eaten only a few times a month.

If your clientele includes a significant number of vegetarians, you may wish to consult a vegetarian pyramid. Several organizations have developed them; the American Dietetic Association's is based on an earlier version of the USDA's Food Guide Pyramid. The main difference is that dried beans, nuts, seeds, peanut butter, and soy products replace meat, fish, and poultry.

Dietary Recommendations for Special Needs

General dietary recommendations are meant to give guidance to individuals who are in generally good health. However, the demands that certain health conditions make of the body may call for more specific eating plans.

Diabetes

For years, people with diabetes were told to avoid foods that contained sugar. Simple carbohydrates were thought to have a greater impact on blood sugar levels than complex carbohydrates. (Soluble fiber slows the rate of digestion, so although all carbohydrates will cause blood sugar levels to increase, eating a meal that includes soluble fiber will cause them to rise more slowly.) Current research indicates that the source of carbohydrates doesn't matter as much as the amount of them. Diabetics are now taught to balance their daily allotment of carbohydrates in each meal and snack while keeping blood sugar under control.

There is no specific "diabetic diet," but the Joslin Diabetes Center offers the following recommendations:

- Keep carbohydrates to 40 percent of total calories per day, and aim for 20 to 35 grams of fiber. The best high-fiber sources are fresh vegetables, fruits, beans, and whole grains.

- Protein should comprise 20 to 30 percent of the day's calories, unless a person has kidney disease.

- Fats should be 30 to 35 percent of the total calories per day, and most fats should be monounsaturated or polyunsaturated.

The Joslin Diabetes Center also encourages a minimum of two and one half to three hours of moderate-intensity exercise every week.

The American Diabetes Association has also created a pyramid for diabetics. Unlike the USDA's pyramid, it groups foods by nutrient content rather than type of food. Potatoes and legumes are grouped with grains and other starches, and cheese is grouped with meats and other proteins rather than with milk. Portion sizes for some carbohydrates are also smaller than in the USDA's Dietary Guidelines, to ensure that carbohydrate counts are consistent.

The Mayo Clinic's recommendations for diabetic calorie distribution allows for 50 to 60 percent of calories from carbohydrates and 15 to 20 percent from protein. Among the servings of carbohydrates, it suggests six or more servings of starches, two to four servings of fruits, two to three servings of milk or milk products, and three to five servings of vegetables, depending on calorie needs.

Hypertension

Created by the United States Department of Health and Human Services, the DASH (Dietary Approaches to Stop Hypertension) eating plan is based on the USDA's Dietary Guidelines. The DASH eating plan has been shown to reduce the likelihood of healthy people developing hypertension, and it can reduce blood pressure levels in people who are hypertensive.

Sodium and high blood pressure are linked. Most people in the United States consume about 3,300 milligrams of sodium per day, far more than the 2,300 to 2,400 most experts recommend. Reducing sodium to this level can bring high blood pressure to healthy levels, and reducing sodium to 1,500 milligrams can reduce it even more.

The DASH eating plan is based on 2,000 calories per day and gives two levels of daily sodium consumption: 2,400 or 1,500 milligrams. It is based on the USDA's Dietary Guidelines, but the amounts of foods to be eaten are given in number of servings, not percentages.

Grains should comprise the bulk of the diet, with 7 to 8 servings per day. Four to 5 servings each of fruits and vegetables and 2 to 3 servings each of low-fat dairy and fats are also recommended. No more than 2 servings of meats, poultry, and fish should be eaten daily. Four to 5 servings per week of nuts, seeds, dried beans, and sweets are recommended.

Dietary Restrictions

Although some people view eating out as an occasion to splurge, many of your customers will not be able to relax their dietary restrictions. People with allergies or chronic digestive conditions such as celiac disease or Crohn's disease must be extremely careful in their food choices to prevent flare-ups, and research indicates that some foods may trigger migraines in people who suffer from them.

Restrictions based on personal goals, such as weight loss, and some that are health-related, such as a diabetic person watching carbohydrate intake or someone with high cholesterol keeping an eye on her saturated fat, might be somewhat more flexible than those based on allergies. But even people who might adapt the rest of their daily diet to allow for a special-occasion meal will appreciate menu choices that take their needs into consideration. Developing menus that are nutritious, balanced, and flavorful should be a priority.

Food Allergies and Intolerances

As of January 2006, all packaged foods that contain major food allergens—milk, eggs, fish, crustacean shellfish, tree nuts (such as almonds, pecans, or walnuts), wheat, peanuts, and soybeans—must have the allergens identified on the label. Foods in their natural state do not need to be labeled. However, dishes on a menu that might contain allergens should be identified, particularly if the ingredient's inclusion might not be apparent from the recipe's name. (To read more about food allergies, see pages 42–43 in Chapter 2 and consult the Recommended Resources and Readings on page 547–48.)

Nutrition Labeling

Nutrition labels contain specific information about food products. Labeling can appear on packaged goods or on menus, or the information may appear in advertisements. The content is created by the food manufacturer or restaurant, but any claims or promises used may be mandated by law.

Deciding which information to communicate to consumers concerning the nutritional content of menu items is a decision that each food-service operator must make. You have the option to say nothing at all, but you may wish to include information about the nutrition or health attributes of your food products in menus or advertising.

Nutrition Facts

Serving Size 1 cup (228g)
Servings Per Container 2

Amount Per Serving

Calories 250   Calories from Fat 110

	% Daily Value*
Total Fat 12g	18%
Saturated Fat 3g	15%
Trans Fat 3g	
Cholesterol 30mg	10%
Sodium 470mg	20%
Potassium 700mg	20%
Total Carbohydrate 31g	10%
Dietary Fiber 0g	0%
Sugars 5g	
Protein 5g	

Vitamin A	4%
Vitamin C	2%
Calcium	20%
Iron	4%

* Percent Daily Values are based on a 2,000 calorie diet. Your Daily Values may be higher or lower depending on your calorie needs.

		Calories:	2,000	2,500
Total Fat	Less than		65g	80g
Sat Fat	Less than		20g	25g
Cholesterol	Less than		300mg	300mg
Sodium	Less than		2,400mg	2,400mg
Total Carbohydrate			300g	375g
Dietary Fiber			25g	30g

Any type of nutrition claim is regulated by the FDA under the Nutrition Labeling and Education Act (NLEA) of 1990. They are updated frequently as new studies add to our share of information, so check the FDA's Web site for the most current regulations. These regulations are complex and run to more than 4,000 pages. Here is a brief overview of them as they apply to food-service operators, with a bit of background first.

A Brief History of Food Labeling in the United States

Since 1906, the U.S. government has developed legislation to inform consumers about the safety and quality of foods by requiring information on food labels. In 1969, the White House Conference on Food, Nutrition, and Health recommended that a system be developed to deliver nutrition information to consumers. For nearly two decades, nutrition labeling was largely voluntary and minimally regulated unless a food contained added nutrients or included a claim about its nutrient content or usefulness in the daily diet. Because information was inconsistent, it was difficult for consumers to make accurate comparisons.

Until fairly recently, there were no rules governing what qualified as "light" or "healthy" and the terms were used indiscriminately. Today, all of those terms have been described and defined in terms. In order to qualify for a nutrition claim, specific standards must be met. The term "light," for example, might only have meant a slight reduction in calories, fat, or sodium. Sometimes, those reductions were nothing more than a manipulation of the serving size recorded on the label. If you see the term light on a label today, you can be sure that it was compared to a reference amount. For a more complete description of nutrition and health claims, see pages 28 and 29 or refer to the Appendix on page 514.

In 1990, Congress enacted the Nutrition Labeling and Education Act (NLEA), which required that standardized nutrition information be included on packaged food labels. Terms like *fat-free*, *low-sodium*, *light*, and *healthy* were clearly defined to ensure that nutrition and health claims were used responsibly and consistently by food producers.

Restaurant menu claims were originally not included in these regulations, but two public advocacy groups, the Center for Science in the Public Interest (CSPI) and Public Citizen, filed suit in 1993 to prevent this exclusion. In 1996, the U.S. District Court issued a ruling that agreed with the plaintiffs, and the court ordered the FDA to amend its regulations. These went into effect in 1997.

How the 1997 Rules Apply to Menus and Advertising

There are several ways to let patrons know which, if any, of the dishes on your menu fit their nutrition parameters. You can describe a dish's ingredients and preparation; consumers who are watching their cholesterol might automatically avoid dishes with *crispy* or *gratinée* in their names and seek out words like *grilled* or *steamed*. You can also use phrases that give clues to nutrient levels, such as *low-fat* and *heart-healthy*.

Opinions differ about whether or not to provide nutrition information directly on a menu. Some operations prefer to make no speecific nutrition or health claims about their menu items. Others want to offer some level of guidance in a form that is familiar to their guests.

A restaurant's menu is in many ways like a label on a food package. Both sell food and convey information, but a menu is not required by the NLEA to provide nutrition information. Restaurants, of course, can choose to provide it, and if they do, the same FDA regulations that govern the language used on food packaging apply to menus and food-service operations. Restaurants and similar operations need to provide information only about specific nutrients referred to in any claim made on the menu or in advertising; they are not required to provide the same exacting nutrition profile as on packaged foods. This information can be provided in any format, but it must be readily available upon request.

Nutrient Content Claims

The FDA established a specific list of words and phrases that may be used to describe the nutrient contents of foods that fit certain criteria (see the Appendix, pages 530–535, for the list and definitions). Nearly all of the criteria are based on standard serving sizes known as *reference amounts* (these are also listed in the Appendix; they can also be found at http://www. cfsan.fda.gov/~lrd/CF101-12.HTML).

According to the FDA, three types of claims may be used to describe the nutrition profile of foods:

An *absolute claim* characterizes the exact amount or range of a nutrient in a particular food. Terms that indicate an absolute claim are *free*, *low*, *reduced*, and *less*. For example, to meet the definition of "low sodium," a food must contain 140 milligrams or less per reference amount. When an absolute claim is made in print, it is not necessary to define it, but the food must meet the established criteria. (Parameters can be found at http://www.cfsan.fda. gov/~dms/flg-6a.html.)

A *relative claim* is a statement made that compares the nutrient content of one food to another food, known as the reference food. (The reference food may be the restaurant's regular product or another restaurant's product; its nutrition values may be derived from a valid database, an average of top national or regional brands, or a market-basket norm.) Words like *reduced* and *less* can also indicate a relative claim; *reduced*, as well as *added* and *light* or *lite*, may be used to compare products that are similar (such as cookies to cookies), whereas *more* and *less* can be used to compare foods within the same category that may be substituted for one another (such as cookies for cake). Definitions of these claims do not need to be in print, but the food must meet the established criteria, including a comparison of the two foods, the percentage of the reduction, and the actual nutrient content of both foods.

Portions, Servings, and "Eating Occasions"

WHEN YOU DISCUSS AMOUNTS OF FOOD, terms like *portion* and *serving* get bandied about. Although they both indicate quantities consumed, they are not synonymous. A *serving* is a prescribed amount of food, but a *portion* is what is actually consumed. Consider soda: A 20-ounce bottle of soda features a Nutrition Facts label claiming each bottle contains 2½ servings. Often, however, the bottle is consumed in one sitting. If that happens, those 2½ servings become one portion. A 12-ounce can of soda lists Nutrition Facts for 12 ounces. In this case, the serving size and portion size are the same.

Reference amounts and *eating occasions* are terms used to determine nutrition and health claims. Reference amounts are often given in metric amounts, and they indicate the quantity of food customarily consumed. An eating occasion may be a meal, a snack, or per use. The reference amount of butter customarily consumed per eating occasion, for example, is one tablespoon; for soda, it is 240 milliliters, or 8 ounces. A more complete listing of reference amounts can be found in the Appendix, pages 541–544.

An *implied claim* is a statement that highlights the presence or absence of an ingredient that is associated with the level of a nutrient. "High in oat bran" carries the implied claim that the food is high in fiber, so any food with this claim must meet the established criteria for high-fiber foods. Other ingredient-nutrient relationships include sugar and calories, oils and total fat, tropical oils and saturated fat, and whole grains or bran and dietary fiber.

Implied claims are difficult to define and can be a source of confusion, and it can be easy to unwittingly make an implied claim. Saying a pizza is "made with low-fat cheese" implies that the pizza is at least "reduced fat" compared to a similar pizza. Such a statement would be prohibited by the FDA if the pizza failed to meet the criteria for a "reduced-fat" food.

Some statements about ingredients are not considered nutrient claims. These are general statements that pertain to ingredients that are perceived to have value (e.g., "made with fresh fruit and honey"), that do not serve nutritive purposes (e.g., "no preservatives"), or that may need to be avoided for various reasons. Additionally, statements in which the ingredient is part of the identity of a food, such as whole-wheat pasta or multigrain bread, are not considered nutrient claims.

Health Claims

A health claim defines the relationship between the nutrient content of a food and a disease or health-related condition. A nutrient content claim refers only to a level or range of a nutrient in a food, while a health claim includes two elements: A reference to the nutrient or substance, and a reference to a disease or health-related condition. Generally, a health claim must:

1. Be complete, truthful, and not misleading.
2. Use *may* or *might* to express the relationship between nutrient and disease.
3. Indicate that the risk of disease depends on many factors.

Health claims may be expressed through statements, icons or symbols, or as a vignette. The form of the claim is not important as long as all the required elements are present. Where space allows, statements may be included such as, "While many factors affect heart disease, diets low in saturated fat and cholesterol may reduce the risk of this disease. Our [recipe name] can be part of such a diet." If an abbreviated claim such as "heart-healthy" or a symbol is used, the restaurant must provide a complete explanation of the claim. It can be featured prominently in the menu or ad, or a statement directing patrons to ask their server can be used if the full claim appears in a brochure or notebook that the restaurant uses to convey nutrition information.

The FDA recognizes eleven nutrient-disease relationships that may be used in health claims:

1. Calcium and osteoporosis
2. Sodium and hypertension
3. Dietary fat and cancer
4. Dietary saturated fat and cholesterol and the risk of heart disease
5. Fiber-containing grain products, fruits, and vegetables and cancer
6. Fruits, vegetables, and grain products that contain fiber, particularly soluble fiber, and the risk of heart disease
7. Fruits and vegetables and cancer
8. Folate and neural tube defects
9. Dietary sugar alcohol and dental caries (cavities)
10. Dietary soluble fiber, such as that found in whole oats and psyllium seed husks, and risk of coronary heart disease
11. Soy protein and risk of coronary heart disease

In order to make any of these health claims, a food, main dish, or meal must meet the following three requirements: First, as shown in the table on page 31, a serving of the food or meal must contain less than the specified levels of four disqualifying nutrients: fat, saturated fat, cholesterol, and sodium. If the item exceeds any one of the four nutrients, a health claim cannot be made. Second, without fortification, the item must contain at least 10 percent of the Daily Value (DV) for at least one of the following six nutrients: vitamin A, vitamin C, calcium, iron, fiber, and protein. Third, in addition to the preceding general requirements, the item must meet the specific criteria for each approved claim. These criteria are detailed in the Appendix (page 536).

Health Claim Nutrient Limits

	TOTAL FAT (GRAMS)	SATURATED FAT (GRAMS)	CHOLESTEROL (MILLIGRAMS)	SODIUM (MILLIGRAMS)
FOOD*	13	4	60	480
MAIN DISH*	19.5	6	90	720
MEAL*	26	8	120	960

Based on the reference amount, as detailed in the Appendix (page 541), or 50 grams when reference amount is 30 grams or less, or 2 tablespoons or less.

Claims about Dietary Guidelines

In addition to nutrient and health claims, food-service operators also have the option of indicating that a particular food falls within dietary guidelines.

A statement that a food or meal meets the dietary guidelines of a recognized dietary authority is not considered a nutrient content or health claim by the FDA, provided that the statement is limited to general dietary guidance and does not characterize the level of a nutrient in a food. Therefore, food-service operators should be cautious of making implied nutrient content or health claims. A statement such as "Meets the National Cancer Institute recommendations for fiber" makes the food subject to nutrient content claim requirements because it characterizes the content of a specific nutrient. If you want to provide information as dietary guidance and not as a health claim, avoid giving undue emphasis to terms or symbols that could be interpreted as an implied claim.

A restaurant can provide general dietary guidance in several ways. A simple statement such as "This entrée is consistent with the Dietary Guidelines for Americans as established by the USDA" is one approach.

Although Dietary Guideline statements are not strictly regulated by the FDA, it is expected that truthfulness will prevail. A food should not be associated with Dietary Guidelines unless it meets with all of the applicable recommendations.

Obtaining Nutrient Information for Recipes

If you wish to make claims regarding the nutrition or health benefits of your products, the FDA requires that you have those foods or recipes analyzed for their nutrient content. There are a number of sources you can turn to for nutrition values.

The simplest way to obtain a recipe analysis is to use recipes that have already been analyzed, such as the ones in this book. This method is inexpensive, it is accepted by the FDA for backing up claims, and the work has already been done.

Recipe analysis can also be computed by hand using nutrition handbooks and food labels. This is extremely time-consuming because the tables give values for specific portion sizes, necessitating conversions and other calculations. For a handful of recipes this method may be cost effective, but it may not be feasible if many recipes need to be analyzed.

You may also wish to purchase software to analyze your recipes in-house. These programs are available with a wide range of options, and many are designed specifically for the food-service industry. These programs provide large databases of food nutrient values and perform the math involved in recipe analysis, and some may even create purchasing lists, spreadsheets, cycle menus, and menus based on allergies, preferences, and dislikes. The choices in the database may be overwhelming, however. One database returned 41 variations of "beef tenderloin" and 149 of "chicken"!

Another option is to hire a consultant to perform the analysis. Fees depend on the complexity of the recipes and the number of nutrients analyzed. This can be a costly approach, but a reliable consultant who is well versed in the intricacies of recipe analysis and is familiar with software and database choices is likely to do the work more accurately, and more rapidly, than someone who is not. Consultants can be found through dietetic associations such as the ADA.

The Variables of Analysis

Many factors come into play when you choose to perform nutrient analyses for recipes. First, you need to determine which nutrients to analyze for. Computer software programs can generate a mind-boggling array of nutrient counts, but for many operators the most relevant are probably calories, fat, saturated fat, cholesterol, sodium, carbohydrates, and fiber.

Ingredient databases or tables may not list all ingredients, especially unusual ones. Some software programs allow you to update the database, using nutrient values derived from Nutrition Facts labels. You may also find information for uncommon foods on the Internet, or by calling a food marketing or advisory council or the food's purveyor, grower, or producer.

Even if all your ingredients are in a database, it is important to remember that nutrient analysis is an estimate, not an actual accounting. Most accepted food nutrient values are averages that reflect the natural variations in foods due to growing conditions, storage, processing, and cooking.

Methods of preparation can affect nutrient analysis. If a marinade is discarded after the soaking, only part of it should be included. The amount discarded can be measured or estimated. If fat content is important, careful attention needs to be paid to which ingredients are selected from a database. "Beef tenderloin, cooked" does not take into account how the beef is cooked or for how long. The amount of fat trimmed from the tenderloin, however, will make a significant difference.

If you make the effort to analyze your recipes, take the steps to ensure that your food products conform to these nutrition profiles. Use standardized recipes and techniques to maintain consistency in preparation. If you use a reliable source in your recipe analysis methods and have made a reasonable effort to adhere to the recipes' preparation methods, the FDA will consider your operation to have a "reasonable basis" for believing that a food meets the requirements for health or nutrition claims and will not hold you legally liable for any minor variations that may occur in production. However, if a product is found to have more or less of a certain nutrient than indicated by a claim, you may receive damaging media attention.

Summary

In the United States, consumers have grown increasingly conscious of the need to make meal choices that are well balanced in order to maintain good health. Pyramids and guidelines have influenced how people select food in restaurants.

Food-service professionals need to be aware of the nutrition concerns of residents and the ways to satisfy their needs. Because food choices are intensely personal, preferences and expectations can vary widely from one group to another. Although health and nutrition are important to many consumers, taste is still primary. The food guide pyramids and Dietary Guidelines are tools that can help develop menu items that are nutritious as well as flavorful and satisfying.

The language that can be used on menus and in advertising to characterize the nutrition and health attributes of foods is regulated by the FDA. Two main categories of claims can be made.

Nutrient content claims describe the nutrition content of a food. The three types of nutrient content claims defined by the FDA are the absolute claim, the relative claim, and the implied claim.

Health claims characterize the relationship between the nutrient content of a food and a disease or health-related condition. Eleven nutrient-disease relationships can be used in health claims.

A menu may also state that a food is consistent with the Dietary Guidelines set up by the USDA or other health organizations. These types of statements are not regulated by the FDA as long as they are restricted to general dietary advice and do not characterize specific nutrient levels.

Any recipe for which health or nutrition claims are made is required by law to be analyzed for nutrient content. There are several methods of analyzing recipes, and many variables will affect their accuracy. If you take the trouble to analyze your recipes, you should also ensure that they conform to their nutrition profiles.

assume that the request for "no garlic" indicates an unevolved palette or an unreasonable food dislike. For the individual suffering from a food allergy, even the merest hint of garlic in your soup can set off a reaction. Some sufferers have a zero tolerance for a given allergen.

As of January 2006, all packaged foods that contain major food allergens must identify them on the label (milk, eggs, fish, crustacean shellfish, tree nuts, wheat, peanuts, and soybeans). So, you must be certain that you have read the label on prepared foods thoroughly. While you may not think about peanuts when you consider which tomato sauce to buy, you should, since peanut oil may well be an ingredient in that sauce. Many manufacturers let their customers know if foods that contain nuts are processed in the same plant as those that do not contain nuts. Depending upon an individual's sensitivity, even the very small amount of allergen left on a piece of equipment and transferred to a food could be enough to set off a reaction.

Since menu items might easily contain allergens that the customer would not be able to identify simply from the name of the dish, it is important that you and your staff, including the front-of-the-house staff, know the ingredients that are used in every dish. People who suffer from an allergy are likely to ask about the foods they cannot eat. You have to be able to answer honestly and completely about the dish in question. You may be able to prepare the dish without the offending ingredient. If not, offer an alternative from the menu that is safe for them to eat.

In the Kitchen

Once a chef has determined which foods to order from which purveyor, he or she needs to ensure that those goods are handled safely after they have been delivered. The importance of food and kitchen safety cannot be overemphasized. Few things are as detrimental to an establishment as an outbreak of food-borne illness.

Causes of Food-Borne Illnesses

Food-borne illnesses are caused by consuming adulterated foods, and their severity depends on the amount of contaminated food eaten as well as on the individual's susceptibility. Children under twelve, the elderly, anyone whose immune system is compromised in any way, and pregnant women and their unborn children are at greater risk than healthy adults.

Contamination can be chemical (insecticides, cleaning substances), physical (bits of glass, rodent hairs), or biological. This last category is responsible for the majority of food-borne illnesses. Biological contaminants include naturally occurring toxins found in some wild mushrooms and rhubarb leaves as well as the microorganisms known as pathogens. Microorganisms are virtually everywhere, and most are helpful or harmless. Among those that are pathogenic, or responsible for causing illness, are fungi, viruses, parasites, and bacteria.

Fungi, which include mold and yeast, are more often responsible for food spoilage than food-borne illness. Viruses include hepatitis; these are introduced to food through poor hand-washing practices after using the restroom or from eating tainted seafood. Once a virus is in the body, it invades a host cell and causes it to reproduce the virus. Parasites include amoebas and various worms, including dysentery and *trichinella spiralis*.

Bacteria are responsible for the majority of incidents of biological contamination. Bacteria may or may not need oxygen to thrive, and different types of bacteria thrive at different temperatures. The most common, and the most dangerous, types of bacteria thrive at temperatures between 60° and 100°F / 16° and 38°C. Although bacteria can survive at temperatures between 32° and 171°F / 0° and 77°C, the "danger zone" for bacterial growth is considered to be between 40° and 140°F / 4° and 60°C. Bacteria reproduce by fission, or splitting: One bacterium divides into two, these two divide into four, the four form into eight, and so on, at a rate of reproducing every twenty minutes. In about twelve hours, one bacterium can multiply into sixty-eight billion bacteria—more than enough to cause illness.

Bacteria require three things to grow: moderate pH, moisture, and protein. Foods such as meats, poultry, seafood, tofu, and most dairy products are all potentially hazardous. Cooked foods such as rice, beans, pasta, and potatoes, as well as sliced melons, sprouts, and garlic-and-oil mixtures are also potentially hazardous.

Foods that contain harmful levels of pathogens may look and smell normal. Cooking will destroy many of the microorganisms, but careless food handling after cooking may introduce more pathogens.

Preventing Food-Borne Illnesses

The keys to reducing the likelihood of food-borne illness are avoiding cross contamination, keeping foods out of the danger zone, and maintaining a clean and sanitized environment.

Cross contamination occurs when food comes into contact with infected surfaces. During the preparation stage, this might occur if bread or produce is used on a cutting board that was not properly cleaned after being used to prepare raw chicken. Separate work areas and equipment should be used for raw and cooked foods, and equipment used with potentially hazardous food should be cleaned and sanitized after each use.

Cross contamination can also occur when food-service operators do not properly wash their hands after they use the restroom, touch their face or hair, eat, smoke, or handle money, dirty dishes, or dirty linens. In addition, bare hands should never be used to handle ready-to-eat foods. Utensils such as tongs, a spatula, or deli tissue, or single-use food-handling gloves, should be used instead.

Pathogens can live at all temperature ranges, but those that are capable of causing food-borne illness thrive at temperatures between 40° and 140°F / 4° and 60°C. Storing foods at temperatures below 40°F / 4°C will slow or interrupt reproduction, and heating foods to 140°F / 60°C will either destroy pathogens or prevent reproduction. (Any toxins that pathogens may have produced, however, are not destroyed by cooking.) As stated in the 2005 FDA Food Code, foods that are left in the danger zone for a period of time longer than four hours are considered adulterated. This period may be cumulative, not just continuous, so every time the food enters the danger zone, the meter is running. Once foods have become adulterated, they cannot be recovered by heating, cooling, or any other method. For more information about specific foods, as well as foods that require both a time and a temperature control for safe holding, consult the 2005 Food Code, availabe on the Internet from the Center for Food Safety and Applied Nutrition (CFSAN).

Foods may also be delivered already contaminated. To reduce this chance, inspect all goods to be sure they arrive in sanitary conditions. Make a habit of checking delivery trucks for unsanitary conditions, such as dirt or pests. Check expiration dates, randomly sample items, and reject any goods that do not meet your standards. Once delivery is accepted, move the items immediately into proper storage conditions.

Foods should be stored at the following temperatures:

Meat and poultry: 32° to 36°F / 0° to 2°C

Fish and shellfish: 30° to 34°F / –1° to 2°C

Eggs: 38° to 40°F / 3° to 4°C

Dairy products: 36° to 40°F / 2° to 4°C

Produce: 40° to 45°F / 4° to 7°C

If separate refrigerators are not available, divide one unit into sections; the back will be the coldest area and the front the warmest.

Cooked foods should be cooled properly before refrigerating, and they should be stored above raw foods to prevent cross contamination by dripping. To cool foods properly, bring them to 70°F / 20°C within two hours, and to 40°F / 4°C within four more hours. Place hot liquids in a metal container (which conducts temperatures better than plastic or glass) then place in an ice water bath. Stir frequently to bring the temperature down more rapidly. Refrigerate solid foods in single layers in shallow containers.

Hot foods should be kept at temperatures at or above 140°F / 60°C, and cold foods should be kept at or below 40°F/4°C. When reheating foods, reheat them to at least 165°F / 74°C for at least 15 seconds.

Clean all surfaces of food particles and soil, then sanitize them to kill pathogens.

Fresh Produce

Fruits, vegetables, and herbs have always been an important part of the human diet, but consumers today are more aware than ever that these foods are nutritional powerhouses. They provide impressive amounts of complex carbohydrates, fiber, water, vitamins, minerals, and phytochemicals, often with very little fat, modest amounts of protein, and no cholesterol. They come in a breathtaking array of flavors, colors, and textures as well.

For the most part, fruits and vegetables do not require the same careful portion budgeting that meats, poultry, and fish do. For this reason, they play a key role in producing the necessary flavor boost and eye appeal that can help dispel the myth of bland and boring nutritious cuisine.

As a healthier alternative to fat- or cream-based sauces, fruits and vegetables can be used in the form of purées, coulis, salsas, chutneys, compotes, and relishes to add flavor and texture to a variety of dishes. Dried fruits in particular are a clever way to introduce an additional plant element to a recipe. They are wonderful in salads, sauces, stuffings, desserts, grain dishes, and breakfast cereals.

Purchasing and Storing Produce

Produce should look fresh: It should be free from bruises, mold, and brown or soft spots; the colors and textures should be appropriate for the type of food; and any attached leaves should be unwilted. Dried fruits should be plump and somewhat flexible.

Traditionally, fresh, local, in-season produce is best. These foods have been minimally handled and shipped, the time between harvest and table is brief, and often the flavors are more pronounced, the colors brighter, and the nutrient levels higher. Sometimes, though, the dictates of common sense make this impractical: It would mean, for example, that many chefs could never use lemons, or could use asparagus or tomatoes only a few months of the year. Foods that have been shipped, frozen, dried, or canned are also acceptable.

Fresh produce should be purchased in sufficient quantities to last between deliveries, with care taken not to purchase too much. Overpurchasing leads to degradation in quality, nutrient content, and eventually a costly loss of raw material.

When purchasing dried, frozen, or canned produce, choose brands of high quality. Be aware that many canned products contain added sodium, and that dried foods tend to be concentrated in calories.

Tomatoes offer a good illustration of the factors to take into account when deciding which form to purchase. Fresh tomatoes, when in season locally, have an incomparable taste. After the local growing season is over, however, you may prefer to use canned tomatoes because they have a better flavor than the pale, watery versions that are engineered to survive early picking, ripening rooms, and long-distance shipping.

Because many nutrients are unstable, fruits and vegetables should be handled with the preservation of nutrient content in mind. Nutrition content starts to decline immediately after harvesting, and this loss continues as the produce ages. To minimize nutrient loss, store produce away from light, air, moisture, and heat. When cooking, be aware that some metals, as well as alkalis and extremely acidic conditions, can affect nutrient content. Additionally, When proper purchasing and storage practices are observed, most food-service establishments do not store fresh produce for more than three or four days.

Storing Produce for Maximum Quality and Safety

Unless noted, store produce at 40° to 45°F / 4° to 7°C and at a relative humidity of 80 to 90 percent. Do not peel, wash, or trim until ready to use. Fruits and vegetables that need to ripen should be stored at room temperature until ripe, then refrigerated.

FOOD	HOW TO STORE
AVOCADOS	Ripen at room temperature, if necessary; refrigerate when ripe.
GARLIC	Store at cool room temperature in a well-ventilated area.
GREENS AND LETTUCES	Store in 40° to 45°F/4° to 7°C temperatures with high relative humidity but no standing water or moisture.
HERBS	Store in 35° to 45°F/2° to 7°C temperatures, wrapped loosely in a damp paper or cloth. If desired, trim roots from leafy herbs and place bunch in a jar of water before covering.
ONIONS, DRY	Store at cool room temperature, away from potatoes (they hasten spoilage) and dairy (it absorbs odors and flavors).
ONIONS, FRESH	Refrigerate away from dairy.
PEACHES	Ripen at room temperature, if necessary; refrigerate when ripe.
POTATOES	Store at cool room temperature, away from onions.
ROOT VEGETABLES WITH TOPS	Remove leaves from carrots, beets, turnips, radishes, etc. to prevent leaves from robbing nutrients from roots. Use leaves immediately; they don't store long. Keep roots at cool room temperature.
TOMATOES	Store at room temperature. Never refrigerate.

Vegetables

Vegetables include a number of foods that botanically are classified as fruits. Tomatoes, peppers, squash, and other seed-bearing foods are really fruits. Because these are often used in savory preparations, their culinary application is the guiding principle for listing them here.

The USDA's Dietary Guidelines divides vegetables into five groups: dark green vegetables, orange vegetables, legumes, starchy vegetables, and other vegetables. Eating a variety of colors—including red cabbage or red bell peppers, yellow sweet corn, white garlic, and deep green spinach—provides fiber and a wide array of vitamins, minerals, and phytochemicals, many of which are found in pigments. Orange and dark green vegetables are good sources of vitamin C and are high in beta carotene, which the body uses to make vitamin A (the chlorophyll in green vegetables masks the carotenoid pigments). Legumes and dark green vegetables are good sources of folate. Potatoes, avocados, and legumes are also high in potassium.

The Dietary Guidelines recommend 2½ cups of vegetables per day for a 2,000-calorie diet, with the following amounts recommended over the course of a week:

Dark green vegetables: 3 cups/week
(broccoli, spinach, most greens)

Orange vegetables: 2 cups/week
(carrots, sweet potatoes, pumpkin, winter squash)

Legumes: 3 cups/week
(dried beans, chickpeas, tofu)

Starchy vegetables: 3 cups/week
(corn, white potatoes, green peas)

Other vegetables: 6½ cups/week
(tomatoes, cabbage, celery, cucumber, lettuce, onions, peppers, green beans, cauliflower, summer squash, mushrooms)

Most people in the United States don't eat anywhere near these recommended intakes, with the possible exception of starchy vegetables, specifically potatoes.

Dark Green Vegetables

Dark green vegetables include most of the crucifers (cabbage family): broccoli, Brussels sprouts, bok choy, kale, and collards; it also includes cooking greens such as Swiss chard, and turnip greens, as well as salad greens such as arugula, leaf lettuce, and spinach. Some of these vegetables, such as kale and Brussels sprouts, are at their best in late fall. Their somewhat pungent flavors mellow after they have been exposed to frost.

These vegetables are extremely low in calories and fat (usually under 1 gram per serving) and contain generous amounts of fiber, vitamin C, beta carotene, iron, calcium, folate, and vitamin B6. Crucifers, including cabbage and cauliflower (see Other Vegetables, page 53), are also high in phytochemicals called glucosinolates, a group that includes indoles, isothiocyanates, and sulforaphane, which are thought to protect against some types of cancer.

It's best not to overcook these vegetables. Doing so causes nutrient loss, and releases the sulfur-containing phytochemicals that cause their unpleasant aromas.

Orange Vegetables

Orange vegetables get their coloring from carotenoid pigments; beta carotene is the one the body converts into vitamin A. Their flesh can range in color from deep yellow (such as butternut squash) to dark orange (carrots), and their peels can be any color. These vegetables are typically very high in fiber and several of the B vitamins as well as vitamins C and even E, and some supply iron and magnesium.

Most of these vegetables store well at cool room temperature, though carrots are better refrigerated.

Legumes

Although most people think of legumes as dried beans, this group includes thousands of plants: a legume has seed pods that split along both sides when ripe, and legumes are classified by whether these pods are edible. The most common include beans and soybeans, lentils, peanuts, and peas. Fresh beans and peas are sweetest and most tender when they are young. Once picked, their natural sugars begin to convert into starch. Garden peas are especially prone to flavor loss.

Most legumes are a good source of protein—for most of the world, they are the primary source of protein—and contain B vitamins like folate and riboflavin, vitamin E, complex carbohydrates, soluble and insoluble fiber, and minerals such as iron, calcium, and magnesium.

Starchy Vegetables

Starchy vegetables are usually roots and tubers that serve as nutrient reservoirs for the upper part of a plant. They are rich in carbohydrates, vitamins, and minerals.

Tubers are enlarged, bulbous roots capable of generating a new plant. Potatoes are the most common tuber, but Jerusalem artichokes, jicama, and yams are others.

If leaves are attached to these vegetables, check to see that the greens are fresh; they should not be wilted or discolored. Remove them before storing and use within a few days. Root vegetables should be stored in a cool, dry place, unpeeled; properly stored, they will maintain their quality for several weeks.

These vegetables can be used to thicken soups, stews, and sauces in place of cream or roux. Pale and blander vegetables like potatoes or celeriac are more versatile than beets for these applications, unless you are preparing borscht.

Other Vegetables

This catchall category includes crucifers that aren't dark green (such as cauliflower and red cabbage), foods that are botanically considered fruits (tomatoes, peppers, cucumbers, and summer squash), as well as the extensive families of mushrooms and onions. These other vegetables vary considerably in nutrients, seasonality, and keeping qualities.

Fruit

Although the Dietary Guidelines do not categorize fruits as they do vegetables, different groups of fruits provide different nutrients. Orange and red fruits like mango, cantaloupe, apricot, watermelon, and red or pink grapefruit are high in carotenoids. Citrus, berries, guava, papaya, kiwi, and cantaloupe are high in vitamin C, while oranges are rich in folate. Fruits like apples and pears aren't especially high in vitamins, but they contain phytochemicals as well as fiber.

Two cups of fruit should be consumed per day for a 2,000-calorie intake. Whole fruits, whether fresh, frozen, canned, or dried, are recommended over fruit juice for the majority of this amount to ensure adequate fiber intake.

Although unripe fruits can be stored at room temperature, most ripe fruit should be refrigerated. Berries in particular are extremely perishable and should be used within a day or two of delivery. Some fruits (including apples, bananas, and melons) emit ethylene gas; this can accelerate ripening in some unripe fruits, but it can also promote spoilage in produce that is already ripe. Store these fruits separately from other foods.

Fruits like lemons and melons emit odors that can permeate other foods; dairy products are prone to absorbing odors, as are fruits such as apples and cherries.

Apples and Pears

The apple, perhaps the United States' most popular fruit, comes in thousands of varieties. The most commonly available are Golden and Red Delicious, McIntosh, Granny Smith, Rome Beauty, Fuji, and Gala, but regional and heirloom varieties like Northern Spy, Greening, and Cameo are worth seeking out.

Pears are to France what apples are to the United States. They also come in many varieties, with the most common being Bartlett, Bosc, Comice, d'Anjou, and Seckel. Pears are extremely fragile and are picked before ripening; they will soften at room temperature.

Fresh apples and pears can be held in climate-controlled cold storage for months without significant loss of quality, so they are readily available year-round.

The flesh of many apples and pears will begin to brown once it is exposed to air. Dousing them in acidulated water will help prevent this but may affect their flavor.

Apples and pears are high in fiber, most of which is soluble, and they supply some vitamin C. Those with red skins contain anthocyanins, a powerful antioxidant pigment.

Berries

Most berries are extremely perishable and are susceptible to bruising, mold, and overripening. Thanks to improved methods of shipping, these once-seasonal fruits are becoming more available, giving chefs the options they need to purchase the berries of the best quality year-round.

Because berries (with the exception of cranberries) are so delicate, the fruit itself and its packaging should be inspected carefully before you accept them. Juice-stained cartons or juice leaking through the carton indicate mishandling or age. Once berries begin to mold, the entire batch goes quickly.

Cranberries are almost always cooked. Other berries can be used fresh or as a flavoring, purée, or sauce; in marinades, dressings, or vinegars; or in preserves, ice creams, or fruit desserts such as pies, tarts, and cobblers. When fresh berries are unavailable, IQF (individually quick-frozen) berries are often a perfectly fine substitute. Dried berries can be used in compotes, stuffings, breads, or other sweet or savory dishes.

Most berries are extremely high in vitamin C, a nutrient that breaks down when exposed to heat and air. Cut berries just before serving, and cook them briefly, if at all, to preserve nutrients.

Grapes

Grapes are technically a berry, but because they come in so many varieties and have so many different uses, they are usually grouped separately.

Grapes may have seeds or not. They are used for eating out of hand, cooking, and wine making, and may be dried into raisins or currants. Harvested at different times in different locales, grapes are usually available throughout the year.

Red and black grapes are higher in nutrients than green grapes. They contain more flavonoids and pigments than green grapes. But green grapes are not nutritionally bankrupt—all grapes supply some vitamin C and B vitamins. Dried into raisins, they supply some iron. To help the body absorb this mineral, use raisins in preparations that contain some vitamin C, such as salads.

There are some classic dishes that use grapes as an ingredient: sole Veronique, a poached fillet of sole in a cream sauce, garnished with peeled seedless grapes, is the most famous. For the most part, grapes are usually used in fruit platters, as an accompaniment to cheese plates, or in salads.

Citrus

Citrus fruits are extremely juicy, with segmented flesh and skins that contain aromatic oils. They can be very sweet to extremely tart. Oranges, grapefruits, lemons, limes, and tangerines are the most common citrus fruits.

Citrus fruits are best known for their high vitamin C content, but they also supply folate, fiber, and phytochemicals. Limonene, which is in the peel, is a phytochemical that may neutralize cancer-causing agents. Oranges and tangerines contain a carotenoid called beta cryptoxanthin, which can inhibit some tumors. Pink and red grapefruit supply lycopene, another antioxidant carotenoid.

Most citrus fruits keep very well. Their fairly thick skins protect them from bruising and decay, and preserve vitamins. Most often used uncooked, citrus can add a sweet-tart note to savory dishes, especially in sauces. They are also used in many desserts.

Melons

Succulent and sweetly aromatic, most melons are related to squashes and cucumbers. The four major types are cantaloupes, watermelons, winter melons (such as honeydew, casaba, and Crenshaw), and muskmelons.

Determining ripeness of melons can be tricky; specific techniques for different types are provided below. Most melons do not ripen after picking, so the challenge is to identify those that were picked when ripe. In general, all melons should be fragrant and feel heavy for their size.

Melons are an exceptional source of soluble fiber, vitamin C, and most B vitamins, as well as different carotenoid pigments.

Firm, uncut melons can be stored at room temperature for two to four days. This will cause their flesh to soften and become juicier. Once they have been cut, they should be refrigerated and used within two days. Don't cut melons until just before using, to preserve vitamin C, and always wash them first so that any bacteria on the skin are not transferred to the flesh.

Stone Fruits

So called because they have one large central pit, or stone, this group of fruits includes peaches, plums, apricots, cherries, and nectarines. They come into peak season throughout the late spring and summer, and they must be handled carefully because they typically have thin skins and flesh that can bruise easily.

Stone fruits are used in preserves, shortcakes, pies, cobblers, as well as in savory dishes. Peaches, cherries, and plums are also used in fruit brandies, wines, and cordials. All stone fruits are available canned, frozen, or dried.

Peaches are sweet and juicy, with a distinctively fuzzy skin. All fall into one of two categories: clingstone or freestone. Clingstone peaches have flesh that clings to the pit, whereas the flesh of freestone peaches separates easily. Peach flesh ranges from pale white to red in color. Peaches are a rich source of soluble fiber, and supply modest amounts of vitamin E.

Other Fruits

A wide variety of fruits falls into this category. Many are tropical fruits that are available seasonally, though some, including mango, papaya, kiwi, and star fruit, are available year-round. Tropical fruits tend to be very high in vitamin C; some supply vitamin E as well. They are often served raw, but some take well to cooked desserts and savory preparations.

Herbs

The leaves of aromatic plants, herbs are used primarily to add flavor to foods. They are available fresh and dried, although sturdier herbs like thyme, bay leaf, and rosemary dry more successfully than others.

Aroma is a good indicator of quality in fresh and dried herbs. Test for smell by rubbing or crumbling leaves between the fingers, then smelling. A weak or stale aroma indicates old, less-potent herbs. Fresh herbs should have good color, fresh-looking leaves and stems, and no wilt or pest damage.

Fresh herbs should be stored loosely wrapped in damp paper or cloth. If desired, they can then be placed in plastic bags to help retain freshness, then stored at 35° to 45°F/2° to 7°C. Leafy herbs like watercress, basil, and parsley can be held by trimming the stems and placing the bunch in a jar of water. Wrap damp toweling around the leaves or cover with a plastic bag. Fresh herbs should be cut as close to serving time as possible and added to a dish toward the end of the cooking time. For uncooked preparations, fresh herbs should be added well in advance of serving so their flavors can blend with the other elements. Fresh herbs also add flavor to salads; parsley, basil, and sorrel can be used to good effect.

Fresh herbs are rarely eaten in large enough quantity for their nutrients to make a significant contribution to meeting daily or weekly recommendations. However, most are high in vitamin C, beta carotene, and iron.

Dried herbs should be stored away from light and heat. They can be added early in the cooking process.

Grains

Grains, breads, and pastas form the foundation of a healthy diet. Their high levels of complex carbohydrates (the body's preferred energy source), vitamins, minerals, and dietary fiber make them the perfect choice to provide the bulk of calories in a meal. Furthermore, their often understated flavors and neutral colors make them a good foil for more highly flavored and colorful foods.

The number of grains typically prepared in a kitchen today is substantially greater than was the case several years ago. In addition to standards such as rice and barley, previously exotic grains such as quinoa, millet, and amaranth are becoming familiar.

Purchasing and Storing

Grains can be whole, cracked, or milled into meals or flours. Whole grains have the bran and germ intact. Because the oils in the grain are concentrated in these parts of the grain structure, whole grains are less stable under long-term storage than processed grains.

In general, the more milling and processing a grain undergoes, the less likely it is to become rancid. However, the germ and bran are also where most of the nutrients are located, making whole grains a better choice from a nutrition standpoint. There is also some benefit to selecting meals and flours that have been stone ground, because this method of milling is less likely to overheat the grain and destroy heat-sensitive nutrients such as thiamin and niacin. However, stone-ground products are often higher in price and may be difficult to find.

Many pastas are available both fresh and dried. Fresh noodles are often made with eggs, but they can also be made quite easily using only egg whites for binding purposes. Commercially available dried pastas are generally made of flour and water. Their chief advantage, apart from their long shelf life, is that they tend to be less expensive than some other foods.

All grains, meals, flours, and pastas should be kept cool, dry, properly covered, and away from exposure to direct light. Their plentiful B vitamins are light-sensitive and degrade over time. Fresh pasta should be tightly wrapped and refrigerated for up to four days, or frozen for up to a month. Some whole grains need to be refrigerated. Grain products can last a long time when properly stored, but if allowed to age too long they become stale and lose flavor and nutritional quality.

Wheat

Wheat comes in a variety of forms. Left whole, it is called wheat berries. Cracked wheat is coarsely crushed; bulgur is a form of cracked wheat. Semolina and farina are polished wheat kernels. Semolina can be whole or ground; couscous is made from it. Farina is a medium-grind wheat. Wheat bran is the outer covering of the kernel, and wheat germ is the embryo.

Wheat flours include whole wheat and graham, all-purpose, bread, cake, pastry, and self-rising. Whole and graham are made from the entire kernel. Cake, pastry, and self-rising flours are made of soft wheat; self-rising flour has baking powder and salt added. Bread flour is made from hard (higher gluten) wheat.

Wheat is a good source of soluble and insoluble fiber, iron, and protein, as well as riboflavin, niacin, thiamin, folate, phosphorus, zinc, and magnesium. The bran and germ contain phytoestrogens, which may reduce the risk for some forms of cancer and heart disease. The germ is also high in vitamin E.

Wheat is one of the foods that may cause an allergic reaction for certain individuals. To learn more about wheat allergies and special dietary concerns for diseases such as Crohn's, consult the Recommended Resources and Readings on page 547.

Rice

Rice is classified as long-, medium-, or short-grain. Long-grain rices include Basmati. Short-grain rices include Arborio, Piedmontese, and Carnaroli, as well as glutinous, or sticky, rice. Brown rice has been hulled, but the bran is intact; white rice has the bran removed. Wild rice is the seed of an aquatic grass and is more closely related to barley than to rice.

Rice provides thiamin, niacin, and vitamin B6 as well as copper, zinc, and magnesium. Brown rice supplies significantly more fiber than white rice, and is higher in vitamins and minerals. It can take twice as long to cook as white rice, however.

Corn

Corn can be eaten as a starchy vegetable or a grain, such as grits, hominy, or polenta. Hulled and degerminated corn kernels are called hominy; grits are ground hominy. Cornmeal is made by grinding hulled kernels. It can be medium or fine ground, and it is white or yellow. Masa is corn processed with lime to remove the hull, then ground; masa harina is ground dried masa. Cornstarch is very finely ground hulled and degerminated kernels.

Corn products are a good source of fiber. Corn is high in niacin, but unless corn is prepared with an acid, such as lime, this vitamin is not available to the body. Yellow cornmeal is a good source of two carotenoids, lutein and zeaxanthin, that may protect against cataracts and macular degeneration.

Barley

Barley has a pleasantly chewy texture. It is most commonly available as pearl barley, which are the polished kernels. Scotch or pot barley are unpolished kernels. Barley meal is made by grinding unpolished kernels.

Barley is an excellent source of iron, selenium, niacin, and fiber. It also supplies thiamin and vitamin B6.

Oats

Of all the grains, oats are notable in that they retain most of their nutrients after hulling, because the bran and germ are not removed. Oats can be left whole (these are called groats) or processed into oatmeal or oat bran. Oatmeal can be steel-cut, rolled, quick-cooking, instant, or made into flakes. They are fairly similar nutritionally, but their textures can be quite different.

Oats are higher in protein than bulgur wheat or brown rice, and they contain thiamin, iron, and selenium. They are also an excellent source of fiber, especially cholesterol-lowering soluble fiber. Oats also supply saponins, which are phytochemicals that appear to regulate blood flow.

Other Grains

Although the grains listed above are the most commonly consumed in the United States, they are by no means the most nutritious, especially when they are milled or processed. All whole grains, including millet, quinoa, rye, and buckwheat, supply complex carbohydrates and fiber, as well as B vitamins. (See Exploring the Unusual, facing page.)

Exploring the Unusual

IN THE UNITED STATES we rely heavily on the old grain standbys of wheat, rice, corn, and oats, but the world is full of other grains that have yet to make a significant mark on American menus. By experimenting and learning how to cook with some of these unusual grains, you can broaden your repertoire immensely. The following are just a few of the grains you may wish to explore.

Amaranth: Once a sacred food of the Aztecs, amaranth is a tiny grain with an aroma and flavor described as corn-like and woodsy. Its high starch content makes it more suitable for soups, stews, and porridges than drier pilaf-style preparations. Toasting the grain first and adding it to already boiling liquid helps prevent it from becoming gummy. Amaranth is high in protein (18 percent), iron, calcium, and vitamin E.

Farro: *Farro* is the Italian word for emmer, or two-grained spelt, an ancient type of wheat. It is traditionally eaten in the Tuscan region of Italy, and it is often combined with cannellini beans for a source of complete protein. Farro contains a starch similar to that found in Arborio rice, but although it releases a creamy binding liquid when cooked, it does not become as starchy as Arborio. Farro is high in vitamins, minerals, and antioxidants.

Job's tears: One of the few nonhybridized grains available today, Job's tears are so named because the unhulled grain resembles a teardrop. This grain is said to have a number of medicinal benefits; as such, it is highly prized in both traditional Chinese medicine and macrobiotic cuisine. Job's tears are high in carbohydrates, iron, and calcium, and are available either polished or unpolished (the unpolished variety has a better nutrition profile). Still rare in this country, Job's tears can be imported and purchased from companies that deal in natural foods and macrobiotic supplies.

Kamut and spelt: These easily digestible ancient forms of wheat can often be tolerated by people with wheat allergies. Both have a better nutrition profile than standard wheat. Spelt and kamut flours substitute well for wheat flour in breads.

Quinoa Pilaf (page 379)

Quinoa: Native to the Andes, quinoa (pronounced keen'-wah) has a mildly nutty flavor and an intriguing texture. The germ, which completely surrounds the rest of the grain, falls away during cooking and remains slightly crunchy, while the grain itself becomes meltingly soft. This duality of texture makes quinoa like two grains in one. Quinoa is one of the quickest-cooking grains and has the highest nutrition profile of any grain. With up to 20 percent high-quality protein, quinoa rivals milk as a source of protein and is also high in vitamin E, iron, zinc, potassium, calcium, and B vitamins.

Teff: Native to Ethiopia, teff is a tiny grain that is only about twice the size of the period ending this sentence. In fact, it derives its name from the Amharic word *tef,* meaning "lost," because it is so easily lost during harvesting and handling. Teff tastes similar to hazelnuts and is often ground into flour from which the traditional Ethiopian flatbread *injera* is made. The whole grain is available in brown, red, and ivory varieties, with the brown being the most flavorful. Teff is high in protein and carbohydrates and is a good source of calcium and iron.

Triticale: A hybrid of wheat and rye, triticale (pronounced trit-i-kay'-lee) is the world's first completely human-engineered grain. Its flavor is pleasantly mild and reminiscent of rye. Triticale was once hailed as the answer to the world's hunger crisis because of its high protein content, high yields, resistance to pests, and field hardiness. Sadly, it has been slow to catch on with growers and consumers, despite the enthusiasm given it by dietitians and scientists.

Adapted from *The Splendid Grain,* by Rebecca Wood. Copyright © 1997 by Rebecca Wood.

Baked Goods and Breads

Whether you serve a bread basket as part of every meal or include breads and baked goods as part of a menu item, you want to be certain that the baked goods you choose are adding as much to the overall nutritional value of the meal as possible. Good choices include whole-grain varieties or versions that include less sugar, butter or shortening, and eggs than traditional renditions, such as we included in this book.

Yeasted breads can be part of a sandwich or can accompany soups or salads. You can improve the profile of any meal that includes a yeasted bread by considering a variety of whole-grain options, including wheat, rye, buckwheat, or millet to replace some or all of the white wheat flour called for in typical yeast bread recipes. A vegetable purée is another way to introduce more nutrients, as well as flavor and moisture. Yogurt can be used instead of milk to add a touch of tang and lightness. Texture is important in baked goods, so select ingredients that are hearty without producing a bread that is too dense, heavy, or wet.

Quick breads can be high in fat, sugar, and sodium. You can opt to use a variety of flours in a quick bread that might be more difficult to work with in a yeasted dough. The quantity of sugar in many quick breads can be cut by 30 to 50 percent without producing a significant change in the taste, texture, or color of your muffins and loaves. Batters made by the well mixing method, rather than the creaming method, include far less butter or shortening. Introducing whole grains such as oats and garnish ingredients like dried fruits or nuts are good ways to bolster most quick bread recipes.

Dried Legumes

Legumes are seeds that grow inside pods. Fresh legumes, such as green beans and peas, are considered vegetables (see page 49). Dried legumes have a much longer shelf life. They are generally mild in flavor and they are a potent source of many nutrients.

Purchasing and Storing

If you purchase dried beans in bags, check to see that the beans are whole and the bags are not torn. Legumes are best when used within six months of purchase. As they age they take longer to cook and thus require more cooking liquid. They should be stored in a cool, dry, well-ventilated area.

Canned beans are a convenient alternative to dried beans—they are already cooked—but they are high in sodium. Draining off the liquid and rinsing the beans can reduce the sodium levels.

Most dried beans are comparable nutritionally. In addition to protein and complex carbohydrates, beans are a rich source of soluble and insoluble fiber and are quite low in fat. Most are a good source of folate; some are high in iron and calcium.

Soyfoods

Soybeans are a rich source of many nutrients. They are an excellent source of high-quality protein, and supply iron, magnesium, vitamin E, riboflavin, thiamin, and folate. However, soybeans are considerably higher in fat than are other legumes. Soy also contains antioxidants called isoflavones, which have been linked to reduced risk for some cancers, osteoporosis, and heart disease. These are found only in soy protein; soy sauce and soybean oil do not confer these benefits.

Soyfoods include edamame and processed products such as tofu, tempeh, miso, and TVP. Soymilk and soy cheese are also available.

Purchasing and Storing

Soyfoods are available in myriad forms and flavors. Most soy products are perishable and should be kept refrigerated. Those packed in aseptic boxes, such as some brands of soymilk, can be stored at room temperature until opened. Some soyfoods can be frozen.

Soy cheese can be made to imitate Cheddar, Parmesan, mozzarella, and cream cheese; those that contain the milk protein casein will melt better than those that contain no animal products. Some brands contain hydrogenated oils.

Soymilk comes in a variety of flavors and can be used instead of milk in most recipes. Fortified soymilks supply vitamins A, B12, and D, riboflavin, zinc, and calcium.

Tempeh is a cake made of fermented soybeans; it has a tender texture and can be used in soups, or marinated and broiled. It is higher in protein and has a more pronounced flavor than tofu.

Textured vegetable protein (TVP) or textured soy protein (TSP) can be substituted for ground beef. They may be frozen or dried. (Dried forms may need to be rehydrated before use.) These can also be processed into meat substitutes for bacon, sausage, hot dogs, and hamburger patties.

Tofu can be soft or water-packed. Soft tofu can be silken, firm, or extra-firm; it is packaged in aseptic boxes. It keeps indefinitely at room temperature but must be refrigerated and used within four to five days once opened. Soft tofu has a custard-like consistency that is ideal in purées, soups, sauces, and dips; it can be used in place of sour cream in some recipes.

Water-packed tofu can be firm or extra-firm. It is usually packed in tubs or plastic cartons and must be refrigerated; once opened, it should be used within four to five days. Water-packed tofu has a dense texture and mild flavor. It is extremely versatile and can be grilled or stir-fried, used to replace eggs in a vegetarian egg salad, or added to stews or baked dishes; it is often marinated before use. Pressing it removes extra liquid, which improves the texture.

Seitan is made of wheat gluten cooked in soy sauce. It is extremely high in protein and has a chewy, firm texture. It can be used like tofu in stir-fries. Seitan is available in tubs or cakes, and in a powdered form that must be mixed with water.

Nuts and Seeds

Nuts and seeds are the fruits of various trees. (Peanuts, although often referred to as nuts, are actually legumes, since they grow underground in the root system of a leguminous plant.) Nuts are available in several forms: in the shell, roasted, shelled, blanched, sliced, slivered, chopped, and puréed into butters.

Nuts are high in vitamins, minerals, and phytochemicals. The favorable nutrition profile in nuts has made them the focus of several clinical studies, all of which showed that nuts may play a role in decreasing the risks for cardiovascular diseases, stroke, diabetes, and cancer.

Approximately 80 percent of the calories in nuts comes from fat, but up to 90 percent of the fat is unsaturated, which has been shown to have a positive effect on serum cholesterol levels. Because they are such a concentrated source of calories, the recommended serving size for most varieties is 1 ounce (roughly ¼ cup).

CANOLA OIL is made from the seeds of the rapeseed plant. There have been several stories about the toxicity of canola oil, and it is true that the rapeseed plant is toxic to humans and animals. The toxic element in canola oil, erucic acid, is present only in very small amounts in most processed canola oils. The oil is light in color, neutral in flavor, and has a healthy proportion of monounsaturated fats. Its smoke point is 420°F / 216°C.

Purchasing and Storing

Nuts are relatively expensive and should be stored carefully, as they can become rancid quickly. Nuts that have not been roasted or shelled keep longer. Shelled nuts may be refrigerated or frozen, or stored in a cool, dry, well-ventilated area. Check periodically to be sure they are still fresh.

Seeds are usually available whole or as a paste and should be stored in the same manner as nuts. Many of the seeds used in the kitchen are considered spices (coriander and fennel seed, for example), while others, such as sunflower and pumpkin seeds, are used more like nuts.

Fats and Oils

Oils are produced by pressing a high-oil food such as olives, corn, avocados, or soybeans. The oil may then be filtered, clarified, or hydrogenated to produce a liquid oil or shortening that has the appropriate characteristics for its intended use.

Hydrogenation causes the oil to remain solid at room temperature; this product is also called shortening. Hydrogenation produces trans fatty acids (see page 12); some shortenings are now trans-fat free.

Purchasing and Storing

Several different oils and shortenings are required for every kitchen. Oils for salads and cold dishes should be of the best possible quality, with a perfectly fresh flavor. Oils used for cooking may have a neutral or a pronounced flavor depending on their application, but those used for frying should have a high smoke point. Oils and shortenings should be stored in a dry place, away from extremes of heat and light. Some extremely perishable oils should be refrigerated but brought to room temperature before use.

Chocolate

Chocolate is produced from cocoa beans, which grow on the cacao tree. It is most commonly associated with sweets and desserts, but it can be used in savory entrées; it is common in Mexico, particularly in mole and other sauces.

Chocolate is naturally bitter; sugar is typically added to make it palatable. Most chocolate also contains varying amounts of cocoa butter, the vegetable fat that occurs naturally in chocolate. Cocoa powder is usually unsweetened. Dutch-process cocoa powder has been treated with an alkali to reduce its acidity.

Chocolate and cocoa powder contain antioxidants, including catechins, the compounds that make tea so beneficial. Dark chocolate has more of these than milk chocolate. Chocolate also supplies minerals such as copper, iron, and zinc. Because chocolate can be high in fat and sugar, however, it should be eaten in moderation.

Chocolate should be stored, well wrapped, in a cool, dry, ventilated area. It should be refrigerated only if it is hot and humid; refrigeration can cause moisture to condense on its surface.

BROWN, ORGANIC, FREE-RANGE, and a variety of nutritionally enhanced eggs are available; they can cost twice as much as generic eggs.

Brown eggs come from hens with red feathers and earlobes. (Hens with white feathers and earlobes lay white eggs.) Brown eggs may be slightly larger than white eggs, but otherwise they are identical nutritionally.

Organic eggs are from hens fed a diet free of pesticides, herbicides, and commercial fertilizers. Organic eggs contain the same amount of nutrients as other eggs, but also contain fewer chemicals. (Hens are not allowed to be fed hormones, so all eggs sold in the United States are hormone-free.)

"Free-range" calls to mind images of birds scratching for feed in front of a chicken coop, but not all free-range eggs are from hens with access to the outdoors. Eggs can be sold as "free-range" if the chickens have access to open areas, even if these areas are indoors. Free-range eggs are nutritionally identical to generic eggs.

Enhanced eggs take a number of different forms. Some brands are higher in omega-3 fatty acids or vitamin E; others are lower in fat or cholesterol than generic eggs. Egg producers can change the nutrient content of an egg by feeding the hens a special diet. A chicken fed a vegetarian diet high in sea algae or kelp will lay eggs that are higher in vitamin E and omega-3 fatty acids, and some nutritionally enhanced eggs contain omega-3s in amounts comparable to such cold-water fish as salmon.

Dairy and Eggs

Most people associate dairy products with calcium—and while they are an excellent source of this important mineral, they can also supply a wealth of other nutrients. Milk and cheese are good sources of protein and vitamin B12; fortified milk also supplies vitamins A and D, riboflavin, and phosphorous.

Although dairy products and eggs are two different products (from a nutrition perspective, eggs fall into the meat-and-bean category of the USDA's pyramid, while milk is a category unto itself), freshness and proper handling are important for both. These foods are highly perishable, so careful purchasing and storage procedures are extremely important.

But dairy products can also be high in fats. Although fat-free milk, yogurt, and sour cream are available, butter, cream and even some cheeses can contain significant amounts of fat, especially saturated fats.

Purchasing and Storing Dairy and Eggs

Eggs should always be inspected carefully upon delivery. The chef should make sure that shells are clean and free of cracks; those with broken shells should be discarded because of the high risk of contamination. Refrigerate eggs promptly and rotate the stock to ensure that only fresh, wholesome eggs are served.

Fresh milk should be stored for about a week. Evaporated milk will maintain its quality for six months unopened; once opened, it should be used in a few days. Sweetened condensed milk and nonfat dry milk can be stored for about three months unopened. Once opened or reconstituted, these foods should be treated as evaporated or fresh milk, respectively.

Ultrapasteurized cream has a fairly long shelf life, as do cultured dairy products such as sour cream, yogurt, crème fraîche, and buttermilk. The less aged a cheese is, the shorter its shelf life.

Careful storage extends beyond food safety. Dairy products in particular are susceptible to absorbing flavors and odors from other foods. Store all milk, cream, and butter away from foods with strong odors. Cheeses should be carefully wrapped in plastic both to keep the cheese from losing moisture and to prevent it from transferring odors and flavors to other foods.

Fish and Shellfish

Fish consumption has doubled in the last few decades as people have become more aware of the health benefits it confers. But many Americans are still reluctant to cook fish at home. It has a reputation for being difficult to cook because it cooks so quickly. For many people, fish is something they order at restaurants.

As fish has become increasingly popular, demand has begun to outstrip supply. Many longtime menu favorites are increasingly unavailable. However, farm-raising of fish, or aquaculture, is growing, and is becoming one of the few reliable sources of fresh fish.

Because fish is typically low in the saturated fats that can cause health problems and may be high in beneficial fats, the American Heart Association recommends eating at least two servings of fish per week, especially fatty fish like mackerel, lake trout, herring, sardines, albacore tuna, and salmon.

Purchasing and Storing Fish

Fish can be categorized in a number of different ways: whether it is freshwater or saltwater, by its skeletal type, and by its fat content.

Finfish can be round, flat, or nonbony. Round fish, such as trout, bass, and salmon, have a backbone along the upper edge, with two fillets on either side, and eyes on either side of their head. Flat fish have a backbone that runs through the center of the fish, with four fillets (two upper and two lower). Flat fish, such as flounders and Dover sole, have eyes on the same side of the head. Nonbony fish include ray, monkfish, and shark; these have cartilage instead of bones.

Lean fish, sometimes called whitefish, are usually sold as fillets; very large lean fish may be cut into steaks. Their flavor is usually quite delicate and mild. These fish are all very low in calories and fat—most have about 2 grams per 3-ounce cooked serving—as well as saturated fat.

Fish that are more than 5 percent fat by weight are called fatty. Fatty fish are low in saturated fats, fairly low in cholesterol, and most are even fairly low in total fat. (Those that supply more than 10 grams of fat per 3-ounce cooked serving are mackerel, salmon, sardines, and shad.) Fatty fish are also extremely rich in omega-3 fatty acids (see table on page 72). These polyunsaturated fats can guard against hypertension and reduce the risk of fatal heart attacks.

All fish are extremely perishable. It is important, therefore, that the chef be able to select absolutely fresh fish of the best quality. A trustworthy purveyor is critically important. Ideally, fish should be purchased only in the amount needed for a day or two. If a purveyor is able to make deliveries only once or twice a week, fish should be stored properly. When it is, it can be held for several days without losing any appreciable quality.

When fish is delivered, it should be inspected carefully for freshness and quality:

- Smell it. Fish should have a clean, briny aroma. A strong odor is a clear indication of old or improperly handled fish.

- If the skin is attached, it should feel slick and moist. Any scales should be firmly attached. Fins and tail should be flexible and full.

- Press the flesh. It should feel firm and elastic, and spring back after you lift your finger.

- Eyes should be clear and full; as fish ages, eyes sink back into the head.

- Gills should be red to maroon, and moist and fresh looking.

The most important test of freshness is smell. No matter how clear the eyes are or how firm the flesh, a fish that smells bad should always be rejected.

To store whole fish, fill the belly cavity with shaved ice, then place the fish, belly down, on a bed of shaved ice in a perforated container. Cover the fish with additional ice. Set the perforated container in another container to catch the water from melting ice. Check the water level and drain it if it appears that the fish is sitting in water. Change the ice daily. Scaling and preparing whole fish should be delayed until close to service.

Fillets or steaks should also be stored in containers set in or on ice, but they should not be in direct contact with ice, because their texture and flavor will suffer.

Omega-3 Content of Fish

(per 100 grams raw fillet)

LESS THAN 0.5 GRAMS	0.6 TO 1.0 GRAM	MORE THAN 1.0 GRAM
Atlantic cod	Channel catfish	Albacore tuna
Atlantic pollock	Chum salmon	Anchovy
Brook trout	Red snapper	Atlantic halibut
Haddock	Spot	Atlantic herring
Northern pike	Swordfish	Atlantic mackerel
Pacific cod	Thread herring	Atlantic salmon
Pacific halibut	Turbot	Bluefin tuna
Pacific whiting	Yellowfin tuna	Coho salmon
Skipjack tuna		Lake trout
Sole		Pacific herring
Striped mullet		Pacific mackerel
Sturgeon		Pink salmon
Walleye		Rainbow trout
		Sardine
		Sockeye salmon

Purchasing and Storing Shellfish

Shellfish can be divided into four categories depending on their skeletal structure. Univalves are single-shelled mollusks such as abalones and sea urchins. Bivalves, which have two shells joined by a hinge, include clams, mussels, oysters, and scallops. Crustaceans have jointed exterior skeletons or shells; lobster, shrimp, and crayfish are examples. Cephalopods, such as squid and octopus, have tentacles attached to the head.

As with finfish, shellfish should be checked carefully upon delivery. Live shellfish like lobsters and crabs should move. Live shellfish should be packed in seaweed or damp paper. If a lobster tank is not available, store them in the shipping containers until they are prepared. Do not allow fresh water to come into contact with lobsters or crabs, as it will kill them.

Bivalves should be tightly closed; they start to open as they age. Tap any that are slightly ajar and reject or discard any that do not snap shut; the shellfish are dead. Reject any delivery that contains many open shells. Clams, mussels, and oysters purchased in the shell should be stored in the bag in which they were delivered. Do not ice them; they last better at temperatures between 35° and 40°F/2° and 7°C. Keep the bag tightly closed and lightly weighted to prevent the shellfish from opening.

Meat and Poultry

In the United States, meat has long been the centerpiece of a meal. Beef has traditionally been the most popular, but as Americans become aware of the effects of eating too much saturated fat, other varieties have made inroads. Pork is leaner than it once was, and it and chicken are the most common alternatives. Lamb, veal, turkey, game hens, and game are eaten less often.

Although red meat in particular can be high in fat, saturated fat, and cholesterol, some cuts are quite lean. By learning which cuts of meat are naturally lean, how to reduce the fat in cuts that aren't, and which source of lean protein can be used in lieu of fattier ones, a chef can create menus that are healthy and delicious.

Purchasing and Storing Meats

Meats should be chosen based on the leanness of particular cuts and trimmed of as much surface fat as possible before cooking. In general, loin and round cuts from meats are the leanest choices.

The grade of meat can be an indication of fat content. The USDA standards for grading rely upon a number of factors. One is the amount of marbling—the streaks of fat found within the muscle. In the case of beef, Choice grade may be a better selection than Prime. The quality is still excellent in Choice, but there is generally less marbling throughout all the cuts.

You may wish to consider specialty brands of beef that come from breeds naturally leaner than regular beef. These breeds, which include Limousin, Belgian Blue, Chianina, and Chiangus, can be substantially lower in fat and calories than standard USDA Choice beef, which must meet standards of quality but does not have to identify the specific breed of meat. To find out if any of these specialty breeds are available in your area, check with your local purveyors. You may also be able to find grass-fed meats, raised in open pasture and free from antibiotics and hormones. Conventionally raised meats are grain-fed and held in pens, known as feedlots, rather than foraging for grass in a pasture. Grass-fed meat is usually organic and free from steroids and antibiotics, as well as lower in total fat and cholesterol. Some studies suggest that these meats have a significantly greater amount of omega-3s. On the negative side, however, grass-fed meats are often described as having strong or unpleasant flavors and aromas, perhaps because we have become accustomed to the relatively mild flavors of conventionally raised meats.

Keep in mind the option of using game instead of "traditional" meats. Many game meats have bolder, more interesting flavors and can be substantially lower in fat and cholesterol than their domestic counterparts. Several game breeds, such as ostrich, emu, venison, and bison, are farm raised and readily available.

All meats should be refrigerated promptly upon delivery. Any marinating should also be done in the refrigerator. Marinades should be discarded after use to prevent contamination.

Purchasing and Storing Poultry

With its mild flavor, reputation for leanness, and versatility, poultry is one of the most popular entrées on menus. Chicken is the most common, but duck and turkey are not unheard of. Cornish game hens, geese, and game birds like quail, squab, and pheasant appear less frequently.

Like meat, poultry is an excellent source of high-quality protein, and it often contains minerals like iron, zinc, phosphorus, and selenium, as well as several B vitamins. Unlike meat, which often has fat marbling the flesh, most of the fat in poultry is in or near the skin. When the skin is removed and discarded before eating, most forms of poultry are exceptionally low in fat and saturated fat.

Poultry is sold by size and age; other marketing terms include *natural, free-range, organic,* and *fresh.* These terms often do not mean what you might think. "Fresh" poultry, for example, may have been stored at temperatures as low as 26°F/–3°C—cold enough to freeze the meat. "Free-range" means that the bird was not penned (see What's in an Egg? on page 69) but it does not automatically mean that the bird is organic.

Seasonings, Condiments, and Beverages

The ingredients and foods in this chapter include prepared sauces and flavoring agents; we cover some of the most common, but our listing is by no means exhaustive. Beverages, particularly those used in the kitchen, are also discussed. These ingredients add flavor and texture to recipes. In some instances they can affect the nutrition profile of a recipe in which they're used; some are high in sugar, and others, in sodium. Brands that contain less sugar or sodium are usually available. Depending on the recipe, these "light" versions can typically be used with excellent results.

Seasonings

Dried herbs, spices, salt, and pepper have been used for centuries to add flavor to foods; salt has been used as a preservative. Although refrigeration has lessened the need for salt-curing foods, salt and all seasonings have important culinary uses. Most seasonings are used in amounts small enough to have a nominal effect on health. Salt, however, contains sodium, an essential mineral that can have a profound effect on health.

Most of the herbs on page 59 are available in dried form. Drying alters their flavors, however, and improper storage compounds the problem of flavor loss. A chef should purchase only the amount of dried herbs that can be used within two or three months and should store them away from heat and out of direct light. Crumbling dried herbs or rubbing them between palm and fingertips before adding them to a dish may reinvigorate their flavors, but musty or "flat" aromas indicate herbs that are past their prime.

Spices are aromatics produced primarily from the bark and seeds of plants. Spices are nearly always sold dried, and may be whole or ground. For optimal flavor, purchase whole spices and grind them as close as possible to the time they are to be used. Spices, like dried herbs, should be stored away from extreme heat and direct light; they will retain their potency for about six months when stored properly.

Pepper was once the most expensive seasoning in the world. Whole peppercorns will retain their flavor almost indefinitely; ground or cracked pepper loses pungency quickly and should be checked often for flavor loss.

Although black peppercorns are the most common, most kitchens require a number of different peppers for different uses. White peppercorns are preferred for pale or light-colored sauces. Pink peppercorns are actually from a rose plant, and Szechwan peppercorns, from a prickly ash tree. Cayenne is made from dried and ground cayenne chiles; chile flakes, sometimes called red pepper flakes, are coarsely ground dried whole chile peppers. Paprika is made by grinding dried pimiento peppers and can be mild, sweet, or hot. Hungarian paprikas are among the best; Spanish paprikas are also high-quality. Some Spanish paprika is smoked.

Salt

Salt contains sodium, an essential mineral that helps maintain the body's normal fluid balance. It has also been linked to hypertension, or high blood pressure. Although consuming a high-salt diet does not cause hypertension in otherwise healthy individuals, it may aggravate a preexisting hypertensive condition, particularly in people who are sensitive to sodium.

Most Americans consume more than 3,000 milligrams of sodium per day. Experts suggest that sodium should be limited to no more than 2,400 milligrams, or about the amount in one teaspoon of table salt. The primary source of sodium, however, isn't salting foods at the table during cooking; it's in processed foods (see Hidden Sources of Sodium below). If you are concerned about reducing the sodium content of your recipes, opt for lower-sodium products whenever possible.

Salt brings its own flavor to foods and, when used wisely in cooking, draws out and enhances the natural flavor of other ingredients. Adding salt early during the cooking process allows for deeper salt penetration and better flavor enhancement. Whenever possible, taste before adding more salt, and be aware that chefs often build up a tolerance to salt and may add more than customers prefer.

Be aware that using less salt in the kitchen may result in dishes that taste bland, causing customers to add more salt at the table. This can result in a superficial contact between the salt and the food, causing more salt to be used to achieve the same level of flavor enhancement than adding salt during the cooking process.

Consider the temperature at which foods will be served: salt tends to be more pronounced in cooler dishes.

Using high-sodium ingredients to replace some of the salt in a recipe allows for the introduction of other flavor elements. Capers, olives, anchovies, soy sauce, fish sauce, pickles, mustard, green peppercorns, and Parmesan and Romano, add a dimension beyond just saltiness.

Hidden Sources of Sodium

TYPE	ROLE
MONOSODIUM GLUTAMATE (MSG)	Flavor enhancer
SODIUM BENZOATE	Preservative
SODIUM CASEINATE	Thickener and binder
SODIUM CITRATE	Buffer, used to control acidity in soft drinks
SODIUM NITRITE	Curing agent in meat
SODIUM PHOSPHATE	Emulsifier, stabilizer
SODIUM PROPIONATE	Mold inhibitor
SODIUM SACCHARIN	Noncaloric sweetener

Types of Salt

SALT IS FOUND IN SEVERAL FORMS, each of which carries different qualities. However, all types of salt, with the exception of light salt, are composed of 40 percent sodium and 60 percent chloride. One teaspoon of table salt or 6 grams of any salt other than light salt contains 2,325 milligrams of sodium.

Table salt is most commonly used in cooking and as a table condiment. It consists of small, dense, granular cubes that adhere poorly to food, dissolve slowly in solution, and are difficult to blend.

Iodized salt is table salt to which iodine has been added as a preventative against goiter, an enlargement of the thyroid gland caused by iodine deficiency.

Kosher salt is granular salt that has been compressed to provide a greater surface area. It is flaky and, compared to table salt, lighter in weight, dissolves more readily, and adheres better to food. Diamond Crystal® kosher salt is formed through an evaporation process similar to that used in the production of sea salt. The size of a grain of Diamond kosher salt is larger than that of other kosher salt. This means that a teaspoon of Diamond kosher salt contains fewer grains of salt and weighs less than a teaspoon of kosher salt. Although both types of kosher salt are typically more expensive than table salt, many chefs prefer to cook almost exclusively with kosher salts.

Sea salt and bay salt are collected through the evaporation of natural salt water and consist of thin, flaky layers. They adhere well to food and dissolve quickly. These salts also contain other trace minerals that occur naturally in the waters from which the salts are collected. As such, sea and bay salts from different areas of the world taste different. All are generally more complex in flavor than table and kosher salts. Sea and bay salts can be purchased in fine grain and larger crystal forms.

Canning and pickling salts contain no additives and are very pure. They are processed specifically to prevent clouding of the brine and discoloration of food undergoing salt curing.

Rock salt is a coarse salt used in crank ice cream makers and as a bed for shellfish. It has a gray tint from the usually harmless impurities it contains. Some rock salt contains arsenic; this type of salt is not safe to use in situations where the foods may come in contact with the salt. Some rock salt is food-grade. Some rock salt is meant only for use in ice cream machines or other applications where it does not come in contact with the food.

Salt substitutes contain either no sodium or a reduced amount (light salt). Potassium chloride is the best known, but too much of this salt substitute can cause an irregular heartbeat in people with kidney problems and people on certain medications. It can also throw off the body's fluid balance. Potassium chloride has a bitter aftertaste and is blander than salt, so people tend to use it with a heavy hand.

A given volume of each type of salt weighs differently. Unless noted otherwise, recipes in this book calling for salt refer to kosher salt, although many recipes are written for use with table salt. To substitute a kosher or sea salt for table salt and achieve the same level of saltiness, 1½ to 2 times the volume of table salt may be necessary. However, you should always start with the original amount stated and taste before adding more.

NONCALORIC OR NONNUTRITIVE SWEETENERS are hundreds of times sweeter than sugar. Because they are so concentrated, they are typically used in such small amounts that they do not add calories to foods. They are typically offered in packets for customers to use in beverages and on foods, and they are found in processed "diet" and sugar-free foods.

Because noncaloric sweeteners are chemically different from sugar, they cannot be used in lieu of sugar in some recipes. Aspartame, for example, breaks down when heated unless it is in a special encapsulated form. In addition, some people find that noncaloric sweeteners have an unpleasant taste.

The noncaloric sweeteners currently in use in the United States include Saccharin, Aspartame, Acesulfame-potassium (also called Acesulfame K or Ace-K), and Sucralose. Sucralose is created through a process that alters sucrose molecules into a form not metabolized by the body. It is heat stable and can be substituted in equal volume for sugar in recipes because a bulking agent, polydextrose, has been added.

There has been significant controversy regarding the safety of noncaloric sweeteners. Aspartame, for example, was approved for use in 1974, then approval was withdrawn for seven years before it was granted again. The label of products containing Aspartame must warn of the presence of phenylalanine, a substance that cannot be metabolized by people who have a medical condition known as phenylketonuria (PKU).

Sweeteners

Humans are born with a preference for sweet flavors. The sugar in foods may occur naturally, as in fruits and milk, or it may be added. Added sugars, otherwise known as refined sugars, are made by concentrating and refining the simple carbohydrates found in other foods, as in the manufacture of table sugar, molasses, corn syrup, and maple syrup. Sugars are sweeteners that are typically granular in texture. Syrups are pourable liquid forms of sugar. Most sweeteners supply few nutrients beyond calories, and experts are nearly unanimous in their recommendations that sugar intake, particularly of refined sugar, be limited.

Vinegars

Vinegars are made from a variety of fermented ingredients. Consideration should be given to the type of vinegar chosen for a recipe because each variety has unique flavor attributes.

Most vinegars contain negligible amounts of nutrients. Some types of vinegar are higher in sugar than others, but even then the amount is usually not significant enough to affect the overall calorie content of a dish.

Condiments

Condiments introduce sharp, piquant, sweet, or hot flavors into foods. They may be used as an ingredient in the kitchen or served on the side for guests to add according to their taste.

As with other prepared dry goods, select high-quality brands of condiments. Avoid those with a variety of fillers or unnecessary ingredients. Store elevated off the floor in a cool, dry room, and rotate stock.

Most condiments should be refrigerated once opened. Canned goods that are not used completely should be transferred to other containers, not stored in cans.

Mustard

Mustards are made by mixing powdered mustard seeds with seasonings and a liquid. Their heat depends on whether they are made from white or brown seeds; white seeds are milder in flavor than brown, but all mustards are typically quite sharp.

Olives

Olives are actually a fruit. They are usually green or black, depending on whether they are harvested and processed before they are ripened or when fully ripe. They can be cured in oil, water, brine, or salt. Like wine and cheese, olives come in hundreds of varieties.

Olives can be quite high in sodium; they are also high in vitamin E and may be high in iron and other minerals. They can be used whole or chopped in a number of dishes, or puréed into a paste that's often called olivada or tapenade.

Capers

Capers are the unopened buds of a shrub native to the Mediterranean. The buds are picked, dried, and then packed in salt or brine. Capers are pungent and quite salty; rinsing them before use can reduce their sodium. The smaller capers, called nonpareil, are considered superior to the larger Italian capers.

Pickled Foods

Pickles and pickled relishes range from the sweet condiment served on hot dogs, to the tiny sour cornichon served with paté, to kimchee, the extraordinarily pungent Korean condiment made of pickled vegetables. Sauerkraut, made of pickled cabbage, is an excellent source of vitamin C. Most pickled foods are high in salt.

Asian Condiments

Soy sauce is a very salty Asian condiment made by fermenting soybeans and wheat; the best ones are brewed. Tamari and fish sauce are similarly salty and pungent but somewhat different in flavor. Tamari is made without wheat, and fish sauce is made of fish. Hoisin sauce is made of fermented soybean paste, garlic, and a variety of spices and chiles; look for brands that list soybeans, not sugar, as the first ingredient. Oyster sauce is made of oysters, soy sauce, and other seasonings. Teriyaki sauce is a marinade made of soy sauce, ginger, sake, sugar, and other seasonings. Chili oil is made by steeping fiery-hot red chiles in vegetable oil; hot chili paste is made of mashed chiles, vinegar, garlic, and other seasonings. Fermented black beans are preserved in a brine and then dried. They can be quite mild in flavor.

Tomato-Based Condiments

In the United States, the love affair with the tomato could be said to begin with ketchup. Traditionally served with burgers, fries, and frankfurters, ketchup may also top everything from prime rib to scrambled eggs. Tomato ketchups are typically high in sugar, as are tomato-based barbecue sauces.

Other Condiments

Prepared condiments like relishes, chutneys, and salsas are similar, and the terms are often used interchangeably on menus. All refer to finely chopped mixtures of ingredients used as a condiment in or on foods. Relishes tend to be uncooked, though they may include cooked ingredients. Chutneys are cooked condiments that are usually fruit-based and include vinegar, sugar, and spices. Mango chutney is the most common. Salsas may be fresh or cooked.

Like chutneys, jams are typically fruit-based; they rarely include spices, though. The flavor a jam adds to a dish depends on the fruit or vegetable it is made of. Most jams are made with refined sugar; others are sweetened with fruit juice. When melted, jams can be used as a glaze.

Chipotles en adobo have become very popular in recent years. Chipotles are dried, smoked jalapeños, and adobo is a thick paste made of jalapeños, onions, vinegar, and spices. Chipotles en adobo can be used whole, or puréed and added to a variety of Mexican dishes.

Worcestershire sauce is de rigueur in the Bloody Mary cocktail; and it also adds savory flair to marinades, sauces, and gravy. Its dominant flavor is tamarind, but soy sauce, garlic, lime, onions, and vinegar may also be ingredients. It should not be used in vegetarian dishes, as it contains anchovies.

Extracts

Chefs can use a variety of flavoring extracts for cooking and baking. These are alcohol-based and are flavored with herbs, spices, nuts, and fruits. Vanilla, lemon, mint, and almond are common flavors.

Extracts lose their potency when exposed to air, heat, or light. Store in dark bottles or jars, away from heat or direct light, tightly capped.

Beverages

Beverages are of great importance to most establishments: Besides their culinary applications, alcoholic and nonalcoholic beverages can be chosen to complement the foods you serve and enhance the overall dining experience. In addition, beverages can be great moneymakers for food-service operations.

The rule of thumb for selecting alcoholic beverages for use in cooking and baking is: if it is not suitable for drinking, it is not suitable for cooking.

Because some people may not consume alcohol for health or religious reasons, its use in any recipe should be mentioned on the menu.

Among the most common alcoholic beverages used in the kitchen are brandies and cognacs, Champagne, dry red and white wines, port, Sauternes, sherry, stouts, ales, beers, and sweet and dry vermouth. Bourbon, crème de cassis, fruit brandies, gin, Kahlúa, rum, and scotch are frequently used in baking.

Alcohol contains seven calories per gram, but not all of these beverages contain just alcohol. Liqueurs, for example, typically contain sugar or sweeteners and will be significantly higher in calories than other beverages.

ALTHOUGH ALCOHOL IS NOT CONSIDERED a nutrient, alcoholic beverages can have a place in a healthy diet. In the United States, alcohol is regarded with a good deal of caution. It is a drug, and when consumed irresponsibly it can be dangerous, even lethal. But like many drugs, alcohol can have a beneficial effect on health when it is consumed in proper doses. In fact, the Dietary Guidelines for Americans include a recommendation to consume alcoholic beverages in moderation.

The modern scientific community first turned its attention to the beneficial attributes of alcohol when it was recognized that the French people have some of the lowest rates of coronary heart disease in the industrialized world even though their cuisine is one of the richest. This contradiction is known as the French Paradox, and although genetics, exercise, and dietary variety with an emphasis on plant foods play a part in the French Paradox, the answer also seems to lie in part in a glass of (red) wine.

Multitudes of studies over nearly fifty years have been conducted concerning the relationship between alcohol and coronary health. A landmark study in 1988 of drinking habits in industrialized nations showed that the countries with the highest per capita wine consumption had the lowest heart disease rates, while those where the least wine was consumed had the highest rates. This study showed that the countries with the lowest heart disease rates also had the highest rates of cirrhosis of the liver, a disease linked to excessive alcohol consumption.

Alcoholic beverages, consumed in moderation, can help to reduce the risk of heart disease. This does not mean that those who do not drink should start, nor does it mean that those who cannot moderate their alcohol consumption should drink. For the general population in good health, moderation is defined as two drinks per day for men and one drink per day for women, with a drink equaling 12 fluid ounces of beer, 5 fluid ounces of wine, or 1½ fluid ounces of liquor.

Although all alcoholic beverages have a beneficial health effect when consumed in moderation, red wine seems to be particularly effective because it contains phenolic compounds, which influence the color and level of tannins in the grape. These compounds are antioxidants that help to lower the level of LDL cholesterol in the blood while increasing the level of HDL cholesterol. They also appear to help prevent blood clots from forming and to reduce genetic damage caused by carcinogens.

Coffee and Tea

Coffee and tea have become part of the ritual of daily life in the United States. These beverages do appear to have health benefits, as long as they do not become a source of extra calories from sugars and fats. A 20-ounce double mochachino topped with whipped cream and chocolate curls could put a serious dent in the day's allotment of calories, clocking in at around 350 calories and over 3.5 grams of fat. Even a "medium" latte made with skim milk (a 14-ounce serving) is more than 100 calories, while a 3-ounce cup of espresso has 0 calories and an 8-ounce cup of regular coffee has about 5 calories.

The coffee and tea you serve deserves as much care in its selection and preparation as any of the other healthy offerings you provide your guests. Organic and "fair-trade" coffees are among the options you face in deciding what types of coffee and tea to buy.

Coffee may be purchased as whole beans or in preground, portioned vacuum packs. Many restaurants brew decaffeinated coffee, and some offer espresso and cappuccino, both regular and decaffeinated. The degree of roasting influences the flavor and aroma of the coffee. Darker roasts tend more to be complex and bitter, while lighter roasts have a milder flavor.

Tea is the most commonly consumed beverage in the world after water. Many of your customers are aware of recent findings about the important health benefits of tea. We are still learning the health benefits of tea, but it is considered a good choice for at least some of the six to eight cups or glasses of fluids recommended daily. Teas come in many varieties, including decaffeinated black teas and herbal teas. Most are blends and are available in single-serving bags or in loose form. The degree of processing determines whether a tea will be green, black, or red. Green teas are the least processed. They are simply steamed quickly before packaging. Black and red teas are partially dried, crushed, and fermented. Herbal teas (or tisanes) may be a blend of teas along with herbs, spices, flowers, and other flavorings. True tisanes do not contain tea; they are often brewed from leaves, bark, flowers, buds, or fruits.

Although coffee and tea keep well, both should be stored properly to maintain flavor. Whole beans and open containers of coffee should be kept cool; tea should be stored in a cool, dry area away from light and moisture.

Summary

Chefs are being held to a higher standard when it comes to the foods they purchase and prepare. As your guests read more about the concerns surrounding issues like organics and sustainability, they will continue to demand that the chef know more about the food: Where was it raised? How was it raised? What steps go into the processing of the food before you purchased it? How do those steps affect the flavor and quality of that specific food. For some kitchens, a shift to foods that are unprocessed or minimally processed may mean learning new preparation techniques. It is the chef's responsibility to learn as much as possible about the role of healthy ingredients as the bedrock of healthy cooking.

Tea Service

Health Benefits of Tea

Tea leaves contain catechins, phytochemicals that can reduce the risk of some cancers and that are thought to boost the immune system. Green tea has become popular recently because it contains higher concentrations of these compounds than black tea.

Although green tea was the first tea studied for its cancer-fighting benefits, research shows that any tea derived from the leaf of a warm-weather evergreen (*Camellia sinensis*) contains chemicals called polyphenols that give tea its antioxidant properties.

Iced teas can provide as much antioxidant power as hot teas. Bottled, prepared iced teas often have a lower antioxidant level, however, because they contain mostly water and sugar.

Formal tea service (top) includes the following setup: two heated tea pots, one for brewing the tea and one to hold hot water, so the guest can adjust the potency of teas brewed with loose tea. Accompaniments for black tea typically include milk and sugar (or honey). Some tea drinkers add lemon to their brewed black teas, although typically not when they add milk to the tea. If tea is brewed from tea bags instead of loose tea, include a caddy and a strainer to hold the spent bag.

Iced tea (center) service can be very casual. Sweeteners can be added at your guests' discretion. Some operations offer a cruet of flavored syrups to add sweetness or additional flavors (fruits, herbs, and spices can all be infused into the syrup). Long-handled spoons—iced tea spoons—should be part of the service setup.

Herbal teas, sometimes more properly referred to as tisanes, are not derived from the same plant and so do not have the same health-promoting polyphenols. What they do provide however, is a caffeine-free beverage that may offer other benefits. Herbs like chamomile or mint, flowers like hibiscus (a major part of the Ruby Slipper tea shown here) or spices such as clove or cinnamon, are brewed and served in the same manner that you would a traditional brewed tea. Some teas are served with a sweetener, like honey or a sugar syrup, plain or infused with flavors.

3

The Techniques of Healthy Cooking

NUTRITIOUS INGREDIENTS are only part of the healthy cooking equation. The cooking method you choose is of equal importance. When the best ingredients are prepared properly, great-tasting, healthy foods are sure to follow.

Fortunately, most cooking techniques are well suited to a menu designed for healthy cuisine. Deep-frying and pan frying are two exceptions; other techniques require a few minor adaptations, but most work as is.

The technique you choose affects the flavor and quality of the finished dish in several different ways. Flavor will be explored in greater detail on pages 114–27 of this chapter. First, we will review various cooking techniques and explore when and why a chef might want to use one or another. The following cooking methods can be used with great success in healthy cooking.

General Cooking Guidelines

Properly cooked foods should be full of flavor and texture. They should also look appealing. You can easily achieve these goals by pairing ingredients and cooking methods to maximize flavor, texture, and appearance. If healthy cooking is a goal, you should also plan to minimize nutrient loss.

In most cases, traditional cooking methods are well suited to healthy cooking. The exceptions are pan frying and deep-frying, for obvious reasons. The key to cooking foods in a healthy manner is to take a literal approach to classic cooking standards and resist the tendency to add butter, cream, and salt.

Some techniques require minor adaptations; others work as is. With each technique, the quality of the finished dish may be increased by selecting the highest-quality ingredients and preparing them properly.

Foods should be cooked with the goal of retaining moisture and succulence. Sauces should be chosen to enhance flavor without sacrificing nutritional benefit. Although ingredients such as butter and cream can be used in small amounts for enrichment, sauces should be based primarily on vegetables, fruits, and low-fat reductions and essences. Coulis, salsas, chutneys, relishes, and fond de veau lié are all good choices.

All foods should be handled with nutrient retention in mind. Nutrient levels may drop when foods are exposed to light or air, subjected to excessively high levels of heat, cooked in too much liquid, cooked for too long, or cooked under alkaline or very acidic conditions. Preparation techniques should therefore limit exposure to these elements.

Preparing foods as close to cooking time as possible is one of the best ways to minimize nutrient loss. Moist-heat cooking methods that rely on steam and dry-heat methods retain more water-soluble nutrients than simmering or boiling, which cause nutrients to leach into the cooking liquid and get discarded. Stewing and braising are also nutrient-conserving methods because the cooking liquid, which is normally served as a sauce, captures those vitamins and minerals that are not destroyed by heat. Using a bit of fat in preparations helps to make fat-soluble vitamins more available to the body. Although cooking decreases the level of some nutrients, others become more available when foods are cooked. Heat breaks down cell walls in ways that digestion cannot, and it concentrates nutrients.

Overcooking should be avoided at all costs. Foods remain juicy and moist if cooked until just done. Overcooked foods, on the other hand, become dry and tough, or soggy and insipid.

Choose your pan for each technique with care. If you steam vegetables in a pan that's too small, for example, they may sit in the water, not above it. In addition, the pan has a great influence on the outcome of a dish. Its shape, the material it is made of, and any surface treatment of the interior all play a role.

Dry-Heat Techniques

Dry-heat cooking techniques include sautéing, stir-frying, broiling and grilling, baking and roasting, and smoke roasting. These techniques permit foods to brown. As the water in them evaporates, the foods develop a crust and their flavors become extremely intricate. Deep-frying and pan frying are dry-heat techniques, but they are not acceptable for healthy cooking—foods simply absorb too much fat. It is possible to approximate the texture of some fried foods with baking or sautéing, but not all foods can be modified successfully.

Heat can be either direct, as on a stovetop or in a deep-fryer, or indirect, as in the oven or occasionally on a grill.

Sautéing

Sautéing is a natural for healthy cooking. Foods prepared in this manner are cooked quickly in a small amount of fat or oil over medium to high heat. Sautéed foods are often cooked à la minute—that is, they are not prepared until an order arrives in the kitchen. Foods that are freshly prepared are higher in nutrients, flavor, and usually eye-appeal than their precooked counterparts that sit on steam tables or under heat lights or covers.

Sautéing requires foods that are tender, portion-sized or smaller, and thin enough to cook quickly without toughening. Smaller pieces of foods are often stirred so they do not brown too quickly; larger pieces are usually turned once or twice.

Steaks and chops, poultry cuts, and fish fillets or steaks often come to mind when we think of sautéing, and they are sometimes said to be "pan-seared" rather than sautéed. They are often sliced, butterflied, or pounded before sautéing. This is done to make the food of even thickness so it cooks evenly, or to make the item thinner so it cooks more rapidly.

Sautéing can be used with fruits and vegetables as well as with precooked grains, pastas, and legumes. Tender fruits and vegetables like apple slices, spinach, and mushrooms can go directly into the sauté pan. Denser items, such as carrots, turnips, and broccoli, should be parcooked before sautéing.

Sautéing presents a number of opportunities to add flavor. All foods should be seasoned before cooking; this seasoning may be a marinade, a dry spice rub, or a simple sprinkling of salt and freshly ground pepper. (Salt should be applied just before cooking to prevent it from leaching out the food's natural juices.)

As meat, poultry, or seafood items are sautéed, their natural juices become concentrated in the drippings that cook down in the pan, forming what is referred to as the fond. Adding a flavorful liquid to the pan after the food has been removed, a process known as deglazing, dissolves the fond and allows the flavors to be recaptured in a sauce. This sauce can be finished in an infinite number of ways. Sauces should be based on vegetables, vegetable or fruit purées, fond de veau lié, or reductions. High-fat ingredients such as butter, cream, or cheese can be used in small amounts to enrich the sauce if the nutrition profile allows.

Sautéed vegetables retain their color beautifully, and when they are coated with a small amount of fat they look very appealing. They can be tossed with herbs, spices, or citrus zest after cooking, or simply served as is.

Sautéing can also be combined with other techniques. Steaks and chops that are too thick to cook to taste on the stove can be sautéed and finished in the oven. Uncooked grains can be sautéed briefly with aromatics before the cooking liquid is added.

ABOUT SAUTÉ PANS Sauté pans should have a flat bottom with sloping sides to encourage juices released into the pan to reduce rapidly, forming the fond.

The metal should be of a gauge heavy enough to prevent warping and hot spots, and it should be responsive to rapid changes in heat. One of the best choices is aluminum lined with stainless steel; other good choices include copper lined with stainless steel, nonstick pans, and cast-iron sauté pans (known as griswolds).

Dark pans retain heat, and foods cooked in them will brown more, and more rapidly, than foods cooked in shiny pans.

Stir-Frying

Generally associated with Asian styles of cooking, stir-frying is similar to sautéing. Foods are cooked using a small amount of fat, but stir-frying takes place over very high heat, and the foods are cut into small strips, dice, or shreds and are kept constantly moving during the cooking process.

Stir-fried dishes are popular with health-conscious diners because they are often based predominantly on vegetables and grains; meat is used in very small amounts. The chef should choose vegetables with an eye toward variety in color and texture.

Sauces that accompany stir-fried foods are traditionally combinations of intensely flavored liquids thickened with a small amount of cornstarch. As long as soy sauce and sesame oil are used judiciously, these sauces are generally healthy.

ABOUT WOKS A wok is the traditional tool for stir-frying because of its shape, although large sauté pans may also be used.

Woks typically have rounded bottoms with steeply sloping sides. This shape concentrates heat in the bottom of the pan. The sides of the wok have varying degrees of heat, creating "zones" that allow a variety of foods to be prepared in a single pan without over- or undercooking any of them.

Woks should be heavy enough to withstand high temperatures without warping, and should be of a metal that conducts heat evenly.

Grilling and Broiling

Strongly associated with healthy cooking, grilling and broiling are techniques that produce a distinctive flavor element and attractive appearance. They require little if any additional fat during cooking, and foods that are grilled or broiled are generally lean.

These techniques are very similar: In grilling, the heat source is below the food, but in broiling it is above. Grilling can be done over wood or charcoal, whereas broiling is done in the oven. With few exceptions, foods that can be grilled can also be broiled and vice versa. Broilers can offer a bit more control than grills, and they can be used to prepare very delicate foods, such as flounder, or to give foods that are not turned a brown crust. Grilled foods may have a smoky flavor that broiled ones don't (see The Flavor of Wood Chips, page 91).

Tender meats, poultry, and seafood are commonly grilled or broiled, but don't overlook pairing foods like fruits, vegetables, or even flatbreads with these techniques. Just about any vegetable, including such unusual choices as fennel, scallions, radicchio, and asparagus, can be grilled or broiled. Dense vegetables like winter squash or sweet potatoes should either be parcooked before grilling or started on the grill and finished by another cooking method. Adding grilled or broiled vegetables to a soup, stew, or pilaf adds an intriguing depth of flavor.

Fruits such as pineapple rings and peach halves can be grilled or broiled successfully. Serve them alongside meats, chop them into a salsa, or use them in a side dish. Fruits can also be glazed with syrup or a sprinkling of sugar before broiling. Broiled grapefruit, sprinkled with brown sugar, makes an elegant breakfast or novel starter.

RECENT RESEARCH INDICATES that marinades do more than just boost flavor. They can yield a significant health benefit.

All high-temperature cooking methods, including grilling, broiling, roasting, and frying, can result in potentially carcinogenic substances forming on foods. Grilling is particularly dangerous, because fat dripping on hot coals creates smoke that rises back to the foods. Scientists at the Lawrence Livermore National Laboratory in California found that marinating foods for as little as five minutes before grilling can dramatically reduce the presence of some carcinogens. The researchers tested commercial marinades as well as a homemade version; all produced the same positive results.

To lessen the potential for formation of carcinogens, foods can be partially cooked by other methods. Poach, simmer, or steam foods before finishing them on the grill, or mark them briefly on the grill and finish them in the oven.

Extremely delicate or small foods can be placed in a hand rack before grilling, or they can be skewered or wrapped in a protective coating such as dampened cornhusks or grape leaves.

Flavors can be added to foods before, during, and after grilling and broiling. Marinades and dry rubs can be used on foods before cooking (see More than Flavoring, sidebar), and a variety of basting sauces can be used during and after. The choice of sauce is an area where the chef has control over a dish's nutrition profile. Sugary sauces such as teriyaki or barbecue sauce, or emulsified, butter-based sauces or compound butters such as béarnaise or ginger-lime butter should be avoided or limited. Coulis, reductions, cold or warm salsas, chutneys, and other relishes are all healthy choices.

In addition to wood chips, use stems, herbs, grapevine trimmings, and other aromatics to add flavor to grilled foods. Take care to consider whether these aromatics will work with the food to be grilled: not all foods stand up to the strong aroma and flavor of mesquite, for example. If you wish to use aromatics, they should be soaked in cold water while the grill heats. When the grill is hot, they can be thrown on top of the coals or firestones, where they smolder and create a smoke bath that surrounds the food.

ABOUT GRILLING AND BROILING EQUIPMENT In order to produce high-quality grilled foods, proper preparation and maintenance of the grill is extremely important. The rack should be scrupulously cleaned every day before it is heated, and it should be scrubbed with a wire brush frequently during service time to prevent flavors from transferring among different types of foods. After each cleaning, the grill should be lightly coated with oil. This facilitates removing food, and lessens the need to apply oil directly to foods.

Baskets and perforated sheets prevent small and delicate foods from falling into the grill; they can also make turning delicate foods easier.

Broiler pans consist of a rack and a pan with shallow sides so that fat can drip off the meat, poultry, or fish during cooking.

Roasting and Baking

Roasting and baking are ideal techniques for the healthy kitchen. Foods emerge from the oven or rotisserie with flavors that cannot be duplicated by any other technique. They are surrounded by hot air, which cooks foods gently through indirect heat (air is less efficient at conducting heat than fats, liquids, or even steam). Although some foods are traditionally coated with fat or high-fat ingredients before roasting, foods do not require additional fat to be roasted or baked, and as long as foods are not overcooked, they remain moist and flavorful.

These techniques are basically the same procedure. In common parlance, large cuts of meat and whole poultry and fish are said to be roasted while smaller pieces are baked. (Conversely, vegetables that are cut into pieces are said to be roasted, whereas when left whole, they are baked.)

While most people associate roasting with meat or poultry, fruits and vegetables take beautifully to this technique. Their juices evaporate slowly, their flavors concentrate, and the heat caramelizes their natural sugars and leaves them soft and tender on the inside and crisply browned on the outside. Roasting is ideal for dense vegetables; root vegetables like potatoes, carrots, and Jerusalem artichokes are commonly roasted, as are squash, garlic, and even fennel. But experiment with less obvious vegetables, such as asparagus spears, broccoli, cauliflower florets, or tomatoes. Soups made from roasted vegetables are unusually delicious and definitely worth trying.

In the past, extremely lean meats and poultry were barded or basted before roasting to keep them from drying out. Adding fat before or during cooking, and serving meats and poultry with high-fat gravies, is not necessary. Properly cooked meats, poultry, and fish retain their moisture perfectly well. Care must be taken that foods are not overcooked, and that technique matches food. Some cuts of meat are simply too dry for roasting and are better braised; other cuts can be brined before roasting to add moisture. Poultry can be roasted with the skin on to retain moisture, but the skin should be removed before service.

Salt is an essential flavoring in roasted and baked foods, and it is critical to the proper execution of these techniques. A judicious seasoning before cooking allows the salt to draw out some moisture, which dissolves the salt and helps it to permeate the food. As the moisture on the surface of the food evaporates in the oven's heat, the food develops the appealing color and crust that are the hallmarks of roasting and baking.

Flavor can also be added with stuffings and sauces, and they do not need to be complicated. Quartered onions or lemons and sprigs of herbs can infuse a roasted chicken with a lovely flavor. Try cutting thin slits or pockets into leg of lamb or pork loin and stuffing them with a paste of herbs or slivered garlic. Grain- and vegetable-based stuffings can take the place of fat-laden ones, and a jus lié or a contemporary accompaniment of puréed fruits or vegetables can take the place of gravy. Before deglazing the roasting pan, the drippings should be clarified; or heat them until the solids and juices drop to the bottom of the pan and the fat rises to the top. Pour or spoon off the fat before adding the deglazing liquid.

Portion-sized baked items are perfect candidates for a flavorful crust. Coating items with seasoned toppings protects them from drying out and creates a crispy coating. Try using dried potato flakes or rice flakes, bread crumbs or panko, cornflake or cracker crumbs, cornmeal, finely ground dried mushrooms, finely chopped nuts, or pastes.

ABOUT ROASTING PANS Roasting pans should have a flat bottom and relatively low sides so that air can circulate. Sheet pans, half-sheet pans, and jelly-roll pans can be used as well, particularly for vegetables, fruits, and individual portions of meat, poultry, or fish. Pans should hold the food comfortably. If the pan is too large, juices will evaporate too quickly and may scorch rather than develop a fond; if the pan is too small, the juices won't evaporate quickly enough and the food will steam. Vegetables should be in a single layer, as they brown best when they are in contact with the hot pan.

Roasting pans should be of a heavy gauge, and a light or shiny interior is better than a dark finish. Dark metals absorb heat and can hasten the evaporation of juices. Any handles should be riveted on. Handles that fold down make storage convenient, but they are difficult to grab when wearing mitts or holding towels. Either avoid handles entirely or opt for those that stay up all the time.

The Flavor of Wood Chips

PART OF THE APPEAL of grilled and smoke-roasted foods is their flavor, and wood chips are often a large part of the taste. Different woods impart vastly different flavors to foods. Use wood chips that complement the food you are cooking for the best results.

- **Alder** has a very mild taste; it is ideal with vegetables and fish.

- **Apple** has a unique fruity flavor that pairs well with fresh ham, frog legs, pork chops, sweet sausages, Cornish hens, and salmon.

- **Cherry** is similar to apple but has a slightly tart aftertaste; it is ideal with lamb, pheasant, duck, venison, and beef.

- **Hickory** has a strong, heavy flavor that is usually associated with bacon; it is ideal for barbecued foods, spicy foods, steaks, and chops.

- **Maple** has a subtle hint of sweetness; use it with turkey, ham, Canadian bacon, beef or pork tenderloin, poultry, and most kinds of game and vegetables.

- **Mesquite** has a Southwestern tang that imparts a slightly hot, burning sensation as an aftertaste. Use it with pork and most red meats.

- **Oak** is a mellower version of mesquite, but it is still quite intense. It is ideal with steaks, hamburgers, and duck.

- **Pecan** has a mellow flavor not unlike hickory; use it with chicken, duck, and most game birds.

- **Sweet birch** leaves a delicate sweetness on the palate. It is ideal with chicken, tuna, salmon, lamb, barbecued pork, and all vegetables, especially those in the onion family.

A rack allows air to circulate on all sides of the food. If you are roasting a whole bird or fish or a large cut of meat, consider using vegetables to elevate the food instead of a rack. Thickly sliced onions or carrots accomplish the same, and add flavor to the fond.

Smoke-Roasting

Smoke-roasting, or pan-smoking, is a technique for hot-smoking foods without special equipment. Foods are roasted in a bath of smoke and emerge from the pan infused with the flavors of whatever aromatics were chosen—hardwood chips, teas, or herbs are most common. Smoke-roasted foods have an advantage over traditionally smoked foods because they do not contain nitrites, and because they are not brined they are generally lower in sodium.

Foods should be marinated or liberally seasoned before smoke-roasting. Thick foods, such as duck breasts, should be partially smoked and finished in the oven. If they are smoke-roasted until they are cooked to doneness, the smoky taste can overwhelm the food's natural flavor.

Moist-Heat Techniques

Moist-heat cooking methods include steaming, shallow poaching, deep poaching, simmering, boiling, stewing, and braising. Foods are cooked in or over liquid. Because water evaporates at temperatures over 212°F/100°C, moist-heat cooking methods keep foods from reaching the temperatures necessary for browning. Foods cooked by these methods retain their natural flavors and often their colors as well.

When foods are put into cold water and then set over heat, their flavors and water-soluble nutrients will leach into the cooking liquid. Foods added to boiling water, though, develop a seal when they come into contact with the hot liquid and retain most of their flavor and nutrients.

Steaming

When people think of healthy cooking, steaming is probably the cooking technique they think of first. Foods most suited to steaming are healthy ones like vegetables, fruits, seafood, and poultry breasts. Steamed foods retain nutrients because they do not come into direct contact with the cooking liquid, and the foods are prepared without the addition of fats or oils.

The primary challenge of steamed foods is keeping the food from tasting dull or bland. Introducing additional flavors with a buttery sauce is anathema to healthy cooking. Adding aromatics to the steaming liquid can help, as can using liquids like broth or juice. Reheating steamed vegetables with a quick sauté, perhaps adding garlic or scallions, is another way to add flavor. Pan steaming and cooking en papillote are two steaming variations that can also solve this problem handily.

Many cuisines have evolved flavorful steaming techniques. Foods can be combined with a sauce or pungent aromatics in a dish, and then set in the steamer. Other options include wrapping foods in banana leaves or corn husks. Some wrappers add a bit of their own flavor, others permit you to introduce seasonings, aromatics, stuffings, and toppings that can be held in place as the food steams.

Large steamers are an effective way to prepare foods in batches, especially for volume operations. It is just as important to assure that foods to be steamed are properly flavored as they cook, as well as after they are fully cooked and ready to be served.

En Papillote

Foods cooked en papillote are encased in parchment paper and baked. The foods are cooked by trapped steam; the parchment puffs up, and the envelope is opened to dramatic effect in front of the guest. Foods that are naturally moist and tender, such as fish, are most successfully prepared en papillote, but any food that can be cooked in a relatively short time can be prepared en papillote.

To make the paper sack for foods made en papillote, cut a large, heart-shaped piece of parchment. Make an aromatic bed from herbs, vegetables, or other aromatic ingredients on one half of the heart, top with the main ingredient, and then moisten with a touch of broth,

juice, or other liquid. These ingredients and their natural juices will combine to form a sauce. Once all the ingredients are assembled, fold the paper heart in half and then make a series of folds around the edge to crimp the paper tightly enough to trap steam as the food cooks.

Some recipes call for the parchment to be oiled. This is not entirely necessary, but it does create a barrier that keeps the liquid from seeping into the paper as quickly. Because the paper, not the food, is oiled, very little fat is added to the dish.

Once the packet is assembled and sealed, it is placed in a very hot oven. Some chefs like to give the dish a bit of a head start by putting it in a pan over direct heat to warm the pan and start generating a bit of steam. You can choose to do this before you put it into a hot oven, or you can simply put the packets on a sheet pan and bake them from start to finish. The paper

heart will puff up into a balloon. Once the packet is broken open, a cloud of aromatic steam escapes, so this is best done at the table in front of the guest.

ABOUT STEAMERS Steaming must take place in a pan with a lid, and the pan must be deep enough to hold the food above the liquid and large enough to allow the steam to circulate. Steamer baskets are ideal for small amounts of foods. Tiered steamers, such as those used in Asian cooking, are best for large amounts of food or for several foods that cook for different lengths of time. Pressure steamers and convection steamers are ideal for very large quantities of foods.

Shallow Poaching

Shallow poaching is a popular method of cooking that is usually used with tender fish and poultry breasts. The food is placed on a bed of aromatic ingredients, then combined with a few ounces of flavorful liquid, covered loosely, and gently simmered until done. The cooking liquid becomes even more flavorful, and it is usually reduced and used as the basis for the accompanying sauce.

Traditionally, the reduced cooking liquid is enriched with butter and cream. A more contemporary approach is to combine it with a vegetable or fruit coulis. Another option is to thicken it with a little cornstarch or arrowroot and add a touch of evaporated milk to approximate the mouthfeel, flavor, and color of cream.

WHETHER YOU CHOOSE nonstick pans, stainless steel–lined pans, or cast iron, you'll need to treat your cookware carefully to maintain it.

Nonstick surfaces are generally the least durable and should be reserved for special purposes, such as making crêpes or egg dishes. They should be cleaned gently without abrasives and stored carefully with a layer of toweling between each pan to prevent the surfaces from becoming marred. Metal utensils or pot scrubbers should not be used, as they will scratch the finish and eventually destroy the nonstick coating.

Pans lined with stainless steel tend to hold up well without much special care. However, their surfaces should be scoured with salt or nylon scrubbers rather than stainless-steel scrubbers to avoid unduly scratching the surface.

Cast-iron pans must be seasoned before the first use. This treatment seals the porous surface by permeating it with oil. A properly seasoned cast-iron pan usually does not need fat added to it, even when sautéing delicate foods. To season a pan, brush or wipe the inside with vegetable oil, then pour in more oil to a depth of one-quarter inch. Heat the pan for 1 hour in a 300°F/149°C oven. Cool the pan, then wipe away any excess oil.

Whenever possible, the seasoned pan should be wiped clean after each use rather than washed. This maintains the protective seal on the pan's interior. If the pan must be washed, dry it thoroughly in an oven or over very low heat to prevent rust from forming, and then wipe the pan with oil before storing. The seasoning will last through several uses as long as the pan is properly cared for, but periodic reseasoning will be necessary.

Deep Poaching, Simmering, and Boiling

These techniques involve fully immersing a food in liquid throughout the cooking. The difference involves the temperature range at which the cooking takes place. Poaching occurs between 160° and 180°F/71° and 82°C, simmering between 185° and 200°F/85° and 93°C, and boiling at or around 212°F/100°C.

Deep poaching is the gentlest of these methods and is best for tender items such as fish and poultry breasts. Simmering acts to tenderize and rehydrate foods, and is best for dense vegetables, grains, beans, whole birds such as stewing hens, and cuts of meat from the shoulder or shank. Boiling is recommended for some vegetables and dried pasta; it can cause other foods to become tough and stringy.

Liquids other than water or broth can be used, and aromatic ingredients like wine, vinegar, and herbs may be added to the liquid to enrich its flavor. Grains, particularly those served for breakfast, take on a subtle sweetness when cooked in cider and a rich, creamy texture cooked in milk. Couscous or rice simmered in diluted orange juice pairs well with Indian or Moroccan flavors; try coconut milk, too. Use caution when cooking grains or legumes in acidic liquids, including those to which tomatoes have been added. The acids keep these foods from becoming tender.

Stewing and Braising

Stewing and braising are techniques in which one or more main ingredients and aromatics are gently simmered in flavorful liquids; the cooking liquid becomes the sauce. Foods can be cooked in the oven, which provides very gentle, even heat, or on the stove.

These techniques are essentially the same; ingredients in a stew are usually cut into bite-sized pieces and are submerged in the cooking liquid, whereas braised items are usually portion-sized or larger and are only partially covered with liquid. These techniques result in very rich flavors and thick sauces. They are often thought of as hearty, but they don't have to be. Ratatouille, the vegetable stew from Provence, and fish stews can be light additions to summer menus.

Flavor development is critical in stews and braises, and demands careful monitoring throughout cooking time. Some stews and braises call for the main ingredient(s) to be cooked to a certain color directly in hot fat, before you add the liquid. This tends to produce a richer, more complex flavor. Others require the main ingredients to be blanched in boiling water or steam; this step can help control or reduce strong flavors or odors that might become overwhelming by the time the dish finishes cooking as well as to give a dish a particular color. Green vegetables look greener, for instance, when they are blanched before you add them to a stew.

The beauty of braises and stews is that nothing is lost in the cooking process. Heat-resistant nutrients and flavors are captured in the sauce. These dishes are best when prepared a day in advance and refrigerated overnight before serving. When they are allowed to rest before serving, their flavors blend and mature; the cooling step also affords the opportunity to remove any fat that rises to the top.

ABOUT PANS FOR BRAISING AND STEWING A heavy-gauge pot with a lid is ideal for stews and braises. It will distribute the heat evenly and help to protect the food from cooking too quickly, and the lid will help to prevent the liquid from evaporating too rapidly.

If any of the ingredients are acidic, choose a pan made of a nonreactive metal, such as anodized aluminum, enameled cast iron, or stainless steel. Materials like copper, cast iron, and aluminum will react with such ingredients as tomatoes and lemon juice to create discolored foods and a metallic taste.

Earthenware or ceramic casseroles are also commonly used for braises and stews, particularly those traditionally prepared in Mexican, Mediterranean, and Spanish kitchens. A tagine is one such casserole. It consists of a glazed dish that holds the food and a conical lid that traps the steam from the food and essentially bastes itself through the cooking time. In Spain and Mexico, earthenware casseroles known as *cazuelas* are common. Be sure to handle this fragile cookware carefully.

COOKING IS THE ACT OF APPLYING HEAT to foods to prepare them for eating. There are three ways that heat is transferred to food: conduction, convection, and radiation.

Conduction is the direct transfer of heat; sautéing and stir-frying are examples. Cooking on a range allows heat to be transferred from the burner to the pan, and then from the pan to the food. If the pan is not in direct contact with the stove, conduction does not occur. Conduction is most efficient in metal (some are better conductors of heat than others); glass and ceramic are poor conductors of heat, as are gases such as air and liquids.

Convection is the transfer of heat through gases and liquids. As the gas or liquid closest to the heat becomes warm it rises, and cooler, less dense portions of gas or liquid replace it. Convection is therefore a combination of conduction and mixing. This mixing can occur when foods are stirred, as on the stove, or when a fan is used in a convection oven.

Radiation is the transference of heat through waves of electromagnetic energy that travel through space. When they come into contact with the food, molecules on its surface begin to move more rapidly, increasing the food's temperature.

There are two types of radiation. Infrared radiation includes coals of a charcoal grill and coils of an electric toaster, broiler, or oven. As the coils or coals heat up, energy travels from them to the foods. Dark, dull, and rough surfaces absorb radiant energy; shiny, smooth, light-colored ones reflect it. Microwave radiation transfers energy through short, high-frequency waves. These cook foods much faster than infrared radiation because they penetrate foods several inches deep, whereas infrared waves are absorbed mainly at the surface.

Special Cooking Tools and Materials

Bamboo, clay, and other materials are used to produce a wide variety of cooking tools. Matching the material of the tool to the cooking technique as well as the foods you are cooking is the mark of a more advanced approach to cooking. Traditional tools have special characteristics.

Bamboo steamers, for instance, are not completely airtight, making it easier to maintain an even, gentle cooking speed for foods with bright, clear colors. The material of the steamer absorbs moisture as the food steams to eliminate the potential for condensation. The bamboo also imparts a subtle flavor of its own. Bamboo steamers should be washed with warm water and a mild detergent by hand, not in a dishwasher. Let them air-dry thoroughly before storing them in a dry, ventilated area.

Clay and ceramic cookware may be glazed or unglazed. Like bamboo steamers, clay cookers also introduce a specific and subtle flavor in foods. Clay holds heat well and releases it slowly for gentle, even cooking. However, clay is fragile and can shatter when exposed to extremes of heat, for instance, putting a hot clay cooker onto a cold surface. Unglazed clay is porous enough to absorb the flavor of detergents, so it is best to scrub the surfaces to remove cooked-on foods. If necessary, you can soak unglazed cookware, but avoid coarse scrubbing pads.

In addition to traditional tools such as the tagine pictured here or a bamboo steamer, chefs are turning to newer technologies as part of their healthy cooking repertoire. Techniques like sous-vide and cook-chill allow the chef to prepare foods that work well in both batch cooking systems and à la carte restaurants.

Other Cooking Methods

Microwave ovens are common in most kitchens. They can be used to cook some foods, but their chief advantage in the healthy kitchen lies in their ability to reheat foods rapidly. Soups, stews, and grain dishes that are prepared in large batches can be cooled, divided into smaller batches or individual portions, and reheated as necessary before garnishing and serving.

Induction cooktops are relatively new. They are made of a smooth ceramic material over an induction coil. The coil creates a magnetic current that heats metal pans quickly, yet the cooktop itself remains cool. Cookware for induction cooktops must contain iron to work properly, and they must be flat on the bottom so they come into contact with the heat. Induction offers the advantage of rapid heating and easy cleanup.

Techniques for Vegetables

Delicious and properly cooked vegetables are vital to any healthy menu. The techniques described on pages 86–99 are all appropriate for vegetables. All vegetables must be rinsed and trimmed, Some of the techniques are best when vegetables are cut into the appropriate size and shape (consult your recipe for guidance). If you are preparing more than one vegeable in a single dish, be sure to add them to the dish at the right time. While time-temperature tables can be misleading, you can consult them for guidance concerning which vegetables to add to the stew first and which to reserve for the final few minutes of stewing time. Pan steaming, and its close relation, oven steaming, are two techniques for vegetables introduced in this section, along with the technique for making vegetable purées. These purées can be used to make the base of a sauce or soup, a thickener, a binder, or a side dish.

Pan Steaming

Pan steaming is most often used with vegetables. They are cooked directly in a very small amount of simmering liquid but are not completely immersed. As the liquid reduces, it creates a glaze and eliminates the need for a sauce. The liquid is usually flavorful, such as broth or juice, and herbs or other aromatics may be added. Carrots are delicious pan steamed in orange juice with fresh ginger; fish can be pan steamed in court-bouillon. Cooking greens also take well to pan steaming. Sauté them with garlic, if desired, then add a small amount of liquid and cover. The steam will tenderize tough leaves like those of kale and collards.

Steam-Roasting Vegetables

While pan steaming is great for leafy vegetables, diced or sliced vegetables, and naturally tender vegetables like peas or asparagus, it doesn't work as well for dense vegetables, or those with heavy rinds. You can roast vegetables like squash or eggplant whole, just as you might do for sweet potatoes. A few additional steps make it faster and easier to cook and prepare these vegetables.

If possible, cut the vegetable in half, as we've done with the squash shown here. Use a heavy knife to cut through the rind and split the vegetable open. Then, use a kitchen or serving spoon to scoop out the seeds. (Some squash seeds are delicious and make a great addition to salads or as a garnish for side dishes or soups, so save them to season and roast, if you wish.) Place the vegetable cut side down in a roasting pan with a little water. Cover the pan with foil or a tight-fitting lid to trap the steam that the water will create when it heats up in the oven.

Steam-roast the vegetable with the cover in place until the flesh is tender. The vegetable usually takes on an appealing golden color and a rich, roasted flavor. The steam also helps to separate the skin or rind from the flesh.

Scoop the cooked flesh out of the vegetable, if necessary, or cut it into pieces. This squash could be puréed and then used in a number of ways: added to a sauce or soup for flavor and color, added to batters for quickbreads or griddle cakes, mixed into a timbale or custard, or finished with seasonings and stock to serve as a side dish.

VEGETABLES ARE OFTEN BOILED, steamed, or baked until they are soft enough to make into a purée. Some are naturally soft or moist enough uncooked to make into a purée. The purée itself can be served as is or it may be used as a base for such dishes as vegetable timbales, custards, croquettes, or soufflés. It may also be used as an ingredient in other dishes or to flavor or color a sauce or soup.

Vegetables purées can range in texture from coarse to very smooth. If necessary or desired, cook the vegetables until the flesh is soft enough to mash easily. Cooked vegetables should be puréed while still very hot. Use a clean towel to protect your hands as you work. Once the vegetables are roasted, cut away heavy or inedible peels, rinds, stems, or roots. Scoop or squeeze out seeds. Remove as little edible flesh as possible. Break or cut the vegetable in pieces sized properly for the puréeing equipment.

Select the equipment to make the purée according to the way it will be used. A food mill, ricer, or sieve will remove fibers, skin, and seeds. These tools produce purées with a rather rough texture. Food processors can make quite smooth purées from cooked or raw vegetables that have already been trimmed, peeled, and seeded. If the vegetable is fibrous, the processor won't necessarily remove the strings, so the purée will need to be pushed through a sieve. Blenders (immersion or countertop) and vertical chopping machines can cut vegetables so finely that they produce a very smooth purée, though they, too, do not remove fibers and strings from some vegetables.

A vegetable purée can be finished by adjusting its seasoning, adding stock or a little touch of cream or butter, or blending it into other preparations. Or it may be cooled and stored for later use. Cool hot purées over an ice bath before wrapping and storing. Reheat cooled purées over gentle heat or in a bain-marie.

Working with Leafy Greens

Leafy greens are prepared by a technique that combines elements of sautéing and pan steaming. Preheat the pan and add a small amount of a flavorful fat such as olive oil or a bit of a well-flavored stock or broth. You can add aromatics like garlic or spices to the pan; add them before you add the greens so they can infuse the entire dish with flavor.

Trim and rinse the greens. Let them drain, but some moisture should still be clinging to them to create steam in the pan (top). Leafy greens are loosely mounded in the pan, then, as they cook, they lose volume quickly and appear wilted and softened. Add seasonings and continue to sauté until the vegetables are fully cooked and flavorful. Some vegetables must be kept in nearly constant motion as they sauté; others develop a better flavor and color when turned only once or twice. Use offset spatulas, tongs, or stir-frying tools to turn and lift vegetables as they sauté. Very tender greens, like baby spinach, usually don't need to be covered as they cook. Heartier greens, like kale or collards, benefit from a bit of steam heat to cook them until tender. Once the greens are softened and wilted, cover the pan and let the greens cook in a steam bath created by the liquid that they release naturally.

As leafy greens cook, their color intensifies. Now is the time to introduce additional flavoring or garnishing ingredients. Pepper is a popular seasoning, but you may also want to add a touch of toasted nuts (pine nuts, walnuts, almonds, or hazelnuts) or dried fruits. You may opt to reserve the oil that might have been used as a cooking medium to introduce as a final flavoring ingredient (bottom). You can get a great flavor from a very small amount, if you add the oil at the end instead of the beginning. Cold-pressed oils made from nuts or olives are too volatile to use at high heat, but they shine as a final seasoning.

NOT LONG AGO, it was an accepted standard practice for a restaurant to prepare single giant batches of the vegetable and starch of the day prior to the beginning of a service period. The batches were left in a steam table, where they degenerated into pallid versions of their original, freshly cooked selves before being heaped onto every plate that left the kitchen, regardless of how well they complemented the main element. Given what we now know about nutrient retention, this type of cooking is anathema to the tenets of healthy cooking.

Kitchens that cook menu items to order may be able to devise practical methods for cooking many types of vegetables to order, or they may elect to prepare small batches several times throughout a service period so that a fresh supply of cooked items is constantly available. This second approach, known as batch cooking, minimizes the unnecessary loss of flavor, texture, nutrients, and color that occurs when cooked vegetables and fruits are held for long periods. Cooking to order and batch cooking further eliminate the need to reheat cooked foods, a process that often requires the addition of fat, and when foods are cooked as needed, costs are often controlled because waste is reduced.

Because of the nutrient loss that occurs when its surface is exposed to air and light, produce should be rinsed, trimmed, and cut as close to cooking time as is practical. Blanching vegetables stops many of the enzymatic reactions that cause nutrient loss. However,

if the vegetables are shocked in cold water to stop the cooking process they should be removed as soon as they are cool so that nutrients don't leach into the water. In fact, holding vegetables in water, before or after cooking, should be avoided unless the vegetable will discolor when exposed to air.

Various knife cuts can be used to add visual interest to the plate. You should also try to take advantage of cooking techniques that allow the fruit or vegetable to be cooked quickly, with as little added liquid as reasonable. Grilling, stir-frying, broiling, roasting, steaming, pan steaming, and microwaving are all healthy cooking techniques that can be applied to vegetables with excellent results. For more information on these cooking methods, review pages 86–99.

Techniques for Fruits

Customarily used in sweet dishes, fruits are used in desserts such as pies and ice creams, served with or without cheese as a classic finale to a meal, or used in soups or salads. But fruits can be used to great effect in savory dishes as well. Fruit is an excellent foil for richly flavored or oily meat, poultry, and fish, Pork and apples, duck and orange, turkey and cranberries, and lamb with dried fruit, particularly apricots, are natural pairings. Dried fruits add flavor and texture to compotes, stuffings, and sauces.

Fruits can be used to great advantage on their own. Consider broiling fresh citrus or other fruit to caramelize the natural sugars.

When using apples, take care to match the variety to the dish. Some hold their shape, while others disintegrate and are better for sauces or purées; some have thick peels that are obtrusive in a cooked dish, while others have thin skins.

Grilling and Roasting Fruits

A fresh fruit plate is a classic end to many meals, but a guest in your restaurant may want something that is more dramatic or unusual. Grilling and roasting enhance the natural sweetness in fruits. These intense, dry-heat cooking methods also change a fruit's texture and color. Certain flavors that are hard to identify in the fresh fruit become more prominent.

Fruits are usually softer than vegetables and you may need to give them a very light coating of oil or put them in a hand rack so they don't stick or tear when you turn them over. Pineapple has a lot of natural sugar and is quite juicy. Be sure the heat is high enough to quickly mark the outside. The grill marks add color and some texture, of course, but they also introduce a pleasantly smoky, bitter taste.

Roasted fruits, like the oranges shown here, are prepared by slicing the fruit thinly enough so that it cooks to the texture and flavor you want. Like grilling, roasting amplifies some of the fruit's natural flavors. It also has a more noticeable effect on the fruit texture, drying it until it is almost leathery. Fruits can be roasted at a low temperature for short periods to soften them slightly, or for a longer period to create crunchy or chewy textures. Roasted fruits are a good garnish for fruit desserts, salads, or as an element in a sauce, compote, or salsa.

Techniques for Grains

The USDA's Dietary Guidelines recommends 6 ounces of grains a day for a 2,000-calorie diet, and at least half of those should be whole grains.

The subtle flavors of many grains and grain-based products make them ideal for carrying the flavors of other foods, and enable them to act as a base for smaller portions of more pungent and highly flavored foods. A mound of steaming couscous served with a spicy stew and piquant harissa sauce does more than fill up the plate. It also offers the diner a chance to calm a tongue burned by hot spices and chiles. A bed of fragrant basmati rice makes a serving of seafood curry appear more bountiful, and each grain can carry the complex flavors of the sauce without losing its own special savor.

Grains have great potential for uses other than side dishes. They can be used in every category of recipe from salads and stuffings to desserts. For breakfast, grains are a natural and appear in hot and cold cereals, waffles, pancakes, French toast, and quick breads. Additionally, the high starch content of some grains, such as amaranth and rice, makes them very useful for thickening soups and sauces.

Items baked with whole-grain flours generally have a darker appearance, a chewier, denser texture, and a nuttier, more pronounced flavor than those made from white wheat flour (which is stripped of its germ and bran before milling). Formulas for whole-grain leavened breads often require the addition of some white flour, which has a higher ratio of gluten protein. Gluten is necessary in yeast doughs for proper rising, which lightens the texture. The greater the proportion of white flour, the lighter the bread. Flatbreads that do not rely on yeast and gluten for leavening can be made entirely from whole-grain flours.

Consider cooking grains in liquids other than water. Broth, juice, or dilutions of both add flavor. Toasting grains or sautéing them with aromatics before adding liquid enhances their inherent nuttiness. Mixing herbs, nuts, or dried fruits into cooked grains adds flavor and texture.

Whole grains take longer to cook than do processed or refined grains. Consult the Cooking Ratios and Times for Selected Grains table on page 108 for specific information.

Whole grains added to waffles

Simmered grains as a hot cereal

Grains take prominence in an appetizer

Pasta

Grains are also used to make pastas and noodles, which are often among the most popular items on a menu. There are hundreds of pastas and noodles in the global pantry. Italian pasta comes in a multitude of shapes; Asian noodles are made from a variety of grain and legume flours, German cuisine has spätzle, and North African people enjoy couscous.

The possibilities with pastas and noodles are as endless as the forms in which they come. Pasta dough can be flavored and colored with various ingredients such as fresh herbs, saffron, spinach, or tomato (these ingredients comprise only a small amount of the actual serving and thus have a negligible impact on nutrient intake). The dough can also be stuffed with sweet or savory fillings; avoid high-fat, high-cholesterol ingredients such as cream, butter, and bacon for these fillings for best nutrition. Vegetables and herbs make much better companions and should be used as much as possible.

Cooking Ratios and Times for Selected Grains

GRAIN	RATIO OF GRAIN TO LIQUID (CUPS)	APPROXIMATE YIELD (CUPS)	COOKING TIME
AMARANTH	1:1	1½	12 to 17 minutes
BARLEY, PEARLED	1:2	4	35 to 45 minutes
BARLEY GROATS	1:2½	4	50 minutes to 1 hour
BUCKWHEAT GROATS (KASHA)	1:1½ to 2	2	12 to 20 minutes
FARRO	1:2	2½	20 to 25 minutes
HOMINY, WHOLE	1:2½	3	2½ to 3 hours
HOMINY GRITS	1:4	3	25 minutes
JOB'S TEARS	1:2	3	1 hour
KAMUT, WHOLE GRAIN	1:1½	2	1 hour
MILLET	1:2	3	30 to 35 minutes
OAT GROATS	1:2	2	45 minutes to 1 hour
CORNMEAL	1:3 to 3½	3	35 to 45 minutes
QUINOA	1:2	3½ to 4	10 to 12 minutes
RICE, ARBORIO (RISOTTO)	1:3	3	20 to 30 minutes
RICE, AROMATIC	1:1½	3	15 to 25 minutes
RICE, CONVERTED	1:1¾	4	25 to 30 minutes
RICE, LONG-GRAIN, BROWN	1:3	4	40 minutes
RICE, LONG-GRAIN, WHITE	1:1½ to 1¾	3	18 to 20 minutes
RICE, SHORT-GRAIN, BROWN	1:2½	4	35 to 40 minutes
RICE, SHORT-GRAIN, WHITE	1:1 to 1½	3	20 to 30 minutes
RICE, WILD	1:3	4	30 to 45 minutes
RICE, WILD, PECAN	1:1¾	4	20 minutes
SPELT, WHOLE GRAIN	1:1½	2	45 minutes
TEFF	1:1	1½	7 minutes
TRITICALE, WHOLE GRAIN	1:3	2½	75 minutes
WHEAT BERRIES	1:3	2	1 hour
WHEAT, BULGUR, PILAF	1:2½	2	15 to 20 minutes
WHEAT, BULGUR, SOAKED	1:4	2	2 hours
WHEAT, CRACKED	1:2	3	20 minutes

Techniques for Legumes

Before using dried legumes, pick through them to remove shriveled, moldy, or damp ones, as well as any small stones that find their way into packages.

All high-fiber foods, including beans, contain complex sugars called oligosaccharides that are indigestible by the human body. When they are ingested, these sugars are consumed by bacteria in the colon. The bacteria then produce carbon dioxide and other gases that lead to the flatulence problem so often associated with beans.

Tolerance for oligosaccharides can be built up by eating high-fiber foods often, but because most people in the United States tend not to eat beans regularly, soaking and discarding the liquid is probably the kindest route. Soaking beans soften their skins, making them less likely to burst while cooking, and it also causes most of the oligosaccharides to leach into the water. However, soaking also causes nutrients, flavor, and color to leach into the water. Discarding the water reduces the level of oligosaccharides and nutrients; using this liquid to cook the beans preserves both.

Before soaking beans, they should be carefully sorted to remove broken or moldy beans or bits of stone and then rinsed in cold water. The long-soak method calls for beans to be soaked in cool water under refrigeration for the appropriate amount of time (see table below). The short-soak method calls for beans to be combined in a pot with enough cold water to cover them generously and brought to a boil. As soon as the liquid boils, turn off the heat, cover the pot, and let the beans soak for one hour.

After soaking the beans, drain and rinse them (if desired) and then cook them at a simmer in plenty of plain, unsalted water. Add flavorings such as a bouquet garni, epazote, or onions during the final thirty minutes or so of cooking, once the beans have stopped producing large amounts of foam on the top of the water.

Approximate Soaking and Cooking Times for Selected Legumes

TYPE	APPROXIMATE SOAKING TIME	APPROXIMATE COOKING TIME	APPROXIMATE CUP YIELD FROM 1 CUP UNCOOKED LEGUMES
ADZUKI BEANS	4 hours	1 hour	2½
BLACK BEANS	4 hours	1½ hours	3
BLACK-EYED PEAS*	NA	1 hour	2½
CHICKPEAS	4 hours	2 to 2½ hours	3
FAVA BEANS	12 hours	3 hours	3
GREAT NORTHERN BEANS	4 hours	1 hour	2¾
KIDNEY BEANS (RED OR WHITE)	4 hours	1 hour	2¾
LENTILS*	NA	30 to 40 minutes	3
LIMA BEANS	4 hours	1 to 1½ hours	3
MUNG BEANS	4 hours	1 hour	3
NAVY BEANS	4 hours	2 hours	2¾
PEAS, SPLIT*	NA	30 minutes	2
PEAS, WHOLE	4 hours	40 minutes	2
PIGEON PEAS*	NA	30 minutes	2¼
PINK BEANS	4 hours	1 hour	3
PINTO BEANS	4 hours	1 to 1½ hours	3¼
SOYBEANS	12 hours	3 to 3½ hours	2¾

*Soaking is not necessary.

Techniques for Nuts and Seeds

Nuts and seeds are full of flavor and have a number of culinary uses. Toasting them in a dry pan or in the oven enhances their flavor. They can be used effectively as a crusting ingredient because their higher oil content reduces the need for oil in the pan. Coatings made of nuts, however, must be handled carefully: the nuts can burn more easily than other crusts, and they must be turned with care. Nut butters can be used for thickening. Nuts and seeds are also naturals for garnishes.

Techniques for Meats, Poultry, Fish, and Shellfish

More than 200 types of fish are caught in and around the United States. Some are naturally lean, others oily; some have a delicate flavor, others are almost meaty.

A fish's skeletal structure helps to determine how it will be cut up for marketing, but its fat content is the most important distinction for cooking. The best way to pair a fish and cooking technique is to consider the flesh. Oily fish, such as bluefish and mackerel, are often prepared by dry-heat techniques. Fish that are moderately fatty, such as salmon and trout, can be prepared in just about any method. Very lean fish, such as flounder or cod, is most successfully poached, sautéed, pan-fried, or deep-fried. They cook very quickly, and their flesh is often quite fragile, so fillets are often coated or breaded before cooking.

Preparing Beef

In the United States, people take their beef very seriously. The United States produces more beef than any other nation, and it is second only to Argentina in per capita consumption of beef.

Flavor and texture of beef depend on which muscle the cut comes from. In general, the more exercise the muscle gets, the tougher the meat will be, and the more fat, whether intramuscular (called marbling) or on the outside of the cut, the more flavorful the meat will be.

No matter which part of the animal the cut comes from, beef is high in protein, iron, and vitamin B12. Portion sizes should be limited to three to four ounces (cooked weight) per serving. Even at this amount, beef can supply nearly 100 milligrams of cholesterol and 10 grams of fat. Using meat as an ingredient—in a stew or tagine, for example, or pasta sauce—allows you to serve portions that are appropriately sized yet don't appear meager.

Steaks and roasts that come from the rib are especially prized for their balance of tenderness and flavor. Loin cuts are extremely tender as well. Cuts from the round are generally less tender, but some, particularly top round, take well to roasting. Flank and skirt steak are quite flavorful and have a fair amount of marbling; they must be cooked carefully and sliced properly to ensure they remain tender. Most cuts from the rib, loin, round, and flank can be roasted, broiled, grilled, pan-fried, or sautéed; short ribs and back ribs, as well as some round cuts, take well to braising.

Cuts such as tripe, tongue, oxtails, heart, and liver are not as popular in the United States as elsewhere in the world. These cuts are generally extremely flavorful and take well to simmering and braising. Organ meats are an excellent source of vitamins and minerals—liver is extremely high in vitamins A and C, as well as iron—but a 3-ounce/85-gram cooked serving supplies almost as much cholesterol as two large eggs.

Whenever possible, broil or grill steaks to allow fat to drip away; setting roasts on a rack does the same. Prepare braises, stews, and pot roasts in advance. Chill the liquid separately from the meat so the fat congeals on the top, then scrape it off before reheating.

Preparing Veal

A fine-textured meat with a delicate flavor, veal has fallen out of favor due to the practices used in raising calves. A full consideration of this issue is beyond the scope of this book. Veal is lower in calories and fat—particularly saturated fat—than beef but it is slightly higher in cholesterol.

Veal shoulder, or chuck, can be prepared in the same way as beef chuck cuts. Shanks are typically braised as well; osso buco is one of the most famous dishes using veal shank.

Cuts from the rib and loin may be bone-in or boneless and rolled; left whole, they are usually roasted. Portion-sized cuts are referred to as chops or medallions. They are often pan-fried, broiled, or grilled.

The leg yields numerous cuts, including the top and bottom round, as well as cutlets.

Veal breast can be braised; it can also be boned and stuffed, then rolled and tied.

Variety meats from veal are especially prized. Sweetbreads, brains, tongue, and heart are less popular in the United States than elsewhere in the world, but calf's liver has its fans. It is significantly lower in cholesterol than beef liver, and it is more tender and milder in flavor. Because antibiotics, fertilizers, and other chemicals can accumulate in an animal's liver as it ages, calf's liver contains lower amounts of these substances than beef liver does.

Preparing Pork

Most pork today is much leaner than it used to be. While some cuts are still extremely high in fat, others are as much as 30 percent leaner than they were twenty-five years ago. This is a boon for health-conscious consumers, but it presents challenges to the chef. Lean pork can become dry and tough if not handled properly.

Pork shoulder goes by many names: Boston butt, butt, picnic ham, or picnic butt are a few. This cut is somewhat higher in fat than other cuts, so it is often used in sausages and charcuterie. It can be roasted, but it is better braised or stewed.

Pork loin is cut much longer than loins from beef, veal, and lamb. It can be roasted, bone-in or boneless. Chops from the loin differ in composition and shape depending on the end of the loin from which they are cut. Shoulder or arm chops are often braised; center and leg chops take well to any dry-heat method. The tenderloin is extremely lean. Left whole, it can be roasted; cut into medallions or noisettes, it can be sautéed, broiled, or grilled.

The ham simply refers to pork leg, which may or may not have been cured. Fresh ham is typically roasted; leaner parts of the ham can be ground or cut into stew meat as well. Ham steaks can be fresh, cured, or smoked. Cured or smoked hams are usually cooked and ready to heat, though roasting enhances tenderness and flavor. Specialty hams such as prosciutto and country ham are also available.

Spareribs are exceptionally fatty: nearly 70 percent of the calories may come from fat. They also have a high proportion of bone. Nevertheless, they are immensely popular.

Ham is not the only part of the pig that is cured or smoked. Pork belly is smoked or cured (or both) to make bacon; Canadian bacon is boneless smoked loin. Ham hocks, pig's feet and knuckles, and even snouts are available fresh, cured, and smoked. They are often used in soups and as flavorings in simmered dishes such as beans and greens.

Preparing Lamb

Increasingly popular, lamb is raised to be consistently lean and tender. It is milder in flavor than in years past, and it is available year-round rather than just in the spring. Choose lamb that is pink to deep pink with pearly white fat; deep red meat indicates an older animal, which will have a much stronger flavor and slightly coarser texture. Older lamb also tends to have more marbling than younger animals and is therefore higher in fat. The layer of external fat can be trimmed off easily; in addition to lowering the fat content, it also lessens the "gamy" flavor lamb may have.

Like veal, lamb is cut into ribs (also known as racks), shoulder, breast, shank, loin, and leg, and can be prepared similarly. Lamb shank is the leanest cut, but it can be tough. It should be braised or stewed.

Preparing Game

Game meats are increasing in popularity, due in part to their nutritional benefits. As a general rule, game meats are exceptionally lean and particularly low in saturated fat. Venison and bison are excellent alternatives to beef for red meat lovers. Both are farm raised, and this type of venison is less gamy and more tender than animals from the wild. Venison, bison, and other farm-raised animals such as rabbit are available throughout the year.

Because game meats are so low in fat—a 3-ounce cooked serving of venison shoulder roast supplies about 3 grams—it must be cooked carefully to prevent it from toughening. As with other animals, cuts from less-exercised parts of the animal, such as the loin and rib, can be prepared with such dry-heat methods as grilling, roasting, and sautéing. Leg or haunch, shank, and shoulder are better braised or stewed; they can also be ground for use in pâtés and charcuterie.

Preparing Poultry

Poultry skin may be left on during roasting and baking, because this helps prevent the loss of natural juices without adding any significant amount of fat to the meat. Tucking herbs or other aromatics under the skin before cooking is a clever way to introduce an extra flavor element. For any cooking method other than roasting or baking, though, the skin should be removed before cooking, and skin should always be removed before service.

Using Marinades

Marinades are effective ways to add flavor to foods before you cook them. To read more about the role of marinades in healthy cooking techniques, see More Than Flavoring, page 89.

Marinades generally contain one or more of the following: oil, acid, and aromatics (spices, herbs, and vegetables). Oils protect food from intense heat during cooking and help hold other flavorful ingredients in contact with the food. Acids, such as vinegar, wine, yogurt, and citrus juices, flavor the food and change its texture. In some cases, acids firm or stiffen foods (e.g., the lime juice marinade that "cooks" the raw fish in seviche).

Marinating times vary according to the food's texture. Tender or delicate foods such as fish or poultry breast require less time. A tougher cut of meat may be marinated for days. The ratio of acid to other ingredients may also affect timing. High-acid marinades such as those used to prepare seviche produce the desired effect within fifteen or twenty minutes of applying them to a food. Others are best left in contact with foods for several hours, while some require several days. Some marinades are cooked before use; others are not. Sometimes the marinade is used to flavor an accompanying sauce or may itself become a dipping sauce. Marinades that have been in contact with raw foods can be used in these ways provided that they are boiled for several minutes first to kill any lingering pathogens.

To use a liquid marinade, add it to the ingredient and turn the ingredient to coat evenly. Cover and marinate, refrigerated, for the length of time indicated by the recipe, the type of meat, poultry, or fish, and the desired result. Brush or scrape off excess marinade before cooking and pat dry, particularly if the marinade contains herbs or other aromatics that burn easily.

The Role of Flavor

Good cooking is the art of capturing the most appropriate flavors in a dish. The first step in mastering this art form lies in understanding exactly what constitutes flavor. Learning how to develop flavors, as well as when to bring them into balance and harmony and when to allow one flavor to dominate in a dish, is a matter of experimentation and tasting.

Flavor is composed of many elements. It begins with choosing the right ingredients and is improved through the chef's skill. The term *flavor dynamics* indicates that two or more flavors have been blended in some way to produce a new flavor experience. Sometimes the dynamics are the result of mixing things together so that you can't easily recognize specific flavors. The term also applies when two or more flavors are put into an unexpected juxtaposition so that one flavor acts to improve the way another flavor is experienced.

Flavor profiles is a kind of culinary shorthand to talk about the specific preferences you might find within a cuisine. An Asian flavor profile includes ginger, garlic, soy sauce, cilantro, and lemongrass, for instance; a Mexican flavor profile includes chiles, pumpkin seeds, cilantro, and cumin. The profiles are influenced by politics, economics, religion, and the environment.

Flavor is something we experience through our senses. All five of our senses provide us with perceptions that, when taken collectively, become "flavor." How we perceive a dish depends on its appearance and texture as much as it does on its aroma and taste.

Defining Flavor

Flavor is nothing if not subjective. What one person thinks is delicious another thinks is anything but, and what one person perceives as much too salty or spicy may be "just right" to someone else. Researchers attribute this to the number of taste buds a person has. People who have several thousand more than normal are called supertasters. They perceive tastes in foods far more than medium tasters and nontasters do and tend to avoid highly flavored foods, whether spicy chiles, bitter coffee, pungent vegetables, sugary beverages, or buttery rich frosting. With fewer taste buds than normal, nontasters are less sensitive to flavoring compounds that others find unappealing. Nontasters are more likely to eat a wide variety of foods so they are more likely to get a broader array of nutrients from food, but they may also eat too much.

Nutrition and flavor are inextricably linked in other ways, too. Humans have an innate preference for sweet foods and an instinctive aversion to bitter foods. Carbohydrates, the body's preferred source of fuel, are sugars. Many toxic plants are high in substances called alkaloids, which make them taste bitter. This biological imperative to seek out sweet foods and to avoid bitter may have helped our ancestors survive.

Preferences for other flavors can develop over time or through repeated exposure. Although humans are not born with an affinity for salty or spicy foods, we often develop a taste for them. Too much exposure to some flavors can result in "flavor fatigue." Over time, people can develop a tolerance for some flavors and may become desensitized to them. Chefs themselves need to be especially careful to guard against this, as they may end up adding far more seasoning to a dish than customers prefer.

The human tongue recognizes only five basic tastes: sweet, sour, salty, bitter, and *umami,* a Japanese word meaning "deliciousness," often described as savory, brothy, or meaty. However, we are capable of discerning incredibly subtle variations on an almost infinite number of combinations of those tastes, in large part due to the aromas of food. Lemon juice and distilled vinegar are both sour, and white sugar and maple syrup are both sweet, but no one would ever confuse these foods for one another.

Most foods have extremely complicated combinations of flavors. The chemical composition of foods give them their flavors—cruciferous vegetables like cabbage and Brussels sprouts contain sulfur compounds that give them a bitter, pungent taste; the acids in citrus fruits provide the tartness that their sugars tame somewhat. Umami appears to be related to glutamate, an amino acid in foods like beef and mushrooms.

Preparation affects the flavor of foods as well. Foods like garlic and onions get their flavor from volatile oils, which are released when the food is cut. Finely minced or crushed garlic has more exposed surfaces to release these oils than sliced garlic, so crushing will impart a stronger garlic taste than slicing. Heat changes the chemical makeup of foods, too. Raw garlic is harsh and pungent. Sauté it quickly and it becomes palatable yet retains a strong, distinctive flavor, but roast it slowly and it becomes sweet and mellow. Another example is white sugar, which has a purely sweet taste. Heat the sugar until it melts and caramelizes, though, and you have a complex array of sweetness, bitterness, and sourness.

Creating Flavor

Individual foods and ingredients often can have complicated flavors on their own. Combining ingredients and then cooking them, whether in a dish or a meal, can heighten or intensify a specific flavor, or may blend them to make the flavors even more intricate. Because flavor is so subjective, no standard formula exists for developing flavors in foods. However, we can begin to analyze individual dishes in order to gain an understanding of flavor relationships and learn how to create pleasing flavor combinations.

The first thing to consider is what attributes each ingredient contributes to the overall flavor profile of the dish. Take one of your favorite recipes and ask yourself why each ingredient is there. For many ingredients, the answer is obvious, but for others, the function may not be immediately clear. As you examine the role of each ingredient, evaluate whether it is a healthy one. How would replacing a less healthy ingredient with a nutrient-rich one affect the dish's flavor profile and nutrition profile?

Imagine how the dish would taste if you replaced the main ingredient. Could you substitute a chicken breast for a pork chop? Brown rice and quinoa for couscous? Similar foods can often be substituted for one another, but look to less obvious substitutions. Duck breast has a rich, savory flavor and succulent texture that stands up well to robust seasonings. Consider using it in a dish that typically features beef.

Next, explore the other ingredients. Does one provide most of the flavor, such as dill in a sauce to accompany salmon? Or do the other ingredients combine to become something completely different from their individual flavors, such as chili powder, cumin, garlic, and onion in chili? How would the flavor of a dressing change if you used sherry vinegar instead of red wine vinegar or lemon juice as the acid? Could you use tapenade or fish sauce in a marinade in place of salt?

If you are cooking grains, how flavorful are they? Simmering them in water allows their flavor to dominate, but not all grains are interesting enough to withstand such exposure. Bland grains may benefit from a more flavorful cooking liquid that enhances their taste, or you may wish to use a different, more flavorful grain.

Take a look at how the technique affects the dish's flavor. Dry-heat cooking methods allow browning to occur. How do the resulting caramelization and crust affect the food? Imagine how the dish might taste if you used a different technique, or a combination of techniques. Steamed broccoli has a much simpler, purer taste than roasted broccoli, for example, and a stew that is made without first browning the meat or sautéing aromatic vegetables will taste quite different from one that uses these techniques.

Timing affects flavor as well. Look at when the ingredients are added to the pot, and at how long they cook. Adding different ingredients at certain times helps to maximize flavor and ensures that each ingredient is cooked just enough. Onions, garlic, and some spices are normally added at the beginning and cooked with a touch of oil or fat to develop their sweetness and allow their flavors to permeate everything else that is eventually added to the pot. Fresh herbs, on the other hand, are often added to foods shortly before serving so their delicate flavors aren't muted and their aromas and colors really stand out.

By adding ingredients in a certain sequence, we create a layering of flavors. A fairly simple example is when you add freshly minced onions to French onion soup just before adding the crouton. The fresh onions impart another dimension to the flavor of onions, and their sharp, pungent note contrasts dramatically with the sweet, mellow caramelized onions.

A more intricate layering occurs when you add several different ingredients. Consider what happens when you cook meat and then make a mushroom sauce. You might dry-sauté beef medallions or filets. After you removed them from the pan, you deglaze it perhaps by first adding fond de veau lié, which releases the bits of meat that are left in the pan into the sauce. The mushrooms are added next so that they can release their essence into the sauce. Aromatic components—fortified wine, fresh herbs, and pepper—are added just before serving so that their volatile compounds are not lost to prolonged cooking.

When we eat this dish, we perceive each of these flavors in nearly the opposite order. First, the bright aromatic quality of the herbs and the spiciness of the pepper become apparent, quickly followed by the darker earth tones of wine, mushrooms, and fond de veau lié. At the base of all this is rich, meaty beef. This inverse linear quality of flavor perception is one of the key elements in composing successful recipes.

Developing Flavor

At every step, a chef controls the flavor of a dish. At the same time every chef is limited by his or her customers' expectations and what they are willing to pay. A chef at a three-star restaurant is expected to use pristinely fresh produce, properly aged meats, well-made cheeses, and high-quality dry goods to produce elegant plates that look like works of art. The prices on the menu are generally high, and the food budget is correspondingly generous. The director of food service for a school will most likely be working with a significantly less lavish budget, but is by no means exempt from the customers' expectation of delicious, flavorful foods. Regardless of what type of budget or kitchen at the chef's command, any cook worth his or her salt knows that a mediocre chef can ruin high-quality, expensive ingredients in any number of ways, but a talented chef can turn ordinary or inexpensive ingredients into something fabulous.

This control begins with selecting the best ingredients the budget allows, from reliable purveyors. Chefs who are concerned with providing healthy, nutritious options would do well to select foods based on their positive attributes. Rather than focus on what should be avoided, chefs should choose healthy ingredients for their flavors, then consider how those ingredients can be integrated into a menu for widest appeal. Say you want to use kale as an

Developing Flavor in Meats, Fish, and Poultry Dishes

When a spice blend is used as a dry rub (also called a dry marinade) to coat food, the food is refrigerated after application to allow it to absorb the flavors. Very often these rubs contain some salt to help intensify all the flavors in the dish. Dry rubs may be left on the food during cooking or they may be scraped away first. Spice blends may also be added to aromatic vegetables as they cook during the initial stages of preparing a braise or stew.

To use a marinade, combine the marinade and meat in a resealable plastic bag or shallow container. Turn the meat to coat it evenly, cover, and marinate it in the refrigerator for thirty minutes to overnight, depending on the size of the pieces and the level of acidity in the marinade. During longer marinating times, turn the meat once or twice. If a recipe calls for using part of the marinade in an accompanying sauce, reserve some of it before adding the meat or boil the marinade for several minutes after removing raw meat.

A pan sauce gives you the chance to incorporate the flavorful drippings released by foods as they cook. Those drippings reduce and collect in the pan. Adding a flavorful liquid, such as a broth, wine, prepared sauce, or coulis, helps to dilute and dissolve those drippings. Classic pan sauces were often thickened with flour, roux, butter, or cream. Chefs today prefer to let natural reduction develop the flavor and leave the sauces with a somewhat lighter body.

THE TEMPERATURE AT WHICH foods are served affects our ability to perceive tastes. According to Harold McGee, in *On Food and Cooking, Second Edition* (2004), we are most sensitive to taste in the temperature range of 72° to 105°F/22° to 41°C. McGee further states that sweet and sour sensations seem to be enhanced at the upper end of this temperature range, while salty and bitter tastes are more pronounced at the lower end. Good chefs intuitively know this to be true, because from experience they have learned that foods served very cold, like ice creams and terrines, need to be especially flavorful or highly seasoned.

A classic example of this dichotomy is potato-leek soup. When served hot, the sweetness of the leeks tends to stand out over the thick, creamy potato base. The same soup served cold, as vichyssoise, is refreshingly salty, and the starchy quality of the potatoes is more apparent.

accompaniment to pork medallions. A side dish of steamed kale is rich in several nutrients, but its fairly pronounced flavor might be too intense for many diners. Preparing it with an Italian-style *agrodolce* sauce or dressing, however, gives it another dimension without detracting from its rich flavors and nutritional benefits, and will complement the richness of the pork better than the unadorned steamed version.

Once the best ingredients have been selected, the chef must make sure they are stored properly. Dairy foods, for example, can absorb odors from pungent foods and should be kept away from citrus and onions. Improperly stored produce may lose nutrients and texture as well as flavor. Flaccid carrots, limp greens, and mushy apples will only detract from a dish. Proper storage does more than preserve flavor and texture; it helps to ensure that foods will not be exposed to contaminants.

Food safety and flavor extend to how food is handled as it is prepared for cooking. Some foods may need to come to room temperature before use to attain the proper texture of flavor when cooked—eggs to be beaten, some cuts of meat before cooking—but the chef should ensure that they are not left out for extended periods.

Foods that are seasoned before cooking taste different from foods that are not. Salt and other spices and marinades can penetrate the food, so even when mixtures are wiped off, as with gravlax, their essence remains. Whether the chef grinds spices fresh every day or relies on containers of ground spices matters, as does whether the spices are toasted before use and when they are added during the cooking process.

One of the biggest areas where chefs influence flavor is in choosing the cooking technique. Heat alters the chemical structure of food, breaking down cell walls, releasing flavor compounds and nutrients, and making the food more tender.

Dry-heat cooking techniques attain temperatures higher than moist-heat methods. These higher temperatures allow foods to brown and develop a crust. Moist-heat cooking methods are typically gentler. Because foods do not brown, their flavors tend to be simpler and purer. Compare the difference between grilled or roasted salmon and poached salmon.

Finally, the chef controls how flavors are perceived in how the food is presented. The texture of foods can affect how their flavors are perceived as well. A silky smooth bisque and a chunky potage may have the same ingredients, but the puréed soup's flavor may be subtler than the latter, where each ingredient remains distinct. Imagine, too, the difference in flavor between a crab cake with large, meaty chunks of crab and one with small shreds. Because all of our senses are involved in tasting (see Sensing Flavor, page 121), food that looks attractive on the plate is more appealing than a carelessly arranged dish.

How long a food stands between the initial preparation and when it is actually eaten also affects flavor. Some foods, such as delicate vegetables, fish, and sautéed meats, are best immediately after they are cooked because the quality of their flavor, texture, and nutrient content begins to degrade quite quickly. Other foods, like soups and braised dishes, benefit from being prepared a day or so before they are to be eaten. The extra time allows their flavors to fully mature.

Finally, temperature can be used to add an unexpected element to a dish. Very hot and very cold foods tend to have less discernable temperatures. Foods like ice cream, cheeses, and fruits have more developed flavors if they have been allowed to sit at room temperature for a while. Piping hot foods and beverages can deaden the palate.

We generally tend to separate hot foods from cold foods to keep the two temperatures from canceling each other out, but by serving hot and cold foods together, an interesting contrast can be created. In cuisines where food is often spicy, this is a time-honored tradition. For example, in Indian cuisine, a mango *lassi* (mangoes, yogurt, spices) might be served as a beverage with a fiery pork *vindaloo* and spicy mango chutney. Some of the ingredients are similar, and several are the same (mango, spices), but the temperature and creamy quality of the chilled drink provide a cooling counterpoint to the hot and spicy pork dish. Dairy is traditionally served with very spicy foods because proteins in milk interfere with pain receptors in the mouth and lessen the burning sensations caused by capsaicin.

Balancing Flavor

Balance is something that we often assume to be the ultimate goal in the creation of pleasing flavor combinations. This is not always the case, however. Colors, sounds, textures, tastes, aromas, and temperatures can either complement or contrast with each other. Sometimes perfectly complementary flavors are desirable, as in the case of a slowly cooked lentil stew. Here, balance is the goal because the desired result is the melding of several ingredients into a singular taste experience that is completely different from the individual ingredients. If the stew isn't cooked long enough, the ingredients may still retain their distinct flavors.

Other times, though, the chef may wish to highlight a particular flavor. In this case, contrasting flavors can be used to let one or more elements come to the forefront of the flavor profile. Pesto, for instance, showcases the flavor of fresh basil or other herbs and uses the contrasting flavors of garlic, pine nuts, Parmesan, and olive oil to round out the flavor profile.

The amount of time that a flavor lingers on the palate after we have swallowed also influences our perception of the dish's overall flavor. We refer to this as the flavor "finish." Consider, for example, a clear soup versus a puréed soup. The clear soup has a lighter and cleaner finish than the thick and creamy puréed soup.

Flavor Profiles

Each ingredient and dish has a flavor profile—a "fingerprint," so to speak, that makes it unique. But the term can also be used to describe the distinctive combination of ingredients and techniques that make each cuisine unique. Cultural, economic, political, religious, and geographic factors play influential roles in the development of flavor profiles.

Climate often makes geographically disparate cuisines somewhat similar. Thai and Mexican cooking both use lime and chiles as flavorings. From there, however, the cuisines diverge. Mexican cuisine uses different chiles and herbs, as well as tomatoes, and Mexico's most common grain is corn. Indian and Moroccan cooking both use "hot" spices like cinnamon, clove, and ginger. Moroccan cooking is associated with tagines and couscous and mint tea, whereas Indian cooking is associated with curries and tandoori. In India, flavor profiles vary considerably from one region to another, but also from cook to cook. Each makes his or her own blend of curry powder and *garam masala,* and thus each cook puts his or her own stamp on dishes that contain these spice blends.

Northern European cooking is significantly different from the cooking of Mediterranean countries. Scandinavian and German foods tend to be heavier in texture, and they rely on fruits and vegetables that thrive in colder climates and that keep well through long winters: cabbages and kale, potatoes, and apples are far more common than tomatoes and citrus fruit. Even within countries, this geographic influence can be seen. Compare the cooking of Brittany and Paris to that of the Côte d'Azur: northern France has more in common with many northern European countries than it does with southern France. This is also seen in Italy. Landlocked and mountainous regions in the north such as Lombardy and Parma have dramatically different culinary traditions from the southern regions of Sicily and Puglia.

Even in the United States, these regional differences can be seen. Agriculture and climate play a part in each region's preference, but immigration does as well. Northern Europeans settled in the upper Midwest; menus in the Dakotas, Minnesota, and Wisconsin may well feature Swedish meatballs, pickled red cabbage, and a number of wursts and sausages. Portuguese fishermen in Rhode Island and Massachusetts added tomatoes to New England's cream-based chowder. Louisiana's famous Creole cooking shows the influence of Choctaw Indians, French and Spanish settlers, African and Caribbean blacks, and Canadians (or Cajuns).

In addition to crops, livestock play a role in flavor profiles—sometimes in unexpected ways. Greece's rocky terrain is more suited to raising sheep than cattle, for example. As a result, Greek dairy foods are typically made with sheep's milk instead of cow's milk, and have a tangier, deeper flavor.

Flavor profiles evolve over time. At first, they are based primarily on the foods indigenous to a region or area. Colonization and exploration can influence them; as foreign powers invade and settle in an area, they bring with them their culinary traditions, including ingredients, equipment, and techniques. Lemongrass, cilantro, mint, chiles, and fish, for example, are

FLAVOR IS MORE THAN A MATTER OF TASTE. We experience flavor with all of our senses. When a plate of food is set before you, you experience it in many ways: You see its colors, you smell its aromas, and you might hear sizzling. You might hear it crunch when you cut into it or when you chew it. In addition to tasting its flavors, you'll feel the temperature of the food, its texture or consistency, and perhaps whether it is cooling, like mint, or fiery from peppers.

Sight gives clues to flavor: for example, you expect vibrantly green sugar snap peas to taste from-the-garden fresh and slices of orange sweet potato bearing grill marks to have a sweet, slightly smoky taste and a dense, melting texture. Sight also adds to the appeal of food in far more subtle ways. Artfully presented food that is carefully arranged is more tempting than if it were casually or even sloppily set on the plate.

We might not think of foods as making sounds, but they do, both as they cook and when we eat them. A sizzling platter of fajitas and a fizzing glass of champagne send flavor cues before the food or beverage reaches the mouth. Some foods become audible when we eat them. When tucking into a crispy-looking, golden piece of herb-breaded baked chicken, you expect that first bite to be accompanied by a hearty crunch. If the coating turns out to be quietly soggy, you will most likely feel disappointed, even cheated somehow, regardless of the actual taste and aroma.

When you touch a food with your fingers or with a utensil, you receive a preview of its texture. A piece of poached salmon that softly flakes under the gentle prodding of a fork hints at the tenderness of the fish. A steak that resists your most insistent sawing tells you that it is dry and lifeless and ought to be sent back to the kitchen.

Smell plays an enormous role in our perception of flavor, as anyone who has ever had a head cold knows. In fact, aroma is perhaps the primary component of flavor. While we are able to perceive a few basic tastes, we are able to distinguish among hundreds of aromas. For example, an orange and a tangerine share the same basic tastes of sweet and sour, but in a blind taste test most people are still able to tell the difference because each fruit has a different set of characteristic aromas and slightly different textures.

When you chew and swallow the first bite, you experience the full flavor of a dish. What we typically think of as "taste" or "flavor" is actually the interaction of taste and smell, combined with the feel of the food in the mouth. Our sense of taste comes from the chemical receptors on our tongues, referred to as taste buds. Additionally, the insides of our mouths feel such sensations as, for example, the burn of hot chiles, the cooling effect of mint, the astringency of tannins in tea or wine, the numbing sensation of cloves, and the fizz of carbonated beverages.

common in both Thai and Vietnamese cooking. But Vietnam was for decades a French colony, and its cuisine bears a distinctively French stamp that Thai cooking does not.

It is difficult to imagine the cuisines of Mediterranean Europe without tomatoes, but this ingredient did not appear in Europe until the sixteenth century, when Spanish explorers brought it home. Tomatoes were was considered poisonous for a few more centuries and did not become widely used until the 1800s. Each country, however, has combined tomatoes with other ingredients that reflect its profile: Italy with basil and mozzarella; Spain with garlic, olive oil, and peppers; Greece with oregano, mint, basil, and dill.

Travel has allowed people to encounter authentic cooking that they seek to enjoy at home. Before World War II, pizza was found only in Italian neighborhoods. But as GIs returned home, they sought out this and other Italian foods. As air travel became affordable in the 1960s, people went to Europe, Africa, and Asia and discovered how different authentic foods could be from the versions served in U.S. restaurants. People came home from their travels and wished to recreate or experience the flavors and textures they discovered on their journeys.

Chefs often return home from traveling to experiment with new ingredients and techniques, coming up with different combinations.

When playing with flavor profiles, it is wise to stay within flavor families when substituting one ingredient for another. Say, for example, you wish to introduce an Italian flavor to a Thai dish. If the recipe contains fish sauce, you might first try replacing it with anchovies. If the change isn't quite what you were looking for, experiment with other salty foods: capers or olives might be acceptable alternatives.

Techniques for Developing Flavor

There are a number of ways that chefs can develop flavor in their dishes. The first approach is to buy foods that are naturally flavorful. You can use the information in Chapter 2 to help you choose wisely. Getting to know what's in season in your location, the purveyors and producers with a reputation for high-quality, often hand-crafted foods, is an important part of assuring that your offerings are as flavorful as possible.

The second tactic is to maximize flavor through proper techniques. Impeccable technique results in foods that have visual, textural, and aromatic appeal. Every technique, from the basic preparations tasks of rinsing, trimming, and cutting, through the selection and execution of culinary techniques like roasting or steaming or stir-frying, and on through the techniques of plating, presentation, and service, plays a part. We've examined many of the basic culinary techniques you may choose from throughout this chapter. Look to specific recipes in this book for more inspiration.

A third tactic is to pay careful attention to how the interplay of flavors, textures, and colors on a plate will affect the flavor of the entire dish. Incorporating fresh, crunchy salsa or salads,

creamy stewed or braised elements, or adding a crisp item is a key aspect of developing flavor in your menu offerings. If there are no contrasting elements on the plate, it is easy for your guest to develop a sort of flavor fatigue. The first few bites of a dish taste wonderful, but the intensity begins to drop off after a few bites. Giving your guests a way to refresh their palates enhances their enjoyment of every part of the dish, not just the "main" item.

The way you choose and use seasoning and flavoring ingredients determines the ultimate flavor of the dish. A fourth tactic is to select and use flavoring ingredients that bring out the flavor of your other ingredients or add a pronounced flavor of their own. Some flavoring ingredients don't require any special monitoring. Toasted, parched, or freshly ground spices and chiles add rich smoky flavors without introducing sodium or fat. Fresh herbs and aromatic ingredients like garlic, lemongrass, ginger, or lime juice add flavor but not calories. Steeping or infusing these ingredients in vinegars or oils produces your own custom blends to use as an ingredient in a dish or as a sauce or dip. High-sodium foods, such as salt, capers, anchovies, and olives do call for strict measuring and proper handling. Sometimes, you may rinse away some of the brine or soak salty foods to reduce the sodium they add to a dish. You can often find low- or reduced-sodium versions of salty condiments like soy or tamari sauce. Salt itself should always be properly and with care.

Salting Foods

Salt is a seasoning that is almost taken for granted. Nearly everyone notices when you leave it out of a dish, because foods taste a little dull and flat. As we continue to learn more about the potential heath risks of a diet high in sodium, chefs and nutritionists alike are looking at salt more closely once again. Adding a little salt before you cook foods can have the effect of bringing out the best flavor in the cooked foods. If you wait until the very end of cooking to add salt, you may be inclined to add too much. Adding more than that adds a salty taste. Humans do crave salt, but our craving appears to be all out of proportion to both our need and our ability to process it once we eat it.

We do not advocate simply eliminating salt, unless there is a specific reason to do so, but we do encourage all cooks and chefs to use salt wisely. Use kosher salt, as we have done in our recipes, wherever salt is called for. The same volume of kosher salt has about half the sodium of table salt. Use your fingertips to apply salt in a more even coat.

Salt isn't the only source of sodium in foods. Processed and prepared foods are often high in sodium, even when they don't actually taste salty. Look for low- or reduced-sodium versions of ingredients like soy sauce, prepared broths or stocks, and condiments.

Blending Flavors

Whenever you combine ingredients in a dish, you are combining flavors. Some flavors are classic combinations that reflect the characteristic seasonings of a particular cuisine. (For instance, the French combination known as *fines herbes* includes herbs you find in typical French cooking—parsley, chives, chervil, and tarragon—while a spice mixture that combines chiles, cinnamon, cumin, and oregano evokes Mexican dishes.)

Toasting and Infusing Spices

Spices, nuts, and seeds store best if they are purchased whole and untoasted. To bring out their rich, aromatic flavors, toast them as close as possible to the time that you want to use them. You can toast more than one spice at a time, as long as you don't overcrowd the pan. There should be just a thin, relatively even layer. If the pan is crowded, the spices won't toast evenly. If there are too few to fill the pan, the pan could heat unevenly and increase your chance of scorching them. Toast small amounts in a dry skillet. For large quantities, use the oven.

Once the spices give off a rich aroma, immediately transfer them from the skillet or sheet pan to a cool container. This keeps them from continuing to brown. Spices are relatively high in oil and toasting brings those oils to the surface. Let them cool before you grind them so you don't end up with an oily mixture. A mortar and pestle grinds them into a relatively even mixture. Spice grinders and even blenders or food processors are also good options, as long as you take care not to overgrind or process them.

Another way to get the flavor of spices and herbs into a dish is making an infusion. There are a variety of ways to treat the flavoring ingredients, described in greater detail on page 126. Take the time to properly cool and store infused mixtures. Some need time to rest so that their flavor develops. If you have included raw ingredients in an infused oil or vinegar, keep them safe by storing them under refrigeration.

Spices, nuts, and seeds can be toasted to bring out more of their flavor. Once toasted, they can be used whole as part of a bouquet garni or a sachet, lightly crushed to add a flavorful crust to foods, or ground into a fine powder to add to dishes as they cook.

Infusing aromatic ingredients including spices, herbs, and some vegetables and fruits into a liquid is another means of developing a specific flavor that you can add to a dish. Flavored oils and vinegars as well as infused stocks or essences (which are essentially a stock made by steeping aromatic ingredients in water or stock) can be used as finishing ingredients or as major components in sauces, dressings, or marinades.

FLAVORED OILS Oils suffused with garlic, fresh herbs, dried herbs, or hot peppers are called "flavored oils" or "infused oils." These oils are simple to prepare and they make the most of the flavor-carrying capability of fat. Flavored oils have a multitude of uses in the kitchen. In the dining room, they make a healthier alternative to butter as a spread for breads.

Flavored oils can, however, become a breeding ground for harmful bacteria, so it is important to exercise caution. Avoid using low-acid, fresh ingredients with a high moisture content, such as raw garlic and blanched fresh herbs, to infuse oil meant to last for some time. When these ingredients are combined with oil, the anaerobic (oxygen-free) environment can encourage the growth of pathogens, such as the organism that causes botulism.

Infused oils made with dried ingredients, like spices and chiles, are much safer than, and just as potent as, those made with fresh products. If you still want to use fresh ingredients for infused oils, either for cooking or as a dip for customers, make it in small quantities that can be used quickly. Oil infused with fresh ingredients may be refrigerated for up to one week before being discarded. Discard immediately if the oil becomes cloudy.

The oil you choose to flavor should be either olive oil or a neutral vegetable oil, such as canola or grapeseed. The following are basic procedures for making spice oil, fresh root oil, and fresh herb oil.

GROUND SPICE OIL For a more complex flavor, toast whole spices before grinding.

1. Mix 3 tablespoons of the desired ground spice with 1 tablespoon water to make a smooth paste. If paste is dry, add a little more water.
2. Place in clear jar, add 2 cups of oil, cover tightly, and let sit for 2 days. You can shake the jar several times at intervals to increase the strength of the oil.
3. When the spice has settled down to the bottom, remove the oil from the top with a ladle.
4. Store the oil, tightly covered, for 2 to 6 months.

FRESH ROOT OIL The intense and fresh flavor of roots and bulbs, such as shallots, garlic, horseradish, and fresh ginger, mix well with oils.

1. Peel and mince the root.
2. For every 3 tablespoons of minced root, use 2 cups of the appropriate oil.
3. Place in a jar and store in the refrigerator for 1 day before using. Store under refrigeration for up to 1 week.

FRESH HERB OIL Any fresh herb, such as basil, chives, cilantro, mint, or parsley, will work well. The finished oil will have a brilliant green color.

1. Blanch the herbs, including their stems, for 5 seconds in simmering water. Refresh them under cold running water and pat dry.
2. Measure the herbs and place in a blender with an equal amount of the desired oil. Blend to a smooth paste, place in a clean jar, and add 3 times the amount of oil.
3. Store in the refrigerator for 1 day.
4. When the herbs have settled, strain the oil through a coffee filter and use immediately or store under refrigeration for up to 1 week.

FLAVORED VINEGAR Making flavored vinegar is extremely easy, and the beauty of it is that you can experiment and create your own combinations. You can use any mixture of fresh herbs, fresh fruit, spices, garlic, shallots, and fruit and herb extracts. The only requirement is that the flavoring ingredients you use be very fresh. The basic recipe is as follows:

1. Wash and rinse a glass jar in boiling water and air-dry thoroughly.
2. In a stainless-steel saucepan, gently heat enough vinegar to fill the jar. Use low heat and do not boil.
3. For an herb-flavored vinegar, use about 1 cup of fresh herbs for every 2 cups of vinegar (the herbs can be on or off the stem). For fruit-flavored vinegars, use about 1 cup of fresh fruit for every 1 cup of vinegar. Clean the herbs or fruit and place in the jar along with any other flavoring ingredients desired. Cover with the warm vinegar and cool before sealing.
4. Allow the vinegar to rest in a cool, dark spot for roughly 10 to 14 days before tasting. If the vinegar is still weak, let it sit for another few days.
5. Once you are satisfied with the flavor of the vinegar, you can either leave the herbs or fruit in or strain the vinegar through a piece of cheesecloth and discard them. Transfer the vinegar to a bottle if you like.

Some suggestions for flavored vinegar combinations include:

- Champagne vinegar with raspberry extract and fresh raspberries
- Cider vinegar with mint and a touch of sugar
- Cider vinegar with fresh dill and dill seed
- Cider vinegar with chile and garlic
- Red wine vinegar with Opal basil and garlic
- Red wine vinegar with fresh blueberries
- Rice vinegar with fresh ginger
- White wine vinegar with rosemary and orange rind
- White wine vinegar with tarragon and lemon balm
- White wine vinegar with crushed dill, celery, coriander, cumin, and caraway seeds
- White wine vinegar with orange slices and orange extract
- White wine vinegar with fresh raspberries
- White wine vinegar with garlic, shallots, and orange zest

Cooking Aromatic Vegetables

Mirepoix will add a distinct aroma to a dish, even if the cut-up vegetables are simply added to the pot as it simmers. Sweating, smothering, or browning them in fat, however, significantly changes their flavor. Start by cooking onions and leeks in just enough fat to coat the bottom of the pan and vegetables, then add the carrots, and finally the celery. (You can omit the fat, especially if you don't want to brown the ingredients, and replace it with a little flavorful liquid.) White stocks or cream soups generally call for cooking the mirepoix over low heat in fat until it starts to give off some juices, known as sweating. If the pot is covered as the aromatics sweat, the technique is known as smothering.

Mirepoix can cook until it turns a deep, rich brown (sometimes referred to as caramelized), either on the stovetop or in the oven. Tomato paste or purée is often added to the mirepoix for added flavor and color. Add it, if required, once the mirepoix ingredients are partly cooked.

Cook carefully until the ingredients are a deep brown with an intense aroma. The tomato paste, if you have added it, will turn rusty brown and develop a sweet aroma. This technique is called pinçage, from the French *pincer,* "to stiffen or pinch," which is a good description of what happens to the tomatoes as they cook in hot fat.

Summary

Good flavor begins with high-quality ingredients. It is developed and enhanced through preparation, cooking technique, and the manner in which the food is served.

All of our senses contribute to our perception of flavor. In addition to taste and smell, we also see, hear, and feel flavor. The experience of flavor is highly subjective, affected by differences in people's ability to sense and interpret flavor cues and in their expectations for the meal.

Several variables affect our perception of flavor. The combination of ingredients, the timing involved in preparing the food, the order in which ingredients are added during the cooking process, and the final serving temperature are some of these variables.

Flavor profiles are like the "fingerprint" of a cuisine—they are characteristics that identify each cuisine's unique combination of ingredients and techniques and are typically based on indigenous ingredients.

Developing flavor in every dish is the chef's primary responsibility in healthy cooking. There are many tools in the chef's arsenal to accomplish this goal, from ingredient selection to choosing the cooking technique. Flavorful ingredients chosen from around the world also give excitement, color, and texture to dishes. Healthy cooking is much more than cutting out calories or serving smaller portions. At its best, healthy cooking delights your guests by feeding all their senses at the same time that it provides them with nourishment and energy.

4

Developing Healthy Recipes and Menus

NUTRITIOUS RECIPES ARE THE FOUNDATION of a healthy menu. Before you take the time to develop new recipes, take a look at the dishes you already offer. Chances are that some of the recipes on your current menu already are healthy ones; other recipes might need some tweaking, and some might not work at all.

There are three ways to add healthy recipes to your menu. You can use existing recipes, whether from a book such as this or from your menu; adapt or modify recipes; or develop original recipes.

This chapter explains the basic methods of evaluating recipes and how to adapt or develop them. It also explores ways to reduce ingredients your customers may wish to avoid, such as saturated fat, salt, refined carbohydrates, and alcohol, without sacrificing texture or flavor. Because there's more to healthy eating than simply avoiding potentially harmful ingredients, you'll also find suggestions for increasing the presence of nutritious foods like whole grains and vegetables.

Reading a Recipe for Nutrition

The first step in evaluating a recipe for a healthy menu is to know how you and your customers are defining the term. Does *healthy* mean low-fat or high-fiber? Low in sodium or high in calcium? Are you planning to make any claims on your menu that will need substantiating, or will you let the descriptions of your dishes allude to their healthful properties?

You will need to consider the roles that fat, salt, and sugar play in your recipes, as well as the type and source of each. Recipes for baked goods are far more difficult to adapt because ingredients such as butter, eggs, salt, sugar, and flours all perform very specific functions. Butter, for example, is unlike other fats in that it contains milk solids. You might be able to replace it with another fat, but you might need to use less of the substitution.

In other recipes, salt, fat, and sugar may be used as flavorings or for texture or mouthfeel. You may be able to swap an unhealthy trans fat or saturated fat for a monounsaturated fat, or build flavor with spices or seasonings other than salt, to make your recipes healthier. Or you may devise a way to remove the fat entirely from a dish without sacrificing flavor or texture. Rather than dip chicken cutlets in beaten eggs, you might dip them in egg whites, or to add more flavor you might use a mixture of Dijon mustard and white wine.

As you read the list of ingredients to identify those that you or your customers might deem "unhealthy," look for ways to add nutrient-rich ingredients and foods. Healthy cooking isn't just about limiting potentially harmful ingredients. To make a recipe truly healthy, you'll want to include beneficial nutrients as well. See Increasing the Nutrition on page 142 for suggestions and ideas.

Next, look at the technique to see if changing it will improve the recipe. As discussed in Chapter 3, many cooking techniques are healthy, so if you cannot change an ingredient, consider whether changing the technique will help to bring a recipe into nutritionally acceptable parameters. Grilling or broiling a pork chop, for example, may allow you to omit the fat that sautéing requires, and roasting vegetables instead of steaming and then sautéing them preserves nutrients and may streamline preparation.

Using Existing Recipes

Before you spend the time, effort, and money adapting or creating recipes, review the ones you currently use. Look to see that they are in line with the standards for a healthy menu you have established for your operation. Evaluate the technique, the ingredients, and the portion size to be sure.

Grilling, broiling, roasting, poaching, steaming, stewing, and baking are all techniques that do not necessarily require additional fat during cooking. Recipes for clear soups, consommés, pilafs, and stir-fries are also normally appropriate.

Next, review the ingredients and their amounts. Whole grains, vegetables, fruits, pasta, fish, lean meats, and skinless poultry indicate a recipe that is potentially healthy. Ingredients for sauces should be low in saturated fat, salt, and refined sugar. If everything appears to be acceptable, review the portion size. Some recipes that are not initially within parameters can be brought in line by being served in a smaller amount.

1. Think strategically about flavor, with an emphasis on leveraging long-term flavor trends, the public's growing interest in world cuisines, and their discovery of "culinary adventure" in order to broaden options and approaches to healthier menu development.

2. Focus on fruits and vegetables first—in a full range of colors and types, and in applications across all day and menu parts—knowing that your customers on average need to double their consumption of produce to promote good health.

3. Highlight the increased use of healthy plant-based oils, eliminate trans fats, and substantially reduce saturated fats.

4. Increase options for healthy protein choices, adding fish, nuts, and legumes if underrepresented on the menu.

5. Emphasize healthy carbohydrates, increase menu presence of whole grains—especially "intact" whole grains—and add food and beverage options with no or little added sugars and other "empty-calorie" sweeteners.

6. Look for opportunities to reduce salt and sodium in food preparation.

7. Provide a wider range of calorie/portion options, and consider menu concepts that change the value proposition for customers from quantity to a focus on quality and culinary differentiation.

8. Leverage small measures of indulgence for maximum, creative impact, and create new categories of options for healthy menu choices.

9. Share nutrition information with customers as appropriate, but emphasize strategies for selling healthier menu options that rely more on the language of flavor and culinary adventure.

10. Engage colleagues and industry partners in a long-term process of discovery to better understand the art and science of healthy menu R&D, and reimagine the operational designs, technologies, human resource strategies, and marketing innovation necessary to successfully sell and deliver these flavors to customers.

PORTION SIZE IS CRITICAL when trying to bring recipes into acceptable nutrition parameters, but it's often overlooked. In recent decades, people in the United States have come to expect enormous helpings of food at mealtime, particularly in entrées and proteins. The standard is normally a large helping of meat, poultry, or fish—and large can be anywhere from 6 to 12 ounces—with smaller portions of vegetable and starch side dishes. Pasta entrées are often 3 to 4 cups. Although the main point of healthy cooking is to move away from meals heavy on protein, fat, and calories and to make whole grains, legumes, fruits, and vegetables the focus of the plate, massive servings of any food should be avoided.

When designing a healthy recipe, start by paying particular attention to the sizes of meat, poultry, and fish; large amounts of these items are often responsible for pushing the dish beyond the limits of good nutrition. Generally, if the portion size of fat- and calorie-dense foods is kept to 3 to 4 ounces (raw weight), menu items will begin to fall in line. You are then free to round out the plate with more generous helpings of vegetables, whole grains, legumes, and fruits, all of which add variety, color, texture, and flavor.

One of the biggest challenges in decreasing portion size is avoiding the consumer perception of decreased value and quality. Even though many people want to eat healthier, they are still accustomed to huge servings of meat and may not yet be comfortable with smaller amounts. Before making adjustments to your recipes, survey your customer base to determine changes that are desired and those that will not be tolerated.

In order to prevent customers from feeling that they are somehow being cheated, there are a number of strategies you can employ. Offering two versions of the same dish, with different-sized portions (at different price points), is one method of determining interest. You're allowing customers to vote, in effect, on which portion size they prefer. After a few months, you can drop the less popular version from your menu.

Another important strategy in preserving value perception is artful presentation. Stuffing a meat, fish, of poultry item with vegetables or grains (or both) adds bulk, improves visual appeal, and increases the apparent portion size. Special knife cuts can be used to give the illusion that less is more. Cutting a salmon fillet on the bias before cooking, for instance, or thinly slicing and fanning cooked meat or poultry on the plate gives the appearance of a larger portion. Pounding or butterflying a piece of meat, fish, or poultry before cooking has the same effect. In the final presentation, height is an important element. Drawing the eye up and away from individual portions of food on the plate prevents customers from feeling that they were given a skimpy portion of meat.

While employing these techniques, it is important to incorporate whole grains and vegetables into the dish. These foods fill the plate, and create a feeling of satiety in diners. Patrons who leave feeling comfortably full are less likely to feel they were given skimpy portions.

Modifying Recipes

The most common method of developing a healthy recipe is to modify a traditional or classic recipe to reduce its calories, sodium, sugar, fats, or cholesterol. The key to successful modification is to imagine comparisons between the modified recipe and the original version. If a modified recipe cannot emulate the flavor and texture of the original but is still tasty, consider calling it by a new name and forgoing any association to the original dish.

In modifying recipes, two areas can be adjusted: techniques and ingredients, and fat is often critical in both areas. To identify recipes that are good candidates for alteration, look at the amount and purpose of fat. Recipes that rely on fat for the majority of their flavor and texture, such as deep-fried foods or sauces like hollandaise or beurre blanc, should be avoided.

Those that have a moderate amount of fat, and that rely on other ingredients to contribute flavor, moisture, and structure, have potential. You may be able to use less fat if you modify the technique. Adaptations may be as simple as relying on the fat naturally present in a food when sautéing, using less fat or a healthier fat in the pan, or using a nonstick pan. Often healthy techniques can be substituted for less healthy ones. Deep-fried chicken may be "oven-fried" to obtain a similar texture with a fraction of the fat content. A game bird can be poached in water or broth rather than poêléed in a bath of butter, and so forth.

Substituting other ingredients requires a bit more thought. The basic elements that made the original dish successful can often be retained if you take an open-minded approach to solving the puzzle and use your imagination. Two considerations that should be addressed are the function of the ingredient and the flavor it provides. Ingredients that are high in fat, calories, or sodium can usually be substituted for or substantially reduced, as long as care is taken to emulate the function of the original ingredient. Heavy cream sauces and cream-style soups can be made using a velouté thickened with a modified starch rather than a roux and "creamed" with evaporated milk or low-fat yogurt. A mixture of nonfat yogurt and ricotta cheese can fill in for a traditional Bavarian cream base. Vegetables can be enhanced with a flavorful thickened vegetable stock and fresh herbs instead of butter. You can also substitute smaller quantities of strongly flavored foods, such as extra-sharp Cheddar or Roquefort for milder Cheddars or Gorgonzola, or spicy chorizo for linguiça or Italian sausage. Try using egg whites for up to half the amount of whole eggs called for in a recipe. Cocoa powder can often substitute for chocolate, as long as a small amount of the chocolate is retained to provide the rich mouthfeel that cocoa butter imparts. (See Cooking with Less Fat, page 137.)

When you find a formula that works for one recipe, apply it to similar recipes. The same changes in techniques and ingredients often work on other foods of the same type. What works for one cream soup, for example, often works for others.

Portion sizes can also be adjusted to help a recipe fall in line. Protein-based and fat-laden foods should often be reduced in size. Putting a generous assortment of properly prepared vegetables on the plate tips the scales in favor of good nutrition. (See Using Standard Portions, page 134.) High-calorie, high-fat, and high-sodium ingredients, such as sour cream, butter, bacon, and guacamole, need not be totally eliminated in healthy cooking; use them in smaller portions so they do not send any dish over the limits you have established.

Creating Original Recipes

The inspiration for a new dish can come from many sources. Perhaps a delivery brings a box of brilliantly colored, fragrant fruits that leads to a new dessert. Or maybe the memory of a dish enjoyed in another country returns when you smell a bouquet of pungent herbs. Or perhaps a new cookbook, a magazine article, or a newspaper clipping from years ago might be the impetus.

No matter what inspires you, the process of inventing a new recipe requires that you understand how ingredients, flavor dynamics, and nutrition interact. By using the freshest ingredients of the highest quality, incorporating a variety of textures, flavors, and temperatures, keeping sauces light and flavorful, and using cooking techniques that are low in fat, you can develop an idea into a wonderful addition to the healthy menu, as illustrated in the hypothetical process that follows.

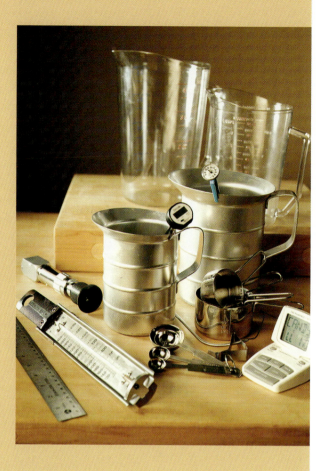

ONCE A STANDARD RECIPE IS ESTABLISHED, it is imperative that kitchen staff adhere to the amounts specified. If a nutrition claim is made about a particular dish, using standard portions ensures that the customer is actually getting the amount of nutrients referred to in the claim. For example, a pizza referred to as low-fat on the menu is not so if the pizza cook habitually uses twice as much cheese as the recipe states. (See Chapter 2 for more on claims and nutrient analysis in recipes.)

You should insist that kitchen staff weigh and measure everything. This is as important for managing costs and inventory, reducing waste, and maintaining product consistency as it is for keeping nutrients in line. Garnishes, flavorings, and other potentially high-fat, high-sodium ingredients should be carefully measured to keep them from upsetting the balance of flavor in a dish. Whenever practical, foods should be preportioned as part of the regular prep routine. Accurate scales are a must in the nutrition-conscious kitchen. Other equipment that can be used to help control portion sizes and amounts of ingredients include ladles, scoops, molds, and pumps that dispense the same amount of product every time.

Once the basics of the recipe are laid down—a dish of steamed fish with an Asian-inspired sauce, for example—it is time to start putting it down on paper or plugging it into a computer. This step is where portion sizes and ingredient measurements come under their first scrutiny.

Perhaps when you first imagined the dish, you envisioned an 8-ounce portion of snapper, but when the recipe was analyzed for its nutrition content this version showed that the calorie count and sodium were unacceptably high. Reducing the portion size to 6 ounces made the calories somewhat better, but reducing it to 4 ounces allowed you a little more leeway in the side dishes you were thinking about. Replacing the tamari sauce with a reduced-sodium version and omitting the added salt in the marinade brought the sodium to a level appropriate for the menu category. When you finished making the adjustments on paper, your next step was to make a few trial dishes.

As each test recipe was prepared, you evaluated not only the nutrition but also the visual appeal, flavor, texture, and interplay of colors. When the consensus was that 4 ounces of fish did not fill the plate enough, you decided to increase the portion to 5 ounces. Finally, to keep the calories in line and to increase the eye appeal, you replaced the rice pilaf with a bed of wilted spinach and baby bok choy, and garnished with julienned carrot.

As this example demonstrates, there are no strict rules that govern the creative process. Developing a new recipe is a game of give and take to reach a balance. In the same way that the inspiration from a dish can come from any of a thousand sources, so the evolution of the recipe might follow a thousand paths.

Cooking with Less Fat

Fats are not equal: Some types are much more desirable than others when creating nutrient-conscious menus. You may be able to improve your recipes by choosing the right type of fat, but sometimes the solution is not as straightforward.

Fat is an essential nutrient, and it performs many important culinary functions. It contributes to the flavor and texture of foods on its own, and it blends the flavors of other ingredients and foods. Nutrients and flavor compounds that are fat-soluble are hidden in foods that are prepared or served without fat. Fat helps to create a crisp texture when used in fried and sautéed foods, helps to tenderize and create a flaky or crumbly texture in baked goods, and helps to retain moisture. It contributes to feelings of satiety and can actually help people to eat less.

Reducing Fat

Reducing fat is one of the most intriguing challenges facing a chef. Although many people want to eat less fat, they are usually unwilling to sacrifice flavor or texture to do so.

The first step in creating low-fat recipes or reducing the fat content of existing recipes is to evaluate whether the recipe can be made with less fat. Sometimes this is easy. Rather than toss butter on vegetables or top a stack of waffles with a pat of butter, another ingredient can

Drain yogurt for a richer mouthfeel.

Add herbs for flavor.

Use to garnish soups instead of high-fat creams.

ALTHOUGH YOU DON'T NEED special equipment for low-fat cooking, having some items on hand can make it much simpler.

Nonstick pans have become much more durable in recent years and are appropriate for professional kitchens. Well-seasoned cast-iron is also useful. Both types of cookware prevent foods from sticking and encourage browning. As long as these pans are cleaned and stored properly (see Caring for and Maintaining Cookware, page 96), they will give you years of use.

Defatting pitchers can be used to remove fat from small amounts of liquid. These have spouts at the bottom that allow the liquid to be poured out when the fat has risen to the top. Defatting ladles can be used to remove fat from large amounts of liquid and are easier to use than regular ladles, which require a very steady hand. Defatting ladles have a raised rim above small slots. The fat flows through the slots and is collected in the bowl of the ladle.

Silicone bake mats are handy for baking. They are nonstick and heat resistant, and can be used to line sheet pans. Parchment serves a similar function, though it is not as effective.

be used. Flavored olive oil or a starch-thickened sauce may complement the vegetables, and a fruit purée adds flavor to breakfast cakes. Sometimes, though, the fat contributes to the finished product in a more complicated manner. The butter in a cake batter, for example, affects the leavening, color, and texture of the finished item.

After the function of the fat is identified, you can figure out your strategy for improving the fat content of a dish. You can use a leaner cut of meat or poultry, or replace a high-fat meat with a meaty fish steak. You can replace meat in a stew with legumes or vegetables. If you are roasting poultry, leave the skin on to help retain moisture; tuck herbs or other aromatics under the skin to introduce another flavor element. Just be sure to remove the skin before serving.

Choose your saturated fats wisely. Bacon provides a unique flavor and can be used as a condiment in some dishes. Render it first and pour off most of the fat before proceeding with the recipe to minimize the amount of saturated fat while taking advantage of its flavor.

You also may have the option to remove unnecessary fat throughout the cooking process. Fat drips off grilled and broiled meats, and is not used in pan sauces. Soups, stews, and braises can be refrigerated overnight. The fat will rise to the top and solidify, making it easy to remove.

Replacing Fat

Many low-fat and fat-free ingredients can be used to replace fat. You'll have no trouble finding high-quality reduced-fat dairy products. Some nonfat dairy products may not be suitable for cooking and baking because they tend to break down when subjected to high heat. Others, however, can be used with great success. The cream cheese in a cheesecake can be replaced with a combination of reduced-fat cream cheese, nonfat yogurt drained of its whey, and puréed low-fat cottage and ricotta cheeses. Evaporated skim milk can be used in place of cream in many dishes. In recipes that call for eggs, several of the egg yolks can often be omitted without anyone noticing.

Reduced-fat dairy foods may curdle because they often lack sufficient fat to inhibit protein coagulation. To avoid this, add the reduced-fat product at the last possible minute and use gentle heat. Or, try mixing a small amount of starch, such as cornstarch or flour, into the dairy product. The starch will swell and block the proteins from coagulating in much the same way that fat would.

The fat in a cream soup can be reduced in a variety of ways. Rather than use a roux to thicken the broth, purée vegetables or starchy ingredients such as potatoes, rice, or legumes. These can also be used in many classic sauces. Gravy, traditionally thickened with a roux, can be made with jus lié. Roasted, braised, fresh, or dried fruits and vegetables can be used in coulis, relishes, and chutneys to give a dish a completely different flavor profile.

Replacing fat in baked goods presents greater challenges because of the complex physical and chemical changes that take place during the baking process. Using cooking spray, a silicone baking mat, or parchment paper to line a pan rather than butter, oil, or shortening reduces the fat somewhat. When replacing the fat in batters and doughs, it is doubly important to consider the function of fat. Fruit purées like applesauce, mashed bananas, lekvar (prune purée), or other fruits with high pectin and sugar levels can be used to replace up to 75 percent of the fat in some recipes. Meringues can be used to provide volume in cake and soufflé batters, and when a cooked meringue is folded with a small amount of whipped heavy cream, the result is a good substitute for full-fat whipped cream. Buttermilk is naturally low in fat; it can be used in lieu of milk or cream in many baking recipes. It adds a pleasant tang to the finished dish, and its high acidity helps to leaven and to create a more tender product.

Cooking with Less Salt

Salt does more than add saltiness to foods. It intensifies the other flavors in a dish, which is why a small amount is often added to desserts and baked goods.

Improperly seasoned foods taste bland and unappealing, but underseasoning foods in the kitchen so customers can add it at the table is unwise. Cooked foods often require more salt to achieve the same amount of flavor than if they had been salted throughout the cooking process. In addition, the majority of the sodium we consume is in processed foods, such as canned goods and snack items, not from salt added before, during, or after cooking.

It's possible to create flavorful dishes without adding a lot of salt or using high-sodium ingredients. Aromatic ingredients such as onions, garlic, shallots, fresh ginger, and scallions are fundamental. They often go into the pot first so their flavors and aromas can infuse everything else in the dish. Look to cuisines from other countries for characteristic flavor profiles that may complement the recipe you are making. Greek cuisine, for example, often uses olive oil, lemon, cinnamon, tomato, and oregano; Asian dishes might begin with ginger, garlic, or scallion. Latin American cooking often uses chiles, lime, and cilantro to build flavor.

Herbs and spices are essential to healthy cooking. Fresh herbs in particular can lift the flavor of any food. Choose those that have intense or unique flavors, such as rosemary and saffron, for the most impact, but add them sparingly so they do not overwhelm the other flavors.

Chiles add a pleasant heat and a piquant zest to foods. Smoked, dried, and fresh chiles are widely available in an array of heat levels.

Pungent ingredients can add bold flavors: Mustard seeds and dry mustard, horseradish, tamarind pods, and wasabi provide a noticeable kick. Soy sauce and fish sauce, Worcestershire sauce, and pastes like tapenade can add a depth of flavor beyond mere saltiness. Be sure to check labels on prepared varieties of these ingredients and avoid those with extremely high sodium levels.

The bright, sharp flavors of acidic foods can often reduce the need for salt. Citrus and flavored vinegars (see page 127) can give recipes a refreshing taste without affecting their sodium content.

By combining and contrasting spices, herbs, and other distinctive flavoring agents, you can moderate sodium levels while enhancing the flavors of the main ingredients.

THERE'S MORE TO COOKING with less sugar than simply using less sweet stuff. Refined grains like white rice and pasta, and starchy vegetables like white potatoes, have an effect on blood sugar that's almost as dramatic as cake or cookies.

Adding whole grains is the obvious solution, but customers may resist unfamiliar flavors and textures. Farro, wheat berries, amaranth, and wild rice are high in nutrients and flavor, but less adventurous diners may be disinclined to try them, and those who do sample them may find their chewier textures and stronger flavors off-putting. You can make these unusual grains more palatable by combining them with familiar grains. Pilafs made of barley and wheat berries, of bulgur and amaranth, or of a blend of rices might find a more receptive audience.

Think of ways to combine unfamiliar and familiar vegetables, too. White potatoes have some nutrients, but they pale in comparison to other root vegetables. Puréeing turnips or sweet potatoes and adding to mashed potatoes boosts nutrition. Stirring cooked greens, toasted nuts, or fruit into a grain dish expands its flavor profile and adds texture and nutrition.

Cooking with Less Sugar

Humans are born with a preference for sweet foods, which can make it difficult to limit the use of refined sugars and to resist desserts. Providing your guests with the option to choose foods that taste delicious but do not contain excessive amounts of sugar is a hallmark of healthy cooking.

Before you turn to refined sugars, try to capitalize on the natural sugars present in many foods. Fruits are a source of sugar, but they also are packed with nutrients. Combining several fruits, or combining the same fruit in different forms (fresh, dried, cooked, or puréed) expands the flavor profile of a dessert.

Caramelizing foods enhances their natural sugars. Cooking foods using a dry-heat method browns them, creating a deep, rich, complex flavor.

Sweeteners other than sugar add flavors beyond just sweetness. Consider how different gingerbread would taste if it were sweetened with maple syrup rather than molasses. Honey often has a flavor that hints of the flower from which it originated; sage and eucalyptus honey are rather bold and somewhat resinous, while orange blossom honey is sweetly citrusy. Like molasses, honey can be used in sweet and savory recipes.

Cooking with Less Alcohol

Many dishes, including entrées, sauces, and desserts, can be enhanced with flavorful spirits. A bottle of beer added to the chili pot adds a depth of flavor some chili aficionados require, and deglazing a sauté or roasting pan with wine or liquor can transform a sauce from ordinary to outstanding.

Alcohol's contribution to the caloric content of a dish depends on how much, if any, of the alcohol evaporates before the dish is served. Careful studies have dispelled the notion that all of the alcohol and its calories are lost; at least a small amount always remains. The rate of evaporation depends on several factors: the degree of heat to which the alcohol is exposed, the length of exposure, and the surface area of the pot in which the alcohol is cooked (a larger surface area results in more evaporation).

In a 1990 study, a pot roast made with burgundy retained just 5 percent of its alcohol after simmering for 2½ hours, while cherries jubilee made with brandy that was heated and quickly ignited still contained 75 percent of its alcohol. In cases where spirits are added at the last moment or when a liqueur is added to a cold preparation, virtually all of the alcohol and its calories are retained.

If you wish to omit alcohol from your recipes, you will need to consider the function of the alcohol. A wine used to deglaze a pan can be replaced with broth or a mixture of water and a small amount of vinegar or lemon juice. Alcohols used for flavoring, such as a fruit-based liqueur, can be replaced with juice or fruit purées.

Of course, recipes for flambés and frozen desserts might not work or will be less successful if you omit the alcohol. Because alcohol freezes at temperatures much lower than water, frozen desserts that contain spirits will have a different texture.

Menu Development

Before you can develop healthy recipes, you need to create a menu for your operation. The number and type of healthy offerings will depend on several interrelated factors that center around the type of establishment and your clientele.

Chefs today work in a variety of non-restaurant venues. You may work at a spa, on a cruise ship, at a resort hotel, as a caterer. You may be the director of food service at a school, office complex, hospital, residential facility, or chain of upscale supermarkets offering home-meal replacements. Even restaurants can vary widely: Do you work at a small, casual bistro or for a large chain of family restaurants?

Where you work determines who your clientele is and the type of food they will expect. Factors such as the number of meals you prepare in a shift, the availability of ingredients, and the amount of storage and equipment you have will affect your menu.

The menu is the medium through which your customers learn what your kitchen is able to offer. Making good nutrition the focus of the menu or offering health-oriented dishes in addition to the more usual fare provides a new level of information to your customers. A menu that places an emphasis on nutrition, no matter how small, tells your customers that your establishment cares about offering them choices to meet their needs.

Sometimes customers' needs may not be the driving force behind creating a healthy menu. Knowing the basics of good nutrition and having the desire to provide foods that have healthful components (that are low in trans fats, high in antioxidants and fiber) may be all the impetus you need.

DEVELOPING HEALTHY RECIPES isn't just about replacing unhealthy fats with healthy ones or using fresh herbs instead of salt. The dishes you devise should supply beneficial nutrients, and they need to be tasty and flavorful as well. You'll find ideas throughout the recipe section, but here are some basic suggestions:

- Build salads with dark greens. Iceberg and Boston lettuces have their place but are low on the list of nutritious salad greens. Darker lettuces and salad greens like romaine, spinach, and arugula contain significantly more vitamins A and C, as well as phytochemical pigments.

- Intensify flavors with variations on a theme. Rather than adding a variety of seasonings to a tomato-based pasta sauce, for example, use several different tomato products, such as canned tomatoes, slow-roasted or sun-dried tomatoes, and fresh tomatoes, to create an intensely rich taste by "layering" the same ingredient. Purée smoked salmon and add to a paste that tops salmon fillets before broiling, or simmer apples in cider when making a sauce.

- Introduce the exotic slowly. Although people in the United States are willing to embrace unusual tastes, you'll have better luck incorporating those tastes if you combine them with the familiar. An entrée of freshly caught grilled sardines might have limited appeal, but add them to a sampler plate that includes olives, marinated vegetables, a pungent cheese, and a grain salad like tabbouleh, and these healthy little fish might find an audience. Kale or mustard greens might be too strongly flavored for a side dish; stir them into a soup or add them to a popular pasta dish on your menu.

- Combine the sweet with the savory. Don't limit fruit to your dessert menu. Toss red or black grapes into savory salads or sauté peach or nectarine slices in the pan drippings after cooking chicken breasts. Look at your sandwich menu to see if a fruit purée can replace mayo as a spread, or consider adding a roast pork sandwich with apple butter and grainy mustard.

- Go nuts. Top mashed sweet potatoes with chopped pecans, stir walnuts into chicken salad, or garnish a Mexican entrée with toasted pumpkin seeds. Serve dishes of spiced nuts at the bar.

Butler service

Appetizers

You may want to use appetizers as a vehicle to introduce a greater array of ingredients onto the menu. Using vegetables as containers for hors d'oeuvre is one way. Cucumber cups, endive spears, and other vegetable "containers" are a good alternative to high-fat crackers or chips.

Appetizers served on a plate as a first course should be thoughtfully garnished. Once again, this is an opportunity to add a greater variety of vegetables, fruits, and other healthful ingredients. These additions can also improve the dish's visual appeal.

Adding a small amount of cheese, meat, or even a rich ingredient like foie gras may be appropriate, as long as you are careful about portioning. However, when you present hors d'oeuvre as part of a buffet, you should select dishes that are lower in calories, fat, and sodium whenever possible.

Plated appetizer as first course

Platter service

Appetizers

Selecting and Preparing Appetizers

Perfectly fresh clams and oysters, shucked as close to service time as possible and served with sauces designed to enhance their naturally briny savor, or a classic shrimp "cocktail," served with a cocktail sauce, salsa, or other pungent sauce, are perennial favorites in any appetizer category. And as long as you are confident that your seafood comes from a reliable source, these simple appetizer foods are fresh, flavorful, and healthy. Foods you might ordinarily try to avoid in other menu categories are appropriate here as long as you are very careful about portioning and presenting the foods.

Smoked fish, meats, or poultry; sausages, pâtés, terrines, and galantines; air-dried hams and beef sliced paper thin—all of these items can be used to create appetizer plates, on their own with a few accompaniments or garnishes or as a sampler plate. Refer to Chapters 6, 7, and 8 for specific recipes and presentation ideas.

Salads are also served as appetizers. You may prefer to change the portion size, substitute a different sauce or garnish to give your menu items a special look, vary it from season to season, or showcase a range of flavors and textures from other cuisines.

Warm and hot appetizers may include small portions of grains or even breads. Broiled or grilled fish, shellfish, or poultry may be featured. Crêpes, blinis, and other similar dishes have been popular in many different cuisines. Meatballs and other highly seasoned ground meat appetizers are also found on today's menus. Swedish meatballs share space in the garde manger's repertoire with *kefta* (spicy kebobs made from ground lamb).

Vegetables are more important than ever as appetizers. Sometimes they are presented very simply; for example, steamed artichokes may be served with a dipping sauce such as a flavored vinaigrette, chilled asparagus may be served drizzled with a flavored oil, or a plate of grilled vegetables may be accompanied by a cold tomato sauce.

Principles for Presenting Appetizers

Keep in mind the following basic principles as you select, prepare, and plate appetizers:

- Serve all appetizers at the proper temperature. Remember to chill or warm plates.

- Season all appetizer items with meticulous care. Appetizers are meant to stimulate the appetite, so seasoning is of the utmost importance.

- Slice, shape, and portion appetizers properly. There should be just enough of any given item to make the appetizer interesting and appealing from start to finish, but not so much on the plate that the guest is overwhelmed.

- Neatness always counts, but especially with appetizers. Your guests will most likely judge their entire meal based on the impression the appetizer gives.

- When offering shared appetizers, consider how they will look when they come to the table. It may be more effective to split a shared plate in the kitchen, rather than expecting the guests to divide it up themselves.

- Color, shape, and "white space" play a role in the overall composition of your plate. Take the time to choose the right size and shape serving pieces and to provide the guest

Soups

Soups can range from light but intensely flavored broths and consommés that are virtually fat free to hearty dishes brimming with vegetables and legumes. Cream soups, bisques, and chowders can present a challenge, but there are techniques you can use to reduce both fat and calories in cream-style soups.

What is most appealing and important in any soup is its flavor and texture. Cream soups have a richer body that remains in your mouth longer than brothy soups. You can take advantage of this by exploiting every technique at your disposal. The first step is creating an aromatic base. We think of cream soups as having a light color, so cook the mirepoix only until it is tender, not until it turns color. This will keep the soup from turning dark and tasting too sweet.

Next, remember that the texture of the soup depends as much upon the garnish ingredients you include as the soup base. A bit of contrast, in the form of a crunchy crouton or other crisp element, makes the soup more interesting. Handle other ingredients correctly so that you don't spoil the velvety look and feel of your soup with unintended additions that might feel stringy or hard. Attention to details, like picking crabmeat to remove shell, is critical.

Some classic cream soups are thickened with roux, then finished with a cream-and-egg–yolk liaison. To avoid those added calories, purée the base until it is very smooth and light. You may wish to strain the soup after you purée it to be sure that all fibers are removed. Then, if you want to finish the soup with a "cream," consider evaporated skim milk. Another alternative is adding a small "puff" or dollop of yogurt, sour cream, or even lightly whipped cream. You can add far less cream this way than if you were to blend it directly into the soup.

Salads

Salads on a healthy menu are a perfect choice, as long as basic menu-planning parameters are observed. You can serve a salad as a first course or as an accompaniment to another dish. Adding a small tossed salad to a plate improves its appearance and makes the main item appear more generous. As you begin to work with portion sizes for high-calorie dishes, this is an important benefit. A simple green salad served as a first course slows the pace of the meal.

Vegetable-, grain-, or legume-based salads can be served alone or combined into a sampler plate. Take care when portioning salads for a sampler. Using a reduced-fat vinaigrette instead of the classic vinaigrette made with three parts oil and one part vinegar means you can be a bit more generous with your portions, but other ingredients in the salad may have to be taken into account as well.

Composed salads can be portioned in such a way that they work as either an appetizer or a main course. Green salads work well as a bed for other ingredients. Avoid adding too many ingredients that are high in calories or fat. A chef salad of sliced meats, cheeses, and eggs is a classic, but you may want to consider cutting those foods into fine julienne or dice so that they are still a strong flavor presence but not the main focus of the salad.

with all the items necessary for the appetizer, including cups for dipping sauces, special utensils, and, if necessary, finger bowls.

Knowing Your Customers

The menu you develop will depend in large part on your market. Are your customers looking to grab a quick sandwich, to impress a date or a client, or to recover from surgery so they can go home? An establishment that caters to executives on expense accounts has a different clientele, with substantially different needs and expectations, than a high-school cafeteria.

Your menu will also depend on logistics. The availability and cost of ingredients, the price you are able to charge customers, and your facilities are factors that affect what you can offer. Chefs who are responsible for all of a person's meals have a greater obligation to provide healthy options than chefs whose patrons are infrequent guests.

Restaurants run the gamut from fast food to haute cuisine, from ten-top independently owned stores to international chains with vast resources. Restaurants may well have the most flexibility in determining a menu. Because a chef really has no control over the other food choices a customer makes in a day, he or she doesn't need to be overly worried with providing balanced nutrition. You should, of course, offer nutritious dishes, but you have no way of knowing how they will fit into a customer's diet. It is the customer's responsibility to make smart choices. You know what your facilities can handle and how much storage you have, and you can plan your purchases, and your menu, accordingly.

A caterer, particularly one who specializes in preparing hot food on location, faces much greater limits. Turning out dozens or hundreds of dishes in a matter of minutes requires a great deal of organization. You may find yourself working under a canopy in a parking lot or in an unfamiliar kitchen. Space and site issues, as well as flavor and nutrition, must be kept in mind when planning a menu with a client.

Chefs who work at institutions have a greater responsibility to keep nutrients in mind, and may face the biggest challenges. The director of food service at a hospital or school will most likely work with a dietician to ensure that menus and recipes fit specific parameters to meet patrons' needs. A sixty-five-year-old quadruple-bypass patient will have distinctly different nutrition needs and food preferences from a child whose tonsils were removed. Sick people often have limited appetites, so creating foods that will tempt them to eat and will help them to heal is the primary goal. What is considered "tempting," however, may vary considerably by age as well as by ethnicity or cultural background. An elderly Chinese immigrant may ignore mashed potatoes, polenta, or cream of wheat, but might welcome a rice dish such as congee.

Cost can be a critical factor at institutions. The chef at a private facility may have a much larger budget than the director of food service for a public school district who charges two dollars for a meal. In addition, school lunch programs serve a customer base with a broad range of caloric and nutrient requirements. A sixteen-year-old boy needs on average about 3,000 calories a day, about 25 percent more than a girl of the same age and almost twice the amount that a first-grader does. Menus with a variety of portion sizes, as well as with options for side dishes, make sense. Appealing choices mean less waste.

The chef at a spa, hotel, or on a cruise ship faces some of the responsibility that an institutional chef does, some of the limitations that a caterer does, and some of the flexibility that a restaurant chef does. When consumers have no choice but to eat your food, particularly for several consecutive meals, you must offer an array of healthy choices. The menu at a spa will reflect the philosophy and mission of the facility; meals may offer dishes at specific calorie ranges or with a limited number of fat grams. A cruise ship might be able to replenish supplies in different ports, but if this is not an option, menus must be designed that take into account storage facilities as well as keeping properties of foods. Guests whose meals are included in their fees expect quality and variety, and they will often expect a high level of service and presentation as well.

Home-meal replacement is one of the fastest-growing segments of the food industry. People who don't have time to cook also might not have time to dine in restaurants, where they must wait for their food to be prepared, but they might not want to eat takeout Chinese or pizza or drive-through fast food every night. Freshly prepared foods, whether from a favorite restaurant or a local supermarket, that can be ordered ahead and eaten at home are finding a wide audience. Allowing customers to build their meals by choosing from a variety of sides ensures that their nutrition needs will be met.

All chefs should keep in mind seasonality and availability of foods. Thanks to faster shipping, virtually every food is available year-round, all over the country. But just because you can get tomatoes in January or apricots in October or apples in April doesn't mean these foods no longer have a "season" or that seasonality doesn't matter. Perishable produce shipped in from far away may have flavors and textures you can barely distinguish from those you buy at the height of the season from a local farmer's market, or they may be nice-looking but tasteless. Regardless of their flavors, the price these imported fruits and vegetables command, however, is usually significantly higher.

Instead, change your menus to reflect the bounty of each season. When local tomatoes are at their peak, create a BLT that reflects your establishment's sensibility: arugula, pancetta, and ciabatta for an Italian restaurant, perhaps. Soft-shell crabs, shad roe, and wild salmon are in season just briefly; it may be easier to add them to your list of specials than to your regular menu.

Even minor modifications can reflect seasonality. Adding asparagus to sautéed mixed vegetables or fresh garden peas to a pasta dish can herald spring. A spinach and goat cheese salad might use blood oranges and olives in the winter, berries and pine nuts in the spring, peaches in the summer, and apples or pears and walnuts in autumn.

Although you might not want to remove signature dishes, consider changing your menu periodically to keep your staff and your customers from getting complacent or bored.

Knowing Your Customers' Needs

When asked, most people will say they want to eat more healthfully. They know that whole grains, lean meats and poultry, fish, and vegetables are good for them, but too often they perceive these foods to be unappealing. Healthy eating is associated with deprivation and food that just doesn't taste "right." No matter what people say, if healthy food doesn't taste good they won't eat it. At the same time, if your menu offers only high-calorie foods that are high in saturated fats and refined carbohydrates, your customers may be resentful at the lack of healthy choices.

The challenge for chefs is to build a menu that incorporates healthy options that look and taste tempting. You cannot control what your customers order, and you may not have any idea what other foods they have eaten that day, but you can offer options that will provide a nutritious meal. Emphasizing the positive—what you do offer—is as important as focusing on what you limit. Some people will interpret a phrase like *low-fat* to mean bland. Rather than highlighting the lack of fat in your recipes, you may wish to spotlight the ingredients and techniques that indicate flavor and nutrition. Instead of positioning foods as a "healthy" option, simply make them available. Add whole-grain breads to your bread baskets, or allow guests to choose white or brown rice as a side dish.

People who are interested in healthy eating usually are able to identify menu items that meet their needs. Thorough descriptions of each dish, including words that describe the side dishes and ingredients in a sauce or coating, will help them spot acceptable choices. Cooking terms like *grilled* or *broiled* let consumers know that a dish is likely to be much lower in fat than a *deep-fried* or *crispy* food. Meat eaters will appreciate knowing whether the steak entrée features a filet, a sirloin, or a porterhouse, and whether the steak is six or sixteen ounces. Even a dessert menu might highlight a flavorful, nutrient-rich triple-berry sauce rather than caramel, crème anglaise, or whipped cream.

A well thought out menu will include a balance of salads (including entrée salads) and pastas, fish, poultry, and vegetarian entrées as well as meats. Allowing guests to order a half portion or to split an entrée gives those with smaller appetites the opportunity to limit portions. Including a variety of appetizers, especially choices that are not fried or high in refined carbohydrates, enables patrons to order items from your starter menu as their main course.

Permitting substitutions of side dishes indicates that you are willing to accommodate guests' nutrition needs and preferences. Although excessive substitutions and special orders can wreak havoc in a busy kitchen and may throw off inventory, ultimately this is information a chef needs to succeed.

Developing a menu and the accompanying recipes is often a work in progress. As each change is introduced, you need to track its reception among your patrons and your staff. If any refinements are needed, they can be made based upon feedback.

Objectives in Creating a Healthy Menu

It can be confusing to keep nutrients in mind while developing menus, but it is not necessary to focus too narrowly on this. Chefs who need to be sure that their menus contain adequate amounts of nutrients in proper balance often work with a dietician to develop menus that are "what the doctor ordered."

If your menu includes recipes with any sort of a health or nutrient claim, you must ensure that the recipes meet specific requirements. These are outlined in Chapter 2 and in the Appendix. Analyzing recipes for their nutrient content will help you to keep on track, and to identify where you may need to adapt a cooking technique, choose a different ingredient or two, reduce the portion size, or even change how the dish is presented.

Healthy recipes should follow certain guidelines. The number of calories and nutrients they should contain will vary depending on whether they are breakfast, lunch, or dinner items, as well as on any parameters you have established that define "healthy."

In the United States, most people also eat far too many calories in a day: Our diets are too high in protein, refined carbohydrates, and saturated and trans fats, and too low in complex carbohydrates and monounsaturated fats. We typically eat a breakfast that is heavy in carbohydrates. Cereal and milk, toast with jam, bagels, pancakes with syrup, and even fresh fruit provide little protein and fat, and might not provide sufficient amounts of complex carbohydrates. Lunches are often too skimpy or too large. A cup of soup or a candy bar from the vending machine won't provide enough nutrients to keep a person going, but a large, heavy lunch can induce lethargy and a mid-afternoon slump. Sugary or salty snacks and sweetened or caffeinated beverages might be chosen to boost energy or fill an empty stomach with equally empty calories. Dinners are usually built around protein, and most of us consider the proper balance to be a piece of meat that covers half the plate, with the remaining half divided between a starchy side and vegetables.

 Because chefs are often at the vanguard of culinary trends, you have the opportunity to influence changes in how people in the United State eat. As a chef, you probably look to other cultures and cuisines for inspiration for flavors and dishes, but consider as well how people in other countries eat. In India, for example, *thali* is a meal without a main course. Meat, legumes, vegetables, rice or bread, salads, and relishes are served in comparable amounts. You may not want to add Indian foods to your menu, but you can certainly borrow this concept in rethinking the balance on a dinner plate.

People in the United States might not be ready for congee or fish soup for breakfast, but perhaps your breakfast or dessert menu might feature blini—made with buckwheat flour, they are higher in fiber than regular pancakes or crêpes. Add kasha to your menu, either as a side dish or mixed into oats as a breakfast food. Rather than a high-fat eggs Benedict or an ersatz version with low-fat hollandaise, you might offer huevos rancheros topped with a zesty salsa or a Spanish frittata-like tortilla.

If you want to have a tuna salad sandwich on your lunch menu, skip the mayo-heavy version and consider a niçoise-inspired salad (minus the potatoes and green beans) or *pan bagnat*. Consider making a whole-grain bread your house bread (but have other options available) for sandwiches and in your breadbaskets.

Look for ways to add nuts to your menu. Can you replace a butter- or cream-based sauce with a one like skordalia or romesco? Perhaps you could use finely ground almonds in a cake batter, or crushed pecans to crust a fish fillet.

If you change your menu often, or if you add dishes that might be unfamiliar to your customers, think about taking a cue from the tapas bars of Spain and add a small-plate option to your menu. Guests will be able to try a variety of dishes and share them among a table, or they can build a meal by ordering a small plate or two with a salad or soup.

When developing a healthy menu, keep flavor in the front of your mind and concentrate on choosing healthy ingredients in appropriate amounts. Focusing on what you can use and what your menu offers is every bit as important as paying attention to what you should limit.

Menu Development for Special Needs

Not only do dietary and cultural preferences come into play with menu development, but different segments of the population have different nutrient needs as well. "Healthy" can vary somewhat depending on the ages, gender, and lifestyle of your customers.

As people grow older, their nutrition requirements change. Chronic health conditions such as type-II diabetes or heart disease often appear as people age. Metabolic rates slow down and calorie needs decrease. Some older people might have adventuresome palates and be willing to try healthy dishes that include unusual flavors or textures. Others will appreciate small portions and healthier versions of traditional favorites.

Children are often forgotten when it comes to providing healthy menu choices. Standard children's menus traditionally offer little more than hot dogs, grilled cheese sandwiches, fried chicken fingers, and French fries. Although children are not known for their willingness to experiment or their passion for bold flavors, familiar foods like pizza, pasta, and sandwiches can be reworked to be kid-friendly and nutrient-rich. Finger foods like grapes, berries, and apple wedges can be dipped into sweetened yogurt sauces for sides or desserts.

Gender is another factor to take into consideration. Overall, both men and women are aware of the negative impact of trans fats and saturated fats and the positive attributes of antioxidants, omega-3 fatty acids, and whole grains. Women are typically more concerned about reducing their consumption of calories and fat. They may ask for grilled foods or salads with sauces and dressings on the side. If your salads feature dressings that use less oil, consider pointing this out. Because women tend to be smaller than men, they typically eat less. Smaller portions, tasting menus, or samplers are likely to appeal.

Men often show more interest in lower-cholesterol and -sodium foods. If your customers tend to be a meat-and-potatoes crowd, offer minor variations on this theme. Highlight leaner cuts of beef on your menu—or replace the beef with a meaty tuna steak or duck breast. Use sweet potatoes and white potatoes in an au gratin side dish, and modify the sauce to include low-fat dairy. Keep portion sizes of proteins to a moderate size, but serve larger helpings of vegetables.

Lifestyle attributes also affect a customer's level of interest in nutrition when dining out. When restaurant meals are reserved for celebrations, customers are more likely to splurge on rich foods; the more often people eat out, the more interested they usually are in healthy menu choices. Businesspeople, families where both parents work, and senior citizens tend to dine in restaurants frequently. Family-style restaurants and establishments that serve a business clientele will want to offer a variety of healthy options. Businesspeople, particularly those who travel frequently, tend to eat out often and are usually well aware of the relationship between diet and overall health.

As people in the United States cook at home less and less often, it becomes increasingly important for restaurants and other food-service providers to offer nutritious options. People in this country are eating more restaurant meals—in 2005, only 58 percent of meals were prepared at home, and the typical individual ate 80 meals in restaurants and nearly 60 meals as carryout—and smaller portions and healthy choices are big concerns.

Vegetarian Menus

Lifestyle can also include vegetarianism. You will find that vegetarian options on your menu appeal to a fairly broad group, including adventurous eaters of all persuasions who have an interest in the ethnic cuisines that are inspiring chefs to include more vegetables, fruits, and plant foods. For many guests, the perception that vegetarian dishes are healthier than traditional meat-based dishes gives them added appeal. .

Developing a vegetable-based menu, or even a few menu items, means more than finding something to replace the meat in a traditional dish or offering a sampler composed of all the side dishes from meat-based entrées. Creativity is paramount here, and the options are limitless. Vegetable-based options can and should be offered in every menu category, but care should be taken not to repeat ingredients. A diner who would like to order several courses won't be happy if every menu option they see contains wild mushrooms.

When designing vegetable-based dishes, the concept of incorporating a variety of foods becomes crucial for both sound nutrition and aesthetic appeal. As with side dishes, vegetarian entrées need to be visualized as a whole to make sure that all of the items are integrated and harmonious.

One of the biggest challenges in creating this type of cuisine is in compensating for the loss of the savory flavors that meats, poultry, and fish provide. Care should be taken to avoid relying heavily on high-fat dairy products and high-sodium ingredients. Instead, ingredients with complex flavors, such as dried chiles or mushrooms and roasted garlic or peppers, can be used. In order to make the dish satisfying and filling, whole grains and legumes should make up the bulk of the calories.

When you devise a vegetarian menu, look to ethnic cuisines that have traditionally relied on plant-based foods for creative inspiration. In addition to the classic dishes they offer, their characteristic spice blends and flavor principles can be adapted for use in original recipes. Look also to dishes on your menu that can be modified; a popular pasta dish, for example, could be offered with or without chicken.

Plant-based cuisine need not be limited to plant foods. Many of the diners who order vegetarian dishes are not traditional vegetarians. They may choose a vegetable-based dish because of the health benefits associated with it or because it sounds delicious. If not all of your customers are strict vegetarians who avoid animal-based foods for ethical or religious reasons, you may have the option of including small amounts of animal foods, such as a bit of bacon in a salad or meat stock in soup, to enhance the flavor profile of a dish.

While there are numerous kinds of vegetarians, the three types that you need to be most concerned with are vegans, lacto vegetarians, and lacto-ovo vegetarians. Vegans adhere to the strictest diets. They do not eat any foods of animal origins, preferring to base their diets exclusively on vegetables, fruits, grains, nuts, and legumes. Lacto vegetarians consume the same foods as vegans, plus dairy products. Lacto-ovo vegetarians eat plant foods, dairy foods, and eggs.

Finally, be sure that any dish billed as vegetarian truly qualifies as such. Some foods that seem vegetarian may contain ingredients of hidden animal origin. An obvious example would be a vegetable soup made with chicken stock. More difficult to identify are ingredients that people often overlook as being animal products. A terrine of grilled vegetables held together with gelatin cannot be considered vegetarian, and anything with honey is off-limits for vegans. Other ingredients to be alert for include eggs in pasta or noodles, and Worcestershire sauce, which includes anchovies. Any dish identified as vegetarian should be vigilantly reviewed for any hidden animal foods used in its preparation.

Communicating

Proper staff training and customer communication techniques are essential in food-service operations. In an establishment where the attempt is made to provide customers with healthy food preparations, they become doubly important.

Well-trained servers are more than just a great sales force; they are also a medium for communicating information about the ingredients and techniques used in the kitchen. Every server should be educated about healthy preparation techniques and menu items as well as how to discuss these subjects with the guest. The kitchen staff should be equally well trained on the nutrition goals of the establishment and the methods used to achieve them.

Many food-service operations also provide nutrition information directly to their customers to help guide them in their selections. In addition to discussing staff training, this chapter highlights some of the ways in which you can communicate nutrition information to your customers. (For more information about nutrient and health claims on the menu, see Chapter 1, page 26.)

The Service Staff

Research has shown that describing foods as "low-fat," "low-calorie," and "healthy" often creates a negative perception and may deter customers from ordering such items. This unfavorable association occurs because these terms focus attention on the absence of something, and customers may associate this absence with a lack of flavor as well.

Because most health-conscious customers are acquainted with the cooking techniques and ingredients that are likely to be healthy, it is often better to teach the service staff to let the foods speak for themselves. For instance, instead of telling a customer who inquires about healthy menu choices that the grilled chicken dish is low in fat and sodium, the server can describe the dish as a boneless, skinless chicken breast marinated in Indian-inspired spices and yogurt before being cooked over a wood-fired grill. In this way, the server actively emphasizes the positive flavor attributes of the dish while implying that because the chicken is a skinless breast and is grilled, it is a healthy choice. Dining room staff should be aware of the location of more specific information on the nutrition content of menu items, in case a customer requests it.

Servers also need to be trained to handle special requests. You should inform your staff about which menu items can be modified and what sorts of adjustments can be made. It is advisable to make the staff aware of which changes are simple to make and which take time. Because it is impossible to anticipate every request, servers should be told to check with you or the person in charge of the kitchen before making promises concerning new requests.

If a customer has certain food preferences, allergies, or dietary restrictions, the server should be taught to gather as much information as possible about what can and can't be eaten. The server should then describe the ingredients in menu selections that may fit the customer's needs and allow the customer to choose. If the server is unsure about whether or not certain ingredients are present in a dish, under no circumstances should he or she ever guess. Taking the extra time to check with the kitchen is not nearly as inconvenient as a lawsuit. In the case that a special dish needs to be created for a customer, the server should be aware that it is just as important to the chef to know what a person can eat as it is to know what he or she cannot.

Once the initial training is complete, steps should be taken to keep the communication channel open between the kitchen and the dining room and to make it a two-way street. Hold preservice meetings as often as necessary to brief the servers on specials and anything else they should know about. Servers should be encouraged to talk to you about their observations in the dining room, particularly concerning customer feedback on menu items.

The Kitchen Staff

Proper technique in the kitchen is paramount in an operation that wants to produce healthy meals. The kitchen staff should be trained in basic nutrition and healthy cooking principles. They should be provided with standardized recipes, and a system for the careful trimming and portioning of all foods should be established to ensure that the customers are getting what they ordered. After all, the intention to create healthy meals means nothing if your line cooks are still using big ladles of oil or giant hunks of butter to grease their sauté pans. It should be emphasized that fat and salt are not the only sources of flavor and that delicious foods can be made easily with controlled amounts of these ingredients.

The kitchen staff should also be trained how to properly handle questions from customers concerning the presence or absence of an ingredient in a particular dish. Although the kitchen staff is aware of the foods that are used in a dish, they should be taught to consider whether or not any prepared products are part of the ingredients. Many prepared products, such as Worcestershire sauce and soup bases, contain ingredients that some customers wish to avoid, but they are often overlooked. If kitchen staff members are unsure of the ingredients in a prepared product, they should always check the label.

Proper training carries with it an advantage beyond superior service and product. Using time and resources to educate your staff usually has the effect of making them feel valuable, resulting in improved productivity and reduced employee turnover.

The Customer

When composing the language of a new menu, every chef is confronted with the dilemma of how much or how little information about the healthfulness of the food to relay to the customer, and what form this communication should take. Because this decision is dependent upon the type of establishment and the clientele, no attempt is made here to spell out every option. Instead, what follows is a summary of types of food-service operations and suggestions for appropriately communicating health and nutrition information to the customer.

Fine Dining Establishments, Bistros, and Executive Dining

Restaurants that cater to a clientele composed mainly of businesspeople and professionals can be relatively certain that their guests are likely to be nutritionally aware. These are people who read about food and nutrition, join health clubs, and, at the same time, enjoy fine dining. While this type of clientele is usually receptive to menu options that are associated with nutrition and health claims, using obvious language like "low in saturated fat" may not be desirable. The following options may be more appropriate in such a situation.

Server training: Teach your dining room sales force to communicate the health and nutrition attributes of certain items to customers.

Standard menu language: Many customers are generally aware of nutrition issues. Using descriptive language like "grilled" or "vegetable coulis" is often enough to tip them off as to the healthfulness of an item.

Icons: Small symbols that indicate a particular ingredient, health, or nutrition attribute are appropriate in some situations. If they are used, their meaning should be clearly explained in the menu. If an icon refers to a health or nutrition claim, written substantiation must be available upon request. A caveat: icons used to indicate "healthy" selections may suggest negative connotations to customers who associate healthy foods with a lack of flavor.

Referrals: A phrase at the bottom of the menu indicating that nutrition information is available on request is a subtle way to infer that the menu includes healthy selections.

Healthy cooking demonstrations: Cooking demonstrations are a great way to encourage people to try your healthy selections and generally promote the operation.

Family-Style Restaurants

Family-style restaurants cater to people who are looking for affordable, wholesome, familiar foods. They often offer a wide variety of menu choices, and chances are they serve some customers who are interested in healthy fare. The informal style of this type of restaurant suggests a more direct approach to nutrition communication.

Special menu sections: Grouping healthy choices into their own menu category makes it easy for customers to identify these selections.

Placemats: Paper placemats can be used as a vehicle for promoting and listing nutrition and health information about certain menu items.

The direct approach: Listing nutrition facts and health claims right on the menu may be an appropriate choice in this type of setting.

Pamphlets: Prominently displayed pamphlets are a great way to communicate the nutrition information for all or some of the menu items.

Home Meal Replacement

Home meal replacement is one of the fastest-growing trends in the food-service industry. It's a sign of the times; people seem to have less leisure time than ever before. Rather than spend those precious few hours on grocery shopping and preparing meals, they often prefer to purchase carryout home-style meals. Because these meals are meant to replace home-cooked foods, they are particularly good candidates for nutrition labeling.

Pamphlets: As in a family-style operation, pamphlets make a visible statement that your establishment cares about providing healthful meals for its customers.

Signage: Menu boards and special posters can be used to indicate which selections are healthy and why.

Labels: On prepackaged foods, nutrition facts labels work very well. Nutrition software packages are available that analyze recipes and create nutrition labels in the FDA format according to your specifications. If these are used, care should be taken to ensure that the portion sizes in the package match the size given on the label.

Spas and Health Resorts

People who patronize spas and health resorts are the most likely of all to be interested in the nutritional content of the foods they are eating. In this type of setting, the most obvious of approaches are suitable.

Special menus: Menus designed to provide a set number of calories and nutrients for each meal period provide the guests with an understanding of healthy ingredients, cooking techniques, and portion sizes. Complete nutrient information can be included on the menu for each course or item, and for the entire meal.

Daily meal plans: These provide the guests with guidelines for making healthy eating choices throughout the day.

Cooking demonstrations: Most guests are interested in learning how to cook healthy meals in their own homes.

Cafeterias, Schools, Hospitals, and Other Institutions

These types of operations serve a diverse clientele in a very informal setting. The self-service approach to the menu offerings suggests a similar treatment of nutrition and health communication.

Kiosks: Although expensive, kiosks containing a self-serve computer database of nutrition information are highly visible and attract the curious.

Nutrition binders: A loose-leaf binder containing the nutrition information is a much cheaper alternative to a computerized system and is also simple to change or update.

Icons: Symbols denoting ingredient, health, or nutrition attributes are particularly appropriate for hospitals and other health care facilities. Their meaning must be clearly explained and the nutrition documentation must be readily available to substantiate claims.

Signage: Small signs next to certain dishes on the serving line work well in a cafeteria setting.

Cooking classes and demonstrations: These are a great way to educate patients and staff in hospitals, and they are wonderful for schoolchildren, who love to watch and be involved.

Fast Food

Although fast-food restaurants are not particularly known for their nutritious selections, many are making an effort to offer more of these options. In the public interest, several fast-food chains make nutrition information on all their menu items available to their customers, regardless of their unhealthy attributes.

Posters: This is an inexpensive way to prominently display nutrition information.

Pamphlets: These can contain a smaller version of a nutrition poster for customers to take home with their carryout meals.

Web sites: Several of the larger fast-food chains maintain Web sites that include complete information on nutrition and ingredients.

Summary

Dining room staff members should be trained to let the foods speak for themselves. Rather than emphasizing that a food is low in fat or calories, for instance, the server should highlight ingredients and cooking methods used in the preparation that are, by definition, healthy. Servers should also be trained on how to handle special requests.

Kitchen staff need to understand the basics of nutrition and the goals of your establishment to provide genuinely healthy menu selections. They should be trained to stick to standard recipes and to carefully portion and trim ingredients.

There are dozens of ways to communicate nutrition information to customers. Individual operators need to choose the method that is most appropriate to the establishment they are running and to their customer base.

5

Soups, Salads, and Appetizers

FIRST COURSE DISHES, even when they are served as the main event, are a good place to start when you want to introduce healthier options on your menu. Soups can be brothy and light, perfect as the first course for a multi-course meal. Some studies have shown that eating soup or a salad before the main course gives individuals the "will power" to resist fat- and calorie-laden entrees (and desserts) by filling them up.

Carefully chosen and measured amounts of ingredients that are typically high in fat, sodium, or calories can give these smaller dishes a significant boost in flavor. Olives and capers add a punch of salty savor and let you cut back on the salt you might otherwise feel compelled to add. A bit of cheese or even bacon piques the appetite without tempting your guests to overindulge.

Appetizers, whether you serve them as a plated first course or "miniaturize" them to serve on a buffet or passed on a tray, give the chef great freedom to experiment with less familiar cuisines and open up a whole new avenue for broadening your repertoire.

Basic Consommé

batch yield: **1 gal / 3.75 L**

servings: **21**

portioning information:
¾ cup / 180 mL

nutrition per serving:
29 calories, 0 g fat, 0 g total
carbohydrate, 7 g protein, 146 mg
sodium, 0 mg cholesterol

CLARIFICATION MIXTURE

1 oignon brûlé

3 lb / 1.35 kg ground lean chicken meat

8 oz / 230 g sliced onion

4 oz / 115 g sliced celery

4 oz / 115 g sliced carrots

12 oz / 340 g tomato concassé

8 large egg whites, lightly beaten

1 Sachet d'Epices (page 544)

5 qt / 4.75 L Chicken Stock (page 490), cold

1. Combine the clarification mixture in a stockpot. Add the cold stock to the mixture and blend well. Slowly bring the consommé to a simmer, stirring frequently until the clarification begins to form a mass, or raft. Once the raft forms, break a small hole in the raft to help you monitor the cooking speed. Baste the raft occasionally with the stock. Simmer gently until the stock is clear and flavorful, about 45 minutes.

2. Drain the consommé through a cheesecloth-lined sieve. Do not disturb the raft if possible. Degrease the consommé by skimming the surface with food-quality paper or cool and remove the solidified fat layer.

Notes

The smaller the vegetables are cut, the more flavor they release into the stock. The vegetables may be ground with the meat.

The choice of meat should complement the flavor of the stock. For example, use ground beef with beef stock. Stock recipes are on pages 489, 490, and 491.

Variations

Beef Consommé

Use lean ground beef to replace the ground chicken in the clarification mixture. Use beef broth to replace the chicken stock.

Fish Consommé

Use ground white-fleshed fish such as flounder to replace the ground chicken in the clarification mixture. Use Fish Fumet (page 491) to replace the chicken stock. For a very light color, you may replace the standard mirepoix in the Basic Consommé recipe above with a White Mirepoix.

Game Hen Consommé

Use ground game hen meat to replace the ground chicken in the clarification mixture. Use Brown Chicken Stock (page 489; made with roasted game hen bones instead of chicken bones, if available) to replace the chicken stock.

Chicken Consommé with Herbed Goat Cheese Ravioli

batch yield: **2 qt / 2 L**

servings: **10**

portioning information:
¾ cup / 180 mL consommé, 1 ravioli, and ½ oz / 14 g tomato

nutrition per serving:
190 calories, 4 g fat, 27 g total carbohydrate, 11 g protein, 750 mg sodium, 5 mg cholesterol

12 oz / 340 g Basic Pasta Dough (page 398)

RAVIOLI FILLING

1½ tsp / 7.5 mL minced shallots

1 tsp / 5 mL minced garlic

½ tsp / 2.5 mL olive oil

1½ oz / 40 g spinach, wilted and chopped (see Note)

2½ oz / 70 g goat cheese

2½ oz / 70 g part-skim ricotta cheese

1 large egg white, lightly beaten

½ oz / 15 g grated Parmesan

1 tsp / 5 mL chopped basil

2 tsp / 10 mL chopped oregano

2 qt / 2 L Basic Consommé (page 160)

GARNISH

5 oz / 140 g julienned tomato

2 tbsp / 30 mL chopped chives

1. Prepare the Basic Pasta Dough as directed, roll it into thin sheets, and cut into 20 circles, about 2 in / 5 cm in diameter. Cover and reserve.

2. To prepare the ravioli filling, sauté the shallots and garlic in the oil until aromatic.

3. Add the remainder of the filling ingredients to the shallots and garlic.

4. To assemble the ravioli, place a small amount of the filling in the center of 10 pasta circles. Brush the edges of the pasta with water and top with the remaining pasta circles. Press to release any trapped air in the pasta and to seal the edges.

5. Cook the ravioli in simmering water until the pasta rises to the surface and is firm to the bite. Drain and reserve.

6. Heat the consommé and the ravioli (by batch or by portion) just before serving.

7. For each portion: Portion ½ oz / 14 g of the tomato and 1 ravioli into a warm bowl. Cover with ¾ cup / 180 mL hot consommé.

Note

Wilt the spinach in the microwave, or pan steam it until tender. Rinse to cool the spinach, drain and squeeze to remove as much moisture as possible before you chop the spinach.

Double Chicken Consommé with Spring Rolls

batch yield: 2 qt / 2 L

servings: 10

portioning information:
¾ cup / 180 mL consommé and 1 spring roll

nutrition per serving:
149 calories, 4 g fat, 15 g total carbohydrate, 6 g protein, 446 mg sodium, 10 mg cholesterol

10 spring rolls

2 qt / 2 L Double Chicken Stock (page 489), cold

CLARIFICATION MIXTURE

18 oz / 500 g ground chicken

2½ oz / 70 g chopped tomatoes

1½ oz / 40 g sliced onion

1 oz / 30 g sliced carrots

1 oz / 30 g sliced celery

¾ oz / 20 g leeks, split lengthwise and sliced thin

5 large whites, lightly beaten

1 thyme sprig

1 bay leaf

2 cloves

1. Prepare a Double Chicken Stock as directed on page 489. Chill the stock completely and degrease it thoroughly.

2. Prepare the spring rolls and keep them chilled until you are ready to serve.

3. To make the Double Chicken Consommé, combine all of the ingredients for the clarification in a large stockpot.

4. Slowly bring the double consommé to a simmer, stirring frequently, until the clarification begins to form a mass, or raft. Break a small hole in the raft to help you monitor the cooking speed. Baste the raft occasionally with the stock.

5. Simmer gently until the stock is clear and flavorful, about 45 minutes.

6. Drain the consommé through a cheesecloth-lined sieve. Do not disturb the raft if possible. Degrease the consommé by skimming the surface with food-quality paper or cool and remove the solidified fat layer.

7. Heat the consommé (by batch or by portion) just before serving. Heat the spring rolls in a steamer or in the microwave until hot.

8. For each portion: Portion 1 spring roll into a warm bowl and cover with ¾ cup / 180 mL hot consommé.

Game Hen Consommé with Roasted Garlic Custards

batch yield: **2 qt / 2 L**

servings: **10**

portioning information:
¾ cup / 180 mL consommé, 1 garlic custard, 2 tsp / 10 mL wild rice, 1 tsp / 5 mL each game hen and prosciutto

nutrition per serving:
149 calories, 4 g fat, 13 g total carbohydrate, 12 g protein, 470 mg sodium, 70 mg cholesterol

ROASTED GARLIC CUSTARDS

1¼ cups / 300 mL skim milk

½ cup / 120 mL evaporated skim milk

2 large eggs

2 large egg whites, lightly beaten

1 head garlic, roasted

¼ tsp / 1.25 mL ground white pepper

Vegetable spray, as needed

2 qt / 2 L Game Hen Consommé (page 160)

GARNISH

1¾ oz / 50 g diced game hen breast, poached

1¾ oz / 50 g diced prosciutto

3½ oz / 100 g cooked wild rice

1. Purée the custard ingredients in a blender until smooth. Strain through a fine-mesh sieve.

2. Use vegetable spray to lightly grease ten 2-oz / 60-g timbales. Fill with the custard and bake in a 170°F / 76°C water bath in a 300°F / 150°C oven until just barely set. Keep the custards warm.

3. Heat the consommé (by batch or by portion) just before serving.

4. For each portion: Arrange the garnish (1 tsp / 5 g each game hen and prosciutto, 2 tsp / 10 mL wild rice) and 1 garlic custard into a warm bowl. Cover with 6 fl oz / 180 mL hot consommé.

Wonton Soup

batch yield: **2 qt / 2 L**

servings: **10**

portioning information:
¾ cup / 180 mL consommé, 2 wontons, 1 oz / 30 g vegetables

nutrition per serving:
172 calories, 2 g fat, 20 g total carbohydrate, 17 g protein, 747 mg sodium, 18 mg cholesterol

CHICKEN WONTONS

7 oz / 200 g soft tofu

14 oz / 400 g cooked chicken

2 oz / 60 g minced ginger

3½ oz / 100 g minced garlic

3½ oz / 100 g hoisin sauce

2 oz / 60 g chopped scallions

1 tbsp / 15 mL tamari

20 (3-in / 7.5-cm) wonton wrappers

2 qt / 2 L Basic Consommé (page 160)

GARNISH

2½ oz / 70 g julienned bok choy

2½ oz / 70 g black mushrooms

2½ oz / 70 g julienned leek

2½ oz / 70 g julienned carrot

¼ oz / 8 g chervil plûches

1. Combine all the wonton ingredients except the wonton wrappers. Mash the ingredients together with a fork.

2. Place a small amount of the filling in the center of each wrapper. Brush the edges of the wrappers with water and fold the wrappers into triangles. Press to release any trapped air and to seal the edges. Twist and press the 2 triangle points together to form wontons.

3. Cook the wontons in simmering water until they rise to the surface and the wonton wrappers are tender and cooked through. Drain and reserve.

4. Heat the consommé and the wontons (by batch or by portion) just before serving.

5. For each portion: Arrange ¼ oz / 7 g each of the vegetable garnish and 2 wontons into a warm bowl. Cover with ¾ cup / 180 mL hot consommé.

Carrot Consommé with Lemongrass, Ginger, Spicy Asian Grilled Shrimp, and Bean Threads

batch yield: **2 qt / 2 L**

servings: **10**

portioning information:
**¾ cup / 180 mL consommé,
2 oz / 57 g grilled shrimp,
¾ oz / 20 g noodles**

nutrition per serving:
152 calories, 1 g fat, 31 g total
carbohydrate, 4 g protein, 177 mg
sodium, 26 mg cholesterol

CARROT CONSOMMÉ

2 qt / 2 L fresh carrot juice

5 large egg whites, lightly beaten

1 lb / 450 g julienned carrots

½ stalk lemongrass, thinly sliced

1 tbsp / 15 mL chopped ginger

5 wild lime leaves, chopped

1 tsp / 5 mL kosher salt

½ tsp / 2.5 mL crushed white peppercorns

8½ oz / 240 g bean thread noodles, cooked, shocked

3 oz / 85 g carrot curls

1 lb 4 oz / 570 g Spicy Asian Grilled Shrimp (page 259), halved

2 tbsp / 30 mL Thai basil chiffonade

2 tbsp / 30 mL mint chiffonade

3 tbsp / 45 mL chopped cilantro

1 tbsp / 15 mL white sesame seeds

1 tbsp / 15 mL black sesame seeds

1. Combine the ingredients for the carrot consommé in a medium soup pot and mix well. Bring the mixture to a simmer, stirring frequently until a raft forms. Break a small hole in the raft, to help you monitor the cooking speed. Baste the raft occasionally with the stock. Simmer just until clear, about 20 minutes.

2. Strain the consommé through a cheesecloth-lined fine-mesh sieve. Season with the salt and pepper. Heat the consommé (by batch or by portion) just before serving.

3. For each portion: In a warm bowl arrange a tight ball of ¾ oz / 20 g noodles and carrot curls surrounded by 2 oz / 57 g grilled shrimp. Pour ¾ cup / 180 mL hot consommé into the bowl and garnish with the herbs and sesame seeds.

Note

Strips of lime zest may be substituted for the lime leaves, and sweet basil for the Thai basil. Rice sticks or capellini may be used instead of the bean threads.

Mushroom Consommé with Shiitake, Bok Choy, and Carrot Curls

batch yield: **2 qt / 2 L**

servings: **10**

portioning information:
**¾ cup / 180 mL consommé,
1 oz / 30 g vegetables**

nutrition per serving:
44 calories, 0 g fat, 3 g total
carbohydrate, 8 g protein, 180 mg
sodium, 0 mg cholesterol

MUSHROOM-INFUSED STOCK

2 qt / 2 L Chicken Stock (page 489)

2 oz / 60 g dried Chinese mushrooms

CLARIFICATION MIXTURE

18 oz / 500 g ground chicken

2½ oz / 70 g tomato concassé

1½ oz / 45 g sliced onion

1 oz / 30 g sliced carrots

1 oz / 30 g sliced celery

1 oz / 30 g leeks, split lengthwise and
sliced thin

5 large egg whites, lightly beaten

1 sprig thyme

1 bay leaf

1 clove

GARNISH

4½ oz / 130 g sliced shiitake mushrooms

3 oz / 85 g carrot curls or julienne

3 oz / 85 g julienned baby bok choy

1. To make the mushroom-infused stock, combine the chicken stock with the mushrooms in a stockpot. Bring to a simmer. Remove from the heat, cover, and steep for 30 minutes. Strain the stock and reserve the mushrooms. Squeeze the mushrooms to extract any excess liquid. Return the liquid to the strained stock and cool completely. Chop the mushrooms and reserve them to add to the clarification.

2. Combine the ingredients for the clarification and the reserved chopped mushrooms in a large stockpot. Add the cold stock to the mixture and blend well.

3. Slowly simmer, stirring frequently until the clarification begins to form a mass, or raft. Break a small hole in the raft, to help you monitor the cooking speed. Baste the raft occasionally with the stock. Simmer gently until the stock is clear and flavorful, about 45 minutes.

4. Drain the consommé through a cheesecloth-lined sieve. Do not disturb the raft if possible. Degrease the consommé by skimming the surface with food-quality paper or cool and remove the solidified fat layer.

5. Sweat the mushrooms, carrots, and bok choy in a small amount of the consommé.

6. Heat the consommé (by batch or by portion) just before serving.

7. For each portion: Ladle out ¾ cup / 180 mL of hot consommé and garnish with 1 oz / 30 g tender vegetables.

Michigan White Bean Soup

batch yield: 2 qt / 2 L

servings: 10

portioning information:
¾ cup / 180 mL

nutrition per serving:
147 calories, 2 g fat, 22 g total carbohydrate, 11 g protein, 233 mg sodium, 7 mg cholesterol

12 oz / 320 g dried northern white beans (see Note)

3 pt / 1.4 L Chicken Stock (page 489)

1½ oz / 45 g minced bacon

2½ oz / 70 g diced leeks

2½ oz / 70 g diced red onion

1 tsp / 10 mL minced garlic

1 thyme sprig

2 bay leaves

½ tsp / 2.5 mL kosher salt

¼ tsp / 1.25 mL ground black pepper

1. Soak the beans for 8 to 12 hours in enough cold water to cover by 3 in / 8 cm (see note).

2. Drain the beans and simmer in the stock until the beans are almost tender, about 30 minutes.

3. Render the bacon to release its fat. Add the leeks, onions, and garlic and sweat until translucent. Add the sautéed onion mixture, thyme, and bay leaves to the beans and simmer until the beans are completely tender. Remove and discard the thyme and bay leaves. The soup is ready to serve now, or it may be properly cooled and stored.

4. Heat the soup (by batch or by portion) just before serving. Season the soup with the salt and pepper and serve.

Note

To reduce the length of soaking time, bring the beans and stock to a boil, remove from the heat, and allow to soak for 1 hour. Continue with the recipe.

Summer-Style Lentil Soup

batch yield: **2 qt / 2 L**

servings: **10**

portioning information:
**¾ cup / 180 mL soup,
½ tsp / 2.5 mL herbs**

nutrition per serving:
200 calories, 4.5 g fat, 28 g total
carbohydrate, 13 g protein, 610 mg
sodium, 10 mg cholesterol

1 oz / 30 g minced bacon

3 oz / 85 g diced onion

¼ oz / 7 g minced garlic

2½ oz / 75 g diced leeks

2 oz / 55 g sliced carrot

1¾ oz / 50 g sliced celery

1 oz / 30 g tomato paste

2 qt / 2 L Chicken or Vegetable Stock (pages
489 and 490)

10 oz / 280 g French lentils

1 Sachet d'Epices (page 490)

3 strips lemon peel

1 tbsp / 15 mL white wine

1 tbsp / 15 mL sherry vinegar

1 tsp / 5 mL kosher salt

¼ tsp / 1.25 mL ground black pepper

HERB GARNISH

1 tbsp / 15 mL chopped chives

1 tbsp / 15 mL chopped parsley

1. Render the bacon to release its fat. Sweat the onions and garlic until translucent.

2. Add the leeks, carrots, and celery. Cover and sweat until the vegetables are tender. Add the tomato paste and sauté until brown. Add the stock, lentils, sachet, and lemon peel strips. Simmer until the lentils are tender, about 20 minutes.

3. Remove and discard the sachet and lemon peel strips. Add the wine, vinegar, salt, and pepper. The soup is ready to serve now, or it may be properly cooled and stored.

4. Heat the soup (by batch or by portion) just before serving. Garnish each portion of soup with chives and parsley.

Potato and Smoked Scallop Soup

batch yield: **2 qt / 2 L**

servings: **10**

portioning information:
¾ cup / 180 mL

nutrition per serving:
167 calories, 5 g fat, 22 g total
carbohydrate, 12 g protein, 233 mg
sodium, 7 mg cholesterol

1 tbsp / 15 mL vegetable oil

4 oz / 115 g pan-smoked scallops

3 oz / 85 g diced carrots

6½ oz / 185 g diced onion

1½ lb / 680 g cabbage chiffonade

1 lb / 450 g diced new potatoes

½ cup / 120 mL cider vinegar

3 pt / 1.44 L Chicken Stock (page 489)

2 tsp / 10 mL caraway seeds

1 tsp / 5 mL kosher salt

¼ tsp / 1.25 mL ground black pepper

1. Heat the oil in a large soup pot. Sear the scallops in the oil. Transfer to absorbent towels.

2. Add the carrots and onions to the oil and sweat until the onions are translucent. Stir in the cabbage and potatoes and cook until the cabbage has wilted. Add the vinegar, and reduce by half. Add the stock and bring to a boil. Simmer the soup until the cabbage and potatoes are tender, about 20 minutes.

3. Stir in the scallops, caraway seeds, salt, and pepper. The soup is ready to serve now, or it may be properly cooled and stored. Heat the soup (by batch or portion) just before serving.

Pan-Smoked Tomato Bisque

batch yield: **2 qt / 2 L**

servings: **10**

portioning information:
¾ cup / 180 mL, 1 slice toast, 1 tsp / 5 mL tapenade, ½ tsp / 2.5 mL saffron aïoli

nutrition per serving:
169 calories, 2 g fat, 33 g total carbohydrate, 5 g protein, 668 mg sodium, 2 mg cholesterol

5 oz / 140 g tomatoes, peeled, seeded, quartered

1½ pt / 720 mL Vegetable Stock (page 490)

2 oz / 55 g diced onion

2 oz / 55 g diced celery

2 oz / 55 g diced leeks

1 oz / 30 g diced parsnips

1¾ lb / 795 g canned plum tomatoes, with juices

8 oz / 225 g tomato purée

1 oz / 30 g sun-dried tomatoes

2 tbsp / 30 mL chopped thyme

4 oz / 115 g cooked white rice

¼ cup / 60 mL balsamic vinegar

GARNISH

5 tsp / 25 mL Saffron Aïoli (page 509)

10 slices French bread, toasted

⅓ oz / 10 g Tapenade (page 484)

1. Place the quartered tomatoes on a rack, in a roasting pan containing a thin layer of hardwood chips. Cover with a tight-fitting lid and place over direct heat. Smoke for 6 to 8 minutes. Small dice the tomatoes and reserve for garnish.

2. Sweat the onions, celery, leeks, and parsnips in a small amount of stock until tender.

3. Stir in the remaining stock, canned tomatoes (with juice), tomato purée, sun-dried tomatoes, and thyme. Simmer until the ingredients are tender, about 30 minutes.

4. Add the rice and simmer until the rice is very tender, an additional 20 to 25 minutes. Purée the soup until smooth. Season the soup with the balsamic vinegar. The soup is ready to serve now, or it may be properly cooled and stored.

5. For each portion: Heat the soup (by batch or by portion) just before serving. Ladle the soup into a heated bowl with a 6-oz / 180-mL ladle and garnish with ½ tsp / 2.5 mL saffron aïoli. Accompany each portion with a slice of French bread spread thinly with tapenade.

Seafood Minestrone

batch yield: **2 qt / 2 L**

servings: **10**

portioning information:
¾ cup / 180 mL

nutrition per serving:
190 calories, 4 g fat, 20 g total
carbohydrate, 14 g protein, 332 mg
sodium, 50 mg cholesterol

4 oz / 115 g dried red kidney beans

16 mussels, scrubbed and debearded

5 tbsp / 75 mL white wine

1½ qt / 1.44 L Fish Fumet (page 491)

½ oz / 14 g slivered bacon

1 tbsp / 15 mL olive oil

4 oz / 115 g sliced onion

5 oz / 140 g leeks, split lengthwise and thinly sliced

1 oz / 30 g sliced celery

½ oz / 14 g minced garlic

1¾ oz / 50 g tomato paste

10 oz / 280 g tomato concassé

1 tsp / 5 mL kosher salt

1 tsp / 5 mL chopped rosemary

1 tsp / 5 mL chopped thyme

⅛ tsp / 0.625 mL ground black pepper

1 bay leaf

1 lemon slice, ½ in / 1 cm thick

2½ oz / 70 g cooked Arborio rice

1¾ oz / 50 g chopped raw shrimp

1. Soak the beans for 8 to 12 hours in enough cold water to cover by 3 in / 8 cm (see Note). Drain the beans and simmer in fresh water until almost tender. Drain and reserve.

2. Steam the mussels in the wine. Remove the mussels, strain the steaming liquid, and add to the fish fumet. Remove the mussels from the shells; roughly chop and reserve.

3. Render the bacon in the oil. Add the onion, leeks, celery, and garlic. Sweat until the onions are translucent. Add the tomato paste and sauté until brown. Add the concassé, salt, herbs, pepper, bay leaf, lemon, and beans. Simmer until the beans are tender.

4. Add the rice, shrimp, and reserved mussels. Continue to simmer until the shrimp are cooked, about 10 minutes. The soup is ready to serve now, or it may be properly cooled and stored.

5. To serve, portion the hot soup into a heated bowl with a 6-oz / 180-mL ladle.

Note

To reduce the length of soaking time, bring the beans and stock to a boil, remove from the heat, and allow to soak for 1 hour. Continue with the recipe.

Louisiana Chicken and Shrimp Gumbo

batch yield: **2 qt / 2 L**

servings: **10**

portioning information:
¾ cup / 180 mL

nutrition per serving:
174 calories, 6 g fat, 16 g total
carbohydrate, 13 g protein, 385 mg
sodium, 47 mg cholesterol

2½ oz / 70 g bread flour

1 oz / 30 g diced andouille sausage

2½ oz / 70 g chopped chicken

2½ oz / 70 g diced bell peppers

2½ oz / 70 g diced celery

2 tbsp / 30 mL diced jalapeños

¼ cup / 60 mL thinly sliced scallions, split lengthwise before slicing

1 tsp / 5 mL minced garlic

1½ qt / 1.44 L Chicken Stock (page 489)

2½ oz / 70 g brown rice

1¼ tsp / 6.25 mL filé powder

1 tsp / 5 mL chopped oregano

1 bay leaf

1 tsp / 5 mL thyme

1 tsp / 5 mL chopped basil

1 tsp / 5 mL ground black pepper

½ tsp / 2.5 mL onion powder

1 tsp / 5 mL kosher salt

2½ oz / 70 g okra

3½ oz / 100 g tomato concassé

1¾ oz / 50 g chopped raw shrimp

1. Toast the flour in a 325°F / 165°C oven until it turns dark brown.

2. Render the sausage in a large soup pot. Add the chicken and sauté until browned. Add the peppers, celery, jalapeños, scallions, and garlic and sauté until aromatic. Add the stock and bring to a boil. Add the rice, filé powder, oregano, bay leaf, thyme, basil, pepper, onion powder, and salt. Simmer until the rice is almost cooked, about 30 minutes. Add the okra and tomato concassé.

3. Place the browned flour in a large bowl. Slowly whisk some of the soup liquid into the flour until smooth. Add the mixture to the pot and simmer until thickened, about 10 minutes. Add the shrimp and simmer until cooked, about 5 minutes.

4. The soup is ready to serve now, or it may be properly cooled and stored. To serve, portion the hot soup into a heated bowl with a 6-oz / 180-mL ladle.

Potato and Vegetable Soup

batch yield: **2 qt / 2 L**

servings: **10**

portioning information:
¾ cup / 180 mL

nutrition per serving:
120 calories, 3.5 g fat, 17 g total
carbohydrate, 7 g protein, 580 mg
sodium, 10 mg cholesterol

5 oz / 140 g sliced Spanish-style chorizo	4 oz / 115 g diced green peppers
1 tbsp / 15 mL olive oil	1½ oz / 40 g tomato paste
3 oz / 85 g diced onions	1 bay leaf
2 tsp / 10 mL minced garlic	½ tsp / 2.5 mL chopped oregano
1 oz / 30 g diced celery	2 tbsp / 30 mL chopped parsley
1½ tsp / 7.5 mL cumin seeds	1 tsp / 5 mL kosher salt
2½ pt / 1.20 L Chicken Stock (page 489)	8 oz / 225 g corn kernels
12 oz / 340 g tomato concassé	¼ tsp / 1.25 mL ground black pepper
5 oz / 140 g potatoes, peeled and diced	2 tbsp / 30 mL chopped cilantro
4 oz / 115 g diced red peppers	

1. Dry sauté the chorizo in a large soup pot until browned, about 10 minutes. Transfer to absorbent towels.

2. Heat the oil in the same pot. Add the onions, garlic, celery, and cumin seeds, and sweat until the onions are translucent. Add the chorizo, stock, tomatoes, potatoes, peppers, tomato paste, bay leaf, oregano, half of the parsley, and the salt. Bring to a boil, reduce heat, and simmer until the potatoes are tender, about 20 minutes. Stir in the corn and black pepper and simmer until thoroughly heated.

3. Discard the bay leaf. The soup is ready to serve now, or it may be properly cooled and stored.

4. To serve, portion the hot soup into a heated bowl with a 6-oz / 180-mL ladle. Garnish each portion with the remaining parsley and the cilantro.

Tortilla Soup

batch yield: **2 qt / 2 L**

servings: **10**

portioning information:
¾ cup / 180 mL

nutrition per serving:
171 calories, 6 g fat, 18 g total
carbohydrate, 12 g protein, 412 mg
sodium, 21 mg cholesterol

4 tsp / 20 mL minced garlic

9 oz / 255 g diced onions

2 qt / 2 L Chicken Stock (page 489)

7 corn tortillas (8-in / 20-cm), cut into julienne

2 tbsp / 30 mL chopped cilantro

9 oz / 255 g tomato purée

1 tbsp / 15 mL ground cumin

2 tsp / 10 mL chili powder

2 bay leaves

GARNISH

¼ cup / 60 mL shredded Cheddar cheese

Toasted tortilla strips (from step 2)

7 oz / 200 g grilled chicken breast, cut into strips

3½ oz / 100 g diced avocado

1. Sweat the garlic and onions in a small amount of stock until translucent. Purée in a blender. Set aside.

2. On a rack in a 200°F / 95°C oven, lightly toast the tortillas until crisp. Set aside ½ cup / 120 mL of the toasted tortillas for a garnish. Crumble the remaining tortillas and reserve.

3. Combine the crushed tortillas, cilantro, onion and garlic purée, and tomato purée in a soup pot. Bring to a simmer. Add the remaining stock, cumin, chili powder, and bay leaves. Simmer until flavorful, about 15 minutes. Purée the soup.The soup is ready to serve now, or it may be properly cooled and stored.

4. For each portion: Ladle the hot soup into a heated bowl with a 6-oz / 180-mL ladle. Garnish with 1 tsp / 5 mL cheese, a scant tablespoon of tortilla strips, ¾ oz / 20 g chicken, and ⅓ oz / 10 g avocado.

Traditional Black Bean Soup

batch yield: **2 qt / 2 L**

servings: **10**

portioning information:
¾ cup / 180 mL

nutrition per serving:
181 calories, 3 g fat, 30 g total carbohydrate, 12 g protein, 348 mg sodium, 6 mg cholesterol

12 oz / 340 g dried black beans

2 qt / 2 L Chicken or Vegetable Stock (pages 489 and 490)

½ oz / 14 g minced bacon

4 oz / 115 g diced onions

½ oz / 14 g minced garlic

⅛ tsp / 0.625 mL ground cumin

1 lemon, thickly sliced

½ oz / 14 g toasted and chopped ancho chiles

1 tsp / 5 mL minced jalapeño

1 oz / 30 g chopped sun-dried tomatoes

1 tsp / 5 mL dried oregano

1 tsp / 5 mL kosher salt

1 tbsp / 15 mL sherry vinegar

1. Soak the beans for 8 to 12 hours in enough cold water to cover by 3 in / 8 cm (see Note). Drain the beans and simmer in the stock until the beans are tender.

2. Render the bacon to release its fat. Add the onions, garlic, and cumin. Sweat until the onions are translucent. Add the sautéed onion mixture, lemon, anchos, jalapeño, tomatoes, oregano, and salt to the beans and simmer until all ingredients are very hot and the soup is flavorful, an additional 15 minutes.

3. Remove and discard the lemon slices. Purée one third of the beans and add the purée back to the soup. Finish the soup by adding the vinegar.

4. The soup is ready to serve now, or it may be properly cooled and stored. To serve, portion the hot soup into a heated bowl with a 6-oz / 180-mL ladle.

Note

To reduce the length of soaking time, bring the beans and stock to a boil, remove from the heat, and allow to soak for 1 hour. Continue with the recipe.

Variation

Cuban Black Bean Soup

When simmering the beans in step 2, add a sachet of 2 cloves, ⅛ tsp / 0.625 mL each allspice berries and toasted cumin seeds, and ¼ tsp / 1.25 mL cracked black peppercorns. Remove the sachet when the beans have cooked.

Combine 2 tbsp / 30 mL Vinaigrette-Style Dressing (page 503), 3 oz / 85 g cooked white rice, 1 oz / 30 g thinly sliced scallions, and ⅔ oz / 19 g wilted spinach chiffonade. Divide this evenly to garnish each portion. (For nutrition information, see Recipe Analysis on page 514.)

Sweet Onion–Radish Soup

batch yield: **2 qt / 2 L**

servings: **10**

portioning information:
¾ cup / 180 mL

nutrition per serving:
105 calories, 5 g fat, 11 g total carbohydrate, 4 g protein, 269 mg sodium, 16 mg cholesterol

½ oz / 14 g butter

2 tsp / 10 mL minced garlic

3 oz / 85 g diced celery

2 oz / 55 g diced leeks

10½ oz / 300 g diced sweet onions (e.g., Vidalia)

1 qt / 1 L Chicken Stock (page 489)

5 oz / 140 g chef's potatoes, peeled, quartered

1 lb 5 oz / 600 g grated red radishes

¼ cup / 60 mL heavy cream

1 tsp / 5 mL kosher salt

¼ tsp / 1.25 mL ground black pepper

2 tbsp / 30 mL fresh lemon juice

½ oz / 14 g chopped herbs (see Notes)

GARNISH

2 oz / 55 g thinly sliced red radishes

1. In a soup pot, melt the butter and sweat the garlic, celery, leeks, and onions until tender. Add the stock and potatoes and bring to a boil. Simmer until the potatoes are tender. Add the radishes and simmer an additional 5 minutes. Purée the soup using a food mill or immersion blender. The soup is ready to finish and serve now, or it may be properly cooled and stored.

2. Heat the soup (by batch or by portion) just before serving. Season the soup with the salt and pepper and serve. Just before serving, bring the cream to a boil (see Notes). Stir the cream, salt, pepper, lemon juice, and herbs into the soup. Garnish each portion with sliced radishes.

Notes

Because radishes have a sharp and peppery taste, herbs with strong flavors best complement the soup. Use chives, cilantro, mint, thyme, or basil.

The cream may be whipped and 2 tsp / 10 mL piped onto each portion of soup.

Cold Asparagus Soup (page 181), Beet-Fennel-Ginger Soup,
Curried Apple-Squash Soup (page 191) served in 2 fl oz / 60 mL
portions as part of a chilled soup sampler.

Beet-Fennel-Ginger Soup

batch yield: **2 qt / 2 L**

servings: **10**

portioning information:
¾ cup / 180 mL

nutrition per serving:
51 calories, 0 g fat, 10 g total
carbohydrate, 3 g protein, 369 mg
sodium, 0 mg cholesterol

1¾ lb / 795 g chopped beets

1 lb / 450 g chopped savoy cabbage

1 lb / 450 g chopped fennel

2 tsp / 10 mL chopped garlic

1½ oz / 45 g chopped ginger

2 qt / 2 L Vegetable Stock (page 490)

1 tsp / 5 mL kosher salt

¼ tsp / 1.25 mL ground black pepper

10 tbsp / 150 mL drained nonfat yogurt

2 tbsp / 30 mL fennel sprigs

1. Combine the beets, cabbage, fennel, garlic, ginger, and stock in a large soup pot. Bring to a boil, cover, and simmer until the vegetables are tender.

2. Strain the soup through a large-holed sieve. Purée the vegetables and a small amount of stock in a blender until smooth. Use the remaining stock to adjust the consistency of the soup. Season the soup with salt and pepper. Chill the soup. The soup is ready to serve once it is completely cooled.

3. To serve, portion the cold soup into a chilled bowl or cup with a 6-oz / 180-mL ladle. Garnish each portion with 1 tbsp / 15 mL yogurt and a few fennel sprigs.

Sweet Potato Soup

batch yield: **2 qt / 2 L**

servings: **10**

portioning information:
¾ cup / 180 mL

nutrition per serving:
160 calories, 4 g fat, 26 g total
carbohydrate, 6 g protein, 350 mg
sodium, 8 mg cholesterol

3 oz / 85 g diced onions

2½ oz / 70 g diced celery

1½ oz / 45 g diced leeks

1 tsp / 5 mL minced garlic

2 qt / 2 L Chicken Stock (page 489)

1½ lb / 680 g sweet potatoes, peeled and diced

1 cinnamon stick

¼ tsp / 1.25 mL ground nutmeg

1 tbsp / 15 mL maple syrup

1 tsp / 5 mL kosher salt

½ cup / 120 mL evaporated skim milk

GARNISH

10 tsp / 50 mL whipped heavy cream

10 tsp / 50 mL slivered almonds, toasted

5 tsp / 25 mL dried currants

1. In a soup pot, sweat the onions, celery, leeks, and garlic in a small amount of the stock until translucent. Add the remaining stock, potatoes, cinnamon, and nutmeg. Simmer until the potatoes are tender. Discard the cinnamon stick and purée the soup, using a food processor, blender, or immersion blender, until smooth and strain through a fine-mesh sieve.

2. Chill for 8 to 12 hours, allowing the flavor to develop. Add the syrup, salt, and milk to the cold soup (by batch or by portion).

3. To serve, portion the cold soup into a chilled bowl or cup with a 6-oz / 180-mL ladle. Garnish with 1 tsp / 5 mL whipped cream, 1 tsp / 5 mL almonds, and ½ tsp / 2.5 mL currants.

Butternut Squash Soup

batch yield: **2 qt / 2 L**

servings: **10**

portioning information:
¾ cup / 180 mL

nutrition per serving:
80 calories, 2.5 g fat, 12 g total
carbohydrate, 3 g protein, 330 mg
sodium, 10 mg cholesterol

2½ tsp / 12 mL minced ginger

2 tbsp / 30 mL white wine

1¾ oz / 50 g diced onion

1¾ oz / 50 g diced celery

1 tsp / 5 ml minced garlic

1¼ pt / 600 mL Chicken Stock (page 489)

2¼ lb / 1 kg butternut squash, peeled, cubed

⅓ cup / 80 mL nonfat plain yogurt

3 tbsp / 45 mL heavy cream

⅓ cup / 80 mL sparkling mineral water

1 tsp / 5 mL kosher salt

¼ tsp / 1.25 mL ground white pepper

GARNISH

2 tbsp / 30 mL chopped chives

1. Steep the ginger in the wine for 30 minutes. Strain and discard the ginger.

2. In a soup pot, sweat the onions, celery, and garlic in a small amount of stock until translucent. Add the remaining stock and the squash. Simmer until the squash is tender. Purée the soup using a food processor, blender, or immersion blender. Chill the soup. The soup is ready to finish and serve once it is completely cooled.

3. Stir the ginger infusion, yogurt, cream, mineral water, salt, and pepper into the cold soup.

4. To serve, portion the cold soup into a chilled bowl or cup with a 6-oz / 180-mL ladle. Garnish each portion of soup with chives.

Serving Suggestion

A small dollop of whipped cream and toasted pumpkin seeds may also be used to garnish the soup.

Cold Asparagus Soup

batch yield: **2 qt / 2 L**

servings: **10**

portioning information:
¾ cup / 180 mL

nutrition per serving:
114 calories, 4 g fat, 14 g total carbohydrate, 7 g protein, 392 mg sodium, 12 mg cholesterol

½ oz / 14 g butter

2 oz / 55 g diced onions

2 tsp / 10 mL minced garlic

2 tsp / 10 mL minced shallots

1 oz / 30 g flour

2¼ lb / 1 kg asparagus stems, peeled and sliced on the diagonal

3 cups / 720 mL Chicken Stock (page 489)

1 tsp / 5 mL grated lemon zest

½ tsp / 2.5 mL kosher salt

½ cup / 120 mL evaporated skim milk

GARNISH

2 tbsp / 30 mL heavy cream, whipped

20 asparagus tips, blanched

1. In a soup pot, melt the butter and sweat the onions, garlic, and shallots until tender.

2. Add the flour, stirring frequently; cook until thick and pasty, about 5 minutes. Add the asparagus stems, stock, and zest. Simmer until the asparagus stems are tender. Purée the soup using a food processor, blender, or immersion blender. Strain the soup through a fine-mesh sieve to remove the asparagus fibers.

3. Stir in the salt and the milk. Chill the soup. The soup is ready to serve once it is completely cooled.

4. To serve, portion the cold soup into a chilled bowl or cup with a 6-oz / 180-mL ladle.

5. For each portion: Garnish with 1 tsp / 5 mL whipped cream and 2 asparagus tips.

Corn Velvet Soup with Crabmeat

batch yield: **2 qt / 2 L**

servings: **10**

portioning information:
¾ cup / 180 mL

nutrition per serving
122 calories, 3 g fat, 14 g total
carbohydrate, 9 g protein, 392 mg
sodium, 22 mg cholesterol

:

7 oz / 200 g corn kernels

1 oz / 30 g butter

4½ oz / 130 g scallions, split lengthwise and thinly sliced

4½ oz / 130 g diced onions

1½ oz / 45 g minced ginger

½ oz / 14 g minced jalapeños

1½ sprigs thyme

2 qt / 2 L Chicken Stock (page 489)

1½ cups / 360 mL evaporated skim milk

¼ cup / 60 mL reduced-sodium soy sauce

½ tsp / 2.5 mL Kosher salt

Pepper to taste

GARNISH

6 oz / 170 g picked lump crabmeat

10 tsp / 50 mL Red Pepper Coulis (page 498)

1. Cut the corn kernels from the cob; reserve the milk.

2. In a soup pot, melt the butter and sweat the scallions, onions, ginger, and jalapeños until tender.

3. Add the corn kernels and sweat for 2 minutes. Add the thyme and stock. Simmer until the vegetables are tender.

4. Purée the soup until smooth using a food processor, blender, or immersion blender. Stir in the evaporated skim milk and the soy. If the soup is too thick, adjust the consistency with more stock. The soup is ready to serve now, or it may be properly cooled and stored.

5. Heat the soup (by batch or by portion) just before serving. Season the soup with the salt and pepper and serve. For each portion: Garnish with ⅔ oz / 17 g crabmeat and 1 tsp / 5 mL pepper coulis just before serving.

Chowder of Corn and Maine Lobster

batch yield: **2 qt / 2 L**

servings: **10**

portioning information:
¾ cup / 180 mL

nutrition per serving:
130 calories, 2.5 g fat, 19 g total
carbohydrate, 9 g protein, 320 mg
sodium, 15 mg cholesterol

½ oz / 14 g butter

3 oz / 85 g scallions, split lengthwise and thinly sliced

1¼ pt / 600 mL skim milk

1¼ pt / 600 mL Chicken Stock, fortified (page 489)

10 oz / 280 g Roasted Smoked Corn (page 368)

8 oz / 225 g Idaho potatoes, peeled and diced

1 sprig thyme

½ tsp / 2.5 mL Worcestershire sauce

½ tsp / 2.5 mL kosher salt

LIAISON

¾ cup / 180 mL evaporated skim milk

½ oz / 14 g arrowroot

LOBSTER GARNISH

5 oz / 140 g sliced lobster tail

1 tbsp / 15 mL chopped chives

1 tbsp / 15 mL chopped parsley

1. Melt the butter in a soup pot. Sweat the scallions in the butter until tender. Add the milk, stock, corn, potatoes, thyme, Worcestershire, and salt. Simmer until the potatoes are tender.

2. Whisk together the ingredients for the liaison. Add to the soup and simmer until thickened, about 2 minutes. The soup is ready to serve now, or it may be properly cooled and stored.

3. To serve, portion the hot soup into a heated bowl with a 6-oz / 180-mL ladle. Garnish each with ½ oz / 14 g lobster, and some chives and parsley before serving.

Crab and Wild Mushroom Chowder

batch yield: **2 qt / 2 L**

servings: **10**

portioning information:
¾ cup / 180 mL

nutrition per serving:
126 calories, 3 g fat, 16 g total
carbohydrate, 10 g protein, 438 mg
sodium, 23 mg cholesterol

1 oz / 30 g arrowroot

1 qt / 950 mL Chicken Stock (page 489)

2 tsp / 10 mL butter

1 tbsp / 15 mL minced garlic

2½ oz / 70 g diced onions

1 oz / 30 g diced celery

1 oz / 30 g diced leeks

12 oz / 340 g diced peeled Idaho potatoes

⅔ cup / 160 mL evaporated skim milk

1 tsp / 5 mL kosher salt

1 tsp / 5 mL crushed black pepper

2 tsp / 10 mL heavy cream

2 tsp / 10 mL dry sherry

1 lb / 450 g sliced wild mushrooms

¾ cup / 180 mL mushroom stock (see Note)

10 oz / 300 g lump crabmeat, picked to remove shells

1. Combine the arrowroot with enough stock to form a paste. Set aside.

2. Melt the butter in a large soup pot. Add the garlic, onions, celery, and leeks and sweat until tender. Add the remaining stock to the vegetables and bring to a simmer. Add the arrowroot mixture to the stock and simmer until thickened, about 2 minutes. Add the potatoes and simmer until tender, about 25 minutes. Remove the pot from the heat and add the milk, salt, pepper, cream, and sherry.

3. In a large sauté pan, sweat the mushrooms in the mushroom stock until tender. Strain the liquid into the soup and reserve the mushrooms. You should have about 7½ oz / 200 g mushrooms.

4. The soup is ready to serve now, or it may be properly cooled and stored.

5. Heat the soup (by batch or by portion) just before serving. For each portion: Spoon 1 oz / 30 g crabmeat and ¾ oz / 20 g mushrooms into a heated bowl. Portion the hot soup into the bowl with a 6-oz / 180-mL ladle and serve.

Note

Simmer the mushroom stems in ¾ cup / 180 mL water to make a mushroom stock.

Chilled Gazpacho

batch yield: **2 qt / 2 L**

servings: **10**

portioning information:
¾ cup / 180 mL

nutrition per serving:
90 calories, 5 g fat, 9 g total carbohydrate, 3 g protein, 300 mg sodium, 5 mg cholesterol

14 oz / 400 g tomato concassé

5 oz / 140 g diced green pepper

2½ oz / 70 g scallions, split lengthwise and thinly sliced

1 oz / 30 g diced jalapeños

1¾ oz / 50 g peeled, seeded, diced cucumber

1¾ oz / 50 g diced celery

3 tbsp / 45 mL chopped basil

1 tbsp / 15 mL chopped tarragon

1 qt / 950 mL Chicken or Vegetable Stock (pages 489 and 490)

1 tbsp / 15 mL extra-virgin olive oil

1 tbsp / 15 mL balsamic vinegar

1 tsp / 5 mL kosher salt

¼ tsp / 1.25 mL ground white pepper

½ tsp / 2.5 mL Tabasco sauce

2 tsp / 10 mL Worcestershire sauce

GARNISH

1 clove garlic, peeled and left whole

2 tsp / 10 mL extra-virgin olive oil

1 oz / 30 g toasted croutons

1. Combine all the ingredients except the garnish and purée with an immersion blender or in batches in a food processor until smooth. Chill for 8 to 12 hours, allowing the flavor to develop.

2. To make the garnish, sauté the garlic clove in the olive oil until aromatic. Add the bread cubes and sauté until crisp and lightly browned. Cool and reserve.

3. To serve, portion the cold soup into a chilled bowl or cup with a 6-oz / 180-mL ladle. Garnish each portion with a few croutons.

Variation

Chilled Gazpacho with Spicy Crayfish

Prepare the soup as directed in step 1 above. Toss 10 cooked and peeled crayfish tails in ¼ cup / 60 mL Balsamic Vinaigrette (page 503) and chill for 8 to 12 hours. Drain all excess vinaigrette from the crayfish.

Serve the cold soup in chilled bowls and garnish with 1 marinated crayfish, 2½ oz / 70 g peeled and diced cucumber, and 2 tbsp / 30 mL chopped fennel tops. (For nutrition information, see Recipe Analysis on page 514.)

Smoked Corn Chowder

batch yield: 2 qt / 2 L

servings: 10

portioning information:
¾ cup / 180 mL

nutrition per serving:
130 calories, 2.5 g fat, 19 g total
carbohydrate, 9 g protein, 320 mg
sodium, 15 mg cholesterol

½ oz / 14 g butter

4 oz / 115 g diced leeks

1¼ pt / 600 mL skim milk

1¼ pt / 600 mL Chicken Stock, fortified
(page 489)

10 oz / 280 g Roasted Smoked Corn (page 368)

8 oz / 225 g diced peeled Idaho potatoes

2 tsp / 10 mL Worcestershire sauce

1 tsp / 5 mL kosher salt

1 Sachet d'Epices (page 490)

¾ cup / 180 mL evaporated skim milk

¼ cup / 60 mL heavy cream

½ oz / 14 g arrowroot

HERB GARNISH

1 tbsp / 15 mL chopped parsley

1 tbsp / 15 mL chopped chervil

1. Melt the butter in a soup pot. Sweat the leeks in the butter until tender. Add the skim milk, stock, corn, potatoes, Worcestershire, salt, and sachet. Simmer until the potatoes are tender. Remove and discard the sachet.

2. Combine the evaporated skim milk, cream, and arrowroot for a liaison. Add to the soup and simmer until thickened, about 2 minutes. The soup is ready to serve now, or it may be properly cooled and stored.

3. Heat the soup (by batch or by portion) just before serving. To serve, portion the hot soup into a heated bowl with a 6-oz / 180-mL ladle. Garnish each portion of soup with parsley and chervil just before serving.

Chilled Melon Soup with California Champagne

batch yield: **2 qt / 2 L**

servings: **10**

portioning information:
¾ cup / 180 mL

nutrition per serving:
114 calories, 1 g fat, 20 g total carbohydrate, 2 g protein, 269 mg sodium, 3 mg cholesterol

3½ lb / 1.60 kg honeydew flesh

⅓ cup / 80 mL half-and-half

2 tsp / 10 mL kosher salt

¼ tsp / 1.25 mL ground white pepper

4 oz / 115 g cantaloupe flesh

3 oz / 85 g papaya flesh

1½ cups / 360 mL dry Champagne

10 mint leaves

30 fresh raspberries

1. Purée the honeydew flesh. Add the half-and-half and season with the salt and pepper. Chill the soup at least 4 and up to 24 hours before serving.

2. Purée the cantaloupe and papaya together. Reserve.

3. Stir the Champagne into the cold honeydew purée just before serving. To serve, portion the cold soup into a chilled bowl or cup with a 6-oz / 180-mL ladle. Garnish each portion with 1 tbsp / 15 mL cantaloupe purée, a mint leaf, and 3 raspberries.

Chilled Red Plum Soup

batch yield: **2 qt / 2 L**

servings: **10**

portioning information:
¾ cup / 180 mL

nutrition per serving:
161 calories, 5 g fat, 31 g total carbohydrate, 2 g protein, 8 mg sodium, 6 mg cholesterol

1 oz / 30 g arrowroot

1 qt / 950 mL apple juice

2½ lb / 1.15 kg chopped peeled red plums

2 oz / 55 g honey

1 Sachet d'Epices (page 490), plus 2 large slices of ginger, 1 cinnamon stick, 8 allspice berries, and 8 black peppercorns

1 tbsp / 15 mL fresh lemon juice

GARNISH

5 oz / 140 g plain nonfat yogurt, drained

1 oz / 30 g slivered almonds, toasted

1. Combine the arrowroot with enough of the apple juice to make a paste.

2. Combine the remaining apple juice, plums, honey, and the sachet in a medium soup pot. Simmer until the plums are tender. Remove and discard the sachet. Purée the soup with an immersion blender or food processor until smooth. Return the soup to the pot and bring to a simmer. Add the arrowroot mixture and simmer until thickened, about 2 minutes. Stir the lemon juice into the soup. Chill the soup at least 4 and up to 24 hours before serving.

3. To serve, portion the cold soup into a chilled bowl or cup with a 6-oz / 180-mL ladle. Garnish each portion with ½ oz / 14 g yogurt and a sprinkle of almonds.

Chilled Seafood Soup

batch yield: **3 qt / 2.88 L**

servings: **10**

portioning information:
10 oz / 285 g

nutrition per serving:
100 calories, 2 g fat, 9 g total
carbohydrate, 12 g protein, 120 mg
sodium, 55 mg cholesterol

1 tbsp / 15 mL tomato paste

6 oz / 170 g chopped fennel

7 oz / 200 g chopped leeks

6 oz / 170 g chopped carrots

7 oz / 200 g chopped onions

1¼ pt / 600 mL water

1 cup / 240 mL dry white wine

1 tsp / 5 mL whole black peppercorns

¼ tsp / 1.25 mL saffron threads

SOUP

9 oz / 255 g shrimp (16–20 count), peeled, deveined

7 oz / 200 g sea scallops

7 oz / 200 g shucked oysters, liquor reserved

½ oz / 14 g gelatin (powder or sheet)

7 oz / 200 g diced leeks, blanched

6 oz / 170 g diced fennel, blanched

6 oz / 170 g diced carrots, blanched

6 oz / 170 g tomato concassé

1 oz / 30 g chopped tarragon

1. To prepare the court bouillon, lightly brown the tomato paste, fennel, leeks, carrots, and onions in a medium sauce pot. Deglaze with the water and wine and simmer until flavorful, about 20 minutes. Add the peppercorns and saffron and simmer an additional 10 minutes. Strain the bouillon and discard the vegetables. Return the bouillon to the pot and simmer gently.

2. Add the shrimp, scallops, and oysters and their liquor to the simmering bouillon. Poach until the seafood is cooked, about 3 minutes. Remove the seafood from the bouillon and refrigerate. Strain the bouillon through a fine-meshed sieve and cool to room temperature.

3. Bloom the gelatin in a small amount of the cooled bouillon for 5 minutes. Dissolve over a double boiler and stir into the reserved bouillon. Stir the seafood, vegetables, and tarragon into the bouillon.

4. Chill the soup at least 4 and up to 24 hours before serving. To serve, portion the cold soup into a chilled bowl or cup with a 6-oz / 180-mL ladle.

Curried Apple-Squash Soup

batch yield: **2 qt / 2 L**

servings: **10**

portioning information:
¾ cup / 180 mL

nutrition per serving:
138 calories, 2 g fat, 27 g total carbohydrate, 4 g protein, 419 mg sodium, 5 mg cholesterol

1 oz / 30 g minced garlic
9½ oz / 270 g diced celery
11 oz / 310 g diced onions
5½ oz / 155 g diced leeks
3 qt / 2.88 L Chicken Stock (page 489)
2 tbsp / 30 mL curry powder
½ tsp / 2.5 mL grated nutmeg
1 tbsp / 15 mL ground cinnamon

2¼ lb / 1 kg chopped butternut squash
4½ lb / 2 kg chopped peeled Jonagold apples
½ tsp / 2½ mL kosher salt
1½ cups / 360 mL buttermilk

GARNISH

6 oz / 170 g diced apples
½ oz / 14 g chopped chives

1. In a soup pot, sweat the garlic, celery, onions, and leeks in a small amount of the stock until the onions are translucent. Add the remaining stock, curry, nutmeg, and cinnamon and bring to a boil. Add the squash and simmer until tender, about 8 minutes. Add the apples and continue to simmer until all the ingredients are tender, about 5 minutes more.

2. Purée the soup using a food mill or immersion blender and add the salt and buttermilk. Chill the soup at least 4 and up to 24 hours before serving. To serve, portion the cold soup into a chilled bowl or cup with a 6-oz / 180-mL ladle. Garnish each portion with ⅔ oz / 19 g apples and some chives.

Grilled Garlic Shrimp and Radish Salad

servings: **10**

portioning information:
2 oz / 55 g shrimp, 3 oz / 85 g radish salad

nutrition per serving:
213 calories, 9 g fat, 17 g total carbohydrate, 16 g protein, 258 mg sodium, 98 mg cholesterol

2 lb / 900 g peeled, deveined shrimp (21–25 count, about 40 each), shells reserved

½ oz / 14 g minced garlic

2 limes, juiced

VINAIGRETTE

1 tbsp / 15 mL olive oil

8 oz / 225 g reserved shrimp shells

½ oz / 14 g minced garlic

¾ oz / 20 g diced shallots

2 oz / 55 g tomato paste

¼ cup / 60 mL brandy

1¾ cups / 420 mL Chicken Stock (page 489)

2 tsp / 10 mL arrowroot

3 tbsp / 45 mL apple cider vinegar

3 tbsp / 45 mL rice vinegar

1 oz / 30 g tahini

2 tbsp / 30 mL reduced-sodium soy sauce

2 tbsp / 305 mL minced jalapeño

1 tbsp / 15 mL sesame oil

1 tbsp / 15 mL peanut oil

RADISH SALAD

5½ oz / 155 g finely julienned daikon

5½ oz / 155 g finely julienned radish

5½ oz / 155 g finely julienned carrots

½ oz / 14 g finely julienned celery

5 oz / 140 g soba noodles

2 oz / 55 g cilantro leaves

¼ tsp / 1.25 mL black sesame seeds

¼ tsp / 1.25 mL white sesame seeds

1. Toss the shrimp with the garlic and lime juice. Thread 4 shrimp (approximately 2 oz / 55 g total) onto a bamboo skewer. Repeat with the remaining shrimp and refrigerate until needed.

2. To make the vinaigrette, heat the oil in a medium saucepan. Add the shrimp shells and sauté until opaque. Add the garlic and shallots and sweat until the shallots are translucent. Add the tomato paste and sauté until rust colored. Deglaze the pan with the brandy and allow to reduce until almost dry. Add the stock and simmer until reduced by half. Strain through a fine-mesh sieve. If necessary, add water or reduce further to yield about ¾ cup / 180 mL. Return to a clean pan and bring to a boil.

3. Combine the arrowroot with enough water to form a slurry. Stir the arrowroot mixture into the boiling stock. Remove the stock from the heat, add the vinegars, and cool completely. Stir the tahini, soy sauce, and jalapeño into the stock. Whisk in the oils.

4. Combine the daikon, radish, carrots, and celery and toss with ⅓ cup / 80 mL of the vinaigrette.

5. Cook the noodles in boiling water until tender to the bite. Drain and cool. Gently toss the noodles with ¾ cup / 180 mL of the vinaigrette.

6. For each portion: Grill a shrimp skewer until the shrimp are cooked, for 3 minutes on each side. Arrange a bed of 1 oz / 30 g noodles on a room-temperature plate and place approximately 2 oz / 55 g radish salad on top of the noodles. Remove the shrimp from the skewer if desired and arrange over the radish salad. Garnish with cilantro leaves and a pinch each of black and white sesame seeds. Drizzle the plate with 1 tbsp / 15 mL of the remaining vinaigrette and serve.

Tuna Carpaccio with Shiitake and Red Onion Salad

servings: **10**

portioning information:
1½ oz / 45 g tuna, 2 oz / 55 g salad

nutrition per serving:
81 calories, 1 g fat, 8 g total carbohydrate, 11 g protein, 246 mg sodium, 20 mg cholesterol

15 oz / 425 g trimmed skinless tuna fillet

2 tbsp / 30 mL sake

SHIITAKE AND RED ONION SALAD

7 oz / 200 g julienned shiitake mushrooms, cooked

3½ oz / 100 g julienned carrot, blanched

3½ oz / 100 g julienned red onion

2 oz / 60 g julienned bok choy

½ cup / 120 mL rice wine vinegar

2 tbsp / 30 mL reduced-sodium soy sauce

WASABI SAUCE

2 tbsp /30 mL reduced-sodium soy sauce

¼ cup / 60 mL plain nonfat yogurt

2 tsp / 10 mL wasabi powder

1. Place the tuna in the freezer until it is partially frozen. Slice the tuna very thinly. Arrange the tuna slices on parchment paper and sprinkle with the sake. Cover and refrigerate for at least 10 minutes.

2. To prepare the salad, combine the shiitakes, carrots, onions, bok choy, vinegar, and soy sauce in a large bowl. Refrigerate for at least 20 minutes.

3. Combine the wasabi sauce ingredients and mix until smooth.

4. For each portion: Arrange 1½ oz / 45 g tuna and 2 oz / 55 g salad on a chilled plate. Serve immediately with 1½ tsp / 7.5 mL of the wasabi sauce.

Serving Suggestion

Garnish with a very fine julienne of cucumber, daikon, and carrots.

Carpaccio of Beef with Fresh Artichokes and Tomato Salad

servings: **10**

portioning information:
1¼ oz / 34 g beef, ¾ oz / 20 g mixed greens, 3½ oz / 100 g artichoke-tomato salad

nutrition per serving:
182 calories, 3 g fat, 8 g total carbohydrate, 11 g protein, 246 mg sodium, 20 mg cholesterol

12 oz / 340 g beef tenderloin, trimmed

1¾ lb / 795 g cooked artichoke hearts, quartered

10 oz / 285 g small-dice peeled, seeded plum tomatoes

1¾ oz / 50 g minced shallots

½ oz / 14 g chopped basil

10 tbsp / 150 mL Balsamic Vinaigrette (page 503)

Mixed salad greens, as needed

Cracked peppercorns, as needed

10 tbsp / 150 mL Anchovy-Caper Dressing (page 508)

1. Chill the beef thoroughly so that it becomes firm enough to slice easily. Slice it very thinly on a slicing machine or with a sharp slicing knife. Lay the slices out on parchment paper as they come off the blade. Do not stack them on top of one another. Cover and refrigerate.

2. Place the artichokes, tomatoes, shallots, and basil in a bowl. Add the vinaigrette and toss to coat evenly. Remove these ingredients with a slotted spoon, allowing the excess vinaigrette to drain back into the bowl. Reserve the vinaigrette to dress the greens.

3. For each portion: Toss ¾ oz / 20 g mixed greens with 1 tbsp / 15 mL of the reserved vinaigrette to coat the leaves lightly. Arrange the dressed greens on a chilled plate and top with 3½ oz / 100 g of the artichoke-tomato mixture. Place 1¼ oz / 34 g sliced beef on the plate and season with a generous amount of cracked black pepper. Drizzle 1 tbsp / 15 mL anchovy-caper dressing over the beef and serve immediately.

Smoked Duck with Red Lentil Salad and Golden Beets

servings: **10**

portioning information:
1¼ oz / 35 g duck, 1½ oz / 45 g lentil salad, 1½ oz / 45 g beets

nutrition per serving:
252 calories, 15 g fat, 15 g total carbohydrate, 14 g protein, 654 mg sodium, 57 mg cholesterol

1 lb / 450 g skinless, boneless duck breast

½ oz / 14 g kosher salt

1 tbsp / 15 mL cracked black peppercorns

2 oz / 55 g grated orange zest

2 oz / 55 g chopped basil

BABY GOLDEN BEETS VINAIGRETTE

1 lb / 450 g baby golden beets, trimmed

½ cup / 120 mL balsamic vinegar

1 oz / 30 g chopped basil, chives, thyme, and parsley

1 tbsp / 15 mL whole-grain mustard

½ cup / 120 mL olive oil

8 oz / 225 oz sliced Maui or other sweet onion

1 lb / 450 g Red Lentil Salad (page 201)

1. Place the duck breast in a medium bowl. Rub the duck with the salt, pepper, orange zest, and basil. Cover tightly with plastic wrap and refrigerate for about 8 hours.

2. Cold-smoke the duck breast for 1½ to 2 hours.

3. Sear the duck breast in a seasoned skillet and roast in a 275°F / 135°C oven to an internal temperature of 165°F / 74°C. Remove from the oven, place on a wire rack, cool, cover, and refrigerate.

4. Cook the beets in simmering acidulated water until tender. Shock the beets, remove their skins, and quarter.

5. Make a vinaigrette by combining the vinegar, herbs, and mustard. Gradually whisk in the oil, or use an immersion blender. Toss the beets and onions with the vinaigrette.

6. For each portion: Arrange about 1¼ oz / 35 g thinly sliced duck breast on a plate. Serve with 1½ oz / 45 g lentil salad and 1½ oz / 45 g beets.

Wild Rice Salad

batch yield: **2¾ lb / 1.25 kg**

servings: **15**

portioning information:
3 oz / 85 g

nutrition per serving:
188 calories, 6 g fat, 30 g total carbohydrate, 7 g protein, 99 mg sodium, 3 mg cholesterol

1 lb / 450 g raw wild rice

1½ qt / 1.45 L Chicken Stock (page 489)

⅔ cup / 160 mL Vinaigrette-Style dressing (page 503) (see Note)

5 oz / 140 g julienned Granny Smith apple

5 oz / 140 g julienned red pepper

1 tsp / 5 mL chopped sage

¾ oz / 20 g minced garlic

½ oz / 14 g minced shallots

3 tbsp / 45 mL apple cider

2 oz / 55 g chopped walnuts, toasted

1. Bring the rice and stock to a boil in a medium sauce pot. Cover the pot tightly and cook in a 350°F / 175°C oven until the rice is tender, about 45 minutes. Drain any excess liquid. While the rice is still hot, add the vinaigrette and toss well. Gently fold the apple, red pepper, and sage into the rice.

2. Sweat the garlic and shallots in the cider until the shallots are translucent. Add the mixture to the rice.

3. Serve at room temperature, garnished with toasted walnuts.

Note

Use walnut oil and cider vinegar in the Vinaigrette-Style Dressing recipe.

Curried Rice Salad

batch yield: **3½ lb / 1.60 kg**

servings: **18**

portioning information:
3 oz / 85 g

nutrition per serving:
130 calories, 3 g fat, 22 g total carbohydrate, 3 g protein, 83 mg sodium, 0 mg cholesterol

½ oz / 14 g curry powder

¾ cup / 180 mL Vinaigrette-Style Dressing (page 503)

2 oz / 55 g golden raisins

2 lb / 910 g cooked long-grain brown rice

8 oz / 225 g cooked peas

4 oz / 115 g diced onion

4 oz / 115 g diced Granny Smith apple

2 oz / 55 g pumpkin seeds, lightly toasted

1 tsp / 5 mL kosher salt

½ tsp / 2.5 mL ground black pepper

1. Lightly toast the curry powder in a small sauté pan over low heat. Remove the pan from the heat and add the vinaigrette and raisins. Allow the mixture to cool.

2. Combine the remaining ingredients and toss with the vinaigrette. Serve chilled or at room temperature.

Red Lentil Salad

batch yield: **2 lb / 910 g**

servings: **10**

portioning information:
3¼ oz / 91 g

nutrition per serving:
103 calories, 6 g fat, 9 g total carbohydrate, 3 g protein, 3 mg sodium, 0 mg cholesterol

1½ oz / 45 g diced red pepper

1 tsp / 5 mL minced jalapeño

2 oz / 55 g diced red onion

2 tbsp / 30 mL minced garlic

2 tbsp / 30 mL olive oil

12 oz / 340 g red lentils, cooked and cooled

1½ oz / 45 g tomato concassé

1½ oz / 45 g diced orange flesh, membranes removed

2 tbsp / 30 mL extra-virgin olive oil

2 tbsp / 30 mL balsamic vinegar

2 tbsp / 30 mL basil chiffonade

1. In a large sauté pan, sweat the red pepper, jalapeño, onion, and garlic in the olive oil until the onion is translucent. Cool.

2. Combine with the remaining ingredients and refrigerate at least 4 and up to 24 hours before serving.

Black Bean Salad

batch yield: **2¼ lb / 1 kg**

servings: **12**

portioning information:
3 oz / 85 g

nutrition per serving:
115 calories, 2 g fat, 18 g total carbohydrate, 6 g protein, 15 mg sodium, 0 mg cholesterol

12 oz / 340 g dried black beans (see Note)

7 oz / 200 g diced bell peppers, assorted colors

1½ oz / 45 g diced red onions

¾ oz / 20 g minced jalapeño

¾ oz / 20 g minced garlic

2 tbsp / 30 mL chopped cilantro

½ cup / 120 mL Lime-Cilantro Vinaigrette (page 504)

1. Soak the beans for 8 to 12 hours in enough water to cover by 3 in / 8 cm. Drain the beans and rinse with cold water.

2. Combine the beans with enough fresh water to cover in a large stockpot. Simmer until the beans are tender, about 1½ hours, adding more water as necessary to keep the beans covered. Drain.

3. Combine the beans with the remaining ingredients for the salad and toss with the vinaigrette.

4. Refrigerate for at least 4 and up to 24 hours before serving.

Note

To reduce the length of soaking time, bring the beans and water to a boil, remove from the heat, and soak for 1 hour. Continue with the recipe.

Barley Salad

batch yield: **3 lb / 1.35 kg**

servings: **16**

portioning information:
3 oz / 85 g

nutrition per serving:
236 calories, 4 g fat, 47 g total
carbohydrate, 6 g protein, 135 mg
sodium, 0 mg cholesterol

1 lb / 450 g pearl barley

2 qt / 2 L Vegetable Stock (page 490)

4 oz / 115 g peeled cipollini onions

2 oz / 55 g ramps, cut into ¼-in / 2-cm lengths

3 navel oranges

4 oz / 115 g currants

4 oz / 115 g golden raisins

2 Thai chiles

1 pt / 480 mL blood orange juice

¾ oz / 20 g curry powder

3 tbsp / 45 mL fresh lemon juice

2 tbsp / 30 mL honey

½ tsp / 2.5 mL kosher salt

4 oz / 120 g shelled pistachios, roasted and chopped

1. Combine the barley and stock in a medium sauce pot. Simmer until the barley is tender. Drain the liquid and cool the barley completely.

2. Roast half of the onions in a 450°F / 230°C oven until dark brown. Small dice both the roasted and raw cipollini onions.

3. Blanch the ramps in 1 qt / 950 mL of boiling water for 2 minutes.

4. Segment each orange and quarter each segment.

5. Combine the currants, raisins, chiles, and blood orange juice in a medium sauce pot. Bring the liquid to a boil and remove the pot from the heat. Steep for a least 30 minutes. Remove the chiles, mince, and return to the juice.

6. In a large bowl, stir together the curry, lemon juice, honey, and salt. Add the barley, onions, ramps, orange segments, and blood orange juice mixture. Toss to combine and marinate for 1 hour before serving.

7. For each serving: Garnish with the pistachios (by batch or by adding about 1 tsp / 5 ml per portion).

Soba Noodle Salad

batch yield: **2 lb / 910 g**

servings: **10**

portioning information:
3¼ oz / 91 g

nutrition per serving:
261 calories, 6 g fat, 47 g total
carbohydrate, 9 g protein, 579 mg
sodium, 0 mg cholesterol

1 lb 4 oz / 565 g soba noodles

1½ tsp / 7.5 mL arrowroot

1 cup / 240 mL Vegetable Stock (page 490)

⅓ cup / 80 mL fresh lime juice

¼ cup / 60 mL rice wine vinegar

2 tbsp / 30 mL reduced-sodium soy sauce

⅔ oz / 19 g minced ginger

⅔ oz / 19 g lime zest

2 tsp / 10 mL minced garlic

2 tbsp / 30 mL sesame oil

½ oz / 14 g chopped cilantro

2 tbsp / 30 mL vegetable oil

4 oz / 115 g julienned shiitake mushrooms

4 oz / 115 g snow peas, blanched

1. Cook the soba noodles in boiling water until tender to the bite. Drain and cool the noodles to room temperature.

2. Combine the arrowroot with enough stock to form a slurry. Bring the remaining stock to a boil. Add the slurry and stir until thickened, about 2 minutes. Cool to room temperature.

3. Combine the lime juice, vinegar, soy sauce, ginger, lime zest, and garlic. Whisk in the thickened stock and sesame oil. Stir in the cilantro.

4. Heat the vegetable oil in a small sauté pan. Add the mushrooms and sauté until almost cooked. Add the snow peas and continue to sauté until the peas are bright green.

5. Toss together the soba noodles, snow peas, mushrooms, and vinaigrette. Serve the salad at room temperature.

Roasted Red Pepper Salad

batch yield: **2 lb / 910 g**

servings: **10**

portioning information:
3¼ oz / 91 g

nutrition per serving:
102 calories, 7 g fat, 10 g total
carbohydrate, 1 g protein, 206 mg
sodium, 0 mg cholesterol

12 oz / 340 g red peppers, halved

2 oz / 55 g golden raisins

¾ cup / 180 mL Balsamic Vinaigrette (page 503)

7 oz / 200 g tomato concassé

2 oz / 55 g julienned red onion

2 oz / 55 g quartered black olives

½ oz / 14 g minced garlic

½ oz / 14 g minced jalapeño

¾ oz / 20 g pine nuts, toasted

⅛ tsp / 0.625 mL cayenne

1. Place the peppers cut side down on a roasting rack and broil or bake in a 500°F / 260°C oven, until the pepper skins turn black and blister.

2. Remove the peppers from the oven and cover with plastic wrap, or place in a paper bag to allow the skins to loosen. When the peppers are cool enough to handle, peel, scraping off any remaining char, and cut into strips.

3. Cover the raisins with warm water and soak until plump, about 15 minutes. Drain.

4. Combine the roasted peppers, raisins, and remaining ingredients in a large bowl. Refrigerate for at least 2 and up to 24 hours before serving.

Note

This salad is an excellent accompaniment to grilled and roasted meat and fish, crusty hearth bread and flatbreads, and pasta salads.

Jícama Salad

batch yield: **2 lb / 910 g**

servings: **10**

portioning information:
3¼ oz / 91 g

nutrition per serving:
89 calories, 5 g fat, 11 g total
carbohydrate, 1 g protein, 238 mg
sodium, 0 mg cholesterol

15 oz / 425 g julienned jícama

6 oz / 170 g Roasted Smoked Corn kernels
(page 368)

3 oz / 85 g sliced red onion

3 oz / 85 g julienned red pepper

3 oz / 85 g julienned yellow pepper

3 oz / 85 g julienned green pepper

1 jalapeño, minced

VINAIGRETTE

2 tbsp / 30 mL red wine vinegar

2 tbsp / 30 mL vegetable oil

2 tbsp / 30 mL water

1 tbsp / 15 mL peanut oil

1 tsp / 5 mL dry mustard

1 tsp / 5 mL kosher salt

1 tsp / 5 mL minced garlic

½ tsp / 2.5 mL cracked black peppercorns

1. Combine the jícama, corn, onions, red and yellow peppers, and jalapeño in a bowl.

2. In a separate bowl, whisk together the vinaigrette ingredients. Pour the vinaigrette over the vegetables to coat evenly. The salad is ready to serve now at room temperature, or it may be chilled for up to 24 hours before serving.

Mexican Corn Salad

batch yield: **2 lb / 910 g**

servings: **10**

portioning information:
3¼ oz / 91 g

nutrition per serving:
90 calories, 2 g fat, 19 g total
carbohydrate, 3 g protein, 70 mg
sodium, 0 mg cholesterol

2 tsp / 10 mL olive oil

1 tsp / 3 g minced garlic

½ oz / 14 g minced shallots

½ tsp / 2.5 mL minced jalapeño

22 oz / 625 g corn kernels

3½ oz / 100 g diced roasted red pepper

3½ oz / 100 g small-dice jícama

3½ oz / 100 g small-dice tomatillo

4 oz / 115 g tomato concassé

1 tbsp / 15 mL chopped cilantro

¼ tsp / 1.25 mL kosher salt

1. Heat the oil in a large sauté pan. Add the garlic, shallots, and jalapeño. Sauté until the shallots are translucent. Add the corn, red pepper, jícama, tomatillo, and tomatoes. Toss over high heat until the mixture is hot. Season with the cilantro and salt. The salad is ready to serve now at room temperature or it may be chilled for up to 24 hours before serving.

Warm Cabbage Salad

batch yield: **2 lb / 910 g**

servings: **10**

portioning information:
3¼ oz / 91 g

nutrition per serving:
58 calories, 2 g fat, 8 g total
carbohydrate, 2 g protein, 55 mg
sodium, 3 mg cholesterol

1½ oz / 45 g minced bacon

3 oz / 85 g diced red onion

1 clove garlic, minced

⅓ cup / 80 mL Chicken Stock (page 489)

3 tbsp / 45 mL tarragon vinegar

3 tbsp / 45 mL dry white wine

4 tsp / 20 mL granulated sugar

2 lb 6 oz / 910 g savoy cabbage chiffonade

¾ tsp / 3.75 mL caraway seeds

1 tbsp / 15 mL chopped parsley

1. Render the bacon in a large skillet until crisp. Remove from the pan, drain, and reserve. Add the onion and garlic to the pan and sauté until the onions are translucent.

2. Combine the stock, vinegar, wine, and sugar in a small bowl. Stir to dissolve the sugar and add to the pan along with the cabbage and caraway seeds. Cook until the cabbage is limp and tender. Remove from the heat and stir in the parsley and reserved bacon.

3. The salad is ready to serve now, warm or at room temperature.

Marinated Asian Vegetable Salad

batch yield: **2 lb / 910 g**

servings: **10**

portioning information:
3 oz / 91 g

nutrition per serving:
113 calories, 8 g fat, 7 g total
carbohydrate, 2 g protein, 97 mg
sodium, 0 mg cholesterol

1 lb / 450 g julienned carrot

1 lb / 450 g julienned daikon

1 oz / 30 g pickled minced ginger

¾ cup / 180 mL Asian Vinaigrette (page 506)

GARNISH

¼ sheet nori seaweed, cut into slivers and toasted

1 tbsp / 15 mL black sesame seeds

1 tbsp / 15 mL white sesame seeds

1. Toss the carrots, daikon, and ginger with the vinaigrette. Refrigerate for at least 1 and up to 24 hours before serving.

2. Drain the salad before serving. Garnish each serving with a sprinkling of nori and sesame seeds.

Marinated Chanterelles

batch yield: **1 lb / 450 g**

servings: **10**

portioning information:
1½ oz / 45 g

nutrition per serving:
42 calories, 1 g fat, 7 g total
carbohydrate, 2 g protein, 151 mg
sodium, 0 mg cholesterol

2 tsp / 10 mL olive oil

1 tsp / 5 mL minced garlic

12 oz / 340 g chanterelles, trimmed, sliced if the caps are large

8 oz / 225 g julienned carrot

6 oz / 170 g julienned fennel

6 oz / 170 g pearl onions, blanched and peeled

⅓ cup / 80 mL Chicken Stock (page 489)

2 tsp / 10 mL white wine

2 tsp / 10 mL sherry vinegar

2 tsp / 10 mL white wine vinegar

2 tsp / 10 mL basil chiffonade

2 tbsp / 30 mL chopped parsley

½ tsp / 2.5 mL kosher salt

¼ tsp / 1.25 mL ground white pepper

1. In a large sauté pan, heat the oil. Add the garlic and sauté until aromatic.

2. Add the chanterelles, carrots, fennel, and onions. Sauté until the mushrooms begin to release their juices. Add the stock, wine, and vinegars. Simmer until the mushrooms are completely cooked. Season with the herbs, salt, and pepper.

3. Allow the mushrooms to cool in their cooking liquid at least 2 and up to 24 hours before serving. Drain before serving.

Fruit Salad with Orange Blossom Syrup

servings: **10**

portioning information:
2½ oz / 70 g salad, 1 tbsp / 15 mL syrup, 1 tsp / 5 mL yogurt

nutrition per serving:
64 calories, 0 g fat, 15 g total carbohydrate, 2 g protein, 27 mg sodium, 1 mg cholesterol

5 fl oz / 150 mL orange blossom water (see Note)

1 oz / 30 g sugar

Zest of 1 orange

7 oz / 200 g medium-dice cantaloupe flesh

6 oz / 170 g medium-dice honeydew melon flesh

6 oz / 170 g medium-dice kiwi

5 oz / 140 g strawberries, quartered

5 oz / 140 g blueberries

10 tbsp / 150 mL nonfat yogurt, drained

3 tbsp / 45 mL spearmint chiffonade

1. To make the syrup, combine the orange blossom water and the sugar in a small saucepan. Heat, stirring occasionally, until the sugar has completely dissolved. Set aside until needed.

2. Peel the zest from the orange and julienne the zest. Place the julienned zest in a small saucepan and cover with cold water. Bring the water to a boil. Drain and repeat the blanching process twice, beginning with cold water each time. Reserve the blanched zest until needed.

3. Combine all of the fruits in a large bowl. Serve immediately or refrigerate until needed.

4. For each portion: Place 2 ½ oz / 70 g fruit salad in a glass or serving dish. Top with 1 tbsp / 15 mL of the syrup and about 1 tbsp / 15 mL of the drained yogurt. Garnish with the blanched orange zest and spearmint chiffonade.

Note

Orange blossom water is generally available from health food stores and wholesalers.

Chinese Long Bean Salad with Tangerines and Sherry-Mustard Vinaigrette

batch yield: **1 lb 8 oz / 680 g**

servings: **8**

portioning information:
3 oz / 85 g

nutrition per serving:
155 calories, 11 g fat, 13 g total
carbohydrate, 4 g protein, 331 mg
sodium, 0 mg cholesterol

8 oz / 225 g Chinese long beans (see Note)

4 tangerines

3 oz / 85 g sliced Vidalia onion

3 oz / 85 g sunflower seeds, toasted

½ tsp / 2.5 mL kosher salt

¼ tsp / 1.25 mL ground black pepper

SHERRY-MUSTARD VINAIGRETTE

1 tsp / 5 mL cornstarch

½ cup / 120 mL Vegetable Stock (page 490)

3 tbsp / 45 mL olive oil

2 tbsp / 30 mL sherry vinegar

2 tbsp / 30 mL fresh tangerine juice

1 tbsp / 15 mL Dijon mustard

½ oz / 14 g light brown sugar

2 tsp / 10 mL minced shallots

1 tsp / 5 mL minced garlic

½ tsp / 2.5 mL kosher salt

¼ tsp / 1.25 mL ground black pepper

1. Trim the beans, cut into 1½-in / 4-cm lengths, and cook in boiling water until barely tender. Drain and cool.

2. Trim the peels from the tangerines. Working over a bowl to catch the juices, cut the segments out from between the membranes, removing seeds, if any. Squeeze the juice from the leftover membranes and reserve for the vinaigrette.

3. Combine the beans, tangerine segments, onions, and sunflower seeds in a large bowl. Season with the salt and pepper.

4. To make the vinaigrette, combine the cornstarch with 1 tsp / 5 mL water to form a slurry. Bring the stock to a boil. Add the slurry and stir until the stock has thickened, about 2 minutes. Cool to room temperature. Combine the remaining vinaigrette ingredients and whisk into the thickened stock.

5. Toss the bean mixture with the vinaigrette. The salad is ready to serve now at room temperature or it may be chilled for up to 24 hours before serving.

Note

Chinese long beans are also known as yard-long beans, though they are seldom left to grow to this length. They are part of the same plant family as the black-eyed pea. Green beans may be substituted if Chinese long beans are unavailable.

Stone Fruits with Mint Syrup

servings: **10**

portioning information:
3 oz / 85 g salad, ¼ cup / 60 mL syrup, 1 tbsp / 15 mL yogurt

nutrition per serving:
136 calories, 0 g fat, 33 g total carbohydrate, 2 g protein, 18 mg sodium, 0 mg cholesterol

5 cups / 1.20 L white grape juice	6 oz / 170 g sliced plums
1½ oz / 45 g raw sugar (Demerara or turbinado)	6 oz / 170 g sliced apricots
½ bunch mint	6 oz / 170 g pitted sweet cherries
6 oz / 170 g sliced nectarines	5 fl oz / 150 mL drained nonfat yogurt
6 oz / 170 g sliced peaches	

1. To make the syrup, combine the grape juice and the sugar in a saucepan. Bring to a boil, stirring occasionally. Continue to boil until the syrup has reduced by half. Remove from the heat.

2. Reserve several of the nicest mint leaves for a garnish and immerse the remaining mint in the hot syrup. Steep for 2 hours, or until the flavor is well developed. Strain the syrup and set aside until needed.

3. Combine all of the fruits in a large bowl. The salad is ready to serve immediately or it may be refrigerated for up to 8 hours.

4. For each portion: Place 3 oz / 85 g of the mixed fruits in a chilled dish. Pour ¼ cup / 60 mL of the syrup over the fruits. Garnish with 1 tbsp / 15 mL of the yogurt and a few mint leaves.

Winter Greens with Warm Vegetable Vinaigrette

servings: **10**

portioning information:
3 oz / 85 g salad, 2 tbsp / 30 mL vinaigrette

nutrition per serving:
153 calories, 11 g fat, 9 g total carbohydrate, 6 g protein, 259 mg sodium, 11 mg cholesterol

1¼ cups / 300 mL Roasted Vegetable Vinaigrette (page 505)	5 oz / 140 g arugula, washed and dried
30 Belgian endive spears	5 oz / 140 g spinach, washed and dried
5 oz / 140 g frisée, washed and dried	20 slices grilled red onion
5 oz / 140 g radicchio, washed and dried	5 oz / 140 g blue cheese
	1¾ oz / 50 g pine nuts, toasted

1. Heat the vinaigrette in a small saucepan. Keep warm.

2. For each portion: Arrange 3 endive spears and ½ oz / 14 g each frisée, radicchio, arugula, and spinach on a plate. Garnish with 2 onion slices, ½ oz / 14 g blue cheese, and a small amount of the pine nuts. Drizzle 2 tbsp / 30 mL of the warm dressing over the salad.

Spinach Salad with Marinated Shiitake Mushrooms and Red Onion

servings: **10**

portioning information:
2½ oz / 70 g salad, 2 tbsp / 30 mL vinaigrette, ¾ oz / 20 g garnish

nutrition per serving:
122 calories, 9 g fat, 9 g total carbohydrate, 2 g protein, 173 mg sodium, 2 mg cholesterol

MARINATED MUSHROOMS

2 tsp / 10 mL walnut oil	1 oz / 30 g diced bacon
10 oz / 280 g sliced shiitake mushrooms	4 oz / 120 g corn kernels (see Note)
4 tsp / 20 mL Veal Stock	4 oz / 115 g diced red onion
2 tsp / 10 mL reduced-sodium soy sauce	10 oz / 280 g trimmed fresh spinach, washed and torn
4 tsp / 20 mL cider vinegar	5 oz / 140 g radicchio chiffonade
⅛ tsp / 0.625 mL salt	1¼ cups / 300 mL Balsamic Vinaigrette (page 503)
⅛ tsp / 0.625 mL ground black pepper	
Dash of Tabasco sauce	

1. To prepare the marinated mushrooms, heat the oil in a sauté pan. Add the mushrooms and sauté for 2 minutes. Add the stock and soy sauce and cook until dry. Remove from the heat and add the vinegar, salt, pepper, and Tabasco. Cool completely.

2. Render the bacon in a small sauté pan until the bacon is crisp. Drain the bacon, reserving 1 tsp / 5 mL of the fat. Sweat the corn and onions in the bacon fat until the onions are translucent and the corn is cooked. Remove from the heat and toss together the bacon, onions, and corn.

3. For each portion: Toss 1 oz / 30 g spinach and ½ oz / 14 g radicchio with 2 tbsp / 30 mL vinaigrette. Place on a chilled plate and top with 1 oz / 30 g of the marinated mushrooms. Garnish with ¾ oz / 20 g of the corn mixture.

Note

Substitute diced yellow pepper if corn is not in season.

Hearty Greens and Wild-Ripened Cheddar with Hazelnut Verjus–Mustard Dressing

servings: **10**

portioning information:
3½ oz / 100 g salad, 2 tbsp / 30 mL dressing

nutrition per serving:
156 calories, 13 g fat, 6 g total carbohydrate, 5 g protein, 323 mg sodium, 15 mg cholesterol

HAZELNUT VERJUS–MUSTARD DRESSING

7 tsp / 70 mL verjus

½ cup / 120 mL Vegetable Stock (page 490)

¼ cup / 60 mL Dijon mustard

½ tsp / 2.5 mL kosher salt

¼ tsp / 1.25 mL ground black pepper

¼ cup / 60 mL hazelnut oil

5 oz / 140 g frisée, washed and dried

5 oz / 140 g radicchio, washed and dried

3½ oz / 100 g arugula, washed and dried

2½ oz / 70 g beet greens, washed and dried

2½ oz / 70 g trimmed spinach, washed and dried

3½ oz / 100 g red seedless grapes, halved

5 oz / 140 g diced Cheddar cheese, wild-ripened if possible

1½ oz / 45 g chopped hazelnuts

1. To prepare the dressing, combine the verjus, stock, mustard, salt, and pepper in a small bowl. Whisk in the oil.

2. Combine all of the greens and refrigerate until needed.

3. For each portion: Toss 2 oz / 55 g mixed greens and 1 tbsp / 15 mL grapes with 2 tbsp / 30 mL of the dressing. Garnish the salad with ½ oz / 14 g of the cheese and a ½ tsp / 2.5 mL of the hazelnuts.

Warm Salad of Wild Mushrooms and Fennel

servings: **10**

portioning information:
3¾ oz / 110 g

nutrition per serving:
158 calories, 8 g fat, 19 g total carbohydrate, 7 g protein, 439 mg sodium, 2 mg cholesterol

5½ oz / 155 g whole garlic cloves

¼ cup / 60 mL extra-virgin olive oil

1 lb 5 oz / 595 g sliced or quartered wild mushrooms

1½ pt / 600 mL Chicken Stock (page 489)

1¾ oz / 50 g drained capers

1¾ oz / 50 g Kalamata olives, pitted and cut into slivers

2 oz / 55 g chopped sun-dried tomatoes

½ oz / 14 g minced sage

1 lb / 450 g sliced fennel

8 oz / 225 g radicchio chiffonade

⅓ cup / 80 mL fresh lemon juice

½ oz / 14 g cracked black peppercorns

3½ oz / 100 g julienned red pepper

1. In a small saucepan, cover the garlic with 1 in / 3 cm of water. Bring to a boil and drain. Repeat and reserve.

2. Heat the oil in a large sauté pan. Add the garlic and sauté until golden brown. Add the mushrooms and sauté until tender. Deglaze the pan with the stock and cook until almost dry. Transfer the mushrooms to a bowl and cool to room temperature. Stir in the capers, olives, tomatoes, and sage.

3. Cook the fennel in boiling water until barely tender. Drain and hold at room temperature.

4. For each portion: Reheat 1½ oz / 45 g of the mushroom mixture in a sauté pan. Place it on a bed of 1½ oz / 45 g fennel tossed with ¾ oz / 20 g radicchio. Drizzle the salad with a little lemon juice. Sprinkle with black pepper and garnish with red pepper julienne.

Mixed Green Salad with Pears, Walnuts, and Blue Cheese

servings: **10**

portioning information:
3½ oz / 85 g salad, 1 tbsp / 15 mL vinaigrette

nutrition per serving:
112 calories, 7 g fat, 9 g total carbohydrate, 2 g protein, 95 mg sodium, 3 mg cholesterol

1 lb 4 oz / 565 g red oak leaf lettuce, washed and dried

5 fl oz / 150 mL Port Wine Vinaigrette (page 504)

15 oz / 425 g ripe Seckel pear quarters (see Note)

1½ oz / 45 g whole walnuts, toasted

1½ oz / 45 g blue cheese, crumbled

1. For each portion: Toss 2 oz / 55 g lettuce with 1 tbsp / 15 mL of the vinaigrette and place on a chilled plate. Top with 1½ oz / 45 g pears and 1 tsp / 5 mL each of the walnuts and blue cheese.

Note

Other pears may be used, depending upon seasonal availability.

Romaine and Grapefruit Salad with Walnuts and Stilton

servings: **10**

portioning information:
3½ oz / 85 g salad, 1 tbsp / 15 mL vinaigrette

nutrition per serving:
153 calories, 11 g fat, 9 g total carbohydrate, 5 g protein, 148 mg sodium, 7 mg cholesterol

¾ tsp / 3.75 mL arrowroot

¼ cup / 60 mL ruby port wine

3 tbsp / 45 mL Vegetable Stock (page 490)

2 tbsp / 30 mL red wine vinegar

2 tbsp / 30 mL grapefruit juice

4 tsp / 20 mL olive oil

1 lb 4 oz / 565 g romaine, chiffonade or bite-sized pieces

1 lb / 450 g white and pink grapefruit sections

3½ oz / 100 g Stilton cheese

3½ oz / 100 g chopped walnuts

1. Combine the arrowroot with the port to form a slurry. Bring the stock to a boil in a small saucepan. Add the slurry and stir until the stock has thickened, about 2 minutes. Remove from the heat; stir in the vinegar and grapefruit juice. Cool completely before slowly whisking in the oil. Reserve.

2. For each portion: Toss 2 oz / 55 g romaine with 1 tbsp / 15 mL of the dressing and place in the center of a chilled plate. Garnish with 1½ oz / 45 g of the grapefruit sections and 2 tsp / 10 mL each of the cheese and walnuts.

Mediterranean Salad and Roasted
Red Pepper Salad (page 204)

Mediterranean Salad

servings: 10

portioning information:
1½ oz / 45 g mixed greens,
1½ oz / 45 g artichoke salad,
2 tbsp / 30 mL vinaigrette

nutrition per serving:
204 calories, 17 g fat, 9 g total
carbohydrate, 6 g protein, 592 mg
sodium, 13 mg cholesterol

1½ oz / 45 g minced anchovy fillets

1¾ cups / 420 mL Vinaigrette-Style Dressing (page 503)

5 oz / 140 g artichoke hearts, cooked and quartered

5 oz / 140 g peas

3½ oz / 100 g julienned carrot

2 oz / 55 g pitted picholine olives

2 oz / 55 g pitted niçoise olives

3½ oz / 100 g Asiago cheese, grated

2 oz / 55 g chopped parsley

1 lb / 450 g baby mixed greens, washed and dried

1. Stir the anchovies into the vinaigrette in a bowl. Add the artichokes, peas, carrots, olives, cheese, and parsley. Toss to coat evenly.

2. For each portion: Place a bed of 1½ oz / 45 g mixed greens in the center of a chilled plate. Top with 1½ oz / 45 g of the artichoke salad (use a slotted spoon to lift the salad so the dressing can drain away). Garnish with a sprinkling of parsley.

Serving Suggestion

In the presentation shown here, Roasted Red Pepper Salad (page 204) is paired with the Mediterranean Salad as part of a seasonal salad sampler plate.

Warm Salad of Hearty Greens, Blood Oranges, and Pomegranate Vinaigrette

servings: **10**

portioning information:
2½ oz / 70 g salad, 2 tbsp / 30 mL vinaigrette

nutrition per serving:
103 calories, 7 g fat, 8 g total carbohydrate, 2 g protein, 36 mg sodium, 0 mg cholesterol

POMEGRANATE VINAIGRETTE

½ oz / 14 g arrowroot

⅓ cup / 80 mL Vegetable Stock (page 490)

½ oz / 14 g minced red onion

¼ cup / 60 mL red wine vinegar

¼ cup / 60 mL pomegranate juice

¼ cup / 60 mL walnut oil

5 oz / 140 g frisée, washed and dried

5 oz / 140 g radicchio, washed and dried

3½ oz / 100 g arugula, washed and dried

2 oz / 55 g beet greens, washed and dried

2 oz / 55 g spinach, washed and dried

7 oz / 200 g blood orange sections

1¾ oz / 50 g slivered almonds, toasted

1. To prepare the vinaigrette, combine the arrowroot with enough stock to form a slurry. In a small saucepan, sweat the onion in the remaining stock until translucent. Add the slurry to the stock and simmer, stirring constantly, until thickened, about 2 minutes. Stir in the vinegar and juice and whisk in the oil. Keep warm.

2. Combine all of the greens and refrigerate until needed.

3. For each portion: Toss 1¾ oz / 50 g mixed greens with 2 tbsp / 30 mL warm vinaigrette and place in the center of a warm plate. Garnish with ¾ oz / 20 g blood orange sections and a small amount of the almonds.

Grilled Chicken and Pecan Salad

servings: **10**

portioning information:
2 oz / 55 g chicken, 2 oz / 55 g salad

nutrition per serving:
291 calories, 16 g fat, 15 g total carbohydrate, 23 g protein, 90 mg sodium, 56 mg cholesterol

1¼ lb / 570 kg boneless, skinless chicken breast

5 oz / 140 g pecan, halves

1¼ cups / 300 mL apple cider

2 tbsp / 30 mL cider vinegar

1 tbsp / 15 mL Worcestershire sauce

1 tbsp / 15 mL Tabasco sauce

1 tbsp / 15 mL chopped thyme

2 tbsp / 30 mL walnut oil

9 oz / 255 g arugula

6 oz / 170 g mixed salad greens

5 oz / 140 g julienned endive

1 lb 4 oz / 570 g sliced Granny Smith apples

1. Grill the chicken breast until thoroughly cooked. Cool and slice thinly.

2. Toast the pecans in a 300°F / 150°C oven until golden brown.

3. Reduce the apple cider by two thirds over high heat. Combine the reduced cider, vinegar, Worcestershire, Tabasco, and thyme. Slowly whisk in the oil away from the heat.

4. Combine the arugula, mixed greens, and endive. Refrigerate until needed.

5. For each portion: Toss 2 oz / 55 g each of the greens and apples with 1 tbsp / 15 mL of the vinaigrette. Place on a room-temperature plate and top with 2 oz / 57 g chicken and ½ oz / 14 g pecans. Drizzle with ½ tsp / 2.5 mL vinaigrette.

Grilled Tuna Niçoise

servings: **10**

portioning information:
2 oz / 55 g tuna, 6 oz / 170 g niçoise salad

nutrition per serving:
382 calories, 20 g fat, 31 g total carbohydrate, 20 g protein, 539 mg sodium, 83 mg cholesterol

1 lb 4 oz / 570 g trimmed tuna fillet

1¼ lb / 570 g small red potatoes

1 pt / 480 mL Vinaigrette-Style Dressing (page 503)

1 lb / 450 g mixed salad greens, washed and dried

1 lb / 450 g haricot verts, cooked

3½ oz / 100 g Tomatillo Salsa (page 485)

1 lb / 450 g halved cherry tomatoes

30 Niçoise olives

3 hard-boiled large eggs, quartered

1. Cut the tuna into 2-oz / 57-g portions. Refrigerate until needed.

2. Roast the potatoes according to the recipe on page 406. Toss the roasted potatoes with ¾ cup / 180 mL of the vinaigrette.

3. For each portion: Grill 1 portion of tuna to the desired doneness. Toss 1½ oz / 45 g greens and 1½ oz / 45 g haricot verts with 2 tbsp / 30 mL vinaigrette. Mound the greens and beans on a plate and top with the tuna. Garnish with 3 tbsp / 45 mL of salsa verde. Arrange 2 oz / 55 g potatoes wedges, 1½ oz / 45 g cherry tomatoes, 3 olives, and 1 egg quarter around the tuna.

Grilled Tuna with Spring Herb Salad and Marinated Tomatoes

servings: **10**

portioning information:
3½ oz / 100 g tuna, 2¾ oz / 80 g salad

nutrition per serving:
204 calories, 9 g fat, 4 g total carbohydrate, 25 g protein, 338 mg sodium, 46 mg cholesterol

MARINATED TOMATOES

6 oz / 170 g tomato concassé

⅓ cup / 80 mL Balsamic Vinaigrette (page 503)

2 tbsp / 30 mL chopped basil

½ tsp / 2.5 mL kosher salt

¼ tsp / 1.25 mL coarse grind black pepper

2¼ lb / 1 kg trimmed yellowfin tuna fillet

1 oz / 30 g chervil leaves

½ oz / 14 g parsley leaves

1 oz / 30 g chives, cut into ½-in / 1-cm lengths

5 oz / 140 g baby arugula, washed and dried

5 oz / 140 g mizuna lettuce, washed and dried

5 oz / 140 g radicchio, washed and dried, chiffonade

½ tsp / 2.5 mL kosher salt

¼ tsp / 1.25 mL coarse grind black pepper

1 cup / 240 mL Balsamic Vinaigrette (page 503)

1. Toss together the tomato concassé, vinaigrette, basil, salt, and pepper and marinate for 1 hour.

2. Cut the tuna into 3½-oz / 100-g portions. Refrigerate until needed.

3. Combine the herbs and lettuces. Refrigerate until needed.

4. For each portion: Season 1 portion of tuna with salt and pepper. Grill to the desired doneness. Toss 1¾ oz / 50 g herb salad with 1 tbsp / 15 mL vinaigrette. Place the grilled tuna on a bed of the herb salad and top with 1 oz / 30 g of marinated tomatoes.

Portobello with Tuscan Bean Salad and Celery Juice

servings: **10**

portioning information:
**2 oz / 60 g mushroom,
3 oz / 85 g bean salad**

nutrition per serving:
103 calories, 6 g fat, 10 g total
carbohydrate, 3 g protein, 290 mg
sodium, 0 mg cholesterol

TUSCAN BEAN SALAD

4 oz / 115 g dried white beans

5 oz / 140 g small-dice carrot

3 oz / 85 g small-dice celery

1½ oz / 45 g small-dice red pepper

1½ oz / 45 g small-dice yellow pepper

1½ oz / 45 g small-dice scallion

1 cup / 240 mL Champagne Vinaigrette (see Note)

2 tbsp / 30 mL chopped chives

2 tbsp / 30 mL chopped parsley

1 tsp / 5 mL kosher salt

½ tsp / 2.5 mL ground black pepper

10 large portobello mushrooms caps, trimmed

1 tbsp / 15 mL olive oil

1¼ cups / 300 mL celery juice

2 oz / 55 g radicchio chiffonade

2 tbsp / 30 mL chopped cilantro

1. To prepare the bean salad, soak the beans until tender according to the instructions on page 108–109. Cool the beans and combine with the remaining salad ingredients. Marinate at room temperature for 2 hours.

2. Place the mushrooms on a baking sheet and brush with the oil. Cover with foil and bake in a 350°F / 175°C oven until tender, 15 to 20 minutes. Remove from the oven and grill for about 2 minutes on each side if desired.

3. For each portion: Slice 1 mushroom on the bias (or see Serving Suggestion below). Spoon approximately 3 oz / 85 g room-temperature bean salad in the center of the plate. Arrange the mushroom slices around the beans and garnish with 2 tbsp / 30 mL celery juice, 1½ tbsp / 22.5 mL radicchio, and ½ tsp / 2.5 mL cilantro.

Note

Substitute Champagne vinegar for red wine vinegar in the Vinaigrette-Style Dressing recipe (page 503).

Serving Suggestion

Garnish with brunoise vegetables for an attractive presentation. In the presentation shown here, the mushroom cap is left whole and topped with the bean salad.

Seared Scallops with Beet Vinaigrette

servings: **10**

portioning information: **3½ oz / 100 g scallops, ½ oz / 15 g salad, 2 tbsp / 30 mL**

nutrition per serving:
156 calories, 2 g fat, 12 g total carbohydrate, 23 g protein, 134 mg sodium, 53 mg cholesterol

BEET VINAIGRETTE

8 oz / 225 g beets

⅓ cup / 80 mL cider vinegar

3 tbsp / 45 mL extra-virgin olive oil

2 tsp / 10 mL chopped dill

1 tsp / 5 mL kosher salt

¼ tsp / 1.25 mL ground black pepper

2¼ lb / 1 kg sea scallops, muscle tabs removed

5 oz / 140 g mixed greens

3 oz / 85 g julienned carrot

3 oz / 85 g julienned daikon

1. Prepare the beet vinaigrette by simmering the beets in acidulated water until tender (see Note). When the beets are cool enough to handle, peel and chop. Place the beets and vinegar in a blender and purée until smooth. Whisk in the oil and season with the dill, salt, and pepper.

2. For each portion: Dry approximately 3½ oz / 100 g scallops with paper toweling and dry-sear in a seasoned sauté pan until brown on both sides and cooked through. Arrange the scallops with ½ oz / 14 g greens and 1 tbsp / 15 mL each of grated carrot and daikon on a room temperature plate. Drizzle with 2 tbsp / 30 mL beet vinaigrette and serve.

Note

For a more intense color and flavor, use a juice machine to juice the raw beets. Combine the juice and vinegar, whisk in the oil, and season with dill, salt, and pepper.

Scallop Seviche in Cucumber Cups

servings: **30**

portioning information:
1½ oz / 45 g

nutrition per serving:
48 calories, 4 g fat, 2 g total
carbohydrate, 0 g protein, 134 mg
sodium, 0 mg cholesterol

6 oz / 170 g sea scallops, cut into brunoise

1 tomato, peeled and seeded, cut into brunoise

1 tsp / 5 mL minced chives

1 tbsp / 15 mL chopped cilantro

½ jalapeño, minced

¼ green pepper, cut into brunoise

1 tbsp / 15 mL olive oil

5 drops Tabasco sauce

1 or 2 limes, juiced, as needed

2 tsp / 10 mL kosher salt

Ground black pepper, as needed

30 cucumber slices, ½ in / 1 cm thick

1½ oz / 45 g sour cream (optional)

2 tsp / 10 mL cilantro leaves (optional)

1. To make the seviche, combine the scallops, tomato, herbs, peppers, oil, and Tabasco. Add enough lime juice to coat the scallops. Season with salt and pepper. Marinate at least 8 hours, stirring occasionally.

2. Trim the cucumber slices with a round cutter to remove the rind. Scoop a pocket out of the middle of the cucumber slices. Do not cut all the way through the slice.

3. Fill the cucumber cups with the seviche. Garnish each seviche cup with a small dot of sour cream and a cilantro leaf, if desired (see page 226.)

Salmon Cakes with Cucumber Relish

servings: **10**

portioning information:
**2 cakes (2⅔ oz / 74 g),
½ oz / 45 g cucumber relish**

nutrition per serving:
179 calories, 7 g fat, 20 g total
carbohydrate, 9 g protein, 278 mg
sodium, 16 mg cholesterol

SALMON CAKES

14 oz / 400 g halved peeled Idaho potatoes

6½ oz / 185 g salmon, poached, cooled, flaked

5 oz / 140 g fresh bread crumbs

5 fl oz / 150 mL skim milk

1¾ oz / 50 g whole-grain mustard

1½ oz / 45 g mayonnaise

¾ oz / 20 g minced smoked salmon

½ oz / 14 g chopped capers

5 tsp / 25 mL chopped chives

5 tsp / 25 mL chopped dill

1 tsp / 5 mL coarse grind black pepper

CUCUMBER RELISH

5½ oz / 155 g diced seedless cucumber, skin on

5½ oz / 155 g tomato concassé

2¾ oz / 78 g diced red onion

1 tbsp / 15 mL minced jalapeño

4 tsp / 20 mL balsamic vinegar

1 tbsp / 15 mL chopped cilantro

2 tsp / 10 mL olive oil

1. Simmer the potatoes in water until tender. Drain and place the potatoes on a sheet pan in a warm oven to steam dry, about 5 minutes.

2. Purée the hot potatoes using a ricer or food mill. Allow the potatoes to cool to room temperature and combine with the remaining salmon cake ingredients. Form into 20 cakes weighing approximately 1⅓ oz / 37 g each.

3. To prepare the cucumber relish, toss the relish ingredients together (see Note).

4. For each portion: Cook 2 cakes in a preheated seasoned skillet until golden brown on each side, about 8 minutes. Serve the salmon cakes on a bed of approximately 1½ oz / 45 g of cucumber relish.

Note

Drain any excess liquid from the relish and reserve it to toss with mixed greens.

Asparagus with Lump Crabmeat and Sherry Vinaigrette

servings: **8**

portioning information:
**3 oz / 25 g vegetables,
1 oz / 30 g crabmeat**

nutrition per serving:
100 calories, 4 g fat, 6 g total
carbohydrate, 19 g protein, 514 mg
sodium, 45 mg cholesterol

1 lb / 500 g asparagus, green, white, or combined, peeled and trimmed

1 cup / 240 mL Vinaigrette-Style Dressing (page 503) (see Note)

8 oz / 250 g lump crabmeat, picked

8 oz /250 g julienned tomato

2 tbsp / 30 mL chopped chives

1. Cook the asparagus until barely tender in a large amount of boiling water. Shock and drain.

2. Gently toss the asparagus with the vinaigrette and marinate for at least 1 and up to 4 hours before serving.

3. For each portion: Arrange 2 oz / 50 g asparagus on a chilled plate and top with 1 oz / 30 g each crabmeat and tomatoes. Drizzle with additional vinaigrette. Scatter chives over each portion to garnish.

Note

Use sherry vinegar in the preparation of the dressing.

Asparagus with Morels

servings: **10**

portioning information:
3 oz / 85 g

nutrition per serving:
69 calories, 2 g fat, 11 g total carbohydrate, 4 g protein, 162 mg sodium, 0 mg cholesterol

2¾ tsp / 13.75 mL arrowroot

1 pt / 480 mL Vegetable Stock (page 490)

1 tbsp / 15 mL extra-virgin olive oil

1 oz / 30 g diced shallots

¾ oz / 20 g minced garlic

10 oz / 280 g fresh morels, cleaned and trimmed

3 lb / 1.35 kg asparagus, peeled and trimmed, blanched

2 tsp / 10 mL fresh lemon juice

1 tbsp / 15 mL chopped parsley

1 tbsp / 15 mL chopped chives

1 tsp / 5 mL kosher salt

¼ tsp / 1.25 mL ground black pepper

1. Combine the arrowroot with enough of the stock to form a smooth paste. Bring the remaining stock to a boil and stir in the arrowroot mixture. Return to a boil and stir constantly until the stock has thickened, about 2 minutes.

2. For each portion: Heat ¼ tsp / 1.25 mL oil in a skillet. Add 1 tsp / 5 mL shallots and ½ tsp / 2.5 mL garlic. Sweat until translucent. Add approximately 1 oz / 30 g morels and sauté until tender. Add approximately 3 oz / 85 g asparagus and 3 tbsp / 45 mL thickened stock; heat thoroughly. Remove the asparagus and arrange in a large heated soup bowl. Season the mushrooms with a dash of lemon juice and a pinch each of the herbs, salt, and pepper. Pour over the asparagus and serve immediately.

Note

This recipe may be prepared in larger batches, but it should be served quickly, as prolonged exposure to lemon will discolor the asparagus.

Prosciutto with Grilled Vegetables

servings: **10**

portioning information:
4½ oz / 135 g grilled vegetables, ¾ oz / 20 g prosciutto

nutrition per serving:
143 calories, 7 g fat, 14 g total carbohydrate, 8 g protein, 376 mg sodium, 14 mg cholesterol

7 oz / 200 g prosciutto

7½ oz / 205 g arugula

1¾ lb / 795 g Grilled Vegetables (page 369)

5 oz / 140 g roasted green peppers, 2- by 3-in / 5- by 8-cm pieces

5 oz / 140 g roasted red peppers, 2- by 3-in / 5- by 8-cm pieces

5 oz / 140 g roasted yellow peppers, 2- by 3-in / 5- by 8-cm pieces

1 lb / 450 g asparagus, peeled and trimmed, blanched

⅓ cup / 80 mL Balsamic Vinaigrette (page 503)

2 oz / 55 g shaved dry Jack cheese

1. Slice the prosciutto into 20 thin pieces.

2. For each portion: Place ¾ oz / 20 g arugula on a plate. Scatter 2½ oz / 70 g Grilled Vegetables, 1 oz / 30 g each roasted green, red, and yellow peppers, and 1½ oz / 45 g asparagus over the arugula.

3. Arrange 2 slices of prosciutto on top of each portion and drizzle the salad with 2 tsp / 10 mL vinaigrette. Garnish with a small amount of shaved cheese and serve.

Wild Mushroom and Goat Cheese Strudel

batch yield: **2 strudels**

servings: **10**

portioning information:
**1 slice (2½ oz / 70 g; ⅕ strudel),
3 tbsp / 45 mL sauce**

nutrition per serving:
118 calories, 5 g fat, 12 g total
carbohydrate, 6 g protein, 183 mg
sodium, 12 mg cholesterol

2 tbsp / 30 mL Vegetable Stock (page 490)

2 oz / 55 g minced shallots

¾ oz / 20 g minced garlic

1 lb / 450 g quartered wild mushrooms

⅓ cup / 80 mL dry white wine

2 oz / 55 g crumbled goat cheese

6 phyllo sheets (14- by 18-in / 35- by 45-cm)

1 oz / 30 g melted butter

SAUCE

1¾ cups / 420 mL Fond de Veau Lié (page 492)

2 tbsp / 30 mL Madeira, port, Marsala, or sherry wine

2 tbsp / 30 mL chopped sage, tarragon, chives, or marjoram

1. Heat the stock in a large sauté pan. Add the shallots and garlic and sweat until the shallots are translucent.

2. Add the mushrooms and sauté until cooked and the juices have reduced.

3. Deglaze the pan with the wine and reduce until almost dry. Remove the pan from the heat and spread the mixture on a sheet pan to cool completely.

4. Combine the goat cheese with the cooled mushrooms.

5. To prepare 1 strudel, stack 3 sheets of phyllo. Brush the top sheet with 1½ tsp / 7.5 mL butter. Mound half the mushroom mixture along the long edge of the dough. Roll the strudel tightly, completely enclosing the mushroom mixture. Brush the top of the strudel with 1½ tsp / 7.5 mL butter. Repeat to assemble the second strudel.

6. Place the strudels on a sheet pan and score to indicate 5 even portions from each strudel. Bake the strudels in a 350°F / 175°C oven until golden brown, about 15 minutes.

7. To prepare the sauce, heat the fond in a small sauce pot. Add the wine and simmer until the alcohol dissipates, about 5 minutes. Remove from the heat and stir in the herbs.

8. For each portion: Serve a slice of strudel on a pool of approximately 3 tbsp / 45 mL heated sauce.

Mussels in Saffron and White Wine Sauce

servings: **10**

portioning information:
12 mussels, ¼ cup / 60 mL sauce

nutrition per serving:
183 calories, 6 g fat, 10 g total carbohydrate, 17 g protein, 435 mg sodium, 46 mg cholesterol

½ oz / 14 g butter

½ oz / 14 g chopped garlic

7 fl oz / 210 mL dry white wine

3 tbsp / 45 mL heavy cream

2 tsp / 10 mL saffron threads

1¾ oz / 50 g thinly sliced scallions

5½ oz / 155 g tomato concassé

2 tbsp / 30 mL fresh lemon juice

1 pt / 480 mL Fish Velouté (page 497)

10 dozen mussels, cleaned and debearded

2 tbsp / 30 mL chopped chives

1. Heat the butter in a large soup pot. Add the garlic and sauté until aromatic. Add the wine, cream, and saffron and simmer 5 minutes.

2. Add the scallions, tomatoes, lemon juice, and velouté. Simmer for 5 minutes, cool, and reserve until needed.

3. For each portion: Bring ¼ cup / 60 mL of the velouté mixture to a simmer in a medium pot. Add 12 mussels and cover the pot. Steam the mussels until their shells open, about 4 minutes. Place the mussels in a heated serving bowl. Stir approximately ½ tsp / 2.5 mL chives into the sauce and pour over the mussels.

Clams Steamed in Beer

servings: **10**

portioning information:
9 clams, 1½ oz / 45 g salsa, 1 slice bread, 1 tsp / 5 mL olivada

nutrition per serving:
224 calories, 3 g fat, 30 g total carbohydrate, 15 g protein, 606 mg sodium, 28 mg cholesterol

1 pt / 480 mL water

1¼ pt / 600 mL beer

90 littleneck clams, scrubbed

1 lb / 450 g Tomato Salsa (page 485)

5 oz / 140 g diced lime flesh, membranes removed

1 oz / 30 g cilantro leaves

10 slices French bread (½ in / 1 cm thick), toasted

10 tsp / 50 mL Olivada (page 484)

1. For each portion: Bring 3 tbsp / 45 mL water and ¼ cup / 60 mL beer to a simmer in a small pot. Add 9 clams and cover the pot. Steam until the clams open, about 5 minutes.

2. Arrange the clams and ¼ cup / 60 mL of the cooking liquid in a large heated soup bowl.

3. Garnish with 1½ oz / 45 g tomato salsa, ½ oz / 14 g diced lime, a few cilantro leaves, and 1 slice of French bread spread with 1 tsp / 5 mL olivada.

Medallions of Lobster with Asian Vegetables

servings: **10**

portioning information:
2 oz / 55 g lobster, 1½ oz / 45 g salad, 2 croutons

nutrition per serving:
167 calories, 6 g fat, 10 g total carbohydrate, 15 g protein, 418 mg sodium, 42 mg cholesterol

2 lobsters (about 1 lb / 450 g each)

1 lb / 450 g Marinated Asian Vegetable Salad (page 206)

1 qt / 1 L Fish Fumet (page 491)

HERB PESTO

2 oz / 55 g spinach

2 tbsp / 30 mL minced basil

4 tsp / 20 mL chopped cilantro

1 tbsp / 15 mL chopped mint

1 tsp / 5 mL minced garlic

½ tsp / 2.5 mL extra-virgin olive oil

½ cup / 120 mL Vegetable Stock (page 490)

½ cup / 120 mL Tomato Coulis (page 498)

20 French Bread Croutons (page 513)

1. Poach the lobsters in a large pot of boiling water until the shells turn bright red, about 8 to 10 minutes. Remove the meat from the shells. Slice the tail meat into 30 even medallions and refrigerate until needed. Dice the claw meat, toss with the Asian vegetable salad, and reserve until needed.

2. Prepare a lobster stock by dry-sautéing the lobster shells in a large stockpot. Cover the shells with the fumet and simmer for 30 minutes. Strain the stock, return it to the pot, and reduce to yield ¼ cup / 60 mL of liquid.

3. Prepare the herb pesto by combining the spinach, herbs, and garlic in a blender. Purée to make a coarse paste. While processing, gradually add the oil and stock until the paste is smooth.

4. For each portion: Decorate a plate by dotting, puddling, or squirting on 2½ tsp / 12.5 mL tomato coulis, 2 tsp / 10 mL pesto, and 1 tsp / 5 mL reduced lobster stock. Mound about 1½ oz / 45 g of the salad in the center of a plate. Arrange 3 medallions of lobster over the salad. Garnish the plate with 2 croutons.

Vietnamese Summer Rolls

servings: 14

portioning information:
1 summer roll, 1 tbsp / 15 mL dipping sauce

nutrition per serving:
152 calories, 0 g fat, 30 g total carbohydrate, 6 g protein, 603 mg sodium, 25 mg cholesterol

DIPPING SAUCE

2 oz / 55 g sugar

¼ cup / 60 mL fish sauce

3 tbsp / 45 mL fresh lemon juice

3 tbsp / 45 mL rice wine vinegar

2 tbsp / 30 mL water

1 tbsp / 15 mL minced garlic

2 tsp / 10 mL chili sauce

FILLING

6 oz / 170 g rice noodles

8 oz / 225 g shrimp (26–30 count)

6 oz / 170 g finely julienned carrots

½ tsp / 2.5 mL kosher salt

4 oz / 115 g iceberg lettuce chiffonade

1½ tsp / 7.5 mL sugar

¼ cup / 60 mL fresh lemon juice

1 oz / 30 g sugar

1 cup / 240 mL warm water

14 rice paper wrappers (8-in / 20-cm)

½ oz / 14 g cilantro leaves

1. Whisk together the dipping sauce ingredients and refrigerate.

2. Cook the rice noodles in boiling water. Shock the noodles in cold water and drain.

3. Blanch the shrimp in boiling water until cooked, about 3 minutes. Shock, peel, and clean the shrimp. Slice the shrimp in half lengthwise.

4. Toss the carrots with the salt and marinate for 10 minutes. Rinse thoroughly and blot any excess moisture from the carrots. Combine the noodles, carrots, lettuce, sugar, and lemon juice.

5. To assemble the summer rolls: Combine the sugar and warm water in a large bowl. Moisten 1 wrapper in the sugar water and place on a clean, flat-weave cloth. Place 2½ oz / 70 g of the noodle mixture, 2 shrimp halves, and a few cilantro leaves in the center of each wrapper. Fold in each end of the wrapper and roll to completely encase the filling. Refrigerate until needed.

6. For each portion: Serve 1 cold summer roll with approximately 1 tbsp / 15 mL dipping sauce.

Mousseline-Style Forcemeat

batch yield: **2¾ lb / 1.25 kg**

servings: **22**

portioning information:
2 oz / 55 g

nutrition per serving:
78 calories, 0 g fat, 6 g total carbohydrate, 12 g protein, 153 mg sodium, 26 mg cholesterol

1½ cups / 360 mL Stock (pages 489, 490, and 491) (see Notes)

4 oz / 115 g raw white rice

2 lb / 910 g lean poultry, fish, or shellfish, cubed

1 tsp / 5 mL kosher salt

½ tsp / 2.5 mL ground white pepper

Seasonings, as needed (see Notes)

1 cup / 240 mL evaporated skim milk, cold

Garnish ingredients, as needed (see Notes)

1. Bring the stock to a boil. Add the rice and simmer gently until the liquid has been absorbed, about 18 minutes. Spread the rice on a sheet pan and refrigerate until thoroughly chilled.

2. Toss the cubed meat or fish with the salt, pepper, and seasonings. Refrigerate until well chilled.

3. Combine the meat mixture with the chilled rice and grind through a medium-hole die.

4. Put the ground mixture and half the milk into a chilled food processor bowl. Purée to form a smooth paste, scraping the sides of the bowl as necessary. Add the remaining milk and pulse just until incorporated. For a very fine texture, push the forcemeat through a drum sieve. Transfer the forcemeat to a metal bowl placed over an ice bath.

5. Poach a small amount of the forcemeat in water to test the consistency and seasoning. Make any necessary adjustments. Add more evaporated skim milk or stock if the forcemeat is too dry, or grind more meat and add if the forcemeat is too loose.

6. Fold the garnish ingredients into the forcemeat. Refrigerated until needed.

Serving Suggestions

Choose the stock to complement the meat or fish you are using. Seasoning choices include herbs, spices, or 2 tbsp / 30 mL of liquor or flavored liquid. Garnish choices include diced meat or fish that has been patted dry; vegetables, dried fruit, or nuts (used sparingly).

Variations

This basic recipe lists the standard ingredient amounts needed to prepare a mousseline-style forcemeat properly. This type of forcemeat can be used in a variety of applications, from pasta filling to terrines. Countless combinations of main ingredients, seasonings, and garnishes (up to 65 percent of a terrine may be garnish) may be used to customize the forcemeat in order to fit your needs.

To make a terrine: Lightly oil the inside of a covered mold, or spray with cooking spray. Line with plastic wrap, leaving a 2-in / 5-cm overhang, and pack with the forcemeat. Fold the overhang over the forcemeat and cover. Place in a 170°F / 75°C water bath and bake in a 325°F / 165°C oven to an internal temperature of 145°F / 62°C for fish or 165°F / 72°C for poultry. Cool the terrine to 120°F / 49°C and cover with foil-wrapped cardboard cut to fit inside the mold. Press with a brick or other heavy object and refrigerate for 8 to 10 hours before serving.

Mediterranean-Style Seafood Terrine

batch yield: **2 lb / 880 g**

servings: **16**

portioning information:
2 oz / 55 g

nutrition per serving:
86 calories, 4 g fat, 1 g total
carbohydrate, 11 g protein, 470 mg
sodium, 83 mg cholesterol

5 fl oz / 150 mL heavy cream

½ tsp / 2.5 mL saffron threads

18 oz / 510 g scallops, muscle tabs removed, quartered

½ tsp / 2.5 mL kosher salt

2 large egg whites

¼ tsp / 1.25 mL ground black pepper

1 lb / 450 g diced shrimp, peeled and deveined

1 tbsp / 15 mL chopped parsley

2 tsp / 10 mL chopped basil

1. Heat the cream to a simmer in a small saucepan. Add the saffron, remove from the heat, and allow to steep for 30 minutes. Chill thoroughly.

2. Place half the scallops and the salt into a chilled food processor bowl. Purée to form a smooth paste, scraping the sides of the bowl as necessary. Combine the chilled saffron cream, egg whites, and pepper. Add the mixture to the puréed scallops in thirds, pulsing the processor to incorporate. Transfer the forcemeat to a metal bowl placed over an ice bath.

3. Poach a small amount of the forcemeat in simmering water to test the consistency and seasoning. Make any necessary adjustments.

4. Pat dry the remaining scallops and the shrimp with paper towels. Fold the scallops, shrimp, parsley, and basil into the forcemeat.

5. Lightly oil the inside of a terrine mold, or spray with cooking spray. Line with plastic wrap, leaving a 2-in / 5-cm overhang, and pack with the forcemeat. Fold the overhang over the forcemeat and cover. Place in a 170°F / 75°C water bath and bake in a 325°F / 165°C oven to an internal temperature of 145°F / 62°C. Cool the terrine to 120°F / 49°C and cover with foil-wrapped cardboard cut to fit inside the mold. Press with a brick or other heavy object and refrigerate for 8 to 10 hours before slicing and serving.

Duck Terrine

batch yield: **4 lb / 1.80 kg**

servings: **32**

portioning information:
2 oz / 55 g

nutrition per serving:
83 calories, 2 g fat, 4 g total carbohydrate, 9 g protein, 59 mg sodium, 31 mg cholesterol

12 duck legs, skinless

3 pints / 1.4 L Chicken Stock (page 489)

1 qt / 750 mL dry red wine

1 Bouquet Garni (page 490)

6 oz / 170 g small-dice carrots

6 oz / 170 g small-dice parsnips

6 oz / 170 g small-dice celeriac

6 oz / 170 g small-dice leeks

1½ cups / 360 mL raspberry vinegar

2 tbsp / 30 mL red wine vinegar

1 oz / 30 g chopped chives

¾ oz / 20 g chopped parsley

½ oz / 14 g chopped rosemary

2½ tsp / 12.5 mL ground black pepper

1. Grill the duck legs just until marked.

2. Place the duck legs, stock, wine, and bouquet garni in a braising pan. Bring to a simmer over medium heat, then braise in a 325°F / 165°C oven until fork tender, about 2½ hours. Discard the bouquet garni. Remove the legs from the braising liquid and reserve.

3. Add the vegetables to the liquid and simmer until tender. Remove the vegetables from the liquid and reserve. Reduce the liquid to 1 cup / 240 mL, or the consistency of syrup.

4. Reduce the raspberry vinegar by half over high heat.

5. When the duck is cool enough to handle, remove the meat from the bones and shred by hand into a large bowl.

6. Add the vegetables, reduced braising liquid and raspberry vinegar, red wine vinegar, herbs, and pepper to the shredded duck meat. Mix to combine.

7. Lightly oil the inside of two 2-lb / 910-g terrine molds, or spray with cooking spray. Line with plastic wrap, leaving a 2-in / 5-cm overhang. Fill each terrine with half the warm duck mixture and cover with the plastic wrap.

8. Cover each terrine with a piece of Styrofoam wrapped in plastic wrap that will fit just inside the lip of the terrine molds. Press each terrine with at least 5 lb / 2.25 kg of weight and refrigerate for 8 to 10 hours before slicing.

Grilled Bell Pepper and Eggplant Terrine

batch yield: 2 lb / 880 g

servings: **16**

portioning information:
2 oz / 55 g

nutrition per serving:
126 calories, 6 g fat, 18 g total
carbohydrate, 4 g protein, 334 mg
sodium, 0 mg cholesterol

1 lb / 450 g sliced eggplant, ¼ in / 6 mm thick

3 lb / 1.35 kg red peppers

3 lb / 1.35 kg yellow peppers

3 lb / 1.35 kg green peppers

½ oz / 14 g gelatin (powder or sheet)

1½ cups / 360 mL Vinaigrette-Style Dressing (page 503)

2 tsp / 10 mL kosher salt

½ tsp / 2.5 mL ground black pepper

1. Grill the eggplant and peppers until the eggplant is tender and the peppers are blackened. Peel and seed the peppers.

2. Lightly oil the inside of a 3-lb / 1.35-kg terrine mold, or spray with cooking spray. Line with plastic wrap, leaving a 2-in / 5-cm overhang. Trim the vegetables to fit the mold.

3. Dissolve the gelatin in the vinaigrette.

4. Layer the peppers and eggplant alternately with the dressing to fill the mold. Sprinkle each layer with salt and pepper. Cover with plastic wrap.

5. Cover the terrine with a piece of Styrofoam wrapped in plastic wrap that will fit just inside the lip of the terrine mold. Press the terrine with at least 5 lb / 2.25 kg of weight and refrigerate for 8 to 10 hours before slicing. The terrine can be properly wrapped and refrigerated for up to 7 days.

Serving Suggestion

Serve each portion with 2 small slices French bread, grated Parmesan, and a small green salad.

Cucumber Granité

batch yield: 2¼ lb / 1 kg

servings: **10**

portioning information:
3½ oz / 100 g

nutrition per serving:
30 calories, 0 g fat, 6 g total
carbohydrate, 1 g protein, 8 mg
sodium, 0 mg cholesterol

2¼ lb / 1 kg chopped, peeled, and seeded cucumber

3 tbsp / 45 mL Champagne vinegar

3 tbsp / 45 mL sugar

1 large egg white, lightly beaten

1. Purée the ingredients in a blender. Pour the purée into a half hotel pan and place in the freezer. Stir frequently as the mixture freezes to form large crystals.

2. Serve as an intermezzo course or as a garnish for Chilled Gazpacho (page 187).

6

Main Dishes for Lunches and Dinners

THE BIG LESSON we all seem to need to learn again and again is that calories count. The chef's challenge is to make them all count for something good. Building an entrée around a big steak is a bad idea from a nutritional standpoint. It is also far from the standards being set in restaurants around the country and around the world. Even when a piece of fish or beef or veal is the showpiece of the plate, you can create healthier menu options by introducing vegetable-laden sauces, whole grain side dishes or stuffings, and a selection of fresh, colorful, seasonal vegetables.

Seared Cod in a Rich Broth with Fall Vegetables, Chive Pasta, and Ginger-Scallion Butter

servings: **10**

portioning information:
3½ oz / 100 g cod, 4 fl oz / 120 mL consommé, 3 oz / 85 g vegetables, 2 oz / 55 g pasta

nutrition per serving:
312 calories, 1 g fat, 47 g total carbohydrate, 27 g protein, 325 mg sodium, 44 mg cholesterol

2¼ lb / 1 kg cod fillet

1 tsp / 5 mL kosher salt

½ tsp / 2.5 mL ground white pepper

4 oz / 115 g dried shiitake mushrooms, ground to a powder

2½ pt / 1.20 L Mushroom Consommé (page 168)

5 oz / 140 g julienned carrots

5 oz / 140 g julienned yellow turnips

5 oz / 140 g julienned white turnips

1 lb / 450 g haricots verts, 1-in / 3-cm lengths

1¼ lb / 570 g Chive Pasta (page 398; see Note)

3 oz / 85 g enoki mushrooms, 1½-in / 4-cm lengths

1 tbsp / 15 mL chives, ½-in / 1-cm lengths

5 tsp / 25 mL Ginger-Scallion Butter (page 510)

1. Portion the cod into 3½-oz / 100-g pieces. Season with the salt and pepper. Dredge the cod in the mushroom powder. Reserve.

2. For each portion: Brown one piece of cod on both sides in a preheated sauté pan. Transfer the cod to a 450°F / 230°C oven and bake until thoroughly cooked, about 5 minutes. Heat 4 fl oz / 120 mL of the consommé in a sauce pot. Add ½ oz / 15 g each of the carrots and turnips, 1½ oz / 45 g of the haricots verts, and 2 oz / 57 g pasta in the consommé and cook at a bare simmer until the vegetables are tender and the pasta is cooked through and tender.

3. Place a piece of cod in a heated soup plate and spoon the consommé, vegetables, and pasta around the cod. Top with the enoki, chives, and a thin slice (½ tsp / 2.5 mL) of ginger-scallion butter.

Note

Chive pasta variation in the Basic Pasta Dough recipe on page 398.

Sautéed Squid and Steamed Mussels with Cannellini Beans, Spinach, and Pancetta

servings: **10**

portioning information:
**3 oz / 85 g bean mixture,
2 oz / 55 g squid, 4 mussels,
1 tsp / 5 mL Parmesan**

nutrition per serving:
320 calories, 10 g fat, 21 g total
carbohydrate, 29 g protein, 830 mg
sodium, 170 mg cholesterol

1¼ lb / 565 g squid

2 lb / 910 g mussels (about 40), scrubbed and debearded

1 pt / 480 mL white wine

2 oz / 55 g sliced pancetta

4½ oz / 125 g sliced red onion

½ oz / 14 g thinly sliced garlic

4 oz / 115 g sliced fennel

14 oz / 400 g cooked cannellini beans

10½ oz / 300 g spinach

13 oz / 370 g tomato concassé

1 tbsp / 15 mL basil chiffonade

1 tbsp / 15 mL chopped oregano

1 tsp / 5 mL kosher salt

¼ tsp / 1.25 mL ground black pepper

1 tbsp / 15 mL olive oil

10 tsp / 50 mL coarsely grated Parmesan

5 tsp / 25 mL chopped parsley

1. Cut the bodies of the squid into thin rings. Leave the tentacles whole. Divide into 2-oz / 6-g portions. Refrigerate.

2. Steam the mussels in the wine. Remove the mussels from the pot and reserve. Strain the cooking liquid and reserve.

3. In a large sauté pan, render the pancetta until crisp. Add the onion, garlic, and fennel and sauté, stirring frequently, until the fennel is tender. Add the beans, spinach, tomatoes, herbs, and enough of the reserved cooking liquid from the mussels to wilt the spinach. Season with the salt and pepper. Reserve.

4. For each portion: heat a pan over high heat. Add just enough oil to barely film the pan. Add one portion of the squid and sauté the squid until opaque, about 2 minutes. In a separate pan, reheat 3 oz / 85 g of the bean mixture. Add 2 tbsp / 30 mL wine. Add 4 mussels, cover the pan, and steam until the mussels open, about 3 minutes.

5. For each portion: Spoon 3 oz / 85 g bean mixture in the center of a soup plate. Lay 3½ oz / 100 g squid on the beans and arrange 4 mussels around the perimeter of the bowl. Garnish with 1 tsp / 5 mL each Parmesan and chopped parsley.

Seared Atlantic Salmon with Corn, Potato, and Arugula Salad

servings: **10**

portioning information:
4½ oz / 135 g salad, 3½ oz / 100 g salmon, 2 tbsp / 30 mL coulis, ½ oz / 12 g cherry tomatoes

nutrition per serving:
411 calories, 20 g fat, 32 g total carbohydrate, 26 g protein, 509 mg sodium, 60 mg cholesterol

CORN, POTATO, AND ARUGULA SALAD

1 tbsp / 15 mL Dijon mustard

1½ fl oz / 45 mL fresh lemon juice

¾ fl oz / 20 mL fresh lime juice

¾ oz / 20 g sugar

2 fl oz / 60 mL peanut oil

2 tbsp / 30 mL extra-virgin olive oil

1¼ lb / 565 g corn kernels

1¼ lb / 565 g Bliss potatoes, cooked and sliced

5 oz / 140 g arugula

2 tbsp / 6 g chopped cilantro

½ tsp / 2.5 mL kosher salt

¼ tsp / 1.25 mL ground black pepper

¼ tsp / 1.25 mL Tabasco sauce

2¼ lb / 1 kg salmon fillet

1 tsp / 5 mL kosher salt

½ tsp / 2.5 mL ground black pepper

1 tbsp / 15 mL chopped chives

10 tsp / 7 g chopped parsley

10 tsp / 7 g chopped chervil

10 fl oz / 300 mL Yellow Tomato Coulis (page 499)

4 oz / 115 g halved cherry tomatoes

1. To prepare the salad, combine the mustard, juices, and sugar. Slowly whisk in the oils. Toss together the corn, potatoes, arugula, cilantro, and dressing. Season with the salt, pepper, and Tabasco.

2. Portion the salmon into 3½-oz / 100-g tranches. Season with the salt and pepper.

3. Heat a large sauté pan. Sear the salmon on 1 side, flip, and finish in a 325°F / °165°C oven until medium doneness.

4. For each portion: Place 4½ oz / 135 g salad in the middle of a warm plate. Sprinkle the chopped herbs on the salad and place a portion of salmon on top of the salad. Pour 2 tbsp / 30 mL coulis around the salmon and garnish with cherry tomatoes.

Lobster Wrapped in Rice Paper with Asian Salad

servings: **10**

portioning information:
2½ oz / 70 g Asian salad, 2 lobster rolls, 1 fl oz / 30 mL vinaigrette

nutrition per serving:
302 calories, 11 g fat, 30 g total carbohydrate, 17 g protein, 728 mg sodium, 45 mg cholesterol

ASIAN SALAD

1 tsp / 5 mL peanut oil

3 oz / 85 g julienned shiitake mushrooms

1½ tbsp / 25 mL reduced sodium soy sauce

4 oz / 115 g julienned carrots

6 oz / 170 g bean sprouts

6 oz / 170 g julienned snow peas

5 oz / 140 g julienned daikon radish

2 oz / 60 g pickled ginger, chopped

2 oz / 60 g scallions, thinly sliced

5 oz / 140 g mixed greens

10 fl oz / 300 mL citrus vinaigrette

5 live lobsters, 1 lb / 450 g each

½ oz / 14 g butter

4 oz / 115 g julienned leek

1½ fl oz / 45 mL brandy

2 tsp / 10 mL kosher salt

½ tsp / 2.5 mL ground black pepper

20 (8-in / 20-cm) rice paper sheets

2 tbsp / 30 mL peanut oil

1. To make the Asian salad, heat the peanut oil in a large sauté pan. Add the shiitake mushrooms and sweat until tender. Add the soy sauce and reduce all the liquid. Chill completely. Combine the mushrooms with the remaining vegetables. Toss with the vinaigrette.

2. Add the lobsters to 3 gal / 11.52 L of boiling water. Boil for 3 minutes, just long enough to release the meat from the shell. Shock in ice water and drain. Remove all the meat from the tails, claws, and knuckles and cut into a medium dice.

3. Heat the butter in a large sauté pan. Add the leek and sweat until tender. Add the lobster meat, brandy, salt, and pepper. Continue to cook another 5 minutes, or until the lobster is cooked.

4. Remove the solids from the pan and reduce any excess liquid to a syrup. Add the reduced liquid to the lobster meat and chill thoroughly.

5. Soften the rice paper sheets in warm water for a few minutes; drain. Place 1½ oz / 45 g of the lobster mixture in each rice paper and roll to completely encase the mixture.

6. Heat the oil in a large skillet. Sauté the lobster rolls until golden brown on 2 sides.

7. Mound 2½ oz / 70 g of the Asian salad in the middle of a plate. Arrange 2 rolls over the greens. Dress the salad with 1 fl oz / 30 mL vinaigrette.

Stir-Fried Scallops

servings: **10**

portioning information:
6 oz/ 170 g stir-fry, 3¼ oz / 90 g rice

nutrition per serving:
292 calories, 9 g fat, 30 g total carbohydrate, 22 g protein, 238 mg sodium, 34 mg cholesterol

2¼ lb / 1 kg bay scallops

2 fl oz / 60 mL peanut oil

½ oz / 14 g minced ginger

½ oz / 14 g minced garlic

5 oz / 140 g julienned celery

2 oz / 55 g julienned red pepper

2 oz / 55 g julienned yellow pepper

2 oz / 55 g julienned green pepper

4 oz / 115 g snow peas

2 oz / 55 g quartered white mushrooms

4 oz / 115 g julienned zucchini

12 fl oz / 360 mL Fish Fumet (page 491)

1½ tsp / 7.50 mL hot bean paste

1 tbsp / 15 mL red bean paste

½ oz / 14 g cornstarch

1 tbsp / 15 mL oyster sauce

2 lb / 900 g cooked brown rice

3½ oz / 100 g thinly sliced scallions

1 oz / 30 g black sesame seeds, toasted

1. Blot excess moisture from the scallops with a paper towel.

2. Heat half of the oil in a wok or large sauté pan. Sear the scallops in the oil. Remove from the pan and reserve.

3. Heat the remaining oil in the pan. Add the ginger and garlic and stir-fry until aromatic.

4. Add the celery, peppers, peas, mushrooms, and zucchini. Stir-fry until the zucchini is almost cooked.

5. Combine the stock, bean pastes, cornstarch, and oyster sauce. Add to the vegetables and bring to a boil while stirring constantly, until the liquid has thickened.

6. Return the scallops to the pan and toss to evenly distribute.

7. For each portion: Serve 6 oz / 170 g stir-fry on 3¼ oz / 90 g rice and garnish with the scallions and sesame seeds.

Seared Cod with Shellfish, Tomato-Fennel Broth, Saffron Pasta, and Chorizo

servings: **10**

portioning information:
**2 oz / 55 g pasta, 2 oz /
55 g cooked cod, 2 littleneck
clams, 7½ oz / 210 g
vegetables and chorizo**

nutrition per serving:
590 calories, 14 g fat, 70 g total
carbohydrate, 41 g protein, 1280 mg
sodium, 75 mg cholesterol

5 oz / 140 g dried chorizo sausage

20 littleneck clams

1¼ lb / 565 g cubed cod fillets

1 tsp / 5 mL kosher salt

¼ tsp / 0.625 mL ground black pepper

8 oz / 225 g flour for dredging

2 tbsp / 30 mL clarified butter

1 tbsp / 15 mL olive oil

2 oz / 55 g minced shallots

1½ qt / 1.45 L Chicken Stock (page 489)

20 mussels

8 oz / 225 g wedge-cut fennel, cooked

8 oz / 225 g tomato concassé

6 oz / 170 g roasted red peppers

6 oz / 170 g roasted yellow peppers

2½ lb / 1.15 kg spinach

1¼ lb / 565 g Saffron Pasta (page 400), cooked

1. Blanch the chorizo in salted water for 1 minute. Cut each sausage in half lengthwise and cut each half into ⅛-in / 3-mm half-moon shapes.

2. Steam the clams in water until they have opened. Drain the clams and reserve.

3. Season the cod with the salt and pepper and dredge in the flour. Heat the butter in a large sauté pan. Brown the cod in the butter until thoroughly cooked.

4. Heat the oil in a large sauce pan. Add the shallots and chorizo and sweat until the shallots are translucent.

5. Add the stock and the mussels. Cover and steam for 1 minute, until the mussels have opened. Add the presteamed clams.

6. Add the fennel, tomatoes, peppers, and spinach. Heat until the spinach is wilted and the other vegetables are hot.

7. For each portion: Place 2 oz / 55 g pasta in the middle of a large soup plate. Place 2 oz / 55 g cooked cod on top of the pasta and spoon 7½ oz / 210 g shellfish and vegetables around the cod.

Salmon with Spinach and Sparkling Wine–Butter Sauce

servings: **10**

portioning information:
1½ oz / 45 g spinach, 1⅔ fl oz / 48 mL sauce, 3½ oz / 100 g salmon

nutrition per serving:
290 calories, 20 g fat, 5 g total carbohydrate, 23 g protein, 600 mg sodium, 80 mg cholesterol

2 fl oz / 60 mL Chicken Stock (page 489)

½ oz / 14 g minced shallots

1 lb / 450 g spinach, wilted and drained

2¼ lb / 1 kg salmon fillet

1 tsp / 5 mL kosher salt

¼ tsp / 0.625 mL ground black pepper

2 tsp / 10 mL olive oil

1 pt / 480 mL Sparkling Wine–Butter Sauce (page 497)

½ oz / 14 g chives, snipped into ½-in / 1-cm lengths

1. Heat the stock in a large sauté pan. Add the shallots and sweat until translucent.

2. Add the spinach and cook until very hot. Drain any excess liquid. Keep warm.

3. Cut the salmon into 3½-oz / 100-g slices. Season with the salt and pepper.

4. Heat the oil in a large sauté pan and sear the salmon on both sides. Cook until medium rare or desired doneness.

5. For each portion: Place 1½ oz / 45 g spinach in the middle of a plate and pour a circle of 1⅔ fl oz / 48 mL sauce around the spinach. Lay a piece of salmon on top and randomly sprinkle the chives in the sauce.

Stir-Fried Shrimp with Lo Mein and Ginger-Sesame Vinaigrette

servings: 10

portioning information:
3½ oz / 91 g stir-fry on a bed of 4 oz / 115 g lo mein noodles

nutrition per serving:
380 calories, 13 g fat, 40 g total carbohydrate, 27 g protein, 707 mg sodium, 155 mg cholesterol

2¼ lb / 1 kg shrimp (25–30 count), peeled, deveined

10 fl oz / 300 mL ginger-sesame vinaigrette

2 lb / 910 g fresh lo mein noodles

1 tbsp / 15 mL peanut oil

10 oz / 280 g julienned green cabbage

7 oz / 200 g julienned carrots

10 oz / 280 g thickly sliced shiitake mushrooms

2 oz / 55 g thinly sliced scallions, cut on the diagonal

1 tbsp / 15 mL white sesame seeds, toasted

1 tbsp / 15 mL black sesame seeds, toasted

1. Toss the shrimp in half the vinaigrette and allow to marinate for at least 2 hours.

2. Cook the noodles in boiling salt water. Shock, drain, and toss in the remaining vinaigrette.

3. Heat the oil in a wok or large sauté pan. Remove the shrimp from the marinade and sear in the hot oil. Remove from the pan and reserve. (Reserve the shrimp marinade and add as necessary when stir-frying the vegetables.)

4. Add the cabbage, carrots, and mushrooms to the hot pan. Stir-fry until the vegetables are tender, adding a little of the reserved marinade to moisten as necessary.

5. Return the shrimp and any remaining reserved marinade to the pan. Toss to evenly distribute and heat thoroughly.

6. For each portion: Serve 6½ oz / 185 g stir-fry on a bed of 3½ oz / 91 g lo mein noodles and garnish with the scallions and sesame seeds.

Broiled Red Snapper with Lime-Cilantro Vinaigrette

servings: 10

portioning information:
5 oz / 140 g salad, 3½ oz / 100 g snapper

nutrition per serving:
250 calories, 11 g fat, 17 g total carbohydrate, 22 g protein, 120 mg sodium, 40 mg cholesterol

2¼ lb / 1 kg red snapper fillets, trimmed

10 fl oz / 300 mL Lime-Cilantro Vinaigrette (page 504)

7 oz / 200 g tomato concassé

2 red grapefruit, cut into suprêmes

2 yellow grapefruit, cut into suprêmes

1 avocado, thinly sliced

1. Score the skin of the fillets. Place the fish, skin side down, on a sizzler platter and brush with 1 fl oz / 30 mL of the vinaigrette.

2. Broil the snapper, turning once during cooking, until just cooked through, 5 to 7 minutes, depending upon the thickness of the fish.

3. Toss the tomatoes, grapefruit, and avocado with the remaining vinaigrette and serve 5 oz / 140 g with each portion of snapper.

Serving Suggestion

Instead of tossing the avocado and grapefruit with the vinaigrette, arrange the slices on the plate and spoon the vinaigrette on top of and around the plate, as shown here. The Black Bean Cake (page 389) adds not only more flavor and texture, but also height for greater visual appeal.

Broiled Red Snapper with Lime-Cilantro
Vinaigrette and Black Bean Cakes (page 389)

Grilled Swordfish with Roasted Red Pepper Salad

servings: **10**

portioning information:
3½ oz / 100 g swordfish, 3¼ oz / 90 g red pepper salad

nutrition per serving:
280 calories, 10 g fat, 23 g total carbohydrate, 25 g protein, 820 mg sodium, 55 mg cholesterol

2¼ lb / 1 kg swordfish

2 limes, thinly sliced

1½ oz / 45 g minced onion

1 tbsp / 15 mL white wine vinegar

1 tsp / 5 mL honey

¼ tsp / 0.625 mL ground white pepper

2 lb / 900 g Roasted Red Pepper Salad (page 204)

1. Cut the swordfish into 3½-oz / 100-g portions.

2. Combine the limes, onion, vinegar, honey, and white pepper and evenly spread on the swordfish. Refrigerate for 30 minutes.

3. Remove the limes from the swordfish, and grill the fish until thoroughly cooked.

4. Serve each portion with 3¼ oz / 90 g red pepper salad.

Grilled Salmon with Savoy Cabbage and Heirloom Bean Sauce

servings: **10**

portioning information:
3½ oz / 100 g salmon, 3¼ oz / 90 g cabbage, 2 oz / 57 g bean sauce

nutrition per serving:
423 calories, 15 g fat, 36 g total carbohydrate, 36 g protein, 700 mg sodium, 78 mg cholesterol

2¼ lb / 1 kg salmon fillet

1 tsp / 5 mL kosher salt

¼ tsp / 1.25 mL ground black pepper

2 lb / 910 g Warm Cabbage Salad (page 205)

1¼ lb / 570 g Heirloom Bean Sauce (page 499)

1. Portion the salmon into 3½-oz / 100-g tranches. Season with the salt and pepper.

2. Lightly grill the salmon on both sides. Finish cooking in a 375°F / 190°C oven until medium doneness.

3. For each portion: Spoon 3¼ oz / 90 g heated cabbage in the middle of a plate. Ladle 2 oz / 57 g bean sauce around the cabbage and lay a piece of salmon on top of the cabbage.

Note

Heirloom beans are from a non-hybridized plant. An alternative to mass-marketed plants, heirlooms are thought to have better flavor than hybrids.

Grilled Halibut with Roasted Red Peppers and Warm Potato Salad

servings: 10

portioning information:
2½ oz / 70 g potato salad,
3½ oz / 100 g grilled halibut,
3¼ oz / 90 g pepper salad

nutrition per serving:
339 calories, 13 g fat, 31 g total
carbohydrate, 25 g protein, 438 mg
sodium, 33 mg cholesterol

2¼ lb / 1 kg halibut

1 tsp / 5 mL kosher salt

½ tsp / 2.5 mL ground black pepper

1½ lb / 680 g Warm Potato Salad (below)

2 lb / 900 g Roasted Peppers with Capers and Cumin

1. Portion the halibut into 3½-oz / 100-g tranches. Season with the salt and pepper and grill to specified doneness.

2. For each portion: Place 2½ oz / 70 g of the room-temperature potato salad in the center of a large plate. Lay a piece of grilled halibut over the potato salad and top with 3¼ oz / 90 g pepper salad.

Warm Potato Salad

servings: 10

portioning information:
3 oz / 85 g

nutrition per serving:
110 calories, 5 g fat, 18 g total
carbohydrate, 2 g protein, 135 mg
sodium, 0 mg cholesterol

2 fl oz / 60 mL extra-virgin olive oil

3 tbsp / 45 mL cider vinegar

3 tbsp / 45 mL chopped parsley

2 tbsp / 30 mL chopped shallots

1 tbsp / 15 mL Dijon mustard

1 tbsp / 15 mL chopped tarragon

½ tsp / 2.5 mL salt

2 lb / 900 g red bliss potatoes

Ground black pepper as needed

1. Combine the oil, vinegar, parsley, shallots, mustard, tarragon, and salt in a bowl.

2. Simmer the potatoes in water until tender. When they are cool enough to handle, slice them ½ inch / 125 mm thick. Immediately add them to the oil and vinegar mixture and toss gently until combined. Season with pepper and serve while still warm.

Grilled Herb Salmon with Southwest White Bean Stew, Jicama Salad (page 204)

Grilled Herbed Salmon with Southwest White Bean Stew

servings: **10**

portioning information:
3½ oz / 100 g salmon, 3 oz / 85 g warm bean stew

nutrition per serving:
268 calories, 9 g fat, 16 g total carbohydrate, 29 g protein, 133 mg sodium, 67 mg cholesterol

2¼ lb / 1 kg salmon fillet

SALMON MARINADE

2 tbsp /30 mL fresh lime juice

1 tbsp / 15 mL chopped parsley

1 tbsp / 15 mL chopped chives

1 tbsp / 15 mL chopped thyme

2 tsp / 10 mL ground black pepper

1 lb 14 oz / 850 g Southwest White Bean Stew (page 392)

1. Cut the salmon into 3½-oz / 100-g portions.

2. Combine the marinade ingredients and evenly spread them on the salmon. Refrigerate for 30 minutes.

3. Grill the salmon until thoroughly cooked. Serve each portion with 3 oz / 85 g warm bean stew.

Note

A mixture of julienned jicama and haricot verts tossed with 1 tsp / 5 mL of Lime-Cilantro Vinaigrette (page 504) is a good accompaniment for the salmon as shown on the facing page. Spoon up to 1 tbsp / 15 mL vinaigrette over the fish if desired for an additional 30 calories per serving.

Grilled Swordfish with Black Pepper Pasta

servings: **10**

portioning information:
**3½ oz / 100 g swordfish,
1½ oz / 45 g pasta, 3 oz /
85 g tomato and olive
mixture**

nutrition per serving:
280 calories, 9 g fat, 23 g total
carbohydrate, 25 g protein, 820 mg
sodium, 55 mg cholesterol

2¼ lb / 1 kg swordfish	1 lb 5 oz / 595 g Smoked Tomatoes (see Note), halved	
½ oz / 14 g dried parsley	5 fl oz / 150 mL balsamic vinegar	
½ oz / 14 g dried chives	2 tsp / 10 mL kosher salt	
½ oz / 14 g dried thyme	1 tsp / 1 g basil chiffonade	
1¾ fl oz / 50 mL olive oil	1 lb / 450 g Black Pepper Pasta (page 398), cooked and drained	
¾ oz / 20 g minced garlic	1¼ pt / 600 mL Fond de Veau Lié (page 492)	
¾ oz / 20 g minced shallots		
3½ oz / 100 g Kalamata olives, pitted and halved		

1. Cut the swordfish into 3½-oz / 100-g portions. Combine the parsley, chives, and thyme and rub the swordfish with the mixture.

2. Heat the oil in a large sauté pan. Add the garlic and shallots and sauté until the shallots are translucent.

3. Add the olives and tomatoes and sauté until heated. Add the vinegar, salt, and basil and toss to fully incorporate. Reserve.

4. Grill the swordfish until thoroughly cooked, about 2 minutes on each side.

5. Toss the pasta and the fond de veau lié together in a sauté pan until the pasta is very hot.

6. For each portion: Lay a piece of swordfish on a bed of 1½ oz / 45 g pasta and top with 3 oz / 85 g tomato and olive mixture.

Note

To smoke the tomatoes, follow the instructions in the recipe for Cassoulet with Smoked Tomatoes, step 1, on page 282.

Spicy Asian Grilled Shrimp

servings: **10**

portioning information:
3½ oz / 100 g shrimp, 2 oz / 57 g salad

nutrition per serving:
200 calories, 9 g fat, 8 g total carbohydrate, 18 g protein, 320 mg sodium, 151 mg cholesterol

2¼ lb / 1 kg shrimp (21–25 count), peeled, butterflied

1½ tsp / 3 g five-spice powder

1 tsp / 5 mL Tabasco sauce

1½ tsp / 4.50 g minced ginger

½ oz / 14 g minced garlic

1 fl oz /30 mL rice wine vinegar

1 tsp / 5 mL fish sauce (nuoc mam)

1 tsp / 5 mL sesame oil

20 oz / 570 g Marinated Asian Vegetable Salad (page 206)

1. Combine the shrimp with the remaining ingredients and marinate, refrigerated, for at least 1 hour.

2. Grill the shrimp until thoroughly cooked, about 2 minutes on each side.

3. For each portion: Serve 3½ oz / 100 g shrimp on a bed of 2 oz / 57 g salad.

Grilled Yellowfin Tuna with Citrus Salad

servings: **10**

portioning information:
3½ oz / 100 g tuna, 5 oz / 140 g citrus salad

nutrition per serving:
233 calories, 8 g fat, 16 g total carbohydrate, 25 g protein, 299 mg sodium, 46 mg cholesterol

2¼ lb / 1 kg yellowfin tuna

1 tbsp / 15 mL olive oil

CITRUS SALAD

14 oz / 400 g pink grapefruit sections

14 oz / 400 g white grapefruit sections

9 oz / 255 g orange sections

1¾ oz / 50 g blood orange sections

2½ oz / 70 g lime sections

¾ oz / 20 g lemon sections

2½ oz / 70 g diced red onion

1 oz / 30 g minced roasted jalapeño

½ tsp / 2.5 mL ground black pepper

1 lb 5 oz / 600 g julienned fennel, blanched

1. Cut the tuna into 3½-oz / 100-g steaks. Brush the tuna with the oil and grill for about 3 minutes on each side.

2. Combine the citrus salad ingredients in a large sauté pan and heat just until warmed.

3. For each portion: Serve 5 oz / 140 g citrus salad with a piece of grilled tuna.

Grilled Soft Shell Crabs

servings: **10**

portioning information:
3½ oz / 100 g crabs, 2 oz / 55 g salsa, 2 oz / 55 g black bean sauce

nutrition per serving:
74 calories, 3 g fat, 1 g total carbohydrate, 8 g protein, 124 mg sodium, 33 mg cholesterol

CRAB MARINADE

4 fl oz / 120 mL fresh lemon juice

2 oz / 55 g minced red pepper

14 fl oz / 420 mL red wine vinegar

14 fl oz / 420 mL dry white wine

3 fl oz / 90 mL extra-virgin olive oil

2 oz / 55 g minced scallions

2 jalapeños, roasted and minced

1 tbsp / 15 mL chopped basil

1 tbsp / 15 mL chopped fennel tops

1 tbsp / 15 mL chopped tarragon

1 tbsp / 15 mL chopped thyme

½ oz / 14 g minced garlic

10 soft-shell crabs (about 2¼ lb / 1 kg), cleaned

20 oz / 560 g Green Papaya Salsa (page 486)

20 oz / 560 g Barley and Wheat Berry Pilaf (page 379)

1. Combine the ingredients for the crab marinade in a shallow pan. Add the crabs, cover, and marinate for at least 2 hours.

2. For each portion, grill 1 crab over medium-high heat until thoroughly cooked, about 2 minutes on each side. Serve with 2 oz / 55 g salsa and 2 oz / 55 g pilaf.

Grilled Swordfish with Lentil Ragoût and Horseradish and Apple Cream Dressing

servings: **10**

portioning information:
3½ oz / 100 g swordfish, 3 fl oz / 90 mL ragoût, 1 tbsp / 15 mL dressing

nutrition per serving:
167 calories, 5 g fat, 8 g total carbohydrate, 22 g protein, 165 mg sodium, 40 mg cholesterol

2¼ lb / 1 kg swordfish

SWORDFISH MARINADE

¾ fl oz / 20 mL fresh lime juice

½ oz / 14 g minced shallots

½ oz / 14 g minced garlic

½ tsp / 2.5 mL chopped chervil

2 lb / 910 mL Lentil Ragoût (page 501)

5 fl oz / 150 mL Horseradish and Apple Cream Dressing (page 509)

1. Cut the swordfish into 3½-oz / 100-g portions.

2. Combine the marinade ingredients and evenly spread them on the swordfish. Refrigerate for 30 minutes.

3. For each portion: Grill a portion of swordfish over medium-high heat until thoroughly cooked. Reheat a 3 fl oz / 90 mL of the ragout and make a bed of the ragoût on a heated plate, top with the swordfish, and finish with 1 tbsp / 15 mL dressing.

Grilled Soft Shell Crabs with Barley
and Wheat Berry Pilaf (page 379)

Broiled Swordfish with Tomatoes, Anchovies, and Garlic

servings: 10

portioning information:
3½ oz / 100 g swordfish, 3 tbsp / 45 mL tomato mixture

nutrition per serving:
162 calories, 6 g fat, 4 g total carbohydrate, 20 g protein, 167 mg sodium, 39 mg cholesterol

2¼ lb / 1 kg swordfish

1 tsp / 5 mL minced garlic

½ oz / 14 g chopped shallots

5 fl oz / 150 mL dry white wine

¾ oz / 20 g minced anchovy fillets

14 oz / 400 g tomato concassé

2 tbsp / 6 g basil chiffonade

1 tbsp / 15 mL olive oil

1. Cut the swordfish into 3½-oz / 100-g steaks. Reserve under refrigeration.

2. In a large sauté pan, sweat the garlic and shallots in the wine until the shallots are translucent. Add the anchovies and tomatoes and heat thoroughly. Remove from the heat, add the basil, and toss to incorporate.

3. For each portion: Brush a swordfish steak with a little oil. Broil until golden brown on both side, about 6 minutes. Spoon 3 tbsp / 45 mL tomato mixture over a swordfish steak.

Pan-Roasted Salmon with Moroccan Spices and Lentil Ragoût

servings: 10

portioning information:
3½ oz / 100 g salmon, 2 fl oz / 60 mL lentil ragoût, ⅔ oz / 17 g caramelized onions, ½ oz / 14 g frisée

nutrition per serving:
248 calories, 10 g fat, 12 g total carbohydrate, 27 g protein, 257 mg sodium, 69 mg cholesterol

2¼ lb / 1 kg salmon fillet

2 tsp / 4 g whole coriander seeds

2 tsp / 4 g whole cumin seeds

2 tsp / 4 g whole caraway seeds

2 tsp / 4 g cardamom seeds

2 tsp / 4 g anise seeds

2 tsp / 4 g whole black peppercorns

4 fl oz / 120 mL Curry Oil (page 512)

1¼ pt / 600 mL Lentil Ragoût (page 501)

6 oz / 170 g Caramelized Pearl Onions (page 374)

5 oz / 140 g frisée, cleaned and torn into pieces

1. Slice the salmon into 3½-oz / 100-g portions.

2. Combine the coriander, cumin, caraway, cardamom, anise, and peppercorns and coarsely grind in a spice grinder. Combine the curry oil with the ground spices. Pour the oil over the salmon and marinate for at least 1 and up to 4 hours.

3. For each portion: Heat a large sauté pan. Remove a portion of salmon from the marinade, letting as much oil drain away as possible. Sear on both sides until golden brown and thoroughly cooked. Be careful to let the oil drain back into the pan before plating the salmon. Pool 2 fl oz / 60 mL lentil ragoût in the middle of the plate. Place a piece of salmon in the middle of the ragoût and garnish the plate with ⅔ oz / 17 g caramelized onions and ½ oz / 14 g frisée.

Scallop Gratin with Wild Mushrooms

servings: **10**

portioning information:
2 oz / 55 g mushroom mixture, 3½ oz / 100 g scallops, 2 fl oz / 60 mL sauce

nutrition per serving:
225 calories, 5 g fat, 22 g total carbohydrate, 22 g protein, 451 mg sodium, 41 mg cholesterol

MUSTARD SAUCE

2½ fl oz / 75 mL dry white wine

½ oz / 14 g minced shallots

1 pt / 480 mL Fish Velouté (page 497)

1¾ oz / 50 g whole-grain mustard

WILD MUSHROOMS

1 oz / 30 g butter

5 oz / 140 g thinly sliced scallions

5 oz / 140 g tomato julienne

10 oz / 285 g julienned shiitake mushrooms

2¼ lb / 1 kg sea scallops, muscle tabs removed

4½ oz / 130 g fresh bread crumbs

1. To make the mustard sauce, heat the wine in a small saucepan. Add the shallots and sweat until translucent. Add the velouté and mustard. Reduce to a coating consistency. Reserve.

2. Heat the butter in a large sauté pan. Add the scallions, tomatoes, and mushrooms and sauté until the mushrooms are tender. Remove from the pan and cool before assembling the gratins.

3. To assemble individual gratins, place 2 oz / 55 g mushroom mixture in an individual gratin dish and top with 3½ oz / 100 g scallops. Coat the scallops evenly with the sauce and top with bread crumbs. Cover and refrigerate until needed.

4. For each portion: Broil or bake in a 500°F / 260°C oven until the bread crumbs are golden brown and the scallops are cooked through, about 5 minutes.

Sautéed Sole with Preserved Mango Chutney and Broiled
Bananas, Wild and Brown Rice Pilaf with Cranberries (page 380)

Sautéed Sole with Preserved Mango Chutney and Broiled Bananas

servings: 10

portioning information:
3½ oz / 100 g sole, 1⅔ oz / 45 g chutney, 2⅓ oz / 68 g bananas

nutrition per serving:
230 calories, 4 g fat, 30 g total carbohydrate, 21 g protein, 110 mg sodium, 55 mg cholesterol

2¼ lb / 1 kg sole fillets, trimmed

3 tbsp / 45 mL skim milk

1 oz / 30 g dry bread crumbs

5 tsp / 25 mL butter

1 lb / 450 g Preserved Mango Chutney (page 480)

1½ lb / 680 g Broiled Bananas (page 466)

1. Trim the sole and divide into 3½ oz / 100 g portions. Reserve. Set up a standard breading setup.

2. For each portion: Dip a portion of sole in the milk. Place the sole immediately into the bread crumbs and coat evenly. Shake off any excess. Sauté a portion of breaded sole in ½ tsp / 2.5 mL butter until just done. Serve at once with 1⅔ oz / 45 g chutney and 2⅓ oz / 68 g bananas.

Bass and Scallops en Papillote

servings: 10

portioning information:
4 oz / 115 g bass and scallops, 7 oz / 200 g vegetable mixture

nutrition per serving:
252 calories, 6 g fat, 25 g total carbohydrate, 19 g protein, 286 mg sodium, 44 mg cholesterol

1 lb / 450 g sea bass fillets

1 lb / 450 g sea scallops, muscle tabs removed

7 fl oz / 210 mL Vegetable Stock (page 490)

3½ fl oz / 105 mL dry vermouth

2 lb / 910 g julienned celeriac

10½ oz / 300 g julienned carrots

1 lb / 450 g thinly sliced Red Bliss potatoes

10½ oz / 300 g julienned cucumbers

1¾ oz / 50 g butter, melted

1½ oz / 45 g Gremolata (page 502)

3 tbsp / 45 mL Fines Herbes (page 538)

1 tsp / 5 mL ground black pepper

1. Divide the bass and scallops into 1½ oz / 45 g portions.

2. Combine the stock and vermouth in a large sauce pot and bring to a simmer. Individually blanch the celeriac, carrots, and potatoes in the stock mixture until tender. Drain the vegetables and toss together with the cucumber.

3. Cut a heart-shaped piece of parchment paper. Brush both sides with butter. Place a bed of 7 oz / 200 g of the mixed vegetables on half of each paper heart. Top the vegetables with a portion of the bass and the scallops. Spoon about ½ tsp / 2.5 mL Gremolata over the fish. Season with a scant 1 tsp / 5 mL Fines Herbes and a pinch of pepper. Fold the empty half of the heart over the fish and vegetables and crimp the edges of the paper to seal tightly. Refrigerate until needed.

4. For each portion: Place a parchment package on a baking sheet and bake in a 375°F / 190°C oven until the paper is puffed and brown, 7 minutes.

Sea Bass in Tomato, Fennel, and Saffron Sauce

servings: **10**

portioning information:
2 oz / 55 g snapper, 4 mussels, 2 oz / 55 g tomato, 3¼ fl oz / 95 mL broth

nutrition per serving:
337 calories, 12 g fat, 20 g total carbohydrate, 30 g protein, 438 mg sodium, 33 mg cholesterol

1 tbsp / 15 mL olive oil	1 bay leaf
1 tbsp / 15 mL minced garlic	½ tsp / 2.5 mL orange zest
4 oz / 115 g julienned leeks	1 tsp / 5 mL kosher salt
4 oz / 115 g diced fennel	¼ tsp / 1.25 mL ground white pepper
1 oz / 30 g tomato paste	1¼ lb / 565 g sea bass fillets
1 qt / 950 mL Fish Fumet (page 491)	40 mussels, scrubbed and debearded
2 fl oz / 60 mL dry white wine	1 lb / 450 g tomato concassé
1 tbsp / 15 mL fresh lemon juice	2 tsp / 10 mL chopped tarragon
½ tsp / 2.5 mL saffron threads	

1. Heat the oil in a large stockpot. Add the garlic and sauté until aromatic. Add the leeks and fennel. Cover the pot and sweat until the vegetables begin to cook. Add the tomato paste and sauté until browned. Deglaze the pan with the fumet, wine, and lemon juice. Add the saffron, bay leaf, zest, salt, and pepper. Simmer until the vegetables are tender, about 30 minutes. Reserve.

2. For each portion, bring 3¼ fl oz / 95 mL broth to a gentle simmer. Add a portion of the fish to the broth and poach until the fish begins to cook. Add 4 mussels, 1½ oz / 45 g concassé, and a pinch of tarragon and simmer until the mussels begin to open.

3. Serve the sea bass in a heated soup or pasta plate. Ladle the broth onto the sea bass. Top with the mussels.

Sunshine Bass with a Ginger Nage

servings: 10

portioning information:
3½ oz / 100 g sea bass, 2 oz /
55 g vegetables, 3¼ fl oz /
95 mL bouillon

nutrition per serving:
172 calories, 5 g fat, 10 g total
carbohydrate, 19 g protein, 307 mg
sodium, 82 mg cholesterol

2¼ lb / 1 kg sea bass fillets

1 qt / 950 mL Court Bouillon (page 491)

2½ fl oz / 75 mL extra-virgin olive oil

5 oz / 140 g julienned shiitake mushrooms (see Note)

5 oz / 140 g julienned red pepper

5 oz / 140 g thinly sliced scallions

5 oz / 140 g quartered baby bok choy

Chervil sprigs, as needed for garnish

1. Cut the bass into 3½-oz / 100-g portions.

2. Bring the court bouillon to a gentle simmer (180° F/82° C).

3. For each portion: Brush a sautoir with a little of the oil. Add the mushrooms, peppers, scallions, and bok choy to the sautoir and top with the bass. Add about 3 fl oz / 90 mL of the simmering bouillon to partially cover the fish. Cover the dish with parchment paper and cook in a 325°F / 165°C oven until the fish is opaque, about 8 minutes. Ladle the boullion and vegetables into a heated soup plate, top with the fish, and garnish each portion with chervil sprigs.

Note

Use the shiitake stems in the court bouillon preparation.

Cioppino

servings: **10**

portioning information:
**2 oz / 55 g swordfish,
2 shrimp, 2 clams, ½ crab,
4 fl oz / 120 mL broth,
1 crouton, 1 tsp / 5 mL aïoli**

nutrition per serving:
321 calories, 9 g fat, 27 g total
carbohydrate, 29 g protein, 287 mg
sodium, 106 mg cholesterol

2 tbsp / 30 mL olive oil

6 oz / 170 g diced onions

2 bunches scallions, diced

2 green peppers, diced

5 oz / 140 g diced fennel

¾ oz / 20 g minced garlic

4 lb / 1.80 kg tomato concassé

8 oz / 225 g tomato purée

8 fl oz / 240 mL dry white wine

1 bay leaf

2 tsp / 10 mL ground black pepper

20 cherrystone clams, scrubbed

5 blue crabs, disjointed

20 shrimp (16–20 count), peeled and deveined

1¼ lb / 565 g swordfish, cubed

3 tbsp / 9 g basil chiffonade

10 Garlic Croutons (page 513)

10 tsp / 50 mL Saffron Aïoli (page 509)

1. Heat the oil in a large stockpot. Add the onions, scallions, peppers, fennel, and garlic. Sauté until the onions are translucent. Add the concassé, purée, wine, and bay leaf. Cover the pot and simmer until thickened and flavorful, about 45 minutes. Season with the pepper. Remove and discard the bay leaf.

2. For each portion: Heat 4 fl oz / 120 mL of the tomato mixture. Add the 2 clams and ½ crab and simmer until the clams have just begun opening, about 4 minutes. Add 2 shrimp and 2 oz / 55 g swordfish and simmer until cooked, about 5 minutes more. Just before serving, stir a pinch of basil into the cioppino. Serve each portion of cioppino with a garlic crouton topped with 1 tsp / 5 mL aïoli.

Bouillabaisse

servings: **10**

portioning information:
8 oz / 225 g seafood, 6 fl oz / 180 mL broth

nutrition per serving:
238 calories, 7 g fat, 4 g total carbohydrate, 28 g protein, 315 mg sodium, 86 mg cholesterol

BOUILLABAISSE STOCK

4 fl oz / 120 mL olive oil

8 oz / 225 g rough-cut onions

4 oz / 115 g rough-cut celery

8 oz / 225 g rough-cut carrots

½ oz / 14 g minced garlic

2 tsp / 10 mL fennel seeds

1 oz / 30 g parsley

1 sprig thyme

4 bay leaves

1 oz / 30 g orange zest

1¾ lb / 795 g canned tomatoes, drained and chopped

1 pt / 480 mL dry white wine

2 tsp / 10 mL saffron threads

¼ tsp / 0.625 mL cayenne

1 gal / 3.75 L Fish Fumet (page 491)

8 oz / 225 g cubed perch fillet

8 oz / 225 g cubed halibut fillet

8 oz / 225 g cubed sea bass fillet

20 littleneck clams, scrubbed

20 mussels, scrubbed and debearded

5 oz / 140 g cubed lobster meat

20 large (16–20 count) shrimp, peeled, deveined

8 oz / 225 g sea scallops, muscle tabs removed

½ oz / 14 g chopped parsley

¼ oz / 7 g chopped tarragon

1. To prepare the bouillabaisse stock, heat the oil in a large soup pot. Add the onions, celery, carrots, garlic, fennel seeds, parsley, thyme, bay leaves, and zest. Sweat until the onions are translucent, about 15 minutes. Add the remaining ingredients and bring to a boil. Simmer until reduced by about one-fourth, 45 minutes. Strain and reserve this stock.

2. Toss together the cubed perch, halibut, and sea bass. Divide into 2-oz / 55 g portions. Reserve.

3. For each portion: Return 9 fl oz / 270 mL stock to the pot and bring to a boil. Add 2 clams and 2 mussels. When their shells have opened, remove from the stock and reserve. Return the stock to a boil. Add the ¾ oz / 20 g lobster, 2 shrimp, scallops and 1½ oz / 45 g of the cubed fish. Simmer until the fish is opaque, about 3 minutes. Return the clams and mussels to the bouillabaisse. Simmer to thoroughly heat. Garnish each portion with parsley and tarragon.

Tenderloin of Beef with Mild Ancho Chile Sauce and Jalapeño Jack Cheese Polenta

servings: 10

portioning information:
3½ oz / 100 g beef, 3 tbsp / 45 mL chile sauce, 3 oz / 90 g slice of polenta, ¼-oz / 7-g slices jalapeño Jack cheese, 1 oz / 30 g zucchini

nutrition per serving:
380 calories, 16 g fat, 27 g total carbohydrate, 33 g protein, 464 mg sodium, 76 mg cholesterol

2¼ lb / 1 kg beef tenderloin, trimmed

2 lb / 900 g prepared Polenta (page 383), cooled

10 slices jalapeño Jack cheese (3½ oz / 100 g total)

1½ lb / 680 g zucchini, cut into "leaves" (see Note)

1 pt / 480 mL Ancho Chile Sauce (page 494)

1. Cut the beef into 10 medallions, about 3½ oz / 100 g each. To maintain an even shape and thickness, tie butcher's twine around the circumference of each medallion. Refrigerate until needed.

2. Slice the polenta into ten 3-oz / 90-g pieces. Top the polenta pieces with a slice of cheese and broil until the cheese has melted.

3. Pan-steam the zucchini until tender and keep hot.

4. For each portion: Dry-sauté a beef medallion in a large skillet to the desired doneness. Remove the meat from the skillet and keep warm in a low-heat oven. Deglaze the skillet with 3 tbsp / 45 mL chile sauce.

5. Serve the beef with the sauce, 1 slice of polenta, and 2½ oz / 75 g zucchini.

Note

Cut the skin of the zucchini away from the flesh in ⅓-in / 1-cm slices. Use a paring knife to cut the skin into leaf shapes.

Tenderloin of Beef with Wild Mushrooms

servings: **10**

portioning information:
3½ oz / 100 g beef, 2 fl oz / 60 mL sauce

nutrition per serving:
360 calories, 11 g fat, 5 g total carbohydrate, 31 g protein, 15 mg sodium, 85 mg cholesterol

2¼ lb / 1 kg beef tenderloin, trimmed

3½ oz / 100 g leek chiffonade

4 fl oz / 120 mL Chicken Stock (page 489)

8 fl oz / 240 mL Fond de Veau Lié (page 492)

1½ lb / 680 g sliced wild mushrooms (see Note)

3½ fl oz / 100 mL Madeira wine

1 tsp / 5 mL chopped sage

2 tsp / 10 mL chopped thyme

½ tsp / 2.5 mL ground black pepper

1. Cut the beef into 10 medallions, about 3½ oz / 100 g each. To maintain an even shape and thickness, tie butcher's twine around the circumference of each medallion. Refrigerate until needed.

2. Stew the leeks in the stock until tender. Drain and reserve.

3. For each portion: In a large skillet, dry-sauté a beef medallions to the desired doneness. Remove the meat from the skillet and keep warm in a low-heat oven.

4. Deglaze the skillet with the fond. Add 1½ oz / 45 g mushrooms and sauté until almost cooked, about 5 minutes. Add 2 tsp / 10 mL wine, and a pinch each of sage, thyme, and pepper. Add about 1 tbsp / 15 mL stewed leeks. Simmer and reduce to sauce consistency. Serve the medallion on a heated plate topped with the mushroom sauce.

Note

Oyster, shiitake, morel, cremini, or domestic mushrooms are a few possibilities. Use any mushroom available for the season.

Sautéed Medallions of Pork with Warm Cabbage Salad

servings: **10**

portioning information:
3½ oz / 100 g pork medallions, 1½ fl oz / 45 mL sauce, 3¼ oz / 92 g warm cabbage salad

nutrition per serving:
243 calories, 9 g fat, 12 g total carbohydrate, 26 g protein, 196 mg sodium, 62 mg cholesterol

2¼ lb / 1 kg pork loin, trimmed

SHERRY VINEGAR SAUCE
1 pt / 480 mL Fond de Veau Lié (page 492)
2 fl oz / 60 mL sherry vinegar

1 oz / 30 g brown sugar

2 lb / 910 g Warm Cabbage Salad (page 205)

1. Cut the pork into 20 medallions, about 1¾ oz / 50 g each. Pound the medallions slightly to even their thickness and shape.

2. Combine the ingredients for the sherry vinegar sauce. Reserve.

3. For each portion: Dry-sauté two pork medallions in a sauté pan. Remove from the pan and keep warm. Deglaze the pan with 2 fl oz / 60 mL sherry vinegar sauce. Allow the sauce to reduce slightly. Serve the pork medallions with 2 fl oz / 60 mL sauce and 3¼ oz / 92 g warm cabbage salad.

Sautéed Veal with Wild Mushrooms and Leeks

servings: **10**

portioning information:
3½ oz / 100 g veal, 3 fl oz / 90 mL sauce, 2 oz / 57 g barley

nutrition per serving:
262 calories, 6 g fat, 24 g total carbohydrate, 29 g protein, 242 mg sodium, 77 mg cholesterol

VEAL RUB
2¼ tsp / 7 g minced garlic
2 tbsp / 12 g ground black pepper
2 tsp / 10 mL chopped thyme

2¼ lb / 1 kg veal top round

MUSHROOM AND LEEK SAUCE
10½ oz / 280 g diced leeks
4 fl oz / 120 mL Vegetable Stock (page 490)
1 lb 5 oz / 595 g sliced wild mushrooms
20 fl oz / 600 mL Fond de Veau Lié (page 492)

1¼ lb / 570 g Stir-Fried Barley (page 386)
2 tsp / 10 mL chopped thyme

1. Make the veal rub by combining the garlic, pepper, and thyme. Rub the veal with the mixture and slice the veal into 3½-oz / 100-g portions.

2. To prepare the sauce, in a large skillet, sweat the leeks in 2 fl oz / 60 mL of the stock until tender. Add the mushrooms and sauté until tender. Add the remaining stock as needed to prevent the mushrooms from burning. Add the fond de veau lié and simmer until heated thoroughly.

3. For each portion: Dry sauté the veal medallions in a large skillet. Serve on a heated plate with 2 fl oz / 60 mL sauce and 2 oz / 57 g barley. Garnish with chopped thyme.

Loin of Lamb with Blood Orange Sauce

servings: **10**

portioning information:
3½-oz / 100-g lamb loin, 2½ fl oz / 70 mL sauce

nutrition per serving:
185 calories, 7 g fat, 10 g total carbohydrate, 20 g protein, 92 mg sodium, 59 mg cholesterol

2¼ lb / 1 kg lamb loin

ORANGE GLAZE

½ oz / 14 g arrowroot

3½ fl oz / 100 mL Vegetable Stock (page 490)

1¾ fl oz / 53 mL orange juice concentrate

2 tsp / 10 mL ground black pepper

BLOOD ORANGE SAUCE

8 fl oz / 240 mL blood orange juice

7 fl oz / 210 mL orange juice

1¾ tsp / 5.25 g arrowroot

5 fl oz / 150 mL Fond de Veau Lié (page 492)

1 tbsp / 15 mL chopped tarragon

1. Cut the lamb into 3½-oz / 100-g portions. Reserve refrigerated.

2. To make the orange glaze, combine the arrowroot with enough stock to form a paste. Bring the remaining stock to a simmer in a small saucepan. Add the arrowroot mixture to the stock and simmer until thickened, about 2 minutes. Add the orange juice concentrate and pepper to the thickened stock. Remove from the heat.

3. Prepare the blood orange sauce by combining the orange juices. Mix the arrowroot with enough juice to form a paste and heat the remaining juices in a small sauce pot. Add the arrowroot mixture to the juices and simmer until thickened, about 2 minutes. Add the fond de veau lié and simmer gently. Add the tarragon just before serving.

4. For each portion: Brush the lamb with the orange glaze and grill until medium rare. Serve the grilled lamb with 2 tbsp / 30 mL sauce.

Lamb Shish Kebob

servings: **10**

portioning information:
3½ oz / 100 g lamb, 2 oz / 55 g peppers and onions, 2 oz / 55 g couscous, one slice of bread

nutrition per serving:
505 calories, 8 g fat, 70 g total carbohydrate, 34 g protein, 202 mg sodium, 75 mg cholesterol

2¼ lb / 1 kg cubed lamb leg

5 oz / 140 g lozenge or paysanne cut red pepper

5 oz / 140 g lozenge or paysanne cut green pepper

5 oz / 140 g lozenge or paysanne cut yellow pepper

5 oz / 140 g lozenge or paysanne cut onion

LAMB MARINADE

8½ fl oz / 255 mL fresh lemon juice

8½ fl oz / 255 mL dry white wine

¾ oz / 20 g minced garlic

1½ tsp / 7.5 mL coriander seeds

1 tbsp / 15 mL chopped parsley

2 tbsp / 30 mL chopped mint

1 tbsp / 15 mL crushed black pepper

1¼ lb / 565 g Couscous (page 382)

10 pieces Chickpea Bread

1. Thread 3½ oz / 100 g lamb and 2 oz / 55 g peppers and onions per skewer.

2. Combine the marinade ingredients in a shallow dish. Add the skewers and marinate, refrigerated, for 30 minutes.

3. For each portion: Remove a skewer from the marinade and grill until the vegetables are tender and the lamb is cooked, about 2 minutes on each side. Serve on a bed of 2 oz / 55 g couscous with a slice of bread.

Grilled Flank Steak with Roasted Shallot Sauce

servings: **10**

portioning information:
**3½ oz / 100 g flank steak,
2 fl oz / 60 mL sauce**

nutrition per serving:
280 calories, 10 g fat, 22 g total
carbohydrate, 24 g protein, 250 mg
sodium, 35 mg cholesterol

2¼ lb / 1 kg flank steak, trimmed

FLANK STEAK MARINADE

1½ pt / 600 mL pineapple juice

8 oz / 225 g chopped fresh pineapple

3½ oz / 100 g thinly sliced red onion

2 tbsp / 30 mL low-sodium soy sauce

1 tbsp / 15 mL red wine vinegar

1 tbsp / 15 mL olive oil

4 limes, sliced

1 bunch cilantro, chopped

½ oz / 14 g minced garlic

2 tsp / 10 mL minced jalapeño

1 tbsp / 15 mL chili powder

3 drops Tabasco sauce

ROASTED SHALLOT SAUCE

1¾ oz / 50 mL unsweetened pineapple juice

2 tbsp / 30 mL lime juice

1 tbsp / 15 mL white wine vinegar

1 tsp / 5 mL cracked black peppercorns

7 oz / 200 g Roasted Shallots (page 288), shredded

1 pt / 480 mL Fond de Veau Lié (page 492)

2 tbsp / 30 mL chopped cilantro

1. Cut the steak into 3½-oz / 100-g portions.

2. Combine all of the ingredients for the marinade. Combine the flank steak with the marinade, cover, and refrigerate for up to 3 hours. Drain well before grilling.

3. To make the sauce, combine the fruit juices, vinegar, and peppercorns. Reduce this mixture by half. Add the shallots and fond. Bring the sauce to a simmer and add the cilantro.

4. For each portion: Grill 1 portion of steak to desired doneness.

5. Let the steak rest while reheating 2 fl oz / 60 mL sauce. Slice steak thinly on the diagonal and serve with the sauce.

Grilled Veal with Blackberries and Vanilla

servings: **10**

portioning information:
3½ oz / 100 g veal, 1½ oz / 45 g pasta, 3 oz / 90 mL sauce, 1 oz / 30 g mushrooms, 1½ oz / 45 g onions

nutrition per serving:
330 calories, 4.5 g fat, 30 g total carbohydrate, 28 g protein, 170 mg sodium, 95 mg cholesterol

VEAL RUB

1 tbsp / 15 mL minced garlic

2 tbsp / 12 g ground black pepper

2 tsp / 10 mL chopped thyme

1 tsp / 5 mL extra-virgin olive oil

2¼ lb / 1 kg veal top round

BLACKBERRY AND VANILLA SAUCE

10½ oz / 300 g blackberries or huckleberries

10½ fl oz / 315 mL black Muscat wine

1¼ pt / 600 mL Fond de Veau Lié (page 492)

1 vanilla bean, split

10½ oz / 300 g quartered chanterelle mushrooms

14 oz / 400 g pearl onions, cooked, peeled

7 fl oz / 210 mL orange Muscat wine

1 lb / 450 g Black Pepper Pasta (page 398), cooked

1. Combine the veal rub ingredients and coat the veal with the mixture.

2. Purée the berries and black Muscat wine in a blender. Simmer gently in a small saucepan until flavorful and thickened. Strain to remove the seeds.

3. Heat the fond de veau lié in a separate sauce pot. Add the vanilla bean, remove the pan from the heat, and steep the vanilla bean in the fond de veau for 10 minutes.

4. Remove the vanilla bean and add the mushrooms and the blackberry-muscat purée to the infused fond. Return the pan to the heat and simmer until the mushrooms are tender.

5. In a large sauté pan, caramelize the pearl onions in the orange Muscat wine.

6. Grill the veal until thoroughly cooked. Slice into 3½-oz / 100-g portions.

7. For each portion: Reheat 1½ oz / 45 g pasta and make into a bed on a heated plate. Top with the sliced veal and coat with the 3 fl oz / 90 mL sauce, 1 oz / 30 g mushrooms, and 1½ oz / 45 g pearl onions.

Indian Grilled Buffalo

servings: **10**

portioning information:
3½ oz / 100 g buffalo

nutrition per serving:
133 calories, 3 g fat, 3 g total
carbohydrate, 23 g protein, 60 mg
sodium, 73 mg cholesterol

INDIAN MARINADE

4 fl oz / 120 mL yogurt

3 oz / 85 g minced onion

¾ oz / 20 g minced ginger

¾ oz / 20 g minced garlic

1 tsp / 5 mL toasted ground cumin seeds

1 tsp / 5 mL ground black pepper

½ tsp / 2.5 mL ground nutmeg

2¼ lb / 1 kg buffalo round, cubed (see Note)

1. Combine the marinade ingredients in a large bowl. Add the buffalo and toss to evenly coat with the mixture. Marinate, refrigerated, for 24 hours.

2. Thread 3½-oz / 100-g portions of the meat onto skewers and grill until medium-rare, about 6 minutes.

Note

Beef or pork may be substituted for the buffalo.

Serving Suggestion

The buffalo skewers may be served with grilled zucchini slices and basmati rice.

Broiled Lamb Chops with Caramelized Root Vegetables and White Bean–Rosemary Sauce

servings: **10**

portioning information:
4 oz / 120 g lamb chops, 3¼ oz / 91 g white bean sauce, 3¼ oz / 91 g root vegetables

nutrition per serving:
326 calories, 12 g fat, 28 g total carbohydrate, 27 g protein, 827 mg sodium, 78 mg cholesterol

MARINADE

3 fl oz / 90 mL reduced-sodium soy sauce

2 tbsp / 30 mL Worcestershire

1 fl oz / 30 mL Dijon mustard

1 tbsp / 15 mL chopped rosemary

1 tbsp / 15 mL chopped thyme

1 tbsp / 15 mL chopped sage

2 tbsp / 30 mL vegetable oil

1 tsp / 5 mL ground black pepper

20 lamb loin chops, trimmed

1 tsp / 5 mL kosher salt

½ tsp / 2.5 mL ground black pepper

2 lb / 910 g Caramelized Root Vegetables (page 375)

2 lb / 910 g White Bean–Rosemary Sauce (page 499)

1 tbsp / 15 mL chopped rosemary

1. Combine the ingredients for the marinade and spread evenly on the lamb chops. Marinate for 30 minutes.

2. Brush any excess marinade off the lamb. Season the chops with salt and pepper and place on a rack in a roasting pan. Broil until medium rare.

3. For each portion: Reheat 3¼ oz / 91 g each vegetables and sauce and plate them with 2 chops and a sprinkle of rosemary.

Tenderloin of Beef with Blue Cheese and Herb Crust

servings: **10**

portioning information:
**3½ oz / 100 g tenderloin,
3 tbsp / 45 mL sauce**

nutrition per serving:
219 calories, 8 g fat, 8 g total
carbohydrate, 27 g protein, 301 mg
sodium, 65 mg cholesterol

2¼ lb / 1 kg beef tenderloin, trimmed

BLUE CHEESE AND HERB CRUST

4 oz / 115 g white bread, dried (see Note)

2 oz / 55 g blue cheese

½ oz / 14 g chopped parsley

½ oz / 14 g chopped chives

⅛ tsp / 0.625 mL ground black pepper

MADEIRA SAUCE

1 pt / 480 mL Fond de Veau Lié (page 492)

2 fl oz / 60 mL Madeira wine

1. Cut the beef into 10 medallions, about 3½ oz / 100 g each. To maintain an even shape and thickness, tie butcher's twine around the circumference of each medallion. Refrigerate until needed.

2. By hand, crumble the ingredients together for the crust to form a coarse paste.

3. Dry-sear the beef medallion in a large skillet. Transfer the meat to a rack in a roasting pan. Coat each medallion with the cheese mixture.

4. Deglaze the skillet with the fond and bring to a simmer. Add the Madeira and reduce to a sauce consistency, about 5 minutes.

5. For each portion: Roast in a 350°F / 175°C oven until cooked to the desired doneness. For rare meat, cook 3 to 5 minutes; for medium-rare, 5 minutes; and for well-done, 10 minutes. Serve with 1½ fl oz / 45 mL sauce.

Note

Leave slices of bread uncovered at room temperature for 8 to 10 hours, or until dry enough to crumble easily.

Roasted Loin of Pork with a Honey-Mustard Pan Sauce

servings: **10**

portioning information:
**3½ oz / 100 g pork loin,
2 fl oz / 60 mL sauce**

nutrition per serving:
212 calories, 8 g fat, 10 g total
carbohydrate, 24 g protein, 540 mg
sodium, 59 mg cholesterol

2¼ lb / 1 kg pork loin, trimmed

HONEY-MUSTARD PAN SAUCE

6 fl oz / 180 mL Chicken Stock (page 489)

½ oz / 14 g minced garlic

½ oz / 14 g minced shallots

1 tbsp / 15 mL chopped thyme

1 oz / 30 g tomato paste

2 fl oz / 60 mL whole-grain mustard

2 tsp / 10 mL ground black pepper

2 fl oz / 60 mL honey

2½ fl oz / 75 mL red wine vinegar

1 pt / 480 mL Fond de Veau Lié (page 492)

2 tsp / 10 mL kosher salt

1. Dry-sear the pork loin in a large sauté pan. Remove the pork from the pan and place it on a rack in a roasting pan. Roast in a 325°F / 165°C oven until an internal temperature of 155°F / 68°C.

2. Prepare the pan sauce while the pork is roasting: Deglaze the sauté pan with the stock. Reduce to about 2 tbsp / 30 mL. Add the garlic and shallots. Sweat until aromatic. Add the thyme, tomato paste, mustard, and pepper. Sauté until the tomato paste has browned. Stir in the honey, vinegar, fond, and salt. Simmer until the mixture has reduced to a sauce consistency, about 10 minutes.

3. Remove the pork from the roasting pan when it is done roasting and let it rest for 15 minutes before carving. Degrease the roasting pan and deglaze the reduced drippings in the pan, if any. Add these drippings to the sauce and simmer to heat and slightly reduce the sauce.

4. Carve the pork into 3½-oz / 100-g portions and serve each portion on a heated plate with 3 tbsp / 45 mL pan sauce.

Variation

Roasted Loin of Pork with a Southwestern-Style Mustard Sauce

Use cilantro in place of the thyme in the sauce (add just before serving), spicy Creole mustard in place of whole-grain mustard, maple syrup or molasses instead of honey, and habanero- or other chile-flavored vinegar instead of red wine vinegar. Garnish the sauce with a fine dice of jalapeños.

Cassoulet with Smoked Tomatoes

servings: **10**

portioning information:
13 oz / 390 g cassoulet

nutrition per serving:
319 calories, 4 g fat, 47 g total carbohydrate, 25 g protein, 384 mg sodium, 29 mg cholesterol

3¼ lb / 1.50 kg tomatoes, peeled, seeded, quartered

9 oz / 255 g duck breast

10 oz / 280 g cubed lean pork

1 qt / 950 mL Chicken Stock (page 489)

2¼ lb / 1 kg thinly sliced onions

5 fl oz / 150 mL red wine

1 tbsp / 15 mL garlic

3½ oz / 100 g tomato paste

2 tsp / 10 mL chopped rosemary

3 tbsp / 45 mL chopped thyme

1 tsp / 5 mL kosher salt

1 lb 10 oz / 735 g tomato concassé

10 fl oz / 300 mL Fond de Veau Lié (page 492)

2 lb / 910 g navy or Great Northern beans, cooked

1 lb / 450 g seasoned ground turkey (see Note)

3½ oz / 100 g fresh bread crumbs

½ tsp / 2.5 mL chopped chives

½ tsp / 2.5 mL chopped parsley

1. Place the tomatoes on a rack in a roasting pan containing a thin layer of hardwood chips. Cover with a tight-fitting lid and place over direct heat. Smoke for 6 to 8 minutes. Small dice the tomatoes.

2. Repeat the same smoking process for the duck breast. Smoke for about 15 to 20 minutes. Dry-sear the smoked duck in a large sauté pan. Julienne the meat.

3. In a medium sauce pot, simmer the pork in the stock until the meat is fork tender. Reserve the meat and the stock separately. Skim any fat from the surface of the stock.

4. Heat a large saucepan and add the onions and 1 fl oz / 30 mL of the wine. Sauté until the onions have browned. Add the garlic and sauté until aromatic. Add the tomato paste and sauté until browned. Deglaze the pan with the remaining wine and allow the wine to reduce to the consistency of heavy syrup. Add half of the smoked tomatoes, the rosemary, and thyme. Cook until the juice released from the tomatoes has cooked away. Add the salt, tomato concassé, fond, and reserved stock. Stew gently for 15 minutes. Add the duck, beans, turkey, and pork. Heat thoroughly, about 20 minutes. Stir in the remaining smoked tomatoes.

5. Toss the breads crumbs with the chives and parsley. Top the stew with the bread crumb mixture and brown in a 500°F / 260°C oven.

Note

Prepare the meat mixture for the Turkey Burger (page 358), but do not form into patties. Sauté the mixture in a large skillet and drain any excess liquid.

Chili Stew

servings: **10**

portioning information:
¾ cup / 177 mL chili stew

nutrition per serving:
217 calories, 8 g fat, 11 g total carbohydrate, 26 g protein, 465 mg sodium, 62 mg cholesterol

2¼ lb / 1 kg beef knuckle, trimmed, cubed

4 oz / 115 g diced onion

1 oz / 30 g minced garlic

2 tbsp / 12 g chili powder

1 oz / 30 g tomato paste

1 pt / 480 mL Chicken Stock (page 489)

1 lb 10 oz / 735 g tomato concassé

9 fl oz / 270 mL Fond de Veau Lié (page 492)

1 tsp / 5 mL cayenne

½ oz / 14 g ancho chiles, toasted and chopped

1 fl oz / 30 mL Tabasco sauce

¾ tsp / 3.75 mL garlic powder

1 tsp / 5 mL onion powder

1 tsp / 5 mL kosher salt

½ tsp / 2.5 mL ground black pepper

1. Dry-sear the beef in a large sauce pot. Remove the meat from the the pan and keep warm.

2. Add the onion and garlic and sauté until the onions are translucent. Add the chili powder and tomato paste. Sauté until the paste has browned. Deglaze the pot with the stock. Return the meat to the pot, and add the tomato concassé, fond, cayenne, chiles, Tabasco, garlic and onion powders, salt, and pepper. Bring to a simmer.

3. Cover the pot and place in a 350°F / 175°C oven. Braise until the meat is fork tender, about 45 to 50 minutes.

Serving Suggestion

The chili may be served in a flour tortilla "bowl" made by baking a 6-in / 15-cm tortilla weighted down with pie weights or dry beans in a ovenproof bowl until crisp. Fill the "bowl" with chili and garnish with Tomato Salsa (page 485), diced red peppers, sliced scallions, grated Cheddar cheese, cooked rice, and sour cream or nonfat yogurt.

(Nutritional information does not include serving suggestions.)

Buffalo Chili

servings: 10

portioning information:
6 oz / 270 g chili, 1 oz / 30 g
rice pilaf, 1 oz / 30 g salsa,
1 oz / 30 g peppers, 1 tortilla

nutrition per serving:
190 calories, 4 g fat, 13 g total
carbohydrate, 27 g protein, 435 mg
sodium, 74 mg cholesterol

2¼ lb / 1 kg buffalo round, trimmed and cubed

5 oz / 140 g diced onion

1½ oz / 45 g minced garlic

1½ oz / 45 g tomato paste

1 oz / 30 g chili powder

12 fl oz / 360 mL Fond de Veau Lié (page 492)

1¾ lb / 795 g tomato concassé

½ oz / 14 g ancho chiles, toasted and chopped

½ oz / 14 g mulato chiles, toasted and chopped

½ oz / 14 g chipotle chiles, toasted and diced

1 tsp / 5 mL kosher salt

½ tsp / 2.5 mL ground black pepper

¾ tsp / 3.75 mL cayenne

GARNISHES

10 (8-in / 20-cm) flour tortillas

10 oz / 280 g Basic Rice Pilaf (page 378)

10 oz / 280 g Tomato Salsa (page 485)

10 oz / 280 g julienned roasted red pepper

3½ oz / 100 g thinly sliced scallions

3½ oz / 100 g grated Cheddar cheese

2 oz / 55 g sour cream replacement

1. Dry-sear the buffalo in a large sauce pot. Add the onion and garlic and sauté until the onions are translucent. Add the tomato paste and chili powder. Sauté until the paste has browned. Deglaze with the fond. Add the tomato concassé, chiles, salt, pepper, and cayenne and bring to a simmer. Cover the pot and place in a 350°F / 175°C oven. Braise until the meat is fork tender, about 40 minutes.

2. Serve the chili in a flour tortilla "bowl" made by baking a tortilla weighted down with pie weights or dry beans in an ovenproof bowl until crisp. Fill the "bowl" with a layer of 1 oz / 30 g rice pilaf and then 6 oz / 170 g chili. Garnish with 1 oz / 30 g salsa, 1 oz / 30 g peppers, scallions, cheese, and Sour Cream Replacement.

Lamb Shanks Braised with Lentils

servings: **10**

portioning information:
**4 oz / 115 g lamb shank,
4 fl oz / 120 mL lentils**

nutrition per serving:
305 calories, 10 g fat, 27 g total
carbohydrate, 27 g protein, 417 mg
sodium, 46 mg cholesterol

10 (4-oz / 115-g) pieces lamb shank, trimmed

1 qt / 950 mL Fond de Veau Lié (page 492)

1 pt / 480 mL dry white wine

12 oz / 340 g lentils

1 Bouquet Garni (page 490)

8 oz / 225 g diced celery

8 oz / 225 g diced carrots

1 tbsp / 15 mL chopped parsley

1 tbsp / 15 mL chopped thyme

¼ tsp / 1.25 mL ground black pepper

1 fl oz / 30 mL fresh orange or lemon juice

1 tsp / 5 mL kosher salt

1. Dry-sear the shanks in a large skillet. Add the fond, wine, lentils, and bouquet garni. Bring to a simmer. Cover the pot and place in a 325°F / 165°C oven. Braise until the lamb and lentils are tender, about 1½ to 2 hours. Remove the shanks and keep them warm.

2. Degrease the braising liquid by skimming the surface. Add the celery and carrots to the sauce and simmer until the vegetables are tender and the sauce has reduced slightly. Season the sauce with the parsley, thyme, pepper, juice, and salt.

3. For each portion: Serve 1 shank with 4 fl oz / 120 mL sauce.

Curried Goat

servings: **10**

portioning information:
**3½ oz / 100 g goat meat,
2½ oz / 70 g sauce**

nutrition per serving:
137 calories, 3 g fat, 1 g total
carbohydrate, 23 g protein, 189 mg
sodium, 59 mg cholesterol

GOAT MARINADE

1 pt / 480 mL red wine

1 tbsp / 15 mL chopped thyme

5 cloves garlic, crushed

1 tbsp / 15 g ground black pepper

2¼ lb / 1 kg goat meat, trimmed and cubed

9 fl oz / 270 mL Fond de Veau Lié (page 492)

1 pt / 480 mL Brown Veal Stock (page 489)

2 tbsp / 12 g Berbere Spice Blend (page 511)

1. Combine the goat marinade ingredients and marinate the goat, refrigerated, for 8 to 10 hours. Remove the goat from the marinade and dry-sear the meat in a large sauce pot. Remove the meat from the pot. Deglaze the pot with the fond and stock. Add the berbere and bring to a simmer.

2. Return the meat to the pot, cover, and place in a 350°F / 175°C oven. Braise until the meat is fork tender, 1½ to 2 hours. Remove the meat from the braising liquid and simmer the liquid over direct heat until it has reduced to a sauce consistency.

3. For each portion: Serve 6 oz / 170 g of the braised goat and braising sauce.

Serving Suggestion

Serve the goat with Curried Teff (page 385) and garnish each portion with Sweet Potato Cakes (page 405) and grilled scallions.

(Nutrition information does not include serving suggestions.)

Chicken Stir-Fry with Soba Noodles

1 oz / 30 g arrowroot

15 fl oz / 450 mL Chicken Stock (page 489)

5 fl oz / 150 mL Fond de Veau Lié (page 492)

1 tsp / 5 mL sesame oil

1½ oz / 45 g minced garlic

1½ oz / 45 g minced ginger

2¼ lb / 1 kg chicken breast, cut into strips

10½ oz / 300 g snow peas

7 oz / 200 g sliced shiitake mushrooms

10½ oz / 300 g julienned red peppers

3½ oz / 100 g thinly sliced scallions

2 lb / 910 g Napa cabbage chiffonade

5 fl oz / 150 mL reduced-sodium soy sauce

1 lb / 450 g soba noodles, cooked

1. To make the stir-fry sauce, combine the arrowroot with enough of the stock to make a smooth paste and reserve. Combine the remaining stock and fond in a small sauce pot and bring to a simmer. Add the arrowroot paste and simmer until the stock has thickened, about 2 minutes. Keep warm.

2. Heat the oil in a wok or large sauté pan. Add the garlic and ginger and stir-fry until aromatic. Add the chicken and stir-fry until the meat is firm and light in color, about 2 minutes.

3. Deglaze the pan with 6 fl oz / 180 mL of the stir-fry sauce. Add the peas, mushrooms, peppers, and scallions. Stir-fry until very hot and almost tender, about 2 minutes. Add the cabbage, soy sauce, and enough of the thickened stock to wilt the cabbage, if necessary.

4. Toss the soba noodles with the remaining thickened stock separately over high heat until the noodles are very hot.

5. For each portion: Serve 6½ oz / 230 g stir-fry on a bed of 1½ oz / 45 g soba noodles.

Duck Breast with Roasted Shallots and a Roasted Onion and Vinegar Sauce

ROASTED SHALLOTS

½ fl oz / 15 mL cider vinegar

8 fl oz / 240 mL Glace de Volaille or Fond de Veau Lié (page 492)

30 shallots

2¼ lb / 1 kg boneless, skinless duck breast

5 oz / 140 g frisée

1¼ pt / 600 mL Roasted Onion and Vinegar Sauce (page 491), warm

½ oz / 14 g chopped chives

1. To prepare the roasted shallots, combine the vinegar and glace. Coat the shallots with the mixture and roast in a 350°F / 175°C oven until tender, about 45 minutes.

2. Dry-sear the duck breast in a large skillet. Remove from the pan and finish cooking in a 350°F / 175°C oven until it reaches an internal temperature of 165°F / 74°C. Allow the meat to rest for 10 minutes before slicing.

3. For each portion: Place 3½ oz / 100 g sliced duck on a bed of ½ oz / 14 g frisée. Drizzle 2 fl oz / 60 mL sauce over the duck and frisée and garnish with 3 roasted shallots and a pinch of chives.

Sautéed Turkey Medallions with Tomato-Basil Jus

servings: 10

portioning information:
3½ oz / 100 g turkey, 2½ fl oz /
75 mL tomato-basil sauce

nutrition per serving:
273 calories, 9 g fat, 12 g total
carbohydrate, 34 g protein, 906 mg
sodium, 70 mg cholesterol

SPICE MIX

1½ oz / 45 g kosher salt

1½ oz / 45 g dry mustard

1 tbsp / 15 mL ground black pepper

1 tbsp / 15 mL dried thyme

1 tbsp / 15 mL dried oregano

1 tbsp / 15 mL ground coriander

1 tbsp / 15 mL ground celery seed

2¼ lb / 1 kg turkey medallions, 1¾ oz / 50 g each

6 oz / 170 g all-purpose flour

2 fl oz / 60 mL peanut oil

20 fl oz / 600 mL Tomato-Basil Jus (page 496)

8 oz / 225 g tomato concassé

3 tbsp / 45 mL basil chiffonade

1. Combine the ingredients for the spice mix. Dredge the turkey medallions in the spice mix and then in the flour.

2. For each portion: Heat a film of peanut oil in a sauté pan. Add 2 turkey medallions and sauté until golden brown on both sides. Remove the medallions from the pan and keep warm.

3. Degrease the pan and deglaze with 2 fl oz / 60 mL jus. Stir ¾ oz / 20 g tomatoes and a pinch of basil into the sauce. Serve the medallions on a heated plate with the tomato-basil sauce.

Serving Suggestion

You can also serve the turkey with sautéed oyster mushrooms, steamed broccoli rabe, and Saffron Pasta (page 400).

(Nutrition information does not include serving suggestions.)

Duck Stir-Fry with Shrimp

servings: **10**

portioning information:
8½ oz / 450 g stir-fry, 1½ oz / 45 g noodles

nutrition per serving:
319 calories, 6 g fat, 40 g total carbohydrate, 29 g protein, 588 mg sodium, 106 mg cholesterol

DUCK MARINADE

1¾ fl oz / 50 mL reduced-sodium soy sauce

1 fl oz / 30 mL sherry vinegar

1 fl oz / 30 mL rice wine vinegar

1 tsp / 5 mL sesame oil

1 tsp / 5 mL minced garlic

1 lb / 450 g duck breast, cut into strips

SHRIMP MARINADE

¼ tsp / 1.25 mL Tabasco sauce

1 tsp / 5 mL minced garlic

1 tsp / 5 mL minced ginger

2 tsp / 10 mL rice wine vinegar

1 tsp / 5 mL fish sauce

¼ tsp / 1.25 mL sesame oil

½ tsp / 2.5 mL five-spice powder

½ fl oz / 15 mL hoisin sauce

1 lb / 450 g shrimp, peeled, split lengthwise

1 oz / 30 g arrowroot

15 fl oz / 450 mL Chicken Stock (page 489)

5 fl oz / 150 mL Fond de Veau Lié (page 492)

1 tsp / 5 mL sesame oil

10½ oz / 300 g snow peas

7 oz / 200 g sliced shiitake mushrooms

10½ oz / 300 g julienned red pepper

3½ oz / 100 g thinly sliced scallions

2 lb / 910 g Napa cabbage chiffonade

5 fl oz / 150 mL reduced-sodium soy sauce

1 lb / 450 g Buckwheat Noodles (page 399), cooked

1. Combine the duck marinade ingredients in a shallow bowl. Add the duck and toss to coat. Combine the shrimp marinade ingredients in a second bowl. Add the shrimp and toss to coat. Marinate the duck and shrimp separately, refrigerated, for 1 hour.

2. Combine the arrowroot with enough of the stock to make a smooth paste. Set aside.

3. Combine the remaining stock and fond in a small sauce pot and bring to a simmer. Add the arrowroot paste and simmer until the stock has thickened, about 2 minutes.

4. Heat the oil in a wok or large sauté pan. Remove the duck and shrimp from the marinades and add both to the hot pan. Stir-fry for about 2 minutes.

5. Deglaze the pan with 6 fl oz / 180 mL of the thickened stock. Add the peas, mushrooms, peppers, and scallions. Stir-fry until almost tender, about 2 minutes.

6. Add the cabbage, soy sauce, and enough of the thickened stock to wilt the cabbage.

7. Toss the buckwheat noodles with the remaining thickened stock and heat in a separate pan if necessary.

8. For each portion: Serve 8½ oz / 450 g stir-fry on a bed of 1½ oz / 45 g buckwheat noodles.

Grilled Chicken and Spicy Pecans

servings: **10**

portioning information:
**7 oz / 200 g chicken salad,
3 tbsp / 45 mL vinaigrette**

nutrition per serving:
300 calories, 17 g fat, 16 g total
carbohydrate, 23 g protein, 90 mg
sodium, 55 mg cholesterol

VINAIGRETTE

10 fl oz / 300 mL apple cider

1¼ fl oz / 40 mL cider vinegar

1 tbsp / 15 mL Worcestershire sauce

1 tbsp / 15 mL Tabasco sauce

1 tbsp / 15 mL chopped thyme

1¼ fl oz / 40 mL walnut oil

5½ oz / 155 g pecan halves

2¼ lb / 1 kg skinless chicken breast

6 oz / 170 g mixed greens

5 oz / 140 g julienned endive

1 lb 5 oz / 595 g thinly sliced Granny Smith
apples

9 oz / 255 g arugula

1. To make the vinaigrette, reduce the apple cider by two thirds. Combine the reduced cider, vinegar, Worcestershire, Tabasco, and thyme. Slowly whisk in the oil.

2. Toast the pecans in a 300°F / 150°C oven until golden brown.

3. Grill the chicken breast until thoroughly cooked. Cool and slice thinly.

4. Toss the pecans, chicken, and remaining ingredients.

5. For each portion: Toss 7 oz / 200 g chicken salad with 3 tbsp / 45 mL vinaigrette and arrange on a room-temperature plate.

Grilled Quail Wrapped in Prosciutto with Figs and Wild Mushrooms

servings: **10**

portioning information:
4 grilled quail halves, 2 fl oz / 60 mL sauce

nutrition per serving:
340 calories, 11 g fat, 10 g total carbohydrate, 46 g protein, 540 mg sodium, 140 mg cholesterol

5 oz / 140 g thinly sliced prosciutto

20 skinless quail, halved

3 fl oz / 100 mL dry sherry

½ oz / 14 g minced garlic

1 tsp / 5 mL ground black pepper

1 oz / 30 g diced shallots

1 pt / 480 mL Fond de Veau Lié (page 492), warm

6 oz / 170 g sliced wild mushrooms

3 oz / 85 g sun-dried figs

1. Wrap a slice of prosciutto around each quail half and thread it onto a skewer.

2. Combine the sherry, garlic, pepper, and half the shallots in a shallow pan. Add the skewered quail and marinate, refrigerated, for 30 minutes.

3. Remove the quail from the marinade and grill until thoroughly cooked, about 2 minutes on each side. Remove from the grill and brush with the fond.

4. Sauté the remaining shallots and the mushrooms in a large nonstick skillet. When the mushrooms begin to release their juices, add the figs and any remaining fond. Gently heat.

5. For each portion: Serve 4 grilled quail halves with 2 fl oz / 60 mL hot sauce.

Grilled Chicken Burritos

servings: **10**

portioning information:
1 tortilla, 3 oz / 85 g guacamole, 3½ oz / 100 g chicken, 2 oz / 56 g tomatillo salsa

nutrition per serving:
279 calories, 9 g fat, 23 g total carbohydrate, 27 g protein, 437 mg sodium, 56 mg cholesterol

CHICKEN MARINADE

½ oz / 14 g minced garlic

2 tsp / 10 mL minced shallots

1 tbsp plus 2 tsp / 5 g chopped cilantro

1 tsp / 5 mL ground black pepper

½ fl oz / 15 mL fresh lime juice

2¼ lb / 1 kg boneless, skinless chicken breast

10 (8-in / 20-cm) whole wheat tortillas

1 lb 14 oz / 850 g Guacamole (page 486)

1¼ lb / 560 g Tomatillo Salsa (page 485)

1. Combine the ingredients for the chicken marinade. Toss the chicken in the marinade and refrigerate for at least 30 minutes.

2. Shake any excess marinade from the chicken and grill until cooked. Slice thinly on a bias.

3. Cover the tortillas with a damp towel and warm in a 250°F / 120°C oven.

4. For each portion: Spread a warmed tortilla with 3 oz / 85 g guacamole and 3½ oz / 100 g chicken. Roll the tortilla into the shape of a cone and serve with 2 oz / 56 g tomatillo salsa.

Grilled Kibbe Kebobs

servings: **10**

portioning information:
3 oz / 85 g kebobs

nutrition per serving:
168 calories, 8 g fat, 13 g total carbohydrate, 10 g protein, 103 mg sodium, 36 mg cholesterol

4 oz / 115 g fine-grind bulghur

1 lb / 450 g ground turkey thigh

6½ oz / 185 g diced onions

2 oz / 55 g minced jalapeño

1 tbsp / 15 mL yogurt

2 tbsp / 30 mL olive oil

1 tbsp / 15 mL chopped parsley

2 tbsp / 30 mL chopped cilantro

1 tbsp / 15 mL chopped mint

2 tsp / 10 mL ground cumin

1 tsp / 5 mL ground allspice

¼ tsp / 1.25 mL cinnamon

½ tsp / 2.5 mL ground black pepper

¼ tsp / 1.25 mL cayenne

GLAZE

1 tbsp / 15 mL molasses

1 tbsp / 15 mL reduced-sodium soy sauce

1 tbsp / 15 mL olive oil

1. Thoroughly rinse the bulghur and soak it in warm water for 10 minutes. Drain in a strainer for 20 minutes. Squeeze any excess moisture from the bulghur.

2. Combine the bulghur with the turkey, onions, jalapeños, yogurt, oil, parsley, cilantro, mint, cumin, allspice, cinnamon, pepper, and cayenne in a food processor. Pulse to fully incorporate.

3. Mold 3-oz / 85-g portions of the meat mixture onto 8-inch (20-cm) wooden skewers that have been soaked in water for 1 hour.

4. Whisk together the glaze ingredients. Brush the meat mixture with the glaze just before grilling.

5. For each portion: Grill 1 skewer for about 3 minutes on each side. Serve on a heated plate.

Jerk Chicken

servings: **10**

portioning information:
3½ oz / 100 g chicken

nutrition per serving:
131 calories, 3 g fat, 4 g total carbohydrate, 20 g protein, 284 mg sodium, 56 mg cholesterol

JERK SEASONING

1 oz / 30 g allspice berries, toasted

1 cinnamon stick, broken into ½-in / 1-cm pieces

¾ tsp / 3.75 mL grated nutmeg

4 scallions, minced

3 oz / 85 g minced onion

1 Scotch Bonnet chile, minced

2 tsp / 10 mL kosher salt

1 tsp / 5 mL ground black pepper

1 tbsp /15 mL dark rum

2¼ lb / 1 kg boneless skinless chicken breast

1. To make the jerk seasoning, grind the toasted berries, cinnamon, and nutmeg to a powder in a spice mill. Transfer the powder to a food processor and add the scallions, onion, chile, salt, pepper, and rum. Process to form a thick paste.

2. Rub the jerk seasoning over the chicken breast and grill for 3 minutes on each side. Continue cooking the breasts on a rack in a roasting pan in a 375°F / 190°C oven until they reach an internal temperature of 165°F / 74°C, about 15 minutes.

Serving Suggestion

Serve 3½ oz / 100 g chicken with Black Bean Sauce (page 500), Green Papaya Salsa (page 486), and plantain chips.

Chicken Breast with Peaches in Zinfandel Wine Sauce

servings: **10**

portioning information:
3½ oz / 100 g chicken, 1 oz / 28 g peaches, 2 fl oz / 30 mL sauce

nutrition per serving:
160 calories, 3 g fat, 7 g total carbohydrate, 24 g protein, 150 mg sodium, 58 mg cholesterol

8 fl oz / 240 mL apple cider

½ oz / 14 g minced shallot

1 tsp / 5 mL minced garlic

¾ fl oz / 20 mL apple cider vinegar

2¼ lb / 1 kg boneless, skinless chicken breast

10 oz / 250 g sliced, pitted, and peeled peaches

1 pt / 480 mL Fond de Veau Lié (page 492)

1¾ fl oz / 50 mL red Zinfandel

1. Combine the cider, shallot, garlic, and vinegar in a shallow bowl. Add the chicken breast and marinate, refrigerated, for 30 minutes.

2. Remove the chicken breasts from the marinade and place in a roasting pan. Roast in a 375°F / 190°C oven until they reach an internal temperature of 165°F / 74°C. Remove the breasts from the pan and rest for 10 minutes.

3. Combine the peaches, fond, and Zinfandel in a small saucepan. Simmer slowly until thoroughly heated and of a good coating consistency.

4. For each portion: Slice 3½ oz / 100 g chicken on a bias and serve with 2 fl oz / 60 mL warm sauce and 1 oz / 28 g peaches.

Jerk Chicken with Preserved Mango Chutney (page 488) and Black Bean Cornmeal Loaf (page 390)

Grilled Pheasant with Asparagus and Black Truffle Butter

servings: **10**

portioning information:
3½ oz / 100 g pheasant, 2¾ oz / 78 g asparagus, 3¼ oz / 91 g risotto, 2 oz / 58 g tomatoes

nutrition per serving:
280 calories, 16 g fat, 6 g total carbohydrate, 27 g protein, 560 mg sodium, 65 mg cholesterol

2¼ lb / 1 kg boneless, skinless pheasant breast

2 tsp / 10 mL kosher salt

1 tsp / 5 mL ground black pepper

3 fl oz / 90 mL vegetable oil

¾ fl oz / 20 mL extra-virgin olive oil

1 lb 4 oz / 550 g tomato concassé

1 lb 11 oz / 780 g asparagus, peeled and trimmed

4 fl oz / 120 mL Chicken Stock (page 489)

2 lb / 910 g Risotto (page 380), warm

5 tsp / 25 mL Truffle Butter (page 510)

1. Season the pheasant with the salt and pepper, and coat lightly with the vegetable oil. Grill the breasts for 3 minutes on each side. Continue cooking the breasts on a rack in a roasting pan in a 375°F / 190°C oven until they reach an internal temperature of 165°F / 74°C, about 10 minutes.

2. Heat the olive oil in a large sauté pan. Add the tomato concassé and heat thoroughly.

3. In a large sauté pan fitted with a lid, pan-steam the asparagus in the stock until tender.

4. For each portion: Fan 2¾ oz / 78 g asparagus from the center of the plate. Spoon 3¼ oz / 91 g risotto in the center of the plate, top with 2 oz / 58 g tomatoes, and rest 3½ oz / 100 g grilled pheasant against the risotto. Top the breast with a dollop of truffle butter (about ½ tsp / 2.5 mL).

Pan-Smoked Chicken Breast with Artichoke and Mustard Sauce

servings: **10**

portioning information:
3½ oz / 100 g chicken breast, 2 fl oz / 60 mL sauce

nutrition per serving:
190 calories, 7 g fat, 7 g total carbohydrate, 25 g protein, 462 mg sodium, 58 mg cholesterol

2¼ lb / 1 kg boneless, skinless chicken breast

2 tsp / 10 mL vegetable oil

1 oz / 30 g diced shallot

10 fl oz / 300 mL Chicken Stock (page 489)

10 fl oz / 300 mL Fond de Veau Lié (page 492)

1 fl oz / 30 mL Dijon mustard

2 fl oz / 60 mL whole-grain mustard

3 tbsp / 45 mL balsamic vinegar

10 cooked artichoke hearts, quartered

5 oz / 140 g pitted halved Kalamata olives

1 tbsp / 15 mL chopped tarragon

1. Lightly pound the chicken breasts to an even thickness.

2. Place the breasts on a rack in a roasting pan containing a thin layer of hardwood chips. Cover with a tight-fitting lid and place over direct heat. Smoke for 6 to 8 minutes. Remove the breasts from the pan and continue cooking on a rack in a roasting pan in a 375°F / 190°C oven until they reach an internal temperature of 165°F / 74°C, about 10 minutes.

3. Heat the oil in a small saucepan. Add the shallot and sauté until translucent. Add the stock and reduce by half. Stir in the fond, mustards, and vinegar. Simmer the sauce until reduced to a sauce consistency. Add the remaining ingredients and heat thoroughly.

4. For each portion: Slice each breast on a bias and serve on a pool of 2 fl oz / 60 mL sauce.

Herb-Breaded Chicken with Creamy Mustard Sauce

servings: **10**

portioning information:
**3½ oz / 100 g chicken,
2 fl oz / 60 mL sauce**

nutrition per serving:
217 calories, 3 g fat, 20 g total
carbohydrate, 25 g protein, 244 mg
sodium, 59 mg cholesterol

2¼ lb / 1 kg boneless, skinless chicken breast

4 oz / 115 g cornmeal

2 oz / 55 g cornflake crumbs

½ oz / 14 g chopped parsley

½ oz / 14 g chopped tarragon

½ oz / 14 g basil chiffonade

½ oz / 14 g chopped chives

8 fl oz / 240 mL buttermilk

20 fl oz / 600 mL Creamy Mustard Gravy
(page 495)

1. Trim any visible fat from the chicken.

2. Combine the cornmeal, cornflakes, and half of the parsley, tarragon, basil, and chives. In another bowl, combine the remainder of the herbs with the buttermilk.

3. Dip the chicken breasts into the buttermilk mixture, and then into the cornmeal mixture. Place the breaded chicken on a rack in a roasting pan. Bake in a 375°F / 190°C oven until cooked, about 20 minutes.

4. For each portion: Gently heat 2 fl oz / 60 mL mustard sauce. Serve 3½ oz / 100 g chicken with the sauce on a heated plate.

Serving Suggestion

Country Corn Bread (page 436) and sugar snap peas and morels pan-steamed in chicken stock are excellent accompaniments to the chicken.

(Nutrition information does not include serving suggestions.)

Whole Wheat Quesadillas with Roasted Chicken, Ancho Chile Caciotta, and Mango Salsa

servings: **10**

portioning information:
2 whole wheat tortillas, 3½ oz / 100 g chicken, 2 oz cheese and pine nut filling, 1 oz / 30 g mango salsa

nutrition per serving:
531 calories, 20 g fat, 51 g total carbohydrate, 33 g protein, 737 mg sodium, 76 mg cholesterol

3 whole chickens (3½ lb / 1.60 kg each)

½ tsp / 2.5 mL kosher salt

½ tsp / 2.5 mL ground black pepper

20 (8-in / 20-cm) whole wheat flour tortillas

8 oz / 225 g scallions, split lengthwise and thinly sliced

3 oz / 85 g pine nuts, toasted

10 oz / 300 g grated ancho chile caciotta cheese

Vegetable oil spray, as needed

10 oz / 300 g Mango Salsa (page 486)

1. Season the chicken with the salt and pepper and roast in a 350°F / 165°C oven to an internal temperature of 165°F / 74°C. Cool, remove all the meat, and shred to yield 2¼ lb / 1 kg meat.

2. Cover the tortillas with a lightly dampened towel and warm in a 225°F / 107°C oven until soft.

3. For each portion: Place 3½ oz / 100 g chicken, some scallions, pine nuts, and 1 oz / 30 g cheese in the center of a tortilla. Top with another tortilla and place in a heated, oil-sprayed sauté pan. Lightly brown on both sides, making certain that the cheese is melted in the middle before removing from the heat. Cut the quesadilla into fourths and serve with 1 oz / 30 g mango salsa.

Duck Breast Crépinette

servings: **10**

portioning information:
**3½ oz / 100 g duck breast,
2 oz / 57 g mousseline,
3 tbsp / 45 mL sauce**

nutrition per serving:
198 calories, 4 g fat, 6 g total
carbohydrate, 33 g protein, 223 mg
sodium, 149 mg cholesterol

10 boneless, skinless duck breasts (about 5 oz / 140 g each)

DUCK MARINADE

1¾ fl oz / 50 mL dry red wine

¾ fl oz / 20 mL Chicken Stock (page 489)

¾ fl oz / 20 mL balsamic vinegar

1 tsp / 5 mL cracked juniper berries

1 bay leaf

1 oz / 30 g diced shallots

20 Savoy cabbage leaves, blanched

DUCK MOUSSELINE

Reserved duck tenderloins (from step 1)

2 egg whites

1 fl oz / 30 mL heavy cream

1 lb / 450 g Duxelles (page 502) , chilled

1 pt / 480 mL Fond de Veau Lié (page 492)

1. Trim the duck breasts and remove the tenderloins. Dice the tenderloins and keep refrigerated.

2. Combine the duck marinade ingredients in a shallow bowl. Add the duck breast and marinate, refrigerated, for 1 hour.

3. While the duck is marinating, make a mousseline forcemeat as follows: Place the diced duck tenderloins, egg whites, and cream in a food processor and process to a form a paste. Transfer the mousseline to a metal bowl set over an ice bath. Gently fold in the chilled duxelles. Keep chilled.

4. Remove the duck breasts from the marinade and place on a rack in a roasting pan containing a thin layer of hickory chips. Cover the pan tightly and place over direct heat. Pan-smoke the breasts for 30 minutes. Remove the breasts from the pan and let rest for 15 minutes before continuing.

5. For each portion: Place a breast on a cabbage leaf. Spread a layer of 2 oz / 57 g mousseline on each breast and wrap the cabbage leaf around the breast. Wrap a second leaf around the breast to completely encase the breast and mousseline.

6. Bake the duck in a 350°F / 175°C oven to an internal temperature of 165°F / 74°C.

7. Heat the fond in a small saucepan and serve 3 tbsp / 45 mL with each crépinette.

Smoked Turkey Breast with Cranberry-Orange Vinaigrette

servings: **10**

portioning information:
3½ oz / 100 g turkey, 2 oz / 60 g endive and frisée, 1 tbsp / 15 mL vinaigrette, 1 oz / 30 g conserve

nutrition per serving:
221 calories, 2 g fat, 35 g total carbohydrate, 14 g protein, 731 mg sodium, 34 mg cholesterol

BRINE FOR TURKEY

3 qt / 2.88 L water

6 oz / 170 g kosher salt

4 oz / 115 g brown sugar

1 tbsp / 15 mL chopped thyme

2 tsp / 10 mL chopped sage

1 tbsp / 15 mL black peppercorns

4 bay leaves

1 tbsp / 15 mL crushed juniper berries

¾ oz / 20 g curing salt

2¼ lb / 1 kg turkey breast

GLAZE FOR TURKEY

2 fl oz / 60 mL whiskey

1 oz / 30 g honey

1½ oz / 45 g brown sugar

10 oz / 300 g Belgian endive

10 oz / 300 g frisée

5 fl oz / 150 mL Cranberry-Orange Vinaigrette (page 503)

10 oz / 300 g Orange and Herb Conserve (page 487)

1. Combine the brine ingredients in a large pot and bring to a boil. Cool completely. Submerge the turkey breast in the brine to cure, refrigerated, for 8 to 10 hours.

2. Remove the turkey from the brine and place on a rack in a roasting pan containing a thin layer of hardwood chips. Smoke-roast the turkey breast in a 350°F / 175°C oven to an internal temperature of 165°F / 74°C.

3. Combine the glaze ingredients in a large pot and bring to a simmer to dissolve the sugars while the turkey is roasting. Baste the turkey with the glaze several times during roasting. Cool the turkey completely and thinly slice.

4. For each portion: Toss 1 oz / 30 g each endive and frisée with 1 tbsp / 15 mL vinaigrette. Arrange 3½ oz / 100 g turkey slices on a bed of greens. Garnish the salad with 1 oz / 30 g conserve.

Poached Chicken Breast in Spicy Broth

2 tsp / 10 mL olive oil

1 tbsp / 15 mL minced garlic

¾ oz / 20 g tomato paste

2 fl oz / 60 mL dry white wine

1 qt / 950 mL Basic Consommé (page 160)

2 tsp / 10 mL chopped tarragon

1 tsp / 5 mL saffron threads

1 large piece orange zest

1 tsp / 5 mL kosher salt

1 bay leaf

3½ oz / 100 g ribbon-cut leeks

3½ oz / 100 g thinly sliced fennel

3½ oz / 100 g sliced okra

1 lb / 450 g tomato concassé

2¼ lb / 1 kg boneless, skinless chicken breast

20 crayfish

1 tbsp / 15 mL fresh lemon juice

¼ tsp / 1.25 mL ground white pepper

1. Heat the oil in a soup pot. Add the garlic and sauté until aromatic. Add the tomato paste and sauté until brown. Deglaze the pot with the wine. Add the consommé, tarragon, saffron, orange zest, salt, and bay leaf. Simmer 15 minutes. Remove and discard the orange zest and bay leaf.

2. Add the leeks, fennel, and okra. Continue to simmer until the vegetables are tender. Add the tomato concassé and simmer until hot. Add the chicken and gently poach until the chicken is cooked thoroughly, about 8 minutes.

3. Add the crayfish in the last 3 minutes of cooking. Just before serving, season with the lemon juice and pepper.

4. For each portion: Put 3½ oz / 100 g chicken, 2 crayfish, and 4 fl oz / 120 mL broth in a warm bowl.

Serving Suggestion

Spread roasted garlic on a crouton and sprinkle with Parmesan cheese. Brown the crouton in the oven. Serve the poached chicken in broth with steamed brown rice and a crouton.

(Nutrition information does not include serving suggestions.)

Poached Cornish Game Hen with Star Anise

servings: **10**

portioning information:
1 cornish game hen, 2 oz / 57 g brown rice, 5 oz / 170 g vegetables

nutrition per serving:
308 calories, 6 g fat, 33 g total carbohydrate, 30 g protein, 564 mg sodium, 112 mg cholesterol

10 Cornish game hens

1 tsp / 5 mL kosher salt

¼ tsp / 1.25 mL ground black pepper

10 bay leaves

10 sprigs thyme

¼ tsp / 1.25 mL caraway seeds

30 stems parsley

1 qt / 950 mL Chicken Stock (page 489), or as needed

20 pieces star anise

10 oz / 300 g carrot batonnet

10 oz / 300 g turnip batonnet

10 oz / 300 g parsnip batonnet

10 oz / 300 g yellow squash batonnet

10 oz / 300 g cucumber batonnet

1¼ lb / 570 g cooked brown rice

2 oz / 60 g thinly sliced scallions, cut on the diagonal

2 oz / 57 g chopped chives

1. Rub each hen with the salt and pepper and season the cavity of each hen with a bay leaf, thyme sprig, a few caraway seeds, and 3 parsley stems. Truss the hens.

2. Place the hens in a deep pot. Cover with the stock and add the star anise. Cover the pot with parchment paper and simmer slowly for 30 minutes.

3. Add the vegetables to the pot and simmer until the vegetables are tender and the hens are cooked, an additional 10 minutes. Stir the rice into the stock and simmer to heat thoroughly.

4. For each portion: Serve 1 Cornish game hen, 2 oz / 57 g brown rice, and 5 oz / 150 g vegetables. Garnish each portion with scallions and chives.

Chicken and Shrimp Pot Pie with Herb-Cracker Crust

servings: 10

portioning information:
7 oz / 200 g stew, 1 oz / 30 g herb crust

nutrition per serving:
367 calories, 10 g fat, 39 g total carbohydrate, 29 g protein, 551 mg sodium, 121 mg cholesterol

1¼ lb / 565 g boneless, skinless chicken breast

2 qt / 2 L Chicken Stock (page 489)

1 lb / 450 g shrimp (16–20 count), peeled and deveined

4 oz / 115 g arrowroot

1 lb 5 oz / 595 g diced potatoes

14 fl oz / 420 mL evaporated skim milk

1 fl oz / 30 mL Dijon mustard

1¾ oz / 50 g butter

3½ oz / 100 g diced onion

3½ oz / 100 g diced celery

3½ oz / 100 g diced carrots

3½ oz / 100 g diced green pepper

1 tbsp / 15 mL chopped rosemary

1 tbsp plus 1 tsp / 15 mL chopped thyme

½ tsp / 2.5 mL ground black pepper

1 fl oz / 30 mL Worcestershire sauce

½ tsp / 2.5 mL Tabasco sauce

10 oz / 300 g Herb-Cracker Crust (page 305)

1. Pound the chicken breasts to an even thickness and cut into 3½-oz / 100-g portions. Roll the chicken into roulades and tie with butcher's twine.

2. Bring the stock to a simmer in a large sauce pot. Add the chicken and poach for 10 minutes. Add the shrimp and continue to poach for another 5 minutes. Remove the chicken and shrimp and skim the surface of the stock.

3. Combine the arrowroot with enough water to form a paste. Add to the stock and simmer until thickened, about 2 minutes. Add the potatoes and simmer until tender.

4. Blend the milk with the mustard and add to the stock and potatoes.

5. Heat the butter in a sauté pan. Add the onion, celery, carrots, and pepper and sweat until tender. Add the herbs, black pepper, Worcestershire, and Tabasco. Simmer for 5 minutes. Add these vegetables to the potato-stock mixture and simmer until all of the ingredients are tender and hot, about 10 minutes. Remove the twine from the chicken and return the chicken and the shrimp to the stew.

6. For each portion: Roll out the cracker crust and cut out to make a "lid" for a crock. Divide the stew evenly among 10 crocks. Top with the crust. Bake in a 425°F / 218°C oven until the crust is crisp, about 10 minutes. Serve at once.

Herb-Cracker Crust

servings: **10**

portioning information:
1 oz / 40 g

nutrition per serving:
80 calories, 2 g fat, 13 g total carbohydrate, 2 g protein, 135 mg sodium, 5 mg cholesterol

5½ oz / 155 g all-purpose flour	2 tbsp / 30 mL chopped basil
1 tsp / 5 mL sugar	2 tbsp / 30 mL chopped parsley
½ tsp / 2.5 mL salt	1 tbsp / 15 mL chopped basil
¼ tsp / 1.25 mL baking powder	4½ fl oz / 130 mL chilled buttermilk
¾ oz / 20 g butter	

1. Sift together the flour, sugar, salt, and baking powder. Cut the butter into the mixture with a fork or pastry knife until mealy. Add the herbs and buttermilk and mix just until a stiff dough forms.

2. Pass the dough through the widest setting of a pasta machine, dusting it with a little flour if necessary to prevent sticking. Fold the dough in thirds, and roll twice more, keeping the dough as rectangular as possible. Continue to pass the dough through the machine, making the settings narrower each time, until the dough is ⅛ in / .315 cm thick. Cut the dough into shapes required to cover pot pies.

Paella Valenciana

servings: **10**

portioning information:
9 oz / 260 g paella

nutrition per serving:
427 calories, 8 g fat, 55 g total carbohydrate, 30 g protein, 265 mg sodium, 76 mg cholesterol

10 skinless game hen legs	¼ tsp / 1.25 mL saffron threads
2 tsp / 10 mL olive oil	1 lb 2 oz / 500 g medium-grain rice
½ oz / 14 g minced garlic	2½ pt / 1.20 L Chicken Stock (page 489)
3½ oz / 100 g diced onion	20 littleneck clams, scrubbed
10 oz / 300 g diced bell peppers, assorted colors	20 mussels, scrubbed and debearded
1½ oz / 45 g minced jalapeño	10 shrimp (16–20 count), peeled and deveined
5 oz / 140 g sliced white mushrooms	10 oz / 300 g peas, fresh or frozen

1. Roast the game hen legs in a 350°F / 175°C oven until medium rare.

2. Heat the oil in a large pot. Add the garlic and onion and sauté until the onions have browned. Add the peppers and jalapeños and cook until tender. Add the mushrooms and sauté until they begin to release their juices. Add the saffron and rice and sauté until the rice grains are coated with the oil.

3. Add the stock and bring to a simmer. Cover and place in a 350°F / 175°C oven for 35 minutes. Add the hen legs, clams, mussels, shrimp, and peas. Cover and continue cooking until the clams and mussels have opened and the shrimp have cooked, about 8 minutes.

4. For each portion: Serve about 9 oz / 260 g of the paella on a heated plate.

Rabbit and Oyster Etouffée

servings: **10**

portioning information:
6 oz / 170 g étouffée, 1½ oz / 45 g rice

nutrition per serving:
340 calories, 9 g fat, 33 g total carbohydrate, 28 g protein, 290 mg sodium, 55 mg cholesterol

SEASONING MIX

7 oz / 200 g all-purpose flour, toasted in the oven

1 tsp / 5 mL hot paprika

½ tsp / 2.5 mL garlic powder

½ tsp / 2.5 mL onion powder

½ tsp / 2.5 mL ground white pepper

½ tsp / 2.5 mL ground black pepper

½ tsp / 2.5 mL dried basil

½ tsp / 2.5 mL filé powder

Pinch cayenne

2¼ lb / 1 kg boneless rabbit, cubed

1 qt / 950 mL Chicken Stock (page 489)

3½ oz / 100 g diced onion

3½ oz / 100 g diced green pepper

2 oz / 55 g diced celery

2 oz / 55 g thinly sliced scallions

2 oz / 55 g tomato concassé

½ oz / 14 g minced garlic

14 oz / 400 g shucked oysters, liquor reserved

1 lb / 450 g Basic Rice Pilaf (page 378)

1 oz / 30 g thinly sliced scallions, cut on the diagonal

1. Combine the seasoning ingredients in a medium bowl. Add the rabbit pieces and turn to coat evenly with the seasoning. Reserve.

2. Heat 2 fl oz / 60 mL of the stock in a large sauce pot. Add the onion, pepper, celery, scallions, tomato, and garlic and sauté until the onions are tender and brown. Shake off any excess spice blend from the rabbit pieces and add them to the pot with the onion mixture. Brown the rabbit evenly on all sides, turning as necessary. Add the remaining stock and bring to a simmer. Cover the pot and cook in a 350°F / 175°C oven until the rabbit is tender, about 30 minutes. Remove the rabbit from the cooking liquid and keep the meat warm.

3. Skim the surface of the cooking liquid and add the oyster liquor. Reduce to a sauce consistency. Add the oysters and rabbit to the sauce and simmer just until the oysters' edges begin to curl, 3 to 4 minutes.

4. For each portion: Serve 6 oz / 170 g étouffée on a bed of 1½ oz / 45 g rice and garnish with sliced scallions.

Asian Buckwheat Noodle Salad with Hot Sesame Chicken

servings: **10**

portioning information:
**3½ oz / 100 g chicken,
4 oz / 120 g salad**

nutrition per serving:
295 calories, 3 g fat, 24 g total
carbohydrate, 7 g protein, 305 mg
sodium, 50 mg cholesterol

1 lb 4 oz / 580 g cooked buckwheat noodles

1 tsp / 5 mL sesame oil

1½ tsp / 7.5 mL peanut oil

11 oz / 315 g sliced shiitake mushrooms

1 tbsp / 15 mL tamari

¼ tsp / 1.25 mL ground black pepper

HOT SESAME CHICKEN

1½ tsp / 7.5 mL peanut oil

1½ tsp / 7.5 mL sesame oil

Pinch red pepper flakes

¼ tsp / 1.25 mL minced ginger

2¼ lb / 1 kg cooked chicken breast, shredded

6 oz / 170 g mixed greens

4 oz / 110 g frisée

5 fl oz / 150 mL Sherry Vinaigrette (page 228)

10 oz / 280 g bean sprouts, washed

5 oz / 140 g julienned carrot

5 oz / 140 g julienned snow peas

6 oz / 170 g thinly sliced scallions, split lengthwise and cut on the diagonal

5 fl oz / 150 mL Asian Vinaigrette (page 506)

2 tsp / 10 mL toasted black sesame seeds

2 tsp / 10 mL toasted white sesame seeds

3 oz / 85 g pickled ginger

1. Toss the noodles with the sesame oil.

2. Heat the peanut oil in a large sauté pan. Add the shiitakes and sauté until tender. Season with the tamari and pepper. Cool completely.

3. Combine the oils, red pepper flakes, and ginger for the hot sesame chicken. Toss with the chicken.

4. Toss the mixed greens and frisée with one third of the vinaigrette.

5. In a bowl, combine the shiitakes, noodles, bean sprouts, carrots, snow peas, and scallions. Toss with the remaining vinaigrette.

6. For each portion: Place a mound of 4 oz / 120 g salad in the center of 1 oz / 30 g greens. Top with 3½ oz / 100 g chicken and garnish with the sesame seeds and pickled ginger.

Mu Shu Vegetables

servings: **8**

portioning information:
**2 mu shu pancakes, 5 oz /
140 g stir-fried vegetables**

nutrition per serving:
246 calories, 6 g fat, 45 g total
carbohydrate, 5 g protein, 328 mg
sodium, 0 mg cholesterol

3 tbsp / 45 mL sesame oil	8 oz / 225 g Napa cabbage chiffonade
½ oz / 14 g minced garlic	10 oz / 285 g julienned red peppers
½ oz / 14 g minced ginger	2 fl oz / 60 mL reduced-sodium soy sauce
8 oz / 225 g julienned celery	3 fl oz / 90 mL hoisin sauce
8 oz / 225 g julienned carrots	16 Mu Shu Pancakes (see below)
8 oz / 225 g julienned fennel	10 oz / 280 g grilled scallions

1. Heat the oil in a wok or large sauté pan. Add the garlic and ginger and stir-fry until aromatic.

2. Add the vegetables in sequence listed (starting with densest vegetable) and stir-fry until tender. Stir in the soy sauce and hoisin.

3. Cover the pancakes with a damp towel and warm in a 250°F / 120°C oven for 4 minutes.

4. For each portion: Place 2½ oz / 70 g stir-fried vegetables in the center of each of 2 warmed pancakes. Fold the ends of the pancakes inward and roll to completely to encase the vegetable mixture. Garnish each roll with 1 oz / 28 g grilled scallions.

Serving Suggestion

Mu shu vegetables and pancakes can be presented on a heated platter to share.

Mu Shu Pancakes

batch yield: **20 pancakes**

servings: **8**

portioning information:
2 pancakes (1 oz / 30 g)

nutrition per serving:
130 calories, 4 g fat, 19 g total
carbohydrate, 3 g protein, 0 mg
sodium, 0 mg cholesterol

9 oz / 250 g all-purpose flour	3 tbsp / 45 mL sesame oil, or as needed
1 cup / 240 mL boiling water, as needed	

1. Sift the flour into a large bowl, add ¾ cup boiling water to the flour, and stir it in immediately, adding a little additional water if necessary to make a dough. Knead the warm dough until smooth. Wrap the dough and let it rest at room temperature for 30 minutes.

2. Turn the rested dough out onto a floured surface. Cut the dough in half. Use a lightly floured rolling pin to roll each half out until it is ¼-inch thick. Use a cookie cutter to cut out 3-inch circles of dough.

3. Brush ½ teaspoon of sesame oil over the tops of 2 dough circles. Lay one pancake on top of another, so that the oiled sides are together. Roll out to form a 6-inch circle. Repeat with the remainder of the pancakes. Use a damp towel to cover the prepared pancakes.

4. Heat a skillet over low heat. Add one of the pancake pairs and cook until barely golden, dry and blistered, about 1 minute. Turn and repeat on the second side. Remove from the pan and pull apart. Repeat with the remainder of the pancakes. Serve immediately or wrap to hold at room temperature. Reheat the pancakes in a steamer or a microwave before serving.

Stir-Fried Garden Vegetables with Marinated Tofu

servings: **12**

portioning information:
7½ oz / 212 g stir fry, 3 oz / 85 g rice

nutrition per serving:
262 calories, 9 g fat, 33 g total carbohydrate, 15 g protein, 558 mg sodium, 0 mg cholesterol

MARINATED TOFU

1 lb / 450 g cubed firm tofu

¾ fl oz / 20 mL reduced-sodium soy sauce

2 tsp / 10 mL minced ginger

2 tsp / 10 mL minced garlic

All-purpose flour, as needed

1½ tsp / 7.50 mL extra-virgin olive oil

¼ tsp / 1.25 mL sesame oil

2 tsp / 10 mL minced ginger

2 tsp / 10 mL minced garlic

1 oz / 30 g thinly sliced scallions

5 lb / 2.25 kg assorted vegetables, bite-sized pieces (see Notes)

8 fl oz / 240 mL Vegetable Stock (page 490)

3½ fl oz / 105 mL reduced-sodium soy sauce

½ oz / 14 g hot red bean paste

½ tsp / 2.5 mL five-spice powder

1 lb 14 oz / 850 g cooked brown rice (see Notes)

½ oz / 14 g sesame seeds

1. Combine the tofu with the soy sauce, ginger, and garlic. Marinate for 20 minutes.

2. Just before serving, remove the tofu from the marinade. Dust the tofu with flour and shake off any excess.

3. Heat the oils a wok or large sauté pan. Add the tofu and stir-fry until golden on all sides. Remove the tofu from the pan and reserve. Add the ginger, garlic, and scallions to the pan and heat until aromatic. Add the vegetables that require the longest cooking time. If necessary, add a small amount of stock to keep the vegetables from burning. Stir-fry until almost tender, then add the remaining vegetables.

4. When all the vegetables are tender, add the soy sauce, bean paste, five-spice powder, and tofu. Toss to heat thoroughly.

5. For each portion: Serve 7½ oz / 212 g stir-fry on a bed of 3 oz / 85 g rice and garnish with the sesame seeds.

Notes

Choose a variety of seasonal vegetables such as sugar snap peas, squashes, broccoli, cauliflower, and bean sprouts.

Other grains such as barley, quinoa, couscous, and basmati rice, or noodles such as soba, lo mein, or cellophane may be used instead of brown rice.

Wild Mushroom and Couscous Parfait

servings: **10**

portioning information:
**2½ oz / 73 g couscous, 1½ oz /
45 g spinach, 4 oz /
115 g mushrooms, 3 oz / 85 g
smoked tomato mixture,
2 fl oz / 60 mL hot demi-glace**

nutrition per serving:
340 calories, 5 g fat, 62 g total
carbohydrate, 15 g protein, 340 mg
sodium, 0 mg cholesterol

COUSCOUS

1 fl oz / 30 mL extra-virgin olive oil

12 oz / 340 g diced red onions

1 oz / 30 g minced shallots

3 lb / 1.35 kg chopped wild mushrooms

1 pt / 480 mL Vegetable Stock (page 490)

1 lb / 450 g dry couscous

1 tbsp / 15 mL basil chiffonade

2 tbsp / 30 mL chopped parsley

1¼ lb / 580 g Smoked Tomatoes (see Note)

4 oz / 120 g sun-dried tomatoes, minced

1 lb / 450 g spinach, steamed and chopped

1¼ pt / 600 mL Vegetarian Demi-Glace
(page 493), hot

1. In a medium sauce pot, heat the oil and sweat the onions and shallots until translucent. Add the mushrooms and sauté until cooked. Add the stock and bring to a boil. Add the couscous and place the mixture in a pan 13 by 9 by 2-in / 33 by 23 by 5-cm. Cover with foil and place in a 350°F / 175°C oven until the couscous has absorbed all the stock. Stir in the herbs. Keep hot.

2. Combine the smoked tomatoes and the sun-dried tomatoes and heat gently in a small saucepan and keep hot.

3. For each portion: Pack 2½ oz / 73 g couscous mixture into a ring mold. Pack a layer of 1½ oz / 45 g spinach on top of the couscous followed by a layer of 4 oz / 115 g mushrooms and 3 oz / 85 g smoked tomato mixture. Unmold the parfait and serve with 2 fl oz / 60 mL hot demi-glace.

Note

To prepare the smoked tomatoes, follow the instructions in the recipe for Cassoulet with Smoked Tomatoes (page 282), step 1.

Risotto Cakes with Green Beans, Wax Beans, and Chanterelles

servings: **10**

portioning information:
4 oz / 120 g risotto cake, 5½ oz / 155 g bean and mushroom mixture, ½ fl oz / 14 g cheese garnish

nutrition per serving:
371 calories, 11 g fat, 46 g total carbohydrate, 17 g protein, 864 mg sodium, 107 mg cholesterol

RISOTTO CAKES

1 tbsp / 15 mL chopped marjoram	1 oz / 30 g minced garlic
2 tsp / 10 mL chopped sage	1½ lb / 680 g quartered chanterelle mushrooms
½ oz / 14 g chopped parsley	1½ lb / 680 g green beans, blanched
2 tbsp plus 1 tsp / 30 mL chopped savory	1½ lb / 680 g wax beans, blanched
2 oz / 55 g grated Parmesan	½ tsp / 2.5 mL kosher salt
2½ lb / 1.15 kg Risotto (page 380)	½ tsp / 2.5 mL ground black pepper
4 eggs, lightly beaten	½ oz / 14 g chopped parsley
	¾ oz / 20 g grated lemon zest
1 oz / 30 g butter	¾ oz / 20 g chopped savory
	5 oz / 140 g grated Parmesan

1. Combine the herbs, Parmesan, and risotto. Spread the risotto onto a parchment-lined sheet pan to cool completely.

2. In a large bowl, combine the beaten eggs with the risotto. Mix thoroughly. Form into 2-oz / 60-g patties. Preheat a large nonstick pan and cook the cakes until golden brown on each side, about 8 minutes total.

3. Heat the butter in a large sauté pan. Add the garlic and sauté until aromatic. Add the mushrooms and sauté until caramelized and tender. Add the beans and heat thoroughly. Season with the salt, pepper, parsley, lemon zest, and savory.

4. For each portion: Place 2 risotto cakes in the center of a plate and spoon 5½ oz / 155 g bean and mushroom mixture around the cakes. Sprinkle ½ oz / 14 g cheese over the vegetables and risotto.

Couscous and Red Lentils with Moroccan-Style Roasted Vegetables in Saffron Broth

servings: 10

portioning information:
3 oz / 85 g couscous and lentils, 3 fl oz / 90 mL saffron broth, 4¾ oz / 135 g vegetables, 1½ oz / 45 g confit

nutrition per serving:
354 calories, 7 g fat, 61 g total carbohydrate, 12 g protein, 327 mg sodium, 1 mg cholesterol

8 oz / 225 g red lentils

3 qt / 2.88 L Vegetable Stock (page 490)

½ oz / 14 g chopped parsley

1 lb / 450 g Couscous (page 382)

1 qt / 950 mL Vegetable Stock (page 490)

1½ tsp / 1.50 g saffron threads

pinch ground allspice

pinch ground cumin

½ oz / 14 g chopped cilantro

3 lb / 1.35 kg Moroccan-Style Roasted Vegetables (page 375), hot

1 lb / 450 g Pearl Onion and Raisin Confit (page 487)

1. Simmer the lentils in 2 qt / 2 L of the stock until just tender. Allow the lentils to cool in the broth before draining. Fold the lentils and parsley into the couscous.

2. To make the saffron broth, combine the remaining stock, saffron, allspice, and cumin. Simmer for 15 minutes to infuse the stock. Stir in the cilantro just before serving.

3. For each portion: Mound 3 oz / 85 g couscous and lentils in the center of an oversized bowl. Ladle 3 fl oz / 90 mL saffron broth around couscous and arrange 4¾ oz / 135 g roasted vegetables in the broth. Top with 1½ oz / 45 g confit.

Barley Risotto Crumble

servings: **10**

portioning information:
7 oz / 200 g barley mixture, 3 sheets phyllo

nutrition per serving:
480 calories, 14 g fat, 75 g total carbohydrate, 15 g protein, 608 mg sodium, 10 g cholesterol

INFUSED WATER

1 qt / 950 mL water

2¼ tsp / 6.75 g crushed garlic

4 sprigs thyme

4 shallots, chopped

2 bay leaves

1 tsp / 5 mL ground black pepper

½ tsp / 2.5 mL kosher salt

4 fl oz / 120 mL sherry vinegar

1 oz / 28 g butter

2 fl oz / 60 mL olive oil

1 lb / 450 g sliced wild mushrooms

12 shallots, sliced

1 oz / 30 g sliced garlic

3½ fl oz / 105 mL dry white wine

14 oz / 400 g pearl barley

2 oz / 60 g grated Parmesan

2 lb / 910 g asparagus, blanched and chopped

½ tsp / 2.5 mL kosher salt

½ tsp / 2.5 mL ground black pepper

30 (11 x 15-in / 27.5 x 37.5-cm) phyllo sheets

1. Combine the infused water ingredients in a medium saucepan and simmer for 15 minutes. Strain and reserve warm.

2. Heat ½ oz / 14 g of the butter and 1 fl oz / 30 mL of the oil in a large skillet. Add the mushrooms and sauté until golden brown. Remove from the heat and reserve.

3. Heat the remaining butter in a large saucepan. Add the shallots and garlic and sauté until lightly browned. Deglaze the pan with the wine and reduce until dry. Add the mushroom mixture and barley to the shallots and garlic. Toss to heat and fully incorporate the ingredients.

4. Stirring constantly over medium to low heat, add the hot infused water in 3 additions, making sure the barley has absorbed each addition of water before the next is added. Remove the barley mixture from the heat and stir in the Parmesan, asparagus, salt, and pepper.

5. Cut the phyllo sheets in half. Use the remaining oil to very lightly brush each sheet. Stack 4 pieces of phyllo and place 7 oz / 200 g barley mixture in the center of the phyllo. Pull the sheets up and around the barley, leaving the edges loose so they look crumpled.

6. For each portion: Arrange the crumbles on a baking sheet lined with parchment paper. Bake in a 350°F / 175°C oven until golden brown, about 15 minutes.

Southwestern Vegetable Lasagna

servings: 10

portioning information:
2 oz / 57 g pasta rounds,
1½ oz / 45 g beans, 3 oz / 85
g onions and peppers, 1 oz /
28 g cheese

nutrition per serving:
470 calories, 13 g fat, 64 g total
carbohydrate, 21 g protein, 580 mg
sodium, 95 mg cholesterol

BLACK BEANS

1 lb / 450 g cooked black beans

1 pt / 480 mL Vegetable Stock (page 490)

1 oz / 30 g minced garlic

½ fl oz / 15 mL jalapeño rum (see Note)

½ fl oz / 15 mL red wine vinegar

½ fl oz / 15 mL habanero vinegar (see Note)

½ oz / 13 g roasted minced jalapeño

⅛ tsp salt, if needed

½ tsp / 2.5 mL ground black pepper

1¼ pt / 600 mL Vegetarian Demi-Glace (page 493)

CORN PASTA

3 oz / 85 g corn flour (masa harina)

13¼ oz / 375 g semolina flour

3 eggs

3 fl oz / 90 mL water

½ tsp / 2.5 mL red pepper flakes (optional)

1 lb / 450 g julienned bell pepper

1 lb / 450 g thinly sliced onions

2 fl oz / 60 mL Vegetable Stock (490)

1 lb / 450 g Vegetarian Refried Beans (page 391)

5 oz / 140 g grated sharp Cheddar cheese

5 oz / 140 g grated jalapeño Jack cheese

1. Simmer the beans in the stock until hot.

2. Add the remaining ingredients and simmer for 15 minutes. Refrigerate until needed.

3. To make the pasta: Combine the ingredients in a mixing bowl. Use a dough hook to knead the dough until it forms a smooth elastic ball. Allow the dough to rest for 30 minutes before rolling into thin sheets. Cut the sheets into thirty 4-in / 10-cm squares or rounds and cook in simmering water.

4. Stew the onions and peppers in the reserved cooking liquid from the beans until tender.

5. Heat the refried beans, onions and peppers, black beans, and pasta circles separately before assembling.

6. For each portion: Lay 1 pasta piece on a large plate. Place 1½ oz / 45 g refried beans on top of the pasta and sprinkle with ½ oz / 14 g Cheddar. Place a second pasta piece on top of the Cheddar. Scatter 3 oz / 85 g onions and peppers over the pasta and top with 1½ oz / 45 g black beans. Sprinkle ½ oz / 14 g Jack cheese over the beans and top with a third pasta piece.

Note

Steep 1 jalapeño per 1 cup of dark rum for at least 1 week. Steep 1 habanero per 1 cup of red wine or malt vinegar for at least 1 week.

Serving Suggestion

For each portion: garnish the plate with Tomato Salsa (page 485), Jicama Salad (page 204), and Guacamole (page 484).

(Nutrition information does not include serving suggestions.)

Yucatán Pumpkin Seed–Sauced "Enchiladas" with Roasted Tomato and Hard-Boiled Egg (Papadzules)

servings: **8**

portioning information:
2 tortillas, ½ oz / 14 g chopped spinach, ½ egg, 2 fl oz / 60 mL pumpkin seed sauce, 2 fl oz / 60 mL tomato-habanero sauce

nutrition per serving:
706 calories, 44 g fat, 53 g total carbohydrate, 41 g protein, 300 mg sodium, 135 mg cholesterol

2 sprigs epazote *or* 8 to 10 sprigs cilantro

4 to 6 habanero chiles, cut in half

1½ lb / 680 g pumpkin seeds (pepitas), toasted

4½ lb / 2 kg ripe tomatoes

1 tbsp / 15 mL corn oil

2 thinly sliced onions

½ tsp / 2.5 mL kosher salt

16 (8-in / 20-cm) corn tortillas

12 oz / 340 g blanched spinach, drained and chopped

4 hard-cooked eggs, chopped

1. To make the epazote broth: Measure 5 cups water into a saucepan. Add the epazote (or the cilantro) and half of the habaneros. Bring to a simmer over medium-high heat. Simmer the broth until flavorful, 12 to 15 minutes. Strain this broth and reserve. Discard the epazote (or cilantro) and habaneros.

2. To make the Pumpkin Seed Sauce: Grind the pumpkin seeds in a mortar and pestle, spice grinder, or food processor, working in batches, until the seeds are pulverized into a very fine powder; set aside. Purée 3 cups of the epazote broth with the pumpkin seed powder in a blender until very smooth. Bring this mixture to a full rolling boil, stirring frequently. (The sauce will be very thick and may appear curdled; that is correct.) Purée the sauce with a stick blender (or purée it in a blender, working in batches) until very smooth.

3. To make the Tomato-Habanero sauce: Broil the tomatoes until the skin is charred and blistered on the first side, about 6 minutes, then flip and broil until the other side is charred. Peel and seed the tomatoes after they have cooled. (Do this over a strainer set in a bowl so that you can collect all the juices.) Purée the tomatoes and the reserved juices in food processor, pulsing the machine off and on just until they form a coarse purée.

4. Heat the oil in a saucepan over medium heat. Add the onion and sauté, stirring often, until golden brown, about 8 minutes. Add the tomatoes and the remaining habaneros. Bring the sauce to a simmer and continue to cook over low heat until thickened, about 20 minutes. Season to taste with the salt and set aside.

5. To assemble the enchiladas: Wrap the tortillas in a clean cloth and steam them until they are soft and pliable, about 5 minutes. Top each tortilla with ½ oz / 14 g chopped spinach (reheat the spinach if necessary), 1 tablespoon chopped egg, and about 1 tbsp / 15 mL of the pumpkin seed sauce to moisten the filling.

6. For each portion: Warm the pumpkin seed sauce and thin it to a light, coating consistency, with a little additional epazote broth. Arrange enchiladas on a warmed plate, coat lightly with 2 fl oz / 60 mL pumpkin seed sauce. Ladle 2 fl oz / 60 mL tomato-habanero sauce over the enchiladas and serve at once garnished with an additional 1 tbsp / 15 mL chopped hard-boiled egg.

Roasted Eggplant Tian

servings: 10

portioning information:
8 oz / 224 g tian

nutrition per serving:
196 calories, 8 g fat, 24 g total carbohydrate, 8 g protein, 333 mg sodium, 11 mg cholesterol

2¾ lb / 1.25 kg thinly sliced peeled eggplant
2¼ lb / 1 kg thinly sliced onions
2 lb / 910 g thinly sliced tomatoes
½ oz / 14 g minced garlic
1 tbsp / 15 mL basil chiffonade
1 tbsp / 15 mL chopped thyme

4½ oz / 130 g grated Parmesan
4 fl oz / 120 mL red wine
1 fl oz / 30 mL extra-virgin olive oil
1¾ oz / 50 g chopped olives
1 oz / 30 g rinsed capers

1. Layer the eggplant, onions, and tomatoes in a 13 x 9 x 2-in / 33 x 23 x 5-cm baking dish. Sprinkle each layer with garlic and herbs. Sprinkle the top layer with the cheese.

2. Whisk together the wine and oil and drizzle over the layered vegetables. Bake in a 300°F / 150°C oven until the vegetables are very tender, about 2½ hours.

3. For each portion: Serve an 8-oz / 224-g portion of the eggplant (reheat in a hot oven or in the microwave, if necessary). Garnish each portion with a little of the olives and capers.

Serving Suggestion

Serve the tian with Grilled Naan (page 440) and a green salad.

(Nutrition information does not include serving suggestions.)

Stuffed Cabbage Roll

servings: 10

portioning information:
**2 cabbage rolls,
3 oz / 85 g ragoût**

nutrition per serving:
320 calories, 6 g fat, 60 g total carbohydrate, 9 g protein, 309 mg sodium, 0 mg cholesterol

5 lb / 2.25 kg savoy cabbage
1½ fl oz / 45 mL vegetable oil
2 oz / 55 g minced onion
½ lb / 565 g brown rice
1 qt / 950 mL Vegetable Stock (page 490)
¾ oz / 20 g grated orange zest

1 tsp / 5 mL chopped thyme
1 tsp / 5 mL kosher salt
½ tsp / 2.5 mL fresh ground pepper
1 lb 14 oz / 850 g Lentil Ragoût (page 501)
2½ oz / 73 g tomato concassé
2 tbsp / 30 mL chopped chives

1. Carefully separate the cabbage leaves. Blanch and shock the leaves. Reserve 20 of the large leaves and julienne 1½ lb / 670 g of the smaller inner leaves.

2. Heat the oil in a medium saucepan. Add the onion and sauté until translucent. Add the rice and toss to coat with the oil. Add the stock, zest, thyme, salt, pepper, and chopped cabbage leaves. Cover the pot tightly and cook in a 325°F / 165°C oven until the rice is tender and has absorbed all the liquid, about 30 minutes.

3. For each portion: Place 2½ oz / 70 g rice mixture on each of 2 large cabbage leaves and roll to completely encase the rice. Serve on a bed of 3 oz / 85 g ragoût and garnish with 1 tbsp / 15 mL tomato concassé and a sprinkling of chives.

Wild Mushroom and Nut Pie

batch yield: two 9-inch / 23-cm pies

servings: 16

portioning information: 4 oz / 115 g

nutrition per serving:
229 calories, 15 g fat, 13 g total carbohydrate, 11 g protein, 172 mg sodium, 47 mg cholesterol (not including garnish)

¾ oz / 20 g dried cèpes

¾ oz / 20 g dried morels

7 oz / 200 g whole blanched almonds

2½ oz / 70 g cashews

1 oz / 30 g butter

6½ oz / 185 g diced onion

½ oz / 14 g minced garlic

8 oz / 225 g minced white mushrooms

2 tbsp / 30 mL chopped parsley

2 tsp / 10 mL chopped thyme

1 tbsp / 15 mL chopped marjoram

1 tsp / 5 mL chopped sage

13 oz / 370 g cooked brown rice

3 oz / 85 g shredded fontina

3 oz / 85 g shredded mozzarella

8 oz / 225 g nonfat cottage cheese

2 eggs

Vegetable oil spray, as needed

1. Reconstitute the dried mushrooms in warm water for about 20 minutes. Drain and chop.

2. Roast the nuts in a 300°F / 150°C oven until golden brown. Cool and grind or chop finely.

3. Heat the butter in a large sauté pan. Add the onion and garlic and sauté until the onions are translucent. Add the fresh mushrooms and cook until their juices have evaporated. Stir in the chopped herbs and remove from the heat.

4. Combine the rice, ground nuts, and cheeses in a large bowl. Add the cooked mushrooms, rehydrated mushrooms, and eggs to the rice mixture. Mix well to incorporate. Spray two 9-in / 23-cm pie tins with vegetable oil . Pack the mushroom mixture into the tins.

5. Bake the pies in a 350°F / 175°C oven until firm and browned, about 1 hour. Allow the pie to rest for 15 minutes before slicing each pie into 8 wedges.

Serving Suggestion

Serve the pie with grilled pineapple, apple, or mango slices or steamed broccoli with lemon zest.

(Nutrition information does not include serving suggestions.)

Barley Risotto with Garden Vegetables

servings: **10**

portioning information: **3 oz / 85 g barley, 6 oz / 170 g vegetables**

nutrition per serving:
180 calories, 2 g fat, 36 g total carbohydrate, 5 g protein, 350 mg sodium, 0 mg cholesterol

1½ qt / 1.44 L Vegetable Stock (page 490)

1½ qt / 1.45 L carrot juice

4 fl oz / 30 mL olive oil

2 oz / 55 g diced shallots

½ oz / 14 g minced garlic

4 oz / 115 g quartered wild mushrooms

1½ lb / 625 g pearl barley

½ tsp / 2.5 mL kosher salt

½ tsp / 2.5 mL ground black pepper

VEGETABLE GLAZE

1 pt / 480 mL Vegetable Stock (page 490)

1 oz / 30 g arrowroot

2 tbsp / 30 mL chopped parsley

2 tbsp / 30 mL chopped chives

14 oz / 400 g baby radishes, blanched

1¼ lb / 565 g quartered artichoke hearts, blanched

14 oz / 400 g haricots verts, blanched

14 oz / 400 g small white turnips, blanched

5 tsp / 25 mL reduced balsamic vinegar (see Note)

1. Bring the stock and carrot juice to a simmer in a small sauce pot.

2. Heat the oil in a medium sauce pot. Add the shallots, garlic, and mushrooms and sweat until the shallots are translucent. Add the barley and sauté until coated with the oil. Stirring constantly over medium heat, add the hot stock mixture in 3 additions, making sure the barley has absorbed each addition of stock before the next is added.

3. Prepare the vegetable glaze by combining the arrowroot with enough stock to make a paste. Bring the remaining stock to a simmer in a small saucepan. Stir in the arrowroot mixture and simmer until the stock has thickened, about 2 minutes. Stir in the herbs. Reheat the blanched vegetables in the hot vegetable glaze.

4. For each portion: Serve 3 oz / 85 g barley garnished with 6 oz / 170 g vegetables and drizzled with reduced balsamic vinegar.

Note

Reduce balsamic vinegar to a syrup by simmering over medium heat.

Farro with Vegetable Ragoût and Parsley and Toasted Almond Salsa

servings: **10**

portioning information:
3¼ oz / 90 g farro, 4 oz / 115 g vegetables

nutrition per serving:
200 calories, 8 g fat, 28 g total carbohydrate, 8 g protein, 347 mg sodium, 0 mg cholesterol

PARSLEY AND TOASTED ALMOND SALSA

1 oz / 30 g diced shallots

1 fl oz / 30 mL red wine vinegar

1¾ oz / 50 g chopped parsley

1 tbsp / 15 mL chopped chervil

1 tbsp / 15 mL chopped basil

1 tbsp / 15 mL capers, rinsed and chopped

1 fl oz / 30 mL extra-virgin olive oil

3 oz / 85 g roasted chopped almonds

2 fl oz / 60 mL Vegetable Stock (page 490)

4 oz / 115 g diced onion

½ oz / 14 g minced garlic

12 oz / 340 g broccoli florets, steamed

12 oz / 340 g cauliflower florets, steamed

7 oz / 200 g sliced turnips, steamed

7 oz / 200 g oblique-cut carrots, steamed

1 fl oz / 30 mL fresh lemon juice

1 tsp / 5 mL kosher salt

½ tsp / 2.5 mL ground black pepper

2 lb / 900 g Farro (page 385)

1. To prepare the parsley and toasted almond salsa, macerate the shallots in the vinegar for 20 minutes. Combine the shallot mixture with the remaining salsa ingredients.

2. Heat the stock in a large saucepan. Add the onion and garlic and sweat until the onions are translucent. Add the steamed vegetables and heat thoroughly. Season with the lemon juice, salt, and pepper.

3. For each portion: Mound 3¼ oz / 90 g farro in the center of a large bowl. Arrange 4 oz / 115 g vegetables around the farro and spoon ¾ oz / 20 g salsa over the vegetables and farro.

Black Bean Chili

batch yield: **2 qt / 950 L**

servings: **10**

portioning information: **6 oz / 50 g**

nutrition per serving:
237 calories, 3 g fat, 4 g total carbohydrate, 13 g protein, 313 mg sodium, 0 mg cholesterol

½ fl oz / 15 mL olive oil

12 oz / 340 g diced onions

½ oz / 14 g minced garlic

4 oz / 115 g diced celery

5 oz / 140 g diced red peppers

4 oz / 115 g diced green peppers

1 minced jalapeño

1 tsp / 5 mL coriander seeds, toasted and ground

2 tsp / 10 mL cumin seeds, toasted and ground

1 tbsp / 15 ml hot paprika

¼ tsp / 1.25 ground cinnamon

1 lb / 450 g cooked black beans

2 lb / 910 g tomato concassé

½ oz / 14 g Mexican chocolate

½ oz / 14 g chopped cilantro

½ tsp / 2.5 mL kosher salt

½ tsp / 2.5 mL ground black pepper

1. Heat the oil in a large sauce pot. Add the onions and garlic and sauté until the onions are translucent. Add the celery and sweat 1 minute. Add the peppers and jalapeño. Sauté until very hot, about 2 minutes. Add the coriander, cumin, paprika, and cinnamon and sauté until aromatic, about 2 minutes.

2. Add the beans and tomatoes. Simmer until the vegetables are tender and the flavors have developed, about 20 minutes.

3. Just before serving, season the chili by adding the chocolate, cilantro, salt, and pepper.

Serving Suggestion

Serve with Brown Rice Pilaf (page 378), Tomatillo Salsa (page 485), and baked tortilla chips.

Vegetable Stew

batch yield: **3 lb / 1.35 kg**

servings: **12**

portioning information:
8 oz / 224 g

nutrition per serving:
186 calories, 5 g fat, 32 g total
carbohydrate, 5 g protein, 309 mg
sodium, 0 mg cholesterol

SPICE BLEND

1 tsp / 2 g dry mustard

1 tsp / 2 g ground coriander

1 tsp / 2 g ground cinnamon

½ tsp / 2.5 mL cayenne

2 tsp / 10 mL Spanish paprika

1 tsp / 2 g cardamom seeds

1 fl oz / 30 mL olive oil

1¼ lb / 565 g diced onions

¾ oz / 20 g minced garlic

1 lb / 450 g diced leeks

1 lb / 450 g diced pumpkin

1 lb / 450 g diced butternut squash

8 oz / 225 g diced zucchini

3 qt / 3 L Vegetable Stock (page 490)

8 oz / 225 g diced carrots

8 oz / 225 g diced celery

1 lb / 450 g diced peeled eggplant

6 fl oz / 180 mL tomato purée

8 oz / 225 g currants

6 oz / 170 g cooked chickpeas

8 oz / 225 g cooked peeled fava beans

1¾ fl oz / 50 mL fresh lemon juice

1 tsp / 5 mL kosher salt

½ tsp / 2.5 mL ground black pepper

5 tsp / 25 mL grated lemon zest

1. Combine the spice blend ingredients and toast lightly in a dry sauté pan over low heat.

2. Heat the oil in a in a large stew pot. Add the onions, garlic, and leeks and sweat until the onions are translucent. Add the spice blend to the onion mixture and sauté until aromatic. Add the pumpkin, squash, zucchini, and enough of the stock to cover the vegetables. Stew for about 10 minutes.

3. Add the carrots, celery, eggplant, tomato purée, currants, and remaining stock. Simmer until all the vegetables are three-quarters cooked, about 25 minutes. Stir in the chickpeas and fava beans. Cover and stew until the vegetables are very tender.

4. Season with the lemon juice, salt, and pepper and garnish each portion with zest.

Serving Suggestion

Serve the stew on a bed of couscous.

(Nutrition information does not include serving suggestions.)

Shrimp-Filled Pasta

batch yield: 60 filled ravioli (or similar filled shapes)

servings: 10

portioning information: 6 ravioli

nutrition per serving:
170 calories, 2 g fat, 45 g total carbohydrate, 5g protein, 42 mg sodium, 19 mg cholesterol

SHRIMP MOUSSELINE FILLING

14 oz / 400 g shrimp, peeled and deveined

2 oz / 55 g part-skim ricotta cheese

1 tbsp / 15 mL basil chiffonade

½ tsp / 2.5 mL kosher salt

pinch ground white pepper

½ tsp / 2.5 mL fresh lemon or lime juice

1 lb / 700 kg Basic Pasta Dough (page 398)

1. Grind the shrimp to a fine paste in a food processor. Add the ricotta and pulse just until the ricotta is incorporated. Remove the shrimp mixture from the processor and place in a metal bowl over an ice bath. Fold in the basil, salt, pepper, and juice.

2. Begin making the ravioli by rolling the pasta dough into thin sheets. Cut 60 2-in / 5-cm circles or squares. Place the cut pasta on baking sheets lined with parchment paper. Cover loosely with plastic wrap when not using to prevent the dough from drying.

3. To assemble the ravioli, place 1 tsp / 5 mL filling in the center of half the pasta circles or squares, Brush the edges of the pasta with water and top with second piece. Press to release any trapped air in the pasta and to seal the edges. Refrigerate until ready to cook.

4. Cook the pasta in simmering water until the pasta rises to the surface and is tender to the bite.

Serving Suggestion

Serve with grilled red endive, peppers, and grilled shrimp on a pool of Red Pepper Coulis (page 498).

(Nutrition information does not include serving suggestions.)

Chorizo-Filled Pasta

batch yield: **8 oz / 225 g**

servings: **8**

portioning information:
6 ravioli

nutrition per serving:
230 calories, 4 g fat, 3 g total
carbohydrate, 14 g protein, 290 mg
sodium, 20 mg cholesterol

CHORIZO FILLING

5 oz / 140 g lean pork, diced

2½ oz / 70 g cooked rice

2¼ tsp / 6.75 g chopped jalapeño

½ oz / 14 g minced garlic

2 oz / 55 g chopped dried chorizo sausage

1 tsp / 5 mL kosher salt

½ tsp / 2.5 mL cayenne

1 tsp / 5 mL chopped oregano

1 tsp / 5 mL cider vinegar

¼ tsp / 1.25 mL red pepper flakes

1 lb / 700 g Basic Pasta Dough (page 398)

1. Thoroughly chill the ingredients.

2. Combine the pork and rice and grind twice through a medium die. Combine the pork mixture with the remaining ingredients and grind for the third time through the medium die. Refrigerate before using.

3. Begin making the ravioli by rolling the pasta dough into thin sheets. Cut 2-in / 5-cm circles or squares. Place the cut pasta on sheet pans lined with parchment paper. Cover with plastic wrap when not using to prevent the dough from drying.

4. To assemble the ravioli, place 1 tsp / 5 mL filling in the center of half the pasta circles or squares. Brush the edges of the pasta with water and top with second piece. Press to release any trapped air in the pasta and to seal the edges. Refrigerate until ready to cook.

5. Cook the pasta in simmering water until the pasta rises to the surface and is tender to the bite.

Serving Suggestion

Serve these ravioli with 2 fl oz / 60 mL Tomato Coulis or Red Pepper Coulis (both on page 498).

Goat Cheese Ravioli

servings: **10**

portioning information:
6 ravioli, 2¼ fl oz / 68 mL sauce

nutrition per serving:
200 calories, 5 g fat, 24 g total carbohydrate, 15 g protein, 344 mg sodium, 50 mg cholesterol

GOAT CHEESE FILLING

½ oz / 14 g minced shallots

1 tsp / 3 g minced garlic

1 tsp / 5 mL olive oil

3 oz / 85 g coarsely chopped spinach

5 oz / 140 g goat cheese

5 oz / 140 g part-skim ricotta

1 egg white

1 oz / 30 g grated Parmesan

1 tbsp / 15 mL basil chiffonade

1 tsp / 5 mL chopped oregano

1½ lb / 700 g Basic Pasta Dough (page 398)

RAVIOLI SAUCE

1 qt / 950 mL Chicken Velouté (page 497)

2 oz / 55 g Pesto (page 502)

5 fl oz / 150 mL heavy cream

1. To make the ravioli filling, sauté the shallots and garlic in the oil until the shallots are translucent.

2. Add the spinach and cook until wilted. Remove from the heat. Stir in the goat cheese, ricotta, egg whites, Parmesan, basil, and oregano. Refrigerate for at least 1 hour.

3. Begin making the ravioli by rolling the pasta dough into thin sheets. Cut 2-in / 5-cm circles or squares. Place the cut pasta on sheet pans lined with parchment paper. Cover with plastic wrap when not using to prevent the dough from drying.

4. To assemble the ravioli, place 1 tsp / 5 mL filling in the center of half of the pasta circles or squares. Brush the edges of the pasta with water and top with second pasta circles. Press to release any trapped air in the pasta and to seal the edges. Refrigerate until ready to cook.

5. Prepare the sauce by heating the velouté, pesto, and cream together in a saucepan.

6. For each serving: Cook 6 ravioli in simmering water until the pasta rises to the surface and is tender to the bite. Drain and serve with 2¼ fl oz / 68 mL hot sauce.

White Bean Ravioli

servings: 10

portioning information:
6 ravioli

nutrition per serving:
170 calories, 8 g fat, 18 g total
carbohydrate, 5 g protein, 250 mg
sodium, 0 mg cholesterol

6½ oz / 185 g dried cannellini beans

1½ pt / 720 mL Vegetable Stock (page 490)

1 bay leaf

4 sprigs thyme

1 oignon piqué

2 fl oz / 60 mL extra-virgin olive oil

1¾ oz / 50 g minced garlic

½ tsp / 2.5 mL fresh lemon juice

½ tsp / 2.5 mL kosher salt

Pinch ground black pepper

1½ lb / 708 g Basic Pasta Dough (page 398)

1. Soak the beans for 8 to 12 hours in enough cold water to cover by 3 in / 8 cm. Drain and simmer the beans in the stock with the bay leaf, thyme, and oignon piqué until tender.

2. Drain the beans, reserving the stock and discarding the bay leaf, thyme, and oignon piqué. Mash the beans with a fork.

3. Heat the oil in a small sauté pan. Add the garlic and sweat until tender.

4. Combine the garlic, lemon juice, salt, and pepper with the mashed beans. Adjust the consistency with the reserved cooking liquid, if necessary. Refrigerate the bean mixture for at least 1 hour.

5. Begin making the ravioli by rolling the pasta dough into thin sheets. Cut sixty 2-in / 5-cm squares. Place the cut pasta on baking sheets lined with parchment paper. Cover with plastic wrap when not using to prevent the dough from drying.

6. Place 1 tsp / 5 mL bean mixture in the center of half of the pieces of pasta. Brush the edges of the pasta with water and top with a second pasta square. Press to release any trapped air in the pasta and to seal the edges. Refrigerate until ready to cook.

7. For each serving: Cook 6 ravioli in simmering water until the pasta rises to the surface and is tender to the bite.

Shrimp and Herb Ravioli with Fennel Sauce

servings: **8**

portioning information:
6 ravoili, 2 fl oz / 60 mL sauce

nutrition per serving:
566 calories, 17 g fat, 64 g total
carbohydrate, 36 g protein, 610 mg
sodium, 155 mg cholesterol

SHRIMP AND HERB FILLING

3 lb / 1.35 kg shrimp (16–20 count)

1½ fl oz / 45 mL Pernod

1½ fl oz /4 mL fresh lemon juice

12 fl oz / 360 mL heavy cream

1 oz / 30 g basil chiffonade

1 oz / 30 g chopped parsley

½ oz / 14 g salt

½ tsp / 2.5 mL cayenne

2 lb / 910 g Basic Pasta Dough (page 398)

FENNEL SAUCE

6 oz / 170 g chopped onions

½ oz / 15 g butter

1 qt / 950 mL water

10 peppercorns

¾ oz / 20 g minced garlic

12 oz / 340 g diced leeks

2¼ lb / 1 kg diced fennel

GARNISH

2 oz / 55 g julienned carrot

12 oz / 360 g julienned fennel

4 oz / 115 g julienned leeks

1 tbsp / 15 mL chopped fennel tops

1 tbsp / 15 mL Pernod

4½ fl oz / 135 mL evaporated skim milk

1. Peel and devein the shrimp and reserve the shells for the sauce. Split the shrimp in half lengthwise and then cut into ½-in / 1-cm pieces.

2. To make the ravioli filling, purée half of the shrimp with the Pernod, juice, and cream in a food processor until a smooth paste forms. Remove the purée from the processor and place in a metal bowl over an ice bath. Fold in the basil, parsley, salt, cayenne, and remaining shrimp.

3. Begin making the ravioli by rolling the pasta dough into thin sheets. Cut 2-in / 5-cm circles or squares. Place the cut pasta on sheet pans lined with parchment paper. Cover with plastic wrap when not using to prevent the dough from drying.

4. To assemble the ravioli, place 1 oz / 20 g of filling in the center of half the pieces of pasta. Brush the edges of the pasta with water and top with second pasta squares. Press to release any trapped air in the pasta and to seal the edges. Refrigerate until ready to cook.

5. Prepare the sauce by first making a shrimp stock. Sauté the onions and reserved shrimp shells in the butter until the shells are opaque. Add the water and peppercorns and simmer uncovered for 1 hour, skimming the surface when necessary. Strain.

6. In a small saucepan, sweat the garlic in the strained shrimp stock. Add the leeks and fennel. Simmer until the vegetables are tender. Purée the sauce until smooth and strain to remove all fibers.

7. Return the sauce to the pot and add the garnish ingredients. Simmer until the vegetables are tender. Stir in the Pernod and milk just before serving.

8. For each portion: Cook 6 ravioli in simmering water until the pasta rises to the surface and is tender to the bite. Drain and serve on a pool of 2 fl oz / 60 mL hot sauce.

Lobster Cappelletti with Ginger Sauce

batch yield: **48 filled cappelletti**

servings: **8**

portioning information: **6 cappelletti, 3 fl oz / 90 mL sauce**

nutrition per serving: 390 calories, 17 g fat, 45 g total carbohydrate, 32 g protein, 500 mg sodium, 100 mg cholesterol

LOBSTER FILLING

10½ oz / 300 g lobster meat

1 egg white

1 fl oz / 30 mL heavy cream

½ oz / 14 g minced shallots

½ oz / 14 g minced garlic

1 tbsp / 15 mL chopped chives

1¼ lb / 565 g Saffron Pasta Dough (page 400)

1½ pt / 720 mL Ginger Sauce (page 495)

GARNISH

½ oz / 14 g lime zest

15 pieces lobster claw

1. To make the lobster filling, purée the lobster, egg white, and cream in a food processor until a smooth paste forms. Remove the purée from the processor and place in a metal bowl over an ice bath. Fold in the shallots, garlic, and chives.

2. Begin making the cappelletti by rolling the pasta dough into thin sheets. Cut into 3-in / 8-cm squares and place on sheet pans lined with parchment paper. Cover with plastic wrap when not using to prevent the dough from drying.

3. To assemble the cappelletti, place 1¾ oz / 50 g of filling in the center of a square of pasta. Brush the edges of the pasta with water and fold into a triangle. Press to release any trapped air and to seal the edges. Twist and press the 2 triangle points together to form cappelletti. Repeat with the remaining pasta and filling. Refrigerate until ready to cook.

4. Gently heat the ginger sauce in a small sauce pot.

5. Place the lime zest in a small pot and cover with cold water. When the water begins to boil, drain and repeat the process 2 more times. Drain and reserve.

6. For each portion: Cook 6 cappelletti in simmering water until the pasta rises to the surface and is tender to the bite. Drain and toss the cappelletti with 3 fl oz / 90 mL hot sauce and garnish each portion with a lobster claw and blanched lime zest.

Gnocchi with Shiitake, Oven-Dried Tomatoes, Zucchini, and Pesto

servings: **20**

portioning information:
5 oz / 14 g gnocchi, 4 oz / 115 g vegetables, ½ oz / 14 g tomatoes, ½ oz / 14 g pesto

nutrition per serving:
300 calories, 13 g fat, 38 g total carbohydrate, 9 g protein, 411 mg sodium, 34 mg cholesterol

1 lb / 450 g halved cherry tomatoes	2¼ lb / 1 kg zucchini batonnet
2 tsp / 10 mL kosher salt	1 lb 11 oz / 765 g halved shiitake mushrooms
6 lb / 2.75 kg Gnocchi (page 401)	10 oz / 285 g Pesto (page 502)
1 tbsp / 15 mL olive oil	2 oz / 55 g shaved Parmesan

1. Place the tomatoes cut side up on a rack in a roasting pan. Salt the tomatoes and bake in a 250°F / 121°C convection oven until they appear dry and have a deep red color, 1 hour.

2. Simmer the gnocchi in water until they float to the surface and are cooked through.

3. Heat the oil in a large sauté pan. Add the zucchini and sauté until tender. Remove from the pan and reserve. Return the pan to the heat, add the shiitakes, and sauté until tender. Remove from the pan and toss with the zucchini.

4. For each portion: Add 5 oz / 140 g gnocchi to a pan and sauté until lightly browned. Add 4 oz / 115 g zucchini and shiitakes, ½ oz / 14 g tomatoes, and ½ oz / 14 g pesto. Toss to thoroughly mix and heat. Garnish with a few curls of shaved Parmesan.

Linguine with Olives, Basil, and Red and Yellow Tomatoes

servings: 10

portioning information:
4 oz / 115 g pasta, 4 oz / 115 g vegetables

nutrition per serving:
383 calories, 11 g fat, 58 g total carbohydrate, 13 g protein, 425 mg sodium, 5 mg cholesterol

3 lb / 1.35 kg linguine

2 fl oz / 60 mL olive oil

½ oz / 14 g minced garlic

2¾ lb / 1.25 kg halved red and yellow cherry tomatoes

4 oz / 115 g finely sliced scallions

4 oz / 115 g sliced pitted Kalamata olives

2 fl oz / 60 mL Vegetable Stock (page 490)

10 tsp / 50 mL basil chiffonade

2 oz / 55 g shaved Parmesan

1. Cook the pasta in boiling water until tender to the bite. Drain and toss with 1 fl oz / 30 mL of the oil.

2. For each portion: Heat a light film of oil in a sauté pan over medium-high heat. Add ¼ tsp garlic and sauté until aromatic. Add 4 oz / 115 g tomatoes and cook just until heated. Add 2 tsp / 10 mL scallions and 2 tsp / 10 mL olives. Add 4 oz / 115 g cooked pasta. If the mixture is too dry, add a little of the stock. Toss to incorporate the ingredients and heat thoroughly.

3. Remove the pan from the heat and toss in 1 tsp / 5 mL basil. Garnish with 1 tsp / 5 mL Parmesan before serving.

Linguine with Clams, Fennel, Leeks, and Saffron

servings: 10

portioning information:
4 oz / 115 g pasta, 4 oz / 115 g clam-and-fennel sauce

nutrition per serving:
417 calories, 5 g fat, 63 g total carbohydrate, 25 g protein, 323 mg sodium, 38 mg cholesterol

1 pt / 480 mL dry white wine

4 sprigs thyme

3 lb / 1.35 kg Manila clams

1 fl oz / 30 mL olive oil

9 oz / 255 g diced leeks

9 oz / 255 g diced fennel

2 tsp / 10 mL minced garlic

¼ tsp / 1.25 mL saffron threads

1 lb / 450 g tomato concassé

1¼ lb / 570 kg linguine

2 tsp / 10 mL kosher salt

¼ tsp / 0.625 mL ground black pepper

¾ oz / 20 g chopped parsley

1. Bring the wine to a boil in a large saucepan. Add the thyme and clams. Cover and steam until the clams fully open. Strain the cooking liquid through a fine-mesh sieve.

2. Heat the oil in a large sauté pan. Add the leeks, fennel, garlic, and saffron. Sweat until the vegetables are tender. Add the reserved clam broth, clams, and tomatoes; heat thoroughly.

3. For each portion, cook 2 oz / 55 g dry pasta in boiling water until tender to the bite. Drain and combine with 4 oz / 115 g of the clam mixture in a sauté pan. Toss over high heat. Season with the salt and pepper and toss to incorporate. Garnish with parsley.

Fedelini with Broccoli Rabe, Pancetta, Parmesan, and Toasted Crumbs

servings: **10**

portioning information:
4 oz / 115 g pasta, 4 oz / 115 g broccoli rabe sauce

nutrition per serving:
495 calories, 8 g fat, 85 g total carbohydrate, 20 g protein, 534 mg sodium, 12 mg cholesterol

TOASTED CRUMBS

1 lb / 450 g rustic bread

Olive oil spray, as needed

1¼ lb / 570 g fedelini pasta

2 oz / 55 g julienned pancetta

12 oz / 340 g diced onions

1 oz / 30 g minced garlic

2 lb / 910 g chopped broccoli rabe

1 tbsp / 15 mL chopped thyme

1 tbsp / 15 mL red pepper flakes

1½ pt / 720 mL Chicken Stock (page 489)

12 fl oz / 360 mL Chicken Velouté-Style Sauce (page 497)

2 tbsp / 30 mL fresh lemon juice

2 oz / 55 g grated Parmesan

¾ oz / 20 g chopped parsley

1. Remove the crust from the bread and discard. Cut the bread into large dice and process in a food processor to a medium-size crumb. Spread the crumbs on a sheet pan and spray with oil. Bake in a 350°F / 175°C oven, turning frequently until golden brown.

2. Cook the pasta in boiling water until tender to the bite. Drain and rinse in cool water to stop the cooking. Drain and reserve.

3. Render the pancetta in a preheated, large sauté pan. Add the onions and garlic and sweat until the onions are translucent.

4. Add the broccoli rabe, thyme, and red pepper flakes. Sauté until the broccoli rabe is tender.

5. Combine the sauce and stock. Stir into the broccoli rabe and reduce to a sauce consistency. Season with the juice. Keep hot.

6. For each portion, reheat 4 oz / 115 g cooked pasta and combine in a saute pan with 4 oz / 115 g broccoli rabe mixture. Toss to incorporate and heat thoroughly. Garnish with the Parmesan, toasted crumbs, and parsley.

Capellini with Grilled Vegetable Ragoût

servings: **10**

portioning information:
4 oz / 115 g pasta, 4 oz / 115 g grilled vegetable sauce

nutrition per serving:
347 calories, 6 g fat, 62 g total carbohydrate, 12 g protein, 215 mg sodium, 0 mg cholesterol

GRILLED VEGETABLES

4 oz / 115 g quartered red peppers

4 oz / 115 g quartered yellow peppers

4 oz / 115 g quartered green peppers

4 oz / 115 g thickly sliced red onions

1 lb / 450 g sliced zucchini, cut on the diagonal

1 lb / 450 g sliced yellow squash, cut on the diagonal

1 fennel bulb, quartered

4 fl oz / 120 mL Balsamic Vinaigrette (page 503)

1 tbsp / 15 mL extra-virgin olive oil

1 tbsp / 15 mL minced garlic

1 oz / 30 g diced shallots

4 fl oz / 120 mL dry white wine

8 oz / 225 g tomato concassé

1 tsp / 5 mL kosher salt

¼ tsp / 1.25 mL ground black pepper

1 fl oz / 30 mL reduced-sodium soy sauce

2 tsp / 10 mL chopped chervil

2 tsp / 10 mL chopped tarragon

2 tsp / 10 mL chopped chives

2 tsp / 10 mL chopped parsley

2 fl oz / 60 mL Vegetable Stock (page 490)

3 lb / 1.35 kg cooked whole wheat capellini pasta

1. Toss the vegetables with the vinaigrette and grill over medium-high heat until tender. When the vegetables are cool enough to handle, cut into large dice. Leave the onions in rings.

2. Heat the oil in a large sauté pan. Add the garlic and shallots and sauté until aromatic. Add the wine and bring to a boil. Add the grilled vegetables, tomatoes, salt, and pepper and heat thoroughly. Stir in the soy sauce and herbs and adjust the consistency with the stock, if necessary. Reserve.

3. For each portion: Reheat 4 oz / 115 g pasta in boiling water until tender to the bite. Drain and toss with 4 oz / 115 g vegetable mixture.

Grilled Asparagus with Morels, Bowtie Pasta, and Spring Peas

servings: **10**

portioning information:
5 oz / 140 g grilled vegetables and sauce, 4½ oz / 130 g pasta

nutrition per serving:
385 calories, 6 g fat, 66 g total carbohydrate, 18 g protein, 410 mg sodium, 9 mg cholesterol

3 lb / 1.35 kg asparagus, peeled and trimmed

1 tbsp / 15 mL olive oil

½ oz / 14 g butter

1½ oz / 45 g minced shallots

12 oz / 340 g halved fresh morels

10 oz / 285 g shelled garden peas (fresh or frozen)

7 oz / 200 g snow peas

7 oz / 200 g snap peas

5 fl oz / 150 mL Vegetable Stock (page 490)

3 lb / 1.35 kg cooked and drained bowtie pasta

1 tbsp / 15 mL chopped marjoram

2 tsp / 10 mL kosher salt

¼ tsp / 1.25 mL ground black pepper

6 oz / 170 g scallions, split lengthwise and thinly sliced on the diagonal

3 oz / 85 g grated dry Jack cheese

1. Toss the asparagus in the oil. Arrange on a grilling rack and grill over medium-high heat until tender and browned. Remove from the grill and slice into 1-in / 3-cm pieces.

2. In a large sauté pan, heat the butter until it begins to turn brown. Add the shallots and morels and sauté until the shallots are translucent. Reserve.

3. For each portion: Add 1 oz / 30 g of the morel mixture to the pan and warm over medium heat. Add the asparagus, garden peas, snow peas, snap peas, stock, pasta, marjoram, salt, and pepper. Cover the pan and pan-steam until the vegetables are tender and the liquid has almost evaporated.

4. Garnish each portion with scallions and grated cheese.

Fettuccine with Corn, Squash, Chile Peppers, Crème Fraîche, and Cilantro

servings: **10**

portioning information:
5 oz / 140 g grilled vegetables and sauce, 5 oz / 140 g pasta

nutrition per serving:
393 calories, 7 g fat, 70 g total carbohydrate, 13 g protein, 355 mg sodium, 20 mg cholesterol

½ oz / 14 g butter	1½ pt / 360 mL Vegetable Stock (page 490)
1 lb / 450 g diced onions	2 tsp / 10 mL kosher salt
1 lb / 450 g diced zucchini	¼ tsp / 1.25 mL ground black pepper
1½ lb / 680 g corn kernels	5 oz / 140 g crème fraîche
2¼ tsp / 6.75 g diced jalapeño	½ oz / 14 g chopped cilantro
½ oz / 14 g minced garlic	3 lb / 1.35 kg cooked whole wheat fettuccine

1. Heat the butter in a large sauté pan. Add the onions and zucchini and sauté until the onions are translucent. Add the corn, jalapeño, and garlic. Cook until the corn is cooked. Add the stock and season with the salt and pepper. When the stock is hot, remove the pan from the heat and stir in the crème fraîche and cilantro.

2. For each portion: Reheat 5 oz / 140 g pasta in boiling water until tender to the bite. Drain and toss with 5 oz / 140 g hot vegetable mixture.

Capellini with Tomatoes, Olives, and Capers

servings: **10**

portioning information:
5 oz / 140 g pasta and 4 oz / 115 g tomato-olive-caper sauce

nutrition per serving:
370 calories, 9 g fat, 63 g total carbohydrate, 13 g protein, 1100 mg sodium, 0 g cholesterol

1 fl oz / 30 mL extra-virgin olive oil

½ oz / 14 g minced garlic

1 lb / 450 g quartered mushrooms

5½ oz / 155 g capers

5½ oz / 155 g sliced green olives

5½ oz / 155 g sliced black olives

3 lb / 1.35 kg tomato concassé

1 lb 9 oz / 700 g halved red and yellow cherry tomatoes

1¾ oz / 50 g basil chiffonade

1 tsp / 5 mL kosher salt

¼ tsp / 1.25 mL ground black pepper

2 fl oz / 60 mL Vegetable Stock (page 490)

3 lb / 1.4 kg cooked whole wheat capellini

1. Heat the oil in a large sauté pan. Add the garlic and mushrooms and sauté until the mushrooms are tender. Add the capers, olives, and concassé. Toss to incorporate the ingredients and to heat thoroughly. Add the cherry tomatoes, basil, salt, and pepper and toss to evenly distribute the ingredients. Cook just until heated. Adjust the consistency with the stock, if necessary.

2. For each portion: Reheat 5 oz / 140 g pasta in boiling water. Drain well and combine in a sauté pan with 4 oz / 115 g tomato mixture over high heat.

Rigatoni in Wild Mushroom Broth with Spring Vegetables

servings: **10**

portioning information:
4½ oz / 130 g pasta and 5 oz / 135 g mushroom and vegetable broth

nutrition per serving:
369 calories, 4 g fat, 69 g total carbohydrate, 13 g protein, 291 mg sodium, 0 mg cholesterol

1 fl oz / 30 mL extra-virgin olive oil

1 oz / 30 g finely sliced scallions

1 oz / 30 g diced shallots

2 tsp / 6 g minced garlic

1 lb / 450 g chopped wild mushrooms

7 oz / 200 g tomato concassé

3½ fl oz / 105 mL dry sherry

1 qt / 950 mL Vegetable Stock (page 490)

1 tsp / 5 mL kosher salt

¼ tsp / 1.25 mL ground black pepper

2 lb / 910 g baby carrots, blanched

10 oz / 280 g sugar snap peas, blanched

3 lb / 1.4 kg cooked whole wheat rigatoni

1¾ oz / 50 g basil chiffonade

1 oz / 30 g chopped parsley

1. Heat the olive oil in a large soup pot. Add the scallions, shallots, and garlic and sweat until the shallots are translucent. Add the mushrooms, tomatoes, sherry, and stock. Simmer for 15 minutes. Keep hot.

2. For each portion: Combine 4 oz / 115 g of the mushroom-tomato broth with 4½ oz / 130 g rigatoni, 3 oz / 85 g carrots, 1 oz / 30 g sugar snap peas, basil, and parsley. Simmer just until very hot. Season with a pinch of salt and pepper if necessary.

Paglio e Fieno with Peas, Smoked Salmon, and Capers

servings: **10**

portioning information:
5 oz / 140 g pasta, 2 oz / 55 g sauce, 1 oz / 30 g salmon

nutrition per serving:
436 calories, 12 g fat, 59 g total carbohydrate, 23 g protein, 771 mg sodium, 37 mg cholesterol

2½ pt / 1.20 L Chicken Stock (page 489)

3 lb / 1.4 kg *paglio e fieno* (hay and straw pasta)

2 oz / 55 g butter

1 lb / 450 g fresh shelled peas

1 tsp / 5 mL kosher salt

¼ tsp / 1.25 mL ground black pepper

3 oz / 85 g crème fraîche

2 fl oz / 60 mL fresh lemon juice

1 lb / 450 g julienned smoked salmon

4 oz / 115 g thinly sliced spring onions or scallions

2 oz / 55 g drained capers

Chervil plûches, as needed

1. Reduce the stock to 1¼ pt / 600 mL.

2. Cook the pasta in boiling water until tender to the bite. Drain.

3. Heat the butter in a large sauté pan. Add the peas, salt, pepper, and reduced stock. Bring to a boil. Add the crème fraîche and juice and return to a boil. Keep warm.

4. For each portion: Reheat 5 oz / 140 g of the pasta in simmering water. Drain and combine in a sauté pan with 3 oz / 85 g sauce. Serve in a heated bowl and garnish with 1½ oz / 45 g smoked salmon, some spring onions, capers, and chervil.

Basic Pizza Dough with Variations

Batch Yield: **2 lb / 910 g**

servings: **10**

portioning information:
3¼ oz / 92 g

nutrition per serving:
245 calories 1 g fat, 50 g total
carbohydrate, 8 g protein, 351 mg
sodium, 0 mg cholesterol

½ fl oz / 15 mL honey

2½ tsp / 10 g dry yeast

14 to 16 fl oz / 420 to 480 mL water

1¼ lb / 565 g bread flour

1½ tsp / 7.5 mL salt

3 oz / 85 g cornmeal

1. Mix the honey, yeast, 4 fl oz / 120 mL of the water, and enough of the flour to make a thin batter. Place the batter in a warm area and cover with plastic wrap or a damp towel. Allow the batter to proof for 1 hour, or until it becomes frothy and increases in bulk.

2. Add 8 fl oz / 240 mL of the water, the remaining flour, and the salt to the batter. Knead with a dough hook at medium speed or by hand, adding the remaining water as necessary until a smooth, elastic dough develops, about 8 to 10 minutes. The dough should cleanly pull away from the sides of the bowl.

3. Place the dough in a warm area and cover with plastic wrap or a damp towel. Allow the dough to rise until it has doubled in bulk and holds an impression for a few seconds when pressed with a finger, about 1 hour.

4. Turn the dough out on a lightly floured work surface and release the air in the dough by kneading briefly. Divide the dough into 10 equal pieces (3 oz / 85 g each) and shape into balls. Cover the dough with plastic wrap and allow to proof a second time, about 1 hour.

5. Flatten each dough ball into a circle 7½ in / 19 cm in diameter. Place each circle on a sheet pan sprinkled with the cornmeal. Garnish as desired and bake in a 550°F / 260°C oven until golden brown and crisp, about 10 minutes.

6. If not using immediately, wrap the dough balls tightly before the final proof in step 4 and refrigerate or freeze. The dough will keep, refrigerated, for 2 days or frozen for up to 1 month. Thaw frozen dough, still wrapped, overnight in the refrigerator. Bring chilled dough to room temperature and allow to proof before using.

Note

This is an alternate mixing method for the dough: Combine the honey, 14 fl oz / 420 mL of the water, and yeast in a mixing bowl. Mix with a dough hook until the yeast has dissolved, about 2 minutes.

Add the flour and salt and knead with a dough hook at medium speed or by hand, adding the remaining water as necessary, until the dough cleanly pulls away from the sides of the bowl and has a smooth, elastic texture, about 5 minutes. Place the dough in a warm area and cover with plastic wrap or a damp towel. Allow the dough to proof for 1 hour, or until it almost doubles in bulk. Continue with step 4.

Variations

Whole Wheat Pizza Dough

Replace one third of the bread flour with whole wheat flour and double the amount of yeast.

Buckwheat Pizza Dough

Replace one third of the bread flour with buckwheat flour and double the amount of yeast.

Pita Bread

Prepare the basic pizza dough or one of the two variations above. Shape the dough as directed above and bake on cornmeal-lined sheet pans in a 550°F / 260°C oven for 10 to 15 minutes. When removed from the oven, the bread will deflate and a pocket will form.

Grilled Bread

Prepare the basic pizza dough or one of the two pizza dough variations above. Shape the dough as directed above and grill over medium-high heat for 3 to 4 minutes on each side, until the bread puffs, blisters, and cooks thoroughly.

Pizza with Roasted Tomatoes and Mozzarella

servings: **10**

portioning information:
1 pizza

nutrition per serving:
411 calories, 12 g fat, 58 g total carbohydrate, 18 g protein, 650 mg sodium, 23 mg cholesterol

1 tbsp / 15 mL olive oil

3 tbsp / 45 g basil

1 tsp / 5 mL chopped oregano

1 oz / 30 g minced garlic

2 lb / 910 g Basic Pizza Dough (page 340)

2¼ lb / 1 kg sliced roasted plum tomatoes

10½ oz / 300 g thinly sliced part-skim mozzarella

10 fl oz / 300 mL Tomato Coulis (page 498)

1½ oz / 45 g grated Parmesan

2 tbsp / 30 mL ground black pepper

1. Mix the oil with 1 tbsp / 15 mL of the basil, all of the oregano and the garlic.

2. For each pizza: Roll out 1 ball of dough as directed in the dough recipe. Spread 1½ tsp / 7.50 mL of the basil-oregano mixture over the dough. Shingle 3½ oz / 100 g tomatoes and 1 oz / 30 g of the mozzarella slices around the outer edge of the pizza (about 10 slices of each). Place 2 tbsp / 30 mL tomato coulis in the center of the pizza. Sprinkle the pizza with a small amount of the Parmesan and a pinch each of the remaining basil and the pepper.

3. Bake the pizza in a 550°F / 260°C oven until the crust is golden brown and crisp, about 10 minutes.

Pizza with Wild Mushrooms and Goat Cheese

servings: **10**

portioning information:
1 pizza

nutrition per serving:
374 calories, 9 g fat, 55 g total
carbohydrate, 17 g protein, 581 mg
sodium, 20 mg cholesterol

1 lb 2 oz / 510 g sliced wild mushrooms

1½ fl oz /45 mL Chicken Stock (page 489)

2 lb / 910 g Basic Pizza Dough (page 340)

10 fl oz / 300 mL Tomato Coulis (page 498)

7 oz / 200 g crumbled goat cheese

1¾ oz / 50 g grated Parmesan

1¾ oz / 50 g minced garlic

2 tsp / 10 mL ground black pepper

1. Sweat the mushrooms in the stock until tender. Drain the excess liquid and reserve the mushrooms until needed.

2. For each pizza: Roll out 1 ball of dough as directed in the dough recipe. Spread the dough with 2 tbsp / 30 mL tomato coulis. Arrange 1 oz / 30 g mushrooms and ¾ oz / 20 g goat cheese on top of the coulis. Sprinkle the pizza with a small amount of the Parmesan, garlic, and pepper.

3. Bake the pizza in a 550°F / 260°C oven until the crust is golden brown and crisp, about 10 minutes.

Smoked Tomato and Provolone Pizza with Black Olives

servings: **10**

portioning information:
1 pizza

nutrition per serving:
403 calories 14 g fat, 55 g total carbohydrate, 14 g protein, 700 mg sodium, 15 mg cholesterol

15 oz / 425 g small-dice smoked tomatoes

2¼ tsp / 6.75 g minced garlic

2 lb / 910 g Basic Pizza Dough (page 340)

1½ fl oz / 45 mL extra-virgin olive oil

3½ oz / 100 g basil leaves

3½ oz / 100 g sliced pitted Kalamata olives

7½ oz / 205 g grated provolone

1. Prepare the smoked tomatoes as described in Step 1 of Cassoulet with Smoked Tomatoes (page 282). Combine the tomatoes with the garlic.

2. For each pizza: Roll out 1 ball of dough as directed in the dough recipe. Brush the dough with ¾ tsp / 3.75 mL oil. Scatter 1½ oz / 45 g smoked tomatoes and 3 tbsp / 9 g basil and 1 tbsp / 9 g olives over the pizza. Cover with ¾ oz / 20 g provolone.

3. Bake the pizza in a 550°F / 260°C oven until the crust is golden brown and crisp, about 10 minutes.

Apple-Cheddar Pizza

servings: **10**

portioning information:
1 pizza

nutrition per serving:
600 calories, 19 g fat, 87 g total carbohydrate, 22 g protein, 650 mg sodium, 30 mg cholesterol

1½ lb / 680 g thinly sliced apples

1½ lb / 680 g thinly sliced mushrooms

1½ fl oz /45 mL Vegetable Stock (page 490)

1 lb / 450 g thinly sliced shallots

2 lb / 910 g Basic Pizza Dough (page 340)

2½ tsp / 7.50 mL chopped rosemary

2½ tsp / 7.50 mL chopped thyme

10 oz / 280 g grated aged sharp Cheddar cheese

5 oz / 140 g pecans, walnuts, or butternuts, toasted and coarsely chopped

1. Cook the apples and mushrooms in the stock until tender. Drain the excess liquid and reserve until needed.

2. Place the shallots on a sheet pan lined with parchment and bake in a 325°F / 165°C oven until soft and slightly caramelized, about 15 minutes. Reserve until needed.

3. For each pizza: Roll out 1 ball of dough as directed in the dough recipe. Scatter the pizza with 1 oz / 30 g roasted shallots and ¼ tsp / 1.25 mL each of the rosemary and thyme. Arrange 3 oz / 85 g of the apple and mushroom mixture on the pizza and top with 1 oz / 30 g Cheddar and ½ oz / 14 g nuts. Bake the pizza in a 550°F / 260°C oven until the crust is golden brown and crisp, about 10 minutes.

Barbecued Chicken Pizza with Tomato Salsa

servings: **10**

portioning information:
1 pizza

nutrition per serving:
599 calories 12 g fat, 93 g total carbohydrate, 31 g protein, 1344 mg sodium, 61 mg cholesterol

1 lb 10 oz / 735 g boneless, skinless chicken breasts, trimmed

1½ pt / 720 mL Barbecue Sauce (page 501)

7 oz / 200 g thinly sliced Monterey Jack cheese

2 lb / 910 g Basic Pizza Dough (page 340)

10 oz / 300 g Tomato Salsa (page 485)

1. Coat the chicken with 8 fl oz / 240 mL of the barbecue sauce and grill to medium-rare. Cool, slice ¼-in / 6-mm thick, and refrigerate until needed.

2. For each pizza: Roll out 1 ball of dough as directed in the dough recipe. Brush the dough with 1½ fl oz / 45 mL barbecue sauce. Place ¾ oz / 20 g cheese around the outer edge of the dough. Arrange 2 oz / 55 g sliced chicken on top of the cheese. Place 1 oz / 30 g salsa in the middle of the pizza.

3. Bake the pizza in a 550°F / 260°C oven until the crust is golden brown and crisp, about 10 minutes.

Lobster and Jalapeño Pizza

servings: **10**

portioning information:
1 pizza

nutrition per serving:
458 calories, 13 g fat, 54 g total carbohydrate, 30 g protein, 808 mg sodium, 61 mg cholesterol

2 lb / 910 g Basic Pizza Dough (page 340)

1½ oz / 45 g extra-virgin olive oil

10 oz / 280 g thinly sliced part-skim mozzarella

1¼ lb / 565 g cooked chopped lobster (from five 1-to-1¼-lb / 450-to-565-g lobsters)

10 oz / 280 g arugula, blanched and coarsely chopped

Fresh lemon juice, as needed

2 oz / 55 g grated Parmesan

2 oz / 55 g minced shallots

1½ oz / 45 g chopped jalapeño

¾ oz / 20 g chopped cilantro

1. For each pizza: Roll out 1 ball of dough as directed in the dough recipe. Brush the dough with ¾ tsp / 3.75 mL oil. Layer 1 oz / 30 g mozzarella around the outer edges of the dough. Top the pizza with 2 oz / 55 g lobster, 1 oz / 30 g arugula, a sprinkling of lemon juice, and a small amount of the Parmesan. Sprinkle with the shallots, jalapeño, and cilantro. Bake the pizza in a 550°F / 260°C oven until the crust is golden brown and crisp, about 10 minutes.

Shrimp and Clam Pizza with Pesto

2 lb / 910 g Basic Pizza Dough (page 340)

10 oz / 280 g Pesto (page 502)

10 oz / 280 g shrimp (16–20 count), peeled, deveined, and halved lengthwise

10 oz / 280 g chopped sun-dried tomatoes

7 oz / 200 g steamed clams (about 12 medium), coarsely chopped

5 oz / 140 g thinly sliced leeks, steamed

1¾ oz / 50 g grated Parmesan

1 tbsp / 15 mL basil chiffonade

2 tsp / 10 mL ground black pepper

1. For each pizza: Roll out 1 ball of dough as directed in the dough recipe. Spread the dough with 1 oz / 30 g pesto. Top with 1 oz / 30 g each shrimp and tomatoes, and ¾ oz / 20 g clams. Arrange ½ oz / 14 g steamed leeks over the seafood. Sprinkle with a small amount of the Parmesan and a pinch each of the basil and pepper. Bake the pizza in a 550°F / 260°C oven until the crust is golden brown and crisp, about 10 minutes.

Smoked Mozzarella, Prosciutto, and Roasted Pepper Pizza

10½ oz / 300 g julienned roasted red pepper

3½ oz / 100 g julienned tomato

3½ oz / 100 g julienned red onion

1 oz / 30 g minced jalapeño

1 oz / 30 g minced garlic

1 tbsp / 3 g basil chiffonade

2 tsp / 10 mL chopped oregano

3½ fl oz / 100 mL Balsamic Vinaigrette (page 503)

2 lb / 910 g Basic Pizza Dough (page 340)

10½ oz / 300 g thinly sliced smoked mozzarella

5 oz / 140 g lean prosciutto, sliced paper thin (see Note)

1. Combine the peppers, tomatoes, onion, jalapeño, garlic, basil, and oregano. Toss with the vinaigrette.

2. For each pizza: Roll out 1 ball of dough as directed in the dough recipe. Arrange 1 oz / 30 g mozzarella and ½ oz / 14 g prosciutto around the outer edge of the dough. Spread 2 oz / 55 g pepper mixture evenly over the pizza. Bake the pizza in a 550°F / 260°C oven until the crust is golden brown and crisp, about 10 minutes.

Note
Partially freezing the prosciutto will make it easier to slice thinly.

Charred Raw Beef or Buffalo Sandwich with Roasted Shallots

servings: **10**

portioning information:
1 sandwich

nutrition per serving:
380 calories, 16 g fat, 35 g total
carbohydrate, 23 g protein, 684 mg
sodium, 56 mg cholesterol

1 lb / 450 g Limousin beef or buffalo strip loin

1 fl oz / 30 mL vegetable oil

2 tsp / 10 mL kosher salt

1 tsp / 2 g ground black pepper

BALSAMIC DRESSING

3 fl oz / 90 mL balsamic vinegar

1 fl oz / 30 mL Fond de Veau Lié (page 492)

6 fl oz / 180 mL extra-virgin olive oil

9 oz / 255 g Roasted Shallots (page 288)

1 tbsp / 15 mL olive oil

20 slices whole-grain bread

1 lb / 450 g arugula

1¼ lb / 565 g thinly sliced dry Jack cheese

1. Cold smoke the meat for 1½ hours (optional).

2. Combine the vegetable oil, salt, and pepper. Coat the meat with the mixture. Char the strip loin on a very hot grill. Remove from the heat, cool, and refrigerate until completely chilled. Slice the meat very thinly.

3. Combine the vinegar and fond in a small bowl. Slowly whisk in the olive oil.

4. Toss the shallots in the olive oil. Roast in a 350°F / 175°C oven until tender, about 30 minutes. Shred by hand when cool enough to handle.

5. For each sandwich: Spread 1 slice of bread with 1 fl oz / 30 mL balsamic dressing. Scatter ¾ oz / 20 g shallots on the dressing and top with 1½ oz / 45 g arugula and 2 oz / 55 g cheese. Arrange 1½ oz / 45 g meat on another slice of bread. Put the 2 halves together and serve.

Vegetable Fajitas

servings: **10**

portioning information:
1 fajitas

nutrition per serving:
296 calories, 8 g fat, 47 g total
carbohydrate, 9 g protein, 426 mg
sodium, 0 mg cholesterol

1 fl oz / 30 mL olive oil

½ oz / 14 g minced garlic

4 oz / 115 g julienned red onion

1 lb / 450 g julienned red pepper

1 lb / 450 g julienned yellow pepper

1 lb / 450 g julienned green pepper

14 oz / 400 g Napa cabbage, chiffonade

2 fl oz / 60 mL Vegetable Stock (page 490)

4 oz / 115 g dried red beans, cooked in
vegetable stock

5 oz / 140 g red chili sauce

20 (8-in / 20-cm) flour tortillas

1. Heat the oil in a large sauté pan. Add the garlic and onions and sauté until the onions are translucent. Add the peppers and cabbage and sauté until tender. Add the stock to help wilt the cabbage, if necessary. Stir in the beans and chili sauce and heat just until warmed.

2. Cover the tortillas with a damp towel and warm in a 250°F / 120°C oven.

3. For each portion: Wrap 3 oz / 85 g vegetable mixture in a warmed tortilla.

Serving Suggestion

Serve the fajitas with Jicama Salad (page 204) and Mexican Corn Salad (page 205).

Crabmeat and Shrimp Sandwich

servings: **10**

portioning information:
1 sandwich

nutrition per serving:
189 calories, 6 g fat, 20 g total carbohydrate, 13 g protein, 376 mg sodium, 65 mg cholesterol

SEAFOOD SANDWICH DRESSING

10½ fl oz / 315 mL mayonnaise

14 oz / 400 g part-skim ricotta cheese

14 fl oz / 420 mL nonfat yogurt

1¾ fl oz / 50 mL white wine vinegar

½ oz / 14 g minced garlic

2 oz / 55 g diced shallots

1 tbsp / 15 mL Worcestershire sauce

1 tsp / 5 mL Tabasco

½ fl oz / 15 mL Dijon mustard

2 tsp / 10 mL kosher salt

8 oz / 225 g cooked shrimp (16–20 count), peeled and deveined

8 oz / 225 g cooked crabmeat

10 pieces Pita Bread (page 341)

8 oz / 225 g thickly sliced tomatoes

3 oz / 85 g thinly sliced avocado

5 oz / 140 g thinly sliced red onions

3 oz / 85 g alfalfa sprouts

1. Combine the dressing ingredients. Add the shrimp and crabmeat and toss to evenly coat.

2. For each portion: Fill a pita with 3 oz / 85 g seafood mixture, ¾ oz / 20 g tomatoes, 1 tbsp / 15 g avocado, ½ oz / 14 g onion, and 1 tbsp / 15 mL alfalfa sprouts.

French Dip Sandwich

servings: **10**

portioning information:
1 sandwich

nutrition per serving:
337 calories, 13 g fat, 30 g total carbohydrate, 25 g protein, 417 mg sodium, 34 mg cholesterol

1¾ lb / 795 g beef top round, tied

10½ fl oz / 315 mL Five-Mustard Vinaigrette (page 506)

10 rolls (1¾ oz / 50 g each), halved lengthwise

10 leaves red leaf lettuce

3½ oz / 100 g alfalfa sprouts

1. Dry-sear the meat in a large skillet. Remove the meat from the pan and place on a rack in a roasting pan. Roast in a 350°F / 175°C oven until cooked to an internal temperature of 160°F / 70°C, about 1 hour.

2. Remove the meat from the oven and allow to rest for 15 minutes before thinly slicing. Degrease the pan drippings and reserve.

3. For each portion: Spread 2 tbsp / 30 mL vinaigrette on one half of a roll. Top with a leaf of lettuce and 1 tbsp / 15 mL alfalfa sprouts. Arrange 2¾ oz / 78 g beef on the other half. Put the 2 halves together and serve with a small bowl of pan drippings.

Grilled Yellowfin Tuna Salad Sandwich

servings: **10**

portioning information:
1 sandwich

nutrition per serving:
235 calories, 6 g fat, 30 g total carbohydrate, 17 g protein, 416 mg sodium, 22 mg cholesterol

DRESSING

3½ fl oz / 105 mL Balsamic Vinaigrette (page 503)

1 tbsp / 15 mL chopped anchovy fillets

½ oz / 14 g julienned Niçoise olives

1 tsp / 5 mL whole-grain mustard

2¼ tsp / 6.75 g minced garlic

1 tsp / 5 mL basil chiffonade

1 tsp / 5 mL chopped thyme

1 tsp / 5 mL chopped oregano

1 tsp / 5 mL chopped chives

1¼ lb / 570 g yellowfin tuna, grilled and cooled

10 oz / 285 g diced roasted red and yellow peppers

10 slices whole wheat bread

10 spears Belgian endive

4 oz / 115 g thinly sliced red onion

10 leaves radicchio

3 oz / 85 g frisée

1. Whisk together the dressing ingredients.

2. Break the tuna into chunks by hand, and combine with the peppers. Add the dressing and toss gently until combined.

3. Toast the bread and cut the slices in half on the diagonal.

4. For each portion: Place a toast triangle in the center of a plate. Top with 1 endive spear, 1 red onion slice, and 2 oz / 55 g tuna mixture. Place a second piece of toast on top of the tuna so that the corners of the second toast point opposite those of the base piece. Top with 1 radicchio leaf, some frisée, and 1 oz / 30 g more tuna.

Grilled Garden Sandwich with Warm Slaw and Crispy Potato Slices

servings: **10**

portioning information:
1 sandwich

nutrition per serving:
410 calories, 7 g fat, 75 g total carbohydrate, 17 g protein, 805 mg sodium, 13 mg cholesterol

15 oz / 425 g part-skim ricotta cheese

12 oz / 340 g thinly sliced red onions

2 fl oz / 60 mL Vegetable Stock (page 490)

8 oz / 225 g sliced mushrooms

6 oz / 170 g julienned red peppers

6 oz / 170 g julienned yellow peppers

½ tsp / 2.5 g kosher salt

⅛ tsp / 0.625 mL ground black pepper

20 slices wheat bread

½ oz / 14 g basil chiffonade

1 lb / 450 g thinly sliced Granny Smith apples

8 oz / 225 g thinly sliced plum tomatoes

1½ lb / 680 g thinly sliced cucumbers

4 oz / 115 g thinly sliced zucchini

1¼ lb / 570 g Warm Cabbage Salad (page 205)

10 oz / 280 g Crispy Potato Slices (page 512)

1. Drain the ricotta in a cheesecloth-lined sieve in the refrigerator for 8 to 10 hours.

2. Grill the onion slices and reserve.

3. Heat the stock in a large sauté pan. Add the mushrooms and peppers and sweat until the vegetables are slightly tender and the stock has completely reduced. Season with the salt and pepper.

4. For each portion: Grill 2 bread slices over a very hot grill. Spread 1 side of a bread slice with ½ oz / 14 g ricotta. Sprinkle basil over the ricotta. Layer 2 oz / 56 g pepper mixture, 1½ oz / 45 g apples, 1 oz / 30 g grilled onions, ¾ oz / 20 g tomatoes, 2½ oz / 70 g cucumber, and 1 tbsp / 15 mL zucchini on top and press together firmly with another slice. Place on a sheet pan and bake in a 350°F / 175°C oven until very hot, 20 to 25 minutes, turning 2 or 3 times while heating.

5. Serve with 2 oz / 55 g warm slaw and 1 oz / 30 g crispy potatoes.

Moroccan Chicken Pita Sandwiches with
Carrot Salad (Msoura)

Moroccan Chicken Pita Sandwiches

servings: **10**

portioning information:
1 sandwich

nutrition per serving:
402 calories, 16 g fat, 28 g total
carbohydrate, 33 g protein, 1050 mg
sodium, 93 mg cholesterol

CHICKEN MARINADE

¼ tsp / 1.25 mL ground cayenne

½ tsp / 2.5 mL Spanish paprika

1 tsp / 5 mL garlic powder

½ tsp / 2.5 mL ground black pepper

½ tsp / 2.5 mL ground cinnamon

½ tsp / 2.5 mL ground cumin

2 tsp / 10 mL kosher salt

¾ fl oz / 20 mL fresh lemon juice

10 skinless chicken legs

1½ fl oz / 45 mL extra-virgin olive oil

8 fl oz / 240 mL Chicken Stock (page 489)

4 oz / 115 g pitted chopped Kalamata olives

1 lb 11 oz / 765 g tomato concassé

1 lb / 450 g diced roasted peppers

1 tsp / 5 mL chopped cilantro

1 tsp / 5 mL chopped parsley

2 tsp / 10 mL kosher salt

10 pieces Pita Bread (page 341)

1. Combine the chicken marinade ingredients in a shallow pan. Add the chicken and toss to evenly coat. Marinate, refrigerated, for at least 2 and up to 12 hours.

2. Heat the oil in a roasting pan. Remove the chicken from the marinade and place it in the roasting pan. Brown the chicken evenly and remove from the pan.

3. Deglaze the pan with the stock and return the legs to the pan. Add the olives, bring to a simmer, cover, and braise until the meat is fork tender. Cool the chicken in the braising liquid. Remove the chicken from the liquid. Degrease the liquid and reserve.

4. Pull the chicken meat from the bones and place in a large bowl. Add the tomatoes, peppers, braising liquid, cilantro, parsley, and salt and toss well.

5. For each portion: Fill a pita bread with 2 oz / 55 g chicken mixture.

Falafel

servings: **10**

portioning information:
3½ oz / 100 g

nutrition per serving:
280 calories, 8 g fat, 40 g total
carbohydrate, 15 g protein, 760 mg
sodium, 40 mg cholesterol

11 oz / 315 g dried chickpeas	1¼ tsp / 2.50 mL ground coriander
11 oz / 315 g dried fava beans	6 cloves garlic, crushed
1 bunch parsley, chopped	1¼ tsp / 6.25 mL baking powder
3 scallions, finely chopped	1 tbsp / 15 mL kosher salt
1 tsp / 5 mL cayenne pepper	
1 tbsp / 15 mL ground cumin	1 qt / 960 mL vegetable oil, or as needed

1. Soak the beans for 8 to 12 hours in enough cold water to cover by 3 in / 8 cm. Drain, and then rinse and dry them.

2. In a food processor, blend all the ingredients together until the mixture is homogenous. (Alternatively, the mixture can be ground twice through a small die until very smooth.) Form into balls (about 1½ in / 3.8 cm in diameter). Slightly flatten the balls.

3. Heat the oil to 350°F / 175°C in a large rondeau or fryer and deep-fry the falafel until crisp and brown, about 4 minutes. Remove from the oil and drain briefly on paper towels. Serve immediately.

Serving Suggestion

Falafel is typically served with pita and a yogurt sauce, along with sliced tomatoes or other fresh vegetable garnishes.

(Nutrition information does not involve serving suggestions.)

Falafel with Cucumber Raita (page 488) and
Pita Bread (page 341)

Turkey Burgers

batch yield: 2 lb / 910 g

servings: **10**

portioning information:
3¼ oz / 92 g

nutrition per serving:
111 calories, 1.5 g fat, 1 g total
carbohydrate, 25 g protein, 290 mg
sodium, 40 mg cholesterol

2¼ lb / 1 kg lean turkey, well chilled

2 tsp / 10 mL kosher salt

1 tsp / 5 mL sugar

½ tsp / 2.5 mL fennel seeds

½ tsp / 2.5 mL ground cinnamon

¼ tsp / 1.25 mL grated nutmeg

¼ tsp / 1.25 mL ground cloves

¼ tsp / 1.25 mL ground cayenne

¼ tsp / 1.25 mL cumin seed

¼ tsp / 1.25 mL chopped rosemary

½ tsp / 2.5 mL chopped thyme

¼ tsp / 1.25 mL ground black pepper

1. Combine the turkey, salt, and sugar. Refrigerate for at least 30 minutes while assembling the grinder. Grind through a large-hole die directly into a bowl set over an ice-water bath.

2. Working by hand with a wooden spoon, stir in the remaining ingredients.

3. Form the meat mixture into 3½-oz / 100-g patties. Arrange on a sheet pan lined with parchment paper and bake in a 475°F / 245°C oven until thoroughly cooked, about 10 minutes.

Chicken and Mushroom Burgers

batch yield: **2¼ lb / 1 kg**

servings: **10**

portioning information:
3½ oz / 100 g

nutrition per serving:
120 calories, 1.5 g fat, 8 g total
carbohydrate, 18 g protein, 360 mg
sodium, 40 mg cholesterol

1½ lb / 680 g boneless, skinless chicken

1 tsp / 5 mL kosher salt

3½ oz / 100 g fresh bread crumbs

9½ oz / 270 g Duxelles (page 502)

¾ tsp / 3.75 mL chopped chives

¾ tsp / 3.75 mL chopped oregano

¾ tsp / 3.75 mL chopped basil

¾ tsp / 3.75 mL chopped rosemary

1. Combine the chicken and salt. Refrigerate for at least 30 minutes while assembling the grinder. Grind through a large-hole die directly into a bowl set over an ice-water bath. Working by hand with a wooden spoon, stir in the remaining ingredients.

2. Form the meat mixture into 3½-oz / 100-g patties. Arrange on a sheet pan lined with parchment paper and bake in a 475°F / 245°C oven until thoroughly cooked, about 10 minutes.

Vegetable Burgers

batch yield: **2¼ lb / 1 kg**

servings: **10**

portioning information:
3½ oz / 100 g

nutrition per serving:
109 calories, 7 g fat, 10 g total
carbohydrate, 3 g protein, 269 mg
sodium, 20 mg cholesterol

1 lb / 450 g grated carrots	4 oz / 115 g minced scallions
2 oz / 55 g grated celery	1 egg, lightly beaten
2 oz / 55 g grated onion	½ tsp / 2.5 mL Tabasco sauce
1 oz / 30 g minced red pepper	1 tsp / 5 mL kosher salt
1 oz / 30 g minced green pepper	¼ tsp / 1.25 mL ground black pepper
3½ oz / 100 g ground walnuts	1 oz / 30 g cracker or matzo meal
4 oz / 115 g minced mushrooms	1 tsp / 5 mL light sesame oil

1. Combine the carrots, celery, onion, and peppers. Press to release any excess liquid. Add the walnuts, mushrooms, scallions, egg, Tabasco, salt, and pepper and stir to thoroughly combine. Add enough cracker meal to make a firm mixture. Form into 3½-oz / 100-g patties. Roll each patty in additional cracker meal.

2. Heat the oil in a large sauté pan. Pan-fry the patties until browned on both sides. Arrange on a sheet pan lined with parchment paper and bake in a 475°F / 245°C oven until thoroughly cooked, about 10 minutes.

7

Side Dishes

MANY OF THE RECIPES in this chapter would be very comfortable at the center of the plate, alone or in combination with other compatible dishes. The sides you choose to feature with your menu items are best when you think about the colors, textures, and flavors of all of the dishes on the plate.

Vegetable cookery is at least as great a culinary challenge as sauce making, perhaps even more so. To get the most out of every side dish, ingredient selection is critically important. Vegetables that are in season and at the peak of flavor will always outshine familiar standbys that have to be trucked or shipped long distances.

Haricots Verts with Walnuts

batch yield: **2 lb / 900 g**

servings: **10**

portioning information:
3¼ oz / 90 g

nutrition per serving:
43 calories, 2 g fat, 7 g total
carbohydrate, 2 g protein, 62 mg
sodium, 0 mg cholesterol

2 lb / 900 g trimmed haricots verts

1 tsp / 5 mL olive oil

¾ oz / 20 g minced shallots

2 cloves garlic, minced

½ oz / 14 g walnuts, toasted and chopped

¼ tsp / 1.25 mL kosher salt

Pinch cracked black peppercorns

1. Blanch the haricots verts in simmering water until tender. Drain the beans, reserving 3 fl oz / 90 mL of the cooking liquid.

2. Heat the oil in a small sauté pan. Add the shallots and garlic. Sauté until the shallots are translucent.

3. Combine the haricot verts with the shallots, garlic, reserved cooking liquid, walnuts, salt, and pepper. Toss to coat, and serve.

Toasting and Chopping Nuts

Nuts hold better if they are purchased raw. Once they are roasted, their oils are driven to the surface, making it easier for them to turn rancid. Toasting nuts right before you want to use them heightens their flavor and improves their texture. You can toast small amounts of nuts in a dry skillet as follows:

Heat a small dry skillet over high heat (cast iron is ideal). Add the nuts and swirl the pan over the heat to keep them from scorching. Continue until the nuts begin to give off a rich, toasted aroma and are just starting to brown, usually about 2 minutes. Immediately transfer them to a bowl to keep them from burning.

Once the nuts are cool, chop them by hand using a chef's knife, or place them in a food processor and pulse it on and off just until the nuts are coarsely chopped.

Asparagus with Toasted Anchovies, Garlic, and Lemon

batch yield: **2 lb / 900 g**

servings: **10**

portioning information:
3¼ oz / 90 g

nutrition per serving:
45 calories, 2 g fat, 4 g total
carbohydrate, 3 g protein, 130 mg
sodium, 3 mg cholesterol

2 lb / 900 g trimmed asparagus

4 tsp / 20 mL extra-virgin olive oil

¾ oz / 20 g thinly sliced garlic

½ tsp / 2.5 mL red pepper flakes

8 anchovy fillets, mashed

⅔ oz / 19 g chopped parsley

3 tbsp / 45 mL fresh lemon juice

1 tsp / 10 mL cracked black peppercorns

1. Pan-steam the asparagus until tender, but not soft, about 3 minutes. Drain on absorbent towels.

2. Heat the oil in a large sauté pan. Add the garlic and red pepper flakes; sauté until the garlic begins to brown. Add the anchovies and sauté until the anchovies begin to brown. Add the asparagus and gently toss to heat. Season with the parsley, lemon juice, and pepper.

Variation

Green beans, cauliflower, or other vegetables may be substituted for the asparagus.

Asparagus

Young asparagus may need no further preparation than a simple trim to remove the very ends of the stalk, and a quick rinse. More mature asparagus may need to have the stalk trimmed a little more and partially peeled to remove the outer skin, which can be tough and stringy.

As asparagus matures, the stalk becomes tough. To remove the woody portion, bend the stalk gently until it snaps. Using a special asparagus peeler or a swivel-bladed peeler, peel the remaining stalk partway up; this enhances palatability and also makes it easier to cook the asparagus evenly.

Asparagus may be tied into loose portion-sized bundles to make it easier to remove them from boiling water when they are blanched or boiled. Don't tie them too tightly, or make the bundles more than a few inches in diameter. Otherwise the asparagus in the middle will not cook properly.

Broccoli Rabe with Garlic and Red Pepper Flakes

batch yield: **2¼ lb / 1 kg**

servings: **10**

portioning information:
3½ oz / 100 g

nutrition per serving:
120 calories, 4 g fat, 14 g total carbohydrate, 7 g protein, 240 mg sodium, 5 mg cholesterol

2 oz / 57 g julienned pancetta

12 oz / 340 g diced onions

1¼ oz / 35 g minced garlic

2 lb / 900 g chopped broccoli rabe

1 tbsp / 15 mL chopped thyme

1 tbsp / 15 mL red pepper flakes

1½ cups / 360 mL Chicken Velouté (page 497)

1½ pt / 720 mL Chicken Stock (page 489)

2 tbsp / 30 mL lemon juice

1. Render the pancetta in a preheated, large sauté pan. Add the onions and garlic and sauté until the onions are translucent. Add the broccoli rabe, thyme, and red pepper flakes. Sauté until the broccoli rabe is tender.

2. Combine the velouté and stock and reduce to a sauce consistency. Stir into the broccoli rabe and season with the lemon juice.

Southern-Style Kale

batch yield: **2 lb / 900 g**

servings: **10**

portioning information:
3¼ oz / 90 g

nutrition per serving:
118 calories, 5 g fat, 15 g total carbohydrate, 6 g protein, 248 mg sodium, 6 mg cholesterol

3 lb / 1.35 kg trimmed chopped kale

3 oz / 85 g diced bacon

4½ oz / 125 g diced onions

1 tsp / 5 mL minced garlic

1 cup / 240 mL Chicken Stock (page 489)

½ tsp / 2.5 mL kosher salt

¼ tsp / 1.25 mL ground black pepper

1. Blanch the kale in a large amount of salted water. Drain well.

2. Render the bacon in a large saucepan. Add the onions and garlic; sauté until the onions are translucent. Add the kale, stock, salt, and pepper. Cook the greens uncovered until tender, about 30 minutes.

Broccoli Rabe with Garlic and Red Pepper
Flakes, Couscous (page 382), Broiled Lamb
Chops (page 279) with Blood Orange Sauce
(page 494)

Brussels Sprouts with Mustard Glaze

Brussels Sprouts with Mustard Glaze

batch yield: **2 lb / 900 g**

servings: **10**

portioning information:
3¼ oz / 90 g

nutrition per serving:
46 calories, 0 g fat, 8 g total
carbohydrate, 4 g protein, 79 mg
sodium, 0 mg cholesterol

2 lb / 900 g trimmed Brussels sprouts

¾ cup / 180 mL Fond de Veau Lié (page 492)
(see Note)

1 tbsp / 15 mL whole-grain mustard

1. Cook the Brussels sprouts in boiling water until tender.

2. Combine the fond with the mustard and heat in a large sauté pan. Add the Brussels sprouts and toss to coat with the mustard mixture.

Note

The fond de veau lié may be replaced with a jus appropriate to the main item that the Brussels sprouts will accompany.

Wild Rice Succotash

batch yield: **2 lb / 900 g**

servings: **10**

portioning information:
3¼ oz / 90 g

nutrition per serving:
63 calories, 2 g fat, 10 g total
carbohydrate, 2 g protein, 193 mg
sodium, 0 mg cholesterol

1 tbsp / 15 mL extra-virgin olive oil

5 oz / 140 g corn kernels

5 oz / 140 g chopped wild mushrooms

10 oz / 280 g tomato concassé

4 oz / 120 g cooked lima beans

4 oz / 120 g cooked wild rice

¼ cup / 60 mL Vegetable Stock (page 490)

1½ oz / 45 g thinly sliced scallions, cut on a bias

¾ tsp / 3.75 mL kosher salt

1 tbsp / 15 mL chopped tarragon

½ tsp / 2.5 mL cracked black peppercorns

1. Heat the oil in a large sauté pan. Add the corn and mushrooms; sauté until tender. Add the tomatoes, lima beans, rice, stock, scallions, and salt. Toss to mix the ingredients and heat thoroughly. Remove the pan from the heat and stir in the tarragon and pepper.

Variation

For a more traditional succotash, omit the wild rice.

Roasted Smoked Corn

batch yield: **2¼ lb / 1 kg**

servings: **10**

portioning information:
3½ oz / 100 g

nutrition per serving:
60 calories, 1 g fat, 14 g total
carbohydrate, 2 g protein, 10 mg
sodium, 0 mg cholesterol

19 ears corn (in the husk)

1 tsp / 10 mL cracked black peppercorns

1 tbsp / 15 mL chopped parsley

1 tbsp / 15 mL chopped chervil

1. Loosen, but do not remove, the husk from the corn. Sprinkle each ear with the pepper and herbs. Tie the husks around the cobs and dampen them with water. Place on a baking sheet and roast in a 400°F / 205°C oven until tender, about 15 minutes.

2. Remove the husks and place the cobs on a rack in a roasting pan containing a thin layer of hardwood chips. Cover with a tight-fitting lid and place over direct heat. Smoke for 6 to 8 minutes. Cut the corn from the cob.

Roasted Corn and Black Beans

batch yield: **2 lb / 900 g**

servings: **10**

portioning information:
3¼ oz / 90 g

nutrition per serving:
107 calories, 1 g fat, 20 g total
carbohydrate, 5 g protein, 67 mg
sodium, 0 mg cholesterol

1 tsp / 5 mL olive oil

1½ oz / 45 g diced red onion

2 cloves garlic, minced

1 tsp / 5 mL minced jalapeño

1 lb / 450 g Roasted Smoked Corn kernels
(previous recipe)

5½ oz / 155 g dried black beans, cooked (page 388) and drained

1¾ oz / 50 g tomato concassé

1 tbsp / 15 mL fresh lime juice

¼ tsp / 1.25 mL kosher salt

1 tbsp / 15 mL chopped cilantro

1. Heat the oil in a large pot. Add the onion, garlic, and jalapeño. Sauté until the onions are translucent. Add the corn, beans, tomatoes, lime juice, and salt. Toss over high heat until the mixture is hot. Remove from the heat and stir in the cilantro.

Grilled Vegetables

batch yield: **2 lb / 900 g**

servings: **10**

portioning information:
3¼ oz / 90 g

nutrition per serving:
47 calories, 2 g fat, 6 g total carbohydrate, 1 g protein, 23 mg sodium, 0 mg cholesterol

10 oz / 280 g ¼-inch / 6-mm slices yellow squash

5 oz / 140 g ¼-in / 6-mm slices zucchini

5 oz / 140 g ¼-in / 6-mm slices Vidalia onions

5 oz / 140 g quartered Belgian endive

4 oz / 120 g scallions, trimmed (3½ in / 9 cm long)

4 oz / 120 g trimmed shiitake mushrooms

3 fl oz / 90 mL Balsamic Vinaigrette (page 503)

1. Toss the vegetables with the vinaigrette and marinate for 30 minutes.

2. Grill the vegetables over medium-high heat until marked on both sides and tender.

Note

A variety of other vegetables, such as eggplant, bell peppers, and tomatoes, may be grilled raw if sliced about ¼ in / 6 mm thick. Denser vegetables, such as fennel, sweet potatoes, and leeks, may burn before cooking fully. Parcooking or blanching is necessary before grilling these types of vegetables.

Pan-Steamed Zucchini and Yellow Squash Noodles

batch yield: **2 lb / 900 g**

servings: **10**

portioning information:
3¼ oz / 90 g

nutrition per serving:
27 calories, 1 g fat, 5 g total carbohydrate, 2 g protein, 14 mg sodium, 1 mg cholesterol

1½ lb / 680 g zucchini

1½ lb / 680 g yellow squash

1 tsp / 5 mL butter

½ oz / 14 g minced shallots

½ tsp / 2.5 mL minced garlic

¼ cup / 60 mL Vegetable Stock (page 490)

1 tbsp / 15 mL minced herbs (see Note)

2 tsp / 10 mL fresh lemon juice

¼ tsp / 1.25 mL cracked black peppercorns

1. Using a mandoline, cut the zucchini and squash lengthwise into ¼-in / 6-mm-thick "noodles." Discard the center of the squashes.

2. Heat the butter in a large sauté pan. Add the shallots and garlic. Sweat until the shallots are translucent. Add the squash noodles and stock. Cover and pan-steam the squash until tender, about 5 minutes. Drain any excess liquid. Season with the herbs, lemon juice, and pepper.

Note

Use a variety of herbs such as basil, tarragon, chives, cilantro, thyme, or oregano.

Ratatouille

batch yield: **2 lb / 900 g**

servings: **10**

portioning information:
3¼ oz / 90 g

nutrition per serving:
30 calories, 1 g fat, 5 g total
carbohydrate, 1 g protein, 90 mg
sodium, 0 mg cholesterol

1 tsp / 5 mL extra-virgin olive oil

2½ oz / 70 g diced red onion

½ oz / 14 g minced garlic

½ oz / 14 g minced shallot

1 oz / 30 g tomato paste

8 oz / 240 g ¼-in / 6-mm slices peeled plum
tomatoes

4 oz / 115 g diced zucchini

4 oz / 115 g diced bell pepper

4 oz / 115 g diced eggplant

3 oz / 85 g diced yellow squash

1 cup / 240 mL Vegetable Stock (page 490)

1 tbsp / 15 mL basil chiffonade

1 tsp / 5 mL chopped oregano

¼ tsp / 1.25 mL kosher salt

¼ tsp / 1.25 mL cracked black peppercorns

1. Heat the oil in a large pot. Add the onion, garlic, and shallots. Sauté until the onions are translucent.

2. Add the tomato paste and sauté until brown. Add the remaining vegetables and the stock. Bring to a gentle simmer and stew, stirring occasionally, until the vegetables are tender, about 15 minutes. Season with the herbs, salt, and pepper.

Serving Suggestion

Combine ratatouille with a grain dish, such as the couscous shown here, for a meatless entrée option.

(Nutrition information does not include serving suggestion.)

Ratatouille with Couscous (page 382)

Artichokes and Mushrooms in White Wine Sauce

batch yield: **2 lb / 900 g**

servings: **10**

portioning information:
3¼ oz / 90 g

nutrition per serving:
79 calories, 3 g fat, 8 g total
carbohydrate, 2 g protein, 274 mg
sodium, 0 mg cholesterol

2 tbsp / 30 mL olive oil	¼ cup / 60 mL fresh lemon juice
1 lb / 450 g halved button mushrooms	½ oz / 14 g tomato paste
½ oz / 14 g minced garlic	½ tsp / 2.5 mL kosher salt
20 artichoke bottom halves	¼ tsp / 1.25 mL coarsely ground black pepper
1½ cups / 360 mL water	1 Sachet d'Epices (page 490), plus 1 tsp / 5 mL coriander seeds and 2 extra bay leaves
1 cup / 240 mL dry white wine	

1. Heat the oil in a medium saucepan. Add the mushrooms. Cook over medium heat until tender, about 4 minutes. Add the garlic and sweat until aromatic. Add the remaining ingredients and mix well. Cover and continue to cook over low heat until the artichokes are tender, 15 to 20 minutes. Drain the vegetables and reduce the cooking liquid to sauce consistency. Return the vegetables to the sauce.

Braised Belgian Endive

batch yield: **2 lb / 900 g**

servings: **10**

portioning information:
3¼ oz / 90 g

nutrition per serving:
37 calories, 1 g fat, 5 g total
carbohydrate, 1 g protein, 239 mg
sodium, 0 mg cholesterol

2 tsp / 10 mL vegetable oil	½ cup / 120 mL white wine
2 oz / 57 g diced onion	¼ cup / 60 mL fresh lemon juice
1 oz / 30 g diced carrot	1 tsp / 5 mL kosher salt
1 oz / 30 g diced celery	2 bay leaves
2 lb / 900 g Belgian endives	4 sprigs thyme
1 qt / 950 mL water	

1. Heat the oil in a large saucepan. Add the onion, carrot, and celery. Sauté until the onions are translucent. Add the remaining ingredients. If necessary, add more water to completely cover the endives. Keep the endives submerged during cooking to avoid oxidation. Simmer until the endives are tender, about 15 minutes. Drain before serving.

Note

The endives may be cooled and stored in the braising liquid for later use or they may be dried and grilled.

Fennel Braised in Chardonnay

batch yield: **2 lb / 900 g**

servings: **10**

portioning information:
3¼ oz / 90 g

nutrition per serving:
39 calories, 0 g fat, 7 g total carbohydrate, 1 g protein, 280 mg sodium, 0 mg cholesterol

2 lb / 900 g fennel bulb, sliced ¼ in / 1 cm thick	1 tsp / 5 mL kosher salt
1 qt / 950 mL water	½ tsp / 2.5 mL coriander seeds
½ cup / 120 mL Chardonnay	2 bay leaves
¼ cup / 60 mL fresh lemon juice	4 sprigs thyme

1. Combine all the ingredients in a large saucepan. Keep the fennel submerged during cooking to avoid oxidation. Simmer until the fennel is tender, about 40 minutes. Drain before serving.

Note

The fennel may be cooled and stored in the braising liquid for later use or it may be drained and grilled.

Saffron Cauliflower and Onions

batch yield: **2 lb / 900 g**

servings: **10**

portioning information:
3¼ oz / 90 g

nutrition per serving:
68 calories, 3 g fat, 8 g total carbohydrate, 2 g protein, 241 mg sodium, 0 mg cholesterol

2 tbsp / 30 mL olive oil	¼ cup / 60 mL fresh lemon juice
1 lb / 450 g peeled pearl onions	1 tsp / 5 mL saffron threads
½ oz / 14 g minced garlic	1 tsp / 5 mL kosher salt
1 lb / 450 g cauliflower florets	¼ tsp / 1.25 mL coarsely ground black pepper
1½ cups / 360 mL water	1 Sachet d'Epices (page 490), plus 1 tsp / 5 mL coriander seeds and 2 extra bay leaves
½ cup / 120 mL dry white wine	

1. Heat the oil in a medium saucepan. Add the onions and cook over medium heat until tender and deep gold color, about 12 minutes. Add the garlic and sauté until aromatic. Stir in the remaining ingredients. Cover and continue to cook over low heat until the vegetables are tender, about 15 minutes.

Caramelized Pearl Onions

batch yield: **2 lb / 900 g**

servings: **10**

portioning information:
3¼ oz / 90 g

nutrition per serving:
50 calories, 1.5 g fat, 10 g total carbohydrate, 1 g protein, 120 mg sodium, 10 mg cholesterol

½ oz / 14 g butter

2 lb / 910 g peeled cooked white pearl onions

1½ tsp / 7.5 mL granulated sugar

½ tsp / 2.5 mL salt

¼ tsp / 1.25 mL ground black pepper

1. Melt the butter in a large sauté pan. Add the onions and caramelize slowly, turning often. Add the sugar and allow the onions to glaze. Season with the salt and pepper.

Cipollini Onions in Brown Sauce

batch yield: **2 lb / 900 g**

servings: **10**

portioning information:
3¼ oz / 90 g

nutrition per serving:
55 calories, 1 g fat, 9 g total carbohydrate, 3 g protein, 74 mg sodium, 1 mg cholesterol

2 tsp / 10 mL olive oil

2 lb / 900 g cipollini onions, trimmed (see Note)

½ cup / 120 mL red wine vinegar

1½ cups / 360 mL Fond de Veau Lié (page 492)

¼ tsp / 1.25 mL ground black pepper

1. Heat the oil in a sauté pan. Add the onions and sauté until brown. Deglaze the pan with the vinegar. Simmer until the vinegar has reduced by half.

2. Add enough of the fond to cover the onions by half. Bring to a simmer. Cover the pan and braise in a 325°F / 165°C oven until the onions are very tender, about 10 minutes. Season with the pepper.

Note

Cipollini onions are about the same size and shape as pearl onions, but they have a much sweeter taste than pearls. To prepare the onions for cooking, trim the root and stem ends and remove the papery skin.

Variation

Cipollini onions may be replaced with leeks. Trim the green portion and stem end of the leeks. Rinse well in plenty of water to remove all sand, and steam briefly before browning in the oil. Continue with the remaining steps of the recipe.

Caramelized Root Vegetables

batch yield: **2 lb / 900 g**

servings: **15**

portion size: **3 oz / 85 g**

nutrition per serving:
50 calories, 2 g fat, 8 g total carbohydrate, 1 g protein, 120 mg sodium, 0 mg cholesterol

2 tbsp / 30 mL olive oil

10½ oz / 300 g diagonal-cut parsnips

10½ oz / 300 g wedge-cut white turnips

10½ oz / 300 g wedge-cut yellow turnips

12 oz / 340 g wedge-cut fennel

½ tsp / 2.5 mL salt

¼ tsp / 1.25 mL ground black pepper

1. Add the olive oil to a roasting pan and preheat in a 350°F / 175°C oven. Add the vegetables and toss in the oil. Roast the vegetables until well caramelized and tender, 25 to 30 minutes. Season with the salt and pepper.

Moroccan-Style Roasted Vegetables

batch yield: **3 lb / 1.35 kg**

servings: **16**

portion size: **3 oz / 85 g**

nutrition per serving:
80 calories, 3.5 g fat, 11 g total carbohydrate, 1 g protein, 90 mg sodium, 0 mg cholesterol

1 lb / 450 g slices red onions (⅓-in / 1-cm)

1 lb / 450 g slices red peppers (⅓-in / 1-cm)

8 oz / 225 g zucchini, quartered lengthwise

8 oz / 225 g leeks, quartered lengthwise

¼ cup / 60 mL extra-virgin olive oil

½ tsp / 2.5 mL salt

½ tsp / 1.25 mL crushed black peppercorns

12 oz / 340 g sweet potatoes, quartered lengthwise

1 tbsp / 15 mL prepared harissa sauce

1. Brush the onions, peppers, zucchini, and leeks with the oil and season with the salt and pepper. Brush the sweet potato wedges with a thin coat of harissa sauce. Roast the vegetables separately in a 400°F / 205°C oven until thoroughly cooked and caramelized.

Pecan Carrots

batch yield: **2 lb / 900 g**

servings: **10**

portioning information:
3¼ oz / 90 g

nutrition per serving:
50 calories, 1 g fat, 10 g total
carbohydrate, 1 g protein, 135 mg
sodium, 0 mg cholesterol

2¼ lb /1 kg oblique-cut carrots

½ oz / 14 g honey

1 tbsp / 15 mL minced shallots (see Note)

½ oz / 14 g toasted chopped pecans

2 tsp / 10 mL sliced chives

¼ tsp / 1.25 mL kosher salt

Pinch ground white pepper

1. Cook the carrots in simmering water until just tender. Drain the carrots (save ½ cup / 120 mL of the cooking liquid), and place in a bowl.

2. Combine the carrots with the honey, shallots, pecans, chives, salt, and pepper in a large pan over medium-high heat. Add enough of the cooking liquid to make a smooth, light, even glaze. Toss to coat evenly and serve.

Note

Raw minced shallots can have a harsh flavor. To give them a more subtle flavor, you can cook them in just enough broth to barely moisten them over low heat, just until they become translucent and the broth cooks away.

Corn Pudding

batch yield: **3 lb / 1.35 kg**

servings: **16**

portioning information:
3 oz / 85 g

nutrition per serving:
129 calories, 1 g fat, 23 g total
carbohydrate, 6 g protein, 490 mg
sodium, 27 mg cholesterol

6 oz / 170 g diced onions

½ oz / 14 g minced garlic

5 oz / 140 g diced red pepper

4 jalapeños, seeded and minced

1 pt / 480 mL Chicken Stock (page 489)

12 oz / 340 g corn kernels

2 tsp / 10 mL chopped thyme

2 tsp / 10 mL chopped oregano

2 tsp / 10 mL chopped rosemary

2 tsp / 10 mL kosher salt

½ tsp / 2.5 mL cracked black peppercorns

1 recipe Country Corn Bread (page 436), crumbled

10 large egg whites

Olive oil spray, as needed

1. In a large stockpot, sweat the onions, garlic, red pepper, and jalapeños in a small amount of the stock. Add the remaining stock and reduce to half its original volume. Add the corn to the reduced stock and allow the mixture to come to a boil.

2. Remove the pot from the heat and add the herbs, salt, and pepper. Allow the mixture to cool slightly and combine with the corn bread and egg whites.

3. Lightly spay sixteen 4-fl oz / 120-mL ramekins with oil. Portion 3 oz / 85 g of the pudding into each ramekin. Bake the puddings in a 170°F / 75°C water bath in a 375°F / 190°C oven until completely set, 25 minutes.

Basic Rice Pilaf

batch yield: **2½ lb / 1.15 kg**

servings: **14**

portioning information:
3 oz / 85 g

nutrition per serving:
151 calories, 1 g fat, 31 g total
carbohydrate, 4 g protein, 250 mg
sodium, 2 mg cholesterol

1½ oz / 45 g diced onion

½ oz / 14 g minced garlic

26 fl oz / 780 mL Chicken Stock (page 489) or
water

14 oz / 400 g long-grain brown rice

2 tsp / 10 mL kosher salt

¼ tsp / 1.25 mL ground white pepper

1 bay leaf

1 sprig thyme

1. In a medium sauce pot, sweat the onions and garlic in ½ cup / 120 mL of the stock until the onions are translucent. Add the rice, remaining stock, salt, pepper, bay leaf, and thyme. Bring the liquid to a boil. Cover the pot tightly and cook in a 350°F / 175°C oven until the rice is tender and has absorbed all the liquid, about 40 minutes.

2. Remove and discard the bay leaf and thyme. Fluff the rice with a fork to separate the grains and release steam.

Notes

The nutritional analysis is for the rice made with stock.

Many other grains can be prepared using the basic pilaf method outlined above. For more information about specific grains, see the table on page 108.

Barley Pilaf

batch yield: **2 lb / 910 g**

servings: **12**

portioning information:
2⅔ oz / 76 g

nutrition per serving:
97 calories, 1 g fat, 19 g total
carbohydrate, 4 g protein, 60 mg
sodium, 2 mg cholesterol

10 oz / 280 g diced onions

¾ oz / 20 g minced garlic

2 qt / 2 L Chicken Stock (page 489)

1 lb 5 oz / 595 g barley

½ tsp / 2.5 mL salt

1. In a medium saucepan, sweat the onions and garlic in a small amount of stock until the onions are translucent.

2. Add the barley and remaining stock. Bring the liquid to a boil and cover the pot tightly.

3. Cook in a 350°F / 175°C oven until the barley is tender and has absorbed all the liquid, about 45 minutes.

Barley Walnut Pilaf

Add 2 oz / 57 g chopped, toasted walnuts to the barley before placing in the oven. When the barley is cooked, stir in another 2 oz / 57 g chopped, toasted walnuts and ½ oz / 14 g each chopped parsley, chives, and thyme.

Barley and Wheat Berry Pilaf

batch yield: **2 lb / 910 g**

servings: **12**

portioning information:
2⅔ oz / 76 g

nutrition per serving:
120 calories, 2 g fat, 23 g total
carbohydrate, 4 g protein, 131 mg
sodium, 3 mg cholesterol

8 oz / 225 g wheat berries	2 oz / 57 g diced celeriac
1½ qt / 1.44 L Chicken Stock (page 489)	1 lb 5 oz / 595 g barley
1 oz / 30 g butter	1 pt / 480 mL amber beer
⅔ oz / 19 g minced shallots	½ tsp / 2.5 mL kosher salt
3 oz / 85 g diced leeks	¼ tsp / 1.25 mL ground black pepper
3 oz / 85 g diced carrots	1 lb / 450 g trimmed chopped collard or mustard greens

1. Soak the wheat berries for 8 to 10 hours in 3 times their volume of water. Drain the berries and combine with 1 qt / 950 mL of the stock. Cover and simmer until tender. Drain any excess stock and reserve.

2. Heat the butter in a medium saucepan. Add the shallots, leeks, carrots, and celeriac and sweat until the vegetables are tender. Add the barley, the remaining 1 pt / 480 mL of stock, the beer, salt, and pepper. Bring the liquid to a boil and cover the pot tightly. Cook in a 325°F / 165°C oven until the barley is tender and has absorbed all the liquid, about 45 minutes.

3. Cook the greens in boiling salted water until deep green and tender, about 7 minutes. Drain very well.

4. Combine the wheat berries, barley, and greens.

Quinoa Pilaf with Red and Yellow Peppers

batch yield: **2 lb / 900 g**

servings: **10**

portioning information:
3¼ oz / 90 g

nutrition per serving:
126 calories, 2 g fat, 22 g total
carbohydrate, 5 g protein, 145 mg
sodium, 1 mg cholesterol

1 oz / 30 g minced shallots	¼ tsp / 1.25 mL ground white pepper
½ oz / 14 g minced garlic	1 bay leaf
1½ pt / 720 mL Chicken Stock (page 489)	1 sprig thyme
12 oz / 340 g quinoa, rinsed	7 oz / 200 g diced roasted red and yellow peppers
½ tsp / 2.5 mL kosher salt	

1. In a medium sauce pot, sweat the shallots and garlic in 2 tbsp / 30 mL of the stock until the shallots are translucent. Add the quinoa, remaining stock, salt, pepper, bay leaf, and thyme. Bring the liquid to a boil. Cover the pot tightly and cook in a 350°F / 175°C oven until the quinoa is tender and has absorbed all the liquid, about 15 minutes.

2. Remove and discard the bay leaf and thyme. Fluff the quinoa with a fork to separate the grains and release steam. Fold in the peppers.

Risotto

batch yield: **2 lb / 910 g**

servings: **10**

portioning information:
3¼ oz / 90 g

nutrition per serving:
159 calories, 2 g fat, 26 g total
carbohydrate, 4 g protein, 84 mg
sodium, 3 mg cholesterol

1½ pt / 720 mL Stock (pages 489, 490, or 491)	10 oz / 280 g raw Arborio rice
¼ tsp / 1.25 mL saffron threads	1 cup / 240 mL white wine
2 tsp / 10 mL olive oil	1 tbsp / 15 mL grated Parmesan
4 oz / 115 g diced onion	

1. Bring the stock to a simmer in a medium saucepan. Add the saffron and steep until the stock takes on a deep golden color. Strain the stock and keep warm.

2. Heat the oil in a medium sauce pot. Sweat the onion in the oil until translucent. Add the rice to the onions and sauté until the rice is coated with the oil. Stirring constantly over medium heat, add the hot stock in 3 additions, making sure the rice has absorbed each addition of stock before the next is added. Add the wine with the final addition of stock. When properly cooked, the rice should have a creamy texture and be firm to the bite.

3. Remove the rice from the heat and stir in the Parmesan.

Note

If making risotto in advance, cook the rice only three-quarters done. Spread the rice thinly on a baking sheet and refrigerate until ready to use. To finish cooking the risotto, place the rice in a saucepan, add the final addition of stock and wine, and stir in the Parmesan.

Wild and Brown Rice Pilaf with Cranberries

batch yield: **2 lb / 900 g**

servings: **10**

portioning information:
3¼ oz / 90 g

nutrition per serving:
190 calories, 1 g fat, 38 g total
carbohydrate, 6 g protein, 68 mg
sodium, 2 mg cholesterol

2 oz / 57 g dried cranberries	**WILD RICE**
¼ cup / 60 mL dry white wine	7 fl oz / 210 mL apple cider
BROWN RICE	1½ cups / 360 mL Chicken Stock (page 489)
1½ oz / 45 g diced onion	6 oz / 170 g wild rice
6 oz / 170 g brown rice	
1½ cups / 360 mL Chicken Stock (page 489)	2 oz / 57 g whole unpeeled shallots
	Coarse salt for a bed

1. Plump the cranberries in the wine for about 20 minutes. Drain the cranberries and reserve the liquid.

2. To make the brown rice, sweat the onion in the reserved cranberry liquid until the onions are translucent. Add the brown rice and stock. Bring the liquid to a boil and cover the pot tightly. Cook in a 350°F / 175°C oven until the rice is tender and has absorbed all the liquid, about 40 minutes.

3. To prepare the wild rice, bring the cider, stock, and wild rice to a boil in a medium sauce pot. Cover the pot tightly, and cook in a 350°F / 175°C oven until the rice is tender and has absorbed all the liquid, about 35 minutes.

4. Place the shallots on a bed of coarse salt in a 375°F / 190°C oven until the exteriors are very crisp, about 20 minutes. Allow the shallots to cool. Remove the skin and shred the flesh.

5. Combine both rices and the plumped cranberries. Garnish with the roasted shallots.

Lemon-Dill Rice

batch yield: **2½ lb / 1.15 kg**

servings: **14**

portioning information:
3 oz / 85 g

nutrition per serving:
117 calories, 1 g fat, 23 g total carbohydrate, 3 g protein, 51 mg sodium, 2 mg cholesterol

1¾ oz / 50 g diced onion	¼ cup / 60 mL fresh lemon juice
26 fl oz / 780 mL Chicken Stock (page 489)	¾ tsp / 7.5 mL grated lemon zest
¼ cup / 60 mL white wine	11 oz / 315 g raw long-grain brown rice
1 bay leaf	1 tbsp / 15 mL chopped dill

1. In a medium saucepan, sweat the onion in ¼ cup / 60 mL of the stock until the onions are translucent. Add the remaining stock, the wine, bay leaf, juice, zest, and rice. Bring the liquid to a boil. Cover the pot tightly and cook in a 350°F / 175°C oven until the rice is tender and has absorbed all the liquid, about 40 minutes.

2. Remove and discard the bay leaf. Fluff the rice with a fork and fold in the dill.

Hoppin' John

Prepare the pilaf as directed above. Stir in 14 oz / 400 g smoked tomatoes, 4 oz / 115 g chopped scallions, and 2 lb / 900 g Smoky Braised Black-Eyed Peas (page 394).

Vegetarian Dirty Rice

batch yield: **2 lb / 900 g**

servings: **10**

portioning information:
3¼ oz / 90 g

nutrition per serving:
156 calories, 3 g fat, 26 g total
carbohydrate, 6 g protein, 101 mg
sodium, 7 mg cholesterol

8 oz / 225 g fresh or frozen cranberries

14 fl oz / 420 mL Vegetable Stock (page 490)

1¾ oz / 50 g diced onion

½ oz / 14 g minced garlic

7 oz / 200 g long-grain brown rice

¾ oz / 20 g tomato paste

1 tbsp / 15 mL habanero vinegar (see Note)

2 tsp / 10 mL minced roasted jalapeño

1 tsp / 5 mL toasted cumin seeds, crushed

1 tsp / 5 mL cracked black peppercorns

1 tsp / 5 mL mild or hot paprika

¼ tsp / 1.25 mL cayenne

2½ oz / 70 g grated aged Cheddar cheese

2½ oz / 70 g Roasted Smoked Corn kernels
(page 368)

10 slices grilled green peppers, ¼ inch / 6 mm
thick

1. Simmer the cranberries in boiling water until tender. Drain and mash with a fork. Reserve.

2. In a medium sauce pot, sweat the onion and garlic in 2 tbsp / 30 mL of the stock until the onions are translucent. Add the rice and sauté briefly. Add the remaining stock, the tomato paste, vinegar, jalapeño, cumin, peppercorns, paprika, and cayenne.

3. Bring the stock to a boil and cover the pot tightly. Cook in a 350°F / 175°C oven until the rice is tender and has absorbed all the liquid, about 40 minutes.

4. Fold the mashed cranberries, cheese, and corn into the rice. Serve each portion topped with a green pepper slice.

Note

*To make habanero vinegar, combine ¼ **tsp** / 1.25 **mL** minced habanero with 1 tbsp / 15 mL cider vinegar.*

Couscous

batch yield: **2 lb / 900 g**

servings: **10**

portioning information:
3¼ oz / 90 g

nutrition per serving:
186 calories, 1 g fat, 37 g total
carbohydrate, 7 g protein, 46 mg
sodium, 1 mg cholesterol

2 oz / 57 g diced onion

½ oz / 14 g minced garlic

1 pt / 480 mL Chicken Stock (page 489)

1 lb / 450 g couscous

1 tbsp / 15 mL chopped mint

2 tbsp / 30 mL chopped parsley

2 tsp / 10 mL coriander seeds

1. In a medium sauce pot, sweat the onion and garlic in ½ cup / 120 mL of the stock until the onions are translucent. Add the remaining stock and bring to a boil. Combine the onions, garlic, and stock with the couscous in a 13 by 9 by 2-in / 33 by 23 by 5-cm pan. Cover with foil and place in a 350°F / 175°C oven until the couscous has absorbed all the stock, about 3 minutes. Just before serving, stir in the herbs and coriander.

Polenta

batch yield: 2½ lb / 1.15 kg

servings: 14

portioning information:
3 oz / 85 g

nutrition per serving:
109 calories, 3 g fat, 15 g total carbohydrate, 5 g protein, 168 mg sodium, 8 mg cholesterol

1 qt / 910 mL Chicken Stock (page 489)

6 oz / 170 g yellow cornmeal

2 oz / 57 g grated Parmesan

¼ tsp / 1.25 mL ground white pepper

1. Heat the stock to a simmer in a medium sauce pot.

2. While whisking constantly, rain the cornmeal into the stock. Cook over low heat, stirring constantly with a wooden spoon, until the polenta pulls away from the sides of the pot, about 35 minutes.

3. Remove from the heat and stir in the Parmesan and pepper.

4. Brush a 13 by 9 by 2-in / 33 by 23 by 5-cm pan with water and pour the polenta onto the pan. Cool, cover with plastic wrap, and refrigerate until firm.

5. Cut the polenta into 3-oz / 85-g portions. Grill or reheat the portions in the oven before serving.

Buckwheat Polenta

batch yield: 2 lb / 900 g

servings: 10

portioning information:
3¼ oz / 90 g

nutrition per serving:
103 calories, 2 g fat, 16 g total carbohydrate, 5 g protein, 156 mg sodium, 6 mg cholesterol

1¾ oz / 50 g butter

1 oz / 30 g minced garlic

3¾ qt / 3.5 L Chicken Stock (page 489)

1 qt / 950 mL skim milk

½ tsp / 2.5 mL kosher salt

½ tsp / 2.5 mL cracked black peppercorns

1 lb / 450 g yellow cornmeal

1 lb / 450 g buckwheat flour

3½ oz / 100 g grated Romano

1. Heat the butter in a large saucepan. Add the garlic and sauté until aromatic. Add the stock, milk, salt, and pepper. Bring to a boil. Whisking constantly, gradually rain the cornmeal and flour into the stock. Lower the heat and simmer for about 45 minutes, stirring frequently. Remove the mixture from the heat and stir in the cheese.

2. Brush a 13 by 9 by 2-in / 33 by 23 by 5-cm pan with water and pour the polenta onto the pan. Cool, cover with plastic wrap, and refrigerate until firm.

3. Cut the polenta into 3-oz / 85-g portions. Grill or reheat the portions in the oven before serving.

Goat Cheese Polenta

batch yield: **3 lb / 1.35 kg**

servings: **16**

portioning information: **3 oz / 85 g**

nutrition per serving:
123 calories, 3 g fat, 20 g total carbohydrate, 5 g protein, 161 mg sodium, 6 mg cholesterol

¾ oz / 20 g minced garlic

2 qt / 2 L Chicken Stock (page 489)

1 lb / 450 g yellow cornmeal

½ tsp / 2.5 mL ground black pepper

½ tsp / 2.5 mL kosher salt

3 oz / 85 g goat cheese

1 tsp / 5 mL chopped chives

1 tsp / 5 mL chopped thyme

1. In a medium sauce pot, sweat the garlic in a small amount of the stock until the garlic is aromatic. Add the remaining stock and heat to a simmer.

2. Combine the cornmeal, pepper, and salt. While whisking constantly, rain the cornmeal mixture into the stock. Cook over low heat, stirring constantly with a wooden spoon, until the polenta pulls away from the sides of the pot, about 35 minutes. Remove from the heat and stir in the cheese and herbs.

3. Brush a 13 by 9 by 2-in / 33 by 23 by 5-cm pan with water and pour the polenta onto the pan. Cover with plastic wrap, cool, and refrigerate until firm.

4. Cut the polenta into 3-oz / 85-g portions. Grill or reheat each portion in the oven before serving.

Pumpkin Risotto

batch yield: **2 lb / 900 g**

servings: **10**

portioning information: **3¼ oz / 90 g**

nutrition per serving:
94 calories, 1 g fat, 16 g total carbohydrate, 3 g protein, 83 mg sodium, 5 mg cholesterol

3½ oz / 100 g diced onion

½ oz / 14 g minced garlic

1 lb / 450 g diced cheese pumpkin or other turban squash

1½ pt / 720 mL Chicken Stock (page 489), hot

8 oz / 225 g Arborio rice

½ cup / 120 mL white wine

2 oz / 57 g grated Romano

1. Sweat the onion, garlic, and pumpkin in a small amount of the stock until the onions are translucent. Add the rice and sauté briefly.

2. Stirring constantly over medium to low heat, add the hot stock in 3 additions, making sure the rice has absorbed each addition of stock before the next is added. Add the wine with the final addition of stock. When properly cooked, the rice should have a creamy texture and be firm to the bite.

3. Remove the rice from the heat and stir in the cheese.

Farro

batch yield: **2 lb / 900 g**

servings: **10**

portioning information:
3¼ oz / 90 g

nutrition per serving:
71 calories, 1 g fat, 15 g total
carbohydrate, 3 g protein, 118 mg
sodium, 0 mg cholesterol

54 fl oz / 1.7 L water	1 Bouquet Garni (page 490)
2 onions, halved	1 lb / 450 g farro
6 oz / 170 g carrots	2 tsp / 10 mL kosher salt

1. Bring the water to a boil in a large pot with the onion, carrot, and bouquet garni.

2. Rinse the farro in 3 to 4 changes of water. Remove any black kernels of grain. Add the farro and salt to the boiling water and simmer uncovered, until the kernels are soft and chewy and have slightly popped open, about 50 minutes. Drain the farro and discard the aromatic vegetables and bouquet.

Curried Teff

batch yield: **2 lb / 900 g**

servings: **10**

portioning information:
3¼ oz / 90 g

nutrition per serving:
138 calories, 2 g fat, 27 g total
carbohydrate, 5 g protein, 51 mg
sodium, 3 mg cholesterol

ETHIOPIAN CURRY	2½ pt / 1.20 L Chicken Stock (page 489)
1 cinnamon stick, broken into pieces	½ oz / 14 g butter
2 tsp / 10 mL fenugreek seeds (see Note)	slice gingerroot, 1
1 tsp / 5 mL cumin seeds	¾ oz / 20 g minced onion
½ tsp / 2.5 mL cardamom seeds	½ tsp / 2.5 mL minced garlic
¼ tsp / 1.25 mL ground turmeric	1½ lb / 680 g teff
⅛ tsp / .625 mL ground nutmeg	1 tbsp / 15 mL basil chiffonade
1 clove	1 tbsp / 15 mL chopped oregano

1. Make the curry by grinding the ingredients to a powder.

2. Heat the stock in a small sauce pot. Stir in the curry powder. Heat the butter in a large saucepan and sweat the ginger, onion, and garlic in the butter until the onions are translucent. Remove the ginger piece. Add the teff and stir to coat with the butter.

3. Add the hot curried stock and simmer until tender, 10 minutes. Stir in the basil and oregano before serving.

Note

Fenugreek is an aromatic plant native to Asia and southern Europe that is known for its pleasantly bitter, slightly sweet seeds.

Kasha with Spicy Maple Pecans

batch yield: **2 lb / 900 g**

servings: **10**

portioning information:
3¼ oz / 90 g

nutrition per serving:
183 calories, 8 g fat, 26 g total
carbohydrate, 5 g protein, 148 mg
sodium, 6 mg cholesterol

2 oz / 57 g butter	2 tsp / 10 mL kosher salt
4 large egg whites, lightly beaten	6 oz / 170 g chopped pecans
1½ lb / 680 g kasha	½ cup / 120 mL maple syrup
1½ qt / 1.44 L Chicken Stock (page 489)	½ tsp / 2.5 mL cayenne

1.   Melt the butter in a medium sauce pot. Add the egg whites and kasha and cook over low heat, stirring constantly, for 2 minutes. Add the stock and salt to the kasha and bring to a boil. Simmer the kasha covered, until the liquid has been absorbed, about 15 minutes.

2.   Remove the kasha from the heat and allow to rest covered for 5 minutes. Remove the cover and fluff the grains with a fork.

3.   Toast the pecans in a small sauté pan. Stir in the maple syrup and cayenne and simmer until the syrup has reduced to a very thick consistency.

4.   Just before serving, scatter the spiced pecans over the kasha.

Note

Kasha is toasted buckwheat groats that have a nutty aroma and taste. Kasha is cooked with egg whites to coat the grains, preventing lumps when it is simmered in liquid.

Stir-Fried Barley

batch yield: **2½ lb / 1.15 kg**

servings: **12**

portioning information:
3 oz / 85 g

nutrition per serving:
95 calories, 3 g fat, 15 g total
carbohydrate, 3 g protein, 49 mg
sodium, 1 mg cholesterol

1¾ oz / 50 g diced shallot	3 tbsp / 45 mL extra-virgin olive oil
3½ oz / 100 g diced bell pepper	2¼ lb / 1 kg Barley Pilaf (page 378)
1¾ oz / 50 g diced carrot	2 tsp / 10 mL chopped thyme
1¾ oz / 50 g diced celery	

1.   In a medium saucepan, sweat the shallot, pepper, carrot, and celery in the oil until tender. Add the barley and thyme and stir-fry until heated thoroughly.

Hazelnut Wild Rice

batch yield: **4 lb / 1.80 kg**

servings: **22**

portioning information:
3 oz / 85 g

nutrition per serving:
193 calories, 5 g fat, 31 g total
carbohydrate, 7 g protein, 87 mg
sodium, 3 mg cholesterol

BROWN RICE

2 oz / 57 g diced onion

1½ pt / 720 mL Brown Chicken Stock
(page 489)

7 oz / 200 g long-grain brown rice

WILD RICE

7 oz / 200 g wild rice

1 cup / 20 mL Brown Chicken Stock (page 489)

2 oz / 57 g chopped scallions

3 oz / 85 g toasted chopped hazelnuts

1. To make the brown rice, sweat the onion in a small amount of stock until the onions are translucent. Add the brown rice and remaining stock. Bring the liquid to a boil and cover the pot tightly. Cook in a 350°F / 175°C oven until the rice is tender and has absorbed all the liquid, about 40 minutes.

2. To prepare the wild rice, bring the wild rice and stock to a boil in a medium sauce pot. Cover the pot tightly, and cook in a 350°F / 175°C oven until the rice is tender and has absorbed all the liquid, about 90 minutes.

3. Combine both rices with the scallions and hazelnuts.

Note

Bloomed *is the term that describes properly cooked wild rice; the tough outer casing of the rice has cracked and the rice is tender.*

Basic Beans

batch yield: **1 lb 14 oz / 850 g**

servings: **10**

portioning information:
3 oz / 85 g

nutrition per serving:
130 calories, 1 g fat, 22 g total
carbohydrate, 8 g protein, 220 mg
sodium, 2 mg cholesterol

12 oz / 340 g dried beans (see Notes)

2 qt / 2 L Stock (pages 489, 490, and 491) or water (see Notes)

1 Bouquet Garni (page 490)

½ oz / 14 g peeled whole cloves garlic

1. Soak the beans for 8 to 12 hours in enough cold water to cover by 3 in / 8 cm. Drain the beans and rinse with cold water.

2. Combine the beans, stock, bouquet garni, and garlic in a large stockpot. Simmer until the beans are tender. Remove and discard the bouquet garni and garlic. Allow the beans to cool in their cooking liquid. Drain and use as desired.

Notes

Most beans will properly cook in the amount of liquid indicated. The table on page 109 gives approximate cooking times of different beans. Add more liquid to the simmering beans if necessary; the age and type of bean determines the length of cooking and amount of cooking liquid.

To reduce the length of soaking time, bring the beans and stock to a boil, remove from the heat, and allow to soak for 1 hour. Continue with the recipe.

Black Bean Cakes

batch yield: **1 lb 14 oz / 850 g**

servings: **10**

portioning information:
2 cakes (3 oz / 85 g), 2 tsp / 10 mL yogurt sauce, 1 oz / 30 g salsa

nutrition per serving:
288 calories, 8 g fat, 40 g total carbohydrate, 15 g protein, 485 mg sodium, 18m g cholesterol

1 lb / 450 g dried black beans

2 qt / 2 L Chicken Stock (page 489)

1 oz / 30 g chopped Spanish-style chorizo sausage

½ oz / 14 g minced garlic

3½ oz / 100 g diced onion

1 jalapeño, seeded and minced

¾ tsp / 7.5 mL cumin seeds, toasted and ground

¾ tsp / 7.5 mL chili powder

2 egg whites, lightly beaten

4 tsp / 20 mL fresh lime juice

2 tbsp / 30 mL chopped cilantro

2 tsp / 10 mL kosher salt

4 oz / 115 g cornmeal

1¾ oz / 50 g butter

3 tbsp / 45 mL drained nonfat yogurt

1¾ oz / 50 g sour cream

10 oz / 280 g Tomato Salsa (page 485)

1. Soak the beans for 8 to 12 hours in enough cold water to cover by 3 in / 8 cm (see Notes on previous page).

2. Drain the beans and simmer in the stock until tender. The beans should absorb almost all the stock.

3. Render the chorizo over low heat in a medium sauté pan. When a small amount of fat has been released, add the garlic, onion, and jalapeño. Sauté until the onions have browned. Add the cumin and chili powder and sauté until aromatic.

4. Combine the chorizo mixture, egg whites, juice, cilantro, salt, and beans. Form the mixture into small 1½-oz / 43-g cakes and lightly dust with cornmeal.

5. Heat the butter in a large sauté pan. Sauté the cakes until golden brown on each side. Keep warm.

6. Combine the yogurt and sour cream.

7. For each portion: Serve 2 cakes with 2 tsp / 10 mL of the yogurt mixture and 1 oz / 30 g of the tomato salsa.

Black Bean and Cornmeal Loaf

batch yield: **1 loaf (3 lb / 1.3 kg)**

servings: **10**

portioning information:
**3 triangles (6 oz / 170 g),
1 oz / 28 g salsa**

nutrition per serving:
151 calories, 3 g fat, 28 g total
carbohydrate, 5 g protein, 333 mg
sodium, 0 mg cholesterol

2 tbsp / 30 mL vegetable oil	¼ tsp / 1.25 mL Tabasco sauce
5 oz / 140 g diced red pepper	1 qt / 950 mL Vegetable Stock (page 490)
5 oz / 140 g diced green pepper	2 tsp / 10 mL kosher salt
6 oz / 170 g diced red onion	½ tsp / 2.5 mL cracked black peppercorns
2 oz / 57 g minced garlic	8 oz / 225 g cornmeal
3 oz / 85 g diced sun-dried tomatoes	Vegetable oil spray, as needed
12 oz / 340 g cooked black beans	2 oz / 57 g all-purpose flour
3 tbsp / 45 mL chopped cilantro	10 oz / 300 g Tomato Salsa (page 485)

1. Heat the oil in a large skillet. Add the peppers, onion, and garlic and sweat until the onions are translucent. Remove from the heat and stir in the tomatoes, beans, cilantro, and Tabasco.

2. Heat the stock, salt, and pepper in a medium sauce pot. While whisking constantly, rain the cornmeal into the stock. Reduce the heat and simmer, stirring constantly, until the mixture pulls away from the sides of the pot, about 20 minutes.

3. Fold the bean mixture into the cornmeal. Place the mixture into a loaf pan sprayed with oil. Refrigerate for 8 to 10 hours.

4. Unmold the loaf and slice into 15 equal pieces. Slice each piece on a diagonal to make 30 triangles. Lightly dust the triangles with flour and sauté in a hot skillet sprayed with oil until golden brown.

5. For each portion: Top 3 triangles with 1 oz / 28 g tomato salsa.

Vegetarian Refried Beans

batch yield: **2 lb / 900 g**

servings: **10**

portioning information:
3¼ oz / 90 g

nutrition per serving:
91 calories, 1 g fat, 16 g total
carbohydrate, 5 g protein, 103 mg
sodium, 0 mg cholesterol

1 lb / 450 g dried pinto beans

1 pt / 480 mL Vegetable Stock (page 490)

1 tsp / 5 mL corn oil

6 oz / 170 g diced onion

1½ oz / 45 g minced garlic

2 Smoked Tomatoes (see Note), diced

½ tsp / 2.5 mL kosher salt

½ tsp / 2.5 mL cumin seeds, toasted, cracked

½ tsp / 2.5 mL chili powder

1. Soak the beans for 8 to 12 hours in enough cold water to cover by 3 in / 8 cm.

2. Drain and place the beans in a medium soup pot and pour in just enough of the stock to cover the beans. Simmer until the beans are tender. Strain and reserve the beans and stock separately.

3. Heat the oil in a large sauté pan. Add the onion and garlic and sweat until the onions are translucent. Add the cooked beans and simmer over low heat, stirring constantly, until very hot. Add the tomatoes, salt, and reserved liquid to keep the beans moist. Season with the cumin and chili powder. Continue to cook, mashing the beans against the side of the pot to thicken them. Keep hot.

4. For each portion: Serve 3¼ oz / 90 g of the hot beans.

Note

Prepare the smoked tomatoes as described in Step 1 of the recipe for Cassoulet with Smoked Tomatoes, page 282.

Chickpea Stew

batch yield: **2 lb / 900 g**

servings: **10**

portioning information:
3¼ oz / 90 g

nutrition per serving:
123 calories, 2 g fat, 20 g total carbohydrate, 6 g protein, 287 mg sodium, 0 mg cholesterol

1¾ lb / 795 g dried chickpeas

SACHET

2 bay leaves

2 sprigs thyme

6 cloves garlic, crushed

4 large strips orange zest

4 oz / 115 g chopped carrots

2 tsp / 10 mL kosher salt

½ tsp / 2.5 mL cayenne

1 tbsp / 15 mL olive oil

12 oz / 340 g diced onions

10 oz / 280 g diced carrots

8 oz / 225 g diced celery

3 tbsp / 45 mL chopped rosemary

¼ cup / 120 mL chopped parsley

1. Soak the beans for 8 to 12 hours in enough cold water to cover by 3 in / 8 cm. Drain.

2. Make the sachet and combine with the chickpeas and water in a large soup pot. Simmer the peas until tender. Remove the sachet and add the salt and cayenne. Reserve about one-third of the beans and liquid and purée the rest. Add the purée back to the reserved third of the stew.

3. Heat the oil in a large skillet. Add the onions, carrots, and celery and sweat until the onions are translucent. Stir the vegetables and herbs into the stew. Keep hot.

4. For each portion: Serve 3¼ oz / 90 g of the hot beans.

Serving Suggestion

Serve with Farro (page 385) and assorted vegetables for a vegetarian entrée. (Nutrition information does not include serving suggestions.)

Southwest White Bean Stew

batch yield: **2 lb / 900 g**

servings: **10**

portioning information:
3¼ oz / 90 g

nutrition per serving:
201 calories, 4 g fat, 31 g total carbohydrate, 12 g protein, 164 mg sodium, 5 mg cholesterol

14 oz / 400 g cooked navy beans, drained

2 tsp / 10 mL safflower oil

4 oz / 115 g diced red onion

4 oz / 115 g diced bell peppers, assorted colors

2 oz / 57 g diced jalapeño

1 oz / 30 g minced garlic

¼ cup / 60 mL sherry vinegar

4 oz / 115 g tomato concassé

2 tbsp / 30 mL chopped cilantro

1. Purée 2 cups of the cooked beans and combine with the whole beans.

2. Heat the oil in a stockpot. Sauté the onion, peppers, jalapeño, and garlic in the oil until the onions are translucent. Add the bean mixture. Stir constantly until the beans are thoroughly heated. Add the vinegar and tomatoes and remove from the heat when hot. Stir in the cilantro just before serving.

Three-Bean Stew

batch yield: **2 lb / 900 g**

servings: **10**

portioning information:
3¼ oz / 90 g

nutrition per serving:
197 calories, 3 g fat, 34 g total
carbohydrate, 11 g protein, 219 mg
sodium, 0 mg cholesterol

8 oz / 225 g dried chickpeas

8 oz / 225 g dried navy or Great Northern beans

8 oz / 225 g dried black or kidney beans

1 tbsp / 15 mL olive oil

½ oz / 14 g minced garlic

2 tsp / 10 mL minced shallot

2½ oz / 70 g diced celery

2½ oz / 70 g diced carrot

4 oz / 115 g diced onion

5 oz / 140 g tomato concassé

2 tsp / 10 mL curry powder

1 tsp / 5 mL cumin seeds, toasted and ground

1 cup / 240 mL Vegetable Stock (page 490)

¾ cup / 180 mL Vegetarian Demi-Glace
(page 493)

1 tsp / 5 mL cracked black peppercorns

1 tbsp / 15 mL chopped parsley

1 tbsp / 15 mL chopped cilantro

1 tbsp / 15 mL chopped mint

1. Separately soak each kind of beans for 8 to 12 hours in enough cold water to cover by 3 in / 8 cm (see Notes).

2. Drain the beans and simmer each kind separately in water until tender. Allow the beans to cool in their cooking liquid and then drain.

3. Heat the oil in a large sauce pot. Add the garlic, shallot, celery, carrot, and onion and sauté until the onions begin to brown. Add the tomato, curry, and cumin and sauté until aromatic, about 2 minutes. Add the beans, stock, and demi-glace. Bring the liquid to a simmer. Cover and stew over direct heat or in a 350°F / 175°C oven until the carrots and celery are tender, about 20 minutes.

4. Just before serving, finish the stew by adding the pepper, parsley, cilantro, and mint.

Notes

To reduce the length of soaking time, bring the beans and stock to a boil, remove from the heat, and allow to soak for 1 hour. Continue with the recipe.

Choose any selection of beans; refer to the table on page 109 for approximate cooking times. A variety of bean colors produces the most attractive finished dish.

To make the stew into a vegetarian entrée, add vegetables such as pumpkin, zucchini, corn, peas, and peppers and serve with grains like rice, quinoa, and barley.

Smoky Braised Black-Eyed Peas

batch yield: **2 lb / 900 g**

servings: **10**

portioning information:
3¼ oz / 90 g

nutrition per serving:
123 calories, 2 g fat, 18 g total carbohydrate, 8 g protein, 78 mg sodium, 4 mg cholesterol

5 oz / 140 g dried black-eyed peas

1 oz / 30 g peeled, seeded, quartered tomatoes

1 pt / 480 mL Chicken Stock (page 489)

½ oz / 14 g minced bacon

1 oz / 30 g thick slices onion

1 bay leaf

1 sprig thyme

1. Soak the beans for 8 to 12 hours in enough cold water to cover by 3 in / 8 cm. Drain.

2. To smoke the tomatoes, place the tomatoes on a rack in a roasting pan containing a thin layer of hardwood chips. Cover with a tight-fitting lid and place over direct heat. Smoke for 6 to 8 minutes. Small dice the tomatoes and reserve.

3. Simmer the black-eyed peas in enough stock to cover by 3 inches. When the peas are tender, drain and reserve the cooking liquid.

4. Render the bacon fat in a large sauce pot. Add the onion and sauté until the onion begins to brown. Add the black-eyed peas, smoked tomatoes, bay leaf, thyme, and enough of the cooking liquid to moisten the mixture. Bring to a simmer. Cover the pot and braise in a 350°F / 175°C oven until the peas have absorbed the liquid and are tender, about 30 minutes. Discard the bay leaf and thyme.

Steamed Spinach with Garlic and Pernod

batch yield: **1¼ lb / 570 g**

servings: **10**

portioning information:
2 oz / 57 g

nutrition per serving:
45 calories, 1.5 g fat, 5 g total carbohydrate, 4 g protein, 160 mg sodium, 0 mg cholesterol

2 tsp / 10 mL extra-virgin olive oil

1 tbsp / 15 mL minced garlic

1 tbsp / 15 mL minced shallot

2¾ lb / 1.25 kg spinach leaves, rinsed and drained

1 tbsp / 15 mL Pernod

½ tsp / 2.5 mL black pepper

¼ tsp / 1.25 mL kosher salt

1. Heat the oil and add the garlic and shallot. Sauté until they are translucent. Add the spinach, along with any water still clinging to the leaves. If the leaves are very dry, add a few spoonfuls of water to the pan. Cover tightly and steam until the leaves are barely wilted. Drain any excess water.

2. Drizzle the Pernod over the spinach and add the salt and pepper. Toss and serve while still very hot.

Smokey Braised Black-Eyed Peas and Steamed Spinach with Garlic and Pernod, served with Herb-Breaded Chicken with Creamy Mustard Gravy (page 495)

Purée of Yellow Split Peas

batch yield: **2 lb / 900 g**

servings: **10**

portioning information:
3¼ oz / 90 g

nutrition per serving:
230 calories, 5 g fat, 35 g total
carbohydrate, 13 g protein, 480 mg
sodium, 0 mg cholesterol

1 tbsp / 15 mL olive oil

12 oz / 340 g minced red onions

1 lb / 450 g yellow split peas, rinsed

2¼ qt / 2.15 L Vegetable Stock (page 490)
or water

1 tsp / 5 mL kosher salt

1 bay leaf

3 tbsp / 45 mL red wine vinegar

2 oz / 57 g chopped scallions

2 tbsp / 30 mL extra-virgin olive oil (to finish
for service)

1. Heat the oil in a sauce pot over medium heat and sauté the onions until tender and translucent, about 6 minutes. Add the split peas and stir until evenly coated with the oil. Pour in enough stock to cover the split peas by 2 inches. Season with the salt and add the bay leaf.

2. Bring the stock to a boil, reduce the heat to low, cover, and simmer slowly until the split peas are completely disintegrated, 1 to 1½ hours. (Add more stock or water during cooking if necessary to keep the mixture from sticking.)

3. Remove the split peas from the heat and remove and discard the bay leaf. Cover the sauce pot and let them stand until set and thickened, about 30 minutes. The mixture should have the consistency of mashed potatoes. Stir in the vinegar to taste.

4. For each portion: Place 2 oz / 57 g in a bowl and top with some scallions and drizzle with a little of the extra-virgin olive oil. Serve immediately.

Basic Pasta Dough with Variations

batch yield: **5 lb / 2.25 kg**

servings: **20**

portioning information:
4 oz / 115 g

nutrition per serving:
301 calories, 1 g fat, 60 g total
carbohydrate, 12 g protein, 25 mg
sodium, 0 mg cholesterol

3 lb 10 oz / 1.65 kg durum semolina flour

10 oz / 280 g egg whites

1¼ to 1½ cups / 330 to 360 mL water

1. In a mixer, combine the ingredients using a dough hook until the mixture is mealy. If necessary, adjust the consistency with more water or flour. The dough should not form a ball, but it should adhere into a ball when pressed together by hand.

2. Press the dough into a ball and wrap tightly with plastic. Allow the dough to rest, refrigerated, for 1 hour before rolling and cutting. If stored in an airtight container, the dough may be stored for 2 days, or frozen for up to 1 month. Thaw frozen dough, still wrapped, overnight in the refrigerator. Bring chilled dough to room temperature before using.

3. To roll out the dough, pass 8-oz / 225-g pieces through the widest setting of a pasta machine. Fold the dough into thirds, repeat 2 more times, trying to achieve a rectangular shape. Pass the dough through successively smaller settings until the desired thickness. Cut into shapes, or use the sheets of dough to make filled pastas.

4. Cook 1 lb / 450 g pasta in 1 gal / 5.75 L boiling water until tender to the bite. If preparing in advance, slightly undercook the pasta. Rinse and drain the pasta to prevent it from sticking. Reheat the pasta in simmering water.

Variations

Spinach Pasta Dough

Add 1¼ lb / 565 g puréed raw spinach to the dough and decrease the water to 5 fl oz / 150 mL.

Pumpkin, Beet, or Carrot Pasta Dough

Cook 1¼ lb / 565 g puréed pumpkin, beets, or carrots in a sauté pan to remove as much moisture as possible without burning. Add the purée to the pasta. Add only enough water to form a smooth, elastic dough.

Tomato Pasta Dough

Cook 8 oz / 225 g tomato paste in a sauté pan to remove moisture and intensify flavor. Add only enough water for a smooth, elastic dough, about 3 fl oz / 90 mL.

Fresh Herb Pasta Dough

Add 3 tbsp / 45 mL chopped fresh herbs to the dough.

Spice Pasta Dough

Add 2 tbsp / 30 mL ground cumin or crushed peppercorns to the dough.

Buckwheat Noodles

batch yield: **4¾ lb / 2.15 kg**

servings: **19**

portioning information:
4 oz / 115 g

nutrition per serving:
306 calories, 1 g fat, 61 g total
carbohydrate, 12 g protein, 127 mg
sodium, 0 mg cholesterol

2¾ lb / 1.25 kg durum semolina flour

12 oz / 340 g buckwheat flour

10½ oz / 300 g egg whites

9 fl oz / 270 mL water

3 tbsp / 45 mL reduced-sodium soy sauce

1. In a mixer, combine the ingredients using a dough hook until the mixture is mealy. If necessary, adjust the consistency with more water or flour. The dough should not form a ball, but it should adhere into a ball when pressed together by hand.

2. Press the dough into a ball and wrap tightly with plastic. Allow the dough to rest, refrigerated, for 1 hour before rolling and cutting.

3. To roll out the dough, pass 8-oz / 225-g pieces through the widest setting of a pasta machine. Fold the dough into thirds, repeat 2 more times, trying to achieve a rectangular shape. Pass the dough through successively smaller settings until the desired thickness. Cut into spaghetti.

Jalapeño Pasta

batch yield: **4 lb / 1.80 kg**

servings: **16**

portioning information:
4 oz / 115 g

nutrition per serving:
301 calories, 1 g fat, 60 g total
carbohydrate, 12 g protein, 25 mg
sodium, 0 mg cholesterol

5 oz / 140 g chopped jalapeños

8 oz / 225 g egg whites

12 oz / 340 g durum semolina flour

2¼ lb / 1 kg bread flour

1. Purée the jalapeños and egg whites in a blender until smooth. Combine the purée and flours in a mixing bowl. Knead with a dough hook to form a mealy dough.

2. Press the dough into a ball and wrap tightly with plastic. Allow the dough to rest, refrigerated, for 1 hour before rolling and cutting.

3. To roll out the dough, pass 8-oz / 225-g pieces through the widest setting of a pasta machine. Fold the dough into thirds, repeat 2 more times, trying to achieve a rectangular shape. Pass the dough through successively smaller settings until the desired thickness. Cut into shapes, or use the sheets of dough to make filled pastas.

Saffron Pasta

batch yield: **5 lb / 2.25 kg**

servings: **20**

portioning information:
4 oz / 115 g

nutrition per serving:
301 calories, 1 g fat, 60 g total
carbohydrate, 12 g protein, 25 mg
sodium, 0 mg cholesterol

½ oz / 14 g saffron threads

10½ fl oz / 315 mL hot water

3 lb 10 oz / 1.65 kg durum semolina flour

10½ oz / 300 g egg whites

2 tbsp / 30 mL grated lemon zest

1. Steep the saffron in the hot water and allow the infusion to cool.

2. Combine the infusion with the remaining ingredients in a mixing bowl. Knead with a dough hook to form a mealy dough.

3. Press the dough into a ball and wrap tightly with plastic. Allow the dough to rest, refrigerated, for 1 hour before rolling and cutting.

4. To roll out the dough, pass 8-oz / 225-g pieces through the widest setting of a pasta machine. Fold the dough into thirds, repeat 2 more times, trying to achieve a rectangular shape. Pass the dough through successively smaller settings until the desired thickness. Cut into shapes, or use the sheets of dough to make filled pastas.

Chile Pepper Pasta

batch yield: **5 lb / 2.25 kg**

servings: **20**

portioning information:
4 oz / 115 g

nutrition per serving:
301 calories, 1 g fat, 60 g total
carbohydrate, 12 g protein, 25 mg
sodium, 0 mg cholesterol

1 lb / 450 g dried chopped chiles (see Note)

5 fl oz / 150 mL hot water

8 oz / 225 g egg whites

3¼ lb / 1.5 kg durum semolina flour

1. Soften the chiles by steeping in the hot water, about 20 minutes. Drain and reserve the water.

2. Purée the chiles and egg whites in a blender until smooth. Combine the chile purée and flour in a mixing bowl. Knead with a dough hook to form a mealy dough. Adjust the consistency with the reserved water if necessary.

3. Press the dough into a ball and wrap tightly with plastic wrap. Allow the dough to rest, refrigerated, for 1 hour before rolling and cutting.

4. To roll out the dough, pass 8-oz / 225-g pieces through the widest setting of a pasta machine. Fold the dough into thirds, repeat 2 more times, trying to achieve a rectangular shape. Pass the dough through successively smaller settings until the desired thickness. Cut into shapes, or use the sheets of dough to make filled pastas.

Note

Use a mild-flavored dried chile such as an Anaheim or poblano. Toast the chile before hydrating.

Spätzle

batch yield: **2¾ lb / 1.25 kg**

servings: **10**

portioning information:
4 oz / 115 g

nutrition per serving:
166 calories, 0 g fat, 32 g total carbohydrate, 8 g protein, 166 mg sodium, 0 mg cholesterol

5 egg whites	Broth or stock as needed
½ cup / 120 mL skim milk	2 tbsp / 30 mL chopped chives
9½ oz / 270 g all-purpose flour	¼ tsp / 1.25 mL kosher salt
⅛ tsp / 0.625 mL ground nutmeg	Pinch ground black pepper

1. Beat together the egg whites, milk, flour, and nutmeg. Add more flour as needed to form a batter with the consistency of heavy cream.

2. Drop through a colander, large-hole sieve, or spätzle maker into a pot of simmering water. When the spätzle rise back to the surface, remove them with a skimmer and drain.

3. To serve, warm the spätzle in a little of the broth and toss the cooked spätzle with a pinch of the chives, a few grains of salt, and some pepper.

Gnocchi

batch yield: **6 lb / 2.75 kg**

servings: **24**

portioning information:
4 oz / 115 g

nutrition per serving:
159 calories, 1 g fat, 32 g total carbohydrate, 5 g protein, 295 mg sodium, 34 mg cholesterol

4½ lb / 2 kg peeled Russet potatoes	½ oz / 14 g kosher salt
4 eggs, beaten	1¼ lb / 570 g all-purpose flour

1. Simmer the potatoes in water until tender. Drain and steam-dry the potatoes on a sheet pan in a warm oven, about 5 minutes. Purée the hot potatoes using a food mill. Allow to cool completely.

2. Combine the potatoes with the eggs and salt. Gradually add the flour to form a smooth ball of dough. Roll the dough into ½-in / 1-cm-thick ropes and cut on the diagonal into ½-in / 1-cm-long pieces.

3. Simmer the gnocchi in water until the gnocchi float to the surface and are cooked.

Roasted Garlic Gnocchi

Replace the 4 eggs with 2 egg yolks and the all-purpose flour with semolina flour. Purée 5 bulbs of roasted garlic and work into the milled potatoes.

Note

These gnocchi can be combined with a variety of sauces and baked or they may be gently heated by sautéing with a variety of wild mushrooms, vegetables, or fresh herbs in a small amount of olive oil. The analysis here does not include any sauces or finishing ingredients you may wish to include.

Saffron Potatoes

batch yield: **2 lb / 900 g**

servings: **10**

portioning information:
30 oz / 90 g

nutrition per serving:
100 calories, 1 g fat, 18 g total
carbohydrate, 4 g protein, 140 mg
sodium, 5 mg cholesterol

1 qt / 950 mL Chicken Stock (page 489)

¼ tsp / 1.25 mL saffron threads

30 pieces tournéed potatoes (about 1 oz /
30 g each)

1 tbsp / 15 mL chopped herbs (see Note)

1. Bring the stock to a simmer in a medium saucepan. Add the saffron and steep until the stock takes on a deep golden color. Add the potatoes to the saffron-infused stock and simmer until the potatoes are tender.

2. Drain the potatoes and toss with the herbs.

Note

Chopped parsley, chives, rosemary, and thyme are a few suggestions.

Rösti Potatoes with Celeriac

batch yield: **2 lb / 900 g**

servings: **10**

portioning information:
3 oz / 90 g

nutrition per serving:
81 calories, 2 g fat, 14 g total
carbohydrate, 2 g protein, 73 mg
sodium, 0 mg cholesterol

1 lb / 450 g peeled Russet potatoes

1 lb / 450 g peeled celeriac

1 tbsp / 15 mL whole-grain mustard

½ tsp / 2.5 mL cracked black peppercorns

4 tsp / 20 mL olive oil

1. Grate the potatoes and the celeriac. Combine them with the mustard and pepper. Form the mixture into 20 cakes, 1½ oz / 45 g each.

2. Heat enough oil to very lightly coat a nonstick skillet. Sauté the cakes until golden brown on each side. Finish the cakes in a 475°F / 245°C oven until thoroughly heated, about 5 minutes.

Potato Pancakes with Roasted Tomato Sauce

batch yield: **2 lb / 900 g**

servings: **10**

portioning information: **3 oz / 90 g**

nutrition per serving:
142 calories, 5 g fat, 19 g total carbohydrate, 6 g protein, 238 mg sodium, 6 mg cholesterol

ROASTED TOMATO SAUCE

8 oz / 225 g chopped Oven-Roasted Tomatoes (page 513)

¼ tsp / 1.25 mL chopped thyme

2 tsp / 10 mL prepared horseradish

3 lb / 1.35 kg quartered peeled Russet potatoes

1 cup / 240 mL nonfat yogurt

4 oz / 115 g grated Parmesan

5 oz / 140 g minced scallions, green parts only

2 egg whites

½ tsp / 2.5 mL kosher salt

¼ tsp / 1.25 mL ground black pepper

1. To prepare the roasted tomato sauce, stir together the tomatoes, thyme, and horseradish.

2. Simmer the potatoes in water until tender. Drain and place the potatoes on a sheet pan in a warm oven to steam dry, about 5 minutes. While the potatoes are still warm, mash them with a fork for a coarse texture. Allow the potatoes to cool slightly.

3. Combine the remaining ingredients with the potatoes. Form the mixture into small 1½ oz / 45 g cakes. Arrange on a sheet pan lined with parchment paper.

4. Bake the cakes in a 475°F / 245°C oven until thoroughly cooked, about 8 minutes.

5. For each portion: Garnish 2 potato cakes with ¾ oz / 20 g roasted tomato sauce.

Fondant Potatoes

batch yield: **2 lb / 900 g**

servings: **10**

portioning information: **3 oz / 90 g**

nutrition per serving:
96 calories, 1 g fat, 19 g total carbohydrate, 3 g protein, 85 mg sodium, 3 mg cholesterol

30 pieces tournéed potato (about 1 oz / 30 g each)

1 pt / 480 mL Chicken Stock (page 489)

¼ cup / 60 mL Glace de Viande

1. Place the potatoes in a 13 by 9 by 2-in / 33 by 23 by 5-cm rectangular pan. Add the stock and cover the pan. Bake in a 350°F / 175°C oven until the potatoes are three-quarters cooked, about 30 minutes. Brush the potatoes with the glace. Uncover the pan, return to the oven, and cook until the potatoes are tender.

Curried Yukon Gold Potatoes

batch yield: **2 lb / 900 g**

servings: **10**

portioning information:
3 oz / 90 g

nutrition per serving:
100 calories, 2 g fat, 19 g total carbohydrate, 2 g protein, 122 mg sodium, 0 mg cholesterol

2 lb / 910 g quartered peeled Yukon Gold potatoes

1 tbsp / 15 mL vegetable oil

1 tbsp / 15 mL minced onion

5 oz / 140 g diced peeled Granny Smith apple

2 tsp / 10 mL curry powder

2 tbsp / 30 mL all-purpose flour

1 qt / 950 mL water

½ tsp / 2.5 mL kosher salt

1. Simmer the potatoes in water until tender. Drain and reserve.

2. Heat the oil in a small sauce pot. Add the onion and apple and sweat until the onions are translucent.

3. Add the curry powder and flour and sauté to lightly toast. Add the water and salt and simmer until thick, 30 minutes. Combine the curry mixture and the potatoes. Simmer until the potatoes are heated through and flavorful.

Sweet Potato Cakes

batch yield: **2 lb / 900 g**

servings: **10**

portioning information:
3 oz / 90 g

nutrition per serving:
191 calories, 4 g fat, 34 g total carbohydrate, 5 g protein, 177 mg sodium, 2 mg cholesterol

12 oz / 340 g quartered peeled Russet potatoes

12 oz / 340 g quartered peeled sweet potatoes

4 oz / 115 g dried bread crumbs

2 tbsp / 30 mL mayonnaise

3 fl oz / 90 mL skim milk

2 tbsp / 30 mL chopped chives

2 tbsp / 30 mL chopped dill

1 tsp / 5 mL cracked black peppercorns

2 tbsp / 30 mL chopped rinsed capers

1. Simmer the Russet and sweet potatoes separately in water until tender. Drain and place the potatoes on a sheet pan in a warm oven to steam dry, about 5 minutes.

2. Purée the hot potatoes using a ricer or food mill. Allow the potatoes to cool slightly. Combine the remaining ingredients with the potatoes. Form the mixture into small 1½ oz / 45 g cakes. Arrange on a baking sheet lined with parchment paper. Bake the cakes in a 475°F / 245°C oven until thoroughly heated, about 8 minutes.

Oven-Roasted Potatoes

batch yield: **2 lb / 900 g**

servings: **10**

portioning information:
3¼ oz / 90 g

nutrition per serving:
92 calories, 2 g fat, 17 g total
carbohydrate, 2 g protein, 121 mg
sodium, 0 mg cholesterol

1 lb 14 oz / 850 g Russet potato wedges	½ oz / 14 g minced garlic
4 tsp / 20 mL olive oil	½ tsp / 2.5 mL kosher salt
2 tsp / 10 mL chopped rosemary	¾ tsp / 7.5 mL cracked black peppercorns

1. Toss the potatoes with the oil, rosemary, garlic, salt, and pepper. Spread the potatoes in a single layer on a sheet pan or roasting pan lined with parchment paper. Roast the potatoes in a 400°F / 205°C oven until the potatoes are golden brown and tender, about 30 minutes.

Variation

Oven-Roasted Sweet Potatoes

Replace the Russet potatoes with sweet potatoes and the rosemary with thyme. Toss the potatoes with the oil, thyme, garlic, 1½ tsp / 7.5 mL minced ginger, 2 tbsp / 30 mL fresh lime juice, salt, and pepper. Continue as directed in steps 2 and 3 above.

Potato Gratin

batch yield: **5 lb / 2.25 kg**

servings: **26**

portioning information:
3 oz / 85 g

nutrition per serving:
153 calories, 4 g fat, 20 g total
carbohydrate, 9 g protein, 271 mg
sodium, 13 mg cholesterol

2 qt / 2 L skim milk	½ oz / 14 g arrowroot
4 lb / 1.80 kg thinly sliced, peeled Russet potatoes	6 oz / 170 g grated Gruyère
¾ oz / 20 g minced garlic	4 oz / 115 g fresh white bread crumbs
2 tsp / 10 mL kosher salt	4 oz / 115 g grated Parmesan

1. Combine the milk, potatoes, garlic, and salt in a large sauce pot. Simmer until the potatoes are three-quarters cooked.

2. Combine the arrowroot with enough water to form a paste. Add to the potato mixture and simmer until thickened, about 2 minutes. Remove the mixture from the heat and stir in the Gruyère. Pour the mixture into a 13 by 9 by 2-in / 33 by 23 by 5-cm rectangular pan.

3. Combine the bread crumbs and Parmesan and scatter evenly over the potatoes. Bake in a 350°F / 175°C oven until golden brown, about 20 minutes. Rest the potatoes for 10 to 12 minutes to set them before slicing into portions.

Celeriac and Potato Purée

batch yield: **2 lb / 900 g**

servings: **10**

portioning information:
3¼ oz / 90 g

nutrition per serving:
114 calories, 5 g fat, 16 g total
carbohydrate, 3 g protein, 299 mg
sodium, 14 mg cholesterol

3 fl oz / 90 mL skim milk

3 tbsp / 45 mL heavy cream

15 oz / 425 g quartered peeled chef's potatoes

15 oz / 425 g large-dice peeled celeriac

1½ oz / 45 g butter

½ oz / 14 g roasted garlic

2 tsp / 10 mL kosher salt

1. Bring the milk, cream, and butter to a simmer in a small saucepan. Keep warm over very low heat.

2. Simmer the potatoes and celeriac separately in water until tender. Drain and place the potatoes and celeriac on a baking sheet in a warm oven to steam dry, about 5 minutes. Purée the hot potatoes and celeriac using a ricer or food mill. Stir in the roasted garlic. Whip the hot milk mixture into the potato mixture. Season with the salt.

Potato Purée with Roasted Eggplant and Garlic

batch yield: **2 lb / 900 g**

servings: **10**

portioning information:
3¼ oz / 90 g

nutrition per serving:
109 calories, 4 g fat, 16 g total
carbohydrate, 2 g protein, 126 mg
sodium, 8 mg cholesterol

12 oz / 340 g eggplant

1 lb 9 oz / 710 g quartered peeled Russet potatoes

¾ oz / 20 g roasted garlic

¼ cup / 60 mL skim milk

¼ cup / 60 mL heavy cream

4 tsp / 20 mL extra-virgin olive oil

½ tsp / 2.5 mL kosher salt

1. To roast the eggplant, slice it in half lengthwise and score the flesh. Place cut side down on a sheet pan lined with parchment paper. Roast in a 400°F / 205°C oven until the flesh is very soft. Remove the eggplant and scoop the flesh from the skin.

2. Simmer the potatoes in water until tender. Drain and place the potatoes on a sheet pan in a warm oven to steam dry, about 5 minutes. Purée the hot potatoes using a ricer or food mill. Combine the roasted eggplant, potatoes, and garlic.

3. Bring the milk, cream, and oil to a simmer in a small saucepan. Whip the hot milk mixture into the potato mixture. Season with the salt.

8

Breakfast and Beverages

BREAKFAST IS OFTEN a hurried affair and according to many studies, is the meal that most of your guests order on "autopilot." This chapter takes familiar breakfast foods, including eggs, pancakes, and waffles, and makes them more interesting, flavorful, and nourishing. We introduce a host of fresh and dried fruits to griddle cakes and cereals, match egg dishes with beans and vegetables, and make a sausage with lean pork and rice for a fresh alternative to traditional breakfast meats that are typically high in sodium and cholesterol. Beverages for breakfast offer another opportunity to explore the flavors of the world, from smoothies to virgin cocktails made with fresh juices and sparkling water.

Granola

batch yield: **2¼ lb / 1 kg**

servings: **24**

portion information:
1½ oz / 45 g

nutrition per serving:
156 calories, 9 g fat, 17 g total
carbohydrate, 5 g protein, 3 mg
sodium, 0 mg cholesterol

2½ oz / 70 g sesame seeds

2½ oz / 70 g slivered almonds

2 oz / 57 g sunflower seeds

4 oz / 115 g unsalted cashews

3 oz / 85 g unsweetened shredded coconut

10½ oz / 300 g rolled oats

4 oz / 115 g honey

3 oz / 85 g dried currants

1. Toast the sesame seeds until golden brown in a dry skillet. Set aside.

2. In the same skillet, toast the almonds until a pale golden color. Add the sunflower seeds and continue to toast until the almonds are golden brown. Add the cashews, coconut, and oats to the skillet. Toast until the cashews are lightly browned. Add the toasted sesame seeds and honey to the skillet. Heat and toss until all the ingredients are coated with the honey.

3. Remove the pan from the heat and stir in the currants. Spread the mixture on a sheet pan lined with parchment paper.

4. Bake the granola in a 350°F / 175°C oven until the granola has a rich golden-brown color, about 15 minutes.

5. Line another sheet pan with several layers of absorbent towels. Spread the granola onto the towels and cover with additional towels. Allow the granola to cool completely. Break the granola into small chunks and store in an airtight container for up to 3 weeks.

Note

Carefully measure each portion since nuts, seeds, and coconut are high in fat. Granola is recommended as a topping rather than a cereal since a 1½-oz / 43-g serving would barely cover the bottom of a small bowl.

Basic Crêpe Batter

batch yield: **30 crêpes**

portion information:
1 crêpe

nutrition per serving:
75 calories, 1 g fat, 12 g total
carbohydrate, 3 g protein, 30 mg
sodium, 0 mg cholesterol

1 cup / 240 mL skim milk, cold

1 cup / 240 mL cold water

6 oz / 170 g all-purpose flour

4 egg whites

1 tbsp / 15 mL vegetable oil

Vegetable oil spray, as needed

1. Place all the ingredients except the vegetable oil spray in the bowl of a food processor and process until smooth. Strain the batter through a fine-mesh sieve. Allow the batter to rest for 15 minutes.

2. Heat a crêpe pan lightly sprayed with vegetable oil. Ladle 1 fl oz / 30 mL of the batter into the pan and cook on the first side until the edges start to look dry. Turn the crêpe once and cook briefly on the second side. Stack crêpes with parchment between the crepes.

Note

Crêpes may be filled with sweet or savory fillings such as vegetables, cheeses, cooked beans, Tomato Salsa (page 485), Apple Strudel Filling (page 456), or fresh fruits.

Breakfast Sausage Patties

batch yield: **5 lb / 2.25 kg**

servings: **26**

portion information:
two 1½-oz / 43-g patties

nutrition per serving:
130 calories, 5 g fat, 11 g total carbohydrate, 10 g protein, 239 mg sodium, 29 mg cholesterol

4 oz / 115 g minced onion

1 qt / 950 mL Chicken Stock (page 489)

8 oz / 225 g raw long-grain white rice

3 lb / 1.35 kg cubed pork loin

2 tsp / 10 mL kosher salt

1 tbsp / 15 mL poultry seasoning

2 tsp / 10 mL ground ginger

2 tsp / 10 mL red pepper flakes

2 fl oz / 60 mL corn syrup

1. In a medium sauce pot, sweat the onions until translucent in 2 fl oz / 60 mL of the stock. Add the rice and 22 fl oz / 660 mL of the stock and bring the liquid to a boil. Cover the pot tightly and cook in a 350°F / 175°C oven until the rice is tender and has absorbed all the liquid, about 18 minutes. Spread the rice on a sheet pan and chill completely in the refrigerator.

2. Combine the pork, salt, poultry seasoning, ginger, and red pepper flakes in a large bowl. Add the cold rice to the meat and grind the mixture through a coarse die into a bowl set in an ice bath. Slowly stir the corn syrup and remaining 1 cup / 240 mL cold stock into the meat mixture.

3. Make a small patty of the sausage and dry sauté to test for seasoning and consistency. If necessary, adjust the seasoning with additional herbs and adjust the consistency with additional stock.

4. Portion the sausage into 1½-oz / 43-g patties. Dry sauté the patties and drain on absorbent towels.

Four-Grain Waffles served with Maple and Apple Butter Syrup (page 416)

Four-Grain Waffles

batch yield: **16 waffles**

servings: **8**

portion information:
two 6-inch-square waffles

nutrition per serving:
365 calories, 9 g fat, 55 g total
carbohydrate, 15 g protein, 456 mg
sodium, 46 mg cholesterol

12 fl oz / 360 mL nonfat buttermilk

1 egg

2 egg whites

2 fl oz / 60 mL vegetable oil

4 oz / 115 g all-purpose flour

3 oz / 85 g whole wheat flour

1½ oz / 45 g cornmeal

2½ oz / 70 g rolled oats

1 tbsp / 15 mL baking powder

1 oz / 30 g sugar

Vegetable oil spray, as needed

1. Combine the buttermilk, egg, egg whites, and oil in a large bowl.

2. Combine the flours, cornmeal, oats, baking powder, and sugar in a separate bowl. Add the dry ingredients to the liquid ingredients and mix just until incorporated.

3. Lightly spray a hot waffle iron with vegetable oil. Ladle 2 fl oz / 60 mL of the batter into the waffle iron and cook until the waffle is golden brown, about 3 minutes.

Serving Suggestion

Serve with fresh fruit and yogurt, Warm Fruit Compote (page 478), Maple and Apple Butter Syrup (page 419), or Cider and Raisin Sauce (page 447).

(Nutrition information does not include serving suggestion.)

Pumpkin or Banana Pancakes

batch yield: **18 pancakes**

servings: **6**

portion information:
three 2-oz / 57-g pancakes

nutrition per serving:
Pumpkin Pancakes: 268 calories,
8 g fat, 47 g total carbohydrate,
12 g protein, 367 mg sodium,
1 mg cholesterol

Banana Pancakes: 285 calories,
8 g fat, 52 g total carbohydrate,
12 g protein, 366 mg sodium,
1 mg cholesterol

4½ oz / 130 g oat bran

5 oz / 140 g all-purpose flour

1 tbsp / 15 mL baking powder

½ oz / 14 g sugar

1 cup / 240 mL nonfat yogurt

4½ oz / 130 g mashed pumpkin or bananas

1 tsp / 5 mL vanilla extract

1 fl oz / 30 mL vegetable oil

3 egg whites

1. Combine the oat bran, flour, baking powder, and sugar in a large bowl.

2. Combine the yogurt, mashed pumpkin or banana, vanilla, and half the oil in a separate bowl. Add the wet ingredients to the dry and mix just until incorporated.

3. Beat the egg whites to medium peaks and fold into the batter.

4. Use the remaining oil to grease a griddle, or use a large seasoned skillet. For each pancake, ladle 2 fl oz / 60 mL of the batter into the heated pan. Flip each pancake when bubbles on the upper surface appear and burst. Cook until golden brown on each side.

Sausage-Stuffed French Toast with Winter Fruit Compote

servings: **8**

portion information:
1 slice with 1½ fl oz / 45 mL compote

nutrition per serving:
375 calories, 11 g fat, 47 g total carbohydrate, 19 g protein, 577 mg sodium, 100 mg cholesterol

1 lb / 450 g Pullman loaf

1 lb / 450 g Breakfast Sausage (page 412)

3 eggs

6 egg whites

5 fl oz / 150 mL skim milk

½ tsp / 2.5 mL ground cinnamon

1 fl oz / 30 mL vegetable oil or butter

12 fl oz / 360 mL Winter Fruit Compote (page 479)

1. Slice the Pullman loaf into eight 1-in / 3-cm-thick pieces. Cut a pocket through 1 side of each piece.

2. Cook the sausage in a large skillet. Drain on absorbent paper towels. Fill each slice of bread with 2 oz / 57 g sausage.

3. Beat together the eggs, egg whites, milk, and cinnamon.

4. Heat a seasoned skillet over medium heat. Dip the French toast into the egg mixture and cook in the hot pan until golden brown on both sides, about 2 minutes on each side.

5. Slice the toast on the diagonal and serve on a pool of 1½ fl oz / 45 mL compote.

Variation

French Toast Stuffed with Fruit

Use the filling mixture for the Apple Strudel (page 456) to replace the cooked sausage.

Maple and Apple Butter Syrup

batch yield: **1 pt / 480 mL**

servings: **16**

portion information:
1 fl oz / 30 mL

nutrition per serving:
61 calories, 0 g fat, 16 g total carbohydrate, 0 g protein, 4 mg sodium, 0 mg cholesterol

6 oz / 170 g apple butter

4 fl oz / 120 mL apple cider

6 fl oz / 180 mL maple syrup

1. Gently heat the apple butter and cider in a small saucepan. Add the syrup and return to a simmer. Serve warm.

Steel-Cut Oats with Cinnamon and Dried Fruit

batch yield: 2 lb / 900 g

servings: 10

portion information:
3¼ oz / 90 g

nutrition per serving:
155 calories, 2 g fat, 32 g total carbohydrate, 4 g protein, 127 mg sodium, 0 mg cholesterol

(The nutritional analysis is for the oats made with water.)

2½ qt / 2.40 L skim milk or water

10 oz / 300 g steel-cut oats (see Notes)

1 tsp / 5 mL kosher salt

5 oz / 140 g dried fruits (see Notes)

1 tsp / 5 mL ground cinnamon

1 oz / 30 g honey

1. Bring the milk or water to a boil in a medium sauce pot. Gradually add the oats, stirring constantly. Simmer the oats, stirring frequently, until thickened, about 20 minutes. Stir the salt, fruits, and cinnamon into the oats and simmer until the oatmeal has absorbed the liquid, an additional 10 minutes.

2. Serve in heated bowls and drizzle ¾ tsp / 3.75 mL honey on each portion.

Notes

Steel-cut oats, Scotch oats, or Irish oatmeal are all names for groats that have been cut into 2 to 3 pieces and not rolled. They take longer to cook than rolled oats and have a chewy texture.

Use a variety of dried fruits such as cherries, blueberries, currants, cranberries, apricots, dates, figs, raisins, or prunes.

Tortillas de Papas

servings: **10**

portion information:
1 tortilla (6 in / 15 cm)

nutrition per serving:
398 calories, 5 g fat, 25 g total
carbohydrate, 11 g protein, 227 mg
sodium, 228 mg cholesterol

4 lb / 1.80 kg red Bliss potatoes

½ fl oz / 15 mL clarified butter

1 tsp / 5 mL kosher salt

Ground black pepper, as needed

3 Spanish onions, sliced with the grain

6 artichokes

4 roasted, peeled, thickly sliced red peppers

4 roasted, peeled, thickly sliced yellow peppers

1½ fl oz / 45 mL Sherry Vinaigrette (page 228)

½ oz / 14 g chopped parsley

2⅔ tbsp / 50 mL chopped thyme

20 egg whites

10 eggs

5 oz / 140 g crumbled goat cheese

Chervil plûches, for garnish

1. Boil the potatoes in water until they are tender. Drain and cool at room temperature. When the potatoes are cooled, cut them into large dice. (Do not remove the skins.)

2. Heat half of the butter in a large sauté pan and add the diced potatoes. Season with ¼ tsp / 1.25 mL of the salt and pepper to taste. Cook until browned and reserve until needed.

3. Heat the remaining butter in another large sauté pan and add the onions. Season with ¼ tsp / 1.25 mL of the salt and pepper to taste. Cook until caramelized. (If onions begin to scorch, add a small amount of water.) Reserve until needed.

4. Trim the stems and thick outer leaves from the artichokes. Cut off all but about 1 in / 3 cm of the inner leaves. Cook the artichoke bottoms in acidulated water until tender. Cool in the cooking liquid.

5. When the artichoke bottoms are cool enough to handle, drain, scoop out the chokes, and slice into small wedges. Combine the artichokes with the peppers, vinaigrette, parsley, thyme, and black pepper to taste. Reserve in a warm area until needed.

6. For each portion: Combine 4 oz / 115 g potatoes and 2 oz / 57 g artichokes in a bowl. Whip 2 egg whites and 1 egg until foamy and fold into vegetables. Heat a seasoned skillet (6 in / 15 cm) over medium high heat and spray or brush with a little oil. Pour in the egg mixture. Cook over medium heat until the bottom is set, about 2 minutes. Sprinkle 1 tbsp / 15 mL goat cheese over the top and finish in a 425°F / 218°C oven until puffed and golden, about 10 minutes. Garnish with chervil plûches.

Piperade Wrap

servings: **10**

portion size: **1 wrap**

nutrition per serving:
150 calories, 5 g fat, 26 g total carbohydrate, 7 g protein, 1080 mg sodium, 10 mg cholesterol

1 fl oz / 30 mL olive oil

7 oz / 200 g paysanne-cut onions

12 oz / 340 g diced or julienned bell peppers, assorted colors

10 oz / 280 g tomato concassé

5 oz / 140 g diced or julienned ham

¼ tsp / 1.25 mL ground white pepper

10 eggs

1½ fl oz / 45 mL water or milk (optional)

1 tsp / 5 mL kosher salt

Ten 8-in / 20-cm whole wheat tortillas

1. Heat a sauté pan over medium-high heat. Add enough oil to very lightly coat the pan. Add the onions and sauté, stirring occasionally, until they are tender and golden, 8 to 10 minutes. Add the peppers and tomatoes and sauté until the all of the ingredients are very hot and the peppers are tender, 6 to 8 minutes. Add the ham and sauté just until the ham is hot, 2 to 3 minutes. Season with pepper to taste in a sauté pan over medium-high heat. Keep hot until ready to serve (or, if made in advance, cool safely and refrigerate in a wrapped and labeled container).

2. For each portion: Whisk 1 egg until it is foamy. Add 2 oz / 57 g of the pepper-and-ham mixture to a seasoned pan and heat over medium heat. Add the egg and continue to cook, stirring constantly, until the egg is set. Heat a tortilla in a skillet or over a grill until soft. Add the egg mixture to the tortilla and wrap into a cylinder.

Spinach Soufflé

servings: **10**

portion information:
1 soufflé (6 oz / 170 g)

nutrition per serving:
180 calories, 10 g fat, 11 g total carbohydrate, 11 g protein, 231 mg sodium, 185 mg cholesterol

2 oz / 57 g butter, plus as needed to coat molds

2½ oz / 70 g all-purpose flour

1½ pt / 720 mL skim milk

½ tsp / 2.5 mL kosher salt

Ground black pepper, as needed

8 egg yolks

2 oz / 57 g grated Parmesan, plus as needed for coating molds

10 oz / 280 g blanched spinach, dried and chopped

10 egg whites

1. To make the soufflé base, heat the butter in a pan over medium heat and stir in the flour. Cook this roux over low to medium heat for 6 to 8 minutes, stirring frequently, to make a blond roux. Add the milk, whisking well until the mixture is very smooth. Add the salt and pepper. Simmer over low heat, stirring constantly, until very thick and smooth, 15 to 20 minutes.

2. Blend the yolks with some of the hot base to temper. Return the tempered yolks to the base mixture and continue to simmer 3 to 4 minutes, stirring constantly. Do not allow the mixture to boil. Adjust the seasoning with salt and pepper, and strain through a sieve if necessary. The base is ready to use now or it may be properly cooled and stored for later use.

3. To make spinach soufflé, prepare ten 6-fl oz / 180-mL soufflé molds by brushing them liberally with softened butter. Lightly dust the interior of each mold with grated Parmesan.

4. For each soufflé, combine 2½ oz / 75 g soufflé base and 1 oz / 30 g spinach. Beat 1 egg white to medium-firm peaks. Bake in a 425°F / 220° oven until puffed and set, about 16 minutes. Serve at once.

Raspberry-Lime Rickey

batch yield: **2 qt / 2 L**

servings: **10**

portion information:
1 drink (7 fl oz / 200 mL)

nutrition per serving:
15 calories, 0 g fat, 4 g total carbohydrate, 0 g protein, 45 mg sodium, 0 mg cholesterol

5 fl oz / 150 mL raspberry purée

5 fl oz / 150 mL lime juice

2 qt / 2 L club soda or sparkling water

8 lime wedges, for garnish

1. Combine the raspberry purée and lime juice in a pitcher. Add the carbonated water and stir 15 to combine. Serve in tall glasses over ice, garnished with lime wedges.

Mediterranean Cooler

batch yield: **3 pt / 1.8 L**

servings: **8**

portion information:
1 drink (6 fl oz / 180 mL)

nutrition per serving:
90 calories, 0 g fat, 21 g total carbohydrate, 1 g protein, 20 mg sodium, 0 mg cholesterol

1 qt / 950 mL tangerine juice

1 pt / 480 mL pomegranate juice

1 pt / 480 mL club soda

1. If using fresh tangerines, juice them and strain the juice to remove any seeds or unwanted pulp. Combine the tangerine juice with the pomegranate juice in a pitcher. Chill.

2. When ready to serve, add the club soda and stir to combine. Serve over ice, if desired.

Bitters and Sparkling Mineral Water

batch yield: **6 fl oz / 180 mL**

servings: **1**

portion information:
1 drink (6 fl oz / 180 mL)

nutrition per serving:
40 calories, 0 g fat, 7 g total carbohydrate, 0 g protein, 2 mg sodium, 0 mg cholesterol

2 to 3 tsp / 10 to 15 mL Angostura bitters

5 fl oz / 150 mL sparkling mineral water

1. Pour the bitters into a chilled wineglass containing several ice cubes.

2. Fill the glass with the mineral water and stir.

Raspberry-Lime Rickey and
Mediterranean Cooler

Juicy Fling

batch yield: **6 fl oz / 180 mL**

servings: **1**

portion information:
6 fl oz / 180 mL

nutrition per serving:
85 calories, 0 g fat, 20 g total carbohydrate, 1 g protein, 2 mg sodium, 0 mg cholesterol

3 fl oz / 90 mL fresh orange juice

1 fl oz / 30 mL fresh grapefruit juice

1 fl oz / 30 mL unsweetened pineapple juice

2 oz / 57 g raspberries

1. Combine the juices in a blender. Blend until very smooth. Serve in tall cocktail glasses filled with ice. Garnish with the raspberries.

Lemonade

batch yield: **1 qt / 950 mL**

servings: **5**

portion information:
6 fl oz / 180 mL

nutrition per serving:
84 calories, 0 g fat, 23 g total carbohydrate, 0 g protein, 2 mg sodium, 0 mg cholesterol

6 fl oz / 180 mL fresh lemon juice

2 oz / 57 g superfine sugar

2 fl oz / 60 mL hot water

1½ pt / 720 mL cold water

1 lemon, thinly sliced

1 lime, thinly sliced

1. Combine the lemon juice, sugar, and hot water. Stir until the sugar has completely dissolved. Add the cold water and sliced lemons and limes and serve over ice.

Seabreeze

batch yield: **6 fl oz / 180 mL**

servings: **1**

portion information:
6 fl oz / 180 mL

nutrition per serving:
65 calories, 0 g fat, 15 g total carbohydrate, 0 g protein, 5 mg sodium, 0 mg cholesterol

3 fl oz / 90 mL fresh grapefruit juice, cold

2 fl oz / 60 mL cranberry juice, cold

1 section grapefruit

1. Combine the juices in a chilled wineglass. Garnish with the grapefruit section.

Cantaloupe Cocktail

batch yield: **36 fl oz / 1 L**

servings: **6**

portion information:
6 fl oz / 180 mL

nutrition per serving:
75 calories, 0 g fat, 18 g total carbohydrate, 1 g protein, 16 mg sodium, 0 mg cholesterol

1¼ lb / 565 g diced cantaloupe

1 pt / 480 mL fresh orange juice

1½ fl oz / 45 mL fresh lime juice

¼ tsp / 1.25 mL vanilla extract

8 to 10 ice cubes

6 slices lime

1. Combine all the ingredients except the lime slices in a blender. Blend until very smooth. Serve in frosted pilsner glasses and garnish with the lime slices.

Gazpacho Cocktail

batch yield: **36 fl oz / 1 L**

servings: **10**

portion information:
6 fl oz / 180 mL

nutrition per serving:
38 calories, 0 g fat, 8 g total carbohydrate, 1 g protein, 133 mg sodium, 0 mg cholesterol

46 fl oz / 1.40 L tomato juice

4 oz / 115 g peeled, seeded, grated cucumber

1½ oz / 45 g minced scallions

2½ fl oz / 75 mL fresh lemon juice

1½ fl oz / 45 mL Worcestershire sauce

¼ tsp / 1.25 mL Tabasco sauce

¼ tsp / 1.25 mL garlic powder

¼ tsp / 1.25 mL ground black pepper

10 sprigs parsley

1. Combine all the ingredients except the parsley in a pitcher. Stir well and refrigerate at least 1 hour. Serve over ice and garnish with the parsley sprigs.

Passion Fruit Cocktail

batch yield: **6 fl oz / 180 mL**

servings: **1**

portion information:
6 fl oz / 180 mL

nutrition per serving:
101 calories, 0 g fat, 24 g total
carbohydrate, 1 g protein, 5 mg
sodium, 0 mg cholesterol

1 passion fruit

1 orange, juiced

Crushed ice, as needed

1 slice orange

1 fresh cherry, pitted

1. Cut the passion fruit in half and scoop out the pulp. Press the pulp through a sieve to remove the seeds. Pour the orange juice through the sieve, pressing the passion fruit seeds to extract their flavor.

2. Fill a tall cocktail glass with crushed ice. Pour the passion fruit and orange juice over the ice. Garnish with the orange slice and cherry.

The American Cocktail

batch yield: **6 fl oz / 180 mL**

servings: **1**

portion information:
6 fl oz / 180 mL

nutrition per serving:
112 calories, 0 g fat, 29 g total
carbohydrate, 1 g protein, 5 mg
sodium, 0 mg cholesterol

6 to 8 seedless green grapes

Crushed ice, as needed

1½ fl oz / 45 mL fresh lime juice

1 pt / 480 mL white grape juice

1. Place the grapes in a chilled champagne flute.

2. Fill a cocktail shaker cup with crushed ice. Add the juices to the cup and stir to chill completely. Strain the juices over the grapes.

Tropical Fruit Smoothie

batch yield: **6 fl oz / 180 mL**

servings: **1**

portion information: **6 fl oz / 180 mL**

nutrition per serving: 97 calories, 0 g fat, 24 g total carbohydrate, 1 g protein, 3 mg sodium, 0 mg cholesterol

6 fl oz / 180 mL unsweetened pineapple juice, cold

6 strawberries

½ banana, sliced

1. Combine all the ingredients except 1 of the strawberries in a blender. Blend until very smooth. Serve in a tall cocktail glass and garnish with the reserved strawberry.

Frozen Cappuccino

batch yield: **6 fl oz / 180 mL**

servings: **1**

portion information: **6 fl oz / 180 mL**

nutrition per serving: 118 calories, 0 g fat, 25 g total carbohydrate, 5 g protein, 86 mg sodium, 3 mg cholesterol

3 fl oz / 90 mL coffee, frozen in cubes

2 fl oz / 60 mL evaporated skim milk

2 tsp / 10 mL sugar

2 tsp / 10 mL coffee-flavored syrup

¼ tsp / 1.25 mL ground cinnamon

1. Combine all the ingredients except the cinnamon in a blender and blend until very smooth. Garnish with the cinnamon.

Chai

batch yield: **1½ qt / 1.44 L**

servings: **8**

portion size: **1 cup / 240 mL**

nutrition per serving:
80 calories, 2 g fat, 12 g total carbohydrate, 3 g protein, 45 mg sodium, 5 mg cholesterol

1½ qt / 1.44 L cool water	¼ tsp / 1.25 mL cloves
12 Darjeeling tea bags	3 to 4 black peppercorns
3 cinnamon sticks, broken into pieces	1 vanilla bean, split
½ oz / 14 g sliced ginger	2 oz / 57 g honey
1 tbsp / 15 mL cardamom pods	1½ pt / 720 mL milk
1½ tsp / 7.5 mL fennel seeds	

1. Bring the water to a boil in a medium saucepan. Add the tea bags, cinnamon, ginger, cardamom, fennel, cloves, peppercorns, and vanilla bean. Reduce the heat and simmer the mixture, stirring occasionally, until aromatic and the mixture is a medium brown, about 10 minutes. Add the honey and milk and stir to dissolve the honey. Bring to a boil and remove from the heat.

2. Strain the liquid through a sieve, pressing on the tea bags and spices to extract as much liquid and flavor as possible. Taste the liquid for sweetness and add more honey if desired.

3. Serve the chai immediately as a hot drink or chill and serve over ice.

Mandarin Frappé

batch yield: **6 fl oz / 180 mL**

servings: **1**

portion information:
6 fl oz / 180 mL

nutrition per serving:
50 calories, 0 g fat, 14 g total carbohydrate, 1 g protein, 0 mg sodium, 0 mg cholesterol

Crushed ice, as needed	1 Mandarin orange, juiced
1 lime, juiced	1 slice lime

1. Fill a cocktail shaker cup with crushed ice. Add the juices to the cup and stir to chill completely.

2. Fill a tall glass with more crushed ice. Strain the juices into the ice-filled glass.

3. Rub the lime slice around the rim of the glass before garnishing.

Chai

Hot Mulled Cider

Hot Mulled Cider

batch yield: **2 qt / 2 L**

servings: **10**

portion information:
6 fl oz / 180 mL

nutrition per serving:
114 calories, 0 g fat, 28 g total
carbohydrate, 0 g protein, 23 mg
sodium, 0 mg cholesterol

1½ qt / 1.44 L apple cider

1 cinnamon stick

3 to 4 cloves

3 to 4 allspice berries

1 orange, zested

10 oranges, thinly sliced

1. Combine all the ingredients except the orange slices in a small sauce pot. Simmer until the flavor of the spices and orange peel are infused into the cider, about 20 minutes.

2. Strain the cider and serve in heated mugs or glasses. Garnish each portion with an orange slice.

Hot Cocoa

batch yield: **2 qt / 2 L**

servings: **10**

portion information:
6 fl oz / 180 mL

nutrition per serving:
202 calories, 2 g fat, 41 g total
carbohydrate, 12 g protein, 140 mg
sodium, 5 mg cholesterol

5 oz / 85 g cocoa powder

7 oz / 200 g sugar

1 tsp / 5 mL ground cinnamon, plus extra
for garnish

1¼ pt / 600 mL evaporated skim milk

2½ pt / 1.20 L skim milk

1. Combine the cocoa, sugar, and cinnamon in a saucepan. Gradually add the evaporated skim milk to form a syrup. Heat to a boil. Whisk in the milk and bring to a simmer. Garnish each portion with cinnamon.

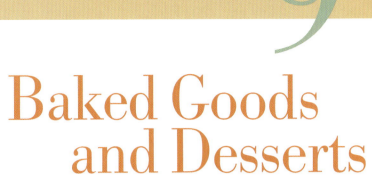

Baked Goods and Desserts

9

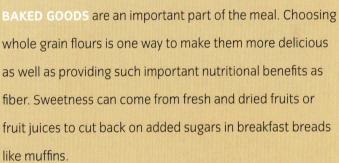

BAKED GOODS are an important part of the meal. Choosing whole grain flours is one way to make them more delicious as well as providing such important nutritional benefits as fiber. Sweetness can come from fresh and dried fruits or fruit juices to cut back on added sugars in breakfast breads like muffins.

Desserts that feature fresh fruits or chocolate are always popular. Whether you introduce special finishing touches, like delicate lace cookies or hippenmasse, or a ricotta-based "glacé" instead of full-fat ice cream, you can "have your cake and eat it too."

Oat Bran and Dried Fruit Muffins

batch yield: **1½ lb / 680 g**

servings: **16 muffins**

portion information:
1½ oz / 45 g

nutrition per serving:
165 calories, 4 g fat, 33 g total carbohydrate, 5 g protein, 212 mg sodium, 0 mg cholesterol

5½ oz / 155 g coarsely chopped assorted dried fruit

4 oz / 115 g oat bran

3 oz / 85 g rolled oats

2½ oz / 70 g all-purpose flour

1½ oz / 45 g brown sugar

¾ oz / 20 g baking powder

1 tsp / 5 mL ground cinnamon

5 oz / 140 g mashed banana

2 tsp / 10 mL grated orange zest

2 fl oz / 60 mL fresh orange juice

1 fl oz / 30 mL vegetable oil

2 egg whites

1 cup / 240 mL skim milk

1. Combine the dried fruit, all dry ingredients, and the banana in a food processor. Process until just evenly mixed. Transfer to a large bowl.

2. In another bowl, combine the zest, juice, oil, egg whites, and milk. Add the orange juice mixture to the dried fruit mixture and fold just until combined.

3. Spoon 1½ oz / 45 g batter into each paper-lined muffin cup and bake in a 400°F / 205°C oven until the surface of the muffins are golden and spring back when lightly pressed, about 20 minutes.

4. Turn the muffins out onto a cooling rack and allow to cool for 10 minutes before serving.

Country Corn Bread

servings: **16**

portion information:
1 square (3 in / 7.5 cm)

nutrition per serving:
160 calories, 2 g fat, 28 g total carbohydrate, 8 g protein, 300 mg sodium, 55 mg cholesterol

10½ oz / 300 g yellow cornmeal

8 oz / 225 g all-purpose flour

1 tbsp / 15 mL baking powder

1 oz / 30 g sugar

1 pt / 480 mL buttermilk

3 eggs

10 oz / 285 g egg whites

Vegetable oil spray, as needed

1. In a large bowl, stir together the cornmeal, flour, baking powder, and sugar with a fork.

2. Beat the buttermilk, eggs, and egg whites together in another bowl. Add the buttermilk mixture to the cornmeal mixture and fold just until combined.

3. Spread the batter in a very lightly oil-sprayed 13 by 9 by 2-inch / 33 by 23 by 5-cm baking pan. Bake in a 350°F / 175°C convection oven until a knife inserted in the center of the corn bread comes out clean, about 15 minutes.

Oat Bran and Dried Fruit Muffins

Black Pepper Biscuits and Country Corn Bread (page 436)

Black Pepper Biscuits

servings: 10

portion information:
1 biscuit (1 oz / 30 g)

nutrition per serving:
62 calories, 4 g fat, 13 g total
carbohydrate, 1 g protein, 110 mg
sodium, 21 mg cholesterol

8 oz / 225 g all-purpose flour

¾ oz / 20 g sugar

2 tsp / 10 mL baking powder

¼ tsp / 1.25 mL baking soda

½ tsp / 2.5 mL salt

2 tsp / 10 mL crushed black peppercorns

1 oz / 30 g butter, cold

6 fl oz / 180 mL buttermilk, plus extra for
glazing biscuits

Vegetable oil spray, as needed

1. Combine the flour, sugar, baking powder, baking soda, salt, and pepper in a large bowl. Cut the butter into the dry ingredients to form a mealy mixture. Make a well in the butter mixture and add the buttermilk. Slowly incorporate the milk. Do not overmix.

2. On a floured surface, roll out the dough to ½ in / 1 cm thick. Use a round biscuit cutter to cut the dough into 1-oz / 30-g portions. Arrange the biscuits on a sheet pan greased with oil spray. Brush the tops of the biscuits with buttermilk and bake in a 375°F / 190°C oven until golden brown, 10 to 12 minutes.

Spiced Graham Muffins

servings: 12

portion information:
1 muffin (1½ oz / 45 g)

nutrition per serving:
162 calories, 4 g fat, 31 g total
carbohydrate, 4 g protein, 110 mg
sodium, 21 mg cholesterol

3½ oz / 100 g raisins

4 fl oz / 120 mL warm water

4 oz / 115 g all-purpose flour

3½ oz / 100 g graham flour (see Note)

2 tsp / 10 mL baking powder

1 tsp / 5 mL ground cinnamon

¼ tsp / 1.25 mL ground cloves

1 egg

2 fl oz / 60 mL nonfat yogurt

1 fl oz / 30 mL vegetable oil

2 oz / 57 g sugar

1. Plump the raisins in the warm water for 20 minutes. Drain and reserve the liquid.

2. Combine the flours, baking powder, cinnamon, and cloves in a small bowl.

3. Beat together the egg, yogurt, oil, sugar, and reserved raisin liquid in a large bowl. Add the dry ingredients to the wet ingredients and mix just until combined. Add the plumped raisins to the batter. Spoon 1½ oz / 45 g batter into each paper-lined muffin cup and bake in a 375°F / 190°C oven until the surface of the muffins are golden brown and spring back when lightly pressed, about 15 minutes.

4. Turn the muffins out onto a cooling rack and allow to cool for 10 minutes before serving.

Note

Graham flour is whole wheat flour that is slightly coarser than regular grind.

Grilled Naan with Eggplant Purée

servings: **10**

portion information:
1 piece naan (about 2 oz / 57 g), 1 oz / 30 g eggplant purée

nutrition per serving:
190 calories, 4 g, 33 total carbohydrate, 7 g protein, 370 mg sodium, 0 mg cholesterol

NAAN

14 oz / 400 g durum semolina flour

1 tsp / 5 mL active dry yeast

6 fl oz / 180 mL warm water

2 fl oz / 60 mL plain yogurt

1 fl oz / 30 mL olive oil

2 egg whites, lightly beaten

½ tsp / 2.5 mL kosher salt

EGGPLANT PURÉE

9 oz / 255 g eggplant

1 tsp / 5 mL kosher salt

4½ oz / 130 g minced onion

1 tsp / 5 mL minced green chile

1 fl oz / 30 mL plain yogurt

1. To prepare the naan, combine the flour and yeast into a large bowl. Stir in the water, yogurt, oil, egg whites, and salt. Add a little additional warm water or flour to make a pliable soft dough, as necessary.

2. Turn the dough out on a lightly floured work surface and knead for about 5 minutes. Transfer the dough to a clean bowl and cover with a floured cloth and leave in a warm area until relaxed, about 3 hours.

3. Deflate the dough by kneading it briefly and divide into ten 2-oz / 57-g pieces. Pull each piece of dough into a 6-in / 15-cm-long teardrop shape.

4. Heat a metal griddle or heavy skillet. Add a piece of dough to the hot pan. Cook on each side until golden brown and slightly puffed, about 4 minutes total.

5. Grill the eggplants until soft and well browned on all sides. Remove the skins and mash the pulp thoroughly. Incorporate the remaining ingredients to make a thick purée.

6. Spread 1 oz / 30 g eggplant purée on each piece of naan. Fold the naan in half and grill on each side until browned.

Grilled Naan with Eggplant Purée
and Red Pepper Coulis (page 498)

Dairy Base for Frozen Glacé and Bavarians

batch yield: **3¼ lb / 1.5 kg**

servings: **14**

portion information:
3½ oz / 100 g

nutrition per serving:
175 calories, 4 g fat, 28 g total
carbohydrate, 7 g protein, 83 mg
sodium, 16 mg cholesterol

See Tables of Nutrition Information,
page 527, for nutritional value of
variations.

1½ lb / 680 g part-skim ricotta cheese

1 pt / 480 mL nonfat yogurt

12 fl oz / 360 mL maple syrup

¾ fl oz / 20 mL vanilla extract

1. Purée the ricotta in a food processor or blender until smooth. Add the remaining ingredients and process until incorporated. Flavor as desired and freeze in an ice cream machine according to the machine's directions.

Variations

Banana Glacé

Add 1 part (by weight) puréed ripe banana to 3 parts dairy base.

Fresh Berry Glacé

Add 1 part (by weight) berries to 3 parts dairy base. The fruit may be whole, sliced, or puréed.

Tropical Fruit Glacé

Add 1 part (by weight) mango, pineapple, passion fruit, or papaya to 3 parts dairy base.

Liqueur-Flavored Glacé

Add 1½ fl oz / 50 mL liqueur, such as amaretto, Kahlúa, or Grand Marnier, to 1 lb / 450 g dairy base.

Pumpkin Glacé

Add 1 lb / 450 g pumpkin purée, 1 tsp / 5 mL ground cinnamon and ¼ tsp / 1.25 mL grated nutmeg to 1 lb / 450 g dairy base.

Cappuccino Glacé

Simmer 1 cup / 240 mL evaporated skim milk, 2 oz / 57 g French-roast coffee beans, and 1 cinnamon stick for 30 minutes. Strain the milk and cool. Continue as directed in the dairy base recipe, but use only 1 cup / 240 mL nonfat yogurt and substitute the coffee-flavored milk for the remainder.

Dried Cherry Glacé

Macerate 1 lb / 450 g dried cherries in 3 fl oz / 90 mL cranberry juice and 1 fl oz / 30 mL kirschwasser for about 8 hours. Combine with 3 lb / 1.35 kg dairy base.

Espresso Praline Glacé

Add ½ fl oz / 15 mL coffee liqueur, 9 fl oz / 270 mL coffee, 1¾ fl oz / 53 mL espresso, and 5½ oz / 155 g Lace Triangles (page 452) to 3¼ lb / 1.5 kg dairy base.

Apple Pie Glacé

batch yield: **2¼ lb / 1 kg**

servings: **10**

portion information:
3½ oz / 100 g

nutrition per serving:
132 calories, 3 g fat, 23 g total carbohydrate, 4 g protein, 50 mg sodium, 11 mg cholesterol

10½ oz / 300 g sliced peeled Granny Smith apples

2¼ tsp / 11.25 mL butter

½ oz / 14 g brown sugar

½ tsp / 2.5 mL ground cinnamon

¼ tsp / 1.25 mL grated nutmeg

2½ fl oz / 75 mL apple cider

1½ lb / 680 g Dairy Base (page 442)

1. Simmer the apples, butter, sugar, cinnamon, and nutmeg in a sauce pot until the apples are tender. Purée the mixture. Add the cider to the purée and chill thoroughly. Combine the purée and dairy base and freeze in an ice cream machine according to the machine's directions.

Note

Serve the glacé with Cinnamon Crisps (page 449) and Caramel Sauce (447).

Pear Sorbet

batch yield: **2¾ lb / 1.25 kg**

servings: **12**

portion information:
3½ oz / 100 g

nutrition per serving:
156 calories, 1 g fat, 36 g total carbohydrate, 1 g protein, 1 mg sodium, 0 mg cholesterol

2¼ lb / 1 kg sliced peeled very ripe pears

9 fl oz / 270 mL water

9 oz / 500 g sugar

6 fl oz / 180 mL pear wine

1 vanilla bean, split

1. Combine all the ingredients in a large stainless-steel sauce pot. Simmer until the pears are very tender.

2. Remove the vanilla bean and purée the pears and the poaching liquid in a food processor or blender until smooth. Strain through a fine-mesh sieve and cool.

3. Freeze the purée in an ice cream machine according to the machine's directions.

Chocolate-Ricotta Bavarian with Biscotti and
Caramel Sauce (page 447)

Chocolate-Ricotta Bavarian

batch yield: **2 lb / 900 g**

servings: **10**

portion information:
1 bavarian (3 oz / 90 g)

nutrition per serving:
158 calories, 5 g fat, 27 g total carbohydrate, 6 g protein, 61 mg sodium, 5 mg cholesterol

Vegetable oil spray, as needed

1 oz / 30 g powdered sugar

3¼ oz / 90 g chopped semisweet chocolate

1 tsp / 5 mL gelatin powder

1½ fl oz / 45 mL water

14 oz / 400 g Dairy Base (page 442)

2 oz / 57 g cocoa powder

1¾ oz / 50 g sugar

6 oz / 170 g egg whites

1. Spray the inside of 3-in / 8-cm diameter ring molds with sides 2-in / 5-cm high with oil and dust with powdered sugar. Place the molds on a sheet pan lined with plastic wrap. Refrigerate until needed.

2. Melt the chocolate over a double boiler.

3. Bloom the gelatin in the water for 5 minutes. Dissolve over a double boiler.

4. Combine the dairy base with the warm chocolate and heat very gently over a double boiler. Add the dissolved gelatin and cocoa powder to the chocolate mixture and whisk until smooth. Cool the mixture to room temperature.

5. Warm the sugar and egg whites together to 100°F / 38°C. Whip the mixture to medium peaks and fold into the chocolate mixture. Pipe 3 oz / 90 g of the mixture into the molds, cover with plastic wrap, and chill for at least 2 hours before serving.

Serving Suggestion

Serve with biscotti (page 451) and Caramel Sauce (page 447).

(Nutrition information does not include serving suggestions.)

Champagne and Lemon Sorbet

batch yield: **1¼ qt / 1.20 L**

servings: **8**

portion information:
5 fl oz / 150 mL

nutrition per serving:
200 calories, 0 g fat, 44 g total
carbohydrate, 0 g protein, 0 mg
sodium, 0 mg cholesterol

1 pt / 480 mL water (divided use)

12 oz / 340 g sugar

12 fl oz / 360 mL Champagne (see Note)

2¼ tsp / 6.75 g grated lemon zest

4 fl oz / 120 mL lemon juice

1. Bring 1 cup / 240 mL of the water and the sugar to a boil in a nonreactive saucepan over medium heat, stirring occasionally, until the sugar is dissolved. Remove from the heat and let cool to room temperature, about 1 hour.

2. Stir in the remaining 1 cup / 240 mL water, the Champagne, zest, and juice.

3. Refrigerate for at least 4 hours or up to overnight. Freeze in an ice cream machine according to the manufacturer's instructions. Pack the sorbet in containers and let ripen in the freezer for 3 to 4 hours before serving. (It keeps well in the freezer for up to 1 month.)

Note

Use other dry sparkling wines, sparkling water, or still water to replace the Champagne if desired.

Apricot Sauce

batch yield: **1½ qt / 1.45 L**

servings: **24**

portion information:
2 fl oz / 60 mL

nutrition per serving:
65 calories, 0 g fat, 17 g total
carbohydrate, 0 g protein, 8 mg
sodium, 0 mg cholesterol

8 oz / 225 g dried apricots

1 pt / 480 mL water

6 oz / 170 g sugar

1 pt / 480 mL fresh orange juice

1. Simmer the apricots, water, and sugar together in a small saucepan for 5 minutes. Remove from the heat and cool completely.

2. In a blender, purée the mixture until smooth.

3. Add the orange juice and strain the sauce through a fine-mesh sieve. The sauce may be stored in the refrigerator for 5 to 8 days, or frozen for 2 to 3 months.

Caramel Sauce

batch yield: **12 fl oz / 360 mL**

servings: **6**

portion information: **2 fl oz / 60 mL**

nutrition per serving:
111 calories, 5 g fat, 15 g total carbohydrate, 1 g protein, 11 mg sodium, 13 mg cholesterol

3 oz / 85 g butter

3½ fl oz / 100 mL water

7 oz / 200 g sugar

4 fl oz / 120 mL evaporated skim milk

2 tsp / 10 mL arrowroot

1 fl oz / 30 mL dark rum, Kahlúa, brandy, cognac, or Grand Marnier

1. Combine the butter, water, and sugar in a medium sauce pot. Heat over moderate heat until the mixture turns a dark brown color. Remove from the heat.

2. Combine the milk, arrowroot, and liqueur in a small bowl. Add to the caramelized sugar, stirring constantly until thoroughly incorporated. Return the sauce to the heat and boil gently while constantly stirring. When the sauce has thickened slightly, about 2 minutes, remove from the heat and cool.

3. The sauce may be stored in the refrigerator for 2 to 3 days.

Note

If the sauce is too thick, add 2 fl oz / 60 mL additional evaporated skim milk.

Cider and Raisin Sauce

batch yield: **1 pt / 480 mL**

servings: **8**

portion information: **2 fl oz / 60 mL**

nutrition per serving:
150 calories, 0 g fat, 31 g total carbohydrate, 0 g protein, 19 mg sodium, 0 mg cholesterol

3 oz / 85 g raisins or dried currants

2 fl oz / 60 mL bourbon

1½ pt / 720 mL apple cider

4 tsp / 20 mL arrowroot

1. In a small bowl, combine the raisins, 1½ fl oz / 45 mL of the bourbon, and enough cider to cover the raisins. Plump the raisins for 25 minutes. Drain and reserve the liquid.

2. Combine the remaining cider and the reserved liquid in a small sauce pot. Over high heat, reduce by half its original volume. Lower the heat to a simmer.

3. Mix the arrowroot with the remaining ½ fl oz / 15 mL of the bourbon to form a smooth paste. Add the diluted arrowroot and the plumped raisins to the liquid. Simmer until the sauce thickens, about 2 minutes.

Fresh Berry Coulis

batch yield: **2½ pt / 1.20 L**

servings: **20**

portion information:
2 fl oz / 60 mL

nutrition per serving:
66 calories, 0 g fat, 14 g total carbohydrate, 0 g protein, 2 mg sodium, 0 mg cholesterol

1 lb / 450 g fresh or frozen raspberries, strawberries, or blueberries (see Note)

1 fl oz / 30 mL kirschwasser

5 fl oz / 150 mL honey

6 fl oz / 180 mL dry or sweet white wine

1. In a blender, purée the berries, kirschwasser, and 3 fl oz / 100 mL each of the honey and wine.

2. Check the consistency and taste of the coulis. The sauce may need to be adjusted depending on the sweetness of the fruit, growing condition, ripeness, and handling and storage during shipping. Add more wine for a smoother texture and more honey for a sweeter taste. Strain the coulis through a fine-mesh sieve to remove the seeds. The coulis may be stored in the refrigerator for 5 to 8 days, or frozen for 2 to 3 months.

Note

Frozen berries should be Individually Quick Frozen (IQF) or low-sugar.

Chocolate Spa Cream

batch yield: **12 oz / 340 g**

servings: **8**

portion information:
1½ oz / 45 g

nutrition per serving:
100 calories, 0 g fat, 14 g total carbohydrate, 7 g protein, 95 mg sodium, 0 mg cholesterol

2 fl oz / 60 mL skim milk

¾ oz / 20 g cocoa powder

¾ tsp / 3.75 mL powdered gelatin

2 fl oz / 60 mL Kahlúa

3½ oz / 100 g nonfat dry milk

1½ oz / 45 g sugar

1 vanilla bean, scraped

2¾ oz / 78 g egg whites

1. Combine the milk and cocoa in a small saucepan. Simmer for 2 minutes. Transfer the mixture to a metal mixing bowl and freeze until the mixture turns to slush, about 40 minutes.

2. In a small saucepan, bloom the gelatin in the Kahlúa and heat until the gelatin has dissolved.

3. Remove the milk mixture from the freezer and add the gelatin mixture, dry milk, 2 tsp / 10 g of the sugar, and the vanilla seeds. Beat until soft peaks form.

4. Combine the remaining sugar and egg whites. Beat to medium peaks. Fold the meringue into the Kahlúa mixture. Cover and chill for at least 15 minutes before serving.

Honey Crisps

batch yield: **7 oz / 200 g**

servings: **14**

portion information:
1 crisp (½ oz / 14 g)

nutrition per serving:
66 calories, 2 g fat, 11 g total carbohydrate, 1 g protein, 6 mg sodium, 6 mg cholesterol

1 oz / 30 g butter

1 oz / 30 g powdered sugar

2 oz / 57 g honey

1 egg white

1½ oz / 45 g all-purpose flour

1. Combine the butter, sugar, and honey in a food processor and process until smooth. Add the egg white and mix until smooth. Add the flour and mix until fully incorporated.

2. Spread a thin layer of batter on the surface of an inverted sheet pan. Bake in a 375°F / 190°C oven until the batter loses its glossy appearance and the edges look dry. Remove from the oven and cut into desired shapes.

Note

To make a shell for glacé and sauces, place a template on an inverted sheet pan and spread the batter thinly, filling the opening of the template. Remove the template and bake as directed above. While the cookie is still hot, lift it from the sheet pan and shape by draping over a rolling pin, inverted cup, or similar object.

Variation

Cinnamon Crisps

Add 1 tsp / 5 mL ground cinnamon to the batter.

Almond-Anise Biscotti

Almond-Anise Biscotti

batch yield: **3 lb / 1.35 kg (144 pieces)**

servings: **48**

portion information: **3 pieces (1 oz / 28 g)**

nutrition per serving: 98 calories, 3 g fat, 15 g total carbohydrate, 2 g protein, 56 mg sodium, 6 mg cholesterol

8 oz / 225 g all-purpose flour	1 tsp / 5 mL almond extract
4½ oz / 130 g sugar	1 oz / 30 g chopped almonds
2 tsp / 10 mL baking powder	½ oz / 14 g anise seeds
2 oz / 57 g butter	Vegetable oil spray, as needed
3 oz / 85 g egg whites	
1 tsp / 5 mL anise extract	

1. Combine the flour, sugar, and baking powder in a large bowl. Cut the butter into the dry ingredients to form a mealy mixture. Stir in the egg whites and extracts. Fold in the almonds and anise seeds.

2. Place the mixture in a pastry bag without a tip and pipe 9 by 2-in / 23 by 5-cm logs onto a parchment-lined, oil-sprayed sheet pan. Bake in a 350°F / 175°C oven until a skewer inserted into the center of the log comes out clean, about 25 minutes.

3. Remove the biscotti from the oven and cool for 10 minutes. Cut each log on a bias ¼ in / 6 mm thick. Place the biscotti on the sheet pan and bake in a 350°F / 175°C oven until dry, about 15 minutes.

Almond Tuiles

batch yield: **4½ lb / 1.5 g**

servings: **150**

portion information: **½ oz / 14 g**

nutrition per serving: 37 calories, 1 g fat, 6 g total carbohydrate, 1 g protein, 5 mg sodium, 0 mg cholesterol

14 oz / 400 g powdered sugar	12 oz / 340 g egg whites
1 lb 5 oz / 595 g almond paste	3 fl oz / 90 mL whole milk
7 oz / 200 g bread flour	

1. Combine the sugar, almond paste, and flour in a food processor and process until the mixture has a grainy texture. Slowly add the egg whites and milk to the sugar mixture while the machine is running. Process until smooth. Transfer the batter to a bowl. Cover and refrigerate the batter for 6 to 8 hours.

2. Spread a thin layer of batter on the surface of an inverted sheet pan. Bake in a 375°F / 190°C oven until the batter loses its glossy appearance and the edges look dry. Remove from the oven and cut into desired shapes (about ½ oz / 14 g each).

Note

To make a shell for glacé and sauces, place a template on an inverted sheet pan and spread the batter thinly, filling the opening of the template. Remove the template and bake as directed above. While the cookie is still hot, lift it from the sheet pan and shape by draping over a rolling pin, inverted cup, or similar object.

Lace Triangles

batch yield: **3 lb / 1.35 kg (144 pieces)**

servings: **48**

portion information:
3 pieces (1 oz / 28 g)

nutrition per serving:
81 calories, 3 g fat, 13 g total carbohydrate, 1 g protein, 3 mg sodium, 9 mg cholesterol

1 lb / 450 g sugar

10½ oz / 300 g butter

10½ oz / 300 g light corn syrup

12¾ oz / 360 g all-purpose flour

2 tsp / 10 mL toasted, coarsely chopped hazelnuts

Vegetable oil spray, as needed

1. Bring the sugar, butter, and corn syrup to a boil in large pot. Remove from the heat and stir in the flour and hazelnuts. Pour the batter into a baking dish to cool.

2. When cool enough to handle, roll the dough into 2-oz / 57-g balls (see Note). Flatten the balls into disks and place 3 in / 7.5 cm apart on an inverted sheet pan sprayed with vegetable oil.

3. Bake in a 375°F / 190°C oven until the cookies stop bubbling completely, about 10 minutes. Remove from the oven. When each cookie is set but still flexible, lift from the pan and cut into 6 wedge-shaped pieces. In a cool dry place, store the cookies between parchment paper in a covered container.

Note

Each 2-oz / 57-g ball will yield 6 triangles. The unbaked batter will keep refrigerated for 1 week.

Chocolate Hippenmasse

batch yield: 5 oz / 140 g

servings: 10

portion information:
1 piece (½ oz / 14 g)

nutrition per serving:
11 calories, 1 g fat, 2 g total carbohydrate, 0 g protein, 9 mg sodium, 0 mg cholesterol

1½ oz / 45 g sugar	⅛ tsp / 0.625 mL kosher salt
1 oz / 30 g almond paste	1 egg white
½ oz / 14 g bread flour	2 tsp / 10 mL heavy cream
2 tbsp / 30 mL cocoa powder	2 tsp / 10 mL skim milk
¼ tsp / 1.25 mL ground cinnamon	

1. Combine the sugar, almond paste, flour, cocoa powder, cinnamon, and salt in a food processor and process until the mixture has a grainy texture. Slowly add the egg white, cream, and milk to the sugar mixture while the machine is running. Process until smooth. Transfer the batter to a bowl. Cover and refrigerate the batter for 6 to 8 hours.

2. Spread a thin layer of batter on the surface of an inverted sheet pan. Bake in a 375°F / 190°C oven until the batter loses its glossy appearance and the edges of the batter look dry. Remove from the oven and cut into desired shapes.

Note

To make a shell for glacé and sauces, place a template on an inverted sheet pan and spread the batter thinly, filling the opening of the template. Remove the template and bake as directed above. While the cookie is still hot, lift from the sheet pan and shape by draping over a rolling pin, inverted cup, or similar object.

Fudge Brownies

batch yield: 1½ lb / 680 g

servings: 12

portion information:
1 piece (2 oz / 58 g)

nutrition per serving:
178 calories, 7 g fat, 34 g total carbohydrate, 4 g protein, 89 mg sodium, 27 mg cholesterol

8 oz / 225 g bread flour	1 lb 1 oz / 480 g sugar
3 oz / 85 g cocoa powder	1 egg
½ tsp / 2.5 mL baking powder	2 egg whites
½ tsp / 2.5 mL kosher salt	1 tsp / 5 mL vanilla extract
5 oz / 140 g butter	Vegetable oil spray, as needed

1. Sift together the flour, cocoa, baking powder, and salt.

2. Melt the butter in a small saucepan. Remove the pan from the heat and sir in the sugar. Add the egg, egg whites, and vanilla to the butter and sugar. Beat the mixture for 1 minute. Stir the dry ingredients into the egg mixture.

3. Pour the batter into an oil-sprayed 10-in / 25-cm cake pan and bake in a 350°F / 175°C preheated oven until set but still moist, about 25 minutes. Remove from the oven and cool completely before unmolding and cutting.

Chocolate Fudge Cookies

batch yield: **1 lb 9 oz / 710 g**

servings: **25**

portion information:
2 cookies

nutrition per serving:
79 calories, 1 g fat, 16 g total carbohydrate, 1 g protein, 52 mg sodium, 0 mg cholesterol

8 oz / 225 g dried prunes	1 oz / 30 g cocoa powder
5½ oz / 155 g chestnut purée	3 oz / 85 g dark chocolate
1 fl oz / 30 mL water	4 oz / 115 g all-purpose flour
1 fl oz / 30 mL rum	2 tsp / 10 mL baking powder
1½ oz / 45 g sugar	Vegetable oil spray, as needed

1. Purée the prunes with a little water (if necessary) until smooth. Combine the prune and chestnut purées and strain through a medium-hole sieve.

2. Combine the water, rum, sugar, and cocoa powder in a small sauce pot. Heat to dissolve the sugar.

3. Place the chocolate in a small metal bowl and melt it over a double boiler.

4. Combine the purées, cocoa mixture, and melted chocolate and mix until smooth. Mix in the flour and baking powder.

5. Drop ½-oz / 14-g portions onto a lightly oil-sprayed sheet pan and bake in a 350°F / 175°C oven until set on the edge but still slightly soft in the center, about 10 minutes. Cool on baking sheet for 10 minutes, then transfer to racks to finish cooling.

Oatmeal-Pear Cookies

batch yield: **1 lb 14 oz / 850 g**

servings: **10**

portion information:
three 1-oz / 28-g cookies

nutrition per serving:
259 calories, 2 g fat, 55 g total carbohydrate, 4 g protein, 16 mg sodium, 3 mg cholesterol

5 oz / 140 g brown sugar	5 oz / 140 g quick-cooking oats
4 oz / 115 g honey	4 oz / 115 g all-purpose flour
½ oz / 14 g butter, soft	4 fl oz / 120 mL pear purée
1 oz / 30 g egg whites	3½ oz / 100 g diced dried pears
½ fl oz / 15 mL evaporated skim milk	Vegetable oil spray, as needed
1 tsp / 5 mL vanilla extract	

1. Cream together the sugar, honey, and butter.

2. Lightly beat together the egg whites, milk, and vanilla and add to the creamed mixture. Fold in the oats and flour. Stir in the pear purée and pears.

3. Drop by 1-oz / 28-g portions onto a lightly oil-sprayed sheet pan and bake in a 350°F / 175°C oven until browned on the edges, about 10 minutes.

Strudel Dough

batch yield: **1½ lb / 565 g**

servings: **20**

portion information:
1 oz / 30 g

nutrition per serving:
37 calories, 1 g fat, 6 g total
carbohydrate, 1 g protein, 5 mg
sodium, 0 mg cholesterol

12 oz / 340 g all-purpose flour

1 tbsp / 15 mL vegetable oil

½ tsp / 2.5 mL kosher salt

1 egg yolk

1 cup / 240 mL cold water

1. Combine all the ingredients in a mixing bowl using a dough hook. Mix at medium speed until the dough forms a smooth ball that is slightly tacky to the touch, about 20 minutes. Cover the dough with plastic wrap and allow to rest for 30 minutes.

2. Over a floured kitchen cloth, stretch the dough with your hands until very thin. Cut the dough into sheets and fill as desired.

3. Freeze the cut sheets of dough by layering between parchment and wrapping tightly with plastic. Allow the dough to defrost for 24 hours in the refrigerator.

Apple Strudel

batch yield: **2 strudels**

servings: **12**

portion information:
1 slice (5 oz / 140 g)

nutrition per serving:
177 calories, 3 g fat, 38 g total
carbohydrate, 1 g protein, 53 mg
sodium, 8 mg cholesterol

1½ oz / 45 g butter

3¾ lb / 1.70 kg sliced peeled Granny Smith apples

3 oz / 85 g golden raisins, plumped in warm water

½ oz / 14 g brown sugar

1 tsp / 5 mL ground cinnamon

¼ tsp / 1.25 mL grated nutmeg

1 recipe Strudel Dough (page 455)

1½ fl oz / 45 mL melted butter

1. Heat the butter in a large sauté pan. Add the apples, raisins, sugar, cinnamon, and nutmeg and sauté until the apples are tender. Cool completely.

2. Make 2 stacks of strudel dough, 3 sheets each. Overlay the stacks ¾ in / 2 cm. Mound half of the apple filling along 1 of the long outer sides of the dough. Roll the dough and place the strudel on a parchment-lined sheet pan, seam-side down. Repeat for the second strudel.

3. Brush the strudels with the butter and score the dough to indicate portions. The strudels may be refrigerated overnight, frozen for about 1 month, or baked immediately in a 450°F / 205°C oven until golden brown. Slice and serve warm.

Serving Suggestion

Serve apple strudel with Caramel Sauce (page 447) and Apple Pie Glacé (page 443).

(Nutrition information does not include serving suggestions.)

Variation

Strawberry and Rhubarb Strudel

Replace the apples with 14 oz / 400 g sliced rhubarb and 2¾ lb / 1.25 kg sliced strawberries. Omit the raisins and add 1½ oz / 45 g toasted chopped pecans. Increase the brown sugar to 3½ oz / 100 g.

Sweet Ricotta Pastry

batch yield: 1 lb 14 oz / 850 g

servings: 20

portion information:
1½ oz / 45 g

nutrition per serving:
124 calories, 3 g fat, 20 g total
carbohydrate, 3 g protein, 92 mg
sodium, 8 mg cholesterol

1 lb / 450 g all-purpose flour

4½ oz / 130 g sugar

1¾ oz / 50 g baking powder

⅛ tsp / 0.625 mL kosher salt

8 oz / 225 g part-skim ricotta cheese, cold

3 fl oz / 90 mL skim milk, cold

2 egg whites, cold

2 oz / 57 g diced butter, cold

1 tbsp / 15 mL vanilla extract

1. Combine the flour, sugar, baking powder, and salt in a food processor. Process briefly to evenly mix the ingredients.

2. Add the remaining ingredients and pulse just until a dough forms. Gather the dough into a ball and wrap tightly with plastic. Refrigerate the dough until firm, at least 1 hour. Roll out the dough to use in pastries as directed.

Variation

Plain Ricotta Pastry

To prepare a dough for savory dishes, omit the sugar and vanilla, and replace the butter with an equal amount of vegetable oil.

Sponge Cake

batch yield: **1 layer**

portion information:
1 oz / 30 g

nutrition per serving:
72 calories, 1 g fat, 14 g total
carbohydrate, 2 g protein, 28 mg
sodium, 2 mg cholesterol

Chocolate Sponge Cake:
72 calories, 2 g fat, 13 g total
carbohydrate, 2 g protein, 28 mg
sodium, 2 mg cholesterol

Vegetable oil spray, as needed

5¼ oz / 150 g cake flour

2½ oz / 70 g arrowroot

1 lb 3 oz / 540 g egg whites

9 oz / 255 g powdered sugar

1 tsp / 5 mL cream of tartar

1 tbsp / 15 mL vanilla extract

1 fl oz / 30 mL melted butter

1. Spray a 10-in / 25-cm cake pan lightly with vegetable oil, dust with 1 tbsp / 15 mL of the flour, and line with parchment paper.

2. Combine the remaining cake flour and the arrowroot and sift 3 times.

3. Whip the egg whites until thick and foamy, but do not hold a peak. Gradually incorporate the sugar and cream of tartar and continue beating to medium peaks. Gently fold the flour mixture into the beaten egg whites. Gently fold in the extract and butter.

4. Pour the batter into the prepared cake pan. Bake in a 350°F / 175°C oven until the cake begins to pull away from the sides of the pan, about 30 minutes.

5. Cool the cakes and use immediately or wrap well and freeze for up to 3 months.

Variation

Chocolate Sponge Cake

Replace 1¼ oz / 35 g of the flour with cocoa powder.

Chocolate Cake

batch yield: **2 cakes**

servings: **16**

portion information:
2 oz / 58 g

nutrition per serving:
298 calories, 11 g fat, 49 g total
carbohydrate, 4 g protein, 163 mg
sodium, 50 mg cholesterol

9 oz / 255 g all-purpose flour

1 oz / 30 g cocoa powder

½ tsp / 2.5 mL baking soda

½ tsp / 2.5 mL baking powder

½ tsp / 2.5 mL g kosher salt

2 eggs

4 egg whites

½ tsp / 2.5 mL espresso paste

2 tsp / 10 mL vanilla extract

6 fl oz / 180 mL buttermilk

1 lb 4 oz / 570 g sugar

6 oz / 170 g butter, soft

Vegetable oil spray, as needed

1. Sift together the flour, cocoa, baking soda, baking powder, and salt.

2. Whisk together the eggs and egg whites.

3. Combine the espresso paste, vanilla, and buttermilk.

4. Cream together the sugar and butter. Slowly add the egg mixture until incorporated. Alternate adding the dry ingredients and buttermilk mixture to the butter mixture. The batter should be smooth.

5. Pour the batter into 2 oil-sprayed 8-in / 20-cm tube pans and bake in a 350°F / 175°C preheated oven until a toothpick inserted in the center of a cake comes out clean, about 40 minutes.

6. Allow the cakes to cool and use immediately or freeze for up to 1 month.

Chocolate Angel Food Cake

batch yield: 1 cake

servings: 12

portion information:
2 oz / 58 g

nutrition per serving:
(cake only) 154 calories, 3 g fat,
29 g total carbohydrate, 5 g protein,
97 mg sodium, 5 mg cholesterol

Vegetable oil spray, as needed	7 oz / 200 g powdered sugar
5¼ oz / 150 g cake flour	1 tsp / 5 mL cream of tartar
1½ oz / 45 g cocoa powder	2 tsp / 10 mL vanilla extract
1 tsp / 5 mL baking powder	1 fl oz / 30 mL melted butter
14 oz / 400 g egg whites	

1. Spray a 10-in / 25-cm tube or springform cake pan lightly with vegetable oil, dust with 1 tbsp / 15 mL of the flour, and line with parchment paper.

2. Combine the remaining cake flour, cocoa, and baking powder and sift twice.

3. Whip the egg whites until thick and foamy, but do not hold a peak. Gradually incorporate the sugar and cream of tartar and continue beating to medium peaks. Gently fold the flour mixture into the beaten egg whites. Gently fold in the extract and butter.

4. Pour the batter into the prepared cake pan. Bake in a 325°F / 165°C oven until the cake begins to pull away from the sides of the pan, about 30 minutes. Cool completely before removing from the pan.

5. Slices of the cake may be grilled briefly and served with Chocolate Spa Cream (page 448).

Chocolate Crêpes

batch yield: Twenty 5-in / 13-cm crêpes

servings: 20

portion information:
1 crêpe (1 oz / 30 g)

nutrition per serving:
96 calories, 6 g fat, 10 g total
carbohydrate, 4 g protein, 222 mg
sodium, 61 mg cholesterol

3 eggs	1 oz / 30 g cocoa powder
10½ fl oz / 300 mL whole milk	1 oz / 30 g sugar
1 fl oz / 30 mL melted butter	2 tsp / 10 mL kosher salt
3 oz / 85 g all-purpose flour	Vegetable oil spray, as needed

1. Blend together all the ingredients except the vegetable oil in a food processor for 1 minute. Scrape down the sides and process an additional 30 seconds. Allow the batter to rest for 15 minutes.

2. Heat a 5-in / 13-cm nonstick pan lightly sprayed with vegetable oil. Ladle 1 fl oz / 30 mL of the batter into the pan and cook on the first side until the edges start to look dry. Turn the crêpe once and cook briefly on the second side.

Serving Suggestion

Use ¾ oz / 20 g Chocolate Spa Cream (page 448) and ¾ oz / 20 g each blackberries, blueberries, strawberries, and raspberries to fill the crêpes. Serve each crêpe in a pool of Fresh Berry Coulis (page 448).

(Nutrition information does not include serving suggestions.)

Rice Pudding

batch yield: **2¼ qt / 2.20 L**

servings: **20**

portion information:
3½ fl oz / 105 mL

nutrition per serving:
142 calories, 1 g fat, 30 g total
carbohydrate, 4 g protein, 53 mg
sodium, 4 mg cholesterol

12½ oz / 355 g short-grain brown rice

1½ qt / 1.45 L water

10½ oz / 300 g golden raisins

¼ tsp / 1.25 mL grated nutmeg

¼ tsp / 1.25 mL ground cinnamon

¼ tsp / 1.25 mL kosher salt

5½ oz / 155 g sugar

1 tbsp / 15 mL fresh lemon juice

10½ oz / 300 g puréed ricotta cheese

1 tbsp / 15 mL vanilla extract

1. Combine the rice, water, raisins, nutmeg, cinnamon, salt, sugar, and lemon juice in a medium saucepan. Cover and simmer until the rice is tender and has absorbed the liquid, about 40 minutes.

2. Transfer the rice to a 13 by 9 by 2-in / 33 by 23 by 5-cm dish to quickly cool. Fold the ricotta and vanilla into the cool rice. Cover and refrigerate for up to 2 days.

Serving Suggestion

Serve with fresh raspberries and Raspberry Sauce (page 448).

(Nutrition information does not include serving suggestions.)

Chocolate Custard

batch yield: **2¾ lb / 1.25 kg**

servings: **12**

portion information:
3½ oz / 100 g

nutrition per serving:
105 calories, 5 g fat, 13 g total
carbohydrate, 5 g protein, 65 mg
sodium, 40 mg cholesterol

1 qt / 950 mL skim milk

1 fl oz / 30 mL heavy cream

1½ oz / 45 g sugar

1 vanilla bean, scraped

2 eggs

2 egg whites

3 oz / 85 g semisweet chocolate

¾ oz / 20 g cocoa powder

Vegetable oil spray, as needed

1. Combine the milk, cream, half the sugar, and the vanilla bean in a medium sauce pot. Bring the mixture to a boil.

2. Whisk together the eggs, egg whites, and remaining sugar.

3. Place the chocolate in a large metal bowl and melt over a double boiler. Stir in the cocoa powder.

4. Strain the hot milk mixture through a fine-mesh sieve into the melted chocolate. Temper the chocolate milk into the egg mixture.

5. Lightly grease twelve 4-fl oz / 120-mL ramekins with the oil spray. Fill each ramekin with 3½ fl oz / 105 mL of the custard. Bake the custards in a hot water bath in a 350°F / 175°C oven until set, about 15 minutes. Chill before serving.

A dessert sampler featuring Chocolate-Yogurt Mousse, Berry Cobbler (page 468), Lemon-Champagne Sorbet with Lace Triangles (page 446), and White Chocolate Cheesecake (page 468). (For a sampler, reduce portion sizes for each component to about one-third portion size suggested in recipes.)

Chocolate-Yogurt Mousse

batch yield: **1¾ lb / 795 g**

servings: **8**

portion information:
3½ oz / 100 g

nutrition per serving:
113 calories, 6 g fat, 20 g total
carbohydrate, 5 g protein, 61 mg
sodium, 1 mg cholesterol

1 pt / 480 mL nonfat yogurt

2 oz / 57 g dark chocolate

1½ oz / 45 g cocoa powder

7 oz / 200 g egg whites

3½ oz / 100 g sugar

1. Drain the yogurt in a cheesecloth-lined sieve in the refrigerator for 24 hours.

2. After the yogurt has drained, allow it to come to room temperature.

3. Melt the chocolate in a stainless-steel bowl over simmering water. Combine the chocolate with the yogurt.

4. Sift the cocoa powder twice. Fold the cocoa into the yogurt mixture and warm over simmering water.

5. Combine the egg whites and sugar in a stainless-steel bowl. Heat to 135°F / 57°C over simmering water. Remove from the heat and beat until the whites form medium peaks. Fold the meringue into the yogurt mixture, mold, and chill until firm.

6. Use ring molds or make molds by cutting 3-in / 8-cm-diameter PVC pipes into 2-in / 5-cm lengths. Spray the molds lightly with vegetable oil and dust with powdered sugar. Place the molds on a sheet pan lined with plastic wrap and fill with the mousse. Chill until set.

Serving Suggestion

To serve, unmold the mousse into a Chocolate Hippenmasse cup (page 453) and serve with Apricot Sauce (page 446) or Fresh Berry Coulis (page 448). Garnish with a rosette of whipped cream, white chocolate curls, or fresh berries. Or, simply pipe the mousse into champagne glasses and garnish with Almond Tuiles (page 451).

(Nutrition information does not include serving suggestion.)

Polenta Soufflé

servings: **10**

portion information:
4 oz / 115 g

nutrition per serving:
138 calories, 1 g fat, 27 g total carbohydrate, 5 g protein, 65 mg sodium, 4 mg cholesterol

Chocolate Polenta Soufflé:
153 calories, 3 g fat, 27 g total carbohydrate, 6 g protein, 66 mg sodium, 4 mg cholesterol

2 tsp / 10 mL skim milk

1 large piece orange peel

4½ oz / 130 g sugar

3 oz / 85 g cornmeal

5 fl oz / 150 mL fruit purée or juice

1 oz / 30 g diced fresh fruit (see Note)

½ oz / 14 g butter

6 egg whites

1. Bring the milk and orange peel to a boil in a small pot. Remove from the heat and steep for 30 minutes. Discard the peel and pour the milk into a medium pot.

2. Bring the milk to a simmer and add 3½ oz / 100 g of the sugar. Slowly add the cornmeal, stirring constantly. Add the fruit purée and diced fruit.

3. Continue to simmer, stirring constantly, until the mixture pulls away from the sides of the pot, about 20 minutes. Transfer the mixture to a 13 by 9 by 2-in / 33 by 23 by 5-cm pan; spread thinly and cover with parchment paper to cool to room temperature.

4. Prepare ten 4-fl oz / 120-mL soufflé dishes by brushing each with the butter and dusting with ½ oz / 15 g of the sugar. Refrigerate until ready to use.

5. Beat the egg whites to soft peaks. Gradually add the remaining ½ oz / 15 g of the sugar and continue to beat to stiff peaks. Fold the egg whites into the polenta.

6. Fill the soufflé dishes three-quarters full and bake in a water bath in a 400°F / 205°C oven until golden brown and well risen, about 25 minutes.

Note

Use naturally soft, ripe fruits such as bananas, berries, and peaches. Other fruits such as apples and pears should be cooked and puréed. Unsweetened pumpkin purée may also be used.

Variation

Chocolate Polenta Soufflé

Add 1 oz / 30 g cocoa powder to the simmering milk with the polenta. Replace the fruit purée and juice with 1¾ oz / 50 g grated baking chocolate. Dust the cooked soufflé with powdered sugar and serve with a sauce made by flavoring the Dairy Base (page 442) with a liqueur or cordial such as Grand Marnier, Kahlúa, or dark or spiced rum. Serve the soufflé with Cappuccino Glacé (page 442).

Apple Cobbler

servings: **10**

portion information:
1 individual cobbler (3¼ oz / 900 g)

nutrition per serving:
121 calories, 4 g fat, 20 g total carbohydrate, 2 g protein, 169 mg sodium, 10 mg cholesterol

BATTER

4 oz / 115 g all-purpose flour

3½ oz / 100 g sugar

1 tbsp / 15 mL baking powder

¼ tsp / 1.25 mL kosher salt

1 cup / 240 mL skim milk

1½ tsp / 7.5 mL vanilla extract

1 tbsp / 15 mL ground cinnamon

1½ oz / 45 g butter

APPLE COBBLER FILLING

1½ lb / 680 g of diced peeled Jonagold apples

3 fl oz / 90 mL cider

1. Combine all the ingredients for the batter except the butter and mix until smooth.

2. Bake 10½ oz / 300 g of apples in a 350°F / 175°C oven until tender and cooked, but not mushy.

3. In a small saucepan, make applesauce by simmering 8 oz / 230 g diced peeled Jonagold apples with cider. Stir in the baked apples.

4. Lightly grease ten 4-fl oz / 120-mL ramekins with the butter.

5. Fill each ramekin with 2 oz / 57 g of filling and top with 1¼ oz / 35 g of the batter. Bake the cobblers in a 350°F / 175°C oven until the batter is browned and the filling is very hot, about 20 minutes.

Serving Suggestions

Serve with Apple Pie Glacé (page 443) and Cinnamon Crisps (page 449) if desired.

(Nutrition information does not include serving suggestion.)

Variation
Berry Cobbler

Use 1 lb / 450 g blueberries, raspberries, or blackberries as the cobbler filling. Sweeten with 1½ oz / 45 g honey or sugar, or more to taste. Season to taste with sweet spices such as cinnamon, cardamom, allspice, mace, and nutmeg.

Grilled or Broiled Bananas

batch yield: **1¼ lb / 570 g**

servings: **10**

portion information:
2 oz / 58 g

nutrition per serving:
107 calories, 4 g fat, 18 g total carbohydrate, 1 g protein, 1 mg sodium, 0 mg cholesterol

5 firm-ripe small bananas (about 4 oz / 115g each)

Few drops of lemon juice

1½ oz / 45 g sugar

1. Slice the bananas into ½-in / 12-mm slices.

2. Sprinkle the bananas evenly with the lemon juice and sugar. Grill them on a hot grill or broil until marked and heated through, about 1 minute per side.

Grilled Bananas with Strawberry Glacé in a Honey Crisp

servings: **10**

portion information:
2 oz / 587 g banana. 2 oz / 57 g glacé, 1 honey crisp

nutrition per serving:
70 calories, 0 g fat, 18 g total carbohydrate, 1 g protein,0 mg sodium, 6 mg cholesterol

5 Grilled or Broiled Bananas (recipe above)

1¼ lb / 570 g Strawberry Glacé (page 442)

10 Honey Crisp cups (page 449)

5 oz / 140 g fine-dice strawberries

1. Grill or broil the banana slices just before assembling the dessert plate.

2. Place a 2-oz / 57 g quenelle of glacé in each cup and top with 2 oz / 57 g of the grilled bananas (about 3 slices).

Serving Suggestion:

Instead of shaping the glacé into a quenelle, freeze it in molds (a cube-shaped mold was used here) for a sophisticated presentation and add a simple fruit salad like the neatly diced strawberries shown on the facing page.

(Nutrition information does not include serving suggestion.)

Grilled Bananas with Strawberry Glacé (page 442) in a Honey Crisp (page 449)

Baked Figs

servings: **10**

portion information:
1 fig

nutrition per serving:
148 calories, 5 g fat, 25 g total
carbohydrate, 2 g protein, 93 mg
sodium, 6 mg cholesterol

10 fresh stemmed figs

1¾ oz / 50 g almond paste

10 sheets phyllo dough (11 by 15 in / 28 by 38 cm)

1 fl oz / 30 mL melted butter

1 oz / 30 g powdered sugar

1. Make a crosswise cut into the top third of each fig.

2. Roll the almond paste into 10 equal balls. Press 1 piece onto the bottom of each fig.

3. Cut each phyllo sheet into quarters and brush with the melted butter. Stack 4 of these quarter pieces, staggering the corners. Place a fig on the center of the stack and wrap the sheets around the fig, making a beggar's purse. Repeat with the other figs.

4. Bake the figs in a 300°F / 150°C oven until they are soft and the phyllo is golden brown, about 30 minutes. Dust with the powdered sugar and serve.

Note

Peeled and cored pears or apples may also be baked this way.

White Chocolate Cheesecake

batch yield: **one 10-in / 25-cm cake**

servings: **24**

portion information:
4 oz / 115 g

nutrition per serving:
200 calories, 6 g fat, 29 g total
carbohydrate, 5 g protein, 150 mg
sodium, 35 mg cholesterol

1¼ lb / 565 g white chocolate

2½ lb / 1.15 kg cream cheese

2 oz / 57 g sugar

2 eggs

2 tsp / 10 mL vanilla extract

Vegetable oil spray, as needed

1. Place the chocolate in a metal bowl and melt over a double boiler.

2. Place the cream cheese in a mixer fitted with a paddle and mix until soft. Add the sugar to the cream cheese and mix well. While the mixer is on low speed, pour the chocolate, eggs, and vanilla into the cream cheese. Mix until smooth.

3. Spray two 10-in / 25-cm springform cake pans lightly with vegetable oil and place on a parchment-lined sheet pan. Divide the cheese mixture between the pans and bake in a 325°F / 165°C oven until set, about 30 minutes. Allow the cheesecakes to cool completely before slicing.

Honey-Vanilla Cheesecake

batch yield: **one 10-in / 25-cm cake**

servings: **12**

portion information: **4 oz / 115 g**

nutrition per serving:
203 calories, 7 g fat, 29 g total carbohydrate, 9 g protein, 232 mg sodium, 42 mg cholesterol

2 oz / 57 g chopped walnuts

4 oz / 115 g graham cracker crumbs

3½ fl oz / 105 mL fresh orange juice

14 oz / 400 g low-fat cottage cheese

7 oz / 200 g part-skim ricotta cheese

1½ fl oz / 45 mL nonfat yogurt, drained (see page 463)

8 oz / 225 g honey

2 eggs

1 egg white

1 oz / 30 g cornstarch

2 large vanilla beans, scraped

1. Put the walnuts in a food processor. Add the graham cracker crumbs, and while the machine is still running, slowly add the orange juice until the mixture begins to adhere.

2. Press the crumb crust evenly over the bottom of a 10-in / 25-cm springform pan. Prebake the crust in a 300°F / 150°C oven until the crust has dried and resembles a cookie, about 15 minutes.

3. Purée the cottage and ricotta cheeses in a food processor until smooth. Add the drained yogurt and remaining ingredients. Continue to purée until smooth.

4. Pour the cheese mixture over the crust and bake in a 300°F / 150°C oven for 15 minutes. Place a bowl of water in the oven below the cheesecake and lower the oven temperature to 200°F / 95°C. Bake until set, 1½ hours more. Allow the cheesecake to cool completely before slicing.

Variation

Chocolate Cheesecake

Replace the walnuts with hazelnuts and add 2½ oz / 70 g cocoa powder in step 3.

Summer Melons with Warm Caramel Sauce

servings: **10**

portion information:
4 oz / 115 g banana, 1 fl oz / 60 mL sauce

nutrition per serving:
150 calories, 5 g fat, 26 g total carbohydrate, 1 g protein, 20 mg sodium, 10 mg cholesterol

10 fl oz / 300 mL Caramel Sauce (page 447) (see Notes)

Forty 1-in / 2.5-cm watermelon balls (10 oz / 285 g)

Forty 1-in / 2.5-cm honeydew balls (10 oz / 285 g)

Forty 1-in / 2.5-cm cantaloupe balls (10 oz / 285 g)

Forty 1-in / 2.5-cm poached pear balls (10 oz / 285 g) (see Notes)

1. Gently warm the caramel sauce in a small saucepan.

2. For each serving: Serve four pieces of each type of fruit in a dish or on a plate. Pour 1 fl oz / 30 mL sauce over the fruit.

Notes

Use Poire William as the liqueur in the caramel sauce recipe.

Use the poached pears from the Poached Pears recipe, cut into balls instead of halved or left whole (page 478).

Berry Napoleon

servings: **10**

portion information:
3 oz / 85 g, 1 oz / 30 g ricotta, 2 crisps

nutrition per serving:
198 calories, 5 g fat, 34 g total carbohydrate, 5 g protein, 44 mg sodium, 15 mg cholesterol

10 oz / 280 g part-skim ricotta cheese

1½ oz / 45 g honey

20 pieces Honey Crisps (page 449)

1 oz / 30 g powdered sugar

10 fl oz / 300 mL Fresh Berry Coulis (page 448)

1¾ lb / 795 g blackberries and/or raspberries

1. Whisk together the ricotta and honey until smooth.

2. Dust the honey crisps with the powdered sugar.

3. For each serving: Coat a large plate with ¾ fl oz / 20 mL coulis. Make a small circle of 1 tbsp / 15 mL ricotta mixture in the center of the plate. Place 1½ oz / 52 g berries on the ricotta mixture and top with 1 honey crisp. Pipe another 1 tbsp / 15 mL of the ricotta mixture on the crisp, followed by 1½ oz / 5 g berries, and top with another crisp.

Glazed Pineapple Madagascar

servings: **10**

portion information:
1¾ oz / 50 g

nutrition per serving:
108 calories, 0 g fat, 20 g total carbohydrate, 1 g protein, 15 mg sodium, 0 mg cholesterol

1 lb 2 oz / 500 g peeled cored pineapple
2 tsp / 10 mL green peppercorns, rinsed
1½ oz / 45 g sugar

2¼ cups / 540 mL fresh orange juice
1½ oz / 45 g honey
3½ oz / 100 mL light rum

1. Slice the pineapple into 1¾-oz / 50-g pieces.

2. Mash the peppercorns using the back of a wooden spoon. Rub the peppercorns on the pineapple slices and sprinkle with the sugar.

3. Combine the orange juice, honey, and rum.

4. Heat a large sauté pan over high heat. Add the pineapple slices to the pan and allow the sugar on both sides of the slices to caramelize. Remove the browned slices from the pan and add the juice mixture to the pan. Reduce the liquid to a maple syrup consistency.

5. For each serving: Drizzle 1 tbsp / 15 mL sauce over 3½ oz / 50 g pineapple.

Tarte Tatin, St. Andrew's Style

servings: **12**

portion information:
5 oz / 140 g

nutrition per serving:
175 calories, 3 g fat, 37 g total carbohydrate, 3 g protein, 61 mg sodium, 8 mg cholesterol

4 oz / 115 g sugar
½ oz / 14 g butter
3 lb / 1.35 kg sliced peeled Granny Smith apples (see Note)

12 oz / 340 g Sweet Ricotta Pastry (page 457)

1. Caramelize the sugar in a 12-in / 30-cm sauté pan until light golden.

2. Add the butter and apples and sauté until the apples are tender and coated with the caramelized sugar. There should not be excess moisture in the bottom of the pan. Remove from the heat. Arrange the apple slices in a concentric circle in the pan.

3. Roll the pastry into a 12-in / 30-cm circle. Transfer the dough to the pan, covering the apples. Score the dough with a knife.

4. Cook the tarte over direct heat until a caramel aroma rises from the pan. Finish cooking the tarte in a 350°F / 175°C oven until the crust is golden brown, about 20 minutes. Loosen the crust from the pan, invert the tarte onto a platter, and allow to cool slightly.

5. Cut into 12 equal pieces and serve warm.

Note

Pears may replace apples in this tarte.

Individual Peach and Blueberry Galettes

servings: **10**

portion information:
1 galette

nutrition per serving:
90 calories, 2 g fat, 18 g total carbohydrate, 2 g protein, 150 mg sodium, 5 mg cholesterol

10 oz / 285 g Sweet Ricotta Pastry (page 457), cold

14 oz / 400 g sliced peeled peaches

4 oz / 115 g fresh blueberries

Few grains grated nutmeg

1. Portion the dough into 2-oz / 57-g pieces and roll each one into a ball. Retaining a round shape, roll out each piece of dough on a floured surface to ⅛ in / 3 mm thick.

2. Arrange about 2 oz / 57 g peaches and 1 tbsp / 15 mL of blueberries on each round of pastry dough, leaving a ½-in / 1-cm border around the edge of the dough.

3. Working gently, fold the edges of the dough up and slightly over the fruit, overlapping the edges and leaving the fruit still exposed in the center of the pastry. If desired, brush a small amount of water onto the dough once each section is folded over to help the overlapping section adhere to it. Grate a small amount of fresh nutmeg over each galette.

4. Gently place the galettes onto a parchment-lined sheet pan, spacing them evenly on the pan.

5. Bake the pastries in a 350°F / 177°C oven until the edges are golden brown, about 25 minutes. Allow them to cool before serving.

6. The galettes can be stored in an airtight container at room temperature for up to 2 days.

Carrot Cake with Cream Cheese Icing

batch yield: **One 10-in / 25 cm cake**

servings: **14**

portion information:
one 3 oz / 85 g slice

nutrition per serving:
220 calories, 8 g fat, 36 g total carbohydrate, 3 g protein, 146 mg sodium, 26 mg cholesterol

5½ oz / 155 g whole wheat flour

1 tsp / 5 mL baking soda

1 tsp / 5 mL baking powder

1 tsp / 5 mL ground cinnamon

4 fl oz / 120 mL vegetable oil

8 oz / 225 g sugar

2 eggs

5 oz / 140 g diced pineapple

1 lb / 450 g grated carrots

3 oz / 85 g raisins

2 egg whites

Vegetable oil spray, as needed

1 oz / 30 g all-purpose flour

CREAM CHEESE FROSTING

12 oz / 340 g nonfat cream cheese, soft

3 oz / 85 g powdered sugar, sifted

2 tsp / 10 mL vanilla extract

1. Combine the whole wheat flour, baking soda, baking powder, and cinnamon.

2. Beat together the oil, sugar, and whole eggs until smooth.

3. Add the dry ingredients to the egg mixture and blend well. Stir in the pineapple, carrots, and raisins.

4. Whip the egg whites to a medium peak and fold into the carrot batter.

5. Lay parchment in a 10-in / 25-cm cake pan. Grease the pan with the oil spray and dust with the all-purpose flour. Pour the batter into the pan and bake in a 350°F / 175°C preheated oven until the cake springs back when lightly pressed, about 40 minutes. Cool the cake in the pan for 10 minutes before unmolding onto a rack to cool completely.

6. To prepare the frosting, combine the frosting ingredients in a food processor, blender, or mixer and mix until smooth. Evenly spread the frosting on the cake after it has completely cooled.

Lemon Tart

batch yield: **one 9-inch tart**

servings: **8**

portion information:
1 slice

nutrition per serving:
306 calories, 5 g fat, 61 g total
carbohydrate, 6 g protein, 240 mg
sodium, 132 mg cholesterol

LEMON CURD

½ oz / 14 g grated lemon zest

12 fl oz / 360 mL fresh lemon juice

11 oz / 315 g sugar

4 eggs, beaten

2 tsp / 10 mL vanilla extract

TART CRUST

4 oz / 115 g all-purpose flour

¼ tsp / 1.25 mL baking powder

1 egg

2 oz / 57 g sugar

¼ tsp / 1.25 mL vanilla extract

½ tsp / 2.5 mL grated lemon zest

½ fl oz / 15 mL corn oil

1. To make the lemon curd, combine the zest, juice, and sugar in a small saucepan and bring to a simmer. Temper the hot lemon mixture into the beaten eggs. Transfer the mixture back to the saucepan and cook, stirring constantly, until the mixture starts to simmer very gently. Strain through a fine-mesh sieve and stir in the vanilla. Cool completely.

2. To make the tartlet crust, whisk together the flour and baking powder. In a separate bowl, beat together the egg, sugar, vanilla, and zest. Whisk the oil into the egg mixture. Add the flour mixture and mix just until combined. The mixture should resemble a thick batter rather than a dough. Cover the batter and refrigerate for at least 20 minutes.

3. Press the batter over the sides and bottom of a 9-in / 23-cm tart pan. Prick the bottom with a fork, line with foil, and weight with dried beans or pie weights.

4. Bake in a 425°F / 220°C oven until golden brown, about 12 minutes. Cool completely before filling with the lemon curd. Cut into 8 equal pieces. Serve.

Warm Strawberries with Frangelico Glacé and Shortcake

servings: **10**

portion information:
1 shortcake, 2½ oz / 73 g strawberry mixture, 1½ oz / 45 g glacé

nutrition per serving:
274 calories, 7 g fat, 45 g total carbohydrate, 6 g protein, 211 mg sodium, 21 mg cholesterol

SHORTCAKES

13½ oz / 385 g all-purpose flour

2½ oz / 70 g sugar

¾ oz / 20 g baking powder

4½ oz / 130 g butter, cold

1 cup / 240 mL skim milk

½ tsp / 2.5 mL grated orange zest

2 fl oz / 60 mL whole milk

Vegetable oil spray, as needed

5 fl oz / 150 mL red port

5 fl oz / 150 mL raspberry purée

2¼ lb / 1 kg strawberries, quartered

1 lb / 450 g Liqueur-Flavored Glacé (page 442; see Note)

1. Combine the flour, sugar, and baking powder in a large bowl. Cut the butter into the dry ingredients to form a mealy mixture. Make a well in the butter mixture and add the skim milk and zest. Slowly incorporate; do not overmix.

2. Roll out the dough to ½ in / 1 cm thick. Use a 1½-in / 4-cm round biscuit cutter to cut the dough into 1-oz / 28-g portions. Arrange the biscuits on a sheet pan greased with the oil spray. Brush the tops of the biscuits with the whole milk and bake in a 375°F / 190°C oven until golden brown.

3. Heat the port in a small saucepan. Stir in the purée and berries.

4. For each serving: Slice a warm biscuit in half, fill with 2½ oz / 73 g warm strawberry mixture and top with 1½ oz / 45 g glacé.

Note

Use Frangelico liqueur to flavor the dairy base.

Warm Fruit Compote

batch yield: **1 pt / 480 mL**

servings: **10**

portion information:
1½ fl oz / 45 mL

nutrition per serving:
32 calories, 0 g fat, 7 g total
carbohydrate, 0 g protein, 1 mg
sodium, 0 mg cholesterol

8 oz / 225 g mixed seasonal fruits (see Note)

4 fl oz /120 mL Fresh Berry Coulis (page 448)

4 fl oz / 120 mL peach or apricot nectar

¾ oz / 20 g orange zest

1. Heat all of the ingredients together in a small saucepan just until warmed; do not boil.

Note

Use a variety of fresh fruits such as cherries, berries, pears, nectarines, apricots, bananas, mangoes, papayas, or pineapples. Select very ripe seasonal fruits that will naturally sweeten the sauce. If the sauce is too sweet, adjust the taste with a few drops of lemon or lime juice.

Poached Pears

batch yield: **2¼ lb / 1 kg**

servings: **10**

portion information:
1 pear

nutrition per serving:
124 calories, 0 g fat, 31 g total
carbohydrate, 1 g protein, 2 mg
sodium, 0 mg cholesterol

2¼ lb / 1 kg pears, about 10

18 fl oz / 540 mL water

1 lb 2 oz / 500 g sugar

13 fl oz / 390 mL pear wine

1 vanilla bean, split

1. Core the pears, leaving them whole or cutting them in half as desired. Peel if desired. Poach the pears by simmering them in the water, sugar, wine, and vanilla bean until the pears are tender, about 15 minutes. Allow the pears to cool in the poaching liquid, drain.

Variation

Trio of Pears

Layer the flavor of pears by serving a poached pear half with Pear Sorbet (page 443), some oven-dried pear slices, and a Lace Triangle (page 452).

Winter Fruit Compote

batch yield: **1 pt / 480 mL**

servings: **10**

portion information:
1½ fl oz / 45 mL

nutrition per serving:
83 calories, 0 g fat, 17 g total
carbohydrate, 0 g protein, 10 mg
sodium, 0 mg cholesterol

4 oz / 115 g dried fruits (see Note)	2 tsp / 10 mL arrowroot
¼ tsp / 1.25 mL white port	2 tsp / 10 mL ground cinnamon
1 pt / 480 mL apple cider	1 tsp / 5 mL grated nutmeg

1. Plump the dried fruits in the wine for 15 minutes. Drain the fruit and reserve the wine.

2. Bring the cider to a boil in a small saucepan.

3. Combine the arrowroot with enough of the reserved wine to form a paste. Add to the cider and simmer until thickened, about 2 minutes. The cider should be the consistency of maple syrup. Add the dried fruit and spices to the thickened cider and simmer for 1 minute.

Note

Use a variety of dried fruits such as cherries, blueberries, currants, cranberries, apricots, dates, figs, raisins, or prunes.

10

Chef's Pantry

A WELL-STOCKED LARDER is one of the chef's most important tools in developing healthier and more exciting menu offerings. Spice blends, marinades, rubs, and coatings can be mixed and matched with a variety of foods, from vegetables to fish to poultry.

Condiments, relishes, dips, and sauces are another way to improve most dishes. Many of these dishes are made from vegetables, nuts, and fresh fruits. Infusing extra-virgin olive oil produces a simple "sauce" that can be drizzled on steamed vegetables or served as a dip.

Moutabel (Roasted Eggplant Spread)

batch yield: **1 lb / 450 g**

servings: **8**

portion information:
2 oz / 57 g

nutrition per serving:
43 calories, 3 g fat, 4 g total
carbohydrate, 1 g protein, 221 mg
sodium, 0 mg cholesterol

1 lb / 450 g roasted eggplant flesh	¾ oz / 20 g tahini
½ fl oz / 15 mL extra-virgin olive oil	1⅜ fl oz / 2¾ tsp minced garlic
½ fl oz / 15 mL fresh lemon juice	½ tsp / 2.5 mL kosher salt

1. Combine all of the ingredients in a food processor and purée until smooth.

2. Adjust the flavor with more lemon juice, if necessary. Serve at room temperature.

Note

Moutabel may be served as a spread, dip, sauce, or sandwich filling.

Variation

Hummus (Chickpea Spread)

Replace the eggplant with 1 lb / 450 g cooked, drained chickpeas. Nutritional information for hummus can be found in the table on page 514.

Skordalia (Greek Garlicky Potato Spread)

batch yield: **1¼ lb / 565 g**

servings: **20**

portion information:
1 oz / 30 g

nutrition per serving:
46 calories, 2 g fat, 6 g total
carbohydrate, 1 g protein, 2 mg
sodium, 0 mg cholesterol

1 lb / 450 g quartered peeled Russet potatoes	1¼ fl oz / 45 mL extra-virgin olive oil
¾ oz / 20 g garlic, mashed to a paste	½ tsp / 2.5 mL crushed black peppercorns
2 fl oz / 60 mL fresh lemon juice	

1. Simmer the potatoes in water until tender. Drain and place the potatoes on a sheet pan in a warm oven to steam dry, about 5 minutes. Purée the hot potatoes using a ricer or food mill.

2. Beat the garlic, juice, oil, and pepper into the potatoes until completely incorporated.

White Bean Purée

batch yield: **1¼ lb / 565 g**

servings: **20**

portion information:
1 oz / 30 g

nutrition per serving:
50 calories, 2 g fat, 6 g total
carbohydrate, 2 g protein, 77 mg
sodium, 0 mg cholesterol

11 oz / 315 g dried Great Northern beans

SACHET

1 oz / 30 g roughly chopped carrot

3 oz / 85 g roughly chopped onion

1 oz / 30 g roughly chopped celery

2 oz / 57 g bacon

½ tsp / 2.5 mL whole black peppercorns

5 cloves garlic, crushed

1 sprig rosemary

1 sprig thyme

1 bay leaf

¼ tsp / 1.25 mL Tabasco sauce

1 tsp / 5 mL kosher salt

¼ tsp / 1.25 mL ground white pepper

1 tbsp / 15 mL chopped garlic

1 tbsp / 15 mL fresh lemon juice

1 tbsp / 15 mL chopped parsley

½ cup / 120 mL extra-virgin olive oil

1. Soak the beans for 8 to 12 hours in enough cold water to cover by 3 in / 8 cm. Drain and place the beans and sachet in a large soup pot. Cover with a generous amount of water and bring to a boil. Gently simmer until the beans are very soft.

2. Discard the sachet and drain the beans, reserving the cooking liquid.

3. Purée the beans, using the reserved cooking liquid to adjust the consistency.

4. Season with the Tabasco, salt, pepper, garlic, and lemon juice.

5. Garnish each portion with parsley and a sprinkle of oil.

6. Serve the spread at room temperature with toasted French bread.

Tapenade

batch yield: **4 oz / 115 g**

servings: **8**

portion information:
½ oz / 14 g

nutrition per serving:
32 calories, 3 g fat, 1 g total
carbohydrate, 1 g protein, 249 mg
sodium, 1 mg cholesterol

1¾ oz / 50 g pitted Niçoise olives

1 oz / 30 g anchovy fillets, rinsed and dried

½ oz / 14 g capers, rinsed

1 tsp / 5 mL minced garlic

1 tsp / 5 mL extra-virgin olive oil

1 tbsp / 15 mL fresh lemon juice

1. Using a mortar and pestle, pound together the olives, anchovies, capers, and garlic to form a coarse paste. Add the oil and lemon juice.

Note

Tapenade is extremely high in sodium; use sparingly or use with recipes that are very low in sodium.

Variation

Olivada

Reduce the amount of Niçoise olives to 1 oz / 30 g and add 1 oz / 30 g of green olives and 1¾ oz / 50 g of sun-dried tomatoes. Nutrition information for Olivada can be found in the Table on page 514.

Guacamole

batch yield: **1 lb 9 oz / 710 g**

servings: **10**

portion information:
2½ oz / 70 g

nutrition per serving:
42 calories, 4 g fat, 3 g total
carbohydrate, 1 g protein, 118 mg
sodium, 0 mg cholesterol

1½ lb / 680 g avocados (4 ripe)

1 oz / 30 g minced scallions

2 tsp / 10 mL minced garlic

¼ cup / 60 mL fresh lime juice

1 tsp / 5 mL minced jalapeño

1 tsp / 5 mL chopped cilantro

1 tsp / 5 mL kosher salt

1. Mash the avocados to a chunky consistency with a fork. Add the scallions, garlic, juice, jalapeño, cilantro, and salt. Stir to blend.

2. Press plastic wrap directly against the guacamole's surface to prevent discoloring. Allow the flavors to blend for 1 hour. Serve immediately.

Note

Use a fork to mash the avocados to a chunky consistency; food processors and blenders will make the mixture too smooth.

Tomato Salsa

batch yield: **1¼ lb / 565 g**

servings: **10**

portion information:
2 oz / 57 g

nutrition per serving:
16 calories, 0 g fat, 4 g total
carbohydrate, 0 g protein, 235 mg
sodium, 0 mg cholesterol

1 lb / 450 g tomato concassé (see Note)

½ oz / 14 g minced jalapeño

3 oz / 85 g minced red onion

3 tbsp / 45 mL chopped cilantro

3 tbsp / 45 mL fresh lime juice

½ tsp / 2.5 mL crushed black peppercorns

1 tsp / 5 mL kosher salt

1. Combine all of the ingredients. Refrigerate for several hours, allowing the flavors to develop. Adjust seasoning if necessary.

Notes

Although fresh tomatoes are the best choice, good-quality canned plum tomatoes may be substituted. The seeds and juice of the tomatoes may be reserved and used as a flavor enhancement in braised dishes, vegetable stock, or vegetarian demi-glace.

Add additional jalapeño peppers, Tabasco, or cayenne for a hotter salsa. A small amount of white wine or sherry vinegar may be added to adjust the flavor. Other ingredients such as parsley, chopped celery, jícama, celeriac, and sweet bell peppers may be added.

Tomatoes are a rich source of fiber, potassium, vitamin C, and lycopene, a powerful cancer fighter.

Tomatillo Salsa

batch yield: **1¼ lb / 565 g**

servings: **10**

portion information:
2 oz / 57 g

nutrition per serving:
17 calories, 0 g fat, 4 g total
carbohydrate, 1 g protein, 235 mg
sodium, 0 mg cholesterol

8 oz / 225 g chopped peeled tomatillos

4 oz / 115 g tomato concassé

4 oz / 115 g diced red onion

½ oz / 14 g chopped roasted jalapeño

1 tbsp / 15 mL fresh lime juice

1 tbsp / 15 mL minced garlic

½ oz / 14 g chopped cilantro

1 tsp / 5 mL chopped oregano

½ tsp / 2.5 mL toasted ground cumin seeds

½ tsp / 2.5 mL crushed black peppercorns

1 tsp / 5 mL kosher salt

1. Combine all of the ingredients and refrigerate until chilled.

Green Papaya Salsa

batch yield: **1 lb 14 oz / 850 g**

servings: **30**

portion information:
1 oz / 28 g

nutrition per serving:
23 calories, 0 g fat, 6 g total carbohydrate, 0 g protein, 168 mg sodium, 0 mg cholesterol

1¼ lb / 565 g diced peeled green papaya

3½ oz / 100 g tomato concassé

3½ oz / 100 g diced Vidalia onion

½ oz / 14 g minced jalapeño

1¾ fl oz / 53 mL fresh orange juice

¾ fl oz / 20 mL fresh lime juice

3 tbsp / 45 mLchopped cilantro

2 tbsp / 30 mL chopped mint

1 tsp / 5 mL kosher salt

1. Combine the papaya, tomatoes, onion, jalapeño, and orange and lime juices in a large skillet and gently warm over medium heat. When the relish is warm, remove from the heat and add the cilantro, mint, and salt.

Parsley and Toasted Almond Salsa

batch yield: **10 oz / 280 g**

servings: **10**

portion information:
1 oz / 28 g

nutrition per serving:
50 calories, 4.5 g fat, 2 g total carbohydrate, 1 g protein, 20 mg sodium, 0 mg cholesterol

1 oz / 30 g diced shallots

2 tbsp / 30 mL red wine vinegar

1¾ oz / 50 g chopped parsley

3 tbsp / 45 mL chopped chervil

3 tbsp / 45 mL chopped basil

1 tbsp / 15 mL rinsed chopped capers

2 tbsp / 30 mL extra-virgin olive oil

3 oz / 85 g roasted chopped almonds

1. Macerate the shallots in the vinegar for 20 minutes. Combine the shallot mixture with the remaining salsa ingredients.

Mango Salsa

batch yield: **1 qt / 950 mL**

servings: **32**

portion information:
1 fl oz / 30 mL

nutrition per serving:
25 calories, 0 g fat, 6 g total carbohydrate, 0 g protein, 0 mg sodium, 0 mg cholesterol

4 ripe mangoes, diced

1 ripe papaya, diced

1 canned chipotle pepper, minced

2½ fl oz / 75 mL fresh orange juice

2 fl oz / 60 mL fresh lime juice

1. Combine all of the ingredients and refrigerate until chilled.

Orange and Herb Conserve

batch yield: **1 pt / 480 g**

servings: **16**

portion information:
1 fl oz / 30 mL

nutrition per serving:
70 calories, 0 g fat, 17 g total
carbohydrate, 0 g protein, 0 mg
sodium, 0 mg cholesterol

2 oranges, halved

1 lemon, halved

8 oz / 225 g sugar

1¾ fl oz / 53 mL sherry

3½ fl oz / 105 mL water

¾ fl oz / 20 mL Champagne vinegar

2 tsp / 10 mL chopped tarragon

2 tsp / 10 mL chopped sage

¾ tsp / 3.75 mL chopped thyme

¾ tsp / 3.75 mL chopped parsley

1. Slice the oranges and lemon thinly and reserve the juices. Combine the sliced citrus, reserved juice, sugar, sherry, and water in a medium sauce pot. Simmer until the citrus rinds are very soft, adding more water as needed. Remove from the heat and add the vinegar and herbs. Chill completely.

Pearl Onion and Raisin Confit

batch yield: **1 lb / 450 g**

servings: **16**

portion information:
1 fl oz / 30 mL

nutrition per serving:
25 calories, 0 g fat, 6 g total
carbohydrate, 0 g protein, 20 mg
sodium, 0 mg cholesterol

6 oz / 170 g peeled pearl onions

2½ oz / 70 g golden raisins

½ oz / 14 g sugar

1 cup / 240 mL Vegetable Stock (page 492)

½ tsp / 2.5 mL saffron threads

Pinch ground allspice

Pinch ground cumin

1. Combine the confit ingredients in small sauce pot. Simmer until the onions are translucent and the liquid has reduced to a thick syrup.

Beet Chutney

batch yield: **1 lb / 450 g**

servings: **21**

portion information:
1 oz / 30 g

nutrition per serving:
20 calories, 0.5 g fat, 3 g total
carbohydrate, 0 g protein, 20 mg
sodium, 0 mg cholesterol

1¼ lb / 565 g beets

1 tbsp / 15 mL minced ginger

2¾ tsp / 13.75 mL diced jalapeño

½ fl oz / 15 mL vegetable oil

1 tbsp / 15 mL chopped cilantro

1 fl oz / 30 mL red wine vinegar

2 tsp / 10 mL fresh lime juice

¼ tsp / 1.25 mL cayenne

1. Place a single layer of beets in a roasting pan. Add enough water to cover the bottom of the pan. Cover the pan with foil and roast the beets in a 375°F / 190°C oven until tender, about 1 hour. Shake the pan every 20 minutes to prevent the beets from sticking or burning. Remove the beets from the oven, peel, and cut into small dice. Combine the beets with the remaining chutney ingredients.

Preserved Mango Chutney

batch yield: **3 lb / 1.35 kg**

servings: **48**

portion information:
1 fl oz / 30 mL

nutrition per serving:
74 calories, 3 g fat, 12 g total
carbohydrate, 1 g protein, 45 mg
sodium, 0 mg cholesterol

2½ lb / 1.15 kg diced fresh mango

7 oz / 200 g brown sugar

6 oz / 170 g diced onion

5 oz / 140 g raisins

1 oz / 30 g walnuts

1 tbsp / 15 mL minced garlic

1 fl oz / 30 mL cider vinegar

1 lemon, zested and juiced

½ oz / 14 g minced ginger

½ oz / 14 g minced jalapeño

½ tsp / 2.5 mL ground mace

¼ tsp / 1.25 mL ground cloves

1. Combine all the ingredients and simmer until reduced and thickened (about 30 minutes). Cool the chutney and taste. Adjust seasoning with additional lemon juice, if necessary. The chutney may be used at this point or refrigerated for 7 to 10 days.

Cucumber Raita

batch yield: **1¼ pt / 600 mL**

servings: **20**

portion information:
1 fl oz / 30 mL

nutrition per serving:
45 calories, 3 g fat, 11 g total
carbohydrate, 0 g protein, 0 mg
sodium, 0 mg cholesterol

1 pt / 480 mL drained nonfat yogurt

9 oz / 255 g diced, peeled, seeded cucumbers

¼ tsp / 1.25 mL kosher salt

Ground white pepper, as needed

1. Combine the yogurt and cucumbers. Season with salt and pepper.

Red Onion Confit

batch yield: **2 lb / 900 g**

servings: **16**

portion information:
2 oz / 57 g

nutrition per serving:
62 calories, 0 g fat, 15 g total
carbohydrate, 1 g protein, 2 mg
sodium, 0 mg cholesterol

2 lb / 910 g julienned red onions

4 oz / 115 g honey

½ cup / 120 mL red wine vinegar

½ cup / 120 mL red wine

¼ tsp / 1.25 mL ground black pepper

1. Simmer the onions in the honey, vinegar, and wine until the mixture is the consistency of marmalade, about 30 minutes. Cool completely. Season with the pepper. Adjust the sweet and sour flavor by adding a small amount of red wine vinegar or honey. The confit may be refrigerated up to 7 days.

Chicken Stock

batch yield: **1 gal / 3.75 L**

portion information:
3 fl oz / 90 mL

nutrition per serving:
56 calories, 2 g fat, 4 g total
carbohydrate, 4 g protein, 201 mg
sodium, 7 mg cholesterol

8 lb / 3.65 kg chicken bones, 3-in / 8-cm lengths

6 qt / 5.75 L cold water

MIREPOIX

8 oz / 228 g rough-cut onions

4 oz / 115 g rough-cut carrots

4 oz / 115 g rough-cut celery

1 Sachet d'Epices (page 490)

1. Rinse the bones with cold water.

2. In a large stockpot, combine the bones with the cold water. Simmer slowly for 5 hours, skimming the surface when necessary. Add the mirepoix and sachet and simmer until flavorful, an additional hour. Strain, cool, and store.

Variations

Game Hen Stock

Replace the chicken bones with an equal amount of game hen bones. Simmer the stock for 7 hours. Add the mirepoix and sachet and simmer an additional hour.

Brown Chicken Stock

Rinse the bones and dry well. Roast the bones in a very hot oven until browned. Simmer the appropriate length of time. Brown the mirepoix with 6 oz / 170 g tomato paste, add to the stock, and simmer an additional hour.

Double Chicken Stock

To make double chicken stock, simmer 4 lb / 1.8 kg chicken legs in each gallon of chicken stock.

Beef Stock

Replace the chicken bones with an equal amount of meaty beef bones (such as short ribs). Simmer for 7 hours before adding mirepoix and sachet. Simmer an additional hour.

Brown Veal Stock

Replace the chicken bones with an equal amount of veal bones. Roast the bones in a hot oven until browned. Simmer the stock for 7 hours. Brown the mirepoix with 600 / 170 g tomato paste, add to the stock, and simmer an additional hour.

Vegetable Stock

batch yield: **1 gal / 3.75 L**

portion information:
3 fl oz / 90 mL

nutrition per serving:
23 calories, 0 g fat, 4 g total
carbohydrate, 1 g protein, 210 mg
sodium, 0 mg cholesterol

2 tsp / 10 mL olive oil	6 oz / 170 g rough-cut celery
½ oz / 14 g chopped garlic	3½ oz / 100 g rough-cut fennel
1 oz / 30 g chopped shallots	3 oz / 85 g rough-cut leeks
7 qt / 6.65 L cold water	1 Bouquet Garni (see below)
1 cup / 240 mL dry vermouth	1 tbsp / 15 mL juniper berries
7 oz / 200 g rough-cut carrots	1 tsp / 5 mL crushed black peppercorns
6 oz / 170 g wild mushrooms	2 bay leaves
5 oz / 140 g button mushrooms	

1. Heat the oil in a large stockpot. Add the garlic and shallots and sauté until the shallots are translucent. Add the remaining ingredients and bring to a boil. Simmer slowly, about 45 minutes, skimming the surface when necessary. Strain, cool, and store.

Note

A variety of vegetables may be used, including parsnips, celeriac, onions, scallions, and green beans. Beets and leafy green vegetables will discolor the stock. Starchy vegetables such as squashes, potatoes, and yams will slightly thicken the stock and give it a cloudy appearance.

Variation

Brown Vegetable Stock

To prepare brown vegetable stock, caramelize the carrots, celery, fennel, and leeks before adding the remaining ingredients.

Sachet d'Epices and Bouquet Garni

A *sachet* is a combination of dried herbs and spices tied up in cheesecloth. The standard ingredients include 3 to 4 chopped parsley stems, ½ tsp / 2.5 mL dried thyme leaves, a bay leaf, and 3 to 4 black peppercorns. Include other herbs and spices as desired for a specific flavor, such as garlic cloves.

A *bouquet garni* is a bundle of fresh herbs and aromatic vegetables tied up with string. The standard combination includes 3 to 4 parsley stems, a sprig of thyme, a bay leaf, a piece of carrot or celery, 2 or 3 black peppercorns held together by a leek leaf.

Fish Fumet

batch yield: 1 gal / 3.75 L

portion information:
3 fl oz / 90 mL

nutrition per serving:
58 calories, 1 g fat, 1 g total
carbohydrate, 3 g protein, 172 mg
sodium, 2 mg cholesterol

11 lb / 5 kg fish bones
¼ cup / 60 mL vegetable oil

MIREPOIX

8 oz / 225 g rough-cut onion
4 oz / 115 g rough-cut leeks

4 oz / 115 g rough-cut celery

10 oz / 280 g mushroom trimmings or stems
5 qt / 4.80 L cold water
1 qt / 950 mL dry white wine
1 Sachet d'Épices (page 490)

1. If using fish bones, trim off the gills, head, and scales.

2. In a large stockpot, heat the oil. Add the bones, mirepoix, and mushroom trimmings and sweat until aromatic. Add the remaining ingredients and simmer slowly 35 to 40 minutes, skimming the surface when necessary. Strain, cool, and store.

Court Bouillon

batch yield: 1 qt / 960 mL

portion information:
3 fl oz / 90 mL

nutrition per serving:
27 calories, 1 g fat, 1 g total
carbohydrate, 1 g protein, 172 mg
sodium, 2 mg cholesterol

2½ pt / 1.20 L water
1¾ lb / 795 g chopped onion
12 oz / 340 g chopped carrots
12 oz / 340 g chopped celery
3½ oz / 100 g thinly sliced ginger

1 fl oz / 30 mL cider vinegar
1 fl oz / 30 mL dry white wine
1 tsp / 5 mL kosher salt
2½ tsp / 12.5 mL whole black peppercorns

1. Combine all the ingredients except the peppercorns in a medium sauce pot. Simmer for 20 minutes. Add the peppercorns and simmer until flavorful, an additional 10 minutes. Strain the bouillon and discard the vegetables. The court bouillon is ready to use now or it may be cooled properly and refrigerated in a covered container for up to 1 week.

Fond de Veau Lié

batch yield: **1½ gal / 5.75 L**

servings: **96**

portion information: **2 fl oz / 60 mL**

nutrition per serving: 58 calories, 0 g fat, 1 g total carbohydrate, 14 g protein, 132 mg sodium, 2 mg cholesterol

MIREPOIX

6 oz / 170 g rough-cut onion

6 oz / 170 g rough-cut carrots

6 oz / 170 g rough-cut leeks

6 oz / 170 g rough-cut celery

25 lb / 11.35 kg veal bones

5 fl oz / 150 mL vegetable oil

10 oz / 280 g tomato paste

1½ qt / 1.45 L red wine

2 cloves garlic

4 bay leaves

½ tsp / 2.5 mL dried thyme

6 gal / 23 L Brown Veal Stock , page 489

9 oz / 255 g arrowroot

1. Place the mirepoix and veal bones in a roasting pan and toss with the oil. Roast in a 450°F / 232°C oven until the mirepoix is caramelized and the bones are a rich brown color, about 30 minutes. Add the tomato paste and continue to roast until brown.

2. Place the roasting pan over direct heat. Deglaze the pan by adding the wine in thirds. Allow the wine to reduce after each addition.

3. Transfer the roasted mirepoix and bones to a stockpot and combine with the garlic, herbs, and stock. Simmer until flavorful, about 6 hours, skimming the surface when necessary. Strain the sauce, pressing the solids to release all the juices.

4. Place the strained sauce in a large saucepan and reduce by half, to yield 1½ gal / 5.75 L (see Notes).

5. Combine the arrowroot with enough water to form a paste. Add to the sauce, bring to a boil, and stir constantly until the stock has thickened, about 2 minutes.

Variations

Glace de Volaille

If the sauce is made with fowl bones and reduced to a syrup, it is called glace de volaille.

Any remaining fat or oil can easily be removed once the sauce has been refrigerated for several hours.

Veal bones may be replaced with other bones (chicken, lamb, venison, pheasant, for example) and simmered in an appropriate stock to make different-flavored fonds.

Glace de Viande

The sauce may be further reduced to a thick syrup called glace de viande, or meat glaze. To prepare glace de viande, continue to simmer the stock in step 4 until reduced to a thick syrup.

Vegetarian Demi-Glace

batch yield: **1 qt / 950 mL**

servings: **16**

portion information:
¼ cup / 60 mL

nutrition per serving:
26 calories, 0 g fat, 5 g total
carbohydrate, 0 g protein, 86 mg
sodium, 0 mg cholesterol

(The nutritional analysis is for the
recipe made with water.)

2 tsp / 10 mL olive oil

4 oz / 115 g rough-cut carrots

4 oz / 115 g rough-cut celery

4 oz / 115 g rough-cut leeks

7 oz / 200 g rough-cut onions

2½ oz / 70 g tomato paste

1 tsp / 5 mL minced shallot

1 tsp / 5 mL minced garlic

1¼ cup / 300 mL red wine

1 bay leaf

1 sprig thyme

1½ qt / 1.45 L water or Vegetable Stock
(page 490)

1¾ oz / 50 g arrowroot

1. Heat the oil in a stockpot. Caramelize the carrots, celery, leeks, and onions. Add the tomato paste, shallots, and garlic and continue cooking until the tomato paste has browned. Deglaze the pan by adding the wine in thirds. Allow the wine to reduce after each addition. Add the bay leaf, thyme, and water. Allow to simmer until reduced by half, skimming the surface when necessary. Strain the sauce, pressing the solids to release all the juices.

2. Combine the arrowroot with enough water to form a paste. Add to the sauce, return to a boil, and stir constantly until the stock has thickened, about 2 minutes.

Notes

Although vegetarian demi-glace will not have the same body and deep flavor as fond de veau lié, it is an excellent flavor enhancement in vegetarian dishes.

Other herbs and spices may be added. For classical dishes, add fine herbs (chives, chervil, tarragon, and parsley) to the sauce. For Asian cuisine, add lemongrass, tamarind, and ginger.

Wild Mushroom Jus

batch yield: **1 qt / 950 mL**

servings: **16**

portion information:
2 fl oz / 60 mL

nutrition per serving:
39 calories, 1 g fat, 5 g total
carbohydrate, 1 g protein, 103 mg
sodium, 0 mg cholesterol

½ fl oz / 15 mL extra-virgin olive oil

6 oz / 170 g diced sweet onion

1¾ tsp / 8.75 mL minced garlic

12 oz / 340 g sliced shiitake mushrooms

12 oz / 340 g sliced portobello mushrooms

12 oz / 340 g sliced cremini mushrooms

1 pt / 480 mL Vegetable Stock (page 490)

½ cup / 120 mL tamari

½ cup / 120 mL dry white wine

½ tsp / 2.5 mL whole wheat flour, roasted

2 tsp / 10 mL chopped oregano

1 tsp / 5 mL kosher salt

½ tsp / 2.5 mL ground white pepper

1. Heat the oil in a medium saucepan. Add the onion and garlic and sweat the onion until translucent. Add the mushrooms and sauté until tender. Add the stock, tamari, and wine. Bring the sauce to a simmer. Stir in the flour to slightly thicken the sauce. Season with the oregano, salt, and pepper.

Ancho Chile Sauce

batch yield: **1 pt / 480 mL**

servings: **10**

portion information:
1½ fl oz / 45 mL

nutrition per serving:
95 calories, 5 g fat, 11 g total
carbohydrate, 4 g protein, 126 mg
sodium, 1 mg cholesterol

3 oz / 85 g ancho chiles

1 fl oz / 30 mL olive oil

4 oz / 115 g diced onion

1⅔ oz / 47 g tomato paste

8 oz / 225 g diced roasted red peppers

½ oz / 14 g roasted garlic

½ oz / 14 g brown sugar

½ fl oz / 15 mL white wine vinegar

½ cup / 120 mL Chicken Stock (page 489)

1 tsp / 5 mL ground cumin

½ tsp / 2.5 mL dried oregano

¼ tsp / 1.25 mL ground cinnamon

⅛ tsp / 0.625 mL cayenne

1 cup / 240 mL Fond de Veau Lié (page 492)

1. Steep the chiles in 2 fl oz / 60 mL of boiling water until soft. Reserve the chiles and discard the water. Remove the stems and seeds of the chiles and chop the flesh.

2. Heat the oil in a medium saucepan. Add the onion and sauté until transparent. Add the tomato paste and cook until rust colored. Add the chiles, peppers, garlic, sugar, vinegar, and stock. Bring the sauce to a simmer. Add the cumin, oregano, cinnamon, and cayenne. Simmer until flavorful and thickened, about 30 minutes.

3. Purée the sauce and combine with the fond. Strain through a large-hole sieve.

Cider Sauce

batch yield: **1 qt / 950 mL**

servings: **16**

portion information:
2 fl oz / 60 mL

nutrition per serving:
62 calories, 0 g fat, 13 g total
carbohydrate, 2 g protein, 109 mg
sodium, 1 mg cholesterol

3 fl oz / 90 mL cider vinegar

1 qt / 950 mL apple cider

1 pt / 480 mL Fond de Veau Lié (page 492)

½ tsp / 2.5 mL kosher salt

¼ tsp / 1.25 mL ground black pepper

1½ lb / 680 g diced peeled Granny Smith apples

1. Combine the vinegar and cider in a large sauce pot and reduce to a heavy syrup consistency. Add the fond and simmer until the sauce is hot. Season with the salt and pepper and garnish with the apples.

Note

Cider sauce complements roasted, grilled, or sautéed pork or chicken.

Variation

Blood Orange Sauce

Replace the apple cider with blood orange juice and omit the apples. Garnish with fine julienne of zest from blood oranges if desired.

Creamy Mustard Gravy

batch yield: **1¼ pt / 600 mL**

servings: **10**

portion information:
2 fl oz / 60 mL

nutrition per serving:
50 calories, 0.5 g fat, 4 g total carbohydrate, 2 g protein, 140 mg sodium, 0 mg cholesterol

¾ oz / 20 g arrowroot

1 pt / 480 mL Brown Chicken Stock (page 489)

⅓ cup / 105 mL evaporated skim milk

1¾ oz / 50 g Dijon mustard

¼ tsp / 1.25 mL ground black pepper

1. Combine the arrowroot with enough of the stock to make a thick paste.

2. Bring the remaining stock to a boil and stir in the arrowroot mixture. Return to a boil and stir constantly until the stock has thickened, about 2 minutes. Remove from the heat and stir in the milk, mustard, and pepper.

Ginger Sauce

batch yield: **1¼ pt / 600 mL**

servings: **10**

portion information:
2 fl oz / 60 mL

nutrition per serving:
63 calories, 4 g fat, 5 g total carbohydrate, 2 g protein, 68 mg sodium, 16 mg cholesterol

½ oz / 14 g minced shallot

½ oz / 14 g minced ginger

¼ cup / 60 mL fresh lime juice

½ cup / 120 mL dry white wine

1 pt / 480 mL Fish Velouté (page 497)

⅓ cup / 105 mL heavy cream

1. Simmer the shallots, ginger, lime juice, and wine in a small stainless-steel saucepan until the mixture has reduced by half. Add the velouté and cream and simmer until reduced to a sauce consistency.

Shrimp Sauce

batch yield: **1½ pt / 720 mL**

servings: **12**

portion information:
¼ cup / 60 mL

nutrition per serving:
79 calories, 5 g fat, 5 g total carbohydrate, 2 g protein, 202 mg sodium, 15 mg cholesterol

½ fl oz / 15 mL olive oil

8 oz / 225 g shrimp shells

½ oz / 14 g minced garlic

¾ oz / 20 g diced shallots

2 oz / 57 g tomato paste

¼ cup / 60 mL brandy

1 cup / 240 mL Chicken Stock (page 489)

1 pt / 480 mL Fish Velouté (page 497)

½ cup / 120 mL heavy cream

1 tsp / 5 mL kosher salt

¼ tsp / 1.25 mL ground white pepper

1. Heat the oil in a medium saucepan. Add the shrimp shells and sauté until opaque. Add the garlic and shallots and sweat until the shallots are translucent. Add the tomato paste and sauté until rust colored. Deglaze the pan with the brandy and allow it to reduce until almost dry. Add the stock and simmer until reduced by half.

2. Strain through a fine-mesh sieve and combine with the velouté and cream in a medium saucepan. Simmer gently to heat and season with the salt and pepper.

Wild Mushroom and Rosemary Sauce

batch yield: **1¼ pt / 600 mL**

servings: **10**

portion information:
¼ cup / 60 mL

nutrition per serving:
32 calories, 0 g fat, 3 g total carbohydrate, 4 g protein, 225 mg sodium, 1 mg cholesterol

1 clove minced garlic

2¼ tsp / 11.25 mL minced shallots

¼ cup / 60 mL Chicken Stock (page 489)

12 oz / 340 g sliced wild mushrooms

1 fl oz / 30 mL dry sherry

1 pt / 480 mL Fond de Veau Lié (page 492)

2 tsp / 10 mL chopped rosemary

1 tsp / 5 mL kosher salt

¼ tsp /1.25 mL ground black pepper

1. In a medium saucepan, sweat the garlic and shallots in the stock until almost dry. Add the mushrooms and sweat until the moisture is released. Continue cooking until the moisture has almost completely evaporated. Deglaze with the sherry. Add the fond and rosemary. Simmer until a sauce texture develops, about 15 minutes. Season with the salt and pepper. Keep hot or cool and store.

Serving Suggestion

This sauce may be served with beef tenderloin.

Variation
Basil-Tomato Jus

Replace the mushrooms with neatly diced plum tomatoes that have been peeled and seeded. Replace the rosemary with 3 sprigs lightly crushed basil (leaves and stems). Remove and discard basil before serving the jus. Finish the sauce with a fine chiffonade of fresh basil, if desired.

Roasted Onion and Vinegar Sauce

batch yield: **1¼ pt / 600 mL**

servings: **10**

portion information:
¼ cup / 60 mL

nutrition per serving:
110 calories, 8 g fat, 6 g total carbohydrate, 3 g protein, 87 mg sodium, 1 mg cholesterol

2¾ fl oz / 80 mL olive oil

3½ oz / 100 g chopped leeks

2 oz / 57 g chopped garlic

7 oz / 200 g chopped onions

13½ fl oz / 400 mL Fond de Veau Lié (page 492)

3¼ fl oz / 95 mL cider vinegar

1. Heat ½ fl oz / 15 mL of the oil in a medium saucepan. Add the leeks, garlic, and onions and toss to coat with the oil. Roast in a 350°F / 175°C oven until caramelized, about 25 minutes. Remove the pan from the oven and deglaze with the fond. Add the vinegar and cool completely before whisking in the remaining 2¼ fl oz / 65 mL of the oil. Reserve at room temperature.

Velouté-Style Sauce/White Sauce

batch yield: **2½ pt / 1.20 L**

servings: **20**

portion information:
¼ cup / 60 mL

nutrition per serving:
29 calories, 1 g fat, 4 g total carbohydrate, 2 g protein, 84 mg sodium, 2 mg cholesterol

Béchamel-Style Sauce: 34 calories, 0 g fat, 6 g total carbohydrate, 3 g protein, 69 mg sodium, 1 mg cholesterol

1½ oz / 45 g arrowroot	1 cup / 240 mL evaporated skim milk
1 qt / 950 mL Chicken Stock (see Variations below)	½ tsp / 2.5 mL kosher salt
	¼ tsp / 1.25 mL ground white pepper

1. Combine the arrowroot with enough stock to form a paste.

2. Bring the remaining stock to a boil in a medium sauce pot. Add the arrowroot mixture and the milk to the boiling stock. Stir constantly until the sauce has thickened, about 2 minutes. Season the sauce with the salt and pepper. Keep hot or cool and store.

Variations

Béchamel-Style Sauce

Replace the stock with an equal amount of skim milk. Simmer gently; do not allow the milk to come to a full boil.

Chicken Veloute

Use Chicken Stock (page 389).

Fish Veloute

Use Fish Fumet (page 491).

Vegetable Veloute

Use Vegetable Stock (page 490).

Sparkling Wine–Butter Sauce

batch yield: **1 pt / 480 mL**

servings: **10**

portion information:
1½ fl oz / 45 mL

nutrition per serving:
78 calories, 2 g fat, 8 g total carbohydrate, 3 g protein, 169 mg sodium, 50 mg cholesterol

¼ cup / 60 mL sparkling wine	4 oz / 115 g butter, cold
4 oz / 115 g tomato purée	2 tsp / 10 mL Dijon mustard
1 fl oz / 30 mL tarragon vinegar	¼ tsp / 1.25 mL Tabasco sauce
1½ oz / 45 g minced shallots	1 tsp / 5 mL kosher salt
6½ fl oz / 195 mL fish Velouté-Style Sauce (above) made with Fish Fumet (page 491)	¼ tsp / 1.25 mL ground black pepper

1. Combine the wine, tomato purée, vinegar, and shallots in a saucepan and completely reduce until dry. Add the velouté and reduce by about two thirds, or until the sauce is syrupy. Whisk in the butter a little at a time; do not allow the sauce to boil. Season with the mustard, Tabasco, salt, and pepper. Strain through a fine-mesh sieve. Keep hot or cool and store.

Red Pepper Coulis

batch yield: 2 qt / 2 L

servings: 32

**portion information:
2 fl oz / 60 mL**

nutrition per serving:
53 calories, 2 g fat, 7 g total
carbohydrate, 2 g protein, 113 mg
sodium, 1 mg cholesterol

6 lb / 2.70 kg chopped red peppers (see Note)

1 jalapeño, minced

8 oz / 225 g chopped onions

½ oz / 14 g minced garlic

¼ cup / 60 mL olive oil

1½ qt / 1.45 L Chicken Stock (page 489)

2 fl oz / 60 mL balsamic vinegar

1 tsp / 5 mL kosher salt

¼ tsp / 1.25 mL ground black pepper

1. Sweat the peppers, jalapeño, onions, and garlic in the oil until the onions are translucent. Add the stock and simmer until almost all of the liquid has reduced, about 12 minutes.

2. Purée the sauce in a blender and strain through a medium-hole sieve. Adjust the consistency by either continuing to reduce, or adding hot stock. Season with the vinegar, salt, and pepper.

Note

For a more intense flavor, use peeled roasted peppers.

Tomato Coulis

batch yield: 3 qt / 2.88 L

servings: 48

**portion information:
2 fl oz / 60 mL**

nutrition per serving:
30 calories, 1 g fat, 5 g total
carbohydrate, 1 g protein, 97 mg
sodium, 0 mg cholesterol

1 oz / 30 g minced garlic

8 oz / 225 g chopped onion

1 fl oz / 30 mL olive oil

1 lb / 450 g tomato paste

6 lb / 2.75 kg tomato concassé

1 Bouquet Garni (page 490)

1 tsp / 5 mL kosher salt

½ tsp / 2.5 mL ground black pepper

1. Sweat the garlic and onions in the oil until the onions are translucent. Add the tomato paste and cook over medium heat until the color deepens, about 3 minutes. Add the tomatoes and bouquet garni and simmer until flavorful, about 2 hours.

2. Remove and discard the bouquet garni. Purée the sauce in a blender. Adjust the consistency by either continuing to reduce, or adding hot stock. Season with the salt and pepper.

Notes

Adding different herbs and flavoring ingredients make red pepper coulis a very versatile sauce; add diced, steamed vegetables such as fennel, leeks, and celery.

Make a "cream" sauce by adding evaporated skim milk.

If fresh plum tomatoes are not available, omit the salt and substitute a No. 10 can of whole plum tomatoes.

Yellow Tomato Coulis

batch yield: **3 qt / 2.88 L**

servings: **48**

portion information:
2 fl oz / 60 mL

nutrition per serving:
70 calories, 1 g fat, 12 g total
carbohydrate, 5 g protein, 270 mg
sodium, 0 mg cholesterol

½ fl oz / 15 mL olive oil

13 oz / 370 g minced onions

2 tsp / 10 mL minced garlic

3 lb / 1.35 kg quartered yellow tomatoes

1 tsp / 5 mL kosher salt

1½ tsp / 7.5 mL sugar

3 bay leaves

¾ tsp / 3.75 mL Tabasco sauce

1. Heat the oil in a large skillet. Add the onions and garlic and sweat until the onions are translucent. Add the remainder of the coulis ingredients and simmer until the mixture is dry, about 30 minutes. Purée the mixture in a blender until smooth. Strain through a large-holed sieve.

White Bean–Rosemary Sauce

batch yield: **1½ pt / 720 mL**

servings: **15**

portion information:
1½ fl oz / 45 mL

nutrition per serving:
101 calories, 1 g fat, 16 g total
carbohydrate, 8 g protein, 316 mg
sodium, 1 mg cholesterol

2 lb / 910 g roasted lamb bones

2 qt / 2 L Veal Stock (page 489)

Cornstarch or arrowroot slurry, as needed

8 oz / 225 g cooked cannellini beans

1 tsp / 5 mL kosher salt

¼ tsp / 1.25 mL ground black pepper

1. Simmer the bones in the stock until very flavorful, about 2 hours. Strain through a fine-mesh sieve and lié with a cornstarch slurry if necessary. Stir in the beans and season with the salt and pepper. Simmer until a sauce texture develops, about 15 minutes.

Heirloom Bean Sauce

batch yield: **4 pt / 2.15 L**

servings: **24**

portion information:
3 fl oz / 90 mL

nutrition per serving:
195 calories, 3 g fat, 32 g total
carbohydrate, 11 g protein, 311 mg
sodium, 7 mg cholesterol

½ oz / 14 g butter

2¼ tsp / 11.25 mL minced garlic

9 oz / 255 g diced leeks

3 oz / 85 g diced celery root

5 oz / 140 g diced Russet potatoes

30 oz / 850 g cooked heirloom beans (flagelot, rice, cadet, Christmas, or others alone or in combination)

2½ pt / 1.20 L Chicken Stock (page 489)

3 fl oz / 90 mL Glace de Viande (page 492)

1 tsp / 5 mL kosher salt

½ tsp / 2.5 mL large-grind black pepper

½ cup / 120 mL fresh lemon juice

1. Heat the butter in a large soup pot. Add the garlic, leeks, celery root, and potatoes and sweat until the vegetables are tender. Add the beans, stock, and glace de viande. Simmer to combine the flavors and reduce to a thick mixture. Season with the salt, pepper, and lemon juice.

Black Bean Sauce

batch yield: **1½ qt / 1.45 L**

servings: **22**

portion information:
2 fl oz / 60 mL

nutrition per serving:
101 calories, 1 g fat, 16 g total carbohydrate, 6 g protein, 160 mg sodium, 3 mg cholesterol

1 lb / 450 g dried black beans (see Notes)	1 tsp / 5 mL ground cumin
½ oz / 14 g diced bacon	2½ qt / 2.40 L Chicken Stock (page 489)
8 oz / 225 g diced onions	1½ oz / 45 g chopped sun-dried tomatoes
2¾ tsp / 13.75 mL minced garlic	1 lemon, thickly sliced
¾ oz / 20 g finely chopped ancho chiles	1 tsp / 5 mL kosher salt
½ tsp / 2.5 mL dried oregano	2 fl oz / 60 mL sherry vinegar

1. Soak the beans for 8 to 12 hours in enough cold water to cover by 3 in / 8 cm (see Notes). Drain and reserve.

2. In a large pot, heat the bacon over low to moderate heat until the fat renders and the bacon begins to crisp. Add the onions, garlic, and chiles. Sweat until the onions are translucent. Add the oregano and cumin and cook for 1 minute more. Add the stock, beans, tomatoes, lemon, and salt. Gently simmer until the beans are tender, about 2 hours.

3. Remove and discard the lemon slices. Purée half of the beans and add the purée back to the sauce. Adjust the consistency with more stock, if necessary.

4. Season with the vinegar.

Notes

Cannellini, navy, Great Northern, and kidney beans are a few substitutions for black beans. The cooking time may need to be adjusted depending on the bean used.

To reduce the length of soaking time, bring the beans and water to a boil, remove from the heat, and allow to soak for 1 hour. Continue with the recipe.

Garnish with chopped cilantro and chopped sun-dried tomatoes, if desired.

Lentil Ragoût

batch yield: **3 qt / 2.88 L**

servings: **45**

portion information:
2 fl oz / 60 mL

nutrition per serving:
46 calories, 1 g fat, 7 g total carbohydrate, 3 g protein, 84 mg sodium, 1 mg cholesterol

1 oz / 30 g diced bacon

8 oz / 225 g diced onions

8 oz / 225 g diced leeks

8 oz / 225 g diced carrots

8 oz / 225 g diced celery

2¾ tsp / 13.75 mL minced garlic

3 oz / 85 g tomato paste

1½ qt / 1.45 L Chicken Stock (page 489)

12 oz / 340 g French or green lentils (see Notes)

1 Sachet d'Épices (page 490) (see Note)

4 fl oz / 120 mL Riesling

2 fl oz / 60 mL sherry vinegar

1 tsp / 5 mL kosher salt

Pinch ground white pepper

6 oz / 180 mL Fond de Veau Lié (page 492) or Vegetarian Demi-Glace (page 493)

1. Render the bacon fat in a soup pot. Sweat the onions, leeks, carrots, celery, and garlic in the fat until the onions are translucent. Add the tomato paste and sauté until rust colored. Add the stock, lentils, and sachet. Simmer until the lentils are tender, about 45 minutes. Remove and discard the sachet. Add the wine, vinegar, salt, pepper, and fond or demi-glace.

2. The ragoût may be properly cooled and stored for up to 1 week refrigerated.

Notes

French or green lentils are the best variety to use in this ragoût because they maintain their shape, preventing the ragoût from becoming thick.

Lemon zest and caraway seeds may be added to the sachet.

Barbecue Sauce

batch yield: **2 qt / 2 L**

servings: **32**

portion information:
2 fl oz / 60 mL

nutrition per serving:
159 calories, 2 g fat, 35 g total carbohydrate, 2 g protein, 622 mg sodium, 0 mg cholesterol

8 oz / 225 g diced onions

1 oz / 30 g minced garlic

1 oz / 30 g minced jalapeño

1 fl oz / 30 mL vegetable oil

1 lb / 450 g tomato paste

1 oz / 30 g chili powder

1 pt / 480 mL brewed coffee

6 fl oz / 180 mL Worcestershire sauce

12 fl oz / 360 mL cider vinegar

12 oz / 340 g brown sugar

12 fl oz / 360 mL apple cider

1½ tsp / 7.5 mL kosher salt

1. Sweat the onions, garlic, and jalapeño in the oil until the onions are translucent. Add the tomato paste and sauté until rust colored. Add the remaining ingredients and bring to a boil. Lower to a simmer until thickened and flavorful, about 15 minutes.

2. When properly cooled and refrigerated, barbecue sauce may be stored for about 2 weeks.

Pesto

batch yield: **5 oz / 140 g**

servings: **10**

portion information:
½ oz / 14 g

nutrition per serving:
77 calories, 7 g fat, 1 g total
carbohydrate, 2 g protein, 45 mg
sodium, 3 mg cholesterol

1¾ oz / 50 g basil leaves, rinsed and dried

1¼ oz / 35 g toasted pine nuts

1½ fl oz / 15 mL olive oil

1 tsp / 5 mL minced garlic

½ fl oz / 15 mL water

1 oz / 30 g grated Parmesan

1. Combine the basil, pine nuts, oil, and garlic in a blender or food processor. Purée to make a coarse paste. Gradually add the water while processing until the paste is smooth. Fold in the cheese by hand.

Note

Pesto is best when it is prepared just before service. However, it can be stored in the refrigerator for up to 24 hours if necessary. To prevent the pesto from darkening during storage, press a piece of parchment or plastic wrap directly on the surface.

Gremolata

batch yield: **1½ oz / 45 g**

servings: **10**

portion information:
1 tbsp / 4.5 g

nutrition per serving:
34 calories, 3 g fat, 1 g total
carbohydrate, 1 g protein, 45 mg
sodium, 3 mg cholesterol

2¾ tsp / 13.75 mL minced garlic

2¾ tsp / 13.75 mL grated lemon zest

2 tbsp / 30 mL chopped parsley

2 tbsp / 30 mL chopped sage

4 tsp / 20 mL chopped rosemary

20 anchovy fillets, chopped

1. Combine the ingredients until they are evenly blended. This may be prepared up to 8 hours in advance. Refrigerate in a tightly covered container until needed.

Duxelles

batch yield: **1 lb / 450 g**

servings: **8**

portion information:
1½ oz / 45 g

nutrition per serving:
33 calories, 0 g fat, 6 g total
carbohydrate, 2 g protein, 16 mg
sodium, 0 mg cholesterol

1 fl oz / 30 mL Chicken Stock (page 489)

2 oz / 57 g minced shallot

1 clove minced garlic

1 lb / 450 g minced mushrooms

1 fl oz / 30 mL Madeira

2 tsp / 10 mL chopped thyme

1. Heat the stock in a large sauté pan. Add the shallot and garlic, and sweat until the shallots are translucent. Add the mushrooms and cook until they begin to release their juices. Continue cooking until the mixture begins to dry. Add the Madeira and thyme and cook until the juices in the pan have completely reduced.

Note

Duxelles may be used as a filling for pasta or a stuffing for meats, poultry, and vegetables.

Vinaigrette-Style Dressing

batch yield: **1 pt / 480 mL**

servings: **16**

portion information:
1 fl oz / 30 mL

nutrition per serving:
67 calories, 7 g fat, 0 g total carbohydrate, 0 g protein, 49 mg sodium, 0 mg cholesterol

8 fl oz / 240 mL Chicken or Vegetable Stock (pages 489 and 490)

1½ tsp / 7.5 mL arrowroot

4 fl oz / 120 mL red wine vinegar

4 fl oz / 120 mL extra-virgin olive oil

½ tsp / 2.5 mL kosher salt

½ tsp / 2.5 mL seasonings (see Notes)

1. Combine the arrowroot with enough cold stock to form a smooth paste.

2. Bring the remaining stock to a boil and stir in the arrowroot mixture. Return to a boil and stir constantly until the stock has thickened, about 2 minutes. Remove from the heat, stir in the vinegar, and cool completely. Gradually whisk in the oil. Add the salt and seasonings.

Variations

Orange-Cranberry Vinaigrette

Replace the stock with orange juice and replace the red wine vinegar with cranberry juice. Garnish with a little orange zest if desired.

Sherry Vinaigrette

Replace the the red wine vinegar with sherry vinegar.

Balsamic Vinaigrette

batch yield: **2 qt / 2 L**

servings: **64**

portion information:
1 fl oz / 30 mL

nutrition per serving:
72 calories, 7 g fat, 1 g total carbohydrate, 0 g protein, 51 mg sodium, 0 mg cholesterol

1 qt / 950 mL Chicken or Vegetable Stock (pages 489 and 490)

¾ oz / 20 g arrowroot

1 pt / 480 mL balsamic vinegar

1 pt / 480 mL extra-virgin olive oil

2 tsp / 10 mL kosher salt

1 tbsp / 15 mL basil chiffonade

1. Combine the arrowroot with enough cold stock to form a smooth paste.

2. Bring the remaining stock to a boil and stir in the arrowroot mixture. Return to a boil and stir constantly until the stock has thickened, about 2 minutes. Remove from the heat, stir in the vinegar, and cool completely. Gradually whisk the oil into the thickened stock. Stir in the salt and basil.

Port Wine Vinaigrette

batch yield: 1¼ pt / 600 mL

servings: 20

portion information:
1 fl oz / 30 mL

nutrition per serving:
74 calories, 7 g fat, 1 g total
carbohydrate, 0 g protein, 44 mg
sodium, 0 mg cholesterol

2¾ tsp / 13.75 mL arrowroot

5 fl oz / 150 mL Vegetable Stock (page 490)

5 fl oz / 150 mL tawny port

5 fl oz / 150 mL red wine vinegar

5 fl oz / 150 mL walnut or hazelnut oil

1 tsp / 5 mL kosher salt

¼ tsp / 1.25 mL crushed black peppercorns

1. Combine the arrowroot with enough cold stock to form a smooth paste.

2. Bring the remaining stock and port to a boil and stir in the arrowroot mixture. Return to a boil and stir constantly until the stock has thickened, about 2 minutes. Remove from the heat, stir in the vinegar, and cool completely. Gradually whisk in the oil. Season with the salt and pepper.

Lime-Cilantro Vinaigrette

batch yield: 1 pt / 480 mL

servings: 16

portion information:
1 fl oz / 30 mL

nutrition per serving:
65 calories, 7 g fat, 1 g total
carbohydrate, 0 g protein, 50 mg
sodium, 0 mg cholesterol

8 fl oz / 240 mL Vegetable Stock (page 490)

1½ tsp / 7.5 mL arrowroot

4 fl oz / 120 mL fresh lime juice

½ tsp / 2.5 mL sugar

2 fl oz / 60 mL sesame oil

2 fl oz / 60 mL peanut oil

½ tsp / 2.5 mL kosher salt

½ tsp / 2.5 mL chopped cilantro

1. Combine the arrowroot with enough cold stock to form a smooth paste.

2. Bring the remaining stock to a boil and stir in the arrowroot mixture. Return to a boil and stir constantly until the stock has thickened, about 2 minutes. Remove from the heat, stir in the lime juice and sugar, and cool completely. Gradually whisk in the oils. Add the salt and cilantro.

Tomato Vinaigrette

batch yield: 1½ qt / 1.45 L

servings: 48

portion information:
1 fl oz / 30 mL

nutrition per serving:
26 calories, 1 g fat, 3 g total
carbohydrate, 0 g protein, 37 mg
sodium, 0 mg cholesterol

1 tbsp / 15 mL minced garlic

¾ oz / 20 g diced shallot

1½ fl oz / 45 mL olive oil

4 oz / 115 g tomato paste

2½ lb / 1.15 kg tomato concassé

½ tsp / 2.5 mL ground white pepper

1 tbsp / 15 mL basil chiffonade

1 tbsp / 15 mL chopped dill

1 tsp / 5 mL chopped tarragon

1½ fl oz / 45 mL balsamic vinegar

1. Sauté the garlic and shallot in the oil until aromatic. Add the tomato paste and sauté until brown. Add the tomatoes and simmer until the mixture is reduced by one quarter, about 20 minutes. Purée until smooth and chill. Add the pepper, fresh herbs, and vinegar.

Ratatouille Vinaigrette

batch yield: **1½ qt / 1.45 L**

servings: **24**

portion information:
2 fl oz / 60 mL

nutrition per serving:
57 calories, 5 g fat, 2 g total carbohydrate, 0 g protein, 55 mg sodium, 0 mg cholesterol

1½ cup / 420 mL Vegetable Stock (page 490)

½ oz / 14 g arrowroot

7 fl oz / 210 mL sherry vinegar

½ fl oz / 15 mL Dijon mustard

7 fl oz / 210 mL extra-virgin olive oil

¾ oz / 20 g minced garlic

1 tbsp / 15 mL diced shallots

6 oz / 170 g diced zucchini

6 oz / 170 g diced red pepper

6 oz / 170 g diced yellow pepper

2 tbsp / 10 mL basil chiffonade

2 tbsp / 30 mL chopped oregano

2 tbsp / 30 mL chopped chervil

1 tsp / 5 mL kosher salt

1. Combine the arrowroot with enough cold stock to form a smooth paste.

2. Bring the remaining stock to a boil and stir in the arrowroot mixture.

3. Return to a boil and stir constantly until the stock has thickened, about 2 minutes. Remove from the heat, stir in the vinegar, and cool completely. Add the mustard to the thickened stock. Gradually whisk in the oil. Stir in the remaining ingredients.

Roasted Vegetable Vinaigrette

batch yield: **1½ pt / 720 mL**

servings: **24**

portion information:
1 fl oz / 30 mL

nutrition per serving:
36 calories, 4 g fat, 1 g total carbohydrate, 0 g protein, 38 mg sodium, 0 mg cholesterol

5½ oz / 155 g chopped carrots

5 oz / 140 g chopped zucchini

5 oz / 140 g chopped yellow squash

5 oz / 140 g chopped bell peppers

7 oz / 200 g chopped tomatoes

5 oz / 140 g chopped onion

5 oz / 140 g chopped celery

5 oz / 140 g chopped leeks

2 fl oz / 60 mL extra-virgin olive oil

5 fl oz / 150 mL red wine vinegar

2 tbsp / 30 mL Dijon mustard

¾ oz / 20 g minced garlic

2½ tsp / 12.5 mL crushed black peppercorns

½ tsp / 2.5 mL kosher salt

3 fl oz / 90 mL extra-virgin olive oil

¾ oz / 20 g chopped parsley, chives, tarragon, chervil

1. Toss the vegetables in the oil and roast in a 350°F / 175°C oven until tender, about 45 minutes. Juice the vegetables using a juicer. The vegetables should yield 10½ fl oz / 315 mL of roasted vegetable juice.

2. Add the remaining ingredients, except the herbs, and purée to evenly incorporate. Thin the consistency of the vinaigrette with vegetable stock, if necessary. Stir the herbs into the vinaigrette.

Five-Mustard Vinaigrette

batch yield: **11 fl oz / 330 mL**

servings: **11**

portion information:
1 fl oz / 30 mL

nutrition per serving:
54 calories, 5 g fat, 1 g total carbohydrate, 0 g protein, 75 mg sodium, 0 mg cholesterol

½ tsp / 2.5 mL arrowroot

9 fl oz / 270 mL Vegetable Stock (page 490)

1½ tsp / 7.5 mL white wine

1 tbsp / 15 mL whole mustard seed

1 tsp / 5 mL dry mustard

1 tbsp / 15 mL Dijon mustard

1½ tsp / 7.5 mL whole-grain mustard

1 tsp / 5 mL Chinese mustard

1 tbsp / 15 mL red wine vinegar

1 tbsp / 15 mL sherry vinegar

1 tbsp / 15 mL cider vinegar

1 tbsp / 15 mL balsamic vinegar

1 tbsp / 15 mL malt vinegar

2 tsp / 10 mL chopped chives

2 tsp / 10 mL chopped tarragon

½ tsp / 2.5 mL kosher salt

¼ tsp / 1.25 mL crushed black peppercorns

1 fl oz / 30 mL extra-virgin olive oil

1 fl oz / 30 mL walnut oil

1 fl oz / 30 mL safflower oil

1. Combine the arrowroot with enough cold stock to form a smooth paste.

2. Bring the remaining stock to a boil and stir in the arrowroot mixture. Return to a boil and stir constantly until the stock has thickened, about 2 minutes. Remove from the heat and cool completely.

3. Bring the wine and mustard seeds to a boil. Remove from the heat and stir in the dry mustard. Add the remaining mustards and stir until smooth. Combine the thickened stock, mustard mixture, vinegars, herbs, salt, and pepper. Gradually whisk in the oils. Chill.

Note

Five-mustard vinaigrette complements wild, bitter greens with bold flavors.

Asian Vinaigrette

batch yield: **1 pt / 480 mL**

servings: **16**

portion information:
1 fl oz / 30 mL

nutrition per serving:
102 calories, 10 g fat, 1 g total carbohydrate, 0 g protein, 78 mg sodium, 0 mg cholesterol

¾ fl oz / 20 mL reduced-sodium soy sauce

½ oz / 14 g minced garlic

½ oz / 14 g diced shallot

3½ tsp / 20 mL whole-grain mustard

3 fl oz / 90 mL rice wine vinegar

6 fl oz / 180 mL sparkling mineral water

6 fl oz / 180 mL peanut oil

2 tbsp / 30 mL chopped chives

1. Combine all the ingredients except the oil and chives in a medium bowl. Slowly whisk the oil into the mixture and stir in the chives.

Note

This vinaigrette makes a flavorful dipping sauce for grilled or broiled fish.

Creamy-Style Dressing

batch yield: 1 qt / 950 mL
servings: 32
portion information:
1 fl oz / 30 mL
nutrition per serving:
21 calories, 1 g fat, 2 g total
carbohydrate, 2 g protein, 22 mg
sodium, 3 mg cholesterol

10 oz / 280 g part-skim ricotta cheese	5 fl oz / 150 mL red wine vinegar
1¼ pt / 600 mL nonfat yogurt	1 tbsp / 15 mL seasonings (see Notes)

1. Purée the ricotta in a food processor or blender until smooth. Add the yogurt and vinegar and process until incorporated. Season as desired and chill.

Notes

Choice of seasonings includes prepared mustards, chopped fresh herbs, capers, onions, garlic, or citrus zest.

Creamy-style dressing may be used as a dipping sauce, an accompaniment to hors d'oeuvres and terrines, or a salad dressing.

If during storage the dressing becomes too thick, it may be thinned with a small amount of buttermilk.

Blue Cheese Dressing

batch yield: 1½ pt / 720 mL
servings: 24
portion information:
1 fl oz / 30 mL
nutrition per serving:
37 calories, 2 g fat, 1 g total
carbohydrate, 3 g protein, 87 mg
sodium, 7 mg cholesterol

10 oz / 285 g part-skim ricotta cheese	2 fl oz / 60 mL cider vinegar
7 fl oz / 210 mL buttermilk	1 tsp / 5 mL roasted garlic
3½ oz / 100 g blue cheese (see Note), crumbled	2 tbsp / 30 mL chopped chives
2 tsp / 10 mL ketchup	½ tsp / 2.5 mL crushed black peppercorns
2 tsp / 10 mL Worcestershire sauce	

1. Using a food processor, blender, or immersion blender, combine all the ingredients except the chives and pepper. Blend until smooth. Fold in the chives and pepper and chill.

Note

Although any quality blue cheese may be used in this dressing, domestically produced cheese, such as Maytag, or Italian-produced blue-veined cheese, such as Gorgonzola, will produce the smoothest texture and boldest flavor.

Ranch Dressing

batch yield: **1½ qt / 1.45 L**

servings: **48**

portion information:
1 fl oz / 30 mL

nutrition per serving:
36 calories, 3 g fat, 2 g total carbohydrate, 1 g protein, 54 mg sodium, 3 mg cholesterol

10½ oz / 300 g part-skim ricotta cheese

10½ fl oz / 315 mL nonfat yogurt, drained

4½ fl oz / 135 mL mayonnaise

13½ fl oz / 405 mL buttermilk

2 fl oz / 60 mL fresh lemon juice

1½ fl oz / 45 mL red wine vinegar

1 tsp / 5 mL minced garlic

2 tbsp plus 2 tsp / 40 mL chopped parsley

2 tbsp plus 2 tsp / 40 mL chopped chives

1 oz / 30 g diced shallots

½ fl oz / 15 mL Dijon mustard

½ tsp / 2.5 mL celery seeds

1½ fl oz / 45 mL Worcestershire sauce

1. Purée the ricotta, yogurt, and mayonnaise in a food processor or blender until smooth. Add the remaining ingredients and purée to evenly incorporate.

Caesar Dressing

batch yield: **2 qt / 2 L**

servings: **64**

portion information:
1 fl oz / 30 mL

nutrition per serving:
71 calories, 6 g fat, 2 g total carbohydrate, 3 g protein, 77 mg sodium, 6 mg cholesterol

1 lb 11 oz / 765 g part-skim ricotta cheese

1½ pt / 720 mL nonfat yogurt, drained

6 fl oz / 180 mL red wine vinegar

3½ fl oz / 105 mL Worcestershire sauce

¾ fl oz / 20 mL Dijon mustard

3½ oz / 100 g grated Parmesan

1¾ oz / 45 g roasted garlic

1 tsp / 5 mL Tabasco sauce

1 oz / 30 g anchovy paste

1. Purée the ricotta in a blender until smooth. Add the yogurt and vinegar and process until incorporated. Add the remaining ingredients and purée to evenly incorporate.

Anchovy-Caper Dressing

batch yield: **1 qt / 950 mL**

servings: **32**

portion information:
1 fl oz / 30 mL

nutrition per serving:
24 calories, 1 g fat, 3 g total carbohydrate, 2 g protein, 137 mg sodium, 3 mg cholesterol

10 oz / 280 g part-skim ricotta cheese

1¼ pt / 600 mL nonfat yogurt, drained

½ cup / 120 mL red wine vinegar

4 oz / 115 g capers

2 anchovy fillets, mashed

2 oz / 57 g minced shallots

½ oz / 14 g minced garlic

½ oz / 14 g chopped chives

½ oz / 14 g chopped parsley

½ oz / 14 g basil chiffonade

1. Purée the ricotta in a food processor or blender until smooth. Transfer the ricotta to a large bowl and whisk in the remaining ingredients.

Horseradish and Apple Cream Dressing

batch yield: **1 lb / 450 g**

servings: **16**

portion information:
1 fl oz / 30 mL

nutrition per serving:
22 calories, 1 g fat, 3 g total carbohydrate, 2 g protein, 24 mg sodium, 3 mg cholesterol

10 oz / 280 g part-skim ricotta cheese
1¼ pt / 600 mL nonfat yogurt, drained
5 fl oz / 150 mL red wine vinegar

1½ oz / 45 g prepared horseradish, well drained
2 oz / 57 g grated peeled Granny Smith apple

1. Purée the ricotta in a food processor or blender until smooth. Add the yogurt and vinegar and process until incorporated.

2. Fold in the horseradish and apples by hand.

Notes

Lemon juice or black pepper may be used to adjust the flavor if desired. Neither ingredient will affect the nutritional data.

Heating the dressing will make it separate.

Serve with cold appetizers, terrines, or seafood sausage.

Saffron Aïoli

batch yield: **1 qt / 950 mL**

servings: **16**

portion information:
2 oz / 57 g

nutrition per serving:
15 calories, 1 g fat, 1 g total carbohydrate, 1 g protein, 66 mg sodium, 7 mg cholesterol

2 tsp / 10 mL nonfat yogurt
½ oz / 14 g arrowroot
1 pt / 480 mL Vegetable Stock (page 490)

1 tsp / 5 mL saffron threads
6 cloves roasted garlic
2 tsp / 10 mL sour cream

1. Drain the yogurt in a cheesecloth-lined sieve in the refrigerator for 24 hours.

2. Combine the arrowroot with enough of the stock to form a paste. Bring the remaining stock to a boil and stir in the arrowroot mixture. Return to a boil and stir constantly until the stock has thickened, about 2 minutes.

3. Remove the thickened stock from the heat, add the saffron, and allow to steep until the stock has cooled.

4. Squeeze the roasted garlic from its skin and place in a blender. Purée the garlic. Gradually add the thickened stock while processing. Transfer the mixture to a mixing bowl and stir in the drained yogurt and sour cream.

Honey-Mustard Glaze

batch yield: **28 fl oz / 840 mL**

servings: **14**

portion information:
2 fl oz / 60 mL

nutrition per serving:
59 calories, 0 g fat, 15 g total
carbohydrate, 1 g protein, 261 mg
sodium, 0 mg cholesterol

2 oz / 57 g minced shallots

1½ oz / 45 g minced garlic

1 fl oz / 30 mL Chicken Stock (page 489)

8 oz / 225 g tomato paste

2 tbsp / 30 mL thyme

8 fl oz / 240 mL Dijon mustard

1 lb / 450 g honey

4 fl oz / 120 mL red wine vinegar

1 tbsp / 15 mL ground black pepper

1 tsp / 5 mL kosher salt

1. Sweat the shallots and garlic in the stock until aromatic. Add the tomato paste and sauté until brown. Add the remaining ingredients and simmer until the glaze is reduced by one third.

2. The glaze may be properly cooled and stored for up to 2 weeks, refrigerated.

Note

The glaze will thicken when chilled. To easily spread it on roasted or grilled foods, warm gently. If necessary, thin the glaze with a small amount of hot water or stock.

Ginger-Scallion Butter

batch yield: **8 oz / 240 g**

servings: **32**

portion information:
½ tsp / 2.5 mL

nutrition per serving:
59 calories, 0 g fat, 15 g total
carbohydrate, 1 g protein, 261 mg
sodium, 0 mg cholesterol

8 oz / 225 g butter, large dice

1 oz / 30 g minced scallions

1 tbsp / 15 mL minced ginger

2 tsp / 10 mL fresh lemon juice

½ tsp / 2.5 mL kosher salt

¼ tsp / 1.25 mL ground black pepper

1. Combine all of the ingredients in a food processor and pulse. Roll the butter in plastic wrap to form a 1-in / 3-cm cylinder. Refrigerate.

Truffle Butter

batch yield: **2 oz / 57 g**

servings: **8**

portion information:
½ tsp / 2.5 mL

nutrition per serving:
50 calories, 6 g fat, 0 g total
carbohydrate, 0 g protein, 80 mg
sodium, 15 mg cholesterol

2 oz / 57 g butter, soft

1 tsp / 5 mL chopped canned or fresh black truffles

¼ tsp / 1.25 mL kosher salt

Pinch crushed black peppercorns

1. Combine the truffle butter ingredients and refrigerate.

Berbere Spice Blend

batch yield: **4 oz / 115 g**

servings: **57**

portion information: **1 tsp / 5 mL**

nutrition per serving: 8 calories, 0.5 g fat, 1 g total carbohydrate, 1 g protein, 26 mg sodium, 0 mg cholesterol

½ tsp / 2.5 mL cardamom seeds

1 tsp / 5 mL cumin seeds

¼ tsp / 1.25 mL coriander seeds

¼ tsp / 1.25 mL ground cinnamon

¼ tsp / 1.25 mL whole black peppercorns

¼ tsp / 1.25 mL fenugreek seeds

2 tbsp / 30 mL red pepper flakes

2 tsp / 10 mL cayenne

1 tbsp / 15 mL paprika

¼ tsp / 1.25 mL ground ginger

Pinch ground allspice

Pinch ground nutmeg

Pinch ground cloves

1. Grind the ingredients together to form a powder. The spice blend is ready to use now or it may be stored in a tightly capped container in a cool, dry area for up to 2 weeks.

Note

Fenugreek, a legume native to Asia and Southern Europe, contains soluble fiber and other compounds that have substantial health benefits. Studies have found that moderate to large doses of fenugreek may improve sugar metabolism in diabetics.

Tandoori Marinade

batch yield: **1 pt / 480 mL**

servings: **8**

portion information: **2 fl oz / 60 mL**

nutrition per serving: 27 calories, 0 g fat, 6 g total carbohydrate, 2 g protein, 355 mg sodium, 1 mg cholesterol

8 fl oz / 240 mL nonfat yogurt

4 fl oz / 120 mL fresh lemon juice

1 oz / 30 g grated ginger

1 tbsp / 15 mL minced garlic

¼ tsp / 1.25 mL cayenne

1 tbsp / 15 mL cumin seeds, toasted, crushed

½ oz / 14 g chopped cilantro

1 tsp / 5 mL kosher salt

1. Combine all of the ingredients in a large bowl.

2. Thickly spread the tandoori marinade on foods and marinate, refrigerated, for 2 to 4 hours.

Note

For 1 whole chicken, use 2 to 3 fl oz / 60 to 85 mL tandoori marinade.

Basil Oil

batch yield: **½ cup / 120 mL**

servings: **24**

portion information:
1 tsp / 5 mL

nutrition per serving:
50 calories, 5 g fat, 0 g total carbohydrate, 0 g protein, 0 mg sodium, 0 mg cholesterol

1 oz / 30 g basil leaves

½ oz / 14 g parsley leaves

½ cup / 120 mL olive oil

1. Blanch the basil and parsley in salted water for 20 seconds. Shock and drain well. Combine the blanched herbs and oil in a blender and purée until smooth.

Curry Oil

batch yield: **1 cup / 240 mL**

servings: **48**

portion information:
1 tsp / 5 mL

nutrition per serving:
50 calories, 6 g fat, 0 g total carbohydrate, 0 g protein, 0 mg sodium, 0 mg cholesterol

1 tbsp plus 2 tsp / 25 mL curry powder

1 tsp / 15 mL water

1 cup / 240 mL olive oil

1. Combine the curry powder and water to make a paste. Whisk in the oil. Allow the oil to sit for 8 to 10 hours at room temperature.

2. Strain through 4 layers of wet cheesecloth and reserve. You will need only ½ cup / 120 mL of curry oil for 10 portions of salmon. The remaining oil can be stored in a cool, dry, place for up to 8 days.

Crispy Potato Slices

batch yield: **3 lb / 1.35 kg**

servings: **48**

portion information:
1 oz / 30 g

nutrition per serving:
20 calories, 0 g fat, 5 g total carbohydrate, 1 g protein, 0 mg sodium, 0 mg cholesterol

3 lb / 1.35 kg thinly sliced peeled Russet potatoes

1. Soak the sliced potatoes in cold water for 1 hour. Drain and arrange on a sheet pan lined with parchment paper. Bake in a 425°F / 220°C convection oven until browned and crisp.

Oven-Roasted Tomatoes

batch yield: **2½ lb / 1.15 kg**

servings: **12**

portion information:
2 oz / 57 g

nutrition per serving:
99 calories, 8 g fat, 7 g total carbohydrate, 1 g protein, 123 mg sodium, 0 mg cholesterol

2¾ lb / 1.25 kg sliced plum tomatoes

2¾ fl oz / 80 mL extra-virgin olive oil

1 oz / 30 g minced garlic

1 oz / 30 g minced shallot

2 tsp / 10 mL basil chiffonade

2 tsp / 10 mL chopped oregano

1 tsp / 5 mL chopped thyme

1 tsp / 5 mL kosher salt

1 tsp / 5 mL crushed black peppercorns

1. Toss together the ingredients to evenly coat the tomato slices. Place the slices on a rack in a roasting pan. Roast the tomatoes in a 275°F / 135°C convection oven until dried and leathery, 3 to 4 hours. Cool and store the tomatoes refrigerated.

French Bread Croutons

batch yield: **10 oz / 280 g**

servings: **20**

portion information:
½ oz / 14 g

nutrition per serving:
22 calories, 0 g fat, 4 g total carbohydrate, 1 g protein, 50 mg sodium, 12 mg cholesterol

10 oz / 285 g French bread, sliced ¼ in / 6 mm thick

6 fl oz / 180 mL Basic Consommé or Chicken Stock (pages 160 and 489)

1. Soak the bread in the consommé until it is saturated. Place the bread on a baking sheet lined with parchment paper. Slowly dry the bread in a 275°F / 135°C oven until the croutons are crisp, about 25 minutes.

Note

If the bread is thickly sliced, it may be dried in the oven for 15 minutes and finished on a hot grill.

Garlic Croutons

batch yield: **10 oz / 280 g**

servings: **20**

portion information:
½ oz / 14 g

nutrition per serving:
59 calories, 2 g fat, 9 g total carbohydrate, 2 g protein, 115 mg sodium, 2 mg cholesterol

1 tbsp / 15 mL extra-virgin olive oil

½ oz / 14 g minced garlic

¼ tsp / 1.25 mL kosher salt

Cracked black pepper, as needed

10 oz / 285 g whole wheat baguette, sliced ¼ in / 6 mm thick

1. Combine the oil, garlic, salt, and pepper. Brush the bread slices evenly and lightly with the oil. Broil or bake in a 350°F / 175°C oven until crisp and lightly browned.

Appendix
Recipe Analysis
Table of Nutrition Information

Item Name	Cals(kcal)	Prot(g)	Carb(g)	Fiber(g)	Sugar(g)	Fat-T(g)	Fat-S (g)	Fat-M (g)	Fat-P (g)	Chol (mg)	Sod(mg)
CHEF'S PANTRY											
Moutabel	43	1	4	2	2	3	—	2	1	—	221
Hummus	121	5	16	4	3	4	1	2	1	—	223
Skordalia	46	1	6	1	—	2	—	2	—	—	2
Tapenade	32	1	1	—	—	3	—	2	—	1	249
Olivada	45	1	5	1	2	3	—	2	—	1	352
Guacamole	42	1	3	2	—	4	1	3	—	—	118
White Bean Purée	50	2	6	2	—	2	—	1	—	—	77
Pesto	77	2	1	—	—	7	2	4	1	3	45
Duxelles	33	2	6	—	3	—	—	—	—	—	16
Yellow Pepper Oil	25	—	1	—	—	2	—	2	—	—	8
Scallion Oil	54	—	1	—	—	6	1	4	1	—	33
Basil Oil	45	—	—	—	—	4.5	0.5	—	—	—	—
Curry Oil	90	—	—	—	—	9	1.5	—	—	—	—
Saffron Aïoli	15	1	1	—	1	1	—	1	—	7	66
Preserved Mango Chutney	62	1	15	1	12	1	—	—	—	—	3
Red Onion Confit	62	1	15	1	11	—	—	—	—	—	2
Tomato Salsa	16	—	4	1	2	—	—	—	—	—	235
Tomatillo Salsa	17	1	4	1	2	—	—	—	—	—	235
Salsa Verde	43	—	1	—	—	4	1	1	—	—	131
Green Papaya Salsa	23	—	6	1	3	—	—	—	—	—	168
Tropical Fruit Salsa	39	—	9	1	6	1	—	—	—	—	74
Mango Salsa	25	—	6	>1	5	—	—	—	—	—	—
Parsley and Toasted Almond Salsa	50	1	2	>1	—	4.5	—	—	—	—	20
Orange and Herb Conserve	70	—	17	>1	16	—	—	—	—	—	—
Pearl Onion and Raisin Confit	25	—	6	—	5	—	—	—	—	—	20
Beet Chutney	20	—	3	>1	2	0.5	—	—	—	—	20
Cucumber Raita	12	1	2	—	1	—	—	—	—	1	43
Red Onion Confit	98	1	23	1	18	—	—	—	—	—	4
Oven-Roasted Tomatoes	99	1	7	2	3	8	1	6	1	—	123
Crispy Potato Slices	20	1	5	—	—	—	—	—	—	—	—
Smoked Tomatoes	11	1	2	1	2	—	—	—	—	—	3
Smoked Roasted Corn	62	2	14	2	2	1	—	—	—	—	10

Item Name	Cals(kcal)	Prot(g)	Carb(g)	Fiber(g)	Sugar(g)	Fat-T(g)	Fat-S (g)	Fat-M (g)	Fat-P (g)	Chol (mg)	Sod(mg)
French Bread Crouton	27	1	5	—	—	—	—	—	—	—	67
Garlic Croutons	138	3	22	2	—	5	1	2	2	—	229
Quatre Epices	5	—	1	—	—	—	—	—	—	—	1
Barbecue Spice Mix	23	1	4	2	1	1	—	—	—	—	604
Chili Powder	21	1	3	2	—	1	—	—	—	—	4
Dry Rub For Roasted Meats & Poultry	17	1	2	1	—	1	—	—	—	—	1442
Gremolata	22	2	1	—	—	1	—	—	—	7	294
Garam Masala	26	1	5	2	—	1	—	—	—	—	5
Curry Powder	23	1	4	2	1	1	—	1	—	—	6
Red Curry Paste	34	—	3	1	1	3	—	2	—	—	139
Ethiopian Curry Powder	10	—	2	1	—	—	—	—	—	—	2
Chinese Five- Spice Powder	22	1	4	2	—	1	—	—	—	—	20
Berbere Spice Blend	2	—	—	—	—	—	—	—	—	—	—
Asian-Style Marinade	84	1	12	1	7	1	—	—	—	1	656
Latin Citrus Marinade	30	1	7	1	4	—	—	—	—	—	467
Cumin Lime Marinade	24	1	7	1	1	—	—	—	—	—	584
Tandoori Marinade	27	2	6	—	2	—	—	—	—	1	355
Chicken Stock	56	4	4	—	2	2	—	1	—	7	201
Vegetable Stock	23	1	4	1	3	—	—	—	—	—	210
Court Bouillon	64	2	15	3	6	—	—	—	—	—	287
Fish Fumet	58	3	1	—	—	1	—	—	—	2	172
Fond de Veau Lié	55	14	1	—	—	—	—	—	—	2	80
Vegetarian Demi-Glace	26	—	5	—	1	—	—	—	—	—	86
Truffle Butter	50	—	—	—	—	6	3.5	—	—	15	80
Ginger-Scallion Butter	59	1	>1	>1	>1	6	4	2	>1	15	261

SAUCES & DRESSINGS

Item Name	Cals(kcal)	Prot(g)	Carb(g)	Fiber(g)	Sugar(g)	Fat-T(g)	Fat-S (g)	Fat-M (g)	Fat-P (g)	Chol (mg)	Sod(mg)
Vinaigrette-Style Dressing	67	—	—	—	—	7	1	5	1	—	49
Balsamic Vinaigrette	72	—	1	—	1	7	1	5	1	—	51
Port Wine Vinaigrette	74	—	1	—	1	7	1	2	4	—	44
Lime-Cilantro Vinaigrette	65	—	1	—	—	7	1	4	2	—	50
Cranberry -Orange Vinaigrette	71	—	8	—	6	4	—	2	1	—	75
Tomato Vinaigrette	26	—	3	—	2	1	—	1	—	—	37
Ratatouille Vinaigrette	57	—	2	—	1	5	1	4	—	—	55
Roasted Vegetable Vinaigrette	36	—	1	—	—	4	—	3	—	—	38
Five-Mustard Vinaigrette	54	—	1	—	—	5	1	3	2	—	75
Asian Vinaigrette	102	—	1	—	—	10	2	5	3	—	78
Asian Citrus Vinaigrette	88	—	4	—	2	8	1	4	3	—	150
Creamy-Style Dressing	21	2	2	—	1	1	—	—	—	3	22
Blue Cheese Dressing	37	3	1	—	1	2	1	1	—	7	87
Ranch Dressing	36	1	2	—	1	3	1	1	1	3	54
Caesar Dressing	71	3	2	—	1	6	2	4	—	6	77
Anchovy-Caper Dressing	24	2	3	—	1	1	—	—	—	3	137

Item Name	Cals(kcal)	Prot(g)	Carb(g)	Fiber(g)	Sugar(g)	Fat-T(g)	Fat-S (g)	Fat-M (g)	Fat-P (g)	Chol (mg)	Sod(mg)
Horseradish and Apple Cream Dressing	22	2	3	—	1	1	—	—	—	3	24
Velouté-Style Sauce	29	2	4	—	2	1	—	—	—	2	84
Bechamel-Style Sauce	34	3	6	—	4	—	—	—	—	1	69
Sparkling Wine Butter Sauce	100	1	3	—	1	9	6	—	—	25	330
Red Pepper Coulis	53	2	7	2	4	2	—	1	—	1	113
Tomato Coulis	30	1	5	1	3	1	—	—	—	—	97
Yellow Tomato Coulis	70	5	12	—	—	1	—	—	—	—	270
Black Bean Sauce	101	6	16	2	3	1	—	—	—	3	160
Heirloom Bean Sauce	195	11	32	2	1	3	—	—	—	7	311
Lentil Ragout	46	3	7	1	1	1	—	—	—	1	84
Barbecue Sauce	159	2	35	2	28	2	—	1	1	—	622
Ancho Chile Sauce	95	4	11	3	3	5	1	—	—	1	126
Cider Sauce	62	2	13	1	11	—	—	—	—	1	109
Ginger Sauce	63	2	5	—	1	4	2	—	—	16	68
Shrimp Sauce	79	2	5	—	2	5	2	2	—	15	202
Creamy Mustard Gravy	50	2	4	—	2	1	—	—	—	2	143
White Bean–Rosemary Sauce	101	8	16	>1	1	1	—	—	—	1	316
Wild Mushroom Jus	40	2	6	1	2	1	—	—	—	—	110
Roasted Onion and Vinegar Sauce	110	3	6	>1	2	8	2	—	—	1	87
Honey-Mustard Glaze	59	1	15	1	13	—	—	—	—	—	261

APPETIZERS

Item Name	Cals(kcal)	Prot(g)	Carb(g)	Fiber(g)	Sugar(g)	Fat-T(g)	Fat-S (g)	Fat-M (g)	Fat-P (g)	Chol (mg)	Sod(mg)
Scallop Seviche in Cucumber Cups	48	1	2	—	—	4	—	—	—	—	134
Seared Scallops with Beet Vinaigrette	156	23	12	1	1	2	1	—	—	53	134
Beet Vinaigrette	48	—	2	—	—	4	1	3	—	—	134
Salmon Cakes with Cucumber Relish	179	9	21	2	3	7	1	3	2	16	278
Cucumber Relish	19	—	2	—	1	1	—	1	—	—	2
Asparagus with Morels	69	4	11	2	4	2	—	1	—	—	162
Asparagus with Lump Crabmeat and Sherry Vinaigrette	120	9	6	3	3	8	1	—	—	30	135
Prosciutto with Grilled Vegetables	143	8	14	4	7	7	2	3	1	14	376
Wild Mushroom and Goat Cheese Strudel	118	6	12	1	2	5	3	1	—	12	183
Sauce for Wild Mushroom Strudel	22	3	1	—	—	—	—	—	—	1	93
Mussels in Saffron and White Wine Sauce	183	17	10	—	2	6	2	2	1	46	435
Clams Steamed in Beer	224	15	30	2	3	3	—	1	1	28	606
French Bread with Olivada	65	2	9	1	2	2.5	—	—	—	—	375
Grilled Tuna with Spring Herb Salad and Marinated Tomatoes	200	25	5	1	2	9	1.5	—	—	45	340
Mousseline-Style Forcemeat	78	12	6	—	1	—	—	—	—	26	153
Mediterranean-Style Seafood Terrine	86	11	1	—	—	4	2	1	—	83	470

Item Name	Cals(kcal)	Prot(g)	Carb(g)	Fiber(g)	Sugar(g)	Fat-T(g)	Fat-S (g)	Fat-M (g)	Fat-P (g)	Chol (mg)	Sod(mg)
Duck Terrine	83	9	4	1	1	2	—	1	—	31	59
Medallions of Lobster with Asian Vegetables	167	15	10	1	2	6	1	2	1	42	418
Herb Pesto	70	2	1	—	—	7	1.5	—	—	—	40
Tomato Coulis	6	—	1	—	1	—	—	—	—	—	19
French Bread Croutons	22	1	4	—	—	—	—	—	—	—	50
Vietnamese Summer Rolls	152	6	30	1	10	—	—	—	—	25	603
Vietnamese Dipping Sauce	25	—	5	—	4	—	—	—	—	—	280
Cucumber Granité	30	1	6	1	5	—	—	—	—	—	8
Portobello with Tuscan Bean Salad and Celery Juice	103	3	10	5	3	6	1	6	1	—	290
Tuscan Bean Salad	103	3	10	4	1	6	1	4	1	—	290
Grilled Bell Pepper and Eggplant Terrine	126	4	18	4	7	6	1	4	1	—	334

SALADS

Item Name	Cals(kcal)	Prot(g)	Carb(g)	Fiber(g)	Sugar(g)	Fat-T(g)	Fat-S (g)	Fat-M (g)	Fat-P (g)	Chol (mg)	Sod(mg)
Grilled Garlic Shrimp and Radish Salad	213	16	17	2	2	9	1	4	3	98	258
Grilled Shrimp	90	2	5	1	1	7	1	3	2	1	150
Radish Salad	17	1	3	1	1	1	—	—	—	—	18
Tuna Carpaccio with Shiitake and Red Onion Salad	81	11	8	1	2	1	—	—	—	20	246
Wild Rice Salad	200	8	30	3	4	6	1	3	2	3	159
Carpaccio of Beef with Fresh Artichokes and Tomato Salad	182	11	8	5	2	3	3	—	—	20	240
Smoked Duck with Red Lentil Salad and Golden Beet Salad	252	14	15	4	7	15	2	11	1	57	654
Golden Beet Salad	137	1	8	2	6	11	2	9	1	—	61
Red Lentil Salad	103	3	9	2	2	6	1	4	1	—	3
Curried Rice Salad	130	3	22	2	4	3	1	2	1	—	83
Red Lentil Salad	103	3	9	2	2	6	1	4	1	—	3
Black Bean Salad	115	6	18	6	1	2	—	1	1	—	15
Barley Salad	236	6	47	7	19	4	1	2	1	—	135
Soba Noodle Salad	261	9	47	1	1	6	1	2	2	—	579
Roasted Red Pepper Salad	102	1	10	1	7	7	1	4	1	—	206
Jicama Salad	89	1	11	3	2	5	1	2	2	—	238
Mexican Corn Salad	90	3	19	3	3	2	—	1	1	—	70
Warm Cabbage Salad	58	2	8	2	4	2	1	1	—	3	55
Marinated Asian Vegetable Salad	113	2	7	1	3	8	1	3	2	—	97
Marinated Chanterelles	42	2	7	2	2	1	—	1	—	—	151
Chinese Long Bean Salad with Tangerines and Sherry-Mustard Vinaigrette	155	4	13	3	2	11	1	5	4	—	331
Fruit Salad with Orange Blossom Syrup	64	2	15	2	11	—	—	—	—	1	27
Stone Fruits with Mint Syrup	136	2	33	2	29	—	—	—	—	—	18
Winter Greens with Warm Vegetable Vinaigrette	153	6	9	3	3	11	3	5	2	11	259
Spinach Salad with Marinated Shiitake Mushrooms and Red Onions	122	2	9	2	3	9	1	6	1	2	173

Item Name	Cals(kcal)	Prot(g)	Carb(g)	Fiber(g)	Sugar(g)	Fat-T(g)	Fat-S (g)	Fat-M (g)	Fat-P (g)	Chol (mg)	Sod(mg)
Hearty Greens and Wild-Ripened Cheddar with Hazelnut Verjus–Mustard Dressing	156	5	6	2	3	13	4	8	1	15	323
Warm Salad of Wild Mushrooms and Fennel	158	7	19	4	4	8	1	5	1	2	439
Mixed Green Salad with Pears, Walnuts, and Blue Cheese	112	2	9	2	5	7	1	1	4	3	95
Romaine and Grapefruit Salad with Walnuts and Stilton	153	5	9	2	5	11	3	3	5	7	148
Mediterranean Salad	204	6	9	3	3	17	4	10	1	13	592
Grilled Tuna Niçoise	382	20	31	6	4	20	3	12	2	83	539
Grilled Tuna with Spring Herb Salad and Marinated Tomatoes	204	25	4	1	2	9	1	6	1	46	338
Warm Salad of Hearty Greens, Blood Oranges, and Pomegranate Vinaigrette	103	2	8	2	3	7	1	3	4	—	36
Grilled Chicken and Pecan Salad	291	23	15	4	10	16	2	7	6	56	90
Asian Buckwheat Noodle Salad with Spicy Sesame Chicken	390	36	21	3	4	17	3	—	—	85	390

SOUPS

Item Name	Cals(kcal)	Prot(g)	Carb(g)	Fiber(g)	Sugar(g)	Fat-T(g)	Fat-S (g)	Fat-M (g)	Fat-P (g)	Chol (mg)	Sod(mg)
Basic Consommé	29	7	—	—	—	—	—	—	—	—	146
Chicken Consommé with Herbed Goat Cheese Ravioli	190	11	27	—	—	—	—	—	—	—	—
Double Chicken Consommé with Spring Rolls	170	11	22	—	—	—	—	—	—	—	—
Mushroom Consommé with Shiitake, Bok Choy, and Carrot Curls	44	8	3	1	1	—	—	—	—	—	180
Game Hen Consommé with Roasted Garlic Custards	190	11	27	—	—	4	4	4	4	5	467
Carrot Consommé with Lemongrass, Ginger, Spicy Grilled Shrimp, and Bean Threads	152	4	31	1	—	1	—	—	1	26	177
Wonton Soup	172	17	21	1	2	2	—	—	1	18	747
Michigan White Bean Soup	147	11	22	6	2	2	—	1	—	7	233
Summer-Style Lentil Soup	120	7	17	5	5	4	1	2	1	9	580
Potato and Smoked Scallop Soup	167	12	22	3	5	5	>1	—	—	7	233
Pan-Smoked Tomato Bisque	169	5	33	4	9	2	—	1	—	2	668
Seafood Minestrone	190	14	20	4	2	4	1	2	1	50	332
Louisiana Chicken and Shrimp Gumbo	174	13	16	1	2	6	2	2	1	47	385
Potato and Vegetable Soup	186	8	19	3	6	9	2	4	1	16	461
Beet-Fennel-Ginger Soup	51	3	10	2	6	—	—	—	—	—	369
Traditional Black Bean Soup	181	12	28	9	3	3	1	1	1	6	348
Tortilla Soup	171	12	18	3	4	6	2	2	1	21	412
Sweet Onion–Radish Soup	105	4	11	3	5	5	3	1	—	16	269
Butternut Squash Soup	80	3	12	2	3	3	1	1	—	8	233
Asparagus Soup	114	7	14	3	5	4	2	1	—	12	392
Corn Velvet Soup with Crabmeat	122	9	14	2	7	3	1	1	—	22	392

Item Name	Cals(kcal)	Prot(g)	Carb(g)	Fiber(g)	Sugar(g)	Fat-T(g)	Fat-S (g)	Fat-M (g)	Fat-P (g)	Chol (mg)	Sod(mg)
Crab and Wild Mushroom Chowder	126	10	16	1	4	3	1	1	—	23	438
Chowder of Corn and Maine Lobster	130	9	19	1	8	2.5	1	—	—	15	320
Sweet Potato Soup	160	6	26	4	11	4	1	1	1	8	350
Smoked Corn Chowder	130	9	19	1	7	3	2	1	—	15	230
Chilled Gazpacho with Spicy Crayfish	96	3	9	1	4	5	1	—	—	5	300
Chilled Melon Soup with California Champagne	114	2	20	3	16	1	1	—	—	3	269
Chilled Red Plum Soup	161	2	31	2	27	5	2	2	1	6	8
Chilled Seafood Soup	120	12	9	1	4	5	1	—	—	55	170
Curried Apple-Squash Soup	138	4	27	4	3	2	—	1	—	5	419
MEAT											
Tenderloin of Beef with Mild Ancho Chile Sauce and Jalapeño Jack Cheese Polenta	380	33	27	4	6	16	6	3	1	76	464
Polenta	109	5	15	1	1	3	1	1	—	8	168
Peppers and Summer Squash	16	1	4	1	2	—	—	—	—	—	4
Ancho Chile Sauce	95	4	11	3	3	5	1	—	—	1	126
Tenderloin of Beef with Wild Mushrooms	360	31	5	1	2	11	4	—	—	85	115
Wild Mushroom Sauce	39	4	6	1	2	—	—	—	—	1	66
Grilled Flank Steak with Roasted Shallot Sauce	280	24	22	1	15	10	3.5	—	—	35	250
Tenderloin of Beef with Blue Cheese and Herb Crust	219	27	8	—	1	8	3	3	—	65	301
Blue Cheese and Herb Crust	51	2	6	—	1	2	1	1	—	4	157
Madeira Sauce	21	3	2	—	—	—	—	—	—	1	99
Sautéed Veal with Wild Mushrooms and Leeks	262	29	24	4	4	6	1	3	1	77	242
Wild Mushroom and Leek Sauce	55	6	8	1	2	—	—	—	—	1	143
Stir-Fried Barley	95	3	15	3	1	3	—	2	—	1	49
Grilled Veal with Blackberries and Vanilla	330	28	30	3	9	4.5	1	—	—	95	170
Sautéed Medallions of Pork with Warm Cabbage Salad	243	26	12	2	7	9	4	4	1	62	196
Sherry Vinegar Sauce	70	—	2	—	—	7	1	—	—	—	60
Warm Cabbage Salad	60	2	8	2	5	2	1	—	—	5	60
Roasted Loin of Pork with a Honey-Mustard Pan Sauce	212	24	10	1	7	8	3	3	1	59	540
Honey-Mustard Sauce	60	1	15	1	13	—	—	—	—	—	210
Broiled Lamb Chops with Caramelized Root Vegetables and White Bean–Rosemary Sauce	326	27	28	10	5	12	5	4	2	78	827
White Bean Rosemary Sauce	101	8	16	6	1	1	—	—	—	1	316
Caramelized Root Vegetables	75	1	12	4	4	3	2	1	—	8	177
Loin of Lamb with Blood Orange Sauce	185	21	10	—	4	7	3	3	—	59	92
Blood Orange Sauce	30	1	6	—	4	—	—	—	—	—	34

Item Name	Cals(kcal)	Prot(g)	Carb(g)	Fiber(g)	Sugar(g)	Fat-T(g)	Fat-S (g)	Fat-M (g)	Fat-P (g)	Chol (mg)	Sod(mg)
Lamb Shish Kebob	505	34	70	6	7	8	2	3	1	75	202
Couscous	107	4	21	1	—	—	—	—	—	1	26
Chickpea Flatbread	220	8	40	3	3	3	—	1	1	—	127
Lamb Shanks Braised with Lentils	305	27	27	6	3	10	4	4	1	46	417
Indian Grilled Buffalo	133	23	3	—	1	3	1	1	—	73	60
Buffalo Chili	190	27	13	2	4	4	1	1	—	74	435
Cassoulet with Smoked Tomatoes	319	25	47	14	7	4	1	1	1	29	384
Chili Stew	217	26	11	2	3	8	2	3	1	62	465
Curried Goat	137	23	1	—	—	3	1	1	—	59	189
Rabbit and Oyster Etouffée	338	28	33	1	3	9	2	3	2	55	291
POULTRY											
Chicken Stir-Fry with Soba Noodles	260	31	25	4	5	3	0.5	—	—	60	800
Grilled Chicken and Spicy Pecans	300	23	16	4	11	17	2	—	—	55	90
Grilled Quail Wrapped in Prosciutto with Figs and Wild Mushrooms	340	46	10	1	5	11	3	—	—	140	540
Grilled Chicken Burritos	279	27	23	5	2	9	2	3	1	56	437
Grilled Kibbe Kebobs	168	10	13	3	2	8	2	5	1	36	103
Jerk Chicken	131	21	4	2	1	3	1	1	1	56	284
Grilled Pheasant with Asparagus and Black Truffle Butter	280	27	6	2	3	16	4	—	—	65	560
Chicken Breast with Peaches in Zinfandel Wine Sauce	160	24	7	—	5	3	1	1	1	58	150
Peaches and Zinfandel Wine Sauce	38	3	4	—	2	—	—	—	—	1	99
Pan-Smoked Chicken Breast with Artichoke and Mustard Sauce	190	25	7	3	2	7	1	3	1	58	462
Artichoke and Mustard Sauce	80	4	7	3	2	4	1	3	—	2	413
Whole Wheat Quesadillas with Roasted Chicken, Ancho Chile Caciotta, and Mango Salsa	531	33	51	6	15	21	6	2	3	76	737
Mango Salsa	58	1	15	2	12	—	—	—	—	—	6
Herb-Breaded Chicken with Creamy Mustard Sauce	217	25	21	1	5	3	1	1	1	59	244
Creamy Mustard Gravy	34	2	6	—	3	1	—	—	—	2	127
Poached Chicken in Spicy Broth	180	28	6	1	2	4	1	2	1	68	284
Chicken and Shrimp Pot Pie with Herb-Cracker Crust	367	29	39	2	10	10	5	3	1	121	551
Poached Cornish Game Hen with Star Anise	308	30	33	5	6	6	1	2	1	112	564
Duck Breast Crépinette	198	33	6	1	3	4	1	1	—	149	223
Fond de Veau Lié	17	3	1	—	—	—	—	—	—	1	92
Duck Breast with Roasted Shallots and a Roasted Onion and Vinegar Sauce	304	28	21	1	4	13	2	7	1	80	199
Roasted Onion and Vinegar Sauce	110	3	6	1	1	8	1	6	1	1	87
Roasted Shallots	66	4	15	—	3	—	—	—	—	1	49

Item Name	Cals(kcal)	Prot(g)	Carb(g)	Fiber(g)	Sugar(g)	Fat-T(g)	Fat-S (g)	Fat-M (g)	Fat-P (g)	Chol (mg)	Sod(mg)
Duck Stir-Fry with Shrimp	319	29	40	4	5	6	1	2	2	106	588
Soba Noodles	104	5	23	1	—	—	—	—	—		63
Sautéed Turkey Medallions with Tomato-Basil Jus	273	34	12	1	5	9	2	3	2	70	906
Tomato-Basil Jus	93	8	8	1	4	3	—	1	—	7	506
Smoked Turkey with Cranberry-Orange Vinaigrette	221	14	35	1	32	2	1	1	1	34	731
Cranberry-Orange Vinaigrette	107	—	27	1	25	—	—	—	—		1
Paella Valenciana	427	30	56	3	5	8	2	3	2	76	265
FISH											
Seared Cod in a Rich Broth with Fall Vegetables, Chive Pasta, and Ginger-Scallion Butter	312	27	47	5	7	1	—	—	—	44	325
Fresh Herb Pasta	149	6	29	2	1	—	—	—	—	—	12
Sautéed Squid and Steamed Mussels with Cannellini Beans, Spinach, and Pancetta	320	29	21	4	2	10	3	—	—	170	830
Seared Atlantic Salmon with Corn, Potato, and Arugula Salad	411	26	32	5	7	21	4	9	6	60	509
Yellow Tomato Coulis	45	2	9	1	2	1	—	1	—	—	151
Corn, Potato, Arugula Salad	175	3	22	3	5	9	1	5	2		179
Seared Cod with Shellfish, Tomato-Fennel Broth, Saffron Pasta, and Chorizo	590	41	70	6	4	14	4.5	—	—	75	1280
Salmon with Spinach and Sparkling Wine Butter Sauce	290	23	5	1	1	20	7	—	—	80	600
Broiled Red Snapper with Lime-Cilantro Vinaigrette	250	22	17	6	9	11	1.5	—	—	40	120
Grilled Herbed Salmon with Southwest White Bean Stew	268	29	16	5	2	9	1	3	3	67	133
Southwest White Bean Stew	100	6	16	5	2	2	—	1	—	3	82
Grilled Salmon with Savoy Cabbage and Heirloom Bean Sauce	423	36	36	10	4	15	4	5	4	78	700
Heirloom Bean Sauce	195	11	32	8	3	3	1	1	—	7	311
Savoy Cabbage	63	2	3	1	1	5	2	2	1	7	222
Pan-Roasted Salmon with Moroccan Spices and Lentil Ragoût	248	27	12	3	3	10	2	3	3	69	257
Caramelized Pearl Onions	20	—	2	—	1	1	1	—	—	3	117
Lentil Ragoût	46	3	7	1	1	1	—	—	—	1	84
Grilled Swordfish with Roasted Red Pepper Salad	280	25	23	3	5	9	1.5			55	820
Pasta	121	5	24	1	1	—	—	—	—	—	10
Grilled Swordfish with Black Pepper Pasta	279	25	23	3	5	9	2	4	2	56	816
Grilled Swordfish with Lentil Ragoût and Horseradish and Apple Cream Dressing	167	22	8	1	2	5	1	2	1	40	165
Lentil Ragoût	46	3	7	1	1	1	—	—	—	1	84
Horseradish and Apple Cream Dressing	22	2	3	—	1	1	—	—	—	3	24

Item Name	Cals(kcal)	Prot(g)	Carb(g)	Fiber(g)	Sugar(g)	Fat-T(g)	Fat-S (g)	Fat-M (g)	Fat-P (g)	Chol (mg)	Sod(mg)
Grilled Tuna with Spring Herb Salad and Marinated Tomatoes											
Broiled Swordfish with Tomatoes, Anchovies, and Garlic	162	20	4	—	2	6	1	3	1	39	167
Grilled Yellowfin Tuna with Citrus Salad	233	25	16	3	10	8	1	3	2	46	299
Citrus Salad	108	1	12	2	10	7	1	3	2	—	130
Grilled Halibut with Roasted Red Pepper and Warm Potato Salad	339	25	31	4	5	13	2	8	2	33	438
Warm Potato Salad	180	3	23	2	2	9	1	6	1	—	155
Peppers with Capers and Cumin	47	1	8	2	3	2	—	1	—	—	112
Sautéed Sole with Preserved Mango Chutney and Broiled Bananas	230	21	30	3	1	4	1.5	—	—	55	110
Sea Bass in Tomato, Fennel, and Saffron Sauce	—	—	—	—	—	—	—	—	—	—	—
Sunshine Bass with a Ginger Nage	172	19	10	2	4	5	1	3	1	82	307
Bass and Scallops en Papillote	252	19	25	4	5	6	3	1	1	44	286
Stir-Fried Scallops	292	22	30	3	2	9	1	3	3	34	238
Brown Rice	101	2	21	2	—	1	—	—	—	—	5
Scallop Gratin with Wild Mushrooms	225	22	22	2	4	5	2	1	—	41	451
Wild Mushrooms	44	1	6	1	2	2	1	1	—	6	4
Lobster Wrapped in Rice Paper and Asian Salad	302	17	30	2	5	11	2	4	3	45	728
Asian Salad	105	2	10	1	5	7	1	3	2	—	234
Stir-Fried Shrimp with Lo Mein and Ginger-Sesame Vinaigrette	380	27	40	2	6	13	2	5	4	155	707
Ginger-Sesame Vinaigrette	90	—	1	—	—	9	1.5	—	—	—	55
Spicy Asian Grilled Shrimp	85	16	1	—	—	1	—	—	1	151	223
Grilled Soft Shell Crabs	74	8	1	—	—	3	—	2	—	33	124
Cioppino	321	29	27	4	8	9	2	4	2	106	287
Crouton	140	3	22	2	—	4.5	0.5	—	—	—	230
Bouillabaisse	238	28	4	—	1	7	1	3	2	86	315

VEGETABLE ENTRÉES

Item Name	Cals(kcal)	Prot(g)	Carb(g)	Fiber(g)	Sugar(g)	Fat-T(g)	Fat-S (g)	Fat-M (g)	Fat-P (g)	Chol (mg)	Sod(mg)
Mu Shu Vegetables	246	5	45	4	5	6	1	2	2	—	328
Ratatouille	30	1	5	1	2	1	—	—	—	—	90
Stir-Fried Garden Vegetables with Marinated Tofu	262	15	33	5	2	9	1	3	4	—	558
Brown Rice	95	2	20	2	—	1	—	—	—	—	1
Wild Mushroom and Couscous Parfait	340	15	62	10	14	5	0.5	—	—	—	340
Risotto Cakes with Green Beans, Wax Beans, and Chanterelles	371	17	46	6	5	11	5	4	1	107	864
Risotto Cakes	244	8	34	1	2	5	2	2	—	91	225
Couscous and Red Lentils with Moroccan-Style Roasted Vegetables in Saffron Broth	354	12	61	9	16	7	1	5	1	1	327

Item Name	Cals(kcal)	Prot(g)	Carb(g)	Fiber(g)	Sugar(g)	Fat-T(g)	Fat-S (g)	Fat-M (g)	Fat-P (g)	Chol (mg)	Sod(mg)
Roasted Vegetables	130	2	18	3	7	6	1	4	1	—	150
Couscous and Red Lentils	173	10	31	5	1	1	—	—	—	1	66
Saffron Broth	10	—	2	—	1	—	—	—	—	—	85
Southwestern Vegetable Lasagna	470	21	64	9	12	13	6	2	2	95	580
Yucatán Pumpkin Seed–Sauced "Enchiladas" with Roasted Tomato and Hard-Boiled Egg	706	41	53	13	12	44	8	—	—	135	300
Roasted Eggplant Tian	196	8	24	5	11	8	3	4	1	11	333
Stuffed Cabbage Roll	320	9	60	10	9	6	1	2	2	—	309
Wild Mushroom and Nut Pie	229	11	13	2	3	15	5	7	2	47	172
Barley Risotto Crumble	480	15	75	10	5	14	4	7	2	11	608
Barley Risotto with Garden Vegetables	480	5	36	8	7	2	>1	1	1	—	350
Garden Vegetables	74	3	16	6	5	—	—	—	—	—	281
Farro with Vegetable Ragoût and Parsley and Toasted Almond Salsa	200	8	28	7	5	8	1	5	—	—	347
Parsley and Toasted Almond Salsa	80	2	3	1	1	7	1	5	1	—	31
Vegetable Ragoût	48	3	10	4	4	—	—	—	—	—	196
Black Bean Chili	327	13	50	8	12	8	1	6	1	—	313
Vegetable Stew	186	5	32	6	7	5	1	3	1	—	309

SANDWICHES

Item Name	Cals(kcal)	Prot(g)	Carb(g)	Fiber(g)	Sugar(g)	Fat-T(g)	Fat-S (g)	Fat-M (g)	Fat-P (g)	Chol (mg)	Sod(mg)
Charred Raw Beef or Buffalo Sandwich with Roasted Shallots	380	23	35	2	1	16	4	9	3	56	684
French Dip Sandwich	337	25	30	3	3	13	3	5	2	34	417
Vegetable Fajitas	296	9	47	6	7	8	2	5	1	—	426
Crabmeat and Shrimp Sandwich	189	13	20	2	2	6	1	1	1	65	376
Grilled Yellowfin Tuna Salad Sandwich	235	17	30	5	5	6	1	3	1	22	416
Grilled Garden Sandwich with Warm Slaw and Crispy Potato Slices	410	17	75	10	17	7	3	2	1	13	805
Warm Slaw	36	1	7	2	3	—	—	—	—	—	228
Crispy Potatoes	115	3	26	2	1	—	—	—	—	—	158
Moroccan Chicken Pita Sandwiches	402	33	28	3	2	16	3	8	3	93	1050
Falafel	280	15	40	14	5	8	0.5	—	—	—	760
Turkey Burgers	111	25	1	—	—	1	—	—	—	40	291
Chicken and Mushroom Burgers	120	18	8	—	1	1.5	—	—	—	40	360
Vegetable Burgers	109	3	10	3	3	7	1	1	5	20	269

PIZZA

Item Name	Cals(kcal)	Prot(g)	Carb(g)	Fiber(g)	Sugar(g)	Fat-T(g)	Fat-S (g)	Fat-M (g)	Fat-P (g)	Chol (mg)	Sod(mg)
Basic Pizza Dough	245	8	50	2	2	1	—	—	—	—	351
Whole Wheat Pizza Dough	240	9	50	3	2	1	—	—	—	—	350
Buckwheat Pizza Dough	250	9	49	4	2	1.5	—	—	—	—	350
Pizza with Roasted Tomatoes and Mozzarella	411	18	58	4	6	12	5	5	1	23	650

Item Name	Cals(kcal)	Prot(g)	Carb(g)	Fiber(g)	Sugar(g)	Fat-T(g)	Fat-S (g)	Fat-M (g)	Fat-P (g)	Chol (mg)	Sod(mg)
Smoked Tomato and Provolone Pizza with Black Olives	403	14	55	4	4	14	5	7	1	15	700
Pizza with Wild Mushrooms and Goat Cheese	374	17	57	4	4	9	5	2	1	20	581
Apple-Cheddar Pizza	600	22	87	5	13	19	7	—	—	30	650
Lobster and Jalapeño Pizza	458	30	54	3	3	13	5	6	1	61	808
Shrimp and Clam Pizza with Pesto	549	28	68	7	13	19	4	9	4	78	1193
Barbecued Chicken Pizza with Tomato Salsa	599	31	93	5	36	12	5	3	2	61	1344
Smoked Mozzarella, Prosciutto, and Roasted Pepper Pizza	400	21	56	3	4	10	4	3	1	27	751
PASTA											
Basic Pasta Dough	301	12	60	3	2	1	—	—	—	—	25
Saffron Pasta Dough	310	12	61	3	2	1	—	—	—	—	25
Spinach Pasta Dough	300	12	60	3	2	1	—	—	—	—	25
Pumpkin, Beet, or Carrot Pasta Dough	330	12	63	4	3	2.5	—	—	—	—	40
Tomato Pasta Dough	310	12	61	3	2	1	—	—	—	—	70
Fresh Herb Pasta Dough	300	12	60	3	2	1	—	—	—	—	25
Spice Pasta Dough	300	12	60	3	2	1	—	—	—	—	25
Jalapeño Pasta	240	10	49	2	1	1	—	—	—	—	20
Chile Pepper Pasta	340	13	70	9	11	2	—	—	—	—	40
Goat Cheese Filling	80	7	2	—	—	5	3.5	—	—	15	135
Shrimp Mousseline Filling	50	9	1	—	—	1	—	—	—	60	180
Chorizo Filling	37	2	2	—	—	2	1	1	—	8	102
White Bean Filling	170	5	18	6	1	8	1	—	—		250
Buckwheat Noodles	306	12	61	4	2	1	—	—	—	—	127
Spätzle	166	8	32	1	1	—	—	—	—	—	166
Gnocchi	159	5	32	2	1	1	—	—	—	34	295
Lobster Cappelletti with Ginger Sauce	390	32	45	2	2	7	4	—	—	100	500
Lobster Filling	60	8	1	—	—	2	1	—	—	30	150
Ginger Sauce	63	2	5	—	2	4	2	1	—	16	68
Shrimp and Herb Ravioli with Fennel Sauce	566	36	64	6	7	17	10	5	1	155	610
Fennel Sauce	84	4	13	3	4	2	1	—	—	6	111
Gnocchi with Shiitake, Oven-Dried Tomatoes, Zucchini, and Pesto	300	9	38	4	4	13	3	8	2	34	411
Linguine with Olives, Basil, and Red and Yellow Tomatoes	383	13	58	4	5	11	2	7	1	5	425
Linguine with Clams, Fennel, Leeks, and Saffron	417	25	63	4	6	5	1	2	1	38	323
Fidelini with Broccoli Rabe, Pancetta, Parmesan, and Toasted Crumbs	495	21	85	4	6	8	3	3	1	12	534
Capellini with Grilled Vegetable Ragoût	347	12	62	5	7	6	1	3	1	—	215

Item Name	Cals(kcal)	Prot(g)	Carb(g)	Fiber(g)	Sugar(g)	Fat-T(g)	Fat-S (g)	Fat-M (g)	Fat-P (g)	Chol (mg)	Sod(mg)
Grilled Asparagus with Morels, Bowtie Pasta, and Spring Peas	385	18	66	8	9	6	3	1	—	9	410
Fettuccine with Corn, Squash, Chile Peppers, Crème Fraîche, and Cilantro	393	13	71	6	9	7	4	2	—	20	355
Capellini with Olives and Capers	370	13	63	7	9	9	1.5	—	—	—	1100
Paglia e Fieno with Peas, Smoked Salmon, and Capers	436	23	59	5	7	12	6	3	2	37	771
Rigatoni in Wild Mushroom Broth with Spring Vegetables	369	13	69	6	12	4	1	2	—	—	291

VEGETABLE SIDES

Item Name	Cals(kcal)	Prot(g)	Carb(g)	Fiber(g)	Sugar(g)	Fat-T(g)	Fat-S (g)	Fat-M (g)	Fat-P (g)	Chol (mg)	Sod(mg)
Wild Rice Succotash	63	2	10	2	2	2	—	1	—	—	193
Haricots Verts with Walnuts	43	2	7	2	3	2	—	—	1	—	62
Asparagus with Toasted Anchovies, Garlic, and Lemon	45	3	4	2	1	2	—	2	—	3	130
Broccoli Rabe with Garlic and Hot Crushed Pepper	120	7	14	1	5	4	1	—	—	5	240
Brussels Sprouts with Mustard Glaze	46	4	8	3	2	—	—	—	—	—	79
Roasted Smoked Corn	62	2	14	2	2	1	—	—	—	—	10
Roasted Corn and Black Beans	107	5	21	5	2	1	—	1	—	—	67
Grilled Vegetables	47	1	6	2	3	2	—	2	—	—	23
Ratatouille	30	1	5	1	2	1	—	—	—	—	90
Pan-Steamed Zucchini and Yellow Squash Noodles	27	2	5	2	3	1	—	—	—	1	14
Artichokes and Mushrooms in White Wine Sauce	79	2	8	2	2	3	—	2	—	—	274
Braised Belgian Endive	37	1	5	3	1	1	—	—	—	—	239
Saffron Cauliflower and Onions	68	2	8	2	3	3	—	2	—	—	241
Fennel Braised in Chardonnay	39	1	7	3	—	—	—	—	—	—	280
Caramelized Pearl Onions	50	1	10	1	4	1.5	1	—	—	5	120
Cipollini Onions in Brown Sauce	55	3	9	2	5	1	—	1	—	1	74
Southern-Style Kale	118	6	15	3	1	5	2	3	1	6	248
Moroccan-Style Roasted Vegetables	80	1	11	2	4	3.5	0.5	—	—	—	90
Caramelized Root Vegetables	50	1	8	2	2	2	—	—	—	—	120
Pecan Carrots	50	1	10	2	6	1	—	—	—	—	135
Steamed Spinach with Garlic and Pernod	45	4	5	3	1	1.5	—	—	—	—	160

GRAINS

Item Name	Cals(kcal)	Prot(g)	Carb(g)	Fiber(g)	Sugar(g)	Fat-T(g)	Fat-S (g)	Fat-M (g)	Fat-P (g)	Chol (mg)	Sod(mg)
Basic Rice Pilaf	151	4	31	—	1	1	—	—	—	2	250
Lemon-Dill Rice	117	3	23	—	1	1	—	—	—	2	51
Vegetarian Dirty Rice	156	6	26	3	1	3	2	1	—	7	101
Hazelnut Wild Rice	193	7	31	3	2	5	1	3	1	3	87
Wild and Brown Rice Pilaf with Cranberries	190	6	38	3	8	1	—	—	—	2	68
Risotto	159	4	26	—	1	2	—	1	—	3	84
Pumpkin Risotto	94	3	16	1	2	1	1	—	—	5	83

Item Name	Cals(kcal)	Prot(g)	Carb(g)	Fiber(g)	Sugar(g)	Fat-T(g)	Fat-S (g)	Fat-M (g)	Fat-P (g)	Chol (mg)	Sod(mg)
Polenta	109	5	15	1	1	3	1	1	—	8	168
Buckwheat Polenta	103	5	16	1	1	2	1	1	—	6	156
Goat Cheese Polenta	123	5	20	1	1	3	1	1	—	6	161
Barley Pilaf	97	4	19	4	1	1	—	—	—	2	60
Stir-Fried Barley	95	3	15	3	1	3	—	2	—	1	49
Barley and Wheat Berry Pilaf	120	4	23	4	1	2	1	1	—	3	131
Couscous	186	7	37	2	1	1	—	—	—	1	46
Farro	71	3	15	2	1	1	—	—	—	—	118
Quinoa Pilaf with Red and Yellow Peppers	126	5	22	2	1	2	—	1	1	1	145
Curried Teff	138	5	27	1	1	2	—	—	—	3	51
Kasha with Spicy Maple Pecans	183	5	26	3	4	8	2	4	2	6	148
Corn Pudding	129	6	23	2	3	1	—	—	—	27	490

POTATOES

Item Name	Cals(kcal)	Prot(g)	Carb(g)	Fiber(g)	Sugar(g)	Fat-T(g)	Fat-S (g)	Fat-M (g)	Fat-P (g)	Chol (mg)	Sod(mg)
Saffron Potatoes	100	4	18	2	2	1	—	—	—	5	140
Rösti Potatoes with Celeriac	81	2	14	2	1	2	—	2	—	—	73
Potato Pancakes with Roasted Tomato Sauce	142	6	19	2	3	5	2	3	—	6	238
Curried Yukon Gold Potatoes	100	2	19	2	2	2	—	1	1	—	122
Fondant Potatoes	96	3	19	2	1	1	—	—	—	3	85
Sweet Potato Cakes	191	5	34	3	4	4	1	—	—	2	177
Oven-Roasted Potatoes	92	2	17	1	1	2	—	2	—	—	121
Potato Gratin	153	9	21	1	4	4	2	1	—	13	271
Celeriac and Potato Purée	114	3	16	2	2	5	3	1	—	14	299
Potato Purée with Roasted Eggplant and Garlic	109	2	16	2	2	4	2	2	—	8	126

LEGUMES

Item Name	Cals(kcal)	Prot(g)	Carb(g)	Fiber(g)	Sugar(g)	Fat-T(g)	Fat-S (g)	Fat-M (g)	Fat-P (g)	Chol (mg)	Sod(mg)
Basic Beans	130	8	22	9	—	1	—	—	—	—	220
Vegetarian Refried Beans	91	5	16	4	2	1	—	—	—	—	103
Smoky Braised Black-Eyed Peas	123	8	18	5	4	2	1	1	—	4	78
Black Bean Cakes	288	15	40	11	3	8	4	2	1	18	485
Black Bean and Cornmeal Loaf	151	5	28	5	4	3	—	1	1	—	333
Southwest White Bean Stew	201	12	31	10	3	4	—	1	1	5	164
Chickpea Stew	123	6	21	5	5	2	—	1	1	—	287
Three Bean Stew	197	11	34	11	3	3	—	1	1	—	219
Purée of Yellow Split Peas	230	13	35	1	3	5	0.5	—	—	—	480

BREAKFAST

Item Name	Cals(kcal)	Prot(g)	Carb(g)	Fiber(g)	Sugar(g)	Fat-T(g)	Fat-S (g)	Fat-M (g)	Fat-P (g)	Chol (mg)	Sod(mg)
Maple and Apple Butter Syrup	61	—	16	—	13	—	—	—	—	—	4
Warm Fruit Compote	32	—	7	1	6	—	—	—	—	—	1
Winter Fruit Compote	83	—	17	1	12	—	—	—	—	—	10
Granola	156	5	17	3	7	9	3	3	2	—	3
Tortillas de Papas	398	25	53	11	10	11	5	3	1	226	5938
Piperade Wrap	150	7	26	3	3	4.5	1	—	—	10	1080
Spinach Soufflé	180	11	11	1	4	10	5	—	—	185	310

Item Name	Cals(kcal)	Prot(g)	Carb(g)	Fiber(g)	Sugar(g)	Fat-T(g)	Fat-S (g)	Fat-M (g)	Fat-P (g)	Chol (mg)	Sod(mg)
Basic Crêpe Batter	75	3	12	—	1	1	—	1	1	—	30
Breakfast Sausage Patties	130	10	11	—	1	5	2	2		29	239
Four-Grain Waffles	365	15	57	5	11	9	2	3	3	46	456
Sausage-Stuffed French Toast	375	19	47	2	12	11	2	4	3	100	577
Pumpkin Pancakes	268	12	47	5	6	8	1	3	3	1	367
Banana Pancakes	285	12	52	6	10	8	1	3	3	1	366
Steel-Cut Oats with Cinnamon and Dried Fruit	155	4	32	4	10	2	—	1	1	—	127

BREAD

Item Name	Cals(kcal)	Prot(g)	Carb(g)	Fiber(g)	Sugar(g)	Fat-T(g)	Fat-S (g)	Fat-M (g)	Fat-P (g)	Chol (mg)	Sod(mg)
Oat Bran and Dried Fruit Muffins	165	5	33	3	13	4	1	1	1	—	212
Spiced Graham Muffins	162	4	31	2	12	4	1	1	1	21	110
Herb Cracker Crust	80	2	13	—	1	2	1	—	—	5	144
Chickpea Flatbread	220	8	40	3	3	3	—	1	1	—	127
Country Corn Bread	160	8	28	2	4	2	0.5	—	—	55	300
Grilled Naan with Eggplant Purée	190	7	33	3	3	3.5	0.5	—	—	—	370
Black Pepper Biscuits	119	3	17	1	2	4	3	1	—	11	224

DESSERT

Item Name	Cals(kcal)	Prot(g)	Carb(g)	Fiber(g)	Sugar(g)	Fat-T(g)	Fat-S (g)	Fat-M (g)	Fat-P (g)	Chol (mg)	Sod(mg)
Dairy Base for Frozen Glacé and Bavarians	175	7	28	—	23	4	2	1	—	16	83
Banana Glacé	137	5	24	1	18	3	2	1	—	10	55
Strawberry Glacé	123	5	21	1	16	3	2	1	—	10	55
Mango Glacé	131	5	23	—	19	3	2	1	—	10	55
Amaretto Glacé	166	5	26	—	21	3	2	1	—	12	65
Pumpkin Glacé	92	4	16	1	11	2	1	1	—	7	39
Cappuccino Glacé	182	8	29	—	24	4	2	1	—	16	95
Dried Cherry Glacé	194	5	38	1	31	3	1	1	—	10	52
Espresso Praline Glacé	155	5	25	—	18	4	2	1	—	14	57
Apple Pie Glacé	132	4	23	1	18	3	2	1	—	11	50
Pear Sorbet	156	1	36	2	30	1	—	—	—	—	1
Champagne and Lemon Sorbet	200	—	44	—	43	—	—	—	—	—	—
Chianti Granita	140	—	28	—	26	—	—	—	—	—	2
Apricot Sauce	65	—	17	1	14	—	—	—	—	—	8
Caramel Sauce	111	1	15	—	15	5	3	1	—	13	11
Cider and Raisin Sauce	150	—	31	1	15	—	—	—	—	—	19
Fresh Berry Coulis	66	—	14	1	12	—	—	—	—	—	2
Chocolate Spa Cream	100	7	14	1	12	—	—	—	—	—	95
Almond Tuiles	37	1	6	—	4	1		1	—		5
Almond-Anise Biscotti	98	2	15	—	7	3	2	1	—	6	56
Honey Crisps	66	1	11	—	7	2	1	1	—	6	6
Lace Triangles	81	1	13	—	7	3	2	1	—	9	3
Chocolate Hippenmasse	11	—	2	—	1	1		—	—	—	9
Fudge Brownies	178	4	34	1	23	7	2	1	—	27	89
Chocolate Fudge Cookies	79	1	16	1	5	1	1	—	—		52

Item Name	Cals(kcal)	Prot(g)	Carb(g)	Fiber(g)	Sugar(g)	Fat-T(g)	Fat-S (g)	Fat-M (g)	Fat-P (g)	Chol (mg)	Sod(mg)
Oatmeal-Pear Cookies	259	4	57	3	30	2	1	1	—	3	16
Apple Strudel	177	1	38	4	29	3	2	1	—	8	53
Sweet Ricotta Pastry	124	3	21	1	6	3	2	1	—	8	92
Sponge Cake	72	2	14	—	8	1	—	—	—	2	28
Chocolate Sponge Cake	72	2	13	—	8	2	—	—	—	2	28
Chocolate Pound Cake	298	4	49	1	36	11	6	3	—	50	163
Chocolate Angel Food Cake	154	5	29	1	17	3	2	1	—	5	97
Chocolate Ricotta Bavarian	158	6	27	2	21	5	3	2	—	5	61
Chocolate Crêpes	96	4	10	1	4	6	2	1	—	61	222
Rice Pudding	142	4	30	1	16	1	1	—	—	4	53
Chocolate Custard	105	5	13	1	11	5	2	1	—	40	65
Polenta Soufflé	138	5	27	1	18	1	1	—	—	4	65
Chocolate Polenta Soufflé	153	6	27	2	18	3	2	1	—	4	66
Chocolate Yogurt Mousse	113	5	20	1	16	6	1	1	—	1	61
Fruit Cobbler Batter	121	2	20	—	11	4	2	1	—	10	169
Apple Cobbler	163	2	31	2	11	4	2	1	—	10	169
Berry Cobbler	167	2	32	2	20	4	2	1	—	10	170
Grilled Bananas	70	1	18	2	11	—	—	—	—	—	—
Baked Figs	148	2	25	2	13	5	2	2	1	6	93
Honey-Vanilla Cheesecake	203	9	29	1	21	7	2	2	3	42	232
Chocolate Cheesecake	220	10	32	3	21	8	2.5	—	—	55	150
Summer Melons with Warm Caramel Sauce	150	1	26	1	23	4.5	3	—	—	10	20
Berry Napoleon	198	5	34	6	22	5	3	1	—	15	44
Glazed Pineapple Madagascar	108	1	20	1	17	—	—	—	—	—	15
Tarte Tatin, St.Andrew's Style	175	3	37	2	25	3	2	1	—	8	61
Individual Peach and Blueberry Galettes	90	2	18	1	9	2	1	—	—	5	150
A Trio of Pears	333	2	75	7	54	4	2	1	—	9	15
Poached Pears	124	1	31	5	22	—	—	—	—	—	2
Pear Sorbet	156	1	36	2	30	1	—	—	—	—	1
Pear Chips	29	—	8	2	5	—	—	—	—	—	—
Lace Triangles	81	1	13	—	7	3	2	1	—	9	3
Carrot Cake	220	3	36	2	22	8	1	3	3	26	146
Cream Cheese Icing	70	5	11	—	9	—	—	—	—	5	190
Warm Strawberries with Frangelico Glacé and Shortcake	274	6	43	3	21	7	4	2	—	21	211
Lemon Tart	306	6	61	1	48	5	1	2	1	132	240

Item Name	Cals(kcal)	Prot(g)	Carb(g)	Fiber(g)	Sugar(g)	Fat-T(g)	Fat-S (g)	Fat-M (g)	Fat-P (g)	Chol (mg)	Sod(mg)
BEVERAGES											
Raspberry-Lime Rickey	15	—	4	1	2	—	—	—	—	—	45
Mediterranean Cooler	90	1	21	—	21	—	—	—	—	—	20
Bitters and Sparkling Mineral Waters	40	—	7	—	—	—	—	—	—	—	2
Juicy Fling	85	1	20	2	12	—	—	—	—	—	2
Seabreeze	65	—	15	—	7	—	—	—	—	—	5
Mandarin Frappé	50	1	14	2	10	—	—	—	—	—	—
Lemonade	84	—	23	1	18	—	—	—	—	—	2
Cantaloupe Cocktail	75	1	18	1	14	—	—	—	—	—	16
Gazpacho Cocktail	38	1	8	1	6	—	—	—	—	—	133
Passion Fruit Cocktail	101	1	24	1	12	—	—	—	—	—	5
The American Cocktail	112	1	29	1	26	—	—	—	—	—	5
Tropical Fruit Smoothie	97	1	24	2	16	—	—	—	—	—	3
Frozen Cappuccino	118	5	25	—	21	—	—	—	—	3	86
Chai	80	3	12	1	10	2	1	—	—	5	45
Hot Cocoa	202	12	41	5	33	2	1	1	—	5	140
Hot Mulled Cider	114	—	28	—	23	—	—	—	—	—	23

Nutrient Content Claims

These are the core terms:

Free

This term means that a product contains no amount of, or only trivial or "physiologically inconsequential" amounts of, one or more of these components: fat, saturated fat, cholesterol, sodium, sugars, and calories. For example, "calorie-free" means fewer than 5 calories per serving, and "sugar-free" and "fat-free" both mean less than 0.5 g per serving. Synonyms for "free" include "without," "no," and "zero." A synonym for fat-free milk is "skim."

Low

This term can be used on foods that can be eaten frequently without exceeding dietary guidelines for one or more of these components: fat, saturated fat, cholesterol, sodium, and calories. Thus, descriptors are defined as follows:

- low-fat: 3 g or less per serving
- low-saturated fat: 1 g or less per serving
- low-sodium: 140 mg or less per serving
- very low sodium: 35 mg or less per serving
- low-cholesterol: 20 mg or less and 2 g or less of saturated fat per serving
- low-calorie: 40 calories or less per serving.

Synonyms for low include "little," "few," "low source of," and "contains a small amount of."

U. S. Department of Health and Human Services
U. S. Food and Drug Administration
Center for Food Safety and Applied Nutrition
A Food Labeling Guide
September, 1994 (Editorial revisions June, 1999)

Lean and extra lean

These terms can be used to describe the fat content of meat, poultry, seafood, and game meats.

- lean: less than 10 g fat, 4.5 g or less saturated fat, and less than 95 mg cholesterol per serving and per 100 g
- extra lean: less than 5 g fat, less than 2 g saturated fat, and less than 95 mg cholesterol per serving and per 100 g

High

This term can be used if the food contains 20 percent or more of the Daily Value for a particular nutrient in a serving.

Good source

This term means that one serving of a food contains 10 to 19 percent of the Daily Value for a particular nutrient.

Reduced

This term means that a nutritionally altered product contains at least 25 percent less of a nutrient or of calories than the regular, or reference, product. However, a reduced claim can't be made on a product if its reference food already meets the requirement for a "low" claim.

Less

This term means that a food, whether altered or not, contains 25 percent less of a nutrient or of calories than the reference food. For example, pretzels that have 25 percent less fat than potato chips could carry a "less" claim. "Fewer" is an acceptable synonym.

Light

This descriptor can mean two things:

First, that a nutritionally altered product contains one-third fewer calories or half the fat of the reference food. If the food derives 50 percent or more of its calories from fat, the reduction must be 50 percent of the fat.

Second, that the sodium content of a low-calorie, low-fat food has been reduced by 50 percent. In addition, "light in sodium" may be used on food in which the sodium content has been reduced by at least 50 percent.

The term "light" still can be used to describe such properties as texture and color, as long as the label explains the intent—for example, "light brown sugar" and "light and fluffy."

More

This term means that a serving of food, whether altered or not, contains a nutrient that is at least 10 percent of the Daily Value more than the reference food. The 10 percent of Daily Value also applies to "fortified," "enriched," "added" "extra," and "plus" claims, but in those cases, the food must be altered.

Alternative spelling of these descriptive terms and their synonyms is allowed—for example, "hi" and "lo"—as long as the alternatives are not misleading.

Healthy

A "healthy" food must be low in fat and saturated fat and contain limited amounts of cholesterol and sodium. In addition, if it's a single-item food, it must provide at least 10 percent of one or more of vitamins A or C, iron, calcium, protein, or fiber. Exempt from this "10-percent" rule are certain raw, canned, and frozen fruits and vegetables and certain cereal-grain products. These foods can be labeled "healthy," if they do not contain ingredients that change the nutritional profile, and, in the case of enriched grain products, conform to standards of identity, which call for certain required ingredients. If it's a meal-type product, such as frozen entrées and multi-course frozen dinners, it must provide 10 percent of two or three of these vitamins or minerals or of protein or fiber, in addition to meeting the other criteria. The sodium content cannot exceed 360 mg per serving for individual foods and 480 mg per serving for meal-type products.

Other Definitions

The regulations also address other claims. Among them:

Percent fat free

A product bearing this claim must be a low-fat or a fat-free product. In addition, the claim must accurately reflect the amount of fat present in 100 g of the food. Thus, if a food contains 2.5 g fat per 50 g, the claim must be "95 percent fat free."

Implied

These types of claims are prohibited when they wrongfully imply that a food contains or does not contain a meaningful level of a nutrient. For example, a product claiming to be made with an ingredient known to be a source of fiber (such as "made with oat bran") is not allowed unless the product contains enough of that ingredient (for example, oat bran) to meet the definition for "good source" of fiber. As another example, a claim that a product contains "no tropical oils" is allowed—but only on foods that are "low" in saturated fat because consumers have come to equate tropical oils with high saturated fat.

Meals and main dishes

Claims that a meal or main dish is "free" of a nutrient, such as sodium or cholesterol, must meet the same requirements as those for individual foods. Other claims can be used under special circumstances. For example, "low-calorie"å means the meal or main dish contains 120 calories or less per 100 g. "Low-sodium" means the food has 140 mg or less per 100 g. "Low-cholesterol" means the food contains 20 mg cholesterol or less per 100 g and no more than 2 g saturated fat. "Light" means the meal or main dish is low-fat or low-calorie.

Standardized foods

Any nutrient content claim, such as "reduced fat," "low calorie," and "light," may be used in conjunction with a standardized term if the new product has been specifically formulated to meet FDA's criteria for that claim, if the product is not nutritionally inferior to the traditional standardized food, and the new product complies with certain compositional requirements set by FDA. A new product bearing a claim also must have performance characteristics similar to the referenced traditional standardized food. If the product doesn't, and the differences materially limit the product's use, its label must state the differences (for example, not recommended for baking) to inform consumers.

Fresh

Although not mandated by NLEA, FDA has issued a regulation for the term "fresh." The agency took this step because of concern over the term's possible misuse on some food labels.

The regulation defines the term "fresh" when it is used to suggest that a food is raw or unprocessed. In this context, "fresh" can be used only on a food that is raw, has never been frozen or heated, and contains no preservatives. (Irradiation at low levels is allowed.) "Fresh frozen," "frozen fresh," and "freshly frozen" can be used for foods that are quickly frozen while still fresh. Blanching (brief scalding before freezing to prevent nutrient breakdown) is allowed.

Other uses of the term "fresh," such as in "fresh milk" or "freshly baked bread," are not affected.

Relative Claims

For all relative claims, percent (or fraction) of change and identity of reference food must be declared in immediate proximity to the most prominent claim. Quantitative comparison of the amount of the nutrient in the product per labeled serving with that in reference food must be declared on information panel.

RELATIVE (OR COMPARATIVE) CLAIMS	ACCOMPANYING INFORMATION
For "Light" claims	Generally, percentage reduction for both fat and calories must be stated. An exception is that percentage reduction need not be specified for "low-fat" products. Quantitative comparisons must be stated for both fat and calories.
For claims characterizing the level of antioxidant nutrients in a food	An RDI must be established for each of the nutrients that are the subject of the claim; each nutrient must have existing scientific evidence of antioxidant activity and the level of each nutrient must be sufficient to meet the definition for "high," "good source," or "high potency" in 21 CFR 101.54(b),(c), or (e). Beta-carotene may be the subject of an antioxidant claim when the level of vitamin A present as beta-carotene in the food is sufficient to qualify for the claim.

Reference Food

"Light" or "Lite"

(1) A food representative of the type of food bearing the claim (e.g., average value of top three brands or representative value from valid data base), (2) Similar food (e.g., potato chips for potato chips), and (3) Not low-calorie and low-fat (except light-sodium foods which must be low-calorie & low-fat).

"Reduced" and "Added"(or Fortified" and "Enriched")

(1) An established regular product or average representative product, and (2) Similar food.

"More" and "Less" (or "Fewer")

(1) An established regular product or average representative product, and (2) A dissimilar food in the same product category which may be generally substituted for the labeled food (e.g., potato chips for pretzels) or a similar food.

Other Nutrient Content Claims

"Lean"

On seafood or game meat that contains less than 10 g total fat, 4.5 g or less saturated fat, and less than 95 mg cholesterol per reference amount and per 100 g.

For meals and main dishes, meets criteria per 100 g and per labeled serving.

For mixed dish not measurable with a cup as defined in Sec. 101.12(b) in table 2, provided that the food contains less than 8 g total fat, 3.5 g or less saturated fat and less than 80 mg cholesterol per reference amount customarily consumed.

"Extra Lean"

On seafood or game meat that contains less than 5 g total fat, less than 2 g saturated fat, and less than 95 mg cholesterol per reference amount and per 100 g.

For meals and main dishes, meets criteria per 100 g and per labeled serving.

"High Potency"

May be used on foods to describe individual vitamins or minerals that are present at 100 percent or more of the RDI per reference amount—or on a multi-ingredient food product that contains 100 percent or more of the RDI for at least 2/3 of the vitamins and minerals with Daily Values, and that are present in the product at 2 percent or more of the RDI (e.g., "High potency multivitamin, multimineral dietary supplement tablets").

"High", "Rich In", or "Excellent Source Of"

Contains 20 percent or more of the Daily Value (DV) to describe protein, vitamins, minerals, dietary fiber, or potassium per reference amount. May be used on meals or main dishes to indicate that product contains a food that meets definition. May not be used for total carbohydrate.

"Good Source of," "Contains," or "Provides"

Ten to 19 percent of the DV per reference amount. These terms may be used on meals or main dishes to indicate that product contains a food that meets definition. May not be used for total carbohydrate.

"More," "Added," "Extra," or "Plus"

10 percent or more of the DV per reference amount. May only be used for vitamins, minerals, protein, dietary fiber, and potassium.

"Modified"

May be used in statement of identity that bears a relative claim (e.g., "Modified Fat Cheese Cake, contains 35 percent Less Fat than our Regular Cheese Cake").

Any Fiber Claim

If food is not low in total fat, must state total fat in conjunction with claim such as "More Fiber."

Implied Claims

Claims about a food or ingredient that suggests that the nutrient or ingredient are absent or present in a certain amount or claims about a food that suggests a food may be useful in maintaining healthy dietary practices and which are made with an explicit claim (e.g., "healthy, contains 3 grams of fat") are implied claims and are prohibited unless provided for in a regulation by FDA. In addition, the Agency has devised a petition system whereby specific additional claims may be considered.

Claims that a food contains or is made with an ingredient that is known to contain a particular nutrient may be made if product is "low" in or a "good source" of the nutrient associated with the claim (e.g., "good source of oat bran").

EQUIVALENCE CLAIMS

"Contains as much [nutrient] as a [food]" may be made if both reference food and labeled food are a "good source" of a nutrient on a per serving basis. (e.g., "Contains as much vitamin C as an 8-ounce glass of orange juice").

The following label statements are generally not considered implied claims unless they are made in a nutrition context:

1) avoidance claims for religious, food intolerance, or other non-nutrition related reasons (e.g., "100 percent milk free");

2) statements about non-nutritive substances (e.g., "no artificial colors");

3) added value statements (e.g., "made with real butter");

4) statements of identity (e.g., "corn oil" or "corn oil margarine"); and special dietary statements made in compliance with a specific Part 105 provision.

5) the terms "Unsweetened" and "Unsalted" as taste claims.

6) the terms "Sugar Free" and "No Added Sugar" claims on dietary supplements only.

Health Claims

APPROVED CLAIMS	FOOD REQUIREMENTS	CLAIM REQUIREMENTS	MODEL CLAIM, STATEMENTS
Calcium and Osteoporosis	- High in calcium	Indicates disease depends on many factors by listing risk factors or the disease: Gender—Female. Race—Caucasian and Asian. Age—Growing older.	Regular exercise and a healthy diet with enough calcium helps teens and young adult white and Asian women maintain good bone health and may reduce their high risk of osteoporosis later in life.
	- Assimilable (Bioavailable)	Primary target population: Females, Caucasian and Asian races, and teens and young adults in their bone-forming years.	
	- Supplements must disintegrate and dissolve	Additional factors necessary to reduce risk: Eating healthful meals, regular exercise.	
	- Phosphorus content cannot exceed calcium content	Mechanism relating calcium to osteoporosis: Optimizes peak bone mass.	
		Foods or supplements containing more than 400 mg calcium must state that total intakes of greater than 2,000 mg calcium provide no added benefit to bone health.	
Sodium and Hypertension	- Low sodium	Required terms: - "Sodium," "High blood pressure" Includes physician statement (Individuals with high blood pressure should consult their physicians) if claim defines high or normal blood pressure.	Diets low in sodium may reduce the risk of high blood pressure, a disease associated with many factors.
Dietary Fat and Cancer	- Low fat (Fish & game meats: "Extra lean")	Required terms: - "Total fat" or "Fat" - "Some types of cancers" or "Some cancers" Does not specify types of fats or fatty acids that may be related to risk of cancer.	Development of cancer depends on many factors. A diet low in total fat may reduce the risk of some cancers.
Dietary Saturated Fat and Cholesterol and Risk of Coronary Heart Disease	- Low saturated fat - Low cholesterol - Low fat (Fish & game meats: "Extra lean")	Required terms: - "Saturated fat and cholesterol" - "Coronary heart disease" or "Heart disease" Includes physician statement (individuals with elevated blood total- or LDL-cholesterol should consult their physicians) if claim defines high or normal blood total— and LDL—cholesterol.	While many factors affect heart disease, diets low in saturated fat and cholesterol may reduce the risk of this disease.

U.S. Food and Drug Administration

Center for Food Safety and Applied Nutrition

A Food Labeling Guide

September 1994 (Editorial revisions June 1999 and November 2000)

APPROVED CLAIMS	FOOD REQUIREMENTS	CLAIM REQUIREMENTS	MODEL CLAIM, STATEMENTS
Fiber-Containing Grain Products, Fruits, and Vegetables and Cancer	- A grain product, fruit, or vegetable that contains dietary fiber - Low fat - Good source of dietary fiber (without fortification)	Required terms: - "Fiber," "Dietary fiber," or "Total dietary fiber" - "Some types of cancer" or "Some cancers" Does not specify types of dietary fiber that may be related to risk of cancer.	Low fat diets rich in fiber-containing grain products, fruits, and vegetables may reduce the risk of some types of cancer, a disease associated with many factors.
Fruits, Vegetables and Grain Products that contain Fiber, particularly Soluble Fiber, and Risk of Coronary Heart Disease	- A fruit, vegetable, or grain product that contains fiber - Low saturated fat - Low cholesterol - Low fat - At least 0.6 grams of soluble fiber per RA (without fortification) - Soluble fiber content provided on label	Required terms: - "Fiber," "Dietary fiber," "Some types of dietary fiber," "Some dietary fibers," or "Some fibers" - "Saturated fat" and "Cholesterol" - "Heart disease" or "Coronary heart disease" Includes physician statement ("Individuals with elevated blood total-or LDL-cholesterol should consult their physicians") if claim defines high or normal blood total— and LDL—cholesterol.	Diets low in saturated fat and cholesterol and rich in fruits, vegetables, and grain products that contain some types of dietary fiber, particularly soluble fiber, may reduce the risk of heart disease, a disease associated with many factors.
Fruits and Vegetables and Cancer	- A fruit or vegetable - Low fat - Good source (without fortification) of at least one of the following: Vitamin A, Vitamin C, or Dietary fiber	Required terms: - "Fiber," "Dietary fiber," or "Total dietary fiber" - "Total fat" or "Fat" - "Some types of cancer" or "Some cancers" Characterizes fruits and vegetables as "Foods that are low in fat and may contain Vitamin A, Vitamin C, and dietary fiber." Characterizes specific food as a "Good source" of one or more of the following: Dietary fiber, Vitamin A, or Vitamin C. Does not specify types of fats or fatty acids or types of dietary fiber that may be related to risk of cancer.	Low fat diets rich in fruits and vegetables (foods that are low in fat and may contain dietary fiber, Vitamin A, or Vitamin C) may reduce the risk of some types of cancer, a disease associated with many factors. Broccoli is high in vitamin A and C, and it is a good source of dietary fiber.
Folate and Neural Tube Defects	"Good source" of folate (at least 40 mcg folate per serving) - Dietary supplements, or foods in conventional food form that are naturally good sources of folate (i.e., only non-fortified food in conventional food form) - The claim shall not be made on products that contain more than 100% of the RDI for vitamin A as retinol or preformed vitamin A or vitamin D - Dietary supplements shall meet USP standards for disintegration and dissolution or otherwise bioavailable - Amount of folate required in N.L.	Required terms: - Terms that specify the relationship (e.g., women who are capable of becoming pregnant and who consume adequate amounts of folate) "Folate," "folic acid," "folacin," "folate a B vitamin," "folic acid, a B vitamin," "folacin, a B vitamin," "neural tube defects," "birth defects, spinal bifida, or anencephaly," "birth defects of the brain or spinal cord—anencephaly or spinal bifida," "spinal bifida or anencephaly, birth defects of the brain or spinal cord." Must also include information on the multifactorial nature of neural tube defects, and the safe upper limit of daily intake.	Healthful diets with adequate folate may reduce a woman's risk of having a child with a brain or spinal cord defect.

APPROVED CLAIMS	FOOD REQUIREMENTS	CLAIM REQUIREMENTS	MODEL CLAIM, STATEMENTS
Dietary Sugar Alcohol and Dental Caries	- Sugar free - The sugar alcohol must be xylitol, sorbitol, mannitol, maltitol, isomalt, lactitol, hydrogenated starch hydrolysates, hydrogenated glucose syrups, erythritol, or a combination. - When a fermentable carbohydrate is present, the food must not lower plaque pH below 5.7.	Required terms: - "does not promote," "may reduce the risk of," "useful [or is useful] in not promoting" or "expressly [or is expressly] for not promoting" dental caries - "sugar alcohol" or "sugar alcohols" or the name or names of the sugar alcohols, e.g., sorbitol - "dental caries" or "tooth decay." Includes statement that frequent between meal consumption of foods high in sugars and starches can promote tooth decay. Packages with less than 15 square inches of surface area available for labeling may use a shortened claim.	Full claim: Frequent between-meal consumption of foods high in sugars and starches promotes tooth decay. The sugar alcohols in [name of food] do not promote tooth decay. Shortened claim(on small packages only): Does not promote tooth decay.
Soluble Fiber from Certain Foods and Risk of Coronary Heart Disease	- Low saturated fat - Low cholesterol - Low fat - Include either (1) one or more eligible sources of whole oats, containing at least 0.75 g whole oat soluble fiber per RA; or (2) psyllium seed husk containing at least 1.7 g of psyllium husk soluble fiber per RA - Amount of soluble fiber per RA declared in nutrition label. Eligible Source of Soluble Fiber: Beta (ß) glucan soluble fiber from oat bran, rolled oats (or oatmeal), and whole oat flour, whole grain barley and certain dry milled barley grain products Oat bran must provide at least 5.5% ß -glucan soluble fiber, rolled oats must provide at least 4% ß -glucan soluble fiber, and whole oat flour must provide at least 4% ß -glucan soluble fiber or psyllium husk wih purity of no less than 95%	Required terms: - "Heart disease" or "coronary heart disease." - "Soluble fiber" qualified by either "psyllium seed husk" or the name of the eligible source of whole oat soluble fiber. - "Saturated fat" and "cholesterol." - "Daily dietary intake of the soluble fiber source necessary to reduce the risk of CHD and the contribution one serving of the product makes to this level of intake." Additional Required Label Statement: Foods bearing a psyllium seed husk health claim must also bear a label statement concerning the need to consume them with adequate amounts of fluids; e.g., "NOTICE: This food should be eaten with at least a full glass of liquid. Eating this product without enough liquid may cause choking. Do not eat this product if you have difficulty in swallowing."	Soluble fiber from foods such as [name of soluble fiber source, and, if desired, name of food product], as part of a diet low in saturated fat and cholesterol, may reduce the risk of heart disease. A serving of [name of food product] supplies __ grams of the [necessary daily dietary intake for the benefit] soluble fiber from [name of soluble fiber source] necessary per day to have this effect.
Soy Protein and Risk of Coronary Heart Disease	- At least 6.25 g soy protein per RA - Low saturated fat - Low cholesterol - Low fat (except that foods made from whole soybeans that contain no fat in addition to that inherent in the whole soybean are exempt from the "low fat" requirement)	Required terms: - "Heart disease" or "coronary heart disease" - "Soy protein" - "Saturated fat" and "cholesterol" Claim specifies daily dietary intake levels of soy protein associated with reduced risk Claim specifies amount of soy protein in a serving of food	(1) 25 grams of soy protein a day, as part of a diet low in saturated fat and cholesterol, may reduce the risk of heart disease. A serving of [name of food] supplies __ grams of soy protein. (2) Diets low in saturated fat and cholesterol that include 25 grams of soy protein a day may reduce the risk of heart disease. One serving of [name of food] provides __ grams of soy protein.

APPROVED CLAIMS	FOOD REQUIREMENTS	CLAIM REQUIREMENTS	MODEL CLAIM, STATEMENTS
Plant Sterol/Stanol Esters and Risk of Coronary Heart Disease	- At least 0.65 g plant sterol esters per RA of spreads and salad dressings or - At least 1.7 g plant stanol esters per RA of spreads, salad dressings, snack bars, and dietary supplements. - Low saturated fat - Low cholesterol - Spreads and salad dressings that exceed 13 g fat per 50 g must bear the statement "see nutrition information for fat content" Salad dressings are exempted from the minimum 10% DV nutrient requirement (see General Criteria below)	Required terms: - "May" or " might" reduce the risk of CHD - "Heart disease" or "coronary heart disease" - "Plant sterol esters" or "plant stanol esters"; except "vegetable oil" may replace the term "plant" if vegetable oil is the sole source of the sterol/stanol ester Claim specifies plant stero/stanol esters are part of a diet low in saturated fat and cholesterol. Claim does not attribute any degree of CHD risk reduction. Claim specifies the daily dietary intake of plant sterol or stanol esters necessary to reduce CHD risk, and the amount provided per serving. Claim specifies that plant sterol or stanol esters should be consumed with two different meals each a day.	(1) Foods containing at least 0.65 gram per serving of vegetable oil sterol esters, eaten twice a day with meals for a daily total intake of at least 1.3 grams, as part of a diet low in saturated fat and cholesterol, may reduce the risk of heart disease. A serving of [name of food] supplies __ grams of vegetable oil sterol esters. (2) Diets low in saturated fat and cholesterol that include two servings of foods that provide a daily total of at least 3.4 grams of plant stanol esters in two meals may reduce the risk of heart disease. A serving of [name of food] supplies __ grams of plant stanol esters.
Whole Grain Foods and Risk of Heart Disease and Certain Cancers	- Contains 51 percent or more whole grain ingredients by weight per RA - Dietary fiber content at least: 3.0 g per RA of 55 g 2.8 g per RA of 50 g 2.5 g per RA of 45 g 1.7 g per RA of 35 g	Required wording of the claim: "Diets rich in whole grain foods and other plant foods and low in total fat, saturated fat, and cholesterol may reduce the risk of heart disease and some cancers."	NA
Potassium and the Risk of High Blood Pressure and Stroke*	- Good source of potassium - Low sodium - Low total fat - Low saturated fat - Low cholesterol	Required wording for the claim: "Diets containing foods that are a good source of potassium and that are low in sodium may reduce the risk of high blood pressure and stroke."	NA

*Claims authorized based on authoritative statements by federal scientific bodies

General Criteria for All Health Claims

All information in one place without intervening material (reference statement permitted).

Only information on the value that intake or reduced intake, as part of a total dietary pattern, may have on a disease or health-related condition.

Enables public to understand information provided and significance of information in the context of a total daily diet.

Complete, truthful, and not misleading.

Food contains, without fortification, 10% or more of the Daily Value for one of six nutrients (dietary supplements excepted):

Vitamin A	500 IU	Calcium	100 mg
Vitamin C	6 mg	Protein	5 g
Iron	1.8 mg	Fiber	2.5 g

Not represented for infants or toddlers less than 2 years of age.

Uses "may" or "might" to express relationship between substance and disease.

Does not quantify any degree of risk reduction.

Indicates disease depends on many factors.

Food contains less than the specified levels of four disqualifying nutrients:

Disqualifying Nutrients	Foods	Main Dishes	Meal Products
Fat	13 g	19.5 g	26 g
Saturated Fat	4 g	6 g	8 g
Cholesterol	60 mg	90 mg	120 mg
Sodium	480 mg	720 mg	960 mg

Abbreviations: RA = reference amount, IU = International Units

Reference Amounts Customarily Consumed Per Eating Occasion

PRODUCT CATEGORY	EXAMPLES	REFERENCE AMOUNT
Bakery products	Biscuits, croissants, bagels, tortillas, soft bread sticks, soft pretzels, corn bread, hush puppies	55 g
	Breads (excluding sweet quick type), rolls	50 g
	Brownies	40 g
	Cakes, heavy-weight (cheese cake; pineapple upside down cake; fruit, nut, and vegetable cakes)	125 g
	Cakes, medium-weight	80 g
	Cakes, light-weight (angel food, chiffon, or sponge)	55 g
	Coffee cakes, crumb cakes, doughnuts, Danish	55 g
	Cookies	30 g
	Crackers	15 g
	Croutons	7 g
	French toast, pancakes	110 g
	Grain-based bars with or without filling, e.g., breakfast bars, granola bars, rice cereal bars	40 g
	Pies, cobblers, fruit crisps, turnovers	125 g
	Pizza crust	55 g
	Taco shells, hard	30 g
Beverages	Carbonated and noncarbonated beverages, wine coolers, water	8 fl oz
	Coffee or tea, flavored and sweetened	8 fl oz
Cereal and Other Grain Products	Breakfast cereals (hot cereal type), hominy grits	1 cup prepared; 40 g plain dry
	Breakfast cereals, ready-to-eat, weighing less than 20 g per cup, e.g., plain puffed cereal grains	15 g
	Breakfast cereals, ready-to-eat weighing 20 g or more but less than 43 g per cup; high fiber cereals containing 28 g or more of fiber per 100 g	30 g
	Breakfast cereals, ready-to-eat, weighing 43 g or more per cup	55 g
	Bran or wheat germ	15 g
	Flours or cornmeal	30 g
	Grains, e.g., rice, barley	140 g prepared; 45 g dry
	Pastas, plain	140 g prepared; 55 g dry
	Pastas, dry, ready-to-eat, e.g., fried canned chow mein noodles	25 g
	Starches, e.g., cornstarch, potato starch, tapioca	10 g
	Stuffing	100 g

PRODUCT CATEGORY	EXAMPLES	REFERENCE AMOUNT
Dairy Products and Substitutes	Cheese, cottage	110 g
	Cheese used primarily as ingredients, e.g., dry cottage cheese, ricotta cheese	55 g
	Cheese, grated hard, e.g., Parmesan, Romano	5 g
	Cheese, all others except those listed as separate for distinct categories—includes cream cheese and cheese spread	30 g
	Cheese sauce—see "Sauces"	
	Cream or cream substitutes	15 mL
	Cream or cream substitutes, powder	2 g
	Cream, half & half	30 mL
	Eggnog	½ cup (120 mL)
	Milk, condensed, undiluted	2 tbsp (30 mL)
	Milk, evaporated, undiluted	2 tbsp (30 mL)
	Milk, milk-based drinks, e.g., instant breakfast meal replacement, cocoa	1 cup (240 mL)
	Shakes or shake substitutes, e.g., dairy shake mixes, fruit frost mixes	1 cup (240 mL)
	Sour cream	30 g
	Yogurt	225 g
Desserts	Ice cream, ice milk, frozen yogurt, sherbet	½ cup
	Frozen flavored and sweetened ice and pops	85 g
	Sundae	1 cup
	Custards, gelatin or pudding	½ cup
Dessert Toppings and Fillings	Cake frostings or icings	35 g
	Other dessert toppings, e.g., fruits, syrups, spreads, marshmallow cream, nuts, dairy and nondairy whipped toppings	2 tbsp
	Pie fillings	85 g
Egg and Egg Sustitutes	Egg mixtures, e.g., egg foo young, scrambled eggs, omelets	110 g
	Eggs (all sizes)	50 g
	Egg substitutes	50 g
Fats and Oils	Butter, margarine, oil	1 tbsp
	Butter replacement, powder	2 g
	Dressings for salads	30 g
	Mayonnaise, sandwich spreads, mayonnaise-type dressings	15 g
	Spray types	0.25 g

PRODUCT CATEGORY	EXAMPLES	REFERENCE AMOUNT
Fish, Shellfish, Game Meats, and Meat or Poultry Substitutes	Bacon substitutes, canned anchovy, caviar	15 g
	Dried, e.g., jerky	30 g
	Entrées with sauce, e.g., fish with cream sauce, shrimp with lobster sauce	140 g
	Entrées without sauce, cooked; e.g., plain or fried fish	85 g
	Fish, shellfish or game meat, canned	55 g
	Substitute for luncheon meat, meat spreads, for distinct pieces	55 g
	Smoked or pickled fish, shellfish, or game meat, fish or shellfish spread	55 g
Fruits and Fruit Juices	Candied or pickled	30 g
	Dried	40 g
	Fruits for garnish or flavor, e.g., maraschino cherries	4 g
	Fruit relishes, e.g., cranberry sauce	70 g
	Fruits used primarily as ingredients, avocado	30 g
	Fruits used primarily as ingredients, others (cranberries, lemon, lime)	55 g
	Watermelon	280 g
	All other fruits	140 g
	Juices, nectars, fruit drinks	240 mL
	Juices used as ingredients, e.g., lemon juice, lime juice	5 mL
Legumes	Bean cake (tofu), tempeh	85 g
	Beans, plain or in sauce	130 g
Miscellaneous Category	Baking powder, baking soda	0.6 g
	Baking decorations, e.g., colored sugars and sprinkles for cookies, by teaspoon	1 tsp (4 g)
	Batter mixes, bread crumbs	30 g
	Cooking wine	30 mL
	Drink mixers (without alcohol)	240 mL
	Salad and potato toppers, e.g., salad crunchies, salad crispins, substitutes for bacon bits	7 g
	Salt, salt substitutes, seasoning salts	¼ tsp
	Spices, herbs	¼ tsp or 0.5 g
Mixed Dishes	Measurable with cup, e.g., casseroles, hash, macaroni and cheese, pot pies, spaghetti with sauce, stews, etc.	1 cup
	Not measurable with cup, e.g., burritos, egg rolls, enchiladas, pizza, rolls, quiche, all types of sandwiches	140 g
Nuts and Seeds	Nuts, seeds, and mixtures, chopped, slivered, and whole	30 g
	Nut and seed butters, pastes, or creams	2 tbsp
	Coconut, nut and seed flours	15 g

PRODUCT CATEGORY	EXAMPLES	REFERENCE AMOUNT
Potatoes and Sweet Potatoes/Yams	French fries, hash browns, skins or pancakes	70 g
	Mashed, candied, stuffed, or with sauce	140 g
	Plain, fresh, canned, or frozen	110 g
Salads	Gelatin salad	120 g
	Pasta or potato salad	140 g
	All other salads, e.g., egg, fish, shellfish, bean, fruit, or vegetable	100 g
Sauces, Dips, Gravies, and Condiments	Barbecue sauce, hollandaise sauce, tartar sauce, other sauces for dipping	2 tbsp
	Major main entrée sauces, e.g., spaghetti sauce	125 g
	Minor main entrée sauces (e.g., pizza sauce, pesto), other sauces used as toppings (e.g., gravy, white sauce, cheese sauce), cocktail sauce	¼ cup
	Major condiments, e.g., ketchup, steak sauce, soy sauce, vinegar, teriyaki	1 tbsp
	Minor condiments, e.g., horseradish, hot sauces, mustards, Worcestershire sauce	1 tsp
Snacks	All varieties, chips, pretzels, popcorns, extruded snacks, fruit- based snacks (e.g., chips), grain-based snack pieces	30 g
Soups	All varieties	245 g
Sugars and Sweets	Baking candies (e.g., chips)	15 g
	Hard candies, breath mints	2 g
	Hard candies, roll-type	5 g
	Hard candies, others	15 g
	All other candies	40 g
	Confectioner's sugar	30 g
	Honey, jams, jellies, fruit butter, molasses	1 tbsp
	Marshmallows	30 g
	Sugar	4 g
Vegetables	Vegetables primarily used for garnish or flavor, e.g., pimiento, parsley	4 g
	Chili pepper, green onion	30 g
	All other vegetables without sauce	85 g
	Vegetable juice	240 mL
	Olives	15 g
	Pickles, all types	30 g
	Pickle relishes	15 g
	Vegetable pastes, e.g., tomato paste	30 g
	Vegetable sauces or purees, e.g., tomato sauce	60 g

Section 21CFR101.12
[Code of Federal Regulations]
[Title 21, Volume 2]
[Revised as of April 1, 2002]
From the U.S. Government Printing Office via GPO Access
[CITE: 21CFR101.12]

Weight Measure Conversions

U.S.	METRIC
¼ ounce	7 grams
½ ounce	14 grams (rounded to 15)
1 ounce	28.35 grams (rounded to 20)
4 ounces	113.4 grams (rounded to 115)
8 ounces (½ pound)	226.8 grams (rounded to 225)
16 ounces (1 pound)	453.6 grams (rounded to 450)
32 ounces (2 pounds)	907.2 grams (rounded to 900)
40 ounces (2 ½ pounds)	1.134 kilograms (rounded to 1.15)

Volume Measure Conversions

U.S.	METRIC
1 teaspoon	4.93 milliliters (rounded to 5)
1 tablespoon	14.79 milliliters (rounded to 15)
1 fluid ounce (2 tablespoons)	29.58 milliliters (rounded to 30)
2 fluid ounces (¼ cup)	59 milliliters (rounded to 60)
8 fluid ounces (1 cup)	236.64 milliliters (rounded to 240)
16 fluid ounces (1 pint)	473.28 milliliters (rounded to 480)
32 fluid ounces (1 quart)	946.56 milliliters (rounded to 950 milliliters or 0.95 liter)
128 fluid ounces (1 gallon)	3.79 liters (rounded to 3.75 liters)

Temperature Conversions

DEGREES FAHRENHEIT (°F)	DEGREES CELSIUS (°C)*
32°	0°
40°	4°
140°	60°
150°	66°
160°	71°
170°	77°
212°	100°
275°	135°
300°	149°
325°	163°
350°	177°
375°	191°
400°	204°
425°	218°
450°	232°
475°	246°
500°	260°

*Celsius temperatures have been rounded.

*About the rounding of converted metric measurements: The recipes in this book were developed and tested using standard U.S. measurements for weight and volume. They have been converted into metric measurements and rounded. In order for the measuring and portioning information to make sense, the rounded metric conversions are as accurate as reasonable, within a range of 5 grams for conversions under 8 ounces, 15 grams up to 20 ounces.

Information, Hints, and Tips for Calculations

1 gallon = 4 quarts = 8 pints = 16 cups (8 fluid ounces) = 128 fluid ounces

1 fifth bottle = approximately 1½ pints or exactly 25.6 fluid ounces

1 measuring cup holds 8 fluid ounces (a coffee cup generally holds 6 fluid ounces)

1 egg white = 2 fluid ounces (average)

1 lemon = 1 to 1¼ fluid ounces of juice

1 orange = 3 to 3¼ fluid ounces of juice

To convert Fahrenheit to Celsius: (°F – 32) × 0.5556 = °C

To convert Celsius to Fahrenheit: (°C + 32) × 1.8 = °F

To convert ounces and pounds to grams: Multiply ounces by 28.35 to determine grams; multiply pounds by 453.59 to determine grams

To convert pounds to kilograms: Divide pounds by 2.2 to determine kilograms

To convert grams to ounces or pounds: Divide grams by 28.35 to determine ounces; divide grams by 453.59 to determine pounds

To convert fluid ounces to milliliters: Multiply fluid ounces by 30 to determine milliliters

To convert milliliters to fluid ounces: Divide milliliters by 30 to determine fluid ounces

Metric Prefixes

kilo = 1,000

hecto = 100

deka = 10

deci = 1/10

centi = 1/100

milli = 1/1,000

Common Equivalencies for U.S. Volume Measures

1 gallon	4 quarts	128 fluid ounces
1 quart	2 pints	32 fluid ounces
1 pint	2 cups	16 fluid ounces
1 cup	16 tablespoons	8 fluid ounces
¾ cup	12 tablespoons	6 fluid ounces
⅔ cup	10 tablespoons + 2 teaspoons	5⅓ fluid ounces
½ cup	8 tablespoons	4 fluid ounces
⅓ cup	5 tablespoons + 1 teaspoon	⅔ fluid ounces
¼ cup	4 tablespoons	2 fluid ounces
1 tablespoon	3 teaspoons	½ fluid ounce

Recommended Resources and Readings

Sanitation and Safety

Applied Foodservice Sanitation Textbook. 4th ed. Educational Foundation of the National Restaurant Association, 1993.

Basic Food Sanitation. The Culinary Institute of America, 1993.

HACCP: Reference Book. Educational Foundation of the National Restaurant Association, 1993.

Chemistry of Cooking

CookWise: The Secrets of Cooking Revealed. Shirley Corriher. Morrow/Avon, 1997.

The Curious Cook. Harold McGee. Macmillan, 1992.

The Experimental Study of Food. 2nd ed. Ada Marie Campbell, Marjorie Porter Penfield, Ruth Mary Griswold. Constable and Co., 1979.

Food Science. 3rd ed. Helen Charley. Prentice Hall Professional, 1994.

On Food and Cooking: The Science and Lore of the Kitchen. Harold McGee. Scribner, 2004.

Nutrition and Nutritional Cookery

Choices for a Healthy Heart. Joseph C. Piscatella. Workman, 1988.

Food and Culture in America: A Nutrition Handbook. Pamela Goyan Kittler and Kathryn P. Sucher. Wadsworth, 1997.

Handbook of the Nutritional Value of Foods in Common Units. U.S. Department of Agriculture. Dover, 1986.

In Good Taste: A Contemporary Approach to Cooking. Victor Gielisse. Simon & Schuster, 1998.

Jane Brody's Good Food Book: Living the High-Carbohydrate Way. Jane Brody. Bantam, 1987.

The Mediterranean Diet Cookbook: A Delicious Alternative for Lifelong Health. Nancy Harmon Jenkins. Bantam, 1994.

The New Living Heart Diet. Michael E. DeBakey, Antonio M. Gotto, Jr., Lynne W. Scott, and John P. Foreyt. Simon and Schuster, 1996.

Nutrition: Concepts and Controversies. 8th ed. Eleanor R. Whitney and Frances S. Sizer. Brooks/Cole, 2003.

General and Classical Cookery

The Chef's Compendium of Professional Recipes. 3rd ed. John Fuller, Edward Renold, and David Foskett. Butterworth-Heinemann, 1992.

Classical Cooking the Modern Way. 3rd ed. Eugene Pauli. John Wiley & Sons, 1999.

Cuisine Actuelle. Victor Gielisse. Taylor Publications, 1992.

Culinary Artistry. Andrew Dornenberg and Karen Page. John Wiley & Sons, 1996.

Dining in France. Christian Millau. Stewart, Workman, 1986.

Escoffier: The Complete Guide to the Art of Modern Cookery. Auguste Escoffier. John Wiley & Sons, 1997.

Escoffier Cook Book. Auguste Escoffier. Crown, 1976.

The Essential Cook Book. Terence Conran, Caroline Conran, and Simon Hopkinson. Stewart, Tabori & Chang, 1980.

Essentials of Cooking. James Peterson. Artisan, 2003.

Garde Manger: The Art and Craft of the Cold Kitchen. The Culinary Institute of America. John Wiley & Sons, 2004.

Gastronomy. Jean Anthelme Brillat-Savarin. Counterpoint, 2000.

The Grand Masters of French Cuisine. Selected and adapted by Celine Vence and Robert Courtine. Putnam, 1978.

Great Chefs of France. Anthony Blake and Quentin Crewe. Harry N. Abrams, 1978.

Guide Culinaire: The Complete Guide to the Art of Modern Cooking. Auguste Escoffier. Translated by H. L. Cracknell and R. J. Kaufmann. John Wiley & Sons, 1979.

Introductory Foods. 11th ed. Marion Bennion. Prentice Hall, 2004.

Jacques Pepin's Art of Cooking. Jacques Pepin. Vols 1 and 2. Knopf, 1987.

James Beard's Theory and Practice of Good Cooking. Running Press Book Publishers, 1997.

Jewish Cooking in America. Joan Nathan. Alfred A. Knopf, 1998.

Ma Gastronomie. Ferdinand Point. Translated by Frank Kulla and Patricia S. Kulla. Lyceum Books, 1974.

The Physiology of Taste, or Meditations on Transcendental Gastronomy. Jean Anthelme Brillat-Savarin. Translated by M.F.K. Fisher, 2000.

Le Répertoire de la Cuisine. Louis Saulnier. Barron's, 1977.

Glossary

acid: A substance that tests lower than 7 on the pH scale. Acids have a sour or sharp flavor. Acidity occurs naturally in many foods, including citrus juice, vinegar, wine, and sour milk products. Acids also act as tenderizers in marinades, helping to break down connective tissues and cell walls.

adulterated food: Food that has been contaminated to the point that it is considered unfit for human consumption.

aerobic bacteria: Bacteria that require the presence of oxygen to function.

à la carte: A menu in which the patron makes individual selections from various menu categories; each item is priced separately.

à la minute: Literally "at the minute." A restaurant production approach in which dishes are not prepared until an order arrives in the kitchen.

albumen: The egg white. Makes up about 70 percent of the egg and contains most of the protein in the egg.

al dente: Literally, "to the tooth"; refers to an item, such as pasta or vegetables, cooked until it is tender but still firm, not soft.

alkali: A substance that tests at higher than 7 on the pH scale. Alkalis are sometimes described as having a slightly soapy flavor and can be used to balance acids. Olives and baking soda are two of the few alkaline foods.

allumette: Vegetable cut usually referring to potatoes cut into pieces the size and shape of matchsticks; ⅛ in by ⅛ in by 1 to 2 in / 3 mm by 3 mm by 3 to 5 cm. Also called *julienne*.

amino acids: The building blocks of proteins. Of the twenty amino acids in the human diet, eight are called "essential" because they cannot be produced by the body and must be supplied through a person's diet.

amuse-gueule: Chef's tasting; a small portion (one or two bites) of something exotic, unusual, or otherwise special that is served when the guests in a restaurant are seated. The amuse is not listed on a menu and is included in the price of an entrée. May also be known as *amuse-bouche*.

anaerobic bacteria: Bacteria that do not require oxygen to function.

antioxidants: Naturally occurring substances that retard the breakdown of tissues in the presence of oxygen. May be added to food during processing or may occur naturally. Help to prevent food from becoming rancid or discolored due to oxidation.

antipasto: Typically, a platter of hot or cold hors d'oeuvre served as part of Italian meal that includes meats, olives, cheeses, and vegetables.

apéritif: A light alcoholic beverage consumed before the meal to stimulate the appetite.

appareil: A prepared mixture of ingredients used alone or in another preparation.

appetizer: Light food served before a meal or as the first course of a meal. It may be hot or cold, plated or served as finger food.

aquaculture: The farm raising of fish or shellfish in natural or controlled marine tanks or ponds.

Arborio: A high-starch, short-grain rice traditionally used in the preparation of risotto.

aromatics: Ingredients, such as herbs, spices, vegetables, citrus fruits, wines, and vinegars, used to enhance the flavor and fragrance of food.

arrowroot: A powdered starch made from the root of a tropical plant of the same name. Used primarily as a thickener. Remains clear when cooked.

aspic: A clear jelly made from stock (or occasionally fruit or vegetable juices) thickened with gelatin. Used to coat foods or cubed and used as a garnish.

as-purchased (AP) weight: The weight of an item as received from the supplier before trimming or other preparation (as opposed to edible-portion [EP] weight).

bacteria: Microscopic organisms. Some have beneficial properties; others can cause food-borne illnesses when contaminated foods are ingested.

bain-marie: The French term for a water bath used to cook foods gently by surrounding the cooking vessel with simmering water. Also, a set of cylindrical nesting pots used to hold foods in a water bath or with a single, long handle used as a double boiler. Also, steam-table inserts.

bake: To cook food by surrounding it with dry heat in a closed environment, as in an oven.

barbecue: To cook food by grilling it over a wood or charcoal fire. Usually some sort of marinade or sauce is brushed on the item during cooking. Also, meat that is cooked in this way.

batch cooking: A cooking technique in which appropriately sized batches of food are prepared several times throughout a service period so that a fresh supply of cooked items is always available.

baton/batonnet: Items cut into pieces somewhat larger than allumette or julienne; ¼ in by ¼ in by 1 to 2 in / 6 mm by 6 mm by 3 to 5 cm. French for "stick" or "small stick."

blanch: To cook an item briefly in boiling water or hot fat before finishing or storing it. Blanching preserves the color, lessens strong flavors, and helps remove the peels of some fruits and vegetables.

blend: A mixture of two or more flavors combined to achieve a particular flavor or quality. Also, to mix two or more ingredients together until combined.

boil: A cooking method in which items are immersed in liquid at or above the boiling point (212°F / 100°C).

bouquet garni: A small bundle of herbs tied with string. It is used to flavor stocks, braises, and other preparations. Usually contains bay leaf, parsley, thyme, and possibly other aromatics wrapped in leek leaves.

braise: A cooking method in which the main item, usually meat, is seared in fat, then simmered at a low temperature in a small amount of stock or another liquid (usually halfway up the meat item) in a covered vessel for a long time. The cooking liquid is then reduced and used as the base of a sauce.

bran: The outer layer of a cereal grain and the part highest in fiber.

brazier/brasier: A pan, designed specifically for braising, that usually has two handles and a tight-fitting lid. Often is round but may be square or rectangular. It is also called a *rondeau*.

brine: A solution of salt, water, and seasonings used to preserve or moisten foods.

broil: To cook by means of a radiant heat source placed above the food.

broiler: The piece of equipment used to broil foods.

broth: A flavorful, aromatic liquid made by simmering water or stock with meat, vegetables, and/or spices and herbs.

brown sauce: A sauce made from a brown stock and aromatics and thickened by roux, a pure starch slurry, and/or a reduction; includes sauce Espagnole, demi-glace, jus de veau lié, and pan sauces.

brown stock: An amber liquid produced by simmering browned bones and meat (usually veal or beef) with vegetables and aromatics (including caramelized mirepoix and tomato purée).

bruise: To partially crush a food item in order to release its flavor.

brunoise: Dice cut of ⅛-in / 3-mm cubes. For a brunoise cut, items are first cut in julienne, then cut crosswise. For a fine brunoise of ¹⁄₁₆-in / 1.50-mm cubes, cut items first in fine julienne.

butterfly: To cut an item (usually meat or seafood) and open out the edges like a book or the wings of a butterfly.

buttermilk: A dairy beverage with a slightly sour flavor similar to that of yogurt. Traditionally, the liquid by-product of butter churning, now usually made by culturing skim milk.

calorie: A unit used to measure food energy. It is the amount of energy needed to raise the temperature of 1 kilogram of water by 1°C.

canapé: An hors d'oeuvre consisting of a small piece of bread or toast, often cut in a decorative shape, garnished with a savory spread or topping.

caramelization: The process of browning sugar in the presence of heat. The caramelization of sugar occurs from 320° to 360°F / 160° to 182°C.

carbohydrate: One of the basic nutrients used by the body as a source of energy. Types include simple (sugars) and complex (starches and fibers).

carbon dioxide: A colorless, tasteless, edible gas obtained through fermentation or from the combination of soda and acid, which acts to leaven baked goods.

carry-over cooking: Heat retained in cooked foods that allows them to continue cooking even after removal from the cooking medium. Especially important to roasted foods.

cellulose: A complex carbohydrate; it is the main structural component of plant cells.

cephalopod: Marine creatures whose tentacles and arms are attached directly to their heads, such as squid and octopus.

chiffonade: Leafy vegetables or herbs cut into fine shreds; often used as a garnish.

chile: The fruit of certain types of capsicum peppers (not related to black pepper), used fresh or dried as a seasoning. Chiles come in many types (e.g., jalapeño, serrano, poblano) and varying degrees of spiciness.

chili: A stewed dish flavored with chili powder, meat, and beans (optional).

chili powder: Dried chiles that have been ground or crushed, often with other ground spices and herbs added.

chine: Backbone or a cut of meat that includes the backbone. Also, to separate the backbone and ribs to facilitate carving.

chinois: A conical sieve used for straining foods through a fine wire mesh.

cholesterol: A substance found exclusively in animal products such as meat, eggs, and cheese (dietary cholesterol) or in the blood (serum cholesterol).

chop: To cut into pieces of roughly the same size. Also, a small cut of meat including part of the rib.

chowder: A thick soup that may be made from a variety of ingredients but usually contains potatoes.

ciguatera toxin: A toxin found in certain species of fish, harmless to the fish, that causes illness in humans when eaten. The poisoning is caused by the fish's diet and is not eradicated by cooking or freezing.

clarification: The process of removing solid impurities from a liquid (such as butter or stock). Also, a mixture of ground meat, egg whites, mirepoix, tomato purée, herbs, and spices used to clarify broth for consommé.

coagulation: The curdling or clumping of proteins, usually due to the application of heat or acid.

coarse chop: A type of preparation in which food is cut into pieces of roughly the same size. Used for items such as mirepoix, where appearance is not important.

cocoa: The pods of the cacao tree, processed to remove the cocoa butter and ground into powder. Used as a flavoring.

collagen: A fibrous protein found in the connective tissue of animals, used to make glue and gelatin. Breaks down into gelatin when cooked in a moist environment for an extended period of time.

combination method: A cooking method that involves the application of both dry and moist heat to the main item (e.g., meats seared in fat then simmered in a sauce for braising or stewing).

complete protein: A food source that provides all of the essential amino acids in the correct ratio so that they can be used in the body for protein synthesis. May require more than one ingredient (such as beans and rice together).

complex carbohydrate: A large molecule made up of long chains of sugar molecules. In food, these molecules are found in starches and fiber.

composed salad: A salad in which the items are carefully arranged separately on a plate, rather than tossed together.

concasser: To pound or chop coarsely. *Concassé* usually refers to tomatoes that have been peeled, seeded, and chopped.

condiment: An aromatic mixture, such as pickles, chutney, and some sauces and relishes, which accompanies food. Usually kept on the table throughout service.

conduction: A method of heat transfer in which heat is transmitted through another substance. In cooking, when heat is transmitted to food through a pot or pan, oven racks, or grill rods.

consommé: Broth that has been clarified using a mixture of ground meat, egg whites, and other ingredients that trap impurities, resulting in a perfectly clear broth.

convection: A method of heat transfer in which heat is transmitted through the circulation of air or water.

convection oven: An oven that employs convection currents by forcing hot air through fans so it circulates around food, cooking it quickly and evenly.

converted rice: Rice that has been pressure-steamed and dried before milling to remove surface starch and retain nutrients. Also known as *parboiled rice*.

cornstarch: A fine, white powder milled from dried corn; used primarily as a thickener for sauce and occasionally as an ingredient in batters.

cottage cheese: A fresh cheese made from the drained curd of soured cow's milk.

coulis: A thick purée of vegetables or fruit, served hot or cold. Traditionally refers to the thickened juices of cooked meat, fish, shellfish purée, or certain thick soups.

court bouillon: Literally "short broth." An aromatic vegetable broth that usually includes an acidic ingredient, such as wine or vinegar; most commonly used for poaching fish.

couscous: Pellets of semolina or cracked wheat usually cooked by steaming, traditionally in a couscoussière. Also, the stew with which this grain is traditionally served.

couscoussière: A set of nesting pots, similar to a steamer, used to cook couscous.

cross contamination: The transference of disease-causing elements from one source to another through physical contact.

crustacean: A class of hard-shelled arthropods with elongated bodies, primarily aquatic, which include edible species such as lobster, crab, shrimp, and crayfish.

cuisson: Shallow poaching liquid, including stock, fumet, or other liquid, which may be reduced and used as a base for the poached item's sauce.

curry: A mixture of spices, used primarily in Indian, Jamaican, and Thai cuisine. May include turmeric, coriander, cumin, cayenne or other chiles, cardamom, cinnamon, clove, fennel, fenugreek, ginger, and garlic. May be dry or a paste. Also, the name for the stew-like dish seasoned with curry.

Daily Values (DV): Standard nutritional values developed by the Food and Drug Administration for use on food labels.

danger zone: The temperature range from 40° to 140°F / 4° to 60°C; the most favorable condition for rapid growth of many pathogens.

debeard: To remove the shaggy, inedible fibers from a mussel. These fibers anchor the mussel to its mooring.

deck oven: An oven in which the heat source is located underneath the deck or floor of the oven and the food is placed directly on the deck instead of on a rack.

deep-fry: To cook food by immersion in hot fat; deep-fried foods are often coated with bread crumbs or batter before being cooked.

deep-poach: To cook food gently in enough simmering liquid to completely submerge the food.

deglaze, déglacer: To use a liquid, such as wine, water, or stock, to dissolve food particles and/or caramelized drippings left in a pan after roasting or sautéing. The resulting mix then becomes the base for the accompanying sauce.

degrease, dégraisser: To skim the fat off the surface of a liquid, such as a stock or sauce.

demi-glace: Literally "half-glaze." A mixture of equal proportions of brown stock and brown sauce that has been reduced by half. One of the "grand" sauces.

dépouillage: To skim the impurities from the surface of a cooking liquid, such as a stock or sauce. This action is simplified by placing the pot off-center on the burner (convection simmer) and skimming impurities as they collect at one side of the pot.

dice: To cut ingredients into evenly sized small cubes (¼ in / 6 mm for small, ½ in / 1 cm for medium, and ¾ in / 2 cm for large is the standard).

die: The plate in a meat grinder through which foods pass just before a blade cuts them. The size of the die's opening determines the fineness of the grind.

direct heat: A method of heat transfer in which heat waves radiate from a source (e.g., an open burner or grill) and travel directly to the item being heated with no conductor between heat source and food. Examples are grilling, broiling, and toasting. Also known as radiant heat.

dredge: To coat food with a dry ingredient such as flour or bread crumbs prior to frying or sautéing.

dressed: Prepared for cooking. A dressed fish is gutted and scaled, and its head, tail, and fins are removed (same as pan-dressed). Dressed poultry is plucked, gutted, singed, trimmed, and trussed. Also, coated with dressing, as in a salad.

dry sauté: To sauté without fat, usually using a nonstick pan.

durum: A very hard wheat typically milled into semolina, which is primarily used in the making of pasta.

dusting: Distributing a film of flour, sugar, cocoa powder, or other such ingredients on pans or work surfaces, or on finished products as a garnish.

Dutch oven: A kettle, usually of cast iron, used for stewing and braising on the stovetop or in the oven.

Dutch process: A method for treating cocoa powder with an alkali to reduce its acidity.

duxelles: An appareil of finely chopped mushrooms and shallots sautéed gently in butter, used as a stuffing, garnish, or as a flavoring in soups and sauces.

edible-portion (EP) weight: The weight of an item after trimming and preparation (as opposed to the as-purchased [AP] weight).

egg wash: A mixture of beaten eggs (whole eggs, yolks, or whites) and a liquid, usually milk or water, used to coat baked goods to give them a sheen.

emulsion: A mixture of two or more liquids, one of which is a fat or oil and the other of which is water based, so that tiny globules of one are suspended in the other. This may involve the use of stabilizers, such as egg or mustard. Emulsions may be temporary, permanent, or semipermanent.

endosperm: The largest portion of the inside of the seed of a flowering plant, such as wheat; composed primarily of starch and protein. This is the portion used primarily in milled grain products.

essence: A concentrated flavoring extracted from an item, usually by infusion or distillation. Includes items such as vanilla and other extracts, concentrated stocks, and fumets.

estouffade: A French stew with wine-moistened pieces of meat. Also, a type of rich brown stock based on pork knuckle and veal and beef bones that is often used in braises.

ethylene gas: A gas emitted by various fruits and vegetables; ethylene gas speeds ripening, maturing, and eventually rotting.

étouffée: Literally "smothered." Refers to food cooked by a method similar to braising, except that items are cooked with little or no added liquid in a pan with a tight-fitting lid. (Also étuver, à l'étuvée.) Also, a Cajun dish made with a dark roux, crayfish, vegetables, and seasonings over a bed of white rice.

evaporated milk: Unsweetened canned milk from which 60 percent of the water has been removed before canning. It is often used in custards and to create a creamy texture in food.

facultative bacteria: Bacteria that can survive both with and without oxygen.

fiber, dietary fiber: The structural component of plants that is necessary to the human diet and is indigestible. Also referred to as roughage.

filé: A thickener made from ground dried sassafras leaves; used primarily in gumbos.

fines herbes: A mixture of herbs, usually parsley, chervil, tarragon, and chives, which lose their flavor quickly. They are generally added to the dish just prior to serving.

first in, first out (FIFO): A fundamental storage principle based on stock rotation. Products are stored and used so that the oldest product is always used first.

fish poacher: A long, narrow pot with straight sides and possibly a perforated rack, used for poaching whole fish.

five-spice powder: A mixture of equal parts ground cinnamon, clove, fennel seed, star anise, and Szechwan peppercorns.

flat fish: A type of fish characterized by its flat body and having both eyes on one side of its head (e.g., sole, plaice, flounder, and halibut).

flattop: A thick plate of cast iron or steel set over the heat source on a range; diffuses heat, making it more even than an open burner.

fold: To gently combine ingredients (especially foams) so as not to release trapped air bubbles. Also, to gently mix together two items, usually a light, airy mixture with a denser mixture. Also, the method of turning, rolling, and layering dough over on itself to produce a flaky texture.

fond: The French term for stock. Also describes the pan drippings remaining after sautéing or roasting food. It is often deglazed and used as a base for sauces.

food-borne illness: An illness in humans caused by the consumption of an adulterated food product. For an official determination that an outbreak of food-borne illness has occurred, two or more people must have become ill after eating the same food, and the outbreak must be confirmed by health officials.

food mill: A strainer with a crank-operated, curved blade. It is used to purée soft foods while straining.

food processor: A machine with interchangeable blades and disks and a removable bowl and lid separate from the motor housing. It can be used for a variety of tasks, including chopping, grinding, puréeing, emulsifying, kneading, slicing, shredding, and cutting into julienne.

fork-tender: Degree of doneness in braised foods and vegetables; fork-tender foods are easily pierced or cut by a fork, or should slide readily from a fork when lifted.

free-range: Refers to livestock that is raised unconfined.

frenching: The process of cutting and scraping meat from rib bones before cooking.

fructose: A simple sugar found in fruits. Fructose is the sweetest simple sugar.

fumet: A type of stock in which the main flavoring ingredient is allowed to cook in a covered pot with wine and aromatics. Fish fumet is the most common type.

garnish: An edible decoration or accompaniment to a dish or item.

gazpacho: A cold soup made from vegetables, typically tomatoes, cucumbers, peppers, and onions.

gelatin: A protein-based substance found in animal bones and connective tissue. When dissolved in hot liquid and then cooled, it can be used as a thickener and stabilizer.

gelatinization: A phase in the process of thickening a liquid with starch in which the starch molecules swell to form a network that traps water molecules.

germ: The portion of the seed of flowering plants, such as wheat, that sprouts to form a new plant; the embryo of the new plant.

glace/glacé: Reduced stock; ice cream.

glucose: A simple sugar found in honey, some fruits, and many vegetables. It has about half the sweetness of table sugar and is the preferred source of energy for the human body.

gluten: A protein present in wheat flour that develops through hydration and mixing to form elastic strands that build structure and aid in leavening.

griddle: A heavy metal cooking surface, which may be either fitted with handles, built into a stove, or heated by its own gas or electric element. Cooking is done directly on the griddle.

grill: A cooking technique in which foods are cooked by a radiant heat source placed below the food. Also, the piece of equipment on which grilling is done. Grills may be fueled by gas, electricity, charcoal, or wood.

grill pan: A skillet with ridges that is used on the stovetop to simulate grilling.

griswold: A pot, similar to a rondeau, made of cast iron; may have a single short handle rather than the usual loop handles.

gumbo: A Creole soup/stew thickened with filé or okra, flavored with a variety of meats and fishes and dark roux.

Hazard Analysis Critical Control Point (HACCP): A monitoring system used to track foods from the time that they are received until they are served to consumers, to ensure that the foods are free from contamination. Standards and controls are established for time and temperature, as well as for safe handling practices.

hominy: Corn that has been milled or treated with a lye solution to remove the bran and germ. Ground hominy is known as grits.

homogenization: A process used to prevent the milk fat from separating out of milk products. The liquid is forced through an ultrafine mesh at high pressure, which breaks up fat globules, dispersing them evenly throughout the liquid.

hors d'oeuvre: Literally "outside the work." An appetizer.

hotel pan: A rectangular metal pan in any of a number of standard sizes, with a lip that allows it to rest in a storage shelf or steam table.

hydrogenation: The process in which hydrogen atoms are added to an unsaturated fat molecule, making it partially or completely saturated and solid at room temperature.

hydroponics: A technique that involves growing vegetables in nutrient-enriched water rather than in soil.

hygiene: Conditions and practices followed to maintain health, including sanitation and personal cleanliness.

induction burner: A type of heating unit that relies on magnetic attraction between the cooktop and metals in the pot to generate the heat that cooks the foods in the pot. Reaction time is significantly faster than with traditional burners.

infection: Contamination by a disease-causing agent, such as bacteria.

infusion: Steeping an aromatic or other item in liquid to extract its flavor. Also, the liquid resulting from this process.

instant-read thermometer: A thermometer used to measure the internal temperature of foods. The stem is inserted in the food, producing an instant temperature read-out.

intoxication: Poisoning. A state of being tainted with toxins, particularly those produced by microorganisms that have infected food.

julienne: Vegetables, potatoes, or other items cut into thin strips; ⅛ in by ⅛ in by 1 to 2 in / 3 mm by 3 mm by 3 to 5 cm is standard. Fine julienne is ¹⁄₁₆ in by ¹⁄₁₆ in by 1 to 2 in / 1.5 mm by 1.5 mm by 3 to 5 cm.

jus: Juice. Refers to fruit and vegetable juices as well as juices from meats. *Jus de viande* is meat gravy. Meat served "au jus" is served with its own juice or jus lié.

jus lié: Meat juice thickened lightly with arrowroot or cornstarch.

kasha: Buckwheat groats that have been hulled and crushed and roasted; usually prepared by boiling.

kosher: Prepared in accordance with Jewish dietary laws.

kosher salt: Pure, refined salt used for pickling. Because it does not contain magnesium carbonate, it does not cloud brine solutions. Also used to prepare kosher items. Also known as *coarse salt* or *pickling salt*.

lactose: The simple sugar found in milk. This disaccharide is the least sweet among the natural sugars.

legume: The seeds of certain pod plants, including beans and peas, which are eaten for their earthy flavors and high nutritional value. Also, the French word for vegetable.

liaison: A mixture of egg yolks and cream used to thicken and enrich sauces. Also loosely used to mean any appareil used as a thickener.

liqueur: A spirit flavored with fruit, spices, nuts, herbs, and/or seeds and usually sweetened. Also known as cordials, liqueurs often have a high alcohol content, a viscous body, and a slightly sticky feel.

low-fat milk: Milk containing less than 2 percent fat.

lozenge cut: A knife cut in which foods are cut into small diamond shapes ½ in by ½ in by ⅛ in / 1 cm by 1 cm by 3 mm thick.

Maillard reaction: A complex browning reaction that results in the particular flavor and color of foods that do not contain much sugar, including roasted meats. The reaction, which involves carbohydrates and amino acids, is named after the French scientist who first discovered it. There are low-temperature and high-temperature Maillard reactions; the high-temperature reaction starts at 310°F / 154°C.

mandoline: A slicing device of stainless steel with carbon steel blades. The blades may be adjusted to cut items into various shapes and thicknesses.

marbling: The intramuscular fat found in meat that makes it tender and juicy.

marinade: An appareil used before cooking to flavor and moisten foods; may be liquid or dry. Liquid marinades are usually based on an acidic ingredient, such as wine or vinegar; dry marinades are usually salt based.

mark on a grill: To rotate a food (without flipping it over) 90 degrees after it has been on the grill for several seconds to create the cross-hatching associated with grilled foods.

medallion: A small, round scallop of meat.

meringue: Egg whites beaten with sugar until they stiffen. Types include regular or common, Italian, and Swiss.

mesophilic: A term used to describe bacteria that thrive in temperatures between 60° and 100°F / 16° and 38°C.

metabolism: The sum of chemical processes in living cells by which energy is provided and new material is assimilated.

millet: A small, round, glutenless grain that may be boiled or ground into flour.

milling: The process by which grain is separated into germ/husk, bran, and endosperm and ground into flour or meal.

mince: To chop into very small pieces.

mineral: An inorganic element that is an essential component of the diet. Provides no energy and is therefore referred to as a noncaloric nutrient. The body cannot produce minerals; they must be obtained from the diet.

minestrone: A hearty vegetable soup that typically includes dried beans and pasta.

mirepoix: A combination of chopped aromatic vegetables—usually two parts onion, one part carrot, and one part celery—used to flavor stocks, soups, braises, and stews.

mise en place: Literally "put in place." The preparation and assembly of ingredients, pans, utensils, and plates or serving pieces needed for a particular dish or service period.

molasses: The dark brown, sweet syrup that is a by-product of sugarcane and sugarbeet refining. Molasses is available as light (the least cooked but sweetest), dark, and blackstrap (the most cooked and most bitter).

mollusk: Any of a number of invertebrate animals with soft, unsegmented bodies usually enclosed in a hard shell; mollusks include gastropods (univalves), bivalves, and cephalopods. Examples include clams, oysters, snails, octopus, and squid.

monosodium glutamate (MSG): A flavor enhancer derived from glutamic acid, without a distinct flavor of its own; used primarily in Chinese and processed foods. It may cause allergic reactions in some people.

monounsaturated fat: A fat with one available bonding site not filled with a hydrogen atom. Helpful in lowering the LDL cholesterol level (the bad cholesterol). Food sources include avocados, olives, and nuts.

nappé: To coat with sauce; thickened. Consistency of a sauce that will coat the back of a spoon.

noisette: A hazelnut or hazelnut-colored. Also, a small portion of meat cut from the rib. *Pommes noisette* are tournéed potatoes browned in butter. *Beurre noisette* is browned butter.

nonbony fish: Fish whose skeletons are made of cartilage rather than hard bone (e.g., shark, skate). Also called *cartilaginous fish*.

nutrient: A basic component of food used by the body for growth, repair, restoration, and energy. Includes carbohydrates, fats, proteins, water, vitamins, and minerals.

nutrition: The process by which an organism takes in and uses food.

oblique cut, roll cut: A knife cut used primarily with long, cylindrical vegetables such as carrots. The item is cut on a diagonal, rolled 180 degrees, then cut on the same diagonal, producing a piece with two angled edges.

oignon brûlé: Literally "burnt onion." A peeled, halved onion seared on a flattop or in a skillet and used to enhance the color of stock and consommé.

oignon piqué: Literally "pricked onion." A whole, peeled onion to which a bay leaf is attached, using a clove as a tack. It is used to flavor béchamel sauce and some soups.

omega-3 fatty acids: Polyunsaturated fatty acids that may reduce the risk of heart disease and tumor growth, stimulate the immune system, and lower blood pressure; they occur in fatty fish, dark, green leafy vegetables, and certain nuts and oils.

omelet: Beaten egg that is cooked in butter in a specialized pan or skillet and then rolled or folded into an oval. Omelets may be filled with a variety of ingredients before or after rolling.

organic leavener: Yeast. A living organism acting to produce carbon dioxide gas, which will cause a batter or dough to rise through the fermentation process.

organ meat: Meat from an organ, rather than the muscle tissue, of an animal. Includes kidneys, heart, liver, sweetbreads, and the like.

paella: A dish of rice cooked with onion, tomato, garlic, vegetables, and various meats, including chicken, chorizo, shellfish, and possibly other types. A paella pan is a specialized pan for cooking paella; it is wide and shallow and usually has two loop handles.

paillard: A scallop of meat pounded until thin; usually grilled or sautéed.

palette knife: A small, long, narrow metal spatula with a rounded tip. May be tapered or straight, offset or flat.

pan broiling: A cooking method similar to dry sautéing that simulates broiling by cooking an item in a hot pan with little or no fat.

pan steaming: A method of cooking foods in a very small amount of liquid in a covered pan over direct heat.

papillote, en: Refers to a moist-heat cooking method similar to steaming, in which items are enclosed in parchment and cooked in the oven.

parchment: Heat-resistant paper used in cooking for such preparations as lining baking pans, cooking items en papillote, and covering items during the process of shallow poaching.

parcook: To partially cook an item before storing or finishing.

parisienne scoop: A small tool used for scooping balls out of vegetables or fruits and for portioning truffle ganache and other such preparations. Also called a *melon baller*.

pasteurization: A process in which milk products are heated to kill microorganisms that could contaminate the milk.

pastry bag: A bag—usually made of plastic, canvas, or nylon—that can be fitted with plain or decorative tips and used to pipe out icings and puréed foods.

pathogen: A disease-causing microorganism.

paysanne or fermier cut: A knife cut in which ingredients are cut into flat, square pieces measuring ¼ in by ¼ in by ⅛ in / 1 cm by 1 cm by 3 mm.

peel: A paddle used to transfer shaped doughs to a hearth or deck oven. Also, to remove the skin from a food item.

pesto: A thick, puréed mixture of an herb, traditionally basil and oil. Used as a sauce for pasta and other foods and as a garnish for soup. Pesto may also contain grated cheese, nuts or seeds, and other seasonings.

pH scale: A scale with values from 0 to 14 representing degree of acidity. A measurement of 7 is neutral, 0 is most acidic, and 14 is most alkaline. Chemically, pH measures the concentration of hydrogen ions.

phyllo/filo dough: Pastry made with very thin sheets of a flour-and-water dough layered with butter and/or bread or cake crumbs; similar to strudel.

physical leavener: The leavening that occurs when steam is trapped in a dough through the introduction of air (vs. a chemical leavener), expanding and causing the cake or bread to rise.

phytochemicals: Naturally occurring compounds in plant foods that have antioxidant and disease-fighting properties.

pilaf: A technique for cooking grains in which the grain is sautéed briefly in butter then simmered in stock or water with various seasonings until the liquid is absorbed. Also called *pilau, pilaw, pullao, pilav.*

pincé: Refers to an item caramelized by sautéing; usually refers to a tomato product.

pluches: Whole herb leaves connected to a small bit of stem; often used as a garnish. Also called *sprigs.*

poach: To cook gently in simmering liquid that is 160° to 185°F / 71° to 85°C.

polenta: Cornmeal mush cooked in simmering liquid until the grains soften and the liquid absorbs. Polenta can be eaten hot or cold, firm or soft.

polyunsaturated fat: A fat molecule with more than one available bonding site not filled with a hydrogen atom. Food sources include corn, cottonseed, safflower, soy, and sunflower oils.

port: A fortified dessert wine. Vintage port is high-quality unblended wine aged in the bottle for at least twelve years. Ruby port may be blended and is aged in wood for a short time. White port is made with white grapes.

pot-au-feu: A classic French boiled dinner that typically includes poultry and beef, along with various root vegetables. The broth is often served as a first course, followed by the meats and vegetables.

prawn: A crustacean that closely resembles shrimp; often used as a general term for large shrimp.

presentation side: The side of a piece of meat, poultry, or fish that will be served facing up.

pressure steamer: A machine that cooks food using steam produced by heating water under pressure in a sealed compartment, allowing it to reach temperatures higher than boiling (212°F / 100°C). The food is placed in a sealed chamber that cannot be opened until the pressure has been released and the steam properly vented from the chamber.

protein: One of the basic nutrients needed by the body to maintain life, supply energy, build and repair tissues, form enzymes and hormones, and perform other essential functions. Protein can be obtained from both animal and vegetable sources.

pulse: The edible seed of a leguminous plant, such as a bean, lentil, or pea. Often referred to simply as legume. Also, the action of turning a food processor or blender on and off to control mixing speed and time.

purée: To process food by mashing, straining, or chopping it very finely in order to make it a smooth paste. Also, a product produced using this technique.

raft: A mixture of ingredients used to clarify consommé. The term refers to the fact that the ingredients rise to the surface and form a floating mass.

ragoût: Stew of meat and/or vegetables.

ramekin/ramequin: A small, ovenproof dish, usually ceramic.

reduce: To decrease the volume of a liquid by simmering or boiling; used to provide a thicker consistency and/or concentrated flavors.

reduction: The product that results when a liquid is reduced.

refresh: To plunge an item into, or run it under, cold water after blanching to prevent further cooking. Also known as *shock*.

risotto: Rice that is sautéed briefly in fat with onions and possibly other aromatics, then combined with stock, which is added in several additions and stirred constantly, producing a creamy texture with grains that are still al dente.

roast: A dry-heat cooking method where the item is cooked in an oven or on a spit over a fire.

roe: Fish or shellfish eggs.

rondeau: A shallow, wide, straight-sided pot with two loop handles often used for braising. It is also known as a *brazier*.

rondelle: A knife cut that produces round or oval flat pieces; used on cylindrical vegetables or items trimmed into cylinders before cutting.

round fish: A classification of fish based on skeletal type, characterized by a rounded body and eyes on opposite sides of its head. Round fish are usually cut by the "up and over" method.

roux: An appareil containing equal parts of flour and fat (usually butter) used to thicken liquids. Roux is cooked to varying degrees (white, blond, or brown), depending on its intended use. The darker the roux, the less thickening power it has, but the fuller the taste.

sachet d'épices: Literally, "bag of spices." Aromatic ingredients, encased in cheesecloth, that are used to flavor stocks and other liquids. A standard sachet contains parsley stems, cracked peppercorns, dried thyme, and a bay leaf.

sanitation: The maintenance of a clean food-preparation environment by healthy food workers in order to prevent food-borne illnesses and food contamination.

sanitize: To kill pathogenic organisms by chemicals and/or moist heat.

saturated fat: A fat molecule whose available bonding sites are entirely filled with hydrogen atoms. These tend to be solid at room temperature and are primarily of animal origin, though coconut oil, palm oil, and cocoa butter are vegetable sources of saturated fat. Animal sources include butter, meat, cheese, and eggs.

sauce: A liquid accompaniment to food, used to enhance the flavor of the food.

sauté: To cook quickly in a small amount of fat in a pan on the range top.

sauteuse: A shallow skillet with sloping sides and a single, long handle. Used for sautéing. Referred to generically as a *sauté pan*.

sautoir: A shallow skillet with straight sides and a single, long handle. Used for sautéing. Referred to generically as a *sauté pan*.

savory: Not sweet. Also, the name of a course (savory) served after dessert and before port in traditional British meals. Also, a family of herbs (including summer and winter savory) that taste like a cross between thyme and mint.

scald: To heat a liquid, usually milk or cream, to just below the boiling point. May also refer to blanching fruits and vegetables.

scale: To measure ingredients by weighing, or to divide dough or batter into portions by weight. Also, to remove the scales from fish.

scaler: Tool used to scrape scales from fish. Used by scraping against the direction in which scales lie flat, working from tail to head.

scallop: A bivalve whose adductor muscle (the muscle that keeps its shells closed) and roe are eaten. Also a small, boneless piece of meat or fish of uniform thickness. Also, a side dish where an item is layered with cream or sauce and topped with bread crumbs prior to baking.

score: To cut the surface of an item at regular intervals to allow it to cook evenly, allow excess fat to drain, help the food absorb marinades, or for decorative purposes.

sear: To brown the surface of food in fat over high heat before finishing by another method (e.g., braising or roasting) in order to add flavor.

sea salt: Salt produced by evaporating seawater. Available refined or unrefined, crystallized or ground. Also known as *sel gris* (French for "gray salt").

seasoning: Adding an ingredient to give foods a particular flavor using salt, pepper, herbs, spices, and/or condiments. Also, the process by which a protective coating is built up on the interior of a pan.

semolina: The coarsely milled hard durum wheat endosperm used for gnocchi, some pasta, and couscous. Semolina has a high gluten content.

shallow poach: To cook gently in a shallow pan of simmering liquid. The liquid is often reduced and used as the base of a sauce.

sheet pan: A flat baking pan, often with a rolled lip, used to cook foods in the oven.

shelf life: The amount of time in storage that a product can maintain its quality.

shellfish: Various types of marine life consumed as food, including mollusks such as univalves, bivalves, cephalopods, and crustaceans.

sherry: A fortified Spanish wine varying in color and sweetness.

sieve: A container made of a perforated material, such as wire mesh, used to drain, rice, or purée foods.

silverskin: The tough connective tissue that surrounds certain muscles. This protein does not dissolve when cooked and must be removed prior to cooking.

simmer: To maintain the temperature of a liquid just below boiling. Also, to cook in simmering liquid. The temperature range for simmering is 185° to 200°F / 85° to 93°C.

simple carbohydrate: Any of a number of small carbohydrate molecules (mono- and disaccharides), including glucose, fructose, lactose, maltose, and sucrose.

skim: To remove impurities from the surface of a liquid, such as stock or soup, during cooking.

skim milk: Milk from which all but 0.5 percent of the milk fat has been removed.

slurry: A starch such as arrowroot, cornstarch, or potato starch dispersed in cold liquid to prevent it from forming lumps when added to hot liquid as a thickener.

smoke point: The temperature at which a fat begins to break (and smoke) when heated.

smoke roasting: A method for roasting foods in which items are placed on a rack in a pan containing wood chips that smolder, emitting smoke, when the pan is placed on the range top or in the oven.

smoking: Any of several methods for preserving and flavoring foods by exposing them to smoke. Methods include cold smoking (in which smoked items are not fully cooked), hot smoking (in which the items are cooked), and smoke roasting.

smother: To cook in a covered pan with little liquid over low heat. The main item is often completely covered by another food item or sauce while it braises.

sodium: An alkaline metal element necessary in small quantities for human nutrition; one of the components of most salts used in cooking.

sorbet: A frozen dessert made with fruit juice or another flavoring, a sweetener (usually sugar), and beaten egg whites, which prevent the formation of large ice crystals.

soufflé: Literally "puffed." A preparation made with a sauce base (usually béchamel for savory soufflés, pastry cream for sweet ones), whipped egg whites, and flavorings. The egg whites cause the soufflé to puff during cooking.

spätzle: A soft noodle or small dumpling made by dropping bits of a prepared batter into simmering liquid.

spice: An aromatic vegetable substance from numerous plant parts, usually dried and used as seasoning.

spider: A long-handled skimmer used to remove items from hot liquid or fat and to skim the surface of liquids.

spit-roast: To roast an item on a large skewer or spit over, or in front of, an open flame or other radiant heat source.

standard breading procedure: The assembly-line procedure in which items are dredged in flour, dipped in beaten egg, then coated with crumbs before being pan fried or deep-fried.

Staphylococcus aureus: A type of facultative bacteria that can cause food-borne illness. It is particularly dangerous because it produces toxins that cannot be destroyed by heat. Staph intoxication is most often caused by transfer of the bacteria from infected food handlers.

steamer: A set of stacked pots with perforations in the bottom of each pot. They fit over a larger pot that is filled with boiling or simmering water. Also, a perforated insert made of metal or bamboo that can be used in a pot to steam foods.

steaming: A cooking method in which items are cooked in a vapor bath created by boiling water or other liquids.

steam-jacketed kettle: A kettle with double-layered walls, between which steam circulates, providing even heat for cooking stocks, soups, and sauces. These kettles may be insulated, spigoted, and/or tilting. The latter are also called *trunnion kettles*.

steel: A tool used to hone knife blades. It is usually made of steel but may be ceramic, glass, or diamond-impregnated metal.

steep: To allow an ingredient to sit in warm or hot liquid to extract flavor or impurities, or to soften the item.

stew: A cooking method nearly identical to braising but generally involving smaller pieces of meat and hence a shorter cooking time. Stewed items also may be blanched, rather than seared, to give the finished product a pale color. Also, a dish prepared by using the stewing method.

stir-frying: A cooking method similar to sautéing in which items are cooked over very high heat, using little fat. Usually this is done in a wok, and the food is kept moving constantly.

stock: A flavorful liquid prepared by simmering meat bones, poultry bones, seafood bones, and/or vegetables in water with aromatics until their flavor is extracted. It is used as a base for soups, sauces, and other preparations.

stockpot: A large, straight-sided pot that is taller than it is wide. Used for making stocks and soups. Some have spigots. Also called a *marmite*.

stone ground: A term used to describe meal or flour milled between grindstones. Because the germ of the wheat is not separated, this method of grinding retains more nutrients than other methods.

strain: To pass a liquid through a sieve or screen to remove particles.

suprême: The breast fillet and wing of chicken or other poultry. Sauce suprême is chicken velouté enriched with cream. Also, a section of citrus without its membrane covering.

sweat: To cook an item, usually vegetables, in a covered pan in a small amount of fat until it softens and releases moisture but does not brown.

table salt: Refined, granulated salt. May be fortified with iodine and treated with magnesium carbonate to prevent clumping.

table wine: Still red, white, and rosé wines containing between 7 and 14 percent alcohol; usually served with a meal.

temper: To heat gently and gradually. May refer to the process of incorporating hot liquid into a liaison to gradually raise its temperature. May also refer to the proper method for melting chocolate.

thermophilic: Heat loving. A term used to describe bacteria that thrive within the temperature range from 110° to 171°F / 43° to 77°C.

thickener: An ingredient used to give additional body to liquids. Arrowroot, cornstarch, gelatin, roux, and beurre manié are examples of thickeners.

tilting kettle: A large, relatively shallow tilting pot used for braising, stewing, and occasionally steaming.

tomato sauce: A sauce prepared by simmering tomatoes in a liquid (water or broth) with aromatics. One of the "grand" sauces.

tourner: To cut items, usually vegetables, into barrel, olive, or football shapes. Tournéed foods should have five or seven sides or faces and blunt ends.

toxin: A naturally occurring poison, particularly those produced by the metabolic activity of living organisms, such as bacteria.

tranche: A slice or cut of meat, fish, or poultry cut on a bias in order to visually increase the appearance of the cut.

Trichinella spiralis: A spiral-shaped parasitic worm that invades the intestines and muscle tissue. Transmitted primarily through infected pork that has not been cooked sufficiently.

truss: To tie up meat or poultry with string before cooking it in order to give it a compact shape for more even cooking and better appearance.

tuber: The fleshy root, stem, or rhizome of a plant, able to grow into a new plant. Some, such as potatoes, are eaten as vegetables.

tuile: Literally "tile." A thin, wafer-like cookie (or food cut to resemble this cookie). Tuiles are frequently shaped while warm and still pliable by pressing them into molds or draping them over rolling pins or dowels.

umami: Describes a savory, meaty taste; often associated with monosodium glutamate (MSG) and mushrooms.

univalve: A single-shelled, single-muscle mollusk, such as abalone and sea urchin.

unsaturated fat: A fat molecule with at least one available bonding site not filled with a hydrogen atom. These may be monounsaturated or polyunsaturated. They tend to be liquid at room temperature and are primarily of vegetable origin.

vegetable soup: A broth- or water-based soup made primarily with vegetables; may include meats, legumes, and noodles and may be clear or thick.

vegetarian: An individual who has adopted a specific diet (or lifestyle) that reduces or eliminates animal products. Vegans eat no foods derived in any way from animals. Lacto-ovo-vegetarians include dairy products and eggs in their diet. Ovo-vegetarians include eggs in their diet.

velouté: A sauce of white stock (chicken, veal, seafood) thickened with white roux. One of the "grand" sauces. Also, a cream soup made with a velouté sauce base and flavorings (usually puréed) that is usually finished with a liaison.

venison: Meat from large game animals in the deer family, but often used to refer specifically to deer meat.

virus: A type of pathogenic microorganism that can be transmitted in food. Viruses cause such illnesses as measles, chicken pox, infectious hepatitis, and colds.

vitamins: Any of various nutritionally essential organic substances that do not provide energy but usually act as regulators in metabolic processes and help maintain health.

wasabi: Root of an Asian plant similar to horseradish. It becomes bright green when mixed with water and is used as a condiment in Japanese cooking.

whip/whisk: To beat an item, such as cream or egg whites, to incorporate air. Also, a special tool for whipping, made of looped wire attached to a handle.

white mirepoix: Mirepoix that does not include carrots and may include chopped mushrooms or mushroom trimmings and parsnips. It is used for pale or white sauces and stocks.

white stock: A light-colored stock made with bones that have not been browned.

whole grain: An unmilled or unprocessed grain.

whole wheat flour: Flour milled from the whole grain, including the bran, germ, and endosperm. Graham flour is a whole wheat flour named after Sylvester Graham, a nineteenth-century American dietary reformer.

wok: A round-bottomed pan, usually made of rolled steel, which is used for nearly all cooking methods in Chinese cuisine. Its shape allows for even heat distribution and easy tossing of ingredients.

yam: A large tuber that grows in tropical and subtropical climates; it has starchy, pale-yellow flesh. The name *yam* is also used for the (botanically unrelated) sweet potato.

yeast: Microscopic fungus whose metabolic processes are responsible for fermentation. It is used for leavening bread and in the making of cheese, beer, and wine.

yogurt: Milk cultured with bacteria to give it a slightly thick consistency and sour flavor.

zest: The thin, brightly colored outer part of citrus rind. It contains volatile oils, making it ideal for use as a flavoring.

Recipe Index

Subject Index

H

Health claims, 30–31
Healthy cooking, general guidelines, 86
Healthy cooking, techniques, 86–99
Heat, 98
Herb tea. See Tea
Herbs, 59, 127, 139
High-density lipoproteins (HDL), 12, 13
Hypertension, 4, 18, 25–26

I

Ingredient selection, 36–43
Intolerances. See Allergies and
    intolerances
Irradiation, 40

J

Job's tears, 63
Juices, fruit, 11

K

Kamut, 63
Kitchen staff, nutrition training, 154

L

Labeling. See Nutrition labeling
Lamb, cooking techniques, 112
Leafy greens, 103
Legumes, 65
    cooking techniques, 108–109
Low-density lipoproteins (LDL), 12, 13

M

Macrominerals, 17–18
"Mad Cow Disease" See Bovine
    Spongiform Encephalopathy
Magnesium, 18
Main dish, defined, 7
Maintenance of cooking equipment, 96, 98
Marinades, 89, 113, 117
Meal, defined, 7
Measuring, importance of, 136
Mediterranean diet, 24
Melons, 57
Menu development, 133, 140–152, 243
Microminerals, 19–20
Minerals, 14–15, 17–20
Mirepoix, 128
Moist-heat cooking techniques, 91–97

N

Noncaloric sweeteners, 78
Nutraceuticals, 19
Nutrient content claims, 28–29
Nutrient density, 22
Nutrient loss, in produce, 48
Nutrients, essential, defined, 8
Nutrients, noncaloric, 13–21

Nutrition, 5–33
    daily needs, 7
    increasing, 142
    labeling, 26–28
Nutritional analysis, 132
    of recipes, 514–529
Nuts and seeds, 66–67
    cooking techniques, 110, 362

O

Oats, 62
Obesity, 4, 12
Obtaining nutrient information, 31–32
Oils, 67
    flavored, 126–127
Omega-3 content of fish (table), 72
Organic foods, 37–38

P

Pan-steaming, 100
Pantry, importance of, 481
Pasta, 107
Pears, 54
Phosphorus, 18
Phytochemicals, 20–21, 51
Poaching
    deep, 96
    shallow, 95
Pork, cooking techniques, 112
Portion size, 29, 134
Potassium, 18
Poultry, cooking techniques, 113
Produce, 46–59
Protein, caloric content, 6, 7
Protein, 9–10
Purchasing and storing
    condiments, 78
    dairy and eggs, 69
    dried legumes, 65
    fats and oils, 67
    fish, 70–71
    fresh produce, 47–49, 54, 55, 56, 57
    grains, 61
    herbs, 59
    meat, 73–74
    nuts and seeds, 67
    poultry, 74
    shellfish, 72
    soyfoods, 65–66
Purées, vegetable, 102
Pyramids, dietary, 24

Q

Quinoa, 63

R

Recipe development, 132–140
Recipe modification, 134–135

Recommended Daily Values. See Daily
    values
Reducing fat, 137–138
"Reference amount", 29
Replacing fat, 138–139
Rice, 62
Roasting, 89–91
    fruit, 105

S

Salads, 146, 159
Salt, 76–77, 123–124
    reducing, 139
Sautéing, 87
Seafood, toxins in, 41
Seasonings and condiments, 75–80
Service staff, communications training, 153
Serving size, 29
Shallow poaching, 95
Side dishes, 361
Simmering, 96
Smoke-roasting, 91
Soaking and cooking times for legumes
    (table), 109
Sodium, 18, 76
Soups, 145, 159–192
Soyfoods, 65–66
Spelt, 63
Spices, 125, 126
Steaming, 92
Steam-roasting, 101
Stewing, 96–97
Stir-frying, 88
Stone fruits, 58
Storage, temperatures, 45
Storing
    chocolate, 68
    coffee and tea, 82
    condiments, 78
    dairy and eggs, 69
    dried legumes, 65
    fats and oils, 67
    fish, 70–71
    fresh produce (table), 49
    fruit, 54, 55, 56, 57
    grains, 61
    herbs, 59
    meat, 73–74
    nuts and seeds, 67
    poultry, 74
    shellfish, 72
    soyfoods, 65–66
Sugar, reducing, 140
Supertasters, 114
Sustainable agriculture, 36–37
Sweeteners, 78